Marius J[?]
St Marks"
Berkeley

R. W. Younkin

THE NATURE OF THE EARLY CHURCH

The Nature
of
The Early Church

By

ERNEST F. SCOTT, D.D.

NEW YORK

Charles Scribner's Sons

1941

PREFACE

The book of Acts was written before the end of the first century, and has been followed by innumerable works on the history of the church. It is strange, however, that while the subject has been studied minutely in all its phases and from every conceivable point of view, the question has seldom been raised of what the church is, in its essential nature. The importance, or even the possibility, of this question has been recognized only in our own day, and various answers to it have been put forward. None of them, it seems to the present writer, is fully adequate. The church, however it may resemble other societies, ancient or modern, is a unique creation, and can be explained only from something unique in the Christian message. An attempt is made in this book to determine how the church was related to the message, as it was understood by the first disciples, in the days immediately following the Lord's departure. It was then that the church arose, and the secret of its formative idea must be sought in that crucial period when it came into being.

The primitive church often has been compared to a tiny rill which was expanded in the course of time by many tributaries until it grew into a mighty river. This analogy is altogether misleading, for in a real sense the church was most fully itself at the very outset. The later movement becomes intelligible only when we go back to that first community which gave aim and motive to all that happened afterwards. It has been impossible, therefore, to limit the enquiry to that brief period with which it is immediately concerned. The problem of the primitive church cannot but broaden out into that of the church as it has always been, and still is today. This will account for much in the book that is not entirely relevant to a strictly historical enquiry.

Amidst the terrible events of the present there may seem to be little place for this investigation of an obscure chapter in the history of the past. The author has felt, however, that in this time when our Christian civilization is in peril its foundations need to be re-examined and tested. The church is the very symbol of those interests which the free nations are struggling to preserve, and there is a practical value in all effort to understand its meaning.

E. F. Scott.

June, 1941

CONTENTS

CHAPTER I

THE SIGNIFICANCE OF THE PRIMITIVE CHURCH

The Christian religion, from the beginning, has identified itself with a community. Before it had any formal creed it found expression in a group of men and women who had followed Jesus in his lifetime and now waited for his return. This group, when it first comes into our view, was made up of a hundred and twenty people, settled in Jerusalem. It steadily grew in numbers and extended its mission over Palestine, then into Syria, Asia Minor and the Western lands. In process of time it became the world-wide church.

It is customary to speak of the church as an institution, but this term is inadequate and misleading. It suggests a society which was formed deliberately, like a club or a business company, with a clearly defined object. The study of church history has been largely vitiated by this underlying assumption. Attempts are made to discover why the church was instituted, and what rules and ordinances were imposed on it. Questions are raised as to whether this institution was necessary, and if so, whether it has now served its purpose and needs to be replaced by something different. The church, however, was not instituted but arose spontaneously, and for some time was hardly conscious of its own existence. It has its true analogy, not in a society created of set purpose, but in a nation. We do not think of Rome or England or America as institutions. They grew of their own accord out of the association of people who were kindred in blood and had the same language and traditions. The nation was formed by a natural process, just as much as the rivers and forests of the land. This was no less true of the church. It was apparent even to pagans that the strange community which had sprung up among them was not one of the formal societies of which there were many in that time. They spoke of the Christians as "this new race of men." An alien people had arisen and was threatening all established rights.

The church is the Christian nation, and no other has had a history so varied and continuous. Our attention is too often absorbed by the mere succession of events, the outstanding leaders, the enterprises that have been achieved from time to time. We are now learning that the real interest even of ordinary history has little to do with these things, when they are taken by themselves. Events are important only as they serve to manifest or to shape the character of the people. We desire to know not so much what happened to them as what they are, and what have been their motives and purposes. This is still more true of the history of the church. Behind all the outward vicissitudes there is an outlook which always has been essentially the same. What is its nature? When we try to determine its ultimate meaning, what is this society which we call the church?

This question as a rule is left unanswered. We are content to know that after Jesus himself had departed those who believed in him united in carrying on his work, and it seems hardly necessary to enquire why they did so. Our concern is not with the dim origins of the Christian community but with the mature results. In the study of English history we do not

linger over the vague migrations of Jutes and Angles in forgotten centuries. It may be admitted that without those obscure preliminaries nothing could have followed; but it is
enough to know that somehow they took place and that the
scene was thus prepared for the true history. In much the same
manner we assume the beginnings of the church.

This is our attitude, too, with regard to its nature and function. For most people it is only a familiar part of the social
order into which they were born. If they were pressed to define
its purpose they would say that besides the ordinary needs men
have a need for religion. They might be satisfied with private
devotion, but the instinct of men is to work together, and they
therefore associate in their religious life. As a result there has
grown up a great society, of which the central object is worship, but which also takes on itself many other duties, connected, more or less directly, with the service of God. The
church is the guardian of morality. It devotes itself to works
of beneficence. It brings its members into friendly intercourse
with each other. In our time, when races and classes are in
acute conflict, it works for mutual understanding. It insists
that every nation should treat the others justly, that labour
should have its due reward, that laws should be humane and
equitable. If it were not for the church all human relations
would be at the mercy of self-interest, as in pagan times, but
this great organization upholds the higher standards, and has
therefore a necessary place in the life of the civilized world.

No one would deny that all this is true. The church is a
great society in which it is possible for all men of good will to
unite their forces and defend the cause of justice and brotherhood in the name of Christ. It is also in a real sense the means

of salvation. Partaking in its worship men are brought into communion with Christ. They are touched with the regenerating influence which flowed from him, and has been transmitted through the long succession of his faithful people. But when all this is said we have not fully explained the church. It is not merely an organization like others, though working for beneficent ends and serving as a channel for the Christian life. It is different in kind from any other society. In order to understand it we have to consider, not so much its activities, moral and social and religious, as the idea which lies at the heart of it.

For this purpose it is necessary to go back to its very beginning. If only we can determine what was in the minds of the first disciples we may hope for some insight into the radical meaning of the church. In all the later effort that first intention has been the vital principle, although it has been so complicated with other interests that it is often difficult to trace. To apprehend it in its simplicity we need to return to the earliest days. This is true, in some measure, of every human society. A nation at the height of its power cherishes the memory of its beginnings, not merely out of a pious sentiment, but in order to explain to itself what has followed. In that remote past it gets down to the bedrock. Here were the conditions which gave it being, and which, in the last resort, must decide its destiny. A social or religious order reveres its founders. They worked on a small scale but for that reason were not distracted from their main purpose. Their memory is the compass by which their successors must continue to steer. In a more definite sense, however, we learn the meaning of the church through the primitive community. The beginnings of a nation are usually shrouded in darkness; nothing can be surely known of the actions of the pioneers and the motives which prompted them. Of the primitive church we know at least the essential facts. We know, too, that the first believers were the immediate disciples of Jesus, and were trying to put into effect what they had learned from him. There is no need to weave myths about them and credit them with motives of which they were not themselves aware. The evidence of their purpose is clearly there, in the recorded message of Jesus.

In all times it has been recognized that the church must study the example of the early days, and seek, if possible, to follow it. Too often, however, a false value has been placed on this example. It has been assumed that in all matters of government and institution the church must model itself on the primitive community. For that brief period at the beginning the church was uncorrupted. It guided itself in all respects by the instruction of Christ himself, and the one test of a true church is its similarity to that primitive one. On this point ecclesiastical controversy has always turned. Each denomination has sought to make out that it alone has remained faithful to the original model. The church of the Apostles was Episcopal or Presbyterian or Congregational, or was more akin to such irregular sects as the Plymouth Brethren or the Salvation Army. Every type of religious organization can be shown, without much difficulty, to have resemblances to the church of the New Testament. But we are now learning to see that all this discussion is beside the mark. The primitive model was one which never can be reproduced, for it answered to conditions which were altogether unique. The community had not yet called itself a church. It had no set order or government. It placed itself wholly under the control of the Spirit, which resided in the group as a whole and in each individual member. Such a community was possible only at the very beginning, when the church was small and was fired with a high enthusiasm. Even within the first year or two the primitive model had to be abandoned, and to return to it now could lead to no other result than sheer anarchy. We cannot revive the New Testament church, nor is this desirable. Jesus himself laid down no directions as to how his followers were to order their society. He only gave them a task to fulfil, and left them to discover for themselves how they might do so most effectually. Again and again the church must organize itself afresh, to meet the requirements of each new time, and according as it is best fitted to the time it gives meaning and reality to its message.

What we need to discover from the study of that first community is not how it was organized and administered, but rather why it came into existence. A society was formed which has ever since maintained itself and has spread over the earth; what was it supposed to be? From its later history this question cannot very well be answered. There was a period in the Middle Ages when the church was everything, and amidst the multiplicity of its interests it is hardly possible to distinguish a central one. In our own time the church is constantly under rebuke for neglecting one duty or another, and can never affirm with certainty that this does not lie within its province. But at the outset there was none of this confusion. The church had its task clearly marked out for it. Its members were possessed with a great conviction which took concrete form in their fellowship. What was this conviction?

Significance of the Primitive Church

It is obvious that the question has an urgent practical importance. The first thing necessary in planning out a journey is to fix the destination. No enterprise can be properly carried through unless the object is known and tenaciously kept in mind. Yet the church, for the most part, has only the vaguest sense of what it is seeking to do. Most of its errors are to be set down, not to moral failure or want of intelligence, but simply to confusion of aim. If it is to fulfil the purpose for which it exists it must first know what that purpose is; and this it can do only by reminding itself of how it began. It had then a clear vision of its calling, and in the light of that vision it must keep itself in the right way.

What do we know, then, about the primitive church? The record might seem to be limited to a few bare facts, preserved for the most part in the book of Acts. Writing after an interval of fifty or sixty years, the author has done his best to collect the stray memories of the primitive time. When allowance is made for his difficulties he has performed his task well. Some of his material would seem to be taken from actual documents. Few records of this kind can have been available, and they would be little more than scanty jottings; but such as they were Luke has sought them out and made the most of them. He has also woven into his narrative a number of reminiscences which had come down by various channels and sometimes had been coloured and worn out of shape in the process. Luke has wisely preserved them just as they had come to him, for the fanciful additions were themselves significant, reflecting, as they do, the ideas and beliefs which were habitual to the first disciples. For the general picture he is himself responsible. He has often been charged with credulity, with writing for effect, with substituting romance for history, but perhaps he has done most justice to the facts where he has used his own imagination. In a wonderful way he has caught the atmosphere of the early church. He has given us not merely the facts, which were often of little moment, but the mood of the actors, the sense of mystery and power which overshadowed the young community. Christ had departed, but his place had now been taken by the Spirit, which was working mightily. It is from this point of view that Luke describes the life of the early church, and the impression which he leaves on us is far more real and convincing than if he had catalogued a great number of facts exactly as they happened.

The account in Acts is supplemented and illuminated by the Epistles of Paul. It is true that Paul wrote after the initial period had come to an end and the church had embarked on the great mission which in large measure changed its character. But again and again he has occasion to glance back on the preceding time, and his notices have a firsthand value which rarely can be claimed for those in the book of Acts. It must be remembered, too, that Paul had himself a close relation to the primitive community. Although he expressed his beliefs in new language they were in substance those of the earlier Apostles. Many of his modern critics, taking their cue unwittingly from the Jewish emissaries who tried to thwart his work, have described him as the adversary of the mother-church. This, as he strongly protested, was not true. He was the spokesman of the church, and when we ask ourselves what it claimed to be we receive the clearest answer from Paul.

Again, we learn much about the early community from the Synoptic Gospels. Their subject is the life of Jesus, but it was the church in Palestine which collected and preserved the records and threw them into their present form. It has been maintained by some scholars that the church was mainly responsible for the substance as well as the form, but this cannot be admitted for a moment. The sayings ascribed to Jesus are, for the most part, self-authenticating, and in many instances are at variance with the ideas of the church. Not only so, but almost always, as we shall see later, they are of such a character that no community could have devised them for its practical guidance. Here and there a strict command has been qualified, and in such cases we may suspect the hand of the church. But these modifications affect only a small part of the teaching and were evidently made when the initial period was over. It is not hard to distinguish the sayings which belong to the earliest stratum of the tradition, and which bear on them the stamp of Jesus' own mind.

We can thus gather from the Synoptic Gospels that the primitive community accepted the teaching of Jesus in its literal form. He had set up a standard which might seem impossible, but this was how he required his followers to live and they must make it their aim to obey him. The Christian rule as we know it in the Gospels was in very fact the rule of the primitive church. Above all, it accepted with a perfect confidence the promise of Jesus that the Kingdom of God would presently set in. This is the central theme of the Gospels. They tell how Jesus had proclaimed the Kingdom, how he had called on men to live for it, how he had suffered as the Messiah who was to bring it in. In the later New Testament writings the conception of the Kingdom tends to fall away. The precise meaning of it had apparently become obscure even in the time when the Gospels were finally put together. But in the minds of the earliest disciples there was no doubt. They knew that the message of Jesus had been that of the Kingdom of God; everything else had been subordinate to this one theme. It was on this message that the community took its stand.

For the understanding of the primitive church the Synoptic Gospels are thus of fundamental value. When Luke set himself to write its history in the book of Acts, he could find little to help him in the way of documents. The early church had been too much occupied with actual living to draw up records of what it had done and thought. But it had preserved the tradition of the message of Jesus, and this is also the self-revelation of the primitive church. For the purpose of its mission it had to tell the world what it believed, why it regarded Jesus as the Messiah, what was the way of life it was trying to follow. Although we had possessed no direct information about the early community we might have formed a picture of it, correct in all that matters, from the evidence of the Gospels alone.

It can hardly be emphasized too much that between the work of Jesus and the church that arose afterwards there was an intimate relation. Too often they have been kept separate, or have even been placed in opposition. Jesus, we are told, had lived and died, and after his death there grew up a community which called itself by his name but otherwise had little connection with him. Sometimes it has been argued that the creation of the church was the primary error which has darkened and nullified the whole meaning of the work of Jesus. He had looked for the Kingdom of God, the new age when men would

be inwardly conformed to God's will. He had believed that in
this coming time all outward authorities and systems would
cease to be, for there would be no further need for them; they
would only stand in the way of a real and immediate fellowship with God. But he had hardly departed when the Kingdom was forgotten and in place of it there appeared the
church, which was only the old mechanical system over again.
This has been singled out as the great apostasy of the Christian
religion, which almost from the outset took a wrong direction
and has been following it ever since. But the truth is that the
church was bound up inseparably with Jesus' own work, and
cannot otherwise be understood. This was recognized by Luke
when he planned a history which should consist of two parts,
integrally united. The first would tell of Jesus' life on earth;
the second would describe the rise and expansion of his church.
Both would have as their theme "the things which Jesus had
done and said"[1]—only the one would deal with his life in the
flesh, the other with his larger invisible life. This earliest of
church historians had a clearer insight into the meaning of the
church than any of his successors. They are content for the
most part to examine the tree apart from the root. They tell us
much of things that happened—successes, persecutions, formation of doctrines, modes of worship—but they have little light
to throw on the inner forces which were at work through all
the changes. The church is severed from the mission of Jesus
himself, apart from which its own mission becomes meaningless.

It is part of the same error that the history of the church is
usually treated as a development. In so far as a place is allowed

[1]Acts 1:1.

for Jesus, he is regarded as giving the initial impulse. Without him the church could never have begun, but his own achievement was relatively small. He was little more, perhaps, than a wandering Rabbi, inspired with wild apocalyptic hopes.[2] He worked for a brief period, two or three years at most, in a remote province of a tiny country, and left at his death a mere handful of disciples, all of them very ordinary men. His significance lies in the tremendous movement to which, by a series of amazing accidents, his work gave rise. The message which in natural course would have been soon forgotten was taken up by a succession of great thinkers, who developed it into a sublime religion, pregnant with high conceptions of which he himself was not more than dimly aware.

For this reading of the history Jesus was in some measure responsible. His parable of the grain of mustard-seed,[3] perverted from its true meaning, has determined almost all our thinking about the church. It is assumed that Jesus himself, hardly knowing what he did, planted a tiny seed, which grew in the course of centuries into a mighty tree which has overshadowed the earth. His parable falls in with our modern idea of evolution, which has proved so fruitful in many fields of knowledge that we apply it everywhere. We assume that in our religion as in all else there must have been a process of growth, a steady unfolding of the germ into ever richer fulfilment. In one sense, no doubt, this has happened. The church has grown enormously larger. Its institutions have been elaborated. The beliefs with which it started have given rise to vast theologies. But all this growth affects our religion only in its

[2]This view is adopted, rather surprisingly, by Otto in his book, *The Kingdom of God.*
[3]Matt. 13:31, 32.

external aspects and has not touched anything that belongs to its essence. The truth is that in things of the spirit the law of development does not apply. Homer is still one of the greatest of poets. There are works of early Egyptian sculpture which have never been surpassed. No later reflection on the mysteries of being has gone deeper than that of ancient India. It has often been noted that in work of a spiritual nature the height is sometimes reached at the beginning. There have been poets and artists who have never repeated what they could do in early youth. Nations have had their golden age in the very dawn of their history. Most of all in religion, the earliest phase, more often than not, is the great and decisive one. A revelation comes suddenly to some inspired prophet, and for ages afterwards his followers reflect on it, and expound it, and embody it in creeds and ceremonies; but it is never again apprehended as it was at the very start. The beginning is also the consummation.

In the study of Christianity, therefore, the theory of development can help us little, and tends only to distort the obvious facts. It requires us to think of Jesus as of little importance, except that he happened to give the initial impulse to a great movement. But he certainly did much more. He created the movement out of his own knowledge of God. None of those later thinkers who are supposed to have advanced on his message had anything essential to add to it. None of them, indeed, were able to comprehend it in anything like the fulness which it had for himself. This can be affirmed with certainty, for we possess the message as he gave it. From the later theologies men have always gone back to those words of Jesus, not merely because he spoke them, but because they are intrinsically greater than anything that came afterwards. As the writer of Hebrews says of him, he was at once the author and the perfecter of faith. It is absurd to speak of his teaching as nothing but the inconspicuous germ out of which the grandeur of Christian thought was finally to develop.

In like manner the primitive church is not to be regarded as a mere grain of mustard-seed; and by thus thinking of it we are blinded to its true significance. No doubt the comparison is just when we reckon by mass and number. The church of the day of Pentecost was assembled in one upper room, and it has since grown into a countless multitude: this expansion of the church has been the miracle of history. Yet on a deeper view there has been no development, for the church in its earliest days was actually more than it ever was to be afterwards. For that little time it answered to its true calling, and was never to rise again to the same level. All reformers in times since have made it their aim to restore the church to at least some semblance of what it was in the primitive days. They have erred, as we have seen, in their emphasis on mere accessories. It does not much matter how the early church was governed, how it selected and ordained its leaders, what forms it adopted in its sacraments or the conduct of its worship. In all such matters it was guided by custom or prudence or circumstance, and for similar reasons we are free to break away from its example. Yet the conception of the primitive church as the model for all later times is far more true to fact than the other view—that it was only a crude experiment, a sort of child's drawing of what a church might be. The true church existed in that primitive community. There has been no development from an imperfect, tentative phase into one of full maturity. For one brief period at the outset the fact, in some measure, corresponded to the ideal.

We cannot speak of a development of the church, and at the same time it is false to think of a deterioration. There never has been a time when Christian men have not complained that the church was declining—that it has grown weak in faith, loose in doctrine, careless in moral standards. More especially in the older Protestantism the study of church history was dominated by the idea of a corruption that had set in after the close of the first century. Until that time the church had been pure. It had been free from all division, intent on its high vocation, firm in its loyalty to the genuine Christian teaching. Then, for various reasons, there had been a falling away. The original Apostles were now dead, and their successors were ignorant and weak. Gentiles had poured into the church, bringing with them their pagan beliefs and practices. Worst of all, a worldly spirit had begun to assert itself. Christians were no longer single-hearted in the cause, but were ambitious and self-seeking, and the church was turned into a half-secular society. Now it cannot be doubted that in this view there was a measure of truth. Even towards the end of the second century earnest men were beginning to feel that something had gone wrong. The Montanist movement, with all its extravagances, won a large following because it offered a necessary protest against the abuses which for many years had been creeping into the church.

Nevertheless, the old theory of a corruption which suddenly began after the New Testament period may now be thrown aside. It can be refuted, for that part, from the New Testament itself. The communities to which Paul wrote his letters were by no means examples of a pure Christianity. Paul has occasion to rebuke jealousies, divisions, even immoralities "such as are not named among the Gentiles."[4] The average standard of conduct in the later church was probably a good deal higher than in the first century. Moral education is always a slow process, and after two or three generations of Christian training a level was reached which was not attainable among converts who had come straight from heathenism. Much the same may be said of belief and doctrine. In the early mission it was difficult to impress the Christian ideas on minds to which they were entirely strange. Paul finds himself obliged to speak, in every Epistle, of lapses into Judaism or pagan speculation. In all the later New Testament books we hear of "false teachings" which had become a grave danger. Those early heresies, too, did not turn, like most of the later ones, on subtle differences of doctrine, but on strange beliefs which struck at the central principles of the Christian faith. It is thus historically false to think of the New Testament church as pure and the later one as subject to a growing corruption. Judging by ordinary standards there was rather a constant improvement. To Christians of the later generations the higher principles, in which they had been nurtured from childhood, were a second nature, and in the fires of persecution which now broke out at intervals the baser elements in the church were burned out. There may have been few conspicuous saints, but the average quality of Christian faith and living was always growing higher.

A change was indeed taking place, of which all thoughtful

[4]I Cor. 5:1.

Christians were keenly aware, but it cannot be properly described as a corruption. Its nature is best indicated in the Epistle to the Hebrews, where the writer deplores the indifference which had come over the church of his generation. It had lost the primitive ardour, the sense of something new and wonderful, the confidence that in Christianity God had given His final revelation. This change, as the writer himself recognizes, was partly due to mere lapse of time.[5] The first enthusiasm had now died down, as it was certain to do. Those who were born into the Christian faith were unable to prize it like the original converts, who had discovered it for themselves. But there were two special causes which had led to the indifference, and it is well to note them, for they have a close bearing on the whole problem of the early church.

On the one hand, the first disciples had looked for the immediate return of Christ to establish his Kingdom on earth. It was on this hope that the church had based itself, and now, to all appearance, it had proved illusory. The writer of Hebrews assures his readers that it still holds good. Years have gone by, but "yet a little while, and the Coming One will come and will not tarry."[6] It was difficult, however, to restore the old vitality to this hope, and the Christian attitude towards it was becoming ever more doubtful. Since the Lord had not yet come, would he ever come? Deeply religious natures were able, like the Fourth Evangelist, to understand the Coming in a spiritual sense and to perceive that Christ had already returned, as an inward presence, to those that loved him. But for ordinary Christians the hope had largely lost its meaning. From habit and training they remained in the church. They

[5]Heb. 5:12; 6:10 f.; 10:32.   [6]Heb. 10:37.

accepted its doctrines, and valued its moral guidance. But their religion was growing cold and perfunctory, since it was no longer quickened by the glorious hope which had inspired the early disciples.

There was another cause, closely related to this one, which acted still more powerfully in changing the character of the church. Since the Lord had not appeared and the Kingdom was not to come in immediately, it was evident that Christians must resign themselves to a continuance of the present age. They had believed at first that this world might be disregarded. It was so near its end that they could hold aloof from it and submit themselves without reserve to that higher law which would prevail in the future. Now it was recognized that this could not be. The existing conditions were to last on, and the Christian, like other men, must conform to them. He must mix with his neighbours and defer to their customs and prejudices. He was involved in a social system which had claims on him, and while holding to his religion he must bring it into some kind of harmony with the earthly life. There were always Christians to whom any concession to this world seemed to be like a betrayal. The writer of Hebrews belonged, apparently, to this Puritan type, and is anxious that the primitive code should still be observed in all its strictness. He declares that after the great renewal by which a man becomes a Christian no second repentance is possible; those who fall away will be irretrievably doomed.[7]

The church at large, however, accepted the fact that it was still in this world, and must allow for human weakness and limitations. As a consequence it ceased to insist on the absolute

[7]Heb. 6:4 f.

Christian rule, and many of its members, at least in the eyes of a rigorous judge, became lukewarm or quite indifferent. But the change was not in any sense a "corruption." Rightly considered, it was inevitable when once the church had begun to realize that it had to continue side by side with the world. We have to think not of a perversion but of an adjustment. After the failure of the original hope the church found itself in a new position, and had to choose one of two alternatives. Either it had to withdraw entirely from the world, or it had to adapt itself as best it could to the world's conditions, which were plainly destined to endure. It chose the second course. Maintaining itself as the community of the Kingdom it sought to make its home in the existing world, and it has pursued this effort for nearly two thousand years.

There is thus a twofold significance in the history of the early church. It reveals to us, on the one hand, what the church was, in its original conception, and must always essentially be. The first disciples looked for the Kingdom which Christ was presently to bring in at his glorious coming. They were the heirs of the Kingdom, which was so close at hand that they could live for it as if it were already here. The present world had ceased to exist for them; they belonged wholly to the world which was to come. On the other hand, we learn from that early history how the church gradually changed its character. It realized that the world was to continue, and that the new community must somehow fit itself into the given framework. Jesus had taught how men were to live in the Kingdom; could not his message be so applied and interpreted that they might live by it on this earth? The church was the community of the Kingdom, and it never ceased to be so; but it sought to be faithful to its high calling and at the same time to acclimatize itself in the present world.

This in all times has been the problem which has confronted the church. It stands for ideals and interests which cannot be realized by earthly beings, and the endeavour to live by them in their full extent is found invariably to defeat itself. Ever and again communities have arisen which have aimed at a perfect compliance with all the precepts of Jesus. They have forbidden any resentment of injuries, any personal desires or possessions. Societies of this kind have always made shipwreck, in a very short time, on the hard facts of the actual world. Individual Christians have set themselves from time to time to follow out literally the teaching of the Gospels, and we owe them an infinite debt. The meaning of Christianity would be quickly forgotten unless there were at least a few in every generation who have sought to bring home to us what the Christian life ultimately involves. Yet this complete obedience has always ended in some kind of disaster. No story is more tragic than that of the aged Tolstoi, broken in health and spirit, alienated from his family and friends, disappointed in all his hopes, dying miserably at last by the roadside—all because he had tried without reserve to follow the way of life which seemed to be enjoined on him by the Gospels. We are familiar in our time with the watchword "Back to Christ." It is continually impressed on us that if Christianity is ever again to become a living power we must throw aside all later interpretations and act, with perfect simplicity, on Jesus' own teaching.

"Christianity," according to Lessing's oft-quoted saying,

"has been practised for eighteen centuries, but the religion of Jesus has never been tried." This is true, and there is a reason for it, but it is not to be found in the perversity of theologians or the blindness and selfishness of the church. The religion of Jesus has never been put into action because it cannot be. It makes demands on us which, in the last resort, are incapable of fulfilment under the given conditions of this world.

Jesus himself was fully aware of the impracticable nature of his message. He admitted that "with man this is impossible" —in the present age the perfect will of God cannot be fulfilled; and this, as he clearly saw, was not due simply to the evil consequences of human greed and folly. Modern reformers are confident that if only we had some new economic system, if the opportunities for a good life were freely open to everybody, all the obstacles to a true Christian society would soon be removed. But Jesus himself was under no such delusion. He perceived that this world, however we may improve it, will still be the world. It is so constituted that so long as it endures men will be debarred from the higher life. A time will indeed come when the poor, the meek, the merciful, the sorrowing will be blessed; but the world, as we now know it, is plainly for the strong, the self-confident, the aggressive. Plants and animals thrive in their own climate, and the man who prospers in this world must always be the worldly man. Jesus pronounced his beatitudes on those who were looking for a different world. When it comes they in their turn will find happiness, but not till then.

We have here the great paradox of Christianity. It answers, like no other religion, to that law which, as Paul says, is written

in the hearts of all men.[8] With our deepest instincts we know
that its demands are right, and that love, truth, goodness,
fidelity have an absolute claim upon us. Yet by all earthly
standards the gospel, as Paul again acknowledges, is foolishness.[9] It runs counter to all maxims of prudence, to all those
courses of action which the world stamps with its approval by
its rewards of wealth, success, reputation, happiness. We have
here a contradiction which was brought, as it were, to a burning focus in the Cross of Christ. By all worldly modes of judgment the Cross was the supreme folly. Jesus had himself to
blame for the disaster. He had paid no heed to public opinion;
he had aroused powerful enemies quite needlessly; he had
taken no thought for his personal safety; he had wilfully
thrown away the happiness that was within his reach and had
aimed at the impossible. His death on the Cross, before his
days were half over, might well be taken as an awful warning
of how men ought not to live, and doubtless it was so used
at the time by many respected teachers. From their own point
of view they were right. If a man desires that all should go
well with him he must exercise ordinary wisdom. Jesus had
defied the principles on which this world is built, and he deserved his death, like a man who rushes blindly into a stream
of traffic, or lives contrary to all the rules of health. Yet the
Cross has appealed to all men since as the very symbol of all
that is highest and most glorious in human life. Jesus was
utterly wrong by all the world's standards; why do we have
that certainty that he was divinely right?

Only one explanation is possible. Belonging to this world
we must submit to its order, but we are conscious of another

[8]Rom. 2:15.   [9]I Cor. 1:23, 24.

world to which we also belong. It has an order of its own, different from the earthly one and most often opposed to it. In his ultimate nature man is a being of that other world, and in obeying its law he realizes his true life. Jesus called on men to live for the higher order. His disciples took up his teaching and sought to put it into effect, and for this purpose they formed the church as a brotherhood in which the new law of living should take the place of the old. But they presently found themselves confronted with an insuperable difficulty. What they had received from Jesus was the law of the higher and future order, and they were bound in by the present one, which is subject to a different law.

It is one of the commonplaces of modern religious teaching that Christianity is a very simple thing, which has been needlessly complicated by doctrine and ritual. Nothing is required of any one who would be truly Christian but to act consistently according to the rules laid down in the Sermon on the Mount. It is assumed that when Christianity is thus understood all the difficulties fall away, and it becomes a practical religion, within the reach of any high-minded man. This, however, is a profound error. If Christianity means obedience to the Sermon on the Mount, no one can ever hope to be a Christian. Not even the best of men could undertake to fulfil a single one of those precepts of Jesus for an hour together. To be absolutely pure and unselfish and sincere; to love one's enemies and forgive without limit; to have no care for tomorrow and trust everything to God; this is indeed Christianity, but who can attain to it? Men have sought to be Christians in many strange and difficult ways. They have remained for years on the top of lofty pillars; they have stood waist-deep the whole day in icy water, reciting prayers; they have forced themselves to believe every article of the most preposterous creeds. All this is easy, compared to a full obedience to the precepts of the Sermon on the Mount.

The law of Christ is manifestly impracticable. It requires that in this world, with our limited capacity as earthly beings, we should live by a rule which cannot be carried out except in a different order of things. The primitive church had thus a problem before it which it attempted to solve. Jesus had called on his disciples to live as in the Kingdom, and in answer to his call the church arose. But it found itself still involved in the earthly order, and its task henceforth was to reconcile the two loyalties. How could it be true to its vocation as the church of Christ, and yet adapt itself to the earthly conditions under which it must exist? In two ways, therefore, the study of the primitive church is of surpassing value. It enables us, on the one hand, to understand the church as it was at the outset, when it took its commission directly from the hands of Jesus. In the light of its beginnings we can perceive the intrinsic nature of the church. On the other hand, we see how the church entered on its task of integrating itself with the present world. The methods which it then devised have proved themselves, by the experience of many centuries, to be the most effective. Our task today is the same as it was then, and in all efforts to accomplish it we find our best guidance in the history of those first days.

CHAPTER II

THE CHURCH AND THE MESSAGE OF JESUS

From the beginning the church called itself by the name of Christ. It was made up of his disciples, and continued his work after his departure. Admission to it was by a rite of baptism in which he was acknowledged as "the Lord." That in some way it owed its existence to him cannot be doubted, and he has commonly been regarded as founding it by his deliberate act.

This belief might seem to be confirmed by the explicit evidence of the famous text, now inscribed in letters of gold over the shrine of St. Peter at Rome. "Thou art Peter, and on this rock I will build my church, and the gates of hell shall not prevail against it." This verse, however, is open to grave question. The passage of which it forms a part (Matt. 16:16–19) may well go back to some authentic utterance of Jesus, for the imagery is strongly Hebraic, and is fully in the manner of his other sayings. Matthew, whose gifts are merely those of a skilful compiler, could not himself have invented an utterance so bold and splendid and characteristic. As it stands, however, it is more than suspicious. Mark, on whom Matthew is dependent throughout the chapter, knows nothing of this addition, and it is quite out of keeping with the incident to which it is attached. Peter had earned no special privilege by his confession, for he had only acted as spokesman for the whole band of disciples. Nor can Jesus have been in the mood to congratulate and reward him, for he was accepting the Messiahship as a terrible burden from which there was no escape.

Apart from this passage there is no indication that Jesus ever contemplated the church in its historical form. One fact alone is sufficient proof that he was not consciously its Founder. When it entered on its career after his death it was obliged at every step to feel its own way, with many misgivings. Differences were constantly arising with regard to government, institutions, forms of worship, and they have continued ever since, with lamentable results to the harmony of the church. If Jesus had foreseen and planned a new community he would have prescribed at least a few simple rules for its guidance, as all religious founders have been careful to do. Apparently he made no such provision. The leaders who followed him were never able to settle any of their controversies on matters of church order by direct appeal to Jesus' own authority. He had often spoken of forgiveness, kindness, helpfulness, willingness to take the lower place. These general sayings with regard to social duties and relations were scrupulously preserved, and now and then they are so applied in our Gospels as to make them serve as rules for the Christian brotherhood. But nothing of a more specific nature could be found in his teaching. He had dealt with broad human relations, and had never, apparently, concerned himself with that particular society which was to take form in the church.

In the strict sense, therefore, Jesus was not the Founder of the church. It may plausibly be argued that a formal organization, with regular officials and stated ordinances, was contrary to his whole intention. He had looked for a time when no external bond would be necessary, and men would serve

God freely and spontaneously because they were in inward sympathy with His will. Nevertheless, the church was the direct outcome of the work of Jesus. This is evident, if from nothing else, from the fact that it had no formal beginning. Luke is aware of the tremendous importance of the new departure, and is anxious to find some definite occasion when the church began. He fixes on the day of Pentecost, with its wonderful manifestations; but whatever happened on that day it is apparent, from Luke's own narrative, that the church was already in being. Its members were actually in session as a church when they received the gift of the Spirit. There was no set day when the church was born. The disciples did not convene a solemn meeting and resolve, after full deliberation, that they would form themselves into a Christian society. They simply continued to live together, as they had done in Jesus' lifetime, and without their knowing the church came to be.

The view has been put forward in recent years,[1] and there is much to be said for it, that the ordinance of the Lord's Supper had a twofold root. It commemorated the Supper which Jesus had held with his disciples on the eve of his death, but this had been only the last of many similar meals which were well remembered. Jesus had been accustomed to close the day with a simple repast, at which he conversed freely with his companions; and it was on these occasions, more than on any others, that they had come near to him and learned to know him. In after days they associated him most vividly with these common meals. This would seem to be the suggestion in the

[1] It is admirably presented by A. B. Macdonald in his book *Christian Worship in the Primitive Church.*

story of the journey to Emmaus, when the two disciples failed to recognize their fellow-traveller until they began a meal with him and "knew him as he distributed the bread."[2] These words can have no reference to the Last Supper, for the two disciples are described as outside the circle of the Twelve. But all who were on terms of friendship with Jesus were familiar with his characteristic actions at the evening meals at which they had sometimes been present.

After his death it was only natural that his followers should maintain the practice of a common supper, and this is expressly mentioned in a significant notice in the book of Acts: "They continued in the fellowship and in the breaking of bread."[3] Jesus was no longer with them, but they could not take part in the accustomed meal without remembering how he had formerly presided at it. They believed that he was still invisibly present, and with the ordinary meal they combined a brief ceremony re-enacting what he had done and said at the Last Supper. In this theory there is much that is attractive, and it offers a natural explanation of how the Supper came to be adopted as a standing ordinance. In a manner it already bore this character. The disciples merely perpetuated the custom which Jesus had taught them, and around this custom the Christian society grew.

So when it is affirmed that Jesus himself was the Founder of the church, a fact of supreme importance is stated in the wrong way. He did not deliberately plan this new society but it originated with him, not merely because he gave the impulse which led to its formation but in a more definite way. It consisted, at the outset, of his personal followers, who aimed

2Luke 24:31.   3Acts 2:42.

at continuing after he was gone the life which they had known in his company. They believed in his promises; they sought to obey his precepts; they maintained the brotherly relation into which he had brought them; they perpetuated his custom of a common meal, and thought of him as still presiding. There was no break with their previous life, no new beginning. The church was simply the group of Jesus' followers, seeking to continue as they had been before. Their numbers grew, but they went on observing the fellowship which had begun under Jesus' direction, and in this manner the church arose. For some time it had no formal organization. Everything was left to the control of the Spirit, which had now taken possession of the community and was believed in some way to represent Jesus himself. Thus no line can be drawn between the company of disciples which Jesus had formed in his lifetime and the church that came into being after his death. It was the same community, expanding and shaping itself, and it had originated with Jesus himself.

Since the church thus arose unconsciously, of its own accord, there is no need to seek its origin in suggestions from the outside. It has been assumed often that Christianity simply took over the Old Testament conception of Israel, the chosen people of God, with the one difference that faith instead of race was made the bond of union. A view of this kind might seem to be adopted in the New Testament itself, and this is not surprising. The disciples were Jews, and knew of no other type of religious association than the Jewish community. They believed that God had made his promises to Abraham and would fulfil his purpose with the world through Abraham's seed. They took for granted, therefore, that the church was Israel, or at least the faithful remnant which in the sight of God, as the prophets had declared, was the true Israel. It is pointed out that the name which the church adopted, apparently from the outset, was "the Ecclesia," a name applied in scripture to the congregation of Israel. Paul in one place[4] speaks explicitly of "the Israel of God," and in the speech of Stephen, perhaps the earliest Christian document which has come down to us, the whole argument turns on the idea that Israel as a nation has been rejected and has surrendered its privileges to the true Israel, the church.

Now it cannot be denied that the Old Testament conception had far-reaching effects on Christian thought. Almost as soon as the church became fully conscious of itself it took the ancient community as its model and sought to bring its own ordinances into line with it. Jewish thinkers, especially in the Dispersion, had already given a spiritual interpretation to the old ritual, and it was not difficult to prove by this method that the church had its temple, its sacrifices, its rite of circumcision, its law and covenant. In all respects it was the Israel of the past, brought at length to its consummation. This line of thought is elaborately worked out in the Epistle to the Hebrews. Yet it is wrong to conceive of the church as breaking away from the old Israel in order to form a new one, similar in character but renovated and purified. So far from regarding itself as a substitute for Israel, its chief anxiety at the outset was to be recognized as a legitimate Jewish sect. So far from trying to repeat the ancient customs it laid all the stress on what was distinctive in its own worship and beliefs and mode of life.

[4]Gal. 6: 16.

It was the "new Israel" in the sense that while it remained part of Israel it was altogether new. Something different had emerged from the old conception of a chosen people.

The truth is that even if the Jewish community had never existed, the church, in all its essential features, was bound to result from the mission of Jesus. Those who believed in him felt themselves to be brethren, and in the effort to follow out his teaching could not but form a new society. As Jews they borrowed much from the example of Israel, but the wonder is that it affected them so little. Instead of copying the Jewish institutions they adopted new ones, springing out of the inherent nature of their new faith. Nothing is more remarkable than this independence which is everywhere manifest in the life of the early church. Perhaps it was due in some measure to the very fact that the disciples continued to be Jews, practising the old religion along with their own. They did not need to devise some equivalent for the Law and the priesthood and the ritual, for in their Jewish faith they had all these things already. Their whole mind was devoted to the discovery of what was required of them by their new beliefs, and they were able to build up the church with a splendid freedom. It was not the Jewish community over again, with a few minor differences, but was a new creation.

The roots of the church are thus to be sought in the Christian message itself, and to determine what the church was we have to consider the nature of that message. Within a generation it came to involve a number of new elements and was formulated by Paul in theological terms. Even when it was thus elaborated it depended for its meaning on one central belief, and this, at the outset, included everything. Jesus had declared that the Kingdom of God was at hand. All his teaching is concerned with this message, and his death also has to be understood in the light of it. The "gospel," as we now employ the term, has a wide variety of meanings, but for Jesus himself it was simply the "good tidings" that the Kingdom, so long expected, was now on the way. The church arose out of this gospel. In the last resort it was nothing but the message of Jesus, expressed in a concrete form.

Jesus never defined the Kingdom of God, partly, no doubt, because he could take for granted that his hearers all knew in a general manner what it signified. Ever since the days of the prophets the hope of Israel had been directed to a future time when God, who was now acknowledged only by His chosen people, would assert His sovereignty over the whole world. The prophets had looked forward to this future age, expecting that God would bring it in through forces that were already operative in human history. But in the century before Christ the hope had taken another direction. It now seemed apparent that in the present world evil had proved triumphant. Israel had been worsted in the struggle with earthly powers. Society was growing more corrupt and contained in it no elements which could possibly make for a better day. If God were to establish His Kingdom He must destroy the present order entirely and replace it with a new one. There can be little doubt that Jesus attached himself to this hope, which pervades the Jewish apocalyptic writings.[5] He took up the message of John

[5] It has been argued very ably by F. C. Grant (*The Gospel of the Kingdom*) that Jesus was little affected by apocalyptic ideas of the Kingdom. This view, however, involves an arbitrary treatment of the Gospel sources.

the Baptist that the Kingdom was at hand, and his message, at least superficially, was similar to that of John. A time of crisis was near in which the whole existing order would be dissolved, and God, by His own immediate act or through His agent the Messiah, would inaugurate the new age.

In one respect, however, the conception of Jesus was different from that of John and the apocalyptic thinkers. Apocalyptic had laid all the stress on the outward attributes of the Kingdom. The earth was to be ten times more fruitful; Israel was to overcome all enemies; pain and danger would disappear; heaven and earth would draw together, and men would be raised to the status of angels. Jesus may have accepted these beliefs, but he hardly touches on them in the whole course of his teaching, and they must have meant little to him. He speaks many parables to explain what the Kingdom would be like, but he never employs that sensuous imagery in which all the apocalyptic writers delight and which is familiar to us from the book of Revelation. His one interest is in the spiritual conditions which will prevail in the new age. Men will have the true knowledge of God; they will obey him gladly and spontaneously; they will be bound in loving service to each other; their aims and motives will be completely different from what they are now. All that belongs to the mere setting of the great future falls into the background; the one thing that matters is the new relation to God, the perfect obedience to His will. For apocalyptic thought the future world is essentially the present one, raised to a higher power, renewed and glorified, but intrinsically the same. Jesus thinks of a world which will be different in kind. The present order of things will give place to another.

It may be questioned indeed whether our modern knowledge of apocalyptic, which is supposed to have thrown a brilliant new light on the thought of Jesus, has not tended rather to obscure it. For the last half century all investigation of the Gospels has turned on the fresh data supplied by the apocalyptic writings. It is assumed that now, with the aid of these long-lost documents, we are in a position to define the real ideas which lay behind Jesus' teaching. We have learned to see that he was one in a succession of Jewish thinkers who were occupied with speculations about the future. His message of the Kingdom of God may be correlated with various passages in the apocalyptic books, and may thus be restored to its authentic meaning. This, however, is to leave out of account the one thing which is vital. By means of what he borrows from apocalyptic Jesus is seeking to express a great conception of his own. It had come to him, not from previous teachers, but by immediate vision; and all that really matters is this significance which the Kingdom had for Jesus himself. To use a very inadequate illustration, it has been proved that when Wordsworth wrote his glorious poem "Tintern Abbey," he had been reading Hartley, a minor philosopher of the eighteenth century, and had been impressed by some of his theories. A critical student of the poem would undoubtedly need to acquaint himself with the work of this forgotten thinker, but it was certainly not from him that the poet had learned to look on nature with "a sense of something far more deeply interfused." There may be ideas and phrases in the poem which can be better elucidated when we have studied the philosophy, but it owes all its splendour and passion to an intense experience which was the poet's own. So we come little nearer to an understanding of Jesus by a knowledge of his apocalyptic background. We run the danger, rather, of mistaking for his real intention what was nothing but its accidental wrapping. He proclaimed the Kingdom as he had himself known it, and as he would have known it although there had been no apocalyptic tradition. He might have expressed himself in different terms, but the substance of his thought would have been the same.

What did he mean, then, by the Kingdom of God, which he describes under those apocalyptic forms which were provided for him by the Jewish thinking of his time? Clearly he has in his mind something which is the highest conceivable good. The Fourth Evangelist does not employ the term "Kingdom of God," but represents Jesus as speaking always of "eternal life," and in some Synoptic passages Jesus himself identifies the Kingdom with life, carried to its perfection in a higher world. His idea is difficult and elusive because it is so comprehensive. In each period of Christian history it has taken on a new meaning, and has been understood as the communion of saints, the future blessedness, the inward fellowship with God, the moral law, the final brotherhood of man. Different as they are, these interpretations are all involved in the thought of Jesus, although each of them by itself is one-sided. They need to be blended together, and even in their sum total they are inadequate, for in Jesus' own mind they are only facets of a larger conception which includes and transcends them.

He was seeking, in fact, to express by the language of Jewish apocalyptic the truth which is fundamental in all religion. Men have always been conscious that over against the visible world there is another, which is the real one. Apart from this conviction man's life has no sense or value; the purposes which he knows in his heart to be the highest all fall to the ground. Religion in its ultimate meaning is nothing but this assurance of a higher, spiritual world. Jesus possessed it in a supreme degree. Living on earth he was continually aware of that higher order for which all things exist. We feel as we listen to his words that he is seeing through all veils to the divine reality. He lives wholly for that higher order which he calls the Kingdom of God.

It has often been disputed whether he thought of the Kingdom as in the future or as already begun. In a number of passages he seems to use the language of the present. He points to the works done by him as evidence that the Kingdom has come. He speaks of John the Baptist as closing an age which has now given place to another. He compares the Kingdom to seed which is already in the ground, although it has still to spring up and grow. The view has been held by some recent scholars that he conceived of his ministry as the actual beginning of the great final drama. Prophets and apocalyptists had looked for a day when God would interpose in human history and establish a new order. Jesus was aware that with him this higher dispensation had begun; and ever since although men have failed to perceive it they have been living under its control.

The theory is an impressive one,[6] but on closer examination it breaks down. For one thing, in spite of sayings that might appear to point the other way, the main emphasis of the

[6]Its best exponent is C. H. Dodd, in his books, *The Parables of the Kingdom* and *The Apostolic Message*.

gospel teaching is on the idea of futurity. The Kingdom is a glorious hope which sustains men in their earthly struggle and offers them a goal towards which they can strive. "Thy Kingdom come" is the central petition of the Lord's Prayer and is meant to define the abiding mood of the Christian life. Jesus was himself supported by this hope of the future Kingdom, and by means of it he seems to have explained to himself the purpose of his death. "I have a baptism to be baptized with, and how am I straitened till it be accomplished."[7] The work appointed to him was the bringing in of the Kingdom, and as yet he could not achieve it. Although the Kingdom was at hand there was some tremendous obstacle which stood in the way of its coming, and till this was removed he could effect nothing. How he conceived of this obstacle we have no means of knowing, and perhaps he never tried to define it, as Paul was to do afterwards. Yet he believed, when he saw his death to be inevitable, that in this way only could the barrier be thrown down. He had proclaimed the Kingdom and prepared men for entering it, but God had so willed that it could not be realized except through his death. This is the train of thought which seems to underlie the account of the Last Supper.

It may be gathered from the whole attitude of the early church that Jesus had described the Kingdom as future. The disciples were acquainted with his mind as we, who know it only through the few sayings preserved to us, cannot pretend to be. They were aware that he had looked forward to a great coming manifestation, and now they eagerly awaited it. The Lord had died and risen again and had thus attained to his

[7]Luke 12:50.

full office as Messiah. Everything was now ready. At any moment he might return from heaven, and the Kingdom which he had promised would become a fact. The mood of the early church is inexplicable unless we can assume that Jesus, by the whole tenor of his teaching, had inspired the disciples with a mighty hope. In the midst of seeming disaster they were able to wait with confidence for the fulfilment which was presently to come.

There is thus little historical basis for the theory that Jesus thought of the Kingdom as now realized; and its religious value is doubtful. As Paul says, when he declares that the Christian salvation is still future, "Hope that is seen is not hope, but if we hope for what we see not, then do we with patience wait for it."[8] His meaning is that hope loses its quality and its moral power when its object is assured. The Christian message must point forward to something not yet attained if it is to bring strength and endurance. In the Middle Ages the idea of the Kingdom as present succeeded for a time in capturing the Christian mind. The church was regarded as itself the Kingdom; whatever the church decreed was to be accepted without question as the final will of God. As a result of this mode of thinking religion was in danger of extinction. It was saved only by the enduring confidence that over against the church on earth there was the church invisible. The true consummation was still in the realm of hope.

For Jesus, therefore, as for the prophets and the apocalyptic teachers, the Kingdom lay in the future. If he seems at times to conceive of it as present this is only because it is so real to him that the brief period before its coming passes almost out

[8]Rom. 8:24, 25.

of sight. Here, it is sometimes held, he fell into a delusion which vitiated his message at its very centre. Not only did he work with apocalyptic ideas which have now lost their meaning, but he expected in the immediate future a fulfilment of which there is still no sign after all these ages. What can be the worth of a religion which was thus based on a palpable error? Now it may be granted that Jesus speaks, in the apocalyptic manner, of a coming age, and imagines it as near at hand. In this he was mistaken, but the mistake was due to nothing else than the clearness and certainty of his vision. The Kingdom was for him so real that he thought of it, not as a vague possibility or an object in the far distance, but as almost near enough to touch. When he says that it is at hand he only expresses his vivid sense of its reality. More than once, for that part, he disclaims any exact knowledge of times and seasons; all this he leaves in the hand of God. What he is sure of is the fact of a higher order, different from that which we know. In the Kingdom the laws of this world are reversed; all aims and desires and ways of living take a new direction; the will of God is perfectly fulfilled.

At a later time Christian thinkers, as they reflected on the message of Jesus, broke away from the apocalyptic scheme. They conceived, not of two ages but of two worlds, over against each other. For Paul and John and the writer to the Hebrews men can seek even now to rise out of the lower world into the higher. Jesus did not state his thought in this manner. He adhered, at least in form, to the apocalyptic tradition, and declared that God was shortly to destroy the present order and establish another in its place. But while he expressed himself in terms of time, his mind was set, as the later writers perceived, on the two opposing worlds. As men are now they cannot apprehend the Kingdom. Something conceals it from them, and the veil may be represented as one of time. Jesus was content to think of it in this manner, and declared that a day was coming when the Kingdom would be made manifest. But his real interest is in the contrast between the higher world and this visible one. Men have accepted the present order and conformed their lives to it, but there is another order of things in which the earthly standards and values cease to have meaning. As children of God men belong to this higher world. They must set their hearts on it and reach forward to it; they must undergo a change of mind so as to live henceforth according to its law. The apocalyptic setting does not affect the real thought of Jesus. When he declared that a crisis was at hand in which this world would come to an end and give place to the Kingdom, he meant, essentially, that the other order was entirely different from this one. All that now appears most certain must be counted as an illusion if we are to follow the true will of God. The teaching of Jesus would have been much the same even if he had known that the Kingdom, which he believed near at hand, would not come for ages. He never expected that it could be realized under earthly conditions. The present order must first come to an end, and it made little difference whether this happened tomorrow or after the lapse of thousands of years. Men could believe in it and set their minds on it and do God's will on earth as it is done in heaven. In this sense, that it might be apprehended as a present reality, the Kingdom was near.

Jesus thus conceived of the Kingdom as the higher order, entirely separate from that of the world we know. It cannot, therefore, proceed from this world but must come supernaturally. The view is often put forward in our day, as almost self-evident, that for the apocalyptic ideas employed by Jesus we must now substitute those of evolution. He looked for a tremendous change, and expected, in accordance with the thought of his time, that it would come suddenly and supernaturally. We have now learned that the great changes are not effected in this manner. The Kingdom is not to come in a moment, but, like everything else, must grow. It will come in, not by way of sudden miracle but gradually, through the silent, continued action of Christian men and women. They are helping it steadily forward by the creation of a better society, by increase of knowledge and mastery of material forces, by the constant amelioration of laws and morals. All this, however, is quite alien to the thought of Jesus—not because he lived in an unenlightened age, but because he drew a clear distinction between the earthly and the divine order. Man cannot bring in the Kingdom any more than he can control the tides and the seasons. It is God's Kingdom and man can do nothing but wait for its coming and prepare himself to receive it. So when Jesus describes it in apocalyptic fashion as appearing unexpectedly and all in a moment, he only uses the traditional language to express a cardinal element in his own conception. God will manifest His Kingdom by a divine act without any co-operation on the part of men. Yet He cannot so manifest it until men are earnestly seeking it, and to this extent they can help Him. They are to pray for the Kingdom; they are to repent and follow the new righteousness. God offers the Kingdom, and by seeking to do His will they respond to Him and prevail on Him to hasten His purpose. They can anticipate the Kingdom by trying to live even now as if it were come.

It has been pointed out by acute scholars in recent years that the teaching of Jesus involves a contradiction. He conceives of the Kingdom as still in the future, and as altogether different from anything we can yet know; but in all his sayings he presupposes the present conditions. He bids men be kind and just and merciful, although in the Kingdom there will be no suffering, no oppression, no weakness or poverty. He insists on the duty of forgiveness, but in the Kingdom there will be nothing to forgive, since no one will wrong his neighbour. He bids us trust in God, even when he seems forgetful, but in the Kingdom, when all will know God as the Father, it will be impossible to doubt Him. The Gospel ethic, it may be fairly argued, will all become meaningless as soon as the Kingdom arrives. It has reference not to the new conditions under which men will live hereafter, but to the present earthly conditions which will have passed away. The view has therefore been held that Jesus meant his teaching to have only an "interim" value. He thought of the Kingdom as coming soon, but not immediately. There would be a period of waiting, and his followers required to know how they should act in this brief but critical interval. No one can yet imagine anything as to the nature of life in the Kingdom. The relations of men to each other will be totally different from what they are now, and Jesus did not presume to lay down rules for that mysterious future. All that he offered was an interim ethic, which indeed made strenuous demands, for in view of the approaching Judgment the standards cannot be pitched too high. Yet the situation which he keeps before him is that of the existing order. According as men discharge their duty in it they will earn the right to enter the Kingdom.

This theory is based on the false conception that what Jesus gave was a number of set rules, which were to be literally obeyed. It is clear, however, when we examine his teaching more closely, that he was concerned not with rules but with principles. The various sayings and parables are intended merely as illustrations of how those principles should be applied. For this purpose he takes his examples from life as it is now, for he could not do otherwise. But the circumstances make no difference to the principles themselves. When the Kingdom comes, love and mercy will find expression in ways which we cannot yet imagine, but in essence they will be the same as they are now. The man who performs an act of kindness is doing God's will as it will be done in the Kingdom. His act, no doubt, is determined by conditions which will one day cease to be. He may be a Samaritan who takes pity on a wounded traveller whom others have passed by, and in the Kingdom of God there will be no robbers who leave men bleeding by the roadside and no selfish priests and levites. But kindness, however it is manifested, has the divine quality. It conforms to the will of God as it must always be.

But the theory of an interim ethic lies open to another and more serious criticism. Jesus cannot have meant his teaching to have only a provisional value, for it could never be put into action, even for the shortest interval. It differs from every other type of ethic precisely in this, that it always insists on the absolute standard. Love must be all-inclusive; forgiveness must have no limit; goodness must be unalloyed, like that of God.

An ethic of this kind is altogether beyond man's reach. In order to follow it man's whole nature and the world he lives in would need to be transformed. The idea that Jesus had nothing in mind but the moral requirements of a few months or years involves an utter misunderstanding. Instead of concentrating on the short time which has still to run, he disregards it altogether. He looks beyond this world to the higher one. The old commandments, as he expressly points out, were meant for the existing state of things. They made concessions to "the hardness of men's hearts," to the earthly hindrances and restrictions to which man's life is subject. A day is coming when all the conditions, inward and outward, will be changed, and Jesus is intent on showing what life will then be. It is not his purpose simply to raise the current morality, so that men may be better prepared for the approaching Judgment. He bids them throw away the present standards and look solely to the absolute will of God as it will be fulfilled in the Kingdom.

Jesus himself makes it clear that this is the nature of his ethic and is never tired of insisting that in the coming age all things will be different from what they are now. They will not only be different, but for the most part opposite. Men will have to reckon with an order in which the principles they have hitherto taken for granted will be reversed. Those who are first will be last. The kind of life which is here the wisest and most profitable will be mere waste and folly. It cannot be affirmed too strongly that what Jesus had in mind was not merely a steady progress by which the world will advance from its present phase to a higher level. All progress since he appeared has indeed been actuated by his teaching, but this does not mean that if we still continue to advance, in the direction to which he pointed, we shall finally attain to the Kingdom. The mariner steers towards the pole-star, but does not expect that if he only sails far enough he will at last reach it. Sailing round the earth he merely advances from one point on earth to another. Jesus bids us seek the Kingdom, and tells us that by seeking it we shall find guidance also in the present life. But the Kingdom itself will always remain unattainable.

We are not to think of Jesus, therefore, as an ethical teacher, whose primary interest is in the right conduct of life under the present conditions. He desires us to look beyond this world and live for the Kingdom. Again and again he says explicitly that the effort to obey him can have no other result than earthly failure. "If any man will come after me, let him take up his cross and follow me." The earthly order, with all its imperfections, is that which we must live in, and those who defy or renounce it are bound to suffer the penalty. This is fully recognized by Jesus. He impresses on his disciples that they must not complain if they meet with trouble, poverty, persecution, for they can expect nothing else. This world reserves its favours for those who accept its order, and this is only just. Nevertheless he calls on men to throw in their lot with the Kingdom of God, and live even now, in spite of all distress and calamity, as if it were come. Losing their life in this world they will find it. It must never be forgotten that when he made this demand he thought of the Kingdom as close at hand. Since the present order had almost run its course it might be left out of account. Men might cut loose from it and identify themselves boldly with the coming order, which was now the only one that mattered. He says in effect, "I demand of you what seems impossible, but the whole nature of things is presently to change, and this course of action, which appears so utterly unreasonable, will soon be the only wise and right one." He required that men should think in terms of the new age. They had grown so accustomed to this one that they could not conceive of anything different, but they must change their minds and become as little children. Even now, while they were subject to the earthly order, they must rise above it and look only to the will of God as it is done in the Kingdom.

It is this which gives greatness to the religion of Jesus. The demands of the higher world were for him so all-important that everything else was of no account. If men could attain to the Kingdom only by the sacrifice of all earthly things, then the sacrifice must be made. "If thine eye offend thee pluck it out and cast it from thee." Nothing must stand in the way of that utter obedience to God's will which is the supreme end of life. No other teacher has dared to make this absolute claim, and it cannot be questioned that in making it Jesus was right. If man is a spiritual being he must live in service to the higher order. Intent on the Kingdom, he will defy the world and the world will crush him; but at all costs he must choose for the Kingdom. Ideally Jesus was right, and his absolute demand will always lie at the heart of Christianity; and yet it will never be capable of a strict fulfilment. So long as he lives on this earth, man is bound up with the earthly order. Whether he will or not he is compelled to submit to its limitations, and they break him when he tries to escape from them. He cannot conduct his life in this world as if he were already in the Kingdom.

Here, then, we are to seek the true relation between Jesus

himself and the church which came into being after his death. In a real sense he was the Founder of the church. It arose directly out of his message of the Kingdom of God. The members of the primitive community were those whom he had called out of the present world to inherit the Kingdom which was now at hand. When they formed themselves into a church they were not conscious of creating something new but were only continuing the life on which they had entered while in Jesus' company. Now that he had died and risen again and was presently to return in his Messianic glory, they were assured, as they could not be in his lifetime, that the Kingdom which he had promised was close at hand. The church was thus the outcome of Jesus' message. It was the fellowship of those who had been called into the Kingdom, who were waiting for it, who were living as if the new order had now displaced the earthly one. This was the idea which called the church into existence, and which must always constitute its inner meaning. It is the community of the Kingdom, made up of those who are living for the higher order. The church as we know it may seem almost to have forgotten those visionary hopes which inspired its first members, but it still rests on that foundation. The Kingdom is at hand and men are to feel already that they are subject to its law. When this ceases to be its meaning the church will disappear.

At the same time there was another purpose in the formation of that early community. Jesus had proclaimed that the Kingdom was just at hand, but time went on and it delayed its coming. The old order which had seemed already to be a thing of the past was continuing, and was plainly destined to continue, no one could tell how long. What was the church to do in face of this unlooked-for difficulty? The law of Christ, to which it had bound itself, was that of the Kingdom, and under the conditions of this world could not be carried into effect. How was it possible, under the old order, to fulfil those demands which were intended for the new? This was the problem with which the church was confronted, almost from the outset; and in the effort to arrive at some solution it took on the character which it has henceforth borne. The church arose out of the message of Jesus, but it may also be said to have arisen out of the apparent failure of the message. Jesus had proclaimed the Kingdom and had created a brotherhood which should live for it and inherit it when it came. But it did not come, and the brotherhood which waited for it had to maintain itself in the present world. Unless it could be fitted somehow into the earthly scheme of things it could not hope to survive and fulfil its divine calling. In all times since the church has had these two aspects. It has stood for the higher order, proclaimed by Jesus, and yet it has fashioned itself as an earthly society, conformed to the order of this world.

CHAPTER III

THE INITIAL PERIOD

According to the book of Acts the church began on the day of Pentecost. On that day, seven weeks after the Passover at which Jesus had died, the little company of his followers was met together and suddenly heard the sound as of a rushing wind. A tongue of fire appeared to rest on the head of each one of them; they were filled with the Spirit and under the influence of this mysterious power went forth to proclaim their message. Luke has purposely invested the occasion with circumstances of awe and wonder, so as to enhance its significance. He wishes us to see in it a counterpart to the giving of the Law on Mount Sinai, when God made a covenant with His chosen people. But beneath the legendary colouring we can trace the memory of an actual event. At one of their meetings, some weeks after Jesus' departure, the disciples first became conscious of those strange powers which were henceforth attributed to the working of the Spirit. This day of Pentecost is selected by the historian as the day on which the church was born.

It must never be forgotten, however, that although a man's life is dated from his birth, it has had an earlier beginning. His birth, indeed, is not a beginning but a completion. That antenatal period through which he has lived unconsciously is by far the most important in his whole lifetime. It has determined for him all that he will henceforth be. He comes into the light a finished human creature, endowed with the faculties, the character, the personality which are to be unfolded during the years that follow. This was no less true of the church. Whatever may have happened on the day of Pentecost it only brought to a head the process which had been leading up to it. If we would discover how the church was made and what it was in its essential nature, we must examine with particular care that dim preliminary period when as yet it had no visible existence. The period was a short one, only a few weeks in duration, and yet it counted for almost everything in the after history of the church.

It may be said that practically nothing is known to us of those earliest days. This, however, is not true, for the memory of at least one tremendous fact has been preserved. It was in those first days that the disciples arrived at the conviction that the Lord had risen from the dead. The story of the Resurrection is beset with endless difficulties—critical, historical, philosophical—but one thing is certain, that the church was fully persuaded of the fact. We have to do, not with a myth created by fancy, or perhaps borrowed from an alien religion, but with a belief which was held by all Christians on grounds which seemed to them indubitable. It may be granted that new elements were drawn from various sources into the original tradition. Within the Gospels themselves we can trace a development from the relatively simple account in Mark to the circumstantial narratives of Matthew, Luke and John. But behind the tradition in all its forms there was the testimony of those who had themselves participated in the events of which they told. Not only so, but it was those primary witnesses who were most firmly convinced of the validity of their experiences. They stood out before the world as the men who could verify the fact of the Resurrection. They made it the central theme of their teaching. They proclaimed it with such evident sincerity that those who heard them were constrained to believe it on their word. Whatever we make of the story that has come down to us, it rested on some fact which for the earliest disciples was so certain that they accepted it as the very cornerstone of their faith.

It is to Paul that we owe the brief account which preserves the tradition in its most primitive and authentic form. He commences the argument of his great chapter on the future life (I Cor. 15) with a statement of how Christ himself had risen. The short passage (verses 4–8) is little more than a catalogue of the appearances of the risen Lord, first to Peter, then to other disciples, in groups or as individuals. Paul expressly says that he reports this list of the appearances as it had come to him, and again affirms, as he closes, that the account which he has given is endorsed by all the Apostles. There could be no nearer approach to firsthand evidence than this passage of Paul, written little more than twenty years after the event and recording the direct testimony of eyewitnesses, most of whom were still alive. The writer, moreover, is able to include himself as one who has shared the experience of which he speaks.

It is to be noted that Paul says nothing of the empty tomb and the incidents connected with it. Even if he knew this part of the tradition, which is questionable, he must have perceived that it was of quite secondary value, for the mere fact that a tomb was found empty could prove nothing. Many reasons why it was empty might be suggested, and none of them could be so improbable as that its occupant had risen from the dead. The only evidence that could carry conviction was that of some actual appearance of Jesus after his death, and Paul lays the whole emphasis on this. He tells how on six different occasions the Lord who had been laid in the grave was seen by his disciples. In view of these manifestations it was impossible to doubt that he was now living. It is highly significant that Paul puts the vision to himself on the same footing as the others. On the way to Damascus he had seen Jesus, not in the body he had worn on earth but in his radiant, heavenly body; and he leaves it to be implied that the visions of the earlier disciples were of a similar character. The whole chapter is written to prove that the new life will involve a new kind of bodily existence. What is sown a natural body will be raised a spiritual one. Those who believe in Christ will assume bodies of glory, and even if they survive till the Lord's coming they must all be changed, casting off their material bodies and receiving the heavenly ones which are the proper vesture of spiritual beings. Christ was thus transformed when he rose from the grave, and it will be the same with those many brethren of whom he was the first fruits.

It may be gathered, therefore, that in the original belief there was no thought of a mere reanimation. The disciples had visions of Jesus, the same in his personality as he had been on earth, but now a being of higher nature, clothed with a heavenly glory. Did those ethereal appearances correspond with something real? In all times since there have been some who would explain them from the heated fancy of the first believers, who cherished the memory of Jesus and persuaded themselves that he had come back to them in his habit as he lived. Modern psychologists have undertaken to trace out the whole experience. They point out that when an idea is intensely present in the mind it tends to visualize itself, as when Macbeth saw the dagger as a palpable object, with the handle towards his hand. So the disciples never doubted that they had seen Jesus, risen from the dead; but what they saw was a projection from their own minds, taking a visual form. The appearances which they believed to be real were only the outcome of their imagination. But the problem cannot be so easily disposed of. Psychology at the best can only explain the mechanism of that conviction which impressed itself on the disciples. Jesus, who had died, was again present to them; this was a fact of which they were certain. He had in some way "broken the bonds of death,"[1] and had made contact from the world beyond with his disciples living on earth. The method by which he had done so did not greatly matter. It might have been by some external manifestation; it might have been by some inward working of his spirit upon theirs, and the visual form may have been supplied by their own phantasy, as the interpretation in terms of sense of an inward perception.

Too much attention has been concentrated on the mere process whereby the appearances of the risen Lord may have been rendered possible. The real question is that of the fact. Did Jesus, by some means, subjective or objective, make himself known to his disciples after his death? They were convinced that he did so; and if this was true the method does not greatly matter. Peter himself probably could have given no coherent account of his state of mind when he received the first vision of Jesus risen from the dead. He could only have

[1]Acts 2:24.

said, as Paul says of his entrance into the third heaven, "whether in the body or out of the body I cannot tell."[2] The whole meaning of the vision for Peter was not in the mode but in the fact. He was conscious that after an interval of parting he had come again into personal relation with the Master whom he had known.

The real difficulty in the story of the Resurrection is not a critical or historical one, but the difficulty which always baffles us when we seek with our earth-bound intelligence to apprehend the nature of the spiritual world. We know that there is such a world, and that we ourselves are in some mysterious manner related to it. Yet it remains hidden from us, and we can never discover how it is linked up with the world we see. What are the conditions under which the soul continues to exist when it is parted from the body? How far can it communicate with those who are still on earth? By what signals can it suggest its presence across the barriers? These are questions which in all ages men have been seeking to answer, and which cannot be answered since they depend on a kind of knowledge which is withheld from us. The Resurrection of Christ is a mystery because it is bound up with that larger mystery of man's relation to the invisible world. All explanations of it are beside the mark so long as we are ignorant even of the first principles of those things which we are trying to explain. Nothing is certain except that the disciples were fully assured that they had seen Jesus in the days following his death. They may have described very imperfectly what they saw; they may not have understood the nature of their experience. But whatever it may have been it was sufficient to

[2]II Cor. 12:2.

convince them of the great fact that Jesus, whom they had known on earth, was still living in the higher world. On the strength of this conviction they built the church.

One thing is particularly noteworthy—that the appearances repeated themselves for only a limited time. Luke says explicitly at the beginning of Acts that "he was seen of them during forty days." In his Gospel he would seem to think of the visions as confined to one day, or at most two or three; but the longer period is undoubtedly in line with the original tradition. It is borne out by Paul's account in I Cor. 15, which allows for a series of incidents, spread out over a considerable time. One of them was the appearance to "above five hundred at once," and this large number could not have come together until the report that the Lord had risen had become generally known among his followers. Paul includes among the visions that which was granted to himself, perhaps a year later; but he admits that it was exceptional. The period within which the Lord had chosen to manifest himself had now come to an end. Why was it that the appearances were thus limited to a definite time, just at the beginning? The limitation cannot have been due to Jesus himself. If he had entered on his eternal life and was clothed with a divine power, he could not have been subject to any temporal constraint. There was no reason why he should not continue, in every time of doubt and difficulty, to appear to his people, and we might have expected that the whole of Christian history would be full of such manifestations as were vouchsafed to the first disciples. It is admitted, however, that even in that miraculous age the visions ceased after a few weeks' time. The favoured few who had received them did not, apparently, have the same experience again. It cannot have been that Christ was now unable to return to them, and the inability must have been in themselves. For a brief time they were sensitive to the Lord's presence, but their responsiveness gradually weakened and died out. Christ might return, and Paul was confident that he had done so to himself, on the way to Damascus, but the disciples were no longer capable of apprehending him.

This fading away of the visions might seem to bear out the theory that they were subjective, arising out of a mood of excitement which in natural course subsided. It is a familiar fact that in moments of high tension men have strange hallucinations; they hear voices and see apparitions, and act as they would never do in ordinary life. Another fact, however, must also be taken into account. What we are wont to call a mental disturbance is the necessary condition of all the highest experiences. In the normal placidity of life they do not come to us; there needs to be the moment of ecstasy in which we grasp in a moment the truth or the beauty which would otherwise be forever beyond our reach. The validity of the experience is not impaired because it is accompanied with that strange condition of mind; on the contrary, it is the very abnormality which makes the experience valid. It has come, as we say, through an inspiration—that is, by the only channel along which the higher knowledge must always reach us. Handel declared that when he wrote the Hallelujah Chorus he felt that he had been transported to heaven and was listening to the song of the angels. That, it might be said, was a delusion; his mind for the time being was disordered, and he ought to have been medically cared for until the fit was over. It may be so; but the sublime Chorus is no delusion, and without the mood of frenzy it could never have come into being. So the visions of the disciples do not in any way lose their value when they are put down to enthusiasts, moved with a wild excitement and hardly responsible for what they thought and saw. This is only another way of saying that they were lifted out of themselves. If intimations were to come to them from a higher world, they were in the state of mind which could respond to them.

It cannot be doubted that this was indeed their mood in the days which immediately followed the Lord's death. For a moment they had been prostrated by the awful calamity, and then came the reaction. They remembered that Jesus had claimed to be the Messiah who was to bring in the Kingdom. His death could be nothing but the means designed by God whereby he would enter on his office. Instead of frustrating His purpose it must in some way have accomplished it. The Kingdom which had hitherto been a distant hope must now be on the very point of fulfilment. One of the distinctive features of the Gospel of Mark is the prediction, repeatedly made by Jesus in the days before the Passion, that he would suffer and die at Jerusalem, only to rise again as the Messiah. It has been argued that these passages were added to the story later, in view of what had actually happened; but there is nothing improbable in the tradition that when Jesus warned his disciples of his impending death he also taught them to look beyond it. At the Last Supper he only repeated by means of symbols what he is said to have predicted in words, giving his solemn pledge to his followers that they would be reunited with him in the Kingdom which was now at hand. When the terrible crisis was over those who had listened to his promises could not but recall them. He had foretold his death, and it had come as he had said; they now awaited the victory which he had also foretold. In Luke's account of the two travellers to Emmaus we may discover a true analysis of the mood of Jesus' followers on the morrow of his death. They were dismayed by the blow which had fallen on them, and yet their faith was only waiting to be revived. When those two had at last recognized their unknown companion they said to one another, "Did not our hearts burn within us while he talked with us on the way?" They were already unconsciously aware of who he was, and in all the disciples during those momentous days there was the same thrill of expectancy. They were waiting for the Resurrection.

It thus belongs to the essence of the whole narrative that the visions came when the minds of those who received them were peculiarly sensitive. A mood of this kind could not be of long duration. Men are so constituted that they cannot escape for more than a brief interval from their ordinary selves, and even then the most trivial accident will at once throw them back again. According to the book of Acts the period of the appearances was about forty days, and the day of Pentecost may thus be taken as closing the initial phase of the church's history and inaugurating a second one, more impressive in its outward results but far less significant. It was in those first days that the church not only came into being but assumed the character which it was ever afterwards to bear. Historians are apt to take for granted that this brief initial time may be almost left out of account. It was only the empty leaf between two chapters of a volume. We may conceive of it, if we will, as occupied with the gradual recovery of Jesus' followers, as in a beneficent sleep, from the disaster which had left them helpless. This view may be justified in so far as the church of those first days had not yet wakened into consciousness. It was guided in its actions not by any clear purpose but by an instinct which it never tried to explain. Yet that short period at the outset was decisive for the whole future. The roots were forming out of which the church was henceforth to grow.

The visions of the risen Lord are not, therefore, to be taken by themselves. They need to be considered as evidence, not only for the Resurrection, but for that exalted mood out of which the church arose. During that short time at the beginning the disciples were in a frame of mind which they had not known before and were never to attain to afterwards. While they were in Jesus' company they had not grasped the full import of his message, and could only think of the Kingdom as remote and uncertain. In their later years it had again receded into the distance, as the present age reasserted itself and closed in around them. But for that brief interval after Jesus' death they stood as it were on a hilltop from which the end of the road lay clear before them. The great act had now been accomplished which would bring God's purposes to fulfilment. Jesus had died and risen again and entered into his glory and would presently return as Lord. The Kingdom was on its way; in everything except the final triumph it was actually come. In the age that followed, the disciples were to achieve great things, but they were never to regain the splendid confidence which inspired them at the very outset. As they ceased to have visions of the risen Lord, so they lost the faculty of apprehending the Kingdom as something that could be almost felt and

seen. But for that little time they were completely lifted out of
the world of sense. They had their being, as Christ's people,
in that higher spiritual order which he had proclaimed. For
once in human history the partition between the seen and the
unseen was broken down. A group of men and women were
seeking to live in the present world as if they were in that other
world where God is King.

It has been the error of most church historians to think of
the church as forming itself by a rational process. They have
asked themselves at every point, "What was the purpose of
this custom or institution? Why did the disciples act in this
particular manner? How is this belief or doctrine to be logically explained?" Endless ingenuity has been expended in trac-
ing back every action of the primitive church to its practical
motive, and in searching the other religions of the time for
analogies and possible influences. No doubt on the face of it
this is the method by which history ought to be investigated.
Man is a rational creature, and behind all his undertakings
there is some design, which he seeks to carry out according to
a reasoned plan. The customs of a savage tribe may seem to
be utterly meaningless, but it can always be shown when we
study them more closely that they are based on some kind of
reason. Rome and London were founded in a dim antiquity,
and we think of them as growing up at haphazard. Yet as we
examine their natural situation we can still make out the purpose which must have been in the mind of their founders, and
the processes by which means were adapted to ends. Columbus
sailed out into unknown waters, but he made his venture on
the ground of calculations, for the most part erroneous, as to
the shape of the earth and the position of the continents. It

is natural to assume that the church was formed in a similar manner. The early disciples created something new and strange, but they went about the work with an object more or less clearly defined, and thought out the methods whereby it might be attained. It seems obvious, therefore, that in order to explain the primitive church we have only to put ourselves into the place of the disciples, and consider what they wished to do, and the means at their disposal, and the models they were able to copy. All that seems obscure in the origin of the church will then become fully intelligible. But a method like this, though it may serve to elucidate most historical problems, cannot be applied to the primitive history of the church. We have here to do with something which was not the product of any design, and all effort to explain it rationally is labour wasted. The disciples in those first days were not deliberating and planning, but were seeing visions of the risen Lord. They were not providing by clever devices for the needs of the future, but were expecting the Kingdom of God to break in at any hour. Their minds were occupied wholly with the heavenly order which was now at hand, and all thought of worldly wisdom appeared to be mere folly. So in the study of the primitive church rational considerations are out of place. At a later time the work was carried forward by far-seeing leaders, who had definite aims before them and carefully thought out their measures; but they followed a course which had been determined for them in the days when everything was left to the free action of the Spirit. The church was like an island which has been thrown up by a convulsion of nature. A time comes when it is settled and cultivated and built upon; but when it first emerged it took on the configuration which it never loses, and which decides the character of all the later changes.

So we cannot understand the church unless we take account of the exalted mood of the first disciples. They waited daily for the return of Christ to bring in the Kingdom. For the time being they were lifted out of the present world, and felt that already they had part in the higher order. Old things had passed away; all things had become new. The church, it may be said, was the creation of an ecstasy. It did not arise from any set purpose to form a society for the promulgation of the new message, or for the replacing of the old Israel by a purely spiritual one. It arose out of a burning conviction that the Kingdom of God was all but come, and that men must break away from the present world and live for the Kingdom. This is the conviction which has lain ever since at the heart of the church, and which makes it different from all other societies. It is the community which stands in this earth for the higher spiritual order. Amidst all the changes which it has undergone in its government and doctrine and modes of worship and practical activities, this is its formative idea, and when it loses this it ceases to be the church. And when we look for the origin of this idea we can only find it in the rapturous mood which possessed the first disciples. They were sensitive in a unique degree to intimations from the higher world. They realized with a passionate faith that it was the one reality, and that they must forget all other things and set their hearts on it. The ecstasy soon passed away. It lasted in its full intensity only for those few weeks in which the visions of the risen Lord repeated themselves. Yet in that brief period the church received the impress which it has retained for nearly twenty centuries. A piece of iron is moulded when it is red-hot. Ever afterwards it remains a vessel, or a ploughshare, or a weapon, but it had to become so in the moment when it was liquid fire. So the church began without any conscious aim or plan as a little group of men who were caught up for an hour into a visionary world. Out of that mood of ecstasy the church as we still know it derived its being.

It arose as a community, and there is a question here which has never been adequately answered. Why is the idea of fellowship inseparable from the practice of Christianity? It is no doubt true that for any important enterprise men must join together, and the church is sometimes regarded as simply an aggregate of people who have found it helpful to unite their effort in the pursuit of a common aim. As members of a great society they can make their influence felt and can set their hand to large undertakings which would otherwise lie beyond their power. They can also encourage and support one another, and become better Christians as they follow the Christian life in congenial company. Thus we are wont to think of the church in terms of the numbers that compose it. It is the collection of Christian people, and the larger it can be made the more it becomes a church. Individuals who are nothing by themselves are transformed into a mighty force according as they are fused together in this great mass of Christian effort. The church, however, is much more than the total sum of its members. Community is an essential element in the Christian life itself. Through his union with others every Christian obtains something for his own soul which he could never have had if he stood alone. The church does not merely receive from each of its members some addition of power and significance.

It gives much more than it gets. It has a life of its own, quite apart from the individuals who happen to belong to it from time to time. As Paul recognized, it is the Body of Christ, and just as a hand or a foot is nothing when separated from the body so the Christian, cut off from the Christian fellowship, loses the vital principle which has made him what he is.

From the very outset the communal idea has been integral to Christianity. When Jesus entered on his ministry his first action was to attach to himself a band of disciples. Without this fellowship he could not have carried on his work, and his message would have lost half its meaning. The saying is ascribed to him, and certainly expresses his authentic thought, "Wherever two or three are gathered together in my name, there am I in the midst of them."[3] It does not matter how small the fellowship may be, but there must be fellowship of some kind, or the spirit of Christ cannot be present. This is an idea which underlies all the teaching of Jesus. He had come, not merely to win over a number of separate persons but to bring into a union those who believed in him. The name which he gave them was "the brethren," implying that there was a family bond which held them together. Most of his precepts are concerned, not so much with their individual duties as with their relations to one another. His final act was to hold a Supper with his disciples, consecrating them as a community which would cherish his memory and would be reunited with him in the Kingdom of God. After his death they continued this fellowship. In the few glimpses we have of them they are always together—in prayer, in study of the scriptures, at the common meal. As in Jesus' lifetime they are not merely a number of

[3]Matt. 18:20.

persons who believe in Jesus and look for his return, but "the brethren."

Why is it that the Christian religion from the outset has involved this idea of community? Many reasons have been suggested, all of them valid and weighty. Apart from the fact that men are by nature social, and must always stand in need of one another, it has to be remembered that in ancient times hardly any place was allowed to the individual. For all purposes of living men were assigned to definite groups and classes, and the man, severed from the group to which he belonged, had virtually no existence. This rule held good in religion as in everything else. Each religion was that of a tribe or city, and by their membership in this community the worshippers were related to their god. The idea of a Christian fellowship was no doubt affected to some extent by this ancient sense of solidarity. Again, it can easily be perceived how the teaching of Jesus led, of its own accord, to the formation of a brotherhood. He called on men to love and serve one another, and they could not do so except in a society. Christianity by its inherent nature has always drawn men into association. The monastic movement began, as the name implies, with "solitaries," who retired into the desert in order to live the Christian life without distraction. But they soon found that it was impossible under these conditions to follow the law of Christ, which called for the exercise of love, forgiveness, helpfulness. In the withdrawal from the world there still had to be community with others who had likewise withdrawn from it. Brotherhood, in some form, was of the essence of Christianity. Once more, it might be shown that faith itself, although it must be personal to every man, has the effect of bringing men into fellowship. "My own belief," said Novalis, "becomes twice as strong when I have found another man who shares it." This is profoundly true, and one of the great functions of the church has been always to provide this strengthening of Christian faith. "One Lord, one faith, one baptism, one God and Father of all."[4] The followers of Christ do not become fully conscious of their personal calling unless they can unite in repeating their confession.

None of these considerations, however, is by itself adequate to explain why the communal idea is so deeply rooted in our religion that the religion seems to dissolve when it is left out of account. Why can there be no Christianity without a Christian church? Perhaps the best answer to this question may be discovered in the light of Paul's conception of Christ as the "second Adam"—the progenitor of a new race of men. This was indeed the significance of the work of Jesus. Other teachers have aimed at some correction or enlargement of the ordinary ways of living. They have given their names to sects or parties, but their followers are distinguished only by their looking at some matters from a peculiar point of view. In all other respects they think and act in much the same manner as their neighbours. The aim of Jesus was to effect a complete transformation. Those who believed in him were to be different in their very nature from what they had previously been. They were to become as little children and enter on a new kind of life, based on a new principle. In other words, Jesus desired to mould humanity according to a different pattern. The "natural man," deriving his attributes from Adam, was to give place to this new type of man.

[4]Eph. 4:5, 6.

From this it followed that the Christian was not merely an individual who had put his faith in Christ. He was to be regarded, rather, as a single example of the new human type. He could not be rightly understood unless he was associated with the type to which he belonged. Now and then, in walking through the streets of a city, one comes on a person who is different in feature and complexion from the rest of the crowd. You know at once that although he is unlike the others he is no mere freak of nature. He is one of a race, and in some distant country there are multitudes like him. You cannot but think of him as lonely and miserable, away from those who speak his language and share his outlook on life. So the Christian is not only an individual but a member of a different race. If a day should ever come when there is only one Christian left in the world, men will indeed be puzzled by him. They will see at once that in all his character and behaviour he is unlike themselves. But they will recognize that although he is solitary he is one of a species. He stands for a race of men from which he has been severed. Somewhere, at some time, there must have been a human type of which this is an example.

Here then we are to seek the ultimate meaning of that instinct which led the Christians, from the very beginning, to form themselves into a community. In the last resort it was nothing but the affinity by which creatures of the same race are drawn to each other. Beneath the unity in hopes and beliefs and activities there was a deeper unity which may be described as one of kind. The Christians were reborn; their natures had undergone a change, so that they now belonged to a new type of humanity. It was only in fellowship with one another that they could rightly live their own individual lives.

The church, therefore, must not be regarded as something that developed later, and in some respects overlaid the message proclaimed by Jesus. His disciples, we are sometimes told, were not content with believing what he had taught. They joined together to form a community which assumed an ever greater importance in their religion, although it was only an afterthought and had little religious value. Christianity is one thing and the church is quite another, and the two must never be confused. The church may disappear, and some day will probably do so, but Christianity, as Jesus himself intended it, will endure. Such criticisms are due to a radical misconception both of Christianity and of the church. The purpose of Jesus was not to inculcate certain ideas about God and man's duty and destiny, so that we have only to cling to these if we would preserve all that is essential in his religion. He came to change man's nature at its centre, and so create an entirely new type of men. And the church is not a society of people who have agreed to accept the ideas of Jesus and maintain and propagate them. It represents that new type of humaniy which Jesus brought into being, and its rise and growth were inevitable, since it was involved in the primary intention of the Christian faith. The message and the community cannot be separated from each other.

So when we ask ourselves how the individual believers came to band themselves together in a church, we create a problem which does not exist. From the very start the community was implicit in the individual. A plant or bird or animal has no existence apart from its species. Its own identity is nothing but the species, manifesting itself in this particular form. A Christian, in like manner, is one with the new race of men which originated with Christ. He exemplifies in his individual life the higher type of humanity, and it is this which makes him a Christian. The church did not arise from the casual association of a number of Christians, for in a true sense the church was prior to its separate members. Jesus had created the new human type, and the Christians were those who were fashioned according to it. As Christians they belonged, by that very fact, to the church of Christ.

The church was thus involved in the Christian message, and there never was a time when the disciples did not think and act together. In his account of the first days at Jerusalem Luke lays emphasis above all on the sense of perfect fellowship. "They were all of one heart and one mind." "No one counted anything to be his own, but they had all things in common." Luke wrote in a time when the church had begun to suffer from division, and it may be that he has exaggerated the unity which had prevailed in an earlier and better day. But there can be little doubt that he has laid hold of a fact which had left an ineffaceable memory. In the days when the people of Christ had the clearest vision of the approaching Kingdom they were drawn most closely together. They were conscious, as they would never be again, that they were a new race of men, belonging to a higher world, and in consequence they felt themselves to be a brotherhood. There could be no surer evidence of how deeply the idea of community is implanted in the Christian religion. It did not grow out of any later reflection or practical necessity, but was given in the initial impulse. In a mood of ecstasy the disciples knew the Kingdom of God to be a reality, and in the same mood they knew that they must live for it as a church.

CHAPTER IV

WORSHIP IN THE EARLY CHURCH

The central thing in religion must always be the act of worship. It is indeed true, as all great teachers have insisted, that forms of devotion are nothing in themselves. There can be no genuine religion which does not express itself in the active service of God. But it is through worship that man becomes conscious of God, that he brings his own life into relation with the divine life. The power which urges him to acts of practical obedience is communicated by the approach to God in worship.

It has been the instinct of men in all ages to join together in their worship of God. Nothing, it might seem, can be more personal than the act in which a man withdraws from the world and presents himself, with his deepest needs and aspirations, before his Maker. This, however, may be the very reason why the sense of fellowship is necessary. In solitude a man is wrapped up in himself, and finds it hard to realize the larger, permanent issues of his life. Through association with others he is able to escape from all that is trivial and accidental. He becomes aware of the great human needs which lie at the roots of his nature, and which he therefore shares with his fellow men. "I pray," says the Apostle, "that I may comprehend with all the saints what is the length and breadth and height of the love of God."[1] The emphasis here is on the communion "with all the saints." By this alone can we rise out of our narrow,

[1] Eph. 3:18.

— 70 —

particular point of view and apprehend God and our own life
in all the dimensions. We make our approach to God with that
which is divinest in ourselves.

The primitive disciples were accustomed to worship in the
Synagogue. This institution was perhaps the most valuable gift
which was made by Israel to the general life of the world. How
it originated we have no means of knowing. It may. have
begun during the exile, as a substitute for the lost services of
the Temple. It may have developed earlier out of the worship
at those local "high places" which were suppressed when all
ritual was centralized at Jerusalem. If it existed in any form
during the ancient period nothing is said about it in the Old
Testament, except incidentally in a late Psalm,[2] where the reference is doubtful. On almost every page the Old Testament
has much to say about the Temple, which as we can now see
was infinitely less important than the Synagogue. With its
priesthood and sacrifices it was merely a survival from primitive times, and had its parallel in all ancient religions. The
Synagogue was a new creation, growing directly out of the
religious genius of Israel. Its purpose was to bring the worship
of God into harmony with those higher conceptions which had
arisen in the minds of the great prophets. God was invisible,
and His worship was made independent of everything that was
sensuous and external. He was the righteous God, and desired
that men should serve Him by moral obedience. They were to
meet before Him to meditate on His will, as it was revealed in
His holy law. The rise of the Synagogue may be compared, in
its historical significance, with the invention of printing, though

[2] Ps. 74:7.

in some ways it marked an even greater revolution. By the art of printing, knowledge was set free, so that all men could have access to what had formerly been the privilege of the few. The Synagogue made it possible for the mass of men to participate in the higher religion. Without it the work of the prophets would have gone for little. Their teaching, like that of the Greek philosophers, would have been intelligible only to small groups of the gifted and cultivated. Through the Synagogue a spiritual religion was brought within the reach of all. Judaism, Christianity, Islam, all religions which have based themselves on the higher conception of God, have modelled their worship on that of the Synagogue. It is bound to continue, under varying forms, as long as men interpret their religion in terms of the moral life.

The Synagogue worship was extremely simple, and consisted of three parts: reading of the Scriptures, in which God spoke to man; prayer and praise, in which man spoke to God; an address, in which man spoke to his fellow man. These must always remain the essential elements of spiritual worship, and the aim of a Christian service is still to allow due place to each of them. Jesus himself worshipped according to the forms of the Synagogue, and they were adopted, as a matter of course, by his disciples. From the outset, however, the church made certain additions to the Jewish forms, and it did so, not from any deliberate purpose, but in the unconscious effort to express the new Christian beliefs. It was through these new elements, grafted on the ordinary service, that the worship of the church assumed its distinctive character.

Before considering these modifications of the service it is

necessary to take account of one peculiar change which goes back to a very early time, and possibly to the beginning. Why was it that the sacred day was put forward from the seventh day of the week to the first? The Sabbath was the cardinal institution of Judaism, and the smallest infringement of the Sabbath law, as we know from the Gospels, was regarded with horror by every pious Jew. It might have been expected that the complete abolition of the Sabbath by the transference of its rights to another day would have been intolerable to those Jewish sentiments which the disciples shared with their countrymen. A change in the Sabbath meant an attack on the very citadel of the Law, and yet we look in vain in the New Testament for even the echo of any protest against this sacrilegious change. The controversy over circumcision almost rent the church asunder, while the transference of the Sabbath came about so quietly that nothing is told us of how and when it was effected. Among Jewish and Gentile Christians alike the custom was established, apparently without demur, of observing the common worship on the first day of the week.

We have here one of the most curious problems in Christian history, and many theories have been put forward for its solution. The customary explanation is that the new day was adopted in memory of the Lord's Resurrection, and there can be no doubt that the day associated with their primary belief was doubly sacred to all Christians. But the change cannot have been due to any mere sentiment. For Christians, as for Jews, the ten commandments were inviolable, and there could be no tampering with the explicit law of God "Remember the seventh day to keep it holy." There is, indeed, no sign that this law ever was set aside, and the change of day, it may be conjectured, has a simple and natural explanation. The primitive believers continued to observe the Jewish custom, and worshipped on the Sabbath in the Synagogue as they had always done. At sunset, however, the Jewish day ended, and there remained a few hours in which every one was still free from labour. Those hours after the close of the Sabbath could be used by the church for its own meeting. The day of rest was still continuing, and yet technically a new day had begun.[3] So after their Sabbath observances were over the brethren met for their common meal, and in conjunction with it held the Lord's Supper and their own Christian service. It followed the general lines of the Synagogue service, but allowed place to those new elements in which the Christian beliefs and emotions found direct expression.

To begin with, therefore, the Christian meeting was a sort of evening service, which rounded off the customary worship of the Sabbath. It was known as the meeting on the first day of the week, and when the mission spread to the Gentile world, and the Gentile reckoning of time was adopted, Sunday became the Christian holy day. This was the more natural as this day was already associated among the Gentiles with religious functions. It was dedicated to the Sun, the first and most glorious of the planets, and from remote times had been set apart for high solemnities. Jewish Christians, wherever they were, would continue to observe the Sabbath, but also met with their Gentile brethren on the first day of the week. Gradually, as the church became completely Gentile, the Sab-

[3]This solution to an old, and perhaps insoluble, problem has not, to my knowledge, been offered before, and may be taken for what it is worth. The best discussion of the general question is that by J. Cotton, *From Sabbath to Sunday*.

bath ceased to differ from other days. Christian reverence attached itself wholly to the Sunday.

It was probably in some way like this that the church was led to change its day of worship, and the character of the worship also underwent a change. For one thing, while the service was modelled on that of the Synagogue, each of its component parts was given a Christian colouring. The passage read from Scripture was no longer a section of the Law, but a prophecy which seemed to point forward to the Messiah and his work. It would appear, too, that from the outset the words of Jesus were placed on the same level as Scripture. The passage of prophecy would be conjoined with sayings of his which brought out its meaning, or with the recital of some incident in his life which had given it fulfilment. Prayer was offered, as in the Synagogue, but not in the stated liturgical form. It was uttered freely, on the impulse of the Spirit, and was presented in the name of Christ, the Intercessor. Christ himself was often directly addressed in prayer. Paul tells the Corinthians how he had "besought the Lord thrice" to relieve him of his bodily affliction, remembering, perhaps, how Jesus had healed the sick while he lived on earth. One of the names by which the Christians described themselves was "those who call upon the name of the Lord," that is, who invoke him in prayer. Hymns were sung, as in the Jewish service, but they were not the traditional Psalms, or later imitations of them. The Christian faith gave rise to hymns of a new character, often produced in the heat of the moment and almost as soon forgotten; but sometimes short lyrics of real beauty which were treasured and repeated. Such hymns are occasionally quoted in the New Testament, as in the verse, "Awake thou that sleepest and arise from the dead, and Christ will give thee light."[4] Paul expressly states that this is a quotation, and it is plainly Christian in origin and can only be part of a hymn. Similar hymns can be traced in the "faithful sayings" of the Pastoral Epistles and in the songs of the book of Revelation and of the opening chapters of Luke's Gospel.

As prayer was addressed to Christ, so he was often the object of hymns of adoration. This was so distinctive a feature of Christian worship that Pliny mentions it in his letter to Trajan as one of the peculiarities of the strange sect which he had encountered in Bithynia. "They meet together and sing a hymn to Christ as a god." This pagan evidence is borne out by some of the fragmentary hymns quoted in the New Testament. To this day, although prayer to Christ has been generally discontinued, he is still addressed personally in many of our most beautiful hymns. Most Christians would feel a hesitancy in offering prayer to him, and the same reluctance grew up, apparently, in the early church. The Fourth Evangelist declares in so many words that Jesus must not be prayed to, but that prayer must be offered to God in his name.[5] It is not easy to explain why prayer to Christ, which in ordinary form offends the Christian instinct, should become entirely natural, indeed necessary and inevitable, when it is expressed in song. From the first the believers used this outlet for their devotion. They held converse with Christ who was invisibly present in their meetings, and prayed to him in improvised hymns.

The worship of the church was thus modelled on that of the

4Eph. 5:14.   5John 16:23.

Synagogue, while at the same time a Christian meaning was impressed on each part of the service. But there were other elements in the worship which were purely Christian in origin. Chief of all these was the observance of the Supper, of which we have already had occasion to speak. This, indeed, was not so much a part of the worship as the vessel which contained all the parts. The purpose of the Christian meeting was to hold the common meal, and to make it a memorial of Jesus' Last Supper with his disciples. That Supper had been his pledge that he would shortly return to establish the Kingdom. In repeating the ordinance the disciples reminded themselves of his promise, and it was this which determined the whole meaning of the acts of worship which followed. The worshippers were filled with a sense of the nearness and certainty of the Kingdom. They were able in some measure to anticipate it. In this meeting of the brotherhood they escaped from the world and were caught up for an hour into the coming age.

The worship was thus ecstatic in its character, and the distinctive feature of it was the exercise of the charismata, or spiritual gifts. Scripture had foretold that the advent of the new age would be marked by the outpouring of a divine power, the Spirit. This had hitherto been bestowed only at rare intervals on men appointed by God to some great task, kings, deliverers, prophets. A day was coming when the power from above would be the common possession of all God's people. "I will pour out my Spirit on all flesh. Your sons and your daughters will prophesy; your young men shall see visions, and your old men shall dream dreams."[6] The primitive disciples were conscious of a faith and ardour which lifted them above them-

[6] Joel 2:28.

selves, and awakened in them mysterious faculties of which they had not hitherto been aware. What could this be but the operation of the promised Spirit? A heavenly power was now manifest in the heirs of the Kingdom.

Of the new gifts the strangest and most impressive was the ability to "speak with tongues"—to express intense emotion in what seemed to be a real though unknown language. The phenomenon was one which has appeared not infrequently in the history of religion, down to our own day. When any emotion becomes so strong that it cannot be put into words, it finds relief in cries or sobs or ejaculations, and this is true also of religious emotion. But for some reason which has never been adequately explained the cries which afford an outlet to religious feeling will sometimes take on the character of an articulate language. It may be that the mind, groping helplessly for words in which to express itself, falls back on a mimicry of words, inventing them on the spur of the moment, and stringing them together in what appear to be sentences. However it may be explained the imitation of language is sometimes so close that even in modern times the *glossolalia* has been mistaken for a foreign tongue, which would be fully intelligible to some race in the past or in a distant part of the world. Luke appears to hold this view, and describes how on the day of Pentecost strangers from all lands were gathered in Jerusalem, and recognized their own languages as they listened to the Apostles.[7] Paul, however, is aware that the new form of speech has nothing to do with any that is used on earth.[8] To man it has no meaning, but is understood by the Spirit, through which it is given. He suggests that the "tongues" are nothing

[7]Acts 2:5–8.   [8]I Cor. 14:2–4.

else than the language of the angels, so that the believer, under the impulse of the Spirit, prays in the very language which is used in heaven.[9] It was never questioned in the early times that the gift was supernatural, and its sudden appearance, so soon after the departure of Jesus, was regarded as a direct confirmation of the Christian hope. The disciples were waiting for the Kingdom, and now they had received the Spirit, which was to be imparted to God's people in the new age. It revealed itself in a manner that could not be mistaken by the gift of tongues, but this was only one of its activities. The believers could feel that in everything they had become new men. They were endowed with a fresh courage, a deeper religious insight, a new apprehension of God and of things unseen. All this had come to them through the Spirit, which Christ had sent upon his church out of the higher world to which he had now ascended. In place of himself he had given the Spirit.

The exercise of the spiritual gifts was thus the characteristic element in the primitive worship. Those gifts might vary in their nature and degree according to the capacity of each individual, but they were bestowed on all and room was allowed in the service for the participation of all who were present. "When you meet together," says Paul, "each of you hath a psalm, a teaching, a tongue, an interpretation."[10] Every member was expected to contribute something of his own to the common worship. In most cases the contribution would be a modest one, a sentence or two of personal confession or adoration, or perhaps a mere "Amen." But there were those who were peculiarly gifted with the Spirit and who prophesied or engaged in ecstatic prayer. It is difficult to make out whether

[9]I Cor. 13:1.   [10]I Cor. 14:20.

a special interval was allowed for those free devotions, or whether they accompanied the service throughout. Paul is himself anxious that they should be confined within due limits. He acknowledges the value of the enthusiasm, but insists that although it breaks out spontaneously it should be held under control, and he declares that this is possible. "The spirits of the prophets are subject to the prophets."[11]

Christian worship had thus a root of its own. It was not merely an outgrowth of Jewish worship but sprang out of the new convictions which had taken possession of the church. Jesus had proclaimed the Kingdom which was just at hand, and the aim of his followers was to throw themselves forward into this higher order. As they met together in worship they could feel themselves set free from the earth-bound life. The Lord had achieved his victory, and for those who believed in him the Kingdom was now a reality. They were able to share in the raptures and speak the very language of that heavenly company in which their own brotherhood would presently be merged. A worship of this kind could not long be maintained. Nothing is more sincere than a high emotion, but it quickly passes, and when the attempt is made to perpetuate it the result too often is some kind of make-believe. All that remains of the original mood is the repetition of forms and words and gestures which no longer have anything real behind them. This was no doubt the reason why *glossolalia* and the other early practices came to be abandoned. There are signs that they lingered on till after the close of the first century.[12] They were never formally suppressed, and again and again they have

[11] I Cor. 14:32.   [12] *E.g.*, various allusions in the Epistles of Ignatius.

been revived; and when the revival has come spontaneously they have had spiritual value as they had at the beginning. But it was felt increasingly that they were produced by a conscious imitation. A simulated enthusiasm is always offensive, and never so much so as in the sphere of religion.

Here, as Jesus himself was always impressing on his hearers, the one thing needed is an utter sincerity. God sees in secret, and knows the real mind of those who profess to be seeking Him. To approach Him with a pretense of fervid longing and devotion is the worst hypocrisy. A time came when the primitive type of worship had ceased to be sincere. Paul could perceive, before the first generation was over, that his converts at Corinth were using the spiritual gifts for parade and self-assertion. It may be inferred that even at that time religious emotion was deliberately cultivated, and before long the phenomena which had once seemed to come supernaturally were produced by a studied technique. This has been the fatal error in many subsequent revivals. They have begun with a genuine fervour, and have brought new life to the church by breaking with the formalism of ordinary worship. But they have ended by replacing it with a worse kind of formalism. Spiritual manifestations in which the Spirit has ceased to be present become a positive hindrance to the true service of God.

An answer may here be found to the charge which is brought so frequently against the historical church. It is alleged that after New Testament times the original faith died out and everything became frigid and external. An official ministry took the place of that of the Apostles and prophets; prayer was offered in liturgical form; laymen were excluded from an active part in the service; the accessories of religion were magnified at the expense of the thing itself. Not only so, but elements of pagan worship crept more and more into Christianity. The ordinances of Baptism and the Supper were assimilated to the rites of heathen cults. Sanctity was attached to symbols and relics and buildings. Art was brought to the aid of devotion, with the result that idolatry came back in all but name. All this, it is held, was indicative of a growing corruption which had changed the Christian religion into something which the first Apostles would have refused to acknowledge.

Now in such a view there is no doubt some measure of truth, but several considerations always must be borne in mind. For one thing, when once the church had undertaken to impress its message on the world, it needed to avail itself of every help which the world could afford it. By adopting symbols and practices which to the pagan mind were the necessary vehicles of religious ideas, it was not false to its own teaching. It was only seeking, in the one practicable way, to make its teaching intelligible. Again, it always has to be remembered that art is a language, just as much as a spoken or written one. To the Mediterranean peoples, with their inborn æsthetic feeling, it was the language which conveyed ideas most expressively. The believers who worshipped in the Catacombs were not conscious of any idolatry when the message of Christ was put before them in pictures. They apprehended it better. As they contemplated the picture of the Good Shepherd they were able to realize more vividly that Christ was still present and was guiding his people. Above all, the new forms of worship were indispensable when the first ardour had spent itself, and the spiritual gifts had lost their spontaneity. The aim of the church was now to cultivate the mood of reverence. Rapture, if it is to mean anything, must come of its own accord and only lasts for a moment, but reverence can be fostered and made habitual. Men can so dispose their minds that at any time they can turn to God and feel that He is near them. The church was intent, in the later time, on devising forms of worship which would produce reverence in place of the earlier enthusiasm. It surrounded its service with impressive ceremony; it threw its prayer into liturgies, couched in grave and noble language; as time went on, it devised beautiful buildings and stately music. All this was external, but the aim was to create the frame of mind in which men might offer a spiritual worship.

It is only right that we should recognize this motive which underlay the increasing emphasis on what might seem mere form and ceremony. As a matter of historical fact the development of ritual went hand in hand with the rise of Christian mysticism; and this was no matter of accident. It was the conscious purpose of the church to change the act of worship into a means of inner communion with God. The worshipper was made to feel, as he took part in the solemn observances, that he was in God's presence. He was called on to perform a number of outward acts, but in so doing he was conscious of an inward experience, and it was in this that his worship consisted. This conception was already familiar to thoughtful Jews of the Dispersion. It underlies the whole thinking of Philo, who seeks, with the aid of allegory, to interpret the Jewish ritual in terms of the inward life. Worship, as he understands it, is in essence a condition of soul, and the external acts have value only as they serve to reflect and to foster this condition.

From an early time Christian thinkers took up this idea,

which was felt to be in harmony with Jesus' own teaching. Paul speaks of a "reasonable service,"[13] that is, one which is offered by the mind. Men are to wait on God with pure thoughts, and hearts attuned to do His will, and only as they attain to this inward disposition do they truly worship Him. The writer to the Hebrews declares that all ritual acts are of the nature of types, pointing to a spiritual reality. Christ has now entered into a heavenly sanctuary and the old ceremonial has disclosed its true purpose. The people of Christ have passed with him through the veil, and have an immediate access to God. It is significant that the writer has nothing to say about any of the specific ordinances of worship. He indeed warns his readers against neglect of the customary meeting, with reference, most likely, to heretical sects which regarded all formal worship as now unnecessary.[14] But he prizes the visible service because it reminds the brethren, as they take part in it, that Christ has now opened for them "a new and living way." This mode of thought comes to its fullest expression in the great declaration of the Fourth Gospel: "God is Spirit, and they that worship Him must worship in Spirit and in truth." The whole of this Gospel may be regarded as an exposition of the idea which is here stated in explicit words. Worship consists in an inward fellowship with God through Christ. Forms and places, all mere external acts, are now subordinate. Christ is present in the heart of each believer, and in communion with him we share in the divine life.

It must never be forgotten, then, that this conception of spiritual worship underlies the apparent formalism of the later time. The early disciples were convinced that the Kingdom

[13]Rom. 12:1.   [14]Heb. 10:25.

was almost come, and this belief determined the nature of their worship. They were conscious of a release from the present life and all its restrictions. They leaped forward in a mood of rapture into the new age, when they would hold immediate fellowship with God. As time went on this mood no longer answered to a real conviction. There was no falling off in faith and devotion, but it was now apparent that the Kingdom was not to come immediately. What was needed was not the ecstatic mood but a settled habit of trust and obedience. It is important to note the change which now took place in the conception of the Spirit. At the outset the Spirit was associated wholly with the strange powers which manifested themselves in sudden visions and utterances. For Paul, however, these had become of secondary value. He thinks of the Spirit as an abiding possession by which the Christian is governed in all his thought and action. The whole of the Christian life is life in the Spirit. Exercise of the spiritual gifts had been the distinctive feature of Christian worship, and in a real sense it continued to be so. But ideas had now changed as to the nature of these gifts. One thinks again of that declaration in the Fourth Gospel: "The hour has come when they who worship the Father must worship in Spirit." For a member of the primitive church these words would have carried a well-defined meaning. They would have suggested that the time was past when worship was confined to a number of set acts and ordinances. Place must be given to the impulses of that new power which was now working in the church, the Spirit which expressed itself in tongues and prophecies. It is in a different way that the Fourth Evangelist understands the worship in the Spirit. He thinks of God as the invisible presence with whom the worshipper can hold communion in the quiet of his own heart. The one object in the later type of worship was to make possible this inward sense of God. Sudden raptures were now held in check, and all was done "decently and in order."[15] The worshipper was enabled without distraction to concentrate his mind on the eternal things. He was assisted in this effort by the accessories now grafted on the service—liturgical forms and symbols, an ordered ceremonial conducted by regular officers. These were only externals, but they served to compose and direct the mind and lift it into a higher atmosphere. There was a spiritual value in the very repetition at every service of the same pious formulæ and observances. Connected as they were with the act of worship and handed down reverently from one generation to another, they acquired a sacredness of which every worshipper was aware. Instead of reducing the service to a dead routine they provided a channel in which Christian feelings and aspirations could naturally flow.

It is thus wrong to assume that after the fervour of the early time, worship became merely formal and ceremonial. The spontaneity may have passed out of it, but in some respects it had grown more truly spiritual. The church had laid to heart Paul's new conception of the Spirit as manifesting itself not in spasmodic outbursts but in a constant mood of Christian faith and living. The primitive type of worship was bound up with the conviction that the world was all but finished and the new age was now breaking in. When this belief had lost its reality the church felt the need of a worship that could be sustained. It was indeed one of the great achievements of the church that when its early anticipations had failed it devised those solemn

[15] I Cor. 14:40.

forms, with the aid of which men could still separate themselves from the world and look forward to the Kingdom of God.

It cannot be denied, however, that the new mode of worship was fraught with a serious danger. Outward forms were employed as a means of awakening and supporting the mood of devotion; and this was wise and necessary. From the time of the prophets onward religious teachers have insisted that worship must be accompanied with the right frame of mind. If this is lacking the most impressive ritual can have no worth, while the publican who only beats his breast in heartfelt repentance will be heard by God. This is profoundly true; yet there has never been a religion which could dispense with forms of devotion. Just as thought must express itself in speech, so religion has need of some outward manifestation or it will wither and die. It is true in religion as in poetry that substance and form must go together. Nevertheless there is always a danger that the forms will take the place of the substance. It is almost a law of religious history that a faith originally vital is smothered at last by the ritual which was intended to preserve it. Noble liturgies have become a mere patter of unmeaning words; devout practices have decayed into superstitious habits; symbols once laden with spiritual import have grown empty. This has happened again and again in the history of Christianity, and almost every reformation has had for its object the discarding of an outworn ritual. The encrusting forms have to be broken before the spirit can be released.

In this work of reformation the watchword has always been, "Back to the primitive church." Worship in those first days was independent of all forms. The brethren simply met in some upper room and surrendered themselves to the higher power which moved within them. They needed no priesthood or traditional rules but offered the free worship of their hearts. But these efforts to revive the primitive practice have never succeeded. This may partly be explained on the general principle that it is never possible to restore what has once been. A custom or mode of thought may at one time have served its purpose admirably, but it was interwoven with the whole fabric of its age and all the old conditions would need to be re-established before it could be the same again. This principle holds good in religion, more perhaps than in anything else. In our relation to God there must be absolute sincerity, and we cannot rightly serve Him when we are living in one age and try to go back into another. Apart, however, from this larger difficulty all revivals of the primitive church are bound to fail, for the same reason that it failed itself. It sought to base worship on a mood of enthusiasm which could not, in the nature of things, endure. The fervid expectation of the Kingdom died away, and the type of worship which answered to it became forced and artificial. The church was saved because it learned in good time to adopt settled modes of worship. It ceased to demand that whenever they met together its members should work themselves into a rapture, and required only that they should wait on God reverently and thus open their hearts to His presence. It taught that this also was worship in the Spirit.

Yet it must never be forgotten that Christianity began as an ecstatic religion. While still in this world men felt themselves lifted into a higher one, and in this condition of mind they had glorious visions, and gave utterance to exultant cries. Religion has its roots in the conviction that beyond this visible sphere of things there is another, and the effort always has been to apprehend it. In hours of high experience or quiet meditation we can assure ourselves of its existence, and feel it pressing in upon our common life; but this is not enough. There is an unquenchable desire to grasp as a reality what we surmise or dream of. The traveller who catches from a hilltop a faint glimpse of the far-off city is filled with the longing to bridge the distance and pass within the gates. How can this desire be satisfied? From the earliest times one method has offered itself and has been practised in many forms. Religion has been associated with ecstasy, induced among the more primitive races by physical means, intoxication, whirling dances, dissonant music. Exciting himself into a frenzy the worshipper has been able to feel that he has broken through the earthly limits and soared into the higher life. Shortly before the Christian era this cruder form of ecstasy had been sublimated by the mysticism which had come in from the East, ultimately perhaps from India. A number of cults had found their way into the Western countries, differing at many points from one another but all turning on the idea of rapture as the one means of entrance into the invisible world. The theory has been widely maintained in recent years that Christianity was closely related to those contemporary cults, and it is more than likely that some Christian teachers, and especially Paul, were influenced by ideas and practices which they had made familiar.

It is certain, however, that Christianity had sprung from sources entirely different from those of the Oriental cults. In its central beliefs and motives it had nothing in common with them. Its character was permanently formed, even in matters of detail, before the alien influences can possibly have begun to operate. Yet early Christianity was akin to the cults in so far as it was, like them, an ecstatic religion. When the brethren met together they prophesied and spoke with tongues. Stephen beheld the heavens opened, and the Son of man standing at the right hand of God. Paul gloried in his visions and revelations. John in the isle of Patmos was in the Spirit on the Lord's day, and saw the things that would be hereafter. The condition of the early Christian worshipper was one of ecstasy, not compelled by artificial methods as in the other religions, but springing of its own accord out of a passionate conviction.

This mood may be illustrated from that which every one has known after the sudden hearing of good news. For the moment you lose consciousness of everything around you. You cannot control your own mind and body, and are hardly responsible for anything you do or say. Paul tells us that a stranger, watching the Christians at their worship, was apt to believe that they were mad;[16] and from Paul's own descriptions and those in the book of Acts a modern reader may get the same impression. Was there not something childish and absurd in those tumultuous meetings, where everybody was trying to speak at the same time, and no one could tell what the others were meaning, or what he meant himself? It seems strange to us, and not a little humiliating, that our religion should have arisen out of such beginnings. Yet we do not think it unnatural that at the siege of Lucknow, when the relieving army was at last heard in the distance, all who were left of the desperate garrison broke out into wild sobs and cries. In this there was nothing unworthy or ridiculous; how could they act otherwise in such a moment?

[16] I Cor. 14:23.

And the primitive worshippers acted in the same way, for the same reason. They had become suddenly aware of a great salvation, and were full of rapture, too intense to find utterance in words.

The ecstasy of early Christian worship was thus inherent in the nature of the message. Christ had won his victory and the Kingdom of God was now on its way. The believers knew themselves to be heirs of the Kingdom; they could feel that they were now standing at its very threshold, that already in some sense they had entered it. As they met together and realized the marvel which had befallen them, they could not but be seized with rapture, and the raptures could find no outlet but in inarticulate cries. The worshippers had ceased for the moment to be normal men and women, expressing themselves in rational language. Their condition was that of Paul when he was caught up into the third heaven, whether in the body or out of the body he could not tell.

The rapturous mood died out as the church abandoned its hope of the Lord's immediate coming, but it was never forgotten that Christian worship originally had been ecstatic. The feeling persisted that it should always be so, and from time to time the effort was made to restore it to its true character. Those revivals, for the most part, were allied with millennarian movements. It was believed that the hour of the Lord's return had only been deferred and was now imminent, and whenever this belief arose it produced a type of worship similar to that of the primitive church. Sometimes the note of rapture was recovered in a different way. For men of deep religious spirit, as for the Fourth Evangelist, the apocalyptic hope in its literal form had little meaning. The Kingdom as they conceived it was to be realized in the soul itself, and they sought to enter it by mystical contemplation. By this means they sought to obtain the beatific vision which would flood their whole being with rapture. At least for an instant they would be transported out of this world and share in the heavenly worship.

These efforts all broke down because they could result in nothing permanent. Worship is a fundamental human need, which cannot be satisfied when it is only possible at rare intervals, when the mind is stirred with a peculiar excitement. A service of reverence may seem cold and external, but it can be sustained and constantly repeated. It may not afford the exultant vision, but it offers a means whereby men may be conscious always, in their common life, of the presence of God. If the ordinary service appears to consist of little else than pious forms it may be answered that this is necessary. Without those forms there could be no stability and continuity in the Christian life. Yet it remains true that Christianity began as an ecstatic religion, and this must always be an essential element of its nature. The primitive belief in the nearness of the Kingdom was no illusion. It took an apocalyptic form, and was so far mistaken, but it corresponded with the fact, proclaimed by Jesus, that there is a higher order in which men are to find their true life. The church exists for the very purpose of witnessing to the nearness and reality of that other world, and if its worshippers could apprehend their faith in its full import they could not but know something of that rapture which possessed the first disciples.

This truth has never ceased to impress itself on the minds of devoted Christians. They have shared in the ordinary worship of the church, but have felt all the time that it was not satisfying. Tertullian was the most intellectual of the Fathers—the man who did more than any other to give strict definition to the Christian doctrines. Yet in his later days he threw in his lot with the wild millennarian sect of the Montanists. He perceived that with all their extravagance they had laid hold of a great truth which the church had forgotten. Christ had come to bring fire on earth. His message was one which kindled and inspired, and those who were content to serve him with a dull, conventional worship had missed his purpose. Edward Irving in modern times was an eloquent preacher who charmed a cultivated audience in London, but it broke in upon him that his methods were all wrong. If the Spirit had once been active in the church and had spoken in tongues and prophecies, why should it now be otherwise? The Spirit must still be present in Christ's people, and ought not to be kept down when it was burning to utter itself. Irving, like Tertullian before him, was disowned by the official church. He exposed himself to ridicule and made shipwreck of a noble life in his vain endeavour to bring back to Christianity that essential thing which, to his mind, it had lost.

It may be granted that these men and others like them were mistaken, in so far as they tried to recover the primitive ardour in just the forms which it had taken in the primitive church. To this extent they were unfaithful to their model, for the early disciples used modes of utterance which came to them spontaneously and which had no meaning when they were consciously imitated. Yet the main perception was a true one, that Christianity is, in its essence, an ecstatic religion. It began with a glorious hope which still burns at the heart of it, like the fires at the earth's centre. The world is passing and the Kingsdom is at hand; old things have passed away, behold all things have become new. This was the Christian message, and this it must always be, and those who have responded to it are lifted out of themselves. They are filled with a rapture which cannot wholly express itself in formal prayer and ritual.

The problem of Christian worship is to make room for this element of ecstasy without which it must always be incomplete. We have come to associate all that is irregular in worship with eccentric sects, or with illiterate people who are governed more by their emotions than by their minds. If their practices were introduced into an ordinary church service, as they were by Irving, intelligent men and women would be shocked and resentful. This in itself might be salutary, but there would be a danger not merely to the sense of decorum, which matters little, but to that of reverence. In the act of worship there must be no distraction. There needs to be order and calm around us if the mind is to withdraw into itself and concentrate on the eternal things. It is easier to draw near to God at a Quaker meeting than amidst the excitement of a so-called revival. Nevertheless it remains true that in the Christian religion there is something volcanic. Those who have caught the vision of a higher world are thrilled with emotions which demand an outlet. It is certain that in every Christian gathering, amidst the crowd of merely formal worshippers, there are some who are touched with rapture; their number is perhaps greater than we ever guess. How can a place be found in our worship for this ecstasy, which is not artificial but at least sometimes is the natural and heartfelt mood of the Christian man? If the mind of our time is growing dull to the meaning of Christianity the reason may be largely this, that in our worship there is so little of that fire, that active manifestation of the Spirit, which was present in the early church and which belongs to the intrinsic nature of our religion.

CHAPTER V

THE ORGANIZING OF THE CHURCH

The book of Acts is a work of history, but it is written, like the historical books of the Old Testament, with a religious purpose. It was planned by Luke as the sequel, or rather the continuation, of his Gospel. In that first part of his work he had recounted the earthly life of Jesus, who had appeared in an obscure province of a remote country and had travelled here and there with a small band of disciples, teaching and healing, until he finally went up to Jerusalem, where he was condemned as a malefactor and put to death. The book of Acts takes up the story where the Gospel had left off. Its theme is still the life of Jesus, but of Jesus risen and glorified. His company of disciples became a great multitude. It spread over Palestine, then into Syria and Asia Minor. Under the leadership of Christ and in the might of his Spirit it made its way into Europe, and found a centre in Rome itself. The movement which had begun so humbly in Galilee was plainly destined, in the fulness of the time, to conquer the world.

The purpose of the book, therefore, is to prove by historical fact that Christ was from God, and that his message was instinct with a divine power. In no other way could the marvellous progress of the new religion be explained. It has been customary, ever since Gibbon wrote his famous chapters,[1] to question this thesis of the book of Acts. Christianity, it is

[1]Chapters XV and XVI of the *Decline and Fall*.

granted, made an almost miraculous progress, but this is mainly to be accounted for by a happy conjunction of natural causes. Everything was in favour of the Christian mission. The world had been unified under the Roman Empire, and was looking for a religion in which men of all races could agree. Greek philosophy and Oriental mysticism were working together, and had created a frame of mind which was highly susceptible to a certain type of religious teaching. Jesus had appeared at just the critical moment, and though he was only the founder of a Jewish sect, which in ordinary course would soon have died out, his message had elements in it which were capable of a wide appeal. By a remarkable chance it was taken up by several men of extraordinary gifts, most notably by the Apostle Paul, who adapted it to the thinking and the social needs of the Gentile world. As a result it became the nucleus around which a universal religion was able eventually to form.

At this distance of time it is not difficult to advance such theories. After any movement has succeeded it always can be shown that the success was inevitable, and all manner of unsuspected forces can be discovered which were working to its advantage. But the truth is that Christianity, through the whole course of its early history, had everything against it. If it had failed instead of succeeding, there would have been no trouble in demonstrating that it was bound to fail. It originated among a people who were generally regarded with disfavour. Its Founder had been executed as a criminal, after trial before a Roman court. Almost from the first it was opposed by all the ruling powers as dangerous to the state. Not only so, but its teaching was hopelessly out of sympathy with the mind of the age. It defied those principles of reason which for all intelligent men of that time had an absolute authority. It stood for a morality which belittled the traditional virtues and threatened to undermine the whole existing order.

When we look at early Christianity with the eyes not of the modern historian but of the ordinary citizen of the first century, we cannot but wonder that it ever survived. All other religions were left free under the tolerant Roman administration; this one alone was persecuted, because it was plainly in conflict with all that men desired or believed. Why was it that in spite of hostility it went on from strength to strength? According to Luke it was because a divine power accompanied the Christian mission. Its Apostles had no help from without, and encountered every sort of difficulty, but the message they proclaimed was from God, and He endued them with His Spirit. This, for Luke, was the clear significance of the marvellous expansion of the church, and however we may choose to express it in modern language this interpretation of the early history is surely the right one. The triumph of Christianity cannot be explained from any combination of external causes. It was due to something inherent in the religion itself. A new power had entered the world through Christ and was working irresistibly through his church.

Luke is thus justified in regarding the outward progress as a visible evidence of the divine character of the message, but he is himself conscious that there was another side to the picture. He recognizes that with all the progress something was lost. In his opening chapters he describes in glowing colours the community of the first days. The disciples were filled with the Holy Spirit. Their faith was certain of itself. All were of one mind and heart, and no one counted anything to be his own. Everywhere in the book we are meant to perceive a contrast between the later church, with its hesitations and divisions, and the ardent brotherhood of the first days. This is no doubt due, in large measure, to the illusion of distance. Luke idealizes the age before him as the subsequent times idealized his own, which to himself appeared degenerate, infested with grievous wolves, not sparing the flock.[2] Yet his contrast between the early church and the later one answered to a fact of which all Christians were sensible. The church as they knew it was no longer what it had been in the opening days. It was prospering outwardly beyond the wildest hopes, but the glow and exaltation had passed out of Christian faith. Their religion for many had become a matter of routine, and almost of indifference. Ventures and sacrifices which had once been made gladly were never attempted.

There are many evidences in the New Testament of this decline which was everywhere apparent in the second and third generations. It may be partly accounted for by the reaction which always follows a tense excitement. Every high enterprise is launched on a wave of enthusiasm, and the most difficult things are done almost without effort. Then comes the ebb, and the work which was once a joy becomes painful, and can be carried forward only by a stern perseverance in some fixed rule. This was certainly the experience of the early church; but besides the natural lassitude it had to reckon with a sense of failure. The first disciples had been confident that the Lord was presently to return. He had died and risen again, and at any hour might appear in the clouds of heaven, bringing in the Kingdom. In this assurance the disciples had been

[2]Acts 20:29.

able to disregard the world they lived in. It had lasted its time and was now as good as over, and they would have part henceforth in that higher order which was to come. For a brief enchanted interval, following the death of Jesus, they lived as if they were already in the Kingdom. But time passed on, and the Lord did not return. The hope of his coming was never abandoned. It was believed that the glorious coming had only been deferred, and that there were those still living who would witness it. Late in his career Paul was confident that he himself would survive until Christ appeared, and that he would be caught up, in a body transformed, to meet him in the air. A generation afterwards the saying went abroad concerning one long-lived disciple that he would not die, but would tarry till the Lord came.[3]

But although the hope was never discarded, and has persisted to this day, it grew ever fainter. The church resigned itself to an indefinite waiting. For years, and perhaps for ages, the world would continue as it was, and there would be no manifestation of the Kingdom of God on earth. To many Christians in the New Testament times this meant nothing less than a shattering of their faith. The writer to the Hebrews laments the carelessness into which his readers had fallen in consequence of their disillusionment. This frame of mind was still more prevalent half a century later, when we hear of doubters who were saying "Where is the hope of his coming: for since the fathers fell asleep all things remain the same as they were from the beginning."[4] The church at large, however, maintained its faith in spite of all disappointment. It frankly accepted the fact that the Kingdom had not come as the first

[3] John 21:23. [4] II Peter 3:4.

believers had anticipated. The world was not to disappear but was to endure as before, with all its hardships and restrictions. Christians had therefore to adjust themselves to these conditions under which they were compelled to live. Instead of trying to assume that the Kingdom was on the point of coming, they must learn to fit their Christianity into the framework of this present world.

The study of Christian origins has always suffered from the failure to define exactly what is meant by "the church." This term may denote the church in its intrinsic character of the holy community, the fellowship of those who have identified themselves with the Kingdom of God. In this sense it owes its existence directly to Jesus, and is bound up with the very idea of Christianity. But when we speak of the church we commonly have in mind the historical organization, with its creeds and rituals and schemes of government. The attempt is made to trace back this ecclesiastical system to Jesus himself. Since it is the church he must have foreseen and planned it, and the structure which arose afterwards was only the realization of his own design. Thus Newman put forward an ingenious theory of "development," using this term in much the same sense as that which it bears in photography. Jesus created the church, just as we know it in later history, but he left everything in miniature. The task of the artificers who came afterwards was to educe the larger picture which was latent in what seemed to be nothing but a blur. All was there, down to the minutest detail, but it took centuries to disclose fully what was hidden. This, however, is to confuse two different things. What Jesus originated was the brotherhood which waited for the Kingdom. This community of his followers survived his death, but it shortly began to assume a shape which he had not contemplated. The church was indeed the consequence of the work of Jesus, and at the core of it there is still the formative idea which it derived from him. But this idea and the visible organization are not to be confused together.

It would hardly be wrong to say that the church, in its historical form, had its origin, not so much in the message of Jesus as in the apparent failure of the message. Jesus had declared that the Kingdom was at hand, and his followers had understood him literally. They united in a fellowship which regarded the present world as in the act of passing, and which lived wholly for the approaching Kingdom. It became increasingly certain that this hope was premature. The Kingdom did not come, and if the fellowship were to continue it had to be placed on a different basis. Since the world was to last on, the believers must accept it. They must constitute themselves as a society similar in character to those around it and able to hold its own in the existing order. One thinks of the old explorers who set out. confidently on the quest for El Dorado. They never doubted that it lay somewhere in front of them, just over the horizon, and on their march they built rude settlements which might serve as resting-places. The Golden City always remained distant, and as the hope of it faded those settlements took on a new importance. They grew in the course of time into the great cities which we know today. It was in much the same manner that the historical church arose and expanded. Like the explorers the early disciples set out with a magnificent hope. They formed the little community, meeting in an upper room, which would presently be reunited with

The Organizing of the Church

Christ in his Kingdom. The Lord did not return, but the community endured and built itself up into the worldwide church.

At some time, then, while it was still confined to Jerusalem, the church underwent a momentous change. Luke, the earliest of church historians, is aware of this change, although he is still too near to perceive its full nature and significance. We can now see, much more plainly than he could do, what was happening in the time succeeding the day of Pentecost. The .community of the Kingdom was transforming itself into an earthly society. Instead of holding separate from the world, the believers had resolved to accept it and to accommodate themselves to its requirements. This ·change of attitude was not effected all at once. The belief that Christ was coming and that with his return a new order would set in was a fixed element in Christian faith, but more and more it fell into the background, or was understood in a purely spiritual sense. With this waning of the primitive hope there came a change in the character of the church. By degrees it took on the form of an ordinary association, modelling itself on others, both Jewish and Gentile, with which it was thrown into contact. At the beginning it had existed solely for the Kingdom, and had acknowledged no other control than that of the Spirit. Now it began to present two aspects, one of them directed to the Kingdom and the other to the world.

The outstanding mark of this change was the growth of an organization. In the initial period there had been no thought of an official ministry, set rules of procedure, a definite creed and method of worship. When the Kingdom came men were to serve God spontaneously because they were in complete harmony with His will, and the church belonged to the Kingdom. It sought to make itself entirely different from earthly societies, which were held together by law and compulsion. "The kings of the Gentiles exercise authority over them, and those that rule them are called benefactors. But ye shall not be so; but he that is greatest among you let him be as the younger, and he that is chief as he that doth serve."[5] This injunction, attributed to Jesus, was put literally into practice. The church proclaimed its affinity with the new age by discarding all the trammels which are imposed by this one. Its members could feel that they were called into a perfect liberty, such as men would know when the Kingdom of God had come in.

For that brief period, when the brethren were few, and all of one heart and mind, and sustained by a high enthusiasm, the ideal was in some measure attainable; but very soon it had to be abandoned. The Kingdom had failed to come, and the growing church had meanwhile to maintain itself amidst the difficulties of the present age. Whether it would or not it had to submit to the restraints which all other societies had found necessary. It had to integrate itself with this world's order, which is based on law. Human society, like the whole frame of things of which it forms a part, must have law for its foundation. Even in a family, however the members may be bound together by mutual affection, there must be parental authority, set hours for meals, duties and possessions assigned to each individual; otherwise everything will go to pieces. The larger the community the more need there is for proper regulation, and in a great society, like a city or a state or an army, it becomes the one thing that matters. This was the truth which gradually

[5]Luke 22:25, 26.

forced itself on the church. It was looking for the new age in which all would be governed harmoniously by the will of God; it was seeking to anticipate this happy day, when system and authority would be things of the past. But it discovered, by hard experience, that so long as it remained in this world it must subject itself to law.

This became the more evident for the very reason that the Christian life, in all its activities, was brought within the sphere of religion. The church was not merely a company which met together for purposes of worship, but a brotherhood in the fullest sense. Its members were associated in everything they did; they ate together, and had the same interests, and were supported by a common fund into which each one had thrown his possessions. By means of this participation they sought to realize their ideal of the perfect society which would exist in the Kingdom of God. But the subjection of everything to the religious motive was perhaps the chief factor in secularizing the life of the church. The Spirit might counsel wisely in the conduct of public worship and the appointment of teachers and missionaries, but when material goods had to be fairly divided, when charity had to be bestowed on the right persons, there needed to be practical administration. Competent officials had to be chosen, books had to be kept as in ordinary business. If these methods were neglected injustice was sure to happen, and the feeling of brotherhood, which it was the aim of the church to foster, could not be preserved. It is in connection with the common fund that we first hear of dissension among the brethren, and of measures taken to introduce system into the affairs of the church. No one doubted as yet that everything must be done according to the will of the Spirit;

but it had grown apparent that the Spirit could not be left wholly to itself. There was a material side to the Christian life, and it required the methods which hold good for the material world.

Little is told us of how an official ministry gradually emerged from the fellowship in which all were equal, but it is easy to see how the way was prepared for it. In every group of equals there is some one who by his gifts or his force of character inevitably takes the lead. This was the position of Peter in the early days of the church, as it already had been during the lifetime of Jesus. Although he held no stated office he was accepted as the counsellor and spokesman of the church, and without him it could hardly have survived the difficult time when it was struggling for bare existence. Of all Jesus' disciples he seems to have been the only one of outstanding intellect, and with his ardent faith and genial temper he was peculiarly fitted to hold a band of enthusiasts together.

With Peter were associated the rest of the twelve disciples. As the personal followers of Jesus they had a claim to precedence which was never disputed, and were known pre-eminently as the Apostles. At an early date, most likely in the days immediately succeeding the death of Jesus, they adopted as their colleague James, the Lord's brother. He makes no appearance during the ministry of Jesus except on the one occasion when he joined with the family in an effort to withdraw his brother from an undertaking which seemed to them insane and dangerous. After the Crucifixion he threw in his lot with the disciples and was soon recognized as one of their leaders. At first this place would be accorded him because of his personal relation to Jesus, and "the Lord's brother" is added to his name as a sort of title of honour. But he gradually asserted himself in his own right. It is noteworthy that while the Twelve drop out of the history, as men are wont to do when their eminence is not due to their intrinsic qualities, James takes an ever more conspicuous place. He finally appears as the acknowledged leader of the church, to whom Peter himself is subordinate.

James has sometimes been called "the first bishop," and although the name is misleading in so far as it suggests a system which had not yet come into existence, it calls attention to a fact. More than any other man James was responsible for the organizing of the church. The place he occupied was not one of moral leadership, like that of Peter, but an official primacy. He appears as the president at church meetings, as the head of a body of "elders" who administer the church under his direction. He sends out delegates in his own name to enquire into the action of distant communities. For nearly a generation the mother church at Jerusalem was ruled by James, who impressed his individual mark on the church at large. From all that we can learn of him he was conservative and somewhat narrow-minded, though it must never be forgotten that with all his zeal for the Law he generously gave the hand of fellowship to Paul, who would otherwise have pursued his mission under serious difficulties. But whatever may have been his shortcomings James possessed in a high degree the organizing gift. Peter was the abler and broader man, and was certainly more in sympathy with the inner principles of Christianity; but for the new task which now confronted the church a man of different type was needed. The enthusiast and visionary gave place to the practically minded man.

It was the growing success of the mission which compelled the church to organize, on an ever wider scale. New converts were steadily pouring in, and without some efficient system the brotherhood would soon have broken up. As a result of this rapid expansion the civil and religious authorities had taken alarm, and the church was in manifest danger unless it could present a united front to all opposition. Above all, it was now starting on its great enterprise of carrying the gospel to the outside world. There are signs that even when the mission was confined to Palestine the field was mapped out, and teachers assigned to definite towns and districts. The leading Apostles, while resident in Jerusalem, visited the daughter churches from time to time, and kept in touch with them by messengers and letters. When Paul went forth to evangelize the Gentiles he followed a system, carefully adapted to his aims and circumstances; but he never suggests that he was the first to plan his work in this fashion. He indicates, rather, that he acted on well-established precedents, and defends himself more than once by appealing to the known practice of missionaries before him.

The growth of the church thus entailed an organization, and was felt to justify it. Paul makes it his grand ambition to have Christian communities planted everywhere, and with this end in view is ready to avail himself of all possible means. He is willing to become all things to all men. He is full of ingenious schemes whereby the new religion may commend itself to every race and class and make its position more secure. We cannot but admire the zeal of the great Apostle, and the statesmanlike method with which he pursued his aim. Yet there is another consideration which must not be left out of sight. In order to expand, the church had to abandon the ground on which it had originally stood. It had claimed to be the community of the Kingdom, and had disowned all rules and programmes which might associate it with the present age. When it set itself to conquer the world it had to make use of worldly means. It ceased to look solely to the Kingdom, and sought alliance with forces and conditions which belonged to the worldly order. We have to allow, in justice to the elder Apostles, that this was partly the reason why they viewed Paul with suspicion. To be sure he was doing a great work. He had carried the gospel to the Gentiles, and the church was multiplying under his hands in a manner that no one could have dreamed of. But the older disciples may well have felt that a success of this kind was dearly bought. A time had been when the church had no ambitions in this world, which was nearly ended, and looked only to the Kingdom of God. Paul, with his scheme for a vast mission, had tacitly denied the hope which gave meaning to the church. He was taking for granted that the world was permanent, and was anxious to win its favour. No doubt by his concessions and adaptations he had increased the numbers and the importance of the church; but had he not betrayed its principles? When we try in this manner to understand the point of view of Paul's opponents we can see that they were not actuated merely by a blind conservatism or a rooted Jewish prejudice. They were concerned for what seemed to them a vital interest of the Christian faith. They were content, and this may surely be counted to their honour, that the church should forego an outward success and remain what it claimed to be, the community of the Kingdom, which asked nothing from the world.

This opposition to Paul, as we shall see later, failed to take account of his true attitude; but it has to be admitted that he was largely responsible for changing the attitude of the church. In his eagerness to advance his mission he was perhaps too ready to compromise. He broke away from the primitive idea that everything should be left to the free motion of the Spirit, and relied on discipline and order. If his communities prospered and were able to maintain themselves during his long absences, it was chiefly because he took pains to organize them. We can see from his Epistles how much of his activity was spent on matters of practical detail. He saw to it that every community should attend to its finances, that it should conduct its meetings in orderly fashion, that it should find appropriate tasks for each of its members. This side of Paul's work was preserved and developed when much of his spiritual teaching was forgotten, and the church took on more and more of the character of an ordinary society. It sought its models deliberately in the guilds and corporations of the day, and before a century had passed a Christian church was almost a replica in miniature of a Roman municipality. It had a body of officers graded like those of the city, clothed in similar vestments and bearing similar titles. The conception of a unique society, representing on earth the new order which would prevail in the Kingdom, seemed almost to have disappeared.

There was another side, however, to this process of conforming the church to the earthly conditions. While it was ordered and governed in much the same manner as any other society, it never gave up its claim to a supernatural calling. Its members were assured that by entering it they had allied themselves with a higher world and were invested with mysterious privileges. This is well illustrated by the Pastoral Epistles, which in their existing form are among the latest of New Testament writings. They come from a time when the organization of the church was far advanced, and seem to have been intended for the very purpose of defining the ordinances which were now considered binding. In the view of this author, writing in the name of Paul, and availing himself, most probably, of brief notes which had come from Paul's hand, the church is no longer a community apart from the world and subject only to the Spirit. It is a fellowship of people who believe in Christ but who also seek to do their duty as good citizens. They pray for the emperor and obey the laws and are interested in the general welfare. They are shrewd in business and have found that godliness is profitable for this world as well as for the hereafter. Yet the writer never doubts that as members of the church they have part in the heavenly order. Living on this earth they look for "that blessed hope and the glorious appearance of the great God and our Saviour Jesus Christ."[6]

It is a singular fact that the secularizing of the church went hand in hand with a growing insistence on its divine function. The more it adapted itself to this world the more it enforced its claim to a supernatural power and dignity. This, indeed, was the danger to which it finally succumbed. While changing itself into a worldly institution it yet magnified its title to be above the world. It required that all those things which belonged to its outward organization—ceremonies, offices, build-

[6]Titus 2:13.

ings, robes and insignia—should be accounted holy. They had been borrowed from the world, to adapt the church to earthly conditions, and now they were revered for their own sake, as part of the higher order. In this manner the primitive conception of the church as representing on earth the Kingdom of God was almost reversed. A mere earthly power was invested with a divine sanction.

It is not surprising, therefore, that later reformers in almost every age have fixed on the organization of the church as the prime cause of all its errors. They have set themselves to break up the whole ecclesiastical system and so recover the original idea of a free brotherhood controlled by the Spirit. In so far as their efforts have been successful they have only resulted in the overthrow of some existing system to put another in its place. However we may strive to restore it, the free community of the primitive days is gone beyond recall. It was only the other side of the belief that this world is on the point of closing and is to be followed almost immediately by the inauguration of the Kingdom. A belief of this kind is now impossible, and had already become so before the first generation was past. The world is here to stay, and we have no choice but to reconcile ourselves to the plain fact. If there is to be a church at all it must somehow be conformed to the present order. Planted in this world it must submit to the world's conditions.

It cannot be denied that when it allowed itself to be organized the church was in many ways a loser. Not only did it surrender much of its freedom but it abandoned what seemed to be vital elements of its faith. It confessed that the Kingdom which it hoped for was still far distant. It acknowledged also that the demands of Jesus were as yet impracticable. He had called for obedience to God's will as it would be done in the Kingdom, but this could be attempted only if the Kingdom were now in sight. If men were still to be subject to the old order they could at best obey the precepts of Jesus in some qualified manner, with due regard to what was possible within the earthly limitations. Here again we have striking evidence of the new Christian attitude in the Pastoral Epistles. The writer addresses himself to a church now fully organized, and seeks to impress on it the ethical principles by which Christians must order their lives. His ethic is indeed a lofty and exacting one, and if all Christians tried to live up to it the church would have good reason to feel satisfied. Yet every one who examines it has the uneasy sense that it is a compromise. This teacher does not say, as Jesus had done, "Forgive without reserve; be absolutely unselfish and sincere and merciful." His demand is rather, "Practise goodness as much as you can; remember that you have part in a higher order, but do not forget that you are tied to this world and must take account of its necessities." As we trace the history of the organized church we can see that at all times it has followed this rule of compromise. Instead of taking its stand on ideal principles it has allowed for circumstances, for opposing forces, for peril that might befall the general welfare if any principle should be pushed too far. The weakness of the church has always been that while it stands for the Kingdom it is also an earthly society, which must keep step with the world at its side. However pure its motives, it cannot but lay itself open to the reproach of inconsistency, lukewarmness, hypocrisy.

Against the loss, however, we must set the gain, which has

been no less indubitable. For one thing, if it had failed to organize itself the church could not have survived. It began with a mighty ardour of faith whereby it was carried triumphantly through the initial dangers which might so easily have crushed it. But all enthusiasms are short-lived, and if it had trusted wholly to that early mood it would soon have dissolved, like so many ecstatic sects in the years since. In good time the brotherhood was changed into a regular society. It was now independent of sudden emotions, which might come and go. It had lost the early inspiration, but each of its members had his task appointed him, and as all worked together, under wise direction, the cause was maintained and went steadily forward. Not only so, but by organizing its life and worship the church made permanent channels for all Christian activity. Sometimes they ran dry, and there was little but the hollow routine of form and custom. But whenever the Spirit revived it found the channel prepared for it, and the life-giving stream was not dissipated and lost.

Again, as an organized society the church was able to throw itself into the active life of the world. If it had held to its first intention and looked solely to the Kingdom which was at hand, it would either have died out or survived as a hermit community. Like the Essenes, to whom they have sometimes been compared, the Christian brethren might have retired to the wilderness, with their message unknown to all outside of their own circle. Instead of that, when they realized that the world would continue they joined hands with the world. They mingled freely with their fellow men. They met the age on its own ground, and took their place as a society, framed on a familiar pattern and working by methods which every one could understand. The church thus made itself an integral part of the world's life, and to this it owed its wonderful expansion. While remaining the holy community it was not aloof and exotic. It shared in the common interests, and built itself into the social structure of the time. In this manner it took hold of the world from within, and was able to permeate and transform it.

Once more, by its change of attitude the church was better qualified, in not a few respects, to carry out the work of Jesus. He had indeed proclaimed a Kingdom which was not of this world, but in his own ministry he had not secluded himself in the desert, like John the Baptist. He had consorted with men in their cities and marketplaces, and had made himself the friend of publicans and sinners. The church could feel that in allying itself with the ordinary life it was faithful to his example. He had become one with men that he might enlighten and save them, and his church must do likewise. From an early time the idea grew up that the church was the new incarnation of Christ. As the divine nature had assumed the form of man, so the holy community, in which Christ reigned, was in outward appearance a society like others. Paul, as we shall see, makes much of this conception of the Body of Christ, and it is significant that he connects it, in the closest manner, with his demand for church organization. The body is made up of many members, each with its peculiar function, and all are so interrelated that they work harmoniously together towards a common purpose. So in the church there are diversities of gifts, and each member of it must be assigned his place according to his special gift. When it is thus knit together as a perfect organism the church becomes truly the Body of Christ, and will represent him in the world and bring his work to fulfilment.

Finally, it is not too much to say that by adapting itself to the earthly conditions the church grew to a fuller knowledge of that Kingdom of God to which it aspired. To apprehend any ideal there must always be some endeavour to realize it in concrete form. No one can understand great painting unless he has himself tried to make a picture. It may be only a wretched daub, but he learns from its very shortcomings what a true picture ought to be. The best reward of attempting any piece of work is the clearer perception of how it should be done, and the power of admiring those who have done it perfectly. Most of all in the moral life there can be no real feeling for goodness without the endeavour to practise it in everyday conduct. The selfish, indolent man may sentimentalize about the saint or hero, but can never even dimly understand him. It is the effort on your own part to act as he did, on however small a scale, which opens your eyes to the vision which he followed. We have here a principle which is too often forgotten in those criticisms of the church with which every one is familiar. It claims to represent the Kingdom of God, but how miserably it has failed. Its history has been little more than a long succession of bigotries and compromises, of infidelities to the high standards which it has professed to honour. Between the aims of the church and the actual performance there has always been a tragic contrast.

All these criticisms are true, but the answer is that by its failures the church has advanced to a better comprehension of what it seeks to be. If it had remained as it was at first, a company of enthusiasts who waited in a rapture for the Kingdom, it would have waited in vain, and would have forgotten in a short time what it was looking for. But when the Kingdom did not come the disciples set themselves to establish the church. They accepted the world as it was, and formed a community which would be part of it, and which would yet strive, under the earthly conditions, to live for the higher order. Luke tells us, in the prelude to his history,[7] how a voice came to the waiting disciples, "Ye men of Galilee, why stand ye gazing up into heaven?" They had begun with the confident hope that a new age was on the point of dawning; then they were disillusioned, and turned to the present world. They seemed to lose sight of the Kingdom as they sought patiently to build up the earthly church, but through this labour on the task before them they learned the meaning of the vision.

[7]Acts 1:11.

CHAPTER VI

TEACHING IN THE EARLY CHURCH

In the thought of Jesus there is almost nothing that properly can be called theological. By picture and parable he sought to reveal the nature of the higher world. He had himself apprehended it by immediate vision, and his aim was to make it real, in the same manner, to others. It is very remarkable that he hardly touches on the problems which have occupied theologians in all ages. He offers no proof of the existence of God, for no doubt of it seems ever to have crossed his mind. He never says whether he conceived of God as transcendent or immanent, as mind or being or energy. He believes in immortality, but makes no attempt to find a ground for it in the nature of the soul. Most of his teaching is concerned with the moral law, but he is content to take it for granted and has nothing to say about its ultimate sanctions.

The whole message of Jesus centred on the Kingdom of God, and it is commonly assumed that he had thought out this conception and formed a consistent theory. The questions are therefore raised "Did he conceive of the Kingdom as present or future? Did he fully accept the apocalyptic view? When and how did he expect the Kingdom to come?" Such questions, however, are beside the mark, for he seems never to have systematized his idea. He simply realized the fact of a higher order which men must live for, and which will finally prevail. It is, indeed, misleading to speak of Jesus as a "teacher."

The term goes back to the Gospels, but there carries the suggestion that he was the bearer of a divine message. It is never meant to signify that his purpose was merely to instruct, imparting to others the fruits of his own reflection. In modern religious literature a great deal is made of the fact that Jesus was a "teacher," and did not claim to be anything else. From this it is inferred that his true place is with the philosophical thinkers, from whom we have much to learn but whose ideas may be rejected when they are insufficiently proved or in conflict with later knowledge. But Jesus never professed to have arrived at certain new ideas which he wished to demonstrate to his hearers. His aim was to impress on men the reality of God and of the unseen world. Mark tells us that he called his disciples "that they might be with him"[1]—not to take in the information which he had to offer but by knowing him to acquire his attitude of mind. He was certain of the Kingdom of God, and sought to inspire his followers with the same confidence.

This assurance of the Kingdom was what Jesus had given to the disciples, and in the power of their faith they formed the brotherhood of those who waited for the Kingdom. New members were continually drawn into it, and were adopted by a rite of baptism. Jesus himself had not practised this rite, but it was employed, apparently from the outset, by his followers. All of them, perhaps, had undergone the baptism of John, as Jesus himself had done, and they assumed as a matter of course that it was necessary for those who aspired to enter the Kingdom. One change, however, was now introduced into the rite. Since Jesus was the Messiah of the Kingdom the convert

[1]Mark 3:14.

was baptized in his name, and was required to utter the confession "Jesus is Lord."[2] In so far as the primitive church had any creed it was limited to this confession, which was not so much a statement of belief as a declaration of loyalty. The Kingdom was to come through Jesus, and he would receive into it those whom he acknowledged as his people. The convert gave his solemn pledge that he was one of them. Nothing but this was necessary for admission into the church. The bond by which its members were held together was not an intellectual or doctrinal one, but a common assurance that Jesus was the Messiah who would presently bring in the Kingdom.

It was evident, however, from the first, that this faith necessitated some kind of teaching. The disciples themselves had acquired the faith unconsciously. In their intercourse with Jesus it had been impressed on them, beyond the possibility of doubt, that his words and actions had carried with them a divine authority. When he had asked them at Cæsarea Philippi "Who say ye that I am?" Peter had at once answered, in the name of all, "Thou art the Messiah." He had never told them so; he had proclaimed the Kingdom, but of himself and his relation to it he had said nothing. Yet the conviction had grown up in them, knowing him as they did, that he could be no other than the promised Messiah. How were they to communicate this faith to those who had never known him, or had seen him only casually? Mere assertion was useless, for at once the question arose, "how can we believe that this is true?" The men whom Jesus had called "that they might be with him" had in some way to prove to others what for themselves required no proof.

[2]Paul's use of this formula clearly indicates that it was the baptismal confession. *Cf.* Rom. 10:9; I Cor. 12:3; Phil. 2:11.

Teaching in the Early Church

Among the records which have come down to us of life in the primitive church, perhaps the most valuable is contained in a single verse of the opening section of Acts: "And they continued stedfastly in the Apostles' teaching, and in fellowship, and in breaking of bread and in prayers."[3] These are singled out as the chief activities of the new community. Its members lived in the closest fellowship with each other; they observed the Supper; they held meetings for prayer, presumably of an ecstatic nature; and along with all of this they received some regular instruction from the immediate disciples. What was the character of this instruction? There was only one subject which the Apostles could be expected to teach. As the personal followers of Jesus they alone could witness, with full authority, to his acts and words. When Peter was ordered by the Council to cease disturbing the people, his answer was: "We cannot but speak the things which we have seen and heard."[4] Here, it can hardly be doubted, we are to seek the fountainhead of the record preserved to us in the Gospels. Luke tells us in his prologue that he derives his knowledge from Christian teachers before him, who in their turn had listened to the eyewitnesses. His object, he says, is to sum up in orderly fashion the instruction which his friend Theophilus had already received. All converts at that later day were required to learn the chief facts of the life of Jesus and his cardinal sayings, and this, we may infer, had been the rule of the church from the beginning. In the earliest time the disciples themselves naturally had been the teachers. They could speak at first hand of the ministry of Jesus and of the impression he had made on those who stood nearest to him. This

[3]Acts 2:42.   [4]Acts 4:20.

presentation of him as he actually had been was the most convincing proof that his claims were true.

There was another proof, however, on which an almost equal emphasis was laid. For the Jewish mind the final test of every belief was the word of Scripture. It has been well said that for the Jews in the time of Christ the Scriptures had much the same place which we now assign to mathematical law. A scientific theory is proved for us when it can be placed on a mathematical basis, and in the same manner a devout Jew was satisfied when the thing he was asked to believe was in correspondence with Scripture. Beyond the word of God Himself there could be no appeal. It was therefore imperative for the early teachers to adduce a scriptural proof for all that they affirmed concerning Jesus. In the Gospel of Matthew almost every incident is accompanied with the formula, "that the Scripture might be fulfilled," and this is no doubt an inheritance from primitive custom. Along with their instruction in the facts of the life of Jesus the disciples tried to demonstrate that in everything he did he gave fulfilment to Old Testament prediction. God, by His own infallible word, had marked him out as the Messiah.

It is important to note that from the very outset one of the chief activities of the church was this one of instruction. The first believers have often been represented as nothing more than a group of enthusiasts, carried away by strange beliefs which they had no means or desire of testing. Later on there appeared teachers like Paul, who sought to discover some kind of basis for the faith, but the original Apostles accepted everything without enquiry. Are we not expressly told that the Jewish Council "perceived them to be unlearned and ignorant men"?[5] This, however, was the judgment of a professional class, accustomed to think slightingly of all outsiders who dared to form opinions without the proper academical training. The same judgment has been pronounced later, by men of the same type, on Shakespeare, Bunyan, Burns, and many others of the greatest minds. The Apostles may never have studied in the Rabbinical schools, but they were men of more than usual intelligence; this must have been one of the reasons why Jesus selected them out of a large number who offered to be his disciples. As the church grew under their supervision they took on them the work of teaching. Not only did they record the facts about Jesus, but they tried to explain these facts in the light of the divine plan. From the very start the church made an appeal to the intelligence. It seemed to be made up of fanatical people, who held tumultuous meetings at which they fell into ecstasies and spoke with tongues; and we cannot but wonder sometimes that this movement began shortly afterwards to produce a succession of great thinkers who linked their beliefs to the loftiest speculations. But this was fully in line with the original tradition. Those primitive enthusiasts were at the same time teachers, intent on finding reasons for their faith. Peter, on the day of Pentecost, was furnished with arguments. Stephen went out among the Synagogues, answering all disputants and more than holding his own. There never was a time when the exercise of the mind was not one of the primary interests of the church.

The earliest teaching, as we know from examples of it in the book of Acts, was all based, in the Jewish manner, on the evidence of Scripture. This does not mean that as yet there was

[5]Acts 4:13.

no effort to think out the message, and that believers were willing to accept it on the bare authority of an Old Testament text. We are familiar in modern times with the Christian "who knows, and knows alone, his Bible true," and while we admire his simple faith and sincerity, we do not take him seriously as a religious thinker. But it needs to be remembered that all thinking among the Jews was scriptural. The Old Testament provided the necessary data with which the intelligence worked, and out of which it constructed the most far-reaching theories. In later times the Jewish mind has done marvellous things in philosophy, science, legal and political enquiry, but perhaps its highest achievement is still to be found in the great literature which enshrines its interpretation of Scripture. Much of the thought is to our minds arbitrary, or hardly intelligible, but there can be no denying its sheer intellectual power. If thought, like art, has a value for its own sake, quite apart from the matter it deals with, some of those Jewish expositors must be classed among the most gifted of all thinkers. In the New Testament itself, most notably in the Epistle to the Hebrews and some sections of Paul's letters, we have splendid examples of religious thinking, accomplished by a purely scriptural method. The earliest teachers confined themselves to this method but addressed themselves just as truly to the intelligence in their presentation of Christian truth.

This is a fact which needs to be emphasized, for in the modern study of Christian origins a sharp distinction is usually drawn between the primitive teaching and that of the age that followed. It is assumed by many writers that the later Christianity had little in common with the earlier except the name. The mind of the primitive church, as they conceive it, was childish and unreflecting. Paul and his successors took hold of the crude, traditional beliefs and thought them out in their deeper implications; and in this process the religion entirely changed its character. Such a view, it may be frankly said, is based on a misunderstanding. The church had always been conscious of deeper meanings in its beliefs. Teachers like Stephen had sought to elucidate them, and had brought to the task an intellectual energy hardly inferior to that of Paul. Again and again, for that part, Paul himself insists that he was no innovator. He declares that he taught the same message as the other Apostles and tried like them to interpret it in the light of the divine purpose. The only difference was that while the older teachers had used the scriptural method Paul had combined it with others, borrowed from Gentile thought. As a Jew of the Dispersion he followed the practice of foreign-born Jews to whom the Gentile modes of reasoning had become as natural as those of the Rabbinical schools. His right to do this was never questioned. The teachers at Jerusalem had misgivings as to his free attitude to the Law, but gave him the right hand of fellowship. They acknowledged that while at some points he differed from them he was a teacher like themselves, continuing in his own manner their task of expounding the gospel.

It is wrong, therefore, to say that Christianity in the later time was theological, while in the earlier days it was not. The only distinction was that theology ceased to be purely scriptural. For Jewish thinkers the word of Scripture was final. God had made His own pronouncement, and what He had said must be accepted as the truth. For Greek thinkers the ultimate criterion was reason. It was the grand achievement of the Greeks that they were the first to perceive that the world is rational, that the mind of man corresponds in some way to the universal mind. Nothing, therefore, could be accepted as true unless it could be reconciled with principles inherent in human reason. This rule was applied by the Greeks in every domain of thought and action, and in the strength of it they built up a new world of knowledge. They demanded that religion itself should conform to rational principles, and in Stoicism, which was the reigning philosophy of the first century, God was identified with reason. There were many religions, worshipping God under different names, but in all of them He was ultimately the mind which pervades the universe and becomes conscious of itself in man. The one task of man, for the Stoics, was to bring the reason which was in himself into harmony with the divine reason. Philo of Alexandria, with his Jewish religious instinct, could not accept this deification of reason. Allowing that it was of divine nature he made it subordinate to God—an outflowing of the absolute Being who Himself transcends the world, which through His reason He has made. Philo is typical of a mode of thought which was gaining ground everywhere in the first century. Just as we are realizing now that there are limitations to science, so in the Greek world there was a reaction against philosophy. Men had grown aware that with all its effort it had failed to answer the fundamental questions, and that no answer to them was possible except through some kind of revelation. The Gentile mind had come half into sympathy with the Jewish position that truth was to be reached only through such enlightenment as God had been pleased to impart through inspired men. Yet there was general agreement with the main contention of the Greek thinkers that reason is the one criterion. Hellenistic Jews could not accept even the word of Scripture unless it was somehow reconciled with ideas that could be rationally proved.

As a result of the Gentile mission the church, while never abandoning the scriptural mode of thought, relied more and more on the methods of Greek philosophy. Paul is eager to make out that the Christian beliefs are foreshadowed in the Old Testament, and never quite feels himself on safe ground unless he can adduce a prophetic text in support of every argument. But more often than not, the text which he quotes has little relevance, and is brought in as an afterthought by way of deference to a conventional authority. His real interest is to prove that the Christian message has its sanction in man's instincts as a rational creature. He tells us, in one place, how the Gentiles, to whom the Law was denied, have yet a law written in their hearts,[6] and it is this inward law, although he affects to disparage it, which governs his thinking. He desires to set forth the gospel in such a manner that it will be recognized as in full accord with principles of reason. This came to be increasingly the aim of Christian teachers, with the result that before the second century was over Christianity was presented as a philosophy, the final outcome of the intellectual quest for God.[7] All the Christian beliefs were formulated as doctrines, stating in terms of reason what was accepted by faith.

It is true, then, that a change came over Christianity when it was set forth in theological forms. The message of Jesus had come to him by revelation, and he desired that others

[6]Rom. 2:14, 15.

[7]This is the position taken by the Apologists, though it must not be forgotten that they wrote expressly for pagan readers.

should apprehend it in like manner. "None hath known the Father but the Son, and he to whomsoever the Son will reveal him."[8] But the church ceased to rely on this immediate knowledge. It required that the truth proclaimed by Jesus should be confirmed and interpreted, and finally fell back on that authority of reason to which this world's knowledge must submit itself. The responsibility for this change has generally been laid on Paul, or at least on that Hellenistic church of which Paul was the spokesman. This may be granted in so far as theology, in its historical form, was a product of the Gentile mission, but the real change had been effected before Paul appeared on the scene. The Jerusalem teachers had sought to justify and explain their message on the ground of Scripture. Their method was different from that of their successors, but the purpose was radically the same. An appeal was made to the human intelligence. A divine message was correlated with modes of thinking which held good for this present world.

This was the decisive step which marked a turning-point in the history of the Christian religion, and it was taken very shortly after the beginning. It was not due, as we are sometimes told, to the intrusion of foreign influences, but followed as a natural consequence from the disappointment of the early hope. The church had grown aware that the coming of the Kingdom had been deferred. For an indefinite time the old order was to continue, and its requirements had now to be taken into account. Just as the church endeavoured by organizing itself to secure a place in the social framework, so it tried to fit its message into the existing forms of thought. A time would doubtless come when all truth would be understood

[8]Matt. 11:27.

immediately; the witness of the Spirit would be sufficient to itself. In some degree the people of Christ were able to walk already by the higher light. But while the present order lasted another kind of testimony was needful. Men were bound in by the earthly horizon, and the message had to be demonstrated and explained in intellectual terms. The wisdom of men is foolishness with God; His purposes cannot be defined by means of it. Yet it was necessary, as the world is now, to express the truth rationally, or it would convey no meaning to the human mind.

Here, it must be noted, we are to seek the true motive of the church's endeavour to frame a theology, whether on a scriptural or a philosophical basis. It sought to make plainer to ordinary minds what would otherwise have been utterly beyond their apprehension. Christianity, we are often told, is extremely simple, but unluckily, at some point in its history, the theologians got hold of it and entangled it in a network of doctrine. A great deal of modern religious teaching is founded on this idea that we must strip away the old theologies and so recover what is termed "the simple gospel." Now the truth is that it is not the theologies but the gospel itself which is difficult. Any one of moderate intelligence can understand a doctrine. Take for instance Justification by Faith, which seems on the face of it rather complicated, and is not very lucidly explained in the Epistle to Romans. But when it is carefully studied and put into clearer language, it is not difficult; certainly not more so than ordinary problems in mathematics or economic theory. As we learn with a little effort to feel at home with other ideas which at first are puzzling, so with those of theology. Doctrine concerns the mind, and is easy; but to believe in God, to know that there is a higher world which is the real one, to accept the Cross as the true way of life—these things are extremely hard. Not one person in ten thousand can honestly affirm that he has grasped their meaning. It is the gospel itself that is difficult, so difficult that few people would make anything of it at all, if it were not for the doctrines. This was why the church put its message into theological form. It aimed at making the Christian beliefs at least partially intelligible. It recognized that if only they were offered to the mind, like ordinary objects of knowledge, the way would be opened for a higher kind of apprehension. Wise teachers from the first perceived the danger that doctrine might be mistaken for religion, and Paul complains of his Corinthians that while they excel in knowledge they have learned little of faith, hope, love. Yet the doctrines did convey some faint impression of what Christ had been, and what he had accomplished. It was possible by way of knowledge to arrive at the Christian frame of mind.

This, then, was the purpose of doctrine—to put the Christian message into rational forms so as to make it plainer to ordinary men. Living as they did under the conditions of this world they required to have the truth conveyed to them through the medium of earthly wisdom. When some one is unresponsive to a great picture or piece of music, you try to explain it to him in words. You show him, as best you can, that by certain colours or chords the artist has expressed a mood of spirit which he seeks in this way to communicate. In itself your description has little value. Painting and music have a language of their own, and the person who is ignorant of it will never take in its meaning from any laboured explanation. Yet if the right kind of feeling is present in him the commentary may serve to awaken it. He will place himself in an attitude of mind which will make it possible for the picture or the melody to speak to him for itself. It is the same with theology —for instance with the various doctrines of the Person of Christ. They describe him as the Messiah, the eternal Word, the Son of God, and these titles are all compressed statements of who he is, and what he will do for those who believe in him. Taken as they stand they do not make Christ more real to us; they might seem rather to make him more remote, substituting an abstract conception for the living Person. Yet they are helpful and indeed necessary to Christian faith. Until we form to ourselves some idea of the significance of Christ we cannot approach him with the right kind of vision. It is for this reason that Mark begins his narrative with the theological statement: "The gospel of Jesus, the Messiah, the Son of God." He is about to describe how Jesus lived and taught, but feels it necessary to impress on his readers at the very outset how they must regard this Jesus. Though to all seeming he was a man like others, he was sent by God, and his work must be considered in the light of this knowledge that it disclosed the divine purpose.

To appreciate anything great the mind must be duly prepared. You look at a star which is nothing to you but one among the myriads; but you are told of its magnitude, its infinite distance, its place in the structure of the universe. This is intellectual knowledge, but it creates in you the wonder and emotion with which you henceforth regard that star. So with theological thinking. We may say, if we please, that it is only an activity of the mind, and has no religious value. This, it must be admitted, has been true of much theology. Its main effect has been to obscure the religious interest and put in its place a merely intellectual one. But this is directly contrary to the true purpose of theology, which is to prepare the way for a more vital religion. It seeks to explain the things we believe so that we may apprehend them better and live by their power and guidance.

At the same time it cannot be affirmed too strongly that theology is not religion. The very word theology involves a contradiction. It denotes the statement of religious truth in terms of reason, and religious truth cannot be so stated. Music, it has been said, is a form of mathematics, and this is true in so far as musical sounds can be reduced to vibrations and can thus be numbered and measured. Yet with mathematics alone you would make little of a piece of music. You might be able to draw up tables of figures, exactly defining the character of the notes and the intervals between them, but this would give no indication of what is conveyed by a symphony to a musical ear. So theology is the attempt to express by reason what is given to faith, and between these two there is no doubt some correspondence, as between mathematics and music. But they are two different modes of knowledge, and the one can never be converted into the other. The rational statement will always leave out the very thing which for religion is essential. Nevertheless we are rational beings, and our instinct is to seek a rational explanation of every fact. Whatever may be its real nature we try, as we say, to "apprehend" it, which means, literally, to take hold of it. The mind is like a hand, which grasps what would otherwise be elusive, and makes it our own.

Not only so, but it is only on the plane of reason that we can communicate with each other. Thought is a kind of currency. Emotions and convictions which are personal to yourself must be changed into this denomination if you wish to impart them to your fellow men.

This parallel, however, serves to illustrate the inadequacy of theological ideas. Everything has its money value, and only on this condition can there be free interchange of goods, but the money does not in any real sense represent the thing. There is nothing in common between a banknote and a horse or a picture, although for commercial purposes it needs to be assumed that the one is the equivalent of the other. Sometimes, indeed, a man arrives at the state of mind in which a horse or a picture means nothing to him except the banknote in which it can be valued; and this is very much the condition of many theologians. They have so accustomed themselves to put the facts of religion into rational conceptions that they finally take these conceptions to be the religious facts. They offer their system of doctrine and say "this is Christianity," although the two things are just as dissimilar as a piece of stamped paper and a race-horse.

Theology, then, is not religion, and no one has perceived this more clearly than Paul, who has been accused, above all others, of turning the gospel into an intellectual code. He declared that the Kingdom of God is not meat or drink, and he insists, no less emphatically, that it is not knowledge, it is not creed or metaphysic. Spiritual things, he says, must be spiritually discerned. No formal doctrine can impart what Jesus sought to give, the trust in God, the sense of an invisible world, the peace and joy and freedom in which the new life consists.

All this was perfectly clear to the early Christian teachers. The New Testament is the fundamental book of our religion, not because it states authoritatively the doctrines to which we must assent, but because it takes us behind the doctrines. We learn from it what the gospel was, in the living experience of the first believers. When he asserts his right to be considered a true Apostle, Paul declares proudly that he had not been taught by men. His knowledge had come to him directly "by revelation of Jesus Christ."[9] Here he lays his finger on what constitutes an Apostle. The founders of the church were not the product of reasoning and instruction. The truth had been revealed to them; they were "filled with the Spirit," and their mood was one of vision and ecstasy.

None the less it was the Apostles who began that work of teaching which had its outcome in the theology of the later church. It is now recognized that our Synoptic Gospels, and in a special degree the earliest Gospel of Mark, are not mere historical narratives, as was formerly assumed, but are suffused with certain ideas which may be termed theological. This has been urged as proof that while they may preserve some genuine traditions, derived from the Apostles, they grew up for the most part out of the thinking of the later church. A view of this kind is quite unwarranted, and rests on the supposition that the church did not begin for nearly a generation to reflect on its beliefs. There is abundant evidence that the process of reflection had begun much earlier. It is apparent in the speeches attributed to Peter in the opening chapters of Acts. It is clearly indicated in various passages of Paul in which he sets his own doctrines against the background of others which

[9]Gal. 1:12.

— 134 —

he had received. The Apostles were teachers, and their teaching was bound in some measure to be theological. Proclaiming Jesus to be the Messiah they were obliged to prove that he was so, and to show what was involved in his Messiahship. The building up of a gospel tradition and the formation of a theology proceeded hand in hand.

Almost from the first, therefore, a movement began which was to have far-reaching consequences. The church had accepted its message on faith, but this was found to be insufficient, and an effort was made to bring in reason in support of faith. Beliefs which had carried with them their own evidence and forced themselves on the soul in moments of rapture were now thrown into intellectual form. The work of the Christian teacher, as Paul says, was to "persuade men."[10] His aim was to win them to the Christian faith, and he found that this must be effected by an appeal to reason. Intellectual assent came more and more to be the acknowledged basis of faith.

It is not difficult to perceive a number of causes which led to this change in the Christian attitude. For one thing, the disciples found it necessary for their own sakes to discover a rational ground for their beliefs. At first they were possessed with a glorious certitude. Jesus was the Messiah and was presently to return, and all doubt was swallowed up in the boundless ardour with which they awaited his coming. But this mood passed away, and there needed to be something else to supply its place. When the light fails you no longer see the point to which you are travelling and must think out the direction in which it lies. When you cease to take a hope for granted you try to assure yourself by discovering reasons why it cannot fail.

[10] II Cor. 5:11.

So in religion men have always fallen back on arguments to demonstrate the beliefs which at one time required no proofs. The poet, lamenting that he has lost the radiant outlook of childhood, consoles himself with the thought of "years which bring the philosophic mind." He knows, however, that his philosophy is a second-best, and this is true most of all in religion. To prove from Scripture that Jesus was the Messiah was a poor substitute for the Resurrection visions. To construct metaphysical theories of his person could not make up for the rapt experience of his invisible presence. It was not on those theories that the disciples rested their faith but on the immediate insight of which they had once been conscious. They could not but be sure of "the things they had seen and heard." Yet the memory of what had been was not enough. Increasingly they felt the need of reason to confirm and renew their faith.

Again, they were compelled to take up the new position for the sake of others. The church had now entered on its mission, and those who had known Jesus, however certain they might be in their own minds, had to make their beliefs intelligible and convincing to others. This could only be done by way of rational proof. The world at large had not shared in the early visions, and could not receive the message in the one manner whereby it could be truly apprehended. It had to be translated into the language of this world. Paul declares passionately that the wisdom of God cannot be expressed in the words which man's wisdom teaches, yet he had no choice but to employ those words.[11] For ordinary men truth has no meaning unless it can be logically proved, and this course had to be followed

[11] I Cor. 2:13.

in the presentation of the Christian message. When Paul says that he had become all things to all men that he might by any means save some, he is thinking chiefly of this rationalizing of the gospel. He argued, now as a Rabbi, now as a Greek philosopher. No one knew better than he did that the message could not be stated intellectually, but how could he preach it otherwise? Men must be approached on their own level; the message must stoop down to the doors which were open to it before it could find entrance.

But the chief cause at work in the making of Christian theology was that which has been indicated already. The church had looked for an immediate coming of the Kingdom, and the Kingdom had not come. Since the old order which had seemed on the point of closing was destined to continue, it had to be reckoned with in the preaching of the gospel, as in all else. In this world the minds of men are so constituted that all truth must be conveyed in rational form. There are other forms, which will some day come to their own. The church had relied on them in its early visions and revelations, and from time to time every man, if only for a moment, has some direct perception of the higher things. But in everyday living, under the world's conditions, all knowledge must be rational, and the Christian message, if men were to accept it, had in some way to rationalize itself. It has often been noted that Christianity never becomes a living force in any nation until it is assimilated to the national modes of thinking. The Indian or Chinaman or African must devise his own religious terms and adapt the gospel to his native culture, or it will remain outside of him. This principle has a wider and much deeper application. Prior to all the racial adjustments there is the need of adapting the divine revelation to the human mind, as it has been moulded in this world of space and time. This was the problem which faced the early church, and which found its answer in the making of a theology. By the law of their present being men apprehend all truth by their reason. Christianity had to change itself into a rational system before it could be acclimatized in the life of the world.

The process by which this was accomplished can be clearly traced in the New Testament. With each new environment in which it was placed the church altered the character of its teaching. This is commonly ascribed to the various "influences" which affected the teachers at different times, but we have to take account, perhaps in still greater measure, of a conscious adaptation. Paul deliberately became all things to all men. When he was called on to address a philosophical audience at Athens he used the ideas and language of Stoicism, and quoted from a Greek poet. It was not that the Stoic thinking had powerfully "influenced" his Christianity, it was simply because those who listened to him were accustomed to think in that manner, and he tried to convey his message in a language they would understand. At an earlier time the Apostles at Jerusalem had searched the Scriptures for proof that Jesus was the Messiah. No doubt as Jews they attached a cardinal value to the word of Scripture, but it was certainly no chance text in an ancient prophet which had convinced them of the claim of Jesus. The scriptural evidences which are adduced in the early speeches in Acts are almost all far-fetched, and this must have been apparent to the speakers themselves. They felt it necessary, however, to employ the sort of argument which carried most weight with thoughtful Jews. Since the world was to last on, the new religion connected itself with those modes of thinking which most appealed to it.

At the outset this was done by way of concession. The church was well aware that its message did not rest on scriptural or philosophical dogma, but consented, in addressing itself to the world, to make the best of the world's wisdom. At a later time the rational evidences were accepted as valid by the church itself. Reason, it was assumed, was of equal value with revelation, or might even be considered the ultimate authority. In the scholastic phrase, "fides quaerit intellectum," faith must have rational proof before it can be certain of itself. This has continued, in one form or another, to be the church's attitude. We are familiar in our day with the effort to reconcile religion with science, with philosophy, with one or another of the new social movements. One cannot but feel at times that this labour is futile and humiliating. If a man cannot believe his religion until it is certified for him by the latest experts in psychology or economics, it cannot have much inherent power. The New Testament teachers, it cannot be too strongly affirmed, never accept the rational proof as final, or even as seriously cogent. They avail themselves of everything in the thought of their time which seems to give support to their message, but always with the reservation that this is "man's wisdom." For the time being men think in this manner, according to principles which hold good for the present order, but a time is coming when everything will be different. Another world will take the place of this one, and all that we now hold certain will have lost its meaning. Faith has its real ground in the revelation of Jesus Christ.

The theology of the New Testament does not profess, therefore, to have an ultimate value. This is evident, if from nothing else, from the variety of doctrines, all conflicting with one another, which are put forward by the different writers, and sometimes by the same one. Paul, for instance, has five or six distinct theories of the meaning of the death of Christ. He is conscious that by his death Christ wrought redemption; this he discerns spiritually, as a religious fact. But when he tries to explain in rational terms why the Cross should have this power, he passes freely from one line of thought to another. It was not the aim of the New Testament writers to prove their beliefs by reason. All that they sought was to ally their message, as far as possible, with the world's manner of thinking. The church belonged to the Kingdom of God but as yet was in this world, and must be prepared to remain in it. The heavenly treasure must be put into earthly vessels.

It has been generally assumed that by the work of its teachers the new religion made a great step forward. What had previously been vague beliefs, founded on apocalyptic hopes, were placed on a firm basis of reason, and the gospel was thus able to disclose its true significance. This view, however, must be regarded as a mistaken one. It was not from a deeper insight into the message of Jesus that the early teachers were led to expound it in rational terms. Their effort was due, rather, to a weakening of the genuine religious apprehension. The day of visions and ecstasies was past, and the church was bent on maintaining itself within the present order. Faith sought to conform itself to human wisdom. The assurance once given by the Spirit was now won painfully by intellectual labour.

Men climbed by a ladder where once they had risen on wings. It may be granted indeed that when reason was thus called in to the assistance of faith, there was a rich development of religious ideas. The beliefs of the primitive church seem crude and meagre when we turn to the high speculations of Paul and the Fourth Evangelist. Yet religious thinking is not religion. It belongs to a lower plane of things and can never represent what may be given in a single flash of direct revelation. Thomas Aquinas, when he was nearing the completion of his *Sum of Theology*, had a mysterious experience, after which he broke off his mighty work. What had happened to him he would not and perhaps could not tell, but when he was urged to resume his task he said "I cannot; I have seen something which makes everything else look vain."[12] Theology at its best is only the attempt to explain religion by means that must always be inadequate, as when a blind man tries to conceive of colour in terms of sound.

So the growth of theology, which had its true origin in the teaching of the primitive church, did not mean a progress and deepening of the Christian religion. In one sense it was a confession of defeat. None the less it was one of the great achievements of the early church to lay the foundations of Christian doctrine. For one thing, if the Apostles had left nothing behind them but the memory of their visions, Christianity would soon have disappeared. A mood of rapture may mean everything to yourself, but you cannot communicate it to others. Whatever revelation it has brought you must be set forth by means of ideas, and these must in some way be demonstrated before other men will take them in. The Apostles were at pains to

[12]The incident is impressively told in Robert Bridges' *Testament of Beauty*, Book I: 485–500.

state intellectually what had come to them in vision, and by the nature of things they could do so only imperfectly. Yet the doctrinal statement was indispensable. If Christianity was to appeal to thinking men it had to be offered in a form which the mind could apprehend.

Again, it was by the creation of a theology, more even than by the tireless zeal of its missionaries, that the church made sure of its victory. It co-ordinated its message with the general thinking of the age. Men were able to respond to the new religion because there was so much in its teaching that they understood already. When Paul appeared in a foreign city he never had any difficulty in obtaining an audience. He was regarded as one of the travelling philosophical lecturers who were a familiar feature in the life of the time, and was listened to respectfully by earnest and intelligent men. This was because he met them on their own ground. He used the language which was current among Platonists and Stoics. He presented Christians truths in the light of ideas which were known, in some degree, to everybody. It made all the difference to the Christian mission that it could thus throw itself into the main current of the world's thought. Men could feel, as they could not have done otherwise, that it had something to offer that was of real and practical concern to them. Not only so, but by bringing itself into line with other movements it was able to borrow from them much that was helpful and enriching. It has always been one of the sources of strength to our religion that it has been ready to avail itself, from time to time, of the growing results of human knowledge. Justin Martyr declared, as early as the second century, "All that has been truly thought among men belongs as a right to us Christians"; and the church has continually acted by this rule. It has justly felt that by welcoming truth from even the most unlikely quarter it is only reclaiming what is its own. When Jesus spoke of the Kingdom of God he had in mind a world of final reality on which everything must converge. All search for truth is directed in the end towards that ideal of Jesus and will help us to understand it better.

Once more, the formation of doctrine was necessary in the interests of faith itself. Paul was the greatest of the early teachers, and again and again in his Epistles he defines the purpose of his teaching as "edification," building up. It was not enough that men should be won over to the faith; they must be established in it, and this could be done only by patient instruction. They might rise now and then into ecstasy, but this could be only for a moment. There must be something stable and continuous. Faith must combine itself with ordinary thinking, and in this way alone could it become a real possession. The writer to Hebrews, enquiring into the cause of the indifference into which his readers were drifting, ascribes it chiefly to this—that they are not thinking hard enough about their religion. They are content to know the bare elements and have no desire to probe into them and explore them further. To excite them to fresh ardour he offers them a new doctrine, one which they will find difficult but which for that reason will brace the mind to strenuous effort.[13] It is a significant fact that the ages of faith have also been pre-eminently the ages of doctrine. One thinks of the New Testament age, the thirteenth century, the periods of the Reformation and of the Puritans. These were times when men passionately believed in their religion, and when

[13]Heb. 5:11; 6:3.

they also sought to explain it, with a fierce intellectual energy. In this there is nothing surprising, for the mind and the affections always react on each other. The lover of flowers wants to know botany as a science; the musician devotes himself to musical theory; the religious man cannot but be interested in theology. In itself it is only an activity of the mind, vainly striving to interpret what must always lie beyond its reach. But religion finds itself compelled to this activity, which leads, in its turn, to a deeper and more stable faith.

This was the experience of the primitive church. It began with a pure enthusiasm, arising from an immediate sense of the reality and the nearness of the Kingdom of God. It responded literally to the demand of Jesus that a man should receive the Kingdom as a little child, asking no questions, requiring no proof or argument, but simply accepting what God, in the fulness of His grace, had offered. But the Kingdom delayed its coming and the world remained; and it was this seeming failure of the Christian hope which gave rise to theology. As enthusiasm died out, men fell back on reason. Knowing that this world would continue they made use of the world's wisdom for the expression of their faith. The effort was a vain one, and doctrine has always been tentative and unsatisfying; the natural man, with his intellectual methods, cannot discern the things of the Spirit. Yet the doctrines have preserved something of the faith out of which they grew, and by their very inadequacy have kept alive the desire for a higher kind of knowledge.

CHAPTER VII

PAUL'S CONCEPTION OF THE CHURCH

Before the advent of Paul the church had taken a firm root, and had grown strong enough to alarm the Jewish authorities. In its worship, its institutions, and to some extent in its teaching, it had assumed the character which it was to bear ever afterwards. As yet, however, it was not fully conscious of itself. It had sprung up of its own accord out of the message proclaimed by Jesus, and hardly suspected that it stood for a new religion. In Paul it found a great man, and the function of a great man is to gather up in himself and bring to clear expression all that is working obscurely in the minds of others. It is sometimes alleged of Paul, as of other great men, that he made little contribution of his own. Although he was foremost in the Gentile mission he did not originate it, as has often been supposed. Although he gave organization to the church he worked on a model which had been prepared by those before him. It may be questioned whether even the theology which we associate with the name of Paul was peculiar to himself. He acknowledges his debt to the elder Apostles, and perhaps had more in common than we know with the ideas which were already current in Gentile Christianity. But through Paul the church came to realize what it was and what it was seeking for. He supplied the key not only to the later history but to the life of the church before him. We cannot rightly understand what was in the minds of the early disciples, and they did not understand it themselves, except by the light of Paul.

It is unfortunate that Paul is so commonly regarded as an alien, who broke in upon the traditions of the church. To many writers it has seemed an almost inexplicable problem that such a man should have come to ally himself with a group which at every point was so little in sympathy with him. The truth is, however, that Paul was a child of the primitive church. When he became a Christian it had been only a short time in existence—no more, perhaps, than a few months or a year—and still was essentially the same as it had been at first. He learned his Christianity from the immediate disciples of Jesus. He was baptized into the primitive community, and worked as one of its accredited teachers. Luke has been sternly criticized for making Jerusalem the centre from which Paul went forth on his several missions, and to which he continued to feel himself responsible. This, we are told, is a palpable misrepresentation, and distorts the whole course of the early history. But while Luke's account may in some ways be artificial, he was acquainted with the facts, and there is no reason to doubt his main assumption. Paul belonged to the primitive community, and although he may not have kept strictly under its supervision he never ceased to regard himself as one of its teachers. Travelling, as he did, into many distant countries he carried with him the spirit and the motives of the brotherhood in Jerusalem.

Through Paul, therefore, we obtain our best insight into the mind of the primitive church. The earlier disciples had never reflected on the nature of the community which had formed under their leadership. If they had sought to describe it they would doubtless have done so in quite different terms from Paul. It is only too evident that in some respects they failed to perceive the true character of the enterprise in which they were engaged, and placed themselves in opposition to Paul. Yet with his gift of ignoring side-issues and penetrating to the heart of every subject, he grasped the real meaning of what his fellow-labourers were doing unconsciously. For the first time he raised the question: "What is this church of which we Apostles are servants?" By his answer he made the church aware of its destiny, and started it on its historical task.

There might seem, at first sight, to be two aspects of Paul's thinking, in sharp contradiction to each other. On the one hand, he is an individualist. Religion, as he conceives it, is a personal relation between the soul and Christ. It rests on the principle of faith, and faith, as he sees it, has no worth or meaning unless it is your own faith. Paul can say of himself that he did not learn his gospel from men, neither was he taught it;[1] he had received it directly from Christ, and for that reason could depend on it with utter certainty. He knows Christ as "my Lord, who loved me and gave himself for me."[2] He is conscious of an immediate union between his soul and Christ, so that he can declare, "I live, yet not I, but Christ lives in me." His aim, therefore, is to bring his converts into that personal fellowship with Christ which he himself has experienced. Christ has made them free, and they are not to put themselves under bondage to men. They are to feel that they have been individually chosen by the grace of God. Their knowledge of God is to be their own, given to them immedi-

[1]Gal. 1:12.   [2]Gal. 1:20.

ately by the indwelling Spirit. This personal note is everywhere present in Paul's teaching, and in all times when religion has become formal and external men have gone back to Paul. He has enabled them to shake themselves free from all human authority, and recover the sense that they may approach God in their own right as His children. Paul may be justly regarded as the very foremost of all the soldiers of liberty.

On the other hand, Paul was an ecclesiastic, the first Christian leader known to us to whom this name may properly be applied. The thought of the church is constantly in his mind, and apparently had been so from the outset. When he became a Christian his first action was to have himself baptized as a member of the church. Wherever he went, in the course of his missionary labours, his object was to form a community, representing in its own locality the one indissoluble church of Christ. We read in the book of Acts how Philip, as he journeyed along a desert coast, fell in with an Ethiopian and sent him back to his native land as a Christian.[3] In the history of Paul there is no similar episode. Wherever he made a convert his first care was to associate him with a community. A Christian who stood all by himself was unthinkable to Paul. Christianity, to his mind, implied membership in the church, and the act of baptism by which a man entered on the new life in the Spirit was at the same time his incorporation in the brotherhood. On one occasion Paul requires that an unworthy member should be excommunicated, and tells how this must be done at a special meeting, solemnly convened. He takes for granted that the man who is thus renounced by the community is in that moment "delivered over to Satan." He has lost

[3]Acts 8:26 f.

his part in the Christian salvation and is thrown back to the prince of this world, who will duly punish him as a deserter, now recaptured.[4] So for Paul the Christian religion is inseparable from the church, and his letters are addressed to churches and deal for the most part with the principles of church conduct and teaching. When the author of the Pastoral Epistles desires at a later time to formulate the necessary rules of church order, he attributes his work to Paul. This was the Apostle who stood out, for all Christians afterwards, as the typical ecclesiastic. Above all others he had concerned himself with the interests of the church, and his directions were to be taken as authoritative.

It is difficult to reconcile these two attitudes which are equally characteristic of Paul. How could the Apostle of individual freedom be likewise the champion of the church, which aims at limiting and controlling that freedom? Paul himself, however, is unconscious of any contradiction, and when his thought is viewed as a whole we can recognize that he is fully consistent. If there is any contradiction it must be found, not in the mind of Paul, but in nature itself. In a previous discussion of the communal idea in Christianity we had occasion to note that what is called an individual is only a separate member of a group or species.[5] To be sure, the individual qualities are all-important, and constitute the identity of the given plant or animal or man. But they are variations of the type, and before we can make anything of the separate creature we must place it within the type to which it belongs. In accordance with this law the people of Christ became a community. They realized from the first that they did not stand separate but all

4I Cor. 5:1 f.   5See Chapter III.

embodied that new type of humanity which had appeared in the world through Christ. If each of them was to develop his own Christian life they must all be bound together in a brotherhood. With Paul this sense of community was peculiarly strong. He was possessed with the idea of a universal scope and value in the work of Christ. "As in Adam all die, even so in Christ shall all be made alive."[6] The one redemption had availed for all men; it had made possible the renewal of all earthly nature. Christ had come to create a new race of men, and each of his disciples must be mindful that what he has received from Christ he shares with others, who have undergone the same change. It follows that no man can become a Christian unless he is included in the community. His Christianity implies that he is one of the new race, apart from which he cannot fulfil his individual Christian life.

There is therefore no conflict between Paul's demand for a personal faith and his other demand for membership in the church. If a man desires to be in the fullest sense himself, he does not attain this end by retiring into solitude. His common humanity is part of himself, by far the greater part of it, and he must exercise and develop it in intercourse with his fellow men. By shutting himself off he does not gain in personality but only shrivels into an ego which is worthless to himself and to everybody. The Christian man, likewise, if he would possess an individual faith, must make himself one with the Christian fellowship. By separating himself he loses all contact with Christ, who is present in him individually because he is present in the whole community of believers.

There is no contradiction between the personal faith of Paul

[6] I Cor. 15:22.

and his devotion to the church. Neither are we to think of them as two different strands which happened to be woven together in his religion. An artist may also be an ardent patriot, and his love of country will probably reflect itself in his art, but between art and patriotism there is no intrinsic connection. So it has been held that Paul combined two interests which had little to do with each other. He was a saint or mystic who was also a born administrator, and with this practical side of his nature was zealous in the service of the church. But the more we examine his thought the more we perceive that his devotion to the church was a vital element in his personal religion; the two interests were fundamentally one and the same. It was because he sought an inward fellowship with Christ that he felt the need of union with the Christian society. This attitude of Paul has had its counterpart in that of many Christian leaders in later times. The term "ecclesiastic" is often used disparagingly, to denote the church politician whose whole concern is with the externals and mere machinery of religion. Yet the truly great ecclesiastics, men like Athanasius, Augustine, Bernard, Calvin, Wesley have been first of all great Christians. It was their insight into the principles of Christianity which made them eager to build up the Christian community. So with ordinary men and women, almost as a general rule, the religious spirit goes hand in hand with loyalty to the church. There always have been those who stood aloof from the church, claiming that they could serve God better in the privacy of their own souls. It may be doubted, however (if a judgment can be formed from outward tokens), whether this isolated religion is very deep or sincere. The Christians of whom we can be certain that their lives are hid with Christ in

God are invariably to be found within the church. They may appear sometimes to attach undue importance to mere details of church custom and ordinance. They lay themselves open, not always unjustly, to the charge of confusing the inward with the outward. Yet the formal devotion does, in some indefinable way,,blend with the spiritual one and deepen it. Love for the community is hardly•to be distinguished from the love of Christ.

Paul, then, is fully conscious of the bond between the church and the inner Christian life. Reference has been made to the Pastoral Epistles, in which ecclesiastical questions are discussed from what is conceived to be the Pauline point of view. On various grounds it is more than probable that those Epistles, though based to some extent on Pauline material, are not the genuine work of Paul; and the weightiest argument is this— that the writer has missed the intangible and yet vital element in Paul's conception of the church. He looks at it in its external aspect as the society which maintains the Christian faith and which therefore must be safeguarded and wisely administered. For Paul himself it is an essential factor in the Christian faith. It is the necessary means whereby the believer participates in the Spirit, and enters into living fellowship with Christ. Paul has indeed much to say about the practical duties of the church, and the methods by which it can perform them more effectually. But his chief concern is always with its inward significance. While it exists as an ordered society, its function is to assist its individual members in that new life which has come to them through Christ. One of the characteristic words of Paul is "communion" (*koinonia*), a word which is difficult to explain, because it always carries with it a twofold meaning. Christians have communion with Christ and also with one another; and these two kinds of fellowship are bound together, and are ultimately the same. The very meaning of •the church, as Paul understands it, is that it is a union of the brethren through which we enter into union with Christ himself.

This is an idea which is presented in various ways throughout Paul's Epistles, but his thought is expressed most clearly by means of two striking images. Like most of Paul's images they are not entirely metaphorical, but are meant rather to be statements in concrete language of spiritual facts.

On the one hand, Paul thinks of the church as the Body of Christ. He set out, apparently, by using this idea as little more than an illustration. His Corinthian converts were making invidious distinctions between the different spiritual gifts, attaching superior value to such endowments as prophecy and speaking with tongues, which bore the evident stamp of a supernatural power. He declares that all activities which further the well-being of the church are due to the Spirit, and that all are equally noble and necessary. The church, he says, is like the human body, which consists of many members, each one with its special function, while all are dependent on one another and operate in harmony. An injury to one is felt by all; the service of one organ may seem inferior to that of another, and yet if it were lacking the whole body would suffer.[7] The analogy was one which had often been used in ancient thought, particularly with reference to the state, which cannot hold together unless all ranks and classes are willing to co-

[7] I Cor. 12:12 f.

operate, each in the place assigned to it. Paul, however, gave a new and profound application to the familiar image. He was the first to apprehend a great principle which has since proved infinitely fruitful in almost every department of knowledge—the principle of unity in difference. In mere uniformity there can be no true unity. A block of sandstone, made up of millions of identical grains, is not really one. The grains are not united but only crushed together, and when they are separated each of them remains what it was before. A plant, with its root and stem and leaves and flower, is a unity; because the parts are different they are all interwoven and serve the indivisible life of the plant. Most of all the human body is the perfection of unity. It consists of thousands of parts which by their difference minister to each other, and blend in the one personality which thinks and wills.

Paul desires that the church should be one as the body is one. He is concerned immediately with the spiritual gifts which are diverse and yet work in harmony; but it cannot be doubted that he would have passed a similar judgment on differences of church order and practice and doctrine. He does so, at least by implication, in an earlier chapter of this same Epistle to the Corinthians.[8] They had broken into parties, calling themselves by the names of leaders, Paul, Apollos, Cephas, who had presented the gospel in different ways. He points out that each leader had made his own contribution to the common cause. Christ is not divided. He makes use of many instruments, and if they are to help on his purpose they need to be different. The varying types of teaching are all in harmony, in so far as each of them is necessary for the full apprehension of the one truth.

[8]I Cor. 3.

In his first intention, then, Paul aimed at showing that the church is an organism, all the more closely knit together because of its diversities. But his conception of the Body of Christ came to possess a much deeper import for his thinking. The body is one because it is pervaded in all its parts by one life-giving principle; what is it that animates the church and holds it together? It can be nothing else than Christ himself, who dwells in the church and uses it in his service. When he lived on earth he manifested himself in a body, and now he has undergone a new incarnation. The church, in a sense, is Christ himself, still visibly present in the world. This idea is most fully set forth in the Epistle to the Ephesians, the authenticity of which has sometimes been denied, on grounds which cannot be deemed adequate. That it represents the view of Paul is indubitable, because its teaching is plainly suggested in other Epistles. In the argument of Ephesians an almost literal meaning is attached to the idea of the Body of Christ. As the soul animates the body, so Christ abides in his church. Each Christian, in virtue of his place in the community, is related to Christ and partakes of his divine life. He can say, as Paul says of himself: "I live, yet not I, but Christ lives in me." Paul's doctrine of the church is thus an essential part of his mysticism. He believes that every Christian has a personal fellowship with Christ and is thus set free from all authority of men. Yet he holds that this personal fellowship is mediated by the Christian community. According as he is a living member of the church the believer has part in Christ himself, who is the vital principle of the body in which he dwells.

Paul expresses his thought from another side by his conception of the church as the earthly counterpart of the higher spiritual order. This idea may be said to underlie all the Epistles, but it is stated most explicitly in a verse of Philippians: "our citizenship is in heaven."[9] Here again we have much more than a vivid and impressive metaphor. Paul thinks of the church as belonging to the heavenly world. To all appearance it is a society like others, made up for the most part of very ordinary men and women; "Few who are noble or wise or mighty have been called."[10] But they have identified themselves with the Kingdom of God. Living in the present world, their true affinities are with a world that lies beyond. A nation may be represented in a foreign country by a handful of traders or soldiers, who mingle with the people around them and adapt themselves to the alien modes of living. Yet their interests are in the distant land from which they came. In times of danger they display their native flag, and feel safe under its protection. Paul has this analogy in his mind and wishes it to be taken literally. The church is placed on earth as an outpost of the heavenly world. Its members are submissive to the present order, but owe their allegiance to another. This is the suggestion which lies always in the background when Paul speaks of "the Lord." Christians are to remind themselves by the use of this name that they belong to a realm in which Christ is sovereign. By their baptism into his church they have transferred their loyalty, and have their citizenship in heaven.

We have here to find the true reason why Christianity, almost from the beginning, was subject to persecution. Pagan society in the early centuries knew little of the Christian teaching, but it was obscurely aware that the followers of Christ, while living in the midst of it, were a foreign people. "These

[9]Phil. 3:20. [10]I Cor. 1:26.

all do contrary to the decrees of Cæsar, saying that there is another king, one Jesus."[11] This judgment was wrong in so far as it condemned the church as a political organization, bent on the destruction of the existing government. Yet it could find its justification in Paul's conception of the nature of the church. He believed, in no mere figurative sense, that it was the advance guard of a different power from that which the world acknowledged. Its members had released themselves from their old allegiance and embraced a new citizenship. This, for Paul, was the very purpose of the church—to stand in this world for that other order of things which is realized in heaven.

From all this it follows that Paul insists on the separateness of the church. This side of his teaching, as we know from his own admission, had caused perplexity among his converts. He had written, "Come out from among them and be ye separate";[12] and they had taken this to mean that they were to have no contact with the world and were to form themselves into some kind of hermit community. They had protested that life under these conditions would be impossible. Paul takes care to assure them that they had mistaken his meaning. So long as this world existed the Christians were to take their part in it, and if they held aloof from their neighbours it must be only from those who were living in notorious sin.[13] None the less he impresses on them that they were a people apart. While sharing in the ordinary life of the city they were to avoid everything that might savour of idolatry. They were to feel that their fellow-Christians were closer to them than others,

[11]Acts 17:7.   [12]II Cor. 6:17.   [13]I Cor. 5:9 f.

and had a special claim on them. All disputes that might arise within the society were to be settled by arbiters of its own appointment, without recourse to the regular law-courts.[14] This injunction is highly significant. Paul had an excessive regard for Roman justice, and believed that in any conflict of interests it was sure to give an impartial decision. Again and again he admonishes his readers to trust the laws and those who administered them, and in this trust he himself made his fatal appeal to Cæsar. Yet he requires that the church, even in worldly matters, should be independent of all outside authority. Christians must never forget that they were citizens of another world.

It is from this point of view that Paul's whole work as a missionary should be understood. His outlook was far wider than that of the primitive disciples, but he never ceased to be faithful to the original conception of the church. It was the community which would inherit the Kingdom. The Judgment was at hand, and the people of Christ would be rescued from the perishing world and would be set apart for eternal life. To a great extent Paul had abandoned this early apocalyptic view. He thought of salvation, not as something reserved for the future, but as given now, in the act of faith. But his object was still to bring men into the holy community and so effect their rescue from this world of perdition. In the view of many people today, the chief value of the church is its leavening influence. Only a small minority may actually belong to it, but they exercise a moral leadership which is everywhere acknowledged. The church is the guardian of all higher standards; it ensures that law should be grounded in right principles, that

[14]I Cor. 6:1 f.

business should be conducted honestly, that the strong should protect the weak, that customs should be seemly and humane. Not so much for its own sake as for this uplifting effect on the general life, the church must be preserved.

A similar judgment is applied to Christian missions. No one, we are told, can seriously believe that the vast populations of India, Japan, China will ever become Christian, and this, per- haps, is not altogether desirable. Missionary effort, in so far as its aim is purely religious, is largely wasted. Its true value con- sists in its civilizing influence. It serves to instil into backward races something of the morality which has grown out of our religion. It leads to the establishment of schools, hospitals, all the helpful institutions which are found in Christian lands. The real benefits of missions are of this indirect kind. Their religious success may be very limited but this does not greatly matter, so long as they raise the general level of culture and imbue non-Christian peoples with some of the beneficent ideas of Christianity.

Much may be said for this conception of the church as a society which diffuses a better spirit through the world around it, even though it does not actually change men into Christians. This, however, was not the conception of Paul. He thought of the church as standing by itself, over against the world, and his one aim as a missionary was to draw men out of the world into the church. There is no sign that he ever had any desire to elevate and improve the heathen society. No charge, indeed, has been so often and so vehemently urged against him as that he never protested against prevailing evils—slavery, the ex- ploitation of subject races, unjust distribution of wealth, the degrading sports of the amphitheatre. Such things must have been utterly repugnant to him, but apparently he never felt himself called on to denounce them. If he had contemplated nothing more than to improve conditions in the world of the first century he would certainly never have undertaken his mission. All the evils as he saw them were inherent in the old order, and were bound to continue, in one form or another, so long as it lasted. Even if it had been possible for him to amend existing institutions it is doubtful whether he would have tried to do so. He would have reasoned that the world, however it was ameliorated, still would be the world. It was intrinsically wrong, and any attempt to make it superficially better would serve only to blind men's eyes to its real nature. The evils of the world must be left as they were. They were less dangerous if they could be plainly seen as part of an order which was wholly contrary to the will of God. Nothing would suffice but that men should be rescued out of this world which was doomed to destruction. So the church, in Paul's view, was not meant to be a leaven or an influence, existing for the sake of human society at large. It represented the higher order of things, and men were to be brought into it. While they remained outside of it, however they might be elevated by some of its gifts to them, it availed them nothing. What they required was the new life which only Christ could bestow on those who were in living fellowship with him through his church.

This attitude of Paul is undoubtedly open to criticism. It has been the glory of the church in past ages, and more than ever in our own, that it has done so much for those who had no part in it, and who often kept deliberately aloof. It has been in the forefront of every battle for liberty, for the relief of pain and poverty, for the humanizing of material and social conditions. Without any direct intention of making men Christians it has ministered to them simply as men, and in so doing it has surely fulfilled the law of Christ. But Paul, in his intense conviction that Christian faith was the one supreme interest, was impatient of all lower ones, and it was this which gave him power to achieve his great mission. The thought was always present to him that the time was short, and that the Kingdom was ready to break in. Men must be saved from this world, which even now was crumbling under their feet, and throw in their lot with the new order. Paul worked at fever heat under the stress of this conviction that he must build up the church as the one city of refuge for mankind.

It has been often pointed out that in his insistence on the separateness of the church he tends to be narrow and exclusive. The virtue which he prizes most is "love of the brethren." He commonly speaks of Christians as "the saints," using this term in its primary meaning of those who are separated from others. In his various accounts of moral duties he has chiefly the life of the community in his mind. Again and again he might seem to restrict the love of Christ to the church, which he purchased with his own blood. It may indeed be granted that we do not find in Paul that all-embracing humanity which attracts us in the teaching of Jesus, to whom God is the Father of all men, sending down His rain and sunshine on the evil and the good alike; but it would be wrong to compare his exclusiveness to that of small-minded sects which confine their sympathies wholly to their own group, and are hardly aware of the people outside of it. He had probably seen more of the world than any other man of his time. He possessed, almost in an excessive degree, the responsive temper which enabled him to become all things to all men. We do not rightly understand his attitude unless we allow for two objects which he had in view when he called on the church to be separate. On the one hand, he wishes to impress on the community that while here in the world it must be always on its guard. Its members must never be forgetful of their high calling. However they mix with others they must carry with them their own motives and standards; they must think of Christ as their one Master. There is a sense in which every high-minded man must be exclusive. He has something which he holds sacred, and at a certain point draws a boundary between himself and the crowd. In the same manner the church must be exclusive. Whatever may be its other interests the religious one is paramount, and if this is to be kept secure its members must fence themselves off from much that pertains to the common life. More than once Paul compares the church to a temple, and in ancient times a temple stood in a walled enclosure, dividing it from the noise and business of the city. The church was the temple of the living God, and must separate itself.

But Paul also desires this separateness for the sake of the world itself. The aim of his mission was to draw men out of the world into the church, and they could not be so drawn unless they could clearly perceive that the church was different. In a number of passages in his letters Paul shows himself anxious, it might seem unduly so, about the world's opinion. The church must expose itself to no ridicule or scandal. It must be careful that its members live up to their profession. It must forbid them to take part in customs and festivities which might bring them too closely into contact with their pagan surroundings. This solicitude for the good name of the church was natural, and was particularly necessary in a time when there were enemies on every side, eager to find some pretext for criticism and slander. But Paul has evidently a further object. He is intent on winning men to his cause, and knows that his labour will go for nothing unless the church stands out from ordinary society. It represents a higher order of things, and this must be made apparent even to the most unthinking. In all that they know of the Christians they must be brought to see that this community does not belong to their world. Paul was well aware that by thus separating itself the church would incur dislike and persecution, for men resent everything that offends the custom of the herd. But he knew that this very aloofness of the church would be its power. The world would find itself confronted with something totally different from itself, and thereby would be attracted. Every city in that age was full of guilds and clubs and friendly societies, and if the church appeared to be merely one of them, it would hardly be worth notice. Men must see at once that it was a new kind of association. The stranger, Paul says, as he looks in upon your meeting, "will be convinced by all and judged by all; the secrets of his heart will be made manifest, and falling down on his face he will worship God, and will report that God is in you of a truth."[15]

Paul insists, then, that the church should be separate, in the sense that it should keep itself distinct from the surrounding life of paganism. Men were to know from its whole attitude and from the character of its members that it belonged to an-

[15] I Cor. 14:24, 25.

other order. At the same time he recognized, apparently from the first, that it must adjust itself to the present age. If it were to answer its purpose as an outpost of the Kingdom it must be willing to submit, for the time being, to the alien conditions. Paul could see this more clearly than the elder Apostles, for although he was a child of the primitive church he had been "born out of due time."[16] He was not confused with memories of the first ecstatic days when the Kingdom seemed already to be breaking in. From the outset of his Christian career he had taken the present order for granted and allowed a place for it in his beliefs. To be sure he shared in the expectation that the end was near, and was confident that he himself would live to witness it; but he counted on many years of activity which were still at his disposal. This is evident from the grandiose plan on which he conducted his mission. He would visit personally all the provinces of the Roman empire, first in the East and then in the West, and establish in each of them at least one community which would be a centre of light for the region round about it. In this manner he would fulfil his intention of preaching the gospel to the whole world.[17] Latterly he seems to have lost his early confidence. As the result, perhaps, of a terrible experience at Ephesus, when he lay for a time under sentence of death,[18] he realized that he would not live to see the Lord's coming. This, however, involved no essential change in his outlook. He became aware that the world would last longer than he had reckoned on, but he had already allowed for its continuance during a space of years.

It was thus clear to Paul that the church must not break

[16] I Cor. 15:8.
[17] This plan is outlined by Paul himself in Rom. 15:18–24.
[18] II Cor. 1:8–10. Also I Cor. 15:32.

with the world. Remaining separate it had yet to take account of the earthly environment, and not only avoid any quarrel with it but use it, as far as possible, for the furtherance of its work. The main object of all the Epistles is to advise the churches on difficulties that have arisen from their twofold relation to the higher order and the earthly one. Paul writes with a view only to the short interval which has still to elapse before the advent of the Kingdom. This interval has now extended to nearly twenty centuries, but Paul faced his problem with such an insight into its nature that his counsels have always remained valid. He may be justly regarded as the great architect of the church. It stands today, in almost everything that concerns its relation to the world, much as we see it in the design of Paul.

The Epistles deal with a large variety of practical questions; each community had difficulties of its own, and Paul examines them carefully, and sometimes in much detail. It might have been expected that his conclusions would be now of little interest, since the matters submitted to him were often local and trivial, and were bound up with old-world conditions which have long ceased to exist. But it was the rare gift of Paul to see the general in the particular. However insignificant may be the case before him he pierces at once to the principle involved in it, and his judgments are therefore of lasting value. These judgments, moreover, are based on certain firm convictions which he had no doubt reached after much pondering on the necessary relations between the church and the world.

He is convinced, for one thing, that the church must constitute itself as an orderly society. Enthusiasm is desirable, and

Paul possessed it in the fullest measure. He could speak in tongues more than them all; he knew what it was to be caught up into the third heaven. But with his capacity for rapture Paul had also the mind of a statesman. Confusion of any kind was abhorrent to him, and he believed that it was so to God. Everything must be done "decently and in order." He was averse, also, to mere fanaticism. He conceives of the Christian life as a race in which the prize will go to him that has staying power, and has disciplined himself, and is "temperate in all things." The true gifts of the Spirit are those which manifest themselves, not in frenzied outbursts, but in practical service and a constant fellowship with God. Love, which is stedfast and can bear up through all discouragements, is the greatest of the spiritual gifts. But Paul's endeavour to organize the church was not due simply to his instinct for order and reality. He saw that nothing enduring could be made out of mere religious fervour, and the church must prepare itself to endure. The return of Christ had been delayed, and the present world was to last on. If the church were not to disappear it must somehow come to terms with the world's conditions. It must take the form of a regular society, able to hold its own in the social structure of the time.

Paul therefore made it his aim to impose some kind of system on his churches. He laid down rules for the conduct of worship, for works of beneficence, for communal and family relations. He provided each group with a staff of officers, and during his absences kept in touch with it through his assistants and by means of letters. The churches were widely scattered, and were all jealous of their independence, but he tried to draw them together. It is possible that in the latter part of his career there floated before his mind the idea of a federation, under the presidency of Jerusalem. Something of this kind seems to be indicated by that scheme for a collection, of which we hear so much in the later Epistles. In any case, by the practical effort to enlist them all in a common enterprise he sought to awaken in his churches a sense of their solidarity. Their ideal unity as the church of Christ was to manifest itself in active co-operation. So in every way Paul set himself deliberately to build up and regulate his communities, and behind all his action we can trace one governing motive. While he thought of the church as a spiritual brotherhood, reflecting the higher order, he perceived that here on earth it must ally itself with the existing order. If it were to survive as the community of the Kingdom, it must also take the form of an organization, fitted to the requirements of this world.

Along with this endeavour to devise rule and system, Paul is anxious, in every way he can think of, to promote friendliness between the church and the world it lives in. Christians in the earlier time had tried to break away from everything that pertained to the present order, which was nearing its end. Paul seeks to bring them back to realities. He impresses on them that they must take their part, as far as conscience permits them, in the ordinary activities. They are to work for their living in the occupations they have been used to follow. If they are slaves they are to obey their masters, although knowing that they have become free men in Christ. Instead of rebelling against existing laws and institutions they must be doubly careful to respect them, and to do so willingly.

It is in this connection that we must understand Paul's attitude to women, which has laid him open to so much misconception in later times. He has been accused of thinking of women disparagingly and going out of his way to lay restrictions on them; but this is certainly far from the truth. He declares that in Christ there is neither male nor female; all human beings are now on an equal footing, and have the same worth in the sight of God. He found perhaps his most valued helpers among women. He gave a place to them in the ministry of the church, recognizing their peculiar gifts as teachers, comforters, agents of charity. It may truly be said that he was one of the great pioneers in the emancipation of women; and this, indeed, is the very reason why he is led at times to speak of them with apparent harshness. He had taught them that they were free, with the result that some of them were inclined to abuse their new-found liberty. For his own part, we can well believe, Paul would not have interfered, but he had to take account of ancient sentiment, especially in Gentile countries, which required a strict decorum on the part of women. Nothing could be more harmful to the church than to have it supposed that its women were forward and domineering, and Paul insists that at least in the formal meetings to which strangers were freely admitted, they should keep in the background, and wear the customary veil. In this, as in other things, he seeks to conciliate the world's opinion. The church must conform its practice to that of ordinary society. It must not wilfully offend the prevailing sentiment, even when this was different from its own. If it was to make its home in the world and win it over, it must be friendly and accommodating.

Paul enforces this rule with a special emphasis whenever he deals with the relation of Christians to the civil power. We come here to a large question which will call for discussion in a separate chapter, but at present it will be enough to note that Paul desires his converts to behave as good citizens. They must submit to the laws of the state, pay all dues and taxes, honour the emperor, and the rulers and magistrates under him. These counsels were obviously wise, in view of the position of the church in the first century. There was much in its teaching that seemed subversive of the established order, and it was notoriously to blame for the breaking up of many families. The riots which interfered from time to time with Paul's own mission were not entirely due to the ignorance of the mob, incited by hostile Jews and agitators. Pagan society had a real case against the church, as representing a dangerous movement which needed to be suppressed before it had gone too far. The situation was aggravated by hotheaded elements in the church itself. When the city of Rome was burned down in 64 A.D. the rumour gained ground that it was the Christians who started the fire. Almost certainly this was due to nothing else than the natural instinct to find a scapegoat for every disaster, but it is significant that in this instance suspicion fell on the Christians. It was known that they looked for the end of the world, and that there were some who held this belief in a fanatical form. Might it not be that they had tried to hasten the end?

We can understand, then, why Paul enjoins obedience to law and authority. He saw that a terrible menace hung over the church, and could be averted only by the utmost circumspection on the part of its members. But this prudential motive is combined for Paul with a much deeper one. He is alive to the fact that although the church is not of the world it must live alongside of it. The end is not to come immediately, and meanwhile the community of the Kingdom must accept the present order. In the teaching of Paul there is much that looks like compromise, and it has been inferred that while he was a Christian enthusiast he was also a shrewd politician, and perhaps something of a timeserver. Charges of this kind were brought against him in his lifetime, and we know from his letters that he bitterly resented them. He was well aware of his true motives. He perceived that if the church was to carry on its task it must come to some agreement with the earthly order, which was evidently to continue, no one could tell how long. Only on this condition could it maintain itself and fulfil its purpose. If it stood wholly apart it would always remain foreign, and those who might have welcomed its message would be repelled. It must find some common ground with the world before the world would accept it.

Paul speaks of himself in one passage as "a wise master-builder" who has planned the foundation of an edifice which those who followed him must complete worthily, with materials which will bear the test of time.[19] Every one would now acknowledge that he has rightly described his work. The church that rose up in the ages that succeeded him was built, in all essentials, according to his plan. He transformed the primitive group of Christians into a great society, which even before his death was spreading itself over the whole extent of the Roman empire. He worked deliberately on a principle without which this vast expansion would never have been possible. While his predecessors had clung to the belief that the world was all but finished, and had sought to guard the church

[19] I Cor. 3:10.

from all contact with it, Paul accepted the world and aimed at adapting the church to its conditions. The primitive brotherhood became in his hands an organization, availing itself of methods and instruments which were frankly borrowed from the world's order. Nevertheless for Paul, as for the earlier Apostles, the church was separate. It was the fellowship of the saints, and stood, amidst the things of time, for the Kingdom of God. "We have died to sin and live unto righteousness." "Our citizenship is in heaven." Christians are to be reconciled to the world they live in, and yet be conscious always of their higher calling. Outwardly they must conform to this passing world, while in their inner being they are set apart as the people of Christ. Paul has so blended these two ideas that they do not conflict, but illuminate and support each other, and it is this which gives permanent value to his teaching on the church.

CHAPTER VIII

THE ETHICAL TASK OF THE CHURCH

To outside observers the church in the primitive days was a group of enthusiasts, intoxicated for the moment with a fanatical hope which would soon prove an illusion. The wisest of contemporary Jews was the Rabbi Gamaliel, whose speech at the Council is recorded in the book of Acts. "I say unto you, Refrain from these men and let them alone; for if this work be of men it will come to nought, but if it be of God ye cannot overthrow it."[1] Gamaliel spoke in guarded fashion, but the idea in his mind is not hard to guess. The work, as he saw it, was of men—one of the ignorant excitements of which he had known many in his time. They had all run their day and been forgotten, and the Council would be foolish to view the matter seriously and perhaps give impetus, by harsh measures, to a movement which would die down in natural course if it were only let alone. This was a sensible attitude, and we still adopt it in face of the new cults and sensations which are constantly bubbling to the surface. They irritate us while they last, but we try to keep our temper and let them fizz themselves out. We can be confident that nothing unsubstantial will trouble us for long.

From the first, however, Christianity was more than an excitement, inspired by wild apocalyptic hopes. Jesus had indeed proclaimed the Kingdom of God, but he had also revealed the

[1]Acts 5:38.

— 172 —

will of God, as it would be done in the Kingdom. He had required of his followers that they should conduct their lives according to that higher pattern, and after his death they had made it their aim to observe his precepts. The earliest name by which they called their movement was "the Way," the new manner of life which had been prescribed by Jesus. Their hope for the Kingdom was combined with a moral activity, and those who looked only to what seemed fanatical in the new beliefs did not allow for this other element. The enthusiasm died down, as might have been expected, but the Christian community was securely anchored to that new righteousness which had been set forth in the Sermon on the Mount.

In all ages this has been the permanent thing in our religion. Theologies have succeeded each other, ritual has passed through many phases, countless sects have arisen, so different in character that it is sometimes hard to distinguish their family likeness. But the Christian ethic has always remained substantially the same. The mediæval saints had many fancies which now appear strange to us, but they practised the Christian virtues, just as we understand them now. A Roman Catholic and a Quaker may seem to be at opposite poles in their worship, but when you ask their judgment on purely moral questions, they answer the same way. Sometimes it is argued that morality has nothing to do with religion, and remains constant, by its own nature, under all forms of belief. This, however, is not true. The old pagan idea of a good man was radically different from the Christian one, and the chief difficulty of the early missionaries was not so much to enforce their doctrines as to change the moral attitude. Even to noble pagans like Marcus Aurelius the behaviour of the Christians appeared foolish or positively wicked.[2] Jesus did not take over the generally accepted ethic but for the most part reversed it, and it was this new morality which impressed itself on his followers, and became the unchanging element in their religion.

The conclusion has often been drawn that the only thing in Christianity which really matters is its ethic. "For forms of faith let fools and bigots fight, He can't be wrong whose life is in the right." A view of this kind has grown increasingly common in our time. We are told that the religion of Jesus was little more than a sheath for the protection of certain moral principles. When these have been secured, the sheath may be thrown away, and our one task now is to give practical effect to those conceptions of justice, kindness, human equality which Jesus brought into the world. He belonged to an ancient time and an eminently religious nation, so it is not surprising that he associated his ethic with the customary beliefs about God. But his vital interest was in moral action, and we can still remain Christians, in the essential meaning of the term, although we dispense with the old beliefs, which have now become a burden.

This, however, is a complete misunderstanding of the purpose of Jesus. His sayings, to be sure, are concerned mostly with the moral and social life, but when we consider them more deeply they are bound up inseparably with his religion. Morality was not his vital interest. On the contrary, he regarded it only as a means towards an end. If one were asked to select the central saying of Jesus, which supplies the key to all the others, it might be found in the verse of the Sermon on

[2]He sees nothing in the death of the martyrs but a "stupid obstinacy."

the Mount, "that ye may be the children of your Father who is in heaven."[3] The motive of all right action is here definitely stated, and it is one which distinguishes the Christian type of morality from all others. Why should I act in the manner I call right? This is the primary moral question, and the answer given to it must always determine the character of an ethical code. Sometimes the ultimate motive is placed in personal advantage, sometimes in social utility, sometimes in the love of virtue for its own sake. Perhaps with the majority of people the motive is nothing but the desire to obey a generally accepted rule. The Greek word "ethic" is closely allied to the word for "custom," and reflects the idea that a man who lives rightly is one who is faithful to all traditional ways. In Judaism, as in most ancient systems, a religious sanction was added to this idea. It was assumed that the traditional law had been divinely given. Why God had so commanded it was not for men to enquire. It was enough to know that this was God's will, revealed to men in a distant past, and that He would punish those who departed from it.

For Jesus also the motive of right action was a religious one, but in a different sense from what it had hitherto been. Indeed it was just at this point that he broke with the religion of his time. Hitherto the act of obedience to the divine command had been sufficient. So long as you obeyed God, whether from love or fear or habit or hope for recompense, you were acting rightly. Jesus transformed this outward submission into an inward one. He taught that you cannot truly obey God unless you believe in Him as your Father and desire to be like Him. He is the righteous God, and you can feel that in acting

[3]Matt. 5:45.

righteously you act as He does. The end of your being is to resemble God your Father, and you attain this end by doing right.

For Jesus, therefore, the motive of right action is to become like God, to possess in oneself more of God's own nature. Jesus has much to say of the benefits conferred on others, of the joy and satisfaction which a man secures for himself, by doing.what is right. All these, however, are subsidiary ends. The grand purpose is always to enter the Kingdom, to win that higher kind of life which is only possible by obedience to the will of God. It is often urged, as the most serious criticism of Jesus' ethic, that it is not disinterested. He never seems to rise to the conception of a goodness practised for its own sake. The emphasis is constantly laid on the "reward" attached to well-doing. Many attempts have been made to qualify or explain away this insistence on reward, which jars on our sense of the purity and loftiness of the ethic. But these well-meant efforts are all futile. The idea of reward is essential in Jesus' teaching. He does not conceive of goodness as practised for itself, and if he had done so his ethic would not have been raised to a higher level, but would have been emptied of its meaning. Our test of the value of anything is the result that flows from it, and are we to believe that goodness, which is the highest thing we know, has no result whatever? Jesus affirms that even when it seems to go for nothing it cannot fail of the richest reward, not, indeed, in any material wealth, but in the attainment of a higher life. By doing the will of God we become more like God, we win for ourselves entrance into His Kingdom. This is the reward, and the desire to obtain it is the one motive of the good life.

The point is a crucial one, for here we are to find the char-acteristic feature of the Christian morality. This term is often used very loosely, to describe any kind of conduct that seems to be in accord with Jesus' teaching. When a man performs some generous action he is said to prove himself a true Chris-tian. He may have been prompted by mere good nature, or a desire for popular esteem. He may have had some higher mo-tive, patriotism, a sense of duty, pity for human suffering. But however we may admire the action in itself, and even the motive out of which it springs, it is not necessarily Christian. In Christian morality there always must be some desire for the higher life, for fellowship with God. This desire may not be a conscious one, for it is one of the marks of Jesus' teaching that he thinks of the purest goodness as unconscious. The will has become so identified with the will of God that it chooses the right as by its own natural impulse. Yet no action is truly Christian unless somewhere at the roots of it there is the re-ligious motive. It is this, indeed, that constitutes the charm and significance of a Christian act. Whatever its character may be it is lifted out of the domain of selfish and worldly ends. Done solely for God's approval, it represents goodness, without alloy.

With Jesus, therefore, morality is not an interest by itself, and to regard him primarily as an ethical teacher is to miss the real purpose of his message. His ethic is certainly more than incidental, for at least three fourths of his recorded sayings are concerned with moral action. This is too often forgotten in those types of Christianity which lay all the stress on doctrines, or acts of worship, or mystical communion. Although Jesus did not reduce religion to morality, he made morality cardinal, for he conceived of God as righteous, and only to be approached by the way of righteousness. Yet righteousness is only the way, and the mind of Jesus is always fixed on the goal. His aim is to waken in men the sense of the Kingdom and the desire to enter it. They will attain to it by the practice of righteousness, but this by itself must not be their primary interest. They must feel themselves to be like travellers who follow the road for the sake of the journey's end.

"Seek ye the Kingdom of God"; that is the theme of Jesus' message, and he dwells on the need of righteousness because this is how the Kingdom must be sought. It follows that the righteousness he calls for is that of the Kingdom. Men must seek the Kingdom by doing God's will now as it is done in heaven. They are to anticipate in this world that higher order in which they will shortly have their part. The moral demands of Jesus are thus absolute in their nature. He looks to the Kingdom and makes no allowance for human limitations and the imperfect conditions of this earthly life. The moral law is set forth in its purity, as it will operate hereafter, when everything is brought into harmony with the will of God. It would hardly be too much to say that Jesus, so far from being exclusively a moral teacher, did not teach an ethic at all. The very purpose of an ethic is to relate man's conduct to the given conditions of his life. Aristotle was the father of ethical science, and supplied the pattern which has been followed in all later systems. Taking man's nature as it is, he tries to discover how man should order his life in the actual world. How are the higher and lower impulses to be kept in equipoise? How can a man co-ordinate himself with the society and the physical en-

vironment into which he has been born? This is the obvious
purpose of an ethical code. It is meant to provide guidance in
living, and must therefore take account of all the hindrances
and disabilities under which we labour as creatures of flesh and
blood. This, however, is not done by Jesus. He takes his stand
on the perfect will of God, which cannot be fulfilled by erring
men amidst the hostile forces of the present world. As Jesus
sees it, this world is shortly to give place to another, and he
calls on men to identify themselves with the coming order.
They are to live now as if the Kingdom were already here,
and in doing so they will find everything against them. They
will be broken against the opposition of this world, which
knows nothing of that higher law by which they have resolved
to act. Nevertheless they must follow it, and by losing their
lives will find them.

So the morality which Jesus taught was that of the Kingdom. He fully recognized that it was not feasible in this world.
Again and again he declares in emphatic language that the
present conditions are directly contrary to those of the coming
age. The world as we know it is made for the powerful, the
calculating, the self-assertive, and it is they who will prosper
in it. They have the right to do so, since they belong to this
world, and thrive in their proper climate. But a time is coming
when everything will be changed. A new order will set in, and
none will have part in the Kingdom except those who are seeking now to conform to its law. Attention has often been called
to the paradoxical character of Jesus' teaching, and it is assumed as self-evident that many things which he said are not
to be taken literally. He cannot have meant seriously that the
poor and sorrowing are blessed, that men should love their

enemies, that they should forgive without limit and abandon all earthly possessions. He only expressed himself, we are told, in the strongest possible language, purposely exaggerating his thought so that no one should overlook it. This, however, is to misunderstand his whole intention. His thought is in its essence paradoxical, for he made demands which in this world are incapable of fulfilment. His eye was always on the Kingdom, which was so real to him that he naturally took its law for granted. But the Kingdom which he contemplated and which he thought so near was still distant. The world of which he hardly took account was a fact, and was going to remain so. This was the real difficulty of his teaching. He called for an absolute ethic which, under the actual conditions, could not be put into practice.

At the outset this difficulty was not realized. The disciples were confident that the Kingdom was at hand; they were all the more confident since Jesus had now passed into the higher world and was sure to return almost immediately as Messiah to complete his work. They took all his precepts in the most literal sense, and tried to live by them. Their effort for a short time was in some measure successful. Every man has resources in him of which he only becomes aware in hours of extreme tension. The soldier in battle, the martyr at the stake, the good man struck by dire calamity, is lifted above himself and for the moment can do the impossible. So the disciples under the impulse of the Resurrection appearances were filled with a mighty ardour. The Kingdom became present for them. They could throw themselves forward into it and forget that they were still in the world. In that glorious springtime of the church the absolute ethic of Jesus appeared the natural one; all were of one heart and mind, and accepted the teaching of Jesus as the rule of their common life. But this outburst of moral energy was followed by the inevitable reaction. It grew apparent that the Kingdom was delayed, that the world was still here and was likely to remain. If the church was to survive within the present order, how was it to maintain the ethic which was meant for a higher one?

This was the problem which confronted the church, and has never ceased to do so. Christianity was the Way, and consisted in observing that new rule of life which had been given by Jesus. But how was the Way to be followed? More and more as it came in conflict with harsh realities the church was made aware that its task was impossible, and there must have been times when it was tempted to despair. The hope of the Lord's return had proved delusive. If the new ethic was in any sense to be fulfilled it had somehow to be adapted to the circumstances of the present world.

This, then, was the task to which the church now set itself, and which, on the whole, it performed successfully. Of all the debts we owe to it this, perhaps, is the greatest. The moral teaching of Jesus, in itself impracticable, was turned into current coin. The ethic of the higher order was made a working ethic for man's ordinary life. We have to consider the methods by which this miracle was accomplished.

In the first place, everything that could be remembered of Jesus' sayings was brought together and put into clear and arresting form. We have no means of knowing by whom or in what manner this collection of the sayings was made, but no doubt it was in process for a considerable time. From a comparison of the three Synoptic Gospels it can be gathered that short collections were gradually merged in larger ones, and that the phrasing of the Sayings was sometimes modified in the course of transmission. Yet a real effort evidently was made to preserve the teaching in something like its original form. It prescribed the mode of living to which the church was committed. Although it might not always be carried into action it had to be kept on record as authoritative. Those precepts of Jesus answered to the standard weights and measures which are laid up at the seat of government in a well-ordered state. All commerce in the last resort depends on them, and in case of doubt there must be access to the authentic pattern.

It may be safely affirmed that criticism has gone far astray in recent theories that the sayings attributed to Jesus grew, for the most part, out of conditions in the early church. The assumption is that from time to time the church encountered some urgent difficulty, and a solution was found for it. This was then embodied in a maxim or parable which was ascribed to Jesus himself, so that it might be valid for all future practice. In this manner, it is held, a body of teaching arose which was finally gathered into our Gospels and has been accepted ever since as the teaching of Jesus, although it had its real origin in the experience and reflection of the community. This theory has been worked out in detail, and scholars have attempted to infer from the nature of every saying the "life-situation" or practical exigency in which it originated.

Now it cannot be denied that some of the recorded sayings are plainly meant to bear a special application to the circumstances of a later time. There are various references, for example, to the behaviour of Christians under persecution, and in Jesus' lifetime the disciples were not persecuted. They were not "cast out of the Synagogues" but welcomed, and Jesus was allowed free use of the Synagogue in his teaching. The later conditions must likewise account for the obvious allusion to the church in some of the parables of the Kingdom. This is particularly evident in the parables reported by Matthew, and it must have been read in by the evangelist himself, for when Jesus spoke his parables the church did not exist. It would be easy to collect similar instances of how later developments have affected the record of the teaching, and this was only natural. The tradition, like a river, had flowed down through a channel which coloured it, but from this it is absurd to argue that there was no fountainhead from which it had sprung.

The theory as a whole can bear no serious examination. Apart from many other objections it leaves wholly out of account the most significant fact about Jesus' sayings. They are all spoken from an absolute point of view. Whatever may have been the occasion which called them forth, they are intended to state the rule which holds good for the Kingdom of God. In the present order of things men do not act by this rule and cannot do so; but here is the will of God, as it is done in heaven. It is entirely out of the question that such sayings were devised by the church to meet one and another of its concrete difficulties. What was needed for such a purpose was some definite, matter-of-fact direction, and this is precisely what is lacking in the Gospel precepts. It has been the chief complaint against them in all ages that they offer nothing but counsels of perfection. We consult them when called upon to make some grave decision, and all that we get is a general principle which we are left to apply for ourselves as best we can. The early Christians, like ourselves, were in need of definite guidance.

Ever and again they had to face a situation which was altogether new, and they would have given much for a finger-post that clearly pointed the way. If the church itself devised maxims for its direction it would never have framed such sayings as are found in the Gospels. There is hardly one of them that could have afforded much practical help. When they are not vague and abstract they advise a line of action which could not possibly be followed. No reason can be conceived for the preservation of the Gospel sayings except that Jesus had actually spoken them. For its everyday needs the church required such pointed counsels as were given later in the Epistles of Paul or James. But it treasured those precepts of Jesus because they were his, and expressed the ideals to which a Christian was bound to aspire.

Now and then, as we have seen, a saying has undergone some modification, so as to make it serviceable as a rule of action. This has happened most often in matters that affect law and discipline, where a general principle was useless until it was reduced to explicit terms. Jesus had said, for instance, that the marriage bond had been ordained by God, and must not be dissolved. This absolute prohibition of divorce was found in practice not to be feasible, and the qualifying clause was introduced, "Except in the case of adultery." In the same manner we must explain the curious passage in Matthew on the treatment of offenders. Jesus had said: "If thy brother trespass against thee rebuke him, and if he repent, forgive him. And if he trespass against thee seven times in a day, and seven times in a day turn again to thee saying, I repent, thou shalt forgive him." This is how Luke reports the saying,[4] and

[4]Luke 17:6.

— 184 —

it cannot be doubted that this version is authentic. Jesus will have nothing but forgiveness, free and unreserved. In Matthew, however, the saying is turned into a formal rule of church discipline. "If thy brother trespass against thee, go and tell him his fault between thee and him alone; if he hear thee thou hast gained thy brother. But if he will not hear thee, take with thee one or two more, that in the mouth of two or three witnesses every word may be established. And if he shall neglect to hear the church, let him be unto thee as a heathen man or a publican."[5] Here we have a clear illustration of how the church took liberties sometimes with sayings of Jesus. It did not put words into his mouth which he had never spoken, but in certain cases it defined his words and gave them specific application. He had called for unlimited forgiveness, but there were those who took advantage of this mercy and were a plague to the church, and grew worse themselves for the lack of wholesome discipline. The demand of Jesus was brought into conformity with actual needs.

In the natural course of things all the sayings might have been qualified in a similar way, for in every case they embodied absolute rules which could not be carried out in ordinary life. The church would have saved itself endless difficulty if it had quietly revised the teaching, and thus furnished itself with a practicable moral code, invested with the authority of Jesus. But it refused to do this. Although it was well aware that the demands, as they stood, were impossible, and that it was manifestly falling short of them, it yet kept on record the Lord's own statement of what was meant by the Christian life. Here we have the convincing proof that the teaching of

[5]Matt. 18:15-17.

Jesus has been preserved, substantially as he gave it. With every temptation to make it different the church allowed it to stand, although it bore continual witness, in those days as in all times since, against the behaviour of Christian men. The problem that faces us in the Gospels is not, "Did the church itself devise the sayings which it ascribed to Jesus?" but rather, "Why did it not do so? Why did it burden itself with a code of morality to which it could not possibly give effect?" The answer can only be that it never ceased to regard the ethic of Jesus as primary and authoritative. In practice it might be necessary to modify those demands, but they set the authentic standards of Christian action. Without them Christianity would lose its meaning. This has been the function of the Gospel sayings in all times. There is hope for a man, however unworthy his life may be, so long as he preserves, somewhere in his mind, an ideal of honour and goodness. There is hope for the church while it treasures, even as a memory, the commands once laid on it by Jesus. They have been often disobeyed, and in spite of the best efforts they cannot be obeyed strictly. It may indeed be argued that a complete obedience would be hurtful, since they were not intended for this imperfect world in which we must play our part. Yet the church must remember at its peril that in the teaching of Jesus it has true Christianity. All moral endeavour must have for its aim the fulfilment, in however poor a measure, of the ideal which is there presented. The early church desired to make this plain, and while it knew that the requirements of Jesus could not be enforced in the actual world, it preserved them as sacred. Every Christian was to feel, when no choice was offered him but to follow the lower rule, "This is not what the

Lord commanded; though I have done the best I can, I am an unprofitable servant."

Again, while the church acknowledged that the ethic of Jesus could not be fulfilled in the present world, it formed itself into a society which was separate from the world. From those who were within this circle it required a way of living which in some degree approximated that conceived by Jesus. It provided, in this fellowship of the church, the necessary conditions under which a true Christian life could at least be attempted. Paul admits that in intercourse with their pagan neighbours his converts have to allow for many things which make the Christian life very difficult. Whether they will or not they must consort with idolators and with people living in open vice. A Christian slave, forced to obey a heathen master, could not follow the dictates of his own conscience. But within the brotherhood the Christian rules can be put into practice. Its members have been selected and set apart. They are united in Christian service, and have bound themselves to encourage and support one another. In this fellowship of kindred spirits the obstacles to a better life have been smoothed away; the Christian virtues can be cultivated as in a walled garden. By its very idea the church was the earthly outpost of the Kingdom, and by living for the church Christians were able, in a sense, to live as in the Kingdom. They could endeavour, in intercourse with the brethren, to obey the higher law as it had been laid down by Christ.

It is from this point of view that we must understand the emphasis in Paul's Epistles and the later New Testament books on "brotherly love." Jesus had declared that all our fellow men without restriction are to be considered our neighbours; we must love even our enemies. When Paul bids his converts do good to all men, he takes care to add, "especially to those who are of the household of faith." The Fourth Evangelist, who is also beyond all reasonable doubt the author of the First Epistle of John, regards love as the very essence of Christianity. To possess love is to share in the divine life, for God is love. Yet the love which he has in mind is chiefly that which prevails in the Christian community. "A new commandment I give unto you, that ye love one another"[6]—that is, your fellow-Christians. "Greater love has no man than this, that a man lay down his life for his friends."[7] To all within the church a Christian owes a boundless devotion. This certainly does not exclude a love to those without, but it must take the priority. It must even overshadow family affection, for with his baptism the convert has entered a new family, which must henceforth be more to him than that into which he was born.

It is easy to criticize the manner in which those early Christians held together, and drew a line between their own group and the rest of mankind. This, indeed, was the principal reason why they were suspected and disliked in their own time. The pagans, with all their faults, were sociable and broad-minded. In the sunny Mediterranean lands they lived in the open air, and were thrown into constant intercourse at festivals and in marketplaces. More than ever in the first century, when Rome was bent on fusing together the diverse races of the empire, anything that made for division was strongly resented. The Christians were morose and clannish. They were wrapped up

[6]John 13:34. [7]John 15:13.

in their own small community, lavish in their care for those who belonged to it and indifferent to all outside. They were often referred to in a popular phrase as "enemies of the human race." Much the same opinion has often been held since, and largely accounts for the common aversion to the church. It is denounced as an exclusive body, concerned with its own interests and its own people, and treating the mass of men as outsiders. This is a prejudiced judgment now, as it was in ancient times, but there has always been a measure of truth in it. The church must needs be separate, as Paul pointed out, because in its essential idea it belongs to another world. If it allows itself to be drawn too much into the general life it forgets its own vocation, and those who have charged it with exclusiveness will be the first to condemn it as worldly-minded. Moreover in the early days it was fighting for its existence and could not hope to survive unless it was inwardly united. If it finally withstood all the powers that were ranged against it this was due, above all, to the intense feeling of brotherhood. Few in numbers and individually weak, the Christians were filled with the same spirit and were knit together in the closest fellowship. For this reason the church was invincible.

But the chief motive which impelled the brotherhood to draw a sharp line between itself and the surrounding world was that which has been already indicated. If the demands of Jesus were to be in any degree fulfilled there needed to be a sphere in which all the conditions were made favourable. Among men in general the Christian could look for no co-operation. If he gave way to others, if he was careless about his own possessions, his action would be construed as folly or weakness. But within the brotherhood the higher law could be put into action. Here was a fellowship in which all believed in Christ, and looked for his coming. They could try, at least among themselves, to exemplify the life of the Kingdom. They could exercise forgiveness and self-denial and kindness in something like the manner that Jesus had desired. The mission of the church was indeed to all mankind, but for that very reason it had to form itself into a distinct society. When a man of science has discovered a new principle by which he hopes to revolutionize all industry, he has first to work it out in his laboratory, isolating its activity from everything that might confuse and impede it. The church had discovered a new rule of life, and was confident that by means of it the world could be transformed; but it had first to demonstrate on the small scale what would some day be effective on the great one. It stood aloof from the world in order to make itself a sort of working model of what all society might become.

This has always been one of the great objects of the church. We are often told, and no doubt with some truth, that the Christian ideal of a world ruled wholly by the highest law is nothing but a dream. The lower impulses are too strong. In the future as in the past men will be guided by their self-interest and look solely to material ends. The church, however, offers itself as a society in which the higher mode of life actually has been achieved. Its members are united by a spiritual bond; they make it their aim to serve one another; they call themselves brothers, and think of love and goodness and compassion as the best rewards of living. Gifted writers in our time have drawn pictures of a future society in which all the evils which we now deplore will have disappeared, as a result of scientific progress and a better economic system. The pictures are imaginary, and usually, as we look at them, we are glad to assure ourselves that they will never be anything more. But without any aid from fancy it is possible to throw our minds into the future and see what the world may yet become. The church may be sadly imperfect, but it does, in the plainest manner, foreshadow a time when there will be no false divisions of race and class. It impresses on its people that they should live for higher ends, and be just and honourable, and devote themselves to generous service on behalf of others. The aim of the church is to realize in its own fellowship the conditions which may some day prevail everywhere. It exhibits in concrete form, and in the world of today, what we often think of as a vain dream.

By means of the church, therefore, the ethic of Jesus was made actual. In its full extent it could be realized only in the Kingdom, and was alien, by its nature, to this world; but a community was formed which tried as far as possible to model itself on the Kingdom. This fellowship of the saints kept separate, so that it might be free from the distracting influences which were always thwarting the law of Christ. Within its borders the new principles could be put into action. They seemed to the common eye to be visionary, but here was a body of men and women who were living by them, and in doing so had found a freedom and a happiness of which they had formerly known nothing. The church was thus a standing challenge to the outside world. Might it not be that this rule of love which had justified itself in the Christian community would produce the same result if it were accepted by the whole race of men?

The church thus set itself to exemplify the ethic of Jesus, but it also claimed the right of interpretation. Jesus had made absolute demands, and in their full import they were just as impracticable for members of the church as for those outside of it. All possible means were offered within the society for making the Christian life normal and attractive, and yet it was found that after baptism men were much the same as before. More than ever when the ecstatic mood of the early days had ceased, the old weaknesses reasserted themselves. Paul has bitter complaints to make of the moral conditions in every church he writes to, and it has sometimes been argued that those converts of whom he was so proud had not become Christians at all. Under a thin veneer of Christian belief they were still pagans at heart, with the old vices and egoisms as active in them as ever. This is certainly not true. Paul knew what he was saying when he told the Corinthians that they had been washed, they had been sanctified, they had been justified.[8] The trouble was not that they were still pagans but that they were still men, who found, like ourselves, that the Christian law was beyond them. They could not fulfil it, however the church might assist them, unless allowances were made for their human weakness and for the earthly forces which held them down.

The church, therefore, took on itself the authority to interpret the will of Christ. This is the meaning of the famous passage: "Thou art Peter, and on this rock I will build my church. And I will give thee the keys of the Kingdom of heaven, and whatsoever thou shalt loose on earth shall be loosed in heaven, and whatsoever thou shalt bind on earth shall be bound in heaven."[9] We have seen that in their present form these words cannot have been spoken by Jesus. How they

[8] I Cor. 6:11.   [9] Matt. 16:18, 19.

originated, and what is their precise application will always be matters of dispute, but the main purpose of the verses is sufficiently clear. Peter is taken as the representative of the church, which declares that it has authority to explain the demands of Jesus, and to decide in what manner they shall be obeyed. In themselves they are general and indefinite, ideal principles and not formal rules. It is the duty of the church to relate them from time to time to changing needs and circumstances, ensuring that the lives of Christians will be conformable, at least in spirit, to the will of Christ.

In the Epistles of Paul we have concrete examples of how this work of interpretation was carried out. Paul has to deal with problems and conditions such as Jesus himself had never contemplated. His mission is to Gentiles, living in great cosmopolitan cities, and for the questions addressed to him he can find no direct answer in the precepts of Jesus. He hardly ever quotes these precepts, and even when he plainly has them in mind he only takes the idea and expresses it in his own way. Believing that he possesses the Spirit, that he is an Apostle speaking in the name of the church, he undertakes to bind and loose, pointing out to his converts how they must act on particular occasions if they would be faithful to the Christian law. We feel, in almost every instance, that Paul's judgment is sound. The course of action which he advocates is that which best accords with Christian principles. If Jesus himself had been called on to answer those questions which had arisen in Corinth or Philippi he would have decided much as Paul does. But it is also true that ever and again Paul qualifies the strict demands of Jesus. He does not look solely to the absolute moral law but allows for what is feasible and prudent, even for custom and public opinion. He recognizes that the Christians are living, not in an order in which the will of God is everything, but in the present order, with all the limitations which it places on human capacity and will.

Has the church any right to that authority which it claimed for itself even in New Testament times? This has always been a matter of bitter controversy. Again and again the church has become tyrannical and has substituted its own will for that of Christ. At other times it has been unworthily submissive. In its interpretation of the Christian law it has taken so much account of human desires and frailties that it has given away almost everything. Reformation always takes the form of rebellion against church authority. Some bold spirit denies that it has any real basis, and calls on men to throw it off and rest their faith on Scripture, or the word of Christ himself, or the inward witness of conscience. It has always been an ill day for Christianity when no one has dared to challenge the claims of the church. Even when they are acknowledged there needs always to be the clear perception that they are not final. The church at best is only representative of a higher power, to which every one has the right of appeal. Without this sense of a limit to church authority there can be no Christian freedom.

Yet the authority of the church was necessary, and has justified itself by results. It was, indeed, the inevitable outcome of the nature of Jesus' teaching. What he gave was the ethic of the Kingdom, and the question could not but arise of how this ideal ethic might be made serviceable for the world. Changes were clearly necessary, but who was to make them? The work could not be left to private judgment, for morality consists in obedience to common standards. If each man is to act on rules of his own making, the idea of an ethic is abandoned. There will no doubt be some who will act nobly, with no other guidance than that of conscience, but even with these all conduct will be arbitrary; for the mass of men the issues of right and wrong will be hopelessly confused. There will quickly be an end, too, of anything that might be called a definitely Christian ethic. Christianity was the Way, the new manner of life which had a character of its own. Other types of morality have always tended to be much alike, so much so that it is difficult to tell from the action of a non-Christian what particular religion he professes. If the distinctiveness of the Christian ethic is to be preserved there must be some authority to safeguard and define it.

Private judgment is not sufficient, neither can the decision of any one man or select group of men be final. Even the best of men can only say how he himself would act in a given situation, and his personal judgment cannot be accepted as valid for others. Paul writes as the director of his churches, but he is careful to make clear that he does not do this as an individual. He appeals to his status as an Apostle, an accredited spokesman of the church; in each of his Epistles he associates one or more of his fellow-workers with himself; he is conscious that he utters the mind of the Spirit, which has been given to him in peculiar measure. When he falls back at times on what he knows to be his personal opinion he frankly indicates that his readers need not be bound by it.

So if there was to be an authority, capable of interpreting the will of Christ, this could be only the church. The judgment which it pronounces is no individual one, but is the consensus of all Christian men, and what all are agreed upon is most likely to be right. This may not be so in scientific or intellectual matters, where the opinion of one man who knows must outweigh that of millions who are ignorant. But on moral issues, which concern everybody and which everybody can test for himself, the common opinion is seldom wrong. It may indeed happen that a whole nation, or for that matter a whole church, may be swept off its feet by a gust of passion, and fall into grave moral error; of this there have been many examples. But the church has a continuous life. In the next generation it can revise the judgments of the last, and in the course of its long history it has collected a great store of moral wisdom, out of which it can speak with confidence. This is acknowledged by the world at large, and the church, however else it may be regarded, stands out as the court of appeal before which all ethical questions come up for decision. A line of action which the church has stamped with its approval is generally accepted as the Christian one.

The task has thus fallen on the church of interpreting the mind of Jesus and presenting his demands in such a form as to make them effectual. This means, in almost every instance, that they have in some way to be qualified. If the world is to live by them they need to be tempered to the world's capacity. When we speak of a Christian ethic we usually have in mind this ethic which the church has evolved out of Jesus' teaching, and which is always to be distinguished from the teaching itself. Some reference was made in a previous chapter to the modern theory that what Jesus gave was an "interim ethic," not the moral law as it would be in the Kingdom but a law that men could live by in the interval before the Kingdom came. As an account of Jesus' own purpose this theory is utterly wrong; but the term "interim ethic" might well be applied to the later morality which was sanctioned by the church. Jesus proclaimed the moral law in its absolute nature, and it cannot be so practised in the present world. When the Kingdom comes the will of God will be done perfectly, but meanwhile it can only be obeyed in part. At every turn we come up against some obstacle, in our own nature or outside of us, which reminds us that we are still in the world, and cannot fulfil the law of Christ. In place of it we need to content ourselves with this Christian ethic, which the church has been moulding for us through all these ages. The principles laid down by Jesus are accepted, but at the same time are adapted to earthly conditions. We are subjected to the Christian law not as it is, but as we are able to practise it.

In this ethic sponsored by the church there are undoubtedly serious dangers. For one thing, it involves a compromise and this is always dangerous, especially in the field of morals. One concession invariably leads to another, until the principle which has once been encroached on is abandoned altogether. This has happened again and again in Christian history, and the church may be pardoned if now and then it takes an unbending attitude in matters that seem of little consequence. It has learned how easily the great interests may be sacrificed along with the small ones. A custom that was valuable a century ago may be meaningless today, and there is certainly need for some new adjustment. But in making it there is always a danger, for the trivial thing may be bound up with something vital. When the process of compromise has once started it too often means the end of a binding moral law.

There is another danger, and perhaps a graver one. In its

effort to adapt the law of the Kingdom to the present world the church is tempted to obscure whatever may seem visionary and extreme in the Christian demands. This, it might be contended, is all to the good. As Aristotle perceived, the key to all virtue is moderation, and the excess of righteousness, like any other excess, is apt to defeat its purpose. It is not necessary that all men should be saints and martyrs, but all have a duty to be good citizens and parents, honest in their dealings, truthful, kindly, conscientious. The church has tried to produce this kind of character, and to a wonderful degree has succeeded. But in its anxiety to foster these plain virtues, which it rightly considers the most desirable, the church too easily loses touch with greatness. Even the ordinary man is aware that there is something amiss and says, in his crude fashion, that the church has identified itself with the middle class. This, if it were true, would be no reproach, for the strength of a people is always to be found in its middle class, which corresponds, in the social order, with the temperate zone, the climate best fitted for the higher purposes of life. In all times, by its moral discipline, the church has tended to place its members in this class. But the real grievance against it is, not that it allies itself with a middle class, but that it favours mediocrity; and this, it must be granted, is too generally true. Christianity by its nature is a heroic religion. Its Founder was the supreme hero of our race, the Captain, as the author of Hebrews calls him, of all who have lived and died by faith. His ethic was that of the Kingdom of God, and is so lofty and exacting that the utmost of human effort can never attain to it. Men are all conscious of this, however dimly; and they cannot but feel the difference between the sublime demands of Jesus and the commonplace morality with which the church is so often satisfied.

It is this mediocrity of its moral aims, more than anything else, which has estranged men from the church. Moderation is an excellent thing, but it is not attractive. There is something in all men which craves for the heroic and responds to it. Our human nature is full of strange inconsistencies, and one of them is this, that men who will not put up with some little discomfort will yet, on occasion, freely offer their lives. They cannot bring themselves to practise an everyday virtue which will cost them little and yield an obvious gain, but are capable of a splendid self-denial. The church has allowed too little for this side of human nature. For the most part it has presented an aspect of dull respectability. It has thought to win men over by keeping its requirements at a minimum, and in this way has defeated its purpose. Jesus himself made impossible demands, and this, in the last resort, has been the secret of his power. From time to time great leaders have rediscovered it. They have asserted the Christian law in its full extent, insisting once more that those who will not follow Christ to the death are not worthy of him. Not by weakening the Christian obligations but by making them sterner and more difficult they have touched the heroic instinct and brought new life to the church.

We owe a tremendous debt to those teachers who have protested against the Christian ethic as it is commonly practised, and have called for a strict obedience to the precepts of Jesus. Our religion is ultimately founded on those lofty precepts, and will crumble and fall if they should ever be forgotten. Yet the church, in its effort to adapt the Gospel teaching to actual conditions, has done a great and necessary service. Men are required as Christians to live as in the Kingdom, but the fact remains that they are in this world, and whether they will or not they must come to terms with it. When they seek to defy the earthly order they arrive, too often, not at a higher Christianity but at some kind of fanaticism. The church, in the early days and in all times since, has sought to make Christianity a working religion for the great mass of men. It asks for a mode of living which may not be Christian in the absolute sense, but yet accords with the Christian principles. Instead of a task which is utterly beyond them men are set to one which is within their compass, and which they cannot without shame leave unattempted.

The church has indeed failed at times even in this restricted aim. It has made doubtful compromises. It contains multitudes of men and women who bear only a faint resemblance to those first disciples for whom the invisible world was more real than this one. Yet it needs, perhaps, to have this miscellaneous character if it is to accomplish its work. Now and then there have been small exclusive sects which have applied rigorous tests and have expelled from their communion all who fall short of the very highest standards. It is not these obscure companies of the elect which have done most for the cause of Christ. The common man, aware of his disabilities, has been frightened away from them. Their own members have fallen into a mood of self-righteousness, and in the anxiety to preserve their holiness have shrunk from all contact with many whom they might have helped. A living church is always one which opens its doors widely. Every sort of man can feel that in its fellowship he will find people like himself, with whom he can struggle forward to that higher life which is beyond him but which he desires. One might almost say that the church has done its best work by freely admitting those who have no obvious right to be there. An army gathers into it many unpromising recruits, but it brings them under a glorious banner and puts them into uniforms and trains them. Professing to be soldiers, they become so, and acquit themselves not unworthily in the day of battle.

CHAPTER IX

THE CHURCH AND THE STATE

Ancient religions were tribal or national. The god was, in the first instance, the guardian of the state, and beyond its territory had no jurisdiction. If he cared for individuals it was only in an indirect fashion, as members of the community which worshipped him. His honour was bound up with the victory and prosperity of his people, and while he sought to promote their welfare they made it their ambition to bring glory to their god. Religion and patriotism, in the ancient world, were almost the same thing.

For centuries the Christian religion had no connection with any state, and for this reason more than any other it appeared sinister and dangerous. It was a principle of Roman government that every people should be left free to practise its own religion. In this respect Rome was more tolerant than any imperial power before or since, and it was largely owing to this wise attitude that the Roman peace was so long maintained. But Christianity, almost from the beginning, was excluded from the general liberty. There was no tribe or nation which acknowledged it, and it could not therefore rank as a religion. Its legal status was that of a "superstition," and as such it had no right to exist. It was far more dangerous than any other superstition, since it was not localized but cut across all national divisions. Not only did it lack any state connection, but it threatened the whole idea of a unified state.

This isolation of Christianity was due to the unexpected turn which its history had taken. The original hope of the disciples was to win over the Jewish people. They did not at first surmise that what Jesus had given was nothing less than a new religion. He had appeared as the Messiah, in whom the hopes of Israel were to reach their consummation, and the nation, although for the moment it had rejected him, was sure in a little time to accept him in his true character. The early mission was concentrated on work in Palestine, with a view to the conversion of Israel. When this was secured Christianity would stand out as Judaism, renewed from within and perfected, and would take its place with other national religions. This early hope was frustrated. It soon became evident that the Jews would have nothing to do with the new message. From mere indifference they passed to open hostility, and the mission gradually abandoned Palestine and sought new fields among the Gentiles. It had now to make its appeal simply as a religion, unconnected with any nationality. This was the cause of all its difficulties, from the time of Paul onward. It had to make its way as best it could without any outward credentials. Wherever it appeared in the Roman world it was much in the position of a man who sets out to travel without a passport.

This trouble was due, however, when we look deeper, to no mere historical accident. The nature of Christianity was such that it could not make itself into a national religion. This, indeed, was the reason why the Jews had rejected it. Their religion was based on the confidence that they were the people chosen by God. They clung to the Law, with its ordinances and customs, which marked them out as a race apart. No one was allowed the privileges of their faith unless he was a Jew by descent, or at least by adoption. But it belonged to the very essence of Jesus' message that he proclaimed all men to be children of God. Although he had confined his work to the Jews, he addressed them not as Jews but simply as men. His religion was inherently universal, and could not but break through all national barriers and find its way to all men, as water rises to its level. The Jews resented the endeavour to force on them a religion which denied their sacred prerogatives. Long before the Christians themselves suspected it, the Jews perceived that this Christianity was not Judaism. It was a new religion altogether, and must be left to itself. Wherever it went, men made the same discovery. The Christian message was incompatible with any kind of national restriction. It was alien to all the ideas with which the name of religion had hitherto been associated.

Jesus himself had never interfered with issues that concerned the state. This sometimes has been taken as evidence that his outlook was narrow and parochial. Living in a remote province he had never turned his mind to large political questions, and was, perhaps, hardly aware of them. A view of this kind is manifestly absurd. The time in which Jesus lived was one of intense political excitement. Palestine was already seething with the discontent which was to break out a generation later in the great revolt, and wherever men met their discussion was sure to lead up to the one burning issue of national right as against the domination of Rome. Galilee, for that part, was by no means the tranquil countryside which it has often been pictured. On the contrary, it was notorious as a centre of civil disturbances. The spirit of Jewish independence was warmer in that small province than anywhere else in Palestine, and in Jesus' own childhood Galilee had been the scene of an uprising which had been ferociously quelled and had left bitter memories.

It was in this atmosphere of political ferment that Jesus had grown up, but it is certain that in his teaching he held studiously aloof from politics. The reason is no doubt partly to be sought in the very fact that they counted for so much in the life of the people. Jesus' message was a religious one, and he knew that its meaning would be fatally obscured if it were mixed up with political debate. Moreover, any allusion to the vexed issue of national right would have been dangerous. If he had once committed himself to one side or another of the quarrel there would have been a speedy end to his work as a public teacher. His ministry was short, and the wonder is that it was allowed to continue so long; this was due only to the consummate prudence with which he avoided those perilous controversies which beset him on every side.

His political aloofness, however, is not to be set down to mere prudential motives. If he had believed that the national issue was in any way a vital one he certainly would have dealt with it, regardless of consequences. He held aloof from politics because he was indifferent to them. The one interest which occupied his mind, to the exclusion of all else, was that of the Kingdom of God. A day was at hand when the present order would come to an end and all the questions which now appeared so important would be emptied of meaning. Even now they had become trivial and unreal in view of the tremendous change that was impending. This, we cannot doubt, was the attitude of Jesus to the party conflicts and patriotic agitations of his time. He saw the men of his generation as children play-

ing in the marketplace, so intent on their foolish game that
they did not see the tempest that was gathering overhead and
would sweep this world away.

On one occasion only does Jesus touch directly on the claims
of the state, and even then he does not speak of his own
volition. His enemies, in their effort to collect evidence against
him during the last week in Jerusalem, asked him to say explicitly whether it was right to pay tribute to Cæsar.[1] However he answered he could not but put himself in danger. If he
said "yes," he would alienate the common people who were
his chief support; if he said "no," he could at once be denounced to the Roman government as a rebel. He eluded the
snare by his famous answer: "Render to Cæsar the things that
are Cæsar's, and to God the things that are God's." The answer has often been criticized as an evasion, and a somewhat
unworthy one. Whatever may have been the purpose of the
question put to him, it was perfectly legitimate and important.
How can religious duty be reconciled with loyalty to the state?
This always has been a crucial problem, and for the Jewish
people at that time it was more urgent than any other. A religious teacher had no right to waive it aside by a platitude or
a verbal quibble, which was all that Jesus offered by way of
answer. But when his words are fairly considered they can be
seen to meet the question in a clear and straightforward manner, so much so that they dispose of it definitely and for all
time.

In that brief saying he makes three distinct pronouncements.
First, he frankly acknowledges the right of the state. It confers

[1]Mark 12:13-17.

certain benefits, and those who accept them must make a due return. This idea is brought out forcibly by the gesture with which Jesus accompanied his answer. He surprised his questioners into showing him a coin, stamped with the image and name of Cæsar. While pretending a doubt as to whether they should submit to the emperor they had his money actually in their possession. Since they availed themselves of what he gave them, they were bound, in common honesty, to pay him back. This is still the valid answer to those who enjoy the protection of the state and would yet refuse to do their part in its service. Again, Jesus makes clear in his answer that the right of the state is limited. It has control only in what pertains to the material life. The things that are Cæsar's are money and property, all that concerns man's safety and well-being in the present world. There are other things, which do not belong to Cæsar. Each man is a spiritual being, with a mind and will of his own, with duties and interests which pertain to his higher life. With this side of man's nature Cæsar has nothing to do. Jesus thus closes with his third pronouncement, which is the decisive one. Man's supreme duty is to God. As a spiritual personality he has part in another order of things, and his earthly life is only the means by which he can fit himself for his true destiny. Whatever authority may be granted to Cæsar it must never interfere with man's higher calling, which is to seek first the Kingdom of God.

The saying of Jesus is thus clear and comprehensive, and is fully in keeping with all else that we can gather as to his political attitude. He was indeed a revolutionary, but not in the sense that he wished to overturn the state. He required for the sake of his mission that the country should be peaceful, and many of his parables would seem to indicate that he approved the firm administration which enabled men to buy and sell and till their fields in security and make plans and investments for the future. With the existing form of government he had no quarrel. He indeed condemned the pride and insolence of officials, and the greed which made use of power for base and selfish ends. But in so far as he condemned the state itself, it was only because he saw in it a necessary part of the worldly order. Resting on force and man-made laws and an exaltation of material things, it was by its nature opposed to the Kingdom of God. Some modern writers have contended that Jesus' activity had a political side, which has been carefully concealed in our Gospels.[2] Of this theory there is not a shred of evidence, and in view of the known facts there could not be. Believing as he did, Jesus could not have been a political zealot. The nationalists, whose cause he is alleged to have favoured, were bent on an earthly empire, centred in Jerusalem. But an imperial Israel would have been just as repugnant to him as an imperial Rome, indeed much more so. Rome was pagan, and did not pretend to anything more than worldly ambitions, while Israel was professedly the people of God. Even to pious Jews like the Pharisees the nationalist position was the betrayal of a sacred trust, and this would undoubtedly be the view of Jesus. What he looked for was the merging of this world's order in that of the Kingdom.

He was indifferent, then, to the state, but the state did not return this indifference. It was instinctively suspicious of him and was directly responsible for his death. There is much that

[2]This view has been carried to absurdity in Robert Eisler's learned but preposterous book, *The Messiah-Jesus*.

is doubtful and obscure in the accounts of Jesus' trial, but it
appears certain that he was condemned on political grounds.
The Roman administration in Palestine did not interfere in
religious matters, and when the chief priests brought Jesus
before the governor they dropped the charges on which he had
been tried previously at the meeting of the Jewish Council.
Pilate knew nothing of the nature of his teaching and had no
interest in it; and the accusers threw all the weight on one fact,
that this man had made himself the leader in a popular movement, claiming in some peculiar sense to be a king. It has been
held sometimes that the case was probably disposed of in a few
minutes, as hardly worth consideration.[3] The accounts, however, are all agreed that Pilate gave time and thought to it,
and that he did so may be taken as certain. To a Roman
magistrate, in a province of doubtful allegiance, a charge of
sedition was a matter of extreme gravity. Jesus himself might
be nothing but a harmless enthusiast, and Pilate was disposed,
apparently, to regard him in this light. Yet he might be an
instrument in the hands of crafty conspirators; his religious
movement, as so often happened among the Jews, might develop into a political one, and the matter needed to be fully
probed.

Pilate finally gave sentence on evidence which he knew to
be insufficient, and for this reason he deservedly stands out forever as the symbol of an unjust judge. The function of a judge
is to make his decision on the ground of facts, and Pilate set
vague suspicions in the place of facts, influenced at the same
time by a wish to gain favour with the Jewish authorities. Yet
he believed, we need not doubt, that he was acting in the in-

[3]This is the opinion of S. J. Case in *Jesus: a Biography*.

terests of the state. His duty as governor was to ensure the Roman supremacy, and this prisoner, though he might be only a religious fanatic, was potentially dangerous as encouraging wild hopes which might possibly lead to sedition. The Fourth Evangelist says of Caiaphas that in counselling the death of Jesus he spoke unwittingly in a spirit of prophecy;[4] and this was still more true of Pilate. He perceived, however dimly and unconsciously, that this Messiah of the Jews had challenged the sovereignty of Cæsar. The state and the new religious movement could not exist together.

It was the decision of Pilate which determined the whole future relation of the church and the state. The Founder of Christianity had been condemned as a rebel; this was the one fact about it which every one knew. Tacitus, in the first reference to the new religion which has come to us in general literature,[5] dwells solely on this fact, and takes for granted, as a Roman, that this is sufficient. The idea was fixed in the public mind that Christianity in some way threatened the stability of the state, and from the very outset the church and the imperial power were opposed to each other. At first there was no regular persecution, and Luke does his best to prove that while the Jews were hostile the Roman administration was friendly. But even on Luke's showing Paul had repeated trouble with the magistrates, and this appears much more clearly in Paul's own letters. Christianity had started under political suspicion, and as time went on and its character was more fully known this was not diminished but increased. There was seen to be something in this new religion which was inimical to the very idea of the state.

[4]John 11:49 f.   [5]Tacitus, *Annales,* XV:38–44.

The Church and the State

All the New Testament writers are confronted with the problem of the relation of the church to the ruling power, and we can distinguish two attitudes, at first sight contradictory. On the one hand, the prevailing sentiment is one of frank hostility. Christians had asked for nothing but to be left alone that they might serve God according to their own conscience. They had gone out of their way to comply with all the obligations which the state laid upon them, and had met with nothing but rebuff and ill-usage. They could not but resent this unreasoning hatred and learned to regard the state as their enemy. This attitude is expressed most emphatically in the book of Revelation, which has for its main theme the judgment which God has decreed and will presently execute on the iniquitous empire. The writer thinks of the world as given over to Satan, who has chosen Rome as the instrument through which he rules. Rome, in the person of its blasphemous emperor, is the Antichrist. The end is approaching, when Christ will descend from heaven, destroy his adversary and establish a new order in place of the old one, which will be blotted out forever. It must never be forgotten that the book was written in a time of persecution, by one of the victims. Allowance must be made for a strain of violence, which was alien to the normal Christian judgment. Yet it commonly happens that in a fit of anger a man blurts out his genuine feelings, hitherto carefully disguised, and we cannot doubt that the author of Revelation discloses the secret mind of multitudes of his fellow-Christians. They conducted themselves in every way as law-abiding citizens, but all the time they regarded the state as their enemy and waited eagerly for the happy day when it would perish.

Over against this attitude of Revelation we have that of

Paul. He was himself a Roman citizen, and was proud of this high privilege. He was also a born statesman, with an instinct for law and order, and could not but admire the splendid achievement of Rome. Out of the old confusion it had created a disciplined state, in which Jew and Greek and Barbarian could live peacefully together. It had established a system of justice, and took care that it should be administered by honest and capable men. So for Paul, Rome is not the Beast or the Antichrist but the instrument of God. Order and peace and justice are divine interests, and the power which upholds them has been divinely appointed. Christians are to render submission to the state "for conscience sake," that is, as part of their religious duty. They are to pray for their rulers. They are to obey the laws, not as a matter of constraint, but with the sense that human law is a reflection of God's own law.

It might thus appear as if Paul were wholeheartedly on the side of the state, and passages from his Epistles have done duty in all times to impress on Christian people that they owe entire subjection to the civil power. But there is another side to Paul's attitude. He indeed acknowledges the right of the state, but always with the reservation that it is only temporary. His real opinion is expressed in guarded language in a cryptic chapter of II Thessalonians, where he speaks of the approaching end.[6] It is not yet here but is not far distant; and will be marked by a terrible outbreak of evil, the supreme effort of Satan to destroy the cause of God. The interval is short and might have been shorter, except for a barrier which stands in the way. There is a power that holds back the forces of evil, which are now mounting to a fury. When this power is removed, Satan

[6]II Thess. 2:3–12.

will have complete mastery, and the present world will fall in ruin. Paul is careful to speak in riddles, but it can hardly be doubted that by the "Restrainer" he means the Roman empire. It has been ordained to repress wickedness by main force, to act as a massive dyke to keep back the anarchy from which human society has been reclaimed, and which is always lying in wait to engulf it again. This work of Rome has been beneficent, but is only for a time. The "Restrainer" will shortly disappear, the empire is doomed to fall. Here we are to find Paul's real estimate of the civil power. He sees that it is necessary, and bids the Christians respect and maintain it, but he allows it nothing but a temporary place. God requires that there should be order, even in a world that is intrinsically evil, and for this reason he has appointed the state to act for him. Nevertheless its title is valid only for the interval before the true Kingdom will come in.

Paul's attitude is thus essentially that of Jesus himself, as revealed in the saying on the tribute money. Cæsar must have his due. Christians are to submit to authority, and to regard it as just and necessary, but always on the condition that they do not accept it as final. They are to live for the Kingdom of God, and to realize that in their inner life they already belong to it. If there is any conflict between the two loyalties to God and to Cæsar, they must not hesitate as to which has the prior claim. Paul, in fact, is in ultimate agreement with the view which dominates the book of Revelation. Although he does not condemn the state as evil he recognizes, like John, that it is bound up with the present order and is one of the old things which will pass away when Christ appears. Our citizenship, as Christians, is in heaven.

One thing is noteworthy in all the New Testament references to the state, even in those passages of Paul which call on Christians to honour and support it. The obedience which is enjoined is all of a passive nature. Taxes are to be paid, laws are to be respected, rulers are to be held in reverence for the sake of their office. But there is no suggestion that Christians are actively to assist the state. We now consider it one of the normal Christian duties to participate, as opportunity offers, in the direction of public affairs. The church must interest itself in the general life of the community. It must point the way to better legislation; it must do what it can to humanize commerce and industry; it must lift up its voice against all aggression and selfish policy. We demand of Christian men that wherever possible they should take their place as leaders in the national and civic and economic life; if this is denied them they should at least be vigilant citizens, always conscious of their responsibility for the common welfare.

Of all this there is nothing in the New Testament. One reason no doubt is that the church in that early time was so inconsiderable that it could exert no influence on the conduct of affairs. Moreover, under the Roman system, all government was in the hands of an official class, which would brook no interference from the outside. If Christians had tried to meddle in politics, or had even drawn up a protest against some abuse, they would only have brought disaster on the church, confirming those suspicions of its character which it was most anxious to allay. Apart, however, from such practical difficulties, the church, in view of its principles, could not render to the state anything but a passive obedience. Looking for the Kingdom which was to come, it stood aloof from the world. To be sure, it had still to remain there, but this could be only for a time and all that was required was patient endurance until the interval of waiting was over. The state, on the other hand, was the power of this world. It might be necessary and beneficent, as Paul was willing to admit, and Christians would do well to support it. In return for the protection it afforded them they must render it scrupulous obedience. But it was not for them to take an active part in an order of things to which they did not belong. They were in the position of aliens in a foreign country, who observe the laws and pay the taxes as faithfully as the native citizens, and are grateful for all the benefits they are allowed to share. They recognize, however, that they have no right to take public office, and must not be too free even in offering their opinions. It is not their own country, and their part is simply to comply with the arrangements it deems best. This, indeed, is the very illustration which is employed more than once in the New Testament. The Christians are reminded that they are "strangers and sojourners," that is, resident aliens in a land which is not theirs. They accept the order in which they find themselves, but know that they must keep their distance. They cannot forget that they are only here for a time.

As it grew apparent that the world was not coming to an end this attitude was changed. The Christians were now in the position of aliens whose sojourn will be permanent. Since this country is to be their home they naturalize themselves, and perhaps interfere too much with matters which they do not fully understand. Within a century of Paul's death we hear of Christians who held official positions in the state. We see the church transforming itself into a society which had more and more to be reckoned with in political affairs. Finally it entered into full partnership with the state, and in great measure controlled it. The community which had held rigorously aloof from the world was now an integral part of the world's order.

This alliance of church and state was helped forward by the ancient conception, which had never died out, that a nation must formally associate itself with a religion. Rome had brought all the separate countries under a single authority, and the external union had gradually become a real and voluntary one. Old divisions had been obliterated, and there had arisen a great international state in which men thought of themselves not as Gauls or Greeks or Syrians, but simply as members of the empire. But this vast society which had everything else in common had no common religion, and while this was lacking it could not feel itself to be in the full sense a nation. Attempts were made to supply the want, by blending all the existing cults in an eclectic system, by replacing the traditional religions by a philosophy, by making the state itself, in the person of its head, the object of worship. These devices were all artificial, and served only to accentuate the need for a genuine religion in which all could unite. Inevitably the choice fell on Christianity. It was identified with no particular nation, and this fatal drawback which had condemned it to persecution now gave it a supreme advantage. By its nature it was not a local but a universal religion, the only one which could serve the purpose of a universal state.

The union of church and state was effected under Constantine, without any clear perception of what it implied; but eventually a basis was found for it in an imposing theory, developed by the great thinkers of the Middle Ages. It was held that God had entrusted the government of the world to two separate powers, which were to work hand in hand. As man is at once an earthly and a spiritual being, so there must be two organs for the maintenance of human society. Material interests are committed to the state, while the church is sovereign in the spiritual realm, and between these two there must be a perfect concord. The mediæval world was built up on this conception. In place of the empire which had now fallen there was established the Holy Roman Empire, under the dual control of pope and emperor. Theoretically they acted in harmony, but in practice they were always in conflict, and Dante attributes to this division all the miseries and calamities of his time. He never questions the theory; he only complains that in their ignorance and malice men have frustrated the plan of God. If the church and the state will each keep its appointed orbit, if they will both act in unison, if there will arise a Christian emperor and a truly Christian pope, then at last the world will be at peace.

In various ways this has been the dream of many thinkers since. They have laboured to show how church and state might so co-operate as to produce the ideal society, the church supplying noble designs which the state would set itself to execute. But the trouble is that the two powers never can be brought to understand each other. As soon as they try to draw together, they seem to spring apart. Every possible means has been contrived to make them united, but the experiment has always failed. It seems obvious and necessary that there should be two institutions, one for the secular, another for the spiritual needs. It seems reasonable, also, to assume that these two institutions, each in its own sphere, may work towards the same end and assist each other. Yet in point of fact they have always been in conflict. With the best will on both sides they have never been able to see with the same eyes and co-ordinate their effort. For the last fifteen hundred years the world's history has turned on the unending quarrel of church and state. Why is it that they can never be reconciled?

For an answer to this question, as to so many others, we need to go back to that early time when the church came into being, in consequence of the message of Jesus. It began as the community of the Kingdom. Renouncing the present world, which was doomed to destruction, it allied itself with the new order, and in the act of joining it men changed their allegiance, and became, in a literal sense, citizens of heaven. From the outset, therefore, there was a radical antagonism between the earthly society and the church, and the earliest Christians were fully aware of this antagonism. They formed a brotherhood which was to be separate and self-contained, acknowledging no control but that of the Spirit, which would rule in the new age. Even when it grew apparent that the world's order would continue, the church refused to submit to it except in part. Its attitude was one of passive endurance. Although it acquiesced in the earthly government it would do nothing that might actively help it. The church must show that it had no portion in this world, and was waiting for the Kingdom.

Thus in early Christianity the opposition of church and state was accepted as self-evident. Thinkers and scholars have laboured hard to discover from the New Testament how the two powers may be reconciled, but however the various texts may be scrutinized and distorted the labour will always be futile. The early church conceived of itself as wholly distinct from the state. While it was submissive and conciliatory it looked for a day when the present order of things would be dissolved. So long as it lasted the state was necessary, but the church represented the Kingdom of God and the state this present world, which is inherently evil. The church could have nothing in common with the alien power to which it had yet to submit, if it was to maintain itself on earth. Its submission was only a part of that "patience of the saints" which would finally be rewarded by the great deliverance.

The state was conscious, however dimly, that this was the Christian attitude. It has often seemed strange that the tolerant Roman government was so bitterly opposed to the Christians, who gave it no trouble and were morally the soundest element in the population. The persecutions have been set down to some blind prejudice, or to the malice of crafty enemies. But from its own point of view the state was justified. It perceived that the Christians did not in their hearts accept its supremacy. Although they offered no active opposition they were enemies of the state. What we now know as passive resistance was making its appearance for the first time, and Rome was puzzled by the new phenomenon. It could see, however, that this want of sympathy might prove more dangerous than open rebellion and gradually undermine the strength of the state. The great persecutions began in the third century, when the empire, after long security, was faced by the menace of invasion, and was finding itself impotent. Something, it was felt, had been eating away the force and loyalty of the people, and what could this be but the new religion, with its insidious promise of another Kingdom? Moreover, although the Christian doctrines were little understood they were known to be subversive of the moral order on which the state was founded. Celsus, who made the first reasoned attack on Christianity in the middle of the second century, was a fair-minded man, who had studied the Gospels at first hand. He gives it as his deliberate opinion that those who followed the teaching of Jesus were bad men. They were humble, and advocated peace, and had no desire for wealth and power, and were friendly to the weak and outcast. But a man's first duty was to the state, and it needed citizens who would assert themselves and increase in wealth and make it their one ambition to be strong. This pagan recognizes, in his own manner, that Christianity stands for a new order, incompatible with the interests of this world.

For the early Christians, then, the church and the state were radically opposed. This view was modified as time went on, and the hostility gave way to an understanding, and finally to an alliance; but the primitive attitude was, on Christian principles, the logical one. The church exists for the Kingdom of God, the state for the present world; and there can be no real affinity between them, although they must live side by side. The state at its best is concerned with earthly ends, which must be attained by earthly means. It has to ensure its own security and assert its might. It must aim at enriching itself, if need be at the expense of others. All this is contrary to the Gospel teaching, and is yet necessary. As a power of this world the state has no choice but to act on principles which are inherent in the world's order. The question of war is the capital instance. There cannot be a doubt that war is the very negation of the gospel; and yet the state must be prepared for it, and is unfaithful to its task if it does not, on a right occasion, en-

gage in it with its utmost might. However noble may be the
purposes of a state it has to achieve them within the limits
of this world's order, in which conflict, of one kind or another,
is a primary law. It may be that some day the struggle will take
a less barbarous form than mutual slaughter, but this is the
utmost that can be hoped for. We shall always be faced by the
paradox that great moral interests must, at a certain point, be
asserted by what seem to be immoral means. What we su-
premely care for and believe in we must be ready to fight for,
and the refusal to do so becomes wrong. The church, however,
stands for an order which is different from the earthly one. In
this higher order the material things are worthless. Each man
looks, not to his own welfare, but to that of others, and the
poor, the meek, the peaceable alone are blessed. For the state
to conform itself to this higher order would be suicidal. It cannot exist as a state unless it keeps step with the earthly order
of which it forms a part.

So between the church and the state there is a radical contradiction. It has been disguised in various ways, and can be at
least partially reconciled. We have seen how Paul himself regards the state, within its own sphere, as an instrument of God.
The world is evil and must shortly come to an end, but while
it lasts it must be saved from anarchy. It is God's will that
order and justice should prevail everywhere, and on this earth
He has committed the duty of enforcing them to the state. The
later church has taken up this New Testament principle, and
has found in it a common ground on which it can co-operate
with the political power. In so far as the state exists for great
moral ends the church has felt justified in upholding it, even
when these ends have to be pursued by doubtful means. Yet

the attempt to harmonize the earthly power with the spiritual one invariably breaks down, and sooner or later results in conflict. As we look back over the last thousand years we can see that the state, at almost every turn, has found the church in its way, and has tried every method of keeping it harmless. Sometimes it has bribed or cajoled, sometimes it has persecuted. In recent years all civilized peoples have been horrified by the revival in Russia and Germany of those scenes of martyrdom which we had come to associate with the dark ages. It may be granted that these nations have indeed reverted to a condition of barbarism, but for their persecution of the church they may plead a real necessity. Church and state belong to two different worlds, and between them there is always a latent antagonism. When the state is determined to make itself everything it finds an unyielding obstacle in the church. This community which stands for a higher world must be broken before the earthly power can be supreme.

How can church and state be so harnessed together that they may work in concord? This is a problem which will never cease to occupy the minds of thinkers and statesmen, but it will never admit of a satisfactory answer. Anything but an external union of church and state is not possible, neither is it desirable. At various times they have seemed to be in full agreement, but this has always been due to a surrender on the part of the church. The evidence is written large in the history of the past that a church thus dominated by the worldly power is dead, and that it only comes to life again when it begins to protest and oppose. It is not too much to say that the true function of the church in relation to the state is this one of unceasing pro-

test. There is no need that Christians should be hostile to the
state, or return to the primitive attitude of a mere passive obedience. Since the state is necessary to this world they live in they
must take their due part in it and work for its stability and
honour. Yet they must never lose the consciousness that there
is something beyond the state, and that its motives and actions
must be judged continually in the light of that other order.
It must perform its task under earthly conditions, and if it lost
sight of them and looked solely to the higher standards it
would come to ruin. None the less, it is these which the church
must ever insist on. It must condemn the state when it falls
short of them, as it cannot but do even when it has tried its
best. This attitude of constant protest is a thankless, and often
it might seem an unreasonable one, but if it takes any other
the church fails in its duty. It represents the Kingdom
of God, and can never simply endorse the actions of the
earthly power.

The state cannot but resent the criticism to which it is thus
subjected, often when it is struggling to do right in the face of
great difficulties. Yet the opposition of the church is necessary
for the welfare of the state itself. The worldly interests of
which it is the guardian are inextricably involved with higher
ones, and if these are neglected it fails even in its more immediate aims. By the presence of the church it is reminded continually that it is doing only half its duty. The protesting voice
may be unwelcome, but when it is silent the state cannot be
truly itself.

For one thing, it must maintain liberty, and this, in the final
issue, is the sense of responsibility to a power above the present
world. So long as men look only to some visible authority they

are not free. They are in bondage to the will of a despot, or the will of the crowd, or the mechanical forces of nature. They attain to freedom only when they can feel themselves to have part in a spiritual order, over which nothing in this world has any control. "We must obey God rather than men"; this must always be the final statement of what is meant by liberty. It is the church which fosters even in its humblest member this frame of mind, and so makes him a free man. By so doing it performs a service which is essential to the very life of the state. It might seem as if the church were forever interfering with laws and methods which on practical grounds are advisable, and short-sighted rulers are anxious, for this reason, to override or suppress it. But the highest interest of the state is liberty, and this is one, in the last resort, with that faith in God which is guarded and sustained by the church.

Again, it is like the mainspring of all impulse to move forward. We read of ancient cities in which no change of law or custom was ever permitted, and this is the natural instinct of the state. Its one aim is to preserve what it has already, and it is nervously afraid of everything that might disturb the settled order which it has been at such pains in creating. There have been nations in the past which have endured for ages with nothing that can be properly called a history. The generations have followed each other, in the same round of simple aims and activities, never venturing on anything new. This, indeed, is the purpose of the state, to provide a fixed framework within which a race of men can maintain its own character and traditions, and when changes take place they are due, not to voluntary action, but to forces from without which break in on the accepted order. The church is a force of this kind which

is constantly operative. It keeps judging the life of the state by
other standards. It denies the value of possessions and achievements on which the state is wont to pride itself. There is thus
a contact not merely with a different culture but with a different world, a cross-fertilization of the earthly order of things
with the higher, spiritual one. The state is intolerant of the
church, which troubles its self-complacency and makes men dissatisfied with the conditions under which they live. But this
discontent is the motive power of all progress. It may be said
confidently that the advances of the last centuries would never
have been dreamed of had it not been that the church kept
constantly before men's eyes the vision of the Kingdom of
God. Whatever was accomplished there was always the desire for something better. Out of this striving towards a world
other than that which we know, all progress has ultimately
sprung.

Once more, it is the church, with its message of the Kingdom, which gives meaning to the life of the state. In the natural order there is no purpose. The stars go round forever;
plants and animals endlessly reproduce their kind. It is only
in the life of man that purpose reveals itself. This, indeed, is
the distinctive quality of man, that his work is consciously
directed to an object, and the worth of his life is measured by
the nature of the object for which he labours. If it is to have a
real value the purpose must, in some sense, be a spiritual one.
This is vouched for by the universal experience that material
things, as soon as they are gained, prove empty. Every age has
echoed the cry of Ecclesiastes, "Vanity of vanities, all is vanity."
Riches, honours, pleasures, appear at a distance to be satisfying, but the moment they are attained the virtue goes out of

them. This is no moral platitude but the grim fact which makes half the tragedy of human life.

And as it is with individual men, so with the community. It has value and meaning only as it works towards a purpose, and the purpose must be a spiritual one. There have been great empires which have come and gone, leaving hardly a name behind them. They aimed at nothing but their own aggrandizement or material well-being, and with all their industry and conquest they accomplished nothing. There have been small nations which seemed to be of no account, and will yet be remembered and revered forever. They were dedicated to some high purpose, to the quest for truth, for beauty, for righteousness, and all that they did has for this reason a lasting significance. So it is the function of the state not merely to maintain itself but to keep before it a spiritual purpose. Without this it is no true state; its existence is futile; its tumultuous doings will appear in retrospect to be nothing but the idle play of waves upon the beach. The church ensures for the state that it is living for a purpose. Its activities may be the common, earthly ones, but they are linked up with the endeavour towards something higher. They have substance in them, and contribute to the final purpose for which man exists on earth.

Between the church and the state there is thus a real relation, but it does not consist in an alliance which will enable them to act in unison. The relation is rather one of opposition, and it is this which constitutes its value. Jesus declared that this world is soon to come to an end and that men should look for that Kingdom of God in which they would find life. The church arose as the community of the Kingdom, and this, in essence, has been its meaning ever since. In the midst of the earthly order it represents the higher one, to which man belongs as a spiritual being. It is thus contrary to the whole nature and intention of the state, which is concerned with man's interests in this world. The church enrols him as a citizen, not of his earthly country, but of another, which obeys a different law. Hence it cannot but divide his loyalty, and must be regarded by the state with a certain fear and suspicion. Yet for this reason it is necessary. Left to itself the state would be blind to man's true nature, and would fail even in its limited task of providing for his earthly welfare. It needs always to have this other power over against it, which reminds it that its authority is partial and continues only for a time.

CHAPTER X

CONCLUSION

Before the end of the first century a movement had begun which was to divide the church for several generations. According to the Gnostic teachers the material world was wholly evil and had arisen through some primal error or catastrophe. Christ had descended from the higher sphere that he might rescue the souls which were imprisoned in the realm of matter. He had made them aware of their bondage, and had sought to restore them to that world of light out of which they had fallen.

This teaching, involved though it was in a fantastic, half-pagan mythology, made a strong appeal to many of the most earnest Christian minds, and it is hard at first sight to account for this attraction. Perhaps it lay chiefly in this—that Gnosticism appeared in its own fashion to reassert the genuine Christian belief, which was in danger of being thrust into the background. Jesus had proclaimed the Kingdom of God and had required of men that they should break with this world, which was unreal and was now nearing its end. The church had been unfaithful to this message. It had given up the hope of the Kingdom as an illusion, and was seeking to reconcile itself to the world.

The Gnostic movement was overcome, but the protest implied in it has been repeated in ever new forms, and is familiar to us at the present day. Later Christianity, we are told, has

— 228 —

been nothing but a confession of defeat. The church has been engaged in the hopeless task of facing both ways. It clings, at least formally, to the original hope for the Kingdom, and is careful all the time to make terms with the world. Secretly aware that its hope is baseless, it refuses to abandon it, and yet in practice accepts the worldly order as the real one. This, it is alleged, is the weakness of Christianity as compared with other religions, or substitutes for religion. They may not profess so much, but they take life honestly, with all its limitations, and are content that it should be well-ordered and that human beings, while they live, should enjoy a reasonable happiness. Even this restricted aim may be difficult to attain, but it does not entail the doubt and failure and disillusionment which cannot but await us as Christians.

It may be answered, however, that the church was not driven to its later attitude by any sense of defeat. When the Kingdom failed to come, in the years that followed Jesus' death, the disciples did not conclude that they had been mistaken. They only inferred that they had misunderstood the "little time" of which he had spoken. His promise of the Kingdom still held good, but it would be necessary, perhaps for ages, to reckon with the present world; and its claims must be duly acknowledged. It was realized, too, that while he had spoken in apocalyptic language, he was thinking not so much of two ages as of two worlds, the visible, material one and the higher spiritual world which is over against it. So it was not owing to any inconsistency that the church continued to preserve its early belief. All that it did was to recognize that two facts are equally certain. The present order of things is real, so also is the Kingdom of God, of which Jesus had spoken.

How can we do our part in this world, and yet live for the Kingdom? Almost from the beginning the church was faced with this problem, and has been striving ever since to find its solution.

The problem might have been evaded if the disciples had simply withdrawn from the world and formed themselves into a holy community, wrapped up in itself. This was the course adopted in the various monastic movements of later times, and it might well have suggested itself to the early believers. Only a day or two's journey from Jerusalem there was a sect which had chosen to dwell apart in the wilderness. The disciples must have known of this sect of the Essenes, and perhaps their first impulse was to follow its example. Although they waited in the city, expecting to meet the Lord on his return, they remained a group by themselves. They shared their possessions and took their meals together; their meetings for worship were private; before the day of Pentecost they apparently had no thought of a mission. Why was it that they gave up their isolation and threw themselves into the world?

One reason may be found in the very confidence with which they awaited the Kingdom. The crisis was regarded as so imminent that it was not worth while to make any change. They were better to remain as they were, in the full assurance that all present arrangements were only for a little time. Paul develops this idea in a graphic passage of I Corinthians where he impresses on his converts that they were to seek no alteration in their worldly circumstances.[1] Those who were single were not to marry; slaves were not to desire their freedom; workmen were to stick to their occupation, whatever it might

[1]I Cor. 7:17-24.

be. The whole scheme of things was soon to become different, and to change one's mode of living would be only a distraction. "In what state soever a man finds himself, therein let him abide with God." This was the general feeling among the early Christians. Being in the world they made no effort to escape from it, since it was presently to dissolve of its own accord. In a sense this has always remained the Christian attitude. The believer follows his ordinary calling, assured that his part in this world is only provisional. He has no need of a hermitage, for his mind is fixed on the Kingdom. Sharing in the earthly interests he can yet sit loose to them, and under all conditions "therein abide with God."

Again, the position of the early church was fully in line with Jesus' own teaching. He had indeed announced that the Kingdom was near, and had summoned men to live for it, detaching themselves from the world. But he thought of the Kingdom in its moral aspects, as the higher order in which the will of God was done perfectly. What was needed for entrance into it was an inward disposition, a will in harmony with God's will. Jesus himself had "come eating and drinking." In all outward respects he had conformed to the world's order, and his separateness had been inward and moral. It is wrong to think of him as a social or political rebel, and it is equally wrong to class him among the ascetics who have despised the world. What he required was the new will. Those who possessed it, although they mingled freely, as he himself had done, with the life around them, were children of the Kingdom.

The Christian relation to the world was further determined by the inherent character of the new religion. It was not national, like the other religions of the time, but universal. At the outset this could not clearly be perceived. The disciples were Jews and had little outlook beyond the confines of their own country. They took for granted that Jesus had fulfilled the hopes of Israel and that his message was in addition to the Law. Baptism was conferred only on members of the Jewish race, or on proselytes who had been adopted into it by circumcision. None the less, the broader scope of the new teaching was apparent from the first. Jesus had limited his work to his own countrymen, but he had taken no part in their feuds and controversies. He had been the friend of publicans and sinners. He had not been a solitary like John the Baptist, who had to be sought out in the wilderness, but had himself approached the people and taught in their fields and villages. So when his followers continued the brotherhood into which he had called them they could not fence it off as a monastic group. Waiting for the Kingdom it yet associated itself with the ordinary life of men. All who would were at liberty to enter it. Paul extended his mission to the Gentile world, but he inherited the missionary impulse from those before him. The church had always been conscious that it was entrusted with a message which must be freely proclaimed to all men, and this was apparent not only to the Church but to the outside world. We learn from the book of Acts how new converts, even in the earliest days, were continually seeking admission. Gentiles were eager to join the brotherhood, in spite of the efforts which were made, for a considerable time, to exclude them. The expansion of the church, it might almost be said, was not due so much to its own initiative as to that of the world itself, which recognized, before the church did, that the Christian message was universal, and insisted that all false barriers should be thrown down.

We can see, then, how the church and the world were brought together from the first. While they waited for the world to end, the disciples remained friendly with it, not only through the necessities of daily living, but because of the principles of their religion. As followers of Jesus they could not but feel in sympathy with their fellow men. So in the later endeavour to reconcile the church with the earthly order there was nothing inconsistent. It answered to the original Christian attitude, with only this difference, that what had always been done unconsciously was now done deliberately. In the days when the disciples were waiting from hour to hour for the Kingdom, they still preserved their human relations with the world around them. Now, when they perceived that the coming of the Kingdom was delayed, they took pains to strengthen these relations. The church did not cease to be the community of the Kingdom, but it sought to make a place for itself within the present order, and took on the form of an earthly society.

This change could not be made without some measure of compromise. Adapting itself to the existing conditions, the church consented in practice to much that was alien to it in theory. Paul admits to the Corinthians that if they strictly fulfilled their calling they would need to go out of the world altogether; and he can do no more than enjoin on them that within their own brotherhood they must try to follow the higher rule.[2] Even with this restriction he is careful not to de-

[2] I Cor. 5:9-11.

mand too much. He makes allowance for weak brethren and for those who are in circumstances of peculiar difficulty. He takes into consideration established laws, public opinion, social conventions, dictates of common prudence. One of his chief interests in all the Epistles is to warn his converts against all avoidable friction with their pagan neighbours. In the Pastoral Epistles, which claim to represent the Pauline tradition, the spirit of compromise is much more evident. The Christian ideal is no longer that of the saint or martyr but that of the pious citizen, honest and diligent, earnest in good works, accepting with thankfulness God's material gifts but temperate and generous in his use of them. Religion, for this writer, is the means of happiness in this world as well as in that to come.[3] He blends the ethic of Jesus with the higher pagan morality of his day. Fervently believing in the coming Kingdom he so interprets its law as to make it fully practicable in the world that is.

Popular Christianity has always been a compromise, and perhaps it is only in this form that the gospel teaching can ever be made intelligible. The Kingdom of God, for most people, implies a betterment of the present order, not an order which is radically different. Protestantism has been especially prone to a confusion between honest service of this world and service of the Kingdom. The principle was laid down by Luther that zeal in his earthly vocation is an essential mark of the Christian man, and the principle is in the main a sound one. But it lies open to grave misunderstanding. On the strength of it men have convinced themselves that by working industriously, often for selfish and material ends, they are in

[3] I Tim. 4:8.

the best sense religious. The success which attends hard work has been extolled as the divine blessing, rightly bestowed on those who have done God's will. It is worth remarking that this glorification of work for its own sake has no sanction in the teaching of Jesus. More often than not he speaks of work disparagingly. He regards it as simply the means whereby life may be sustained from day to day; when it is pushed further it has no moral value, and serves only to gratify pride and earthly desires. The demand of Jesus is always, "Seek first the Kingdom of God, and the other things will be added." When life is directed primarily to work for those other things it misses its true purpose. One cannot but feel that the so-called "gospel of work" has obscured for many people the real meaning of Christianity. It has been preached by Carlyle and other modern prophets with tremendous earnestness, and has been acclaimed as the one religion which is safe and practical. Rightly considered it is the negation of religion. It rests on the assumption that this world is everything, and that labour for it will serve as an equivalent for doing the will of God.

The church, then, tried to adapt the demands of Jesus to the worldly conditions. This it saw to be necessary if it was to maintain itself in the present order of things, which was likely to continue indefinitely. It saw, moreover, that if it was to prosecute its mission and win the world to accept its teaching, it had to meet the world halfway. No one can deny that this course adopted by the church was more than justified by the result. If it had held without any compromise to its original message it could never have been more than a small hermit community, of little significance for the great mass of mankind. It could never have accomplished the work it has done indirectly for the cause of freedom, for education, for art and philosophy, for the spread of a purer morality. As we survey the history of the past centuries we realize how vast has been the influence of the church in every field of human enterprise, and this has been possible only by its co-operation with the world. But it may also be contended that by this co-operation the church itself has grown more truly Christian. When all is said, the world is not a mere obstacle in the way of the higher life, but contributes to it, and thereby has a religious value of its own. This was urged powerfully by the Christian thinkers who assailed the Gnostic position in the second century. They argued that the world had not arisen in consequence of some fatal error, but had been planned and created by God. He had set His people in it that they might serve Him, that they might learn to trust Him, that through shadows and symbols they might rise to knowledge of Himself. If the church was to become fully aware of its own nature and calling, it had to accept its place in the world.

The church was thus justified in organizing itself as an earthly society, and also in its apparent compromise with aims and standards which fell short of the gospel teaching. Jesus had required an absolute obedience to God's will, and within the limitations of man's present existence this could not be. If the gospel precepts were to be carried into action they needed to be made practicable. Men cannot live in this world as if they were in the Kingdom, but they can at least keep before them the principles which Jesus had laid down, and try, according to their capacity, to follow them. It is easy to accuse the church of inconsistency, showing that in every age it has contented itself with the second-best, and has never lived up to the full stature of the religion which it has professed. All this is true, but surely it is something to have made Christianity a working rule of life. Only a few rare saints have ever been able to attempt entire obedience to the law of Christ, and even they have confessed their failure. Of all men, indeed, they have been most bitterly conscious that his law cannot be fulfilled. But millions of men and women have understood the Christianity taught by the church, and have put it into practice. The Christian life has been brought within their compass, so that they admit themselves to be without excuse when they fall short of it. The religion set before them may be only a poor reflection of that of Jesus, but it does represent, however imperfectly, what he had in mind. This, indeed, is the chief glory of the church, that it has made the law of the Kingdom effectual in the everyday life of the world.

In its ultimate nature, however, the church is opposed to this world's order. It had its origin in Jesus' message of the Kingdom and is nothing else than the brotherhood of those who live for the Kingdom. In the midst of the earthly order it stands for a higher one, in which all present values are reversed. The first disciples thought apocalyptically, and looked for a visible return of Christ and a sudden transformation of the whole existing order. But the apocalyptic ideas were only accidental. What the primitive church believed in was the reality of a higher world, and this, however we may conceive it, is still the fundamental belief of the church. It is the standing protest against the world as it is. It is always in conflict with the wisdom of the age, with the current morality, with the social and political institutions. The very reason of its existence is to condemn the order of this world, in which for the time being it must remain. All through its history, even when it has been most corrupt, it has preserved some knowledge of its true calling.

This faith in a visionary world might seem to be its weakness. It calls on men to look away from present realities and set their hearts on things invisible and aims which in their nature are unattainable. Almost from the outset it found itself compelled to qualify its message, and adjust the absolute demands of Jesus to actual conditions. In our days, more than ever, we have grown impatient of everything that seems merely visionary. So much has been accomplished by taking facts as they are and carefully building on them, that everything else is thrown aside as futile. The church, with its reliance on the unseen and intangible, appears to be nothing else than a survival from a credulous age. Conscious that it is thus regarded it grows anxious to compete with the world on its own ground, and gives an ever larger place to its practical activities. By devotion to man's welfare in this world it seeks to demonstrate that it does not live among the clouds, but has its feet planted, like other communities, on the solid earth.

Now it cannot be denied that all beneficent action falls legitimately within the sphere of the church. In the past it has taken the lead in every struggle for liberty, justice, relief of poverty and suffering. If it ever ceases to interest itself in these causes the life will go out of it. But most of the practical work has now been taken out of its hands. It has so far leavened the mass of men with Christian sympathies that other organizations have arisen which attend to man's earthly needs more skilfully and efficiently than it can pretend to do. The church can aim at little more than at imparting the Christian spirit to men and women who will train themselves, in the necessary manner, for all good works. There is one thing, however, which only the church can do. Its true function consists, as it has always done, in bearing witness for the Kingdom of God. In the midst of the earthly order it asserts the fact of a spiritual order, and makes it a reality in the minds of men.

The church is indispensable for the very reason that it concerns itself with things that can never be realized in this world. It might thus seem to have no value for the ordinary conduct of human life, but the opposite is true. Man is so made that he cannot pursue even his normal tasks unless he has a goal before him which is unattainable. The artist seeks for beauty, the scholar for knowledge, the saint for righteousness—all of them aware that however far they travel there is something beyond. It is this which gives meaning to their quest, and will and energy to persevere in it, for everything loses its worth when you know that there is a fixed limit. A theory has lately been put forward that the universe is finite. To be sure, it extends on every side for more millions of miles than there are grains of dust on this planet; but it is a circle with a line drawn round it, and somewhere at the back of the Milky Way it comes to an end. The mind instinctively shrinks from this suggestion. If the universe is finite, it is not worth living in; it begins to feel stuffy; there is no room in it for a man to stretch himself. That he cannot but think in this way is the proof of man's greatness. His life, as we know too well, is frail and transient, occupied with little earthly things; but he cannot live it without the abiding conviction that it is linked up with the eternal.

The church is rooted in this human need for a contact with

the higher world. It is an earthly society, subject to material conditions, but it is also the community of the Kingdom. It originated in those days of rapture, when Jesus had died and risen again, and the Kingdom was apprehended for a little time as a present reality. The group of believers, looking from hour to hour for the Lord's return, could feel that already they had done with the world and had entered on the new age. As the time of waiting was prolonged this mood of ecstasy passed away, and the church accepted the world's conditions. Yet it never ceased to be conscious that amidst the visible order it stood for the higher one; and this, in all times, has been the principle of its being. If the church is to live on, it must therefore remind itself, ever and again, how it first arose, out of the message of Jesus. The little company at Jerusalem has grown into a multitude that cannot be numbered, with interests so many and various that the central one is too easily forgotten. In those primitive days we see the church in its essential nature, as the brotherhood which waited on earth for the Kingdom of God.

A SHORT LIST OF BOOKS

The literature which deals with the early church, in its various aspects, is enormous, and almost every work of Christian scholarship might be included in it. In this brief bibliography the author has confined himself, as far as possible, to books which have a special bearing on the subjects he has discussed, which are accessible in English, and which have been published within the last few years. He has tried, also, to select books which are typical of different points of view, and has therefore omitted many which may be deemed superior, on their intrinsic merits, to some which are here mentioned.

Among older books which are still of the highest value are

Harnack, Adolf von, *The Mission and Expansion of Christianity*.
Pfleiderer, Otto, *Primitive Christianity*.
Renan, Ernest, *Les Origines du Christianisme*.
Weiss, J., and Knopf, R., *History of Primitive Christianity*.
McGiffert, A. C., *The Apostolic Age*.
Loisy, A. F., *The Gospel and the Church.*

On the early Christian history generally there have been a number of admirable recent books. It will be enough to mention:

Lietzmann, Hans, *The Beginnings of the Christian Church*.
Latourette, K. S., *The Expansion of Christianity* (Vols. I and II).
Moffatt, James, *The First Five Centuries*.

The *Life of Jesus* has been critically investigated in many recent books, of which the most important are those of the French scholars, Maurice Goguel and C. A. H. Guignebert. Both of them have been translated into English. The "Lives" by W. B. Denny and P. Gardner-Smith are on a smaller scale but well worth study. A book of special interest is Joseph Klausner's *Jesus of*

Nazareth, written by a Jewish scholar from an orthodox Jewish point of view. Conrad Noel has presented the Life as it appears to a modern Socialist. Mention should be made of *Jesus the Unknown* by the Russian Dmitri Merejkowski, a wildly extravagant book, but full of flashes of genius.

The *Teaching of Jesus* is treated in its more general aspects by A. G. Widgery, *Christian Ethics in History and Modern Life,* and by A. Wilder, *Eschatology and Ethics in the Teaching of Jesus.*

On Jesus' conception of *The Kingdom of God* there have been several recent books of great value: Rudolf Otto, *The Kingdom of God;* F. C. Grant, *The Gospel of the Kingdom;* H. C. Dodd, *The Parables of the Kingdom;* C. E. Raven, *The Gospel and the Church.* Nearly a generation has passed since George Tyrrell wrote *Christianity at the Cross-roads,* but it is still a book which cannot be neglected.

All previous work on the *Book of Acts* has been superseded by the great Commentary in five volumes, edited by F. J. F. Jackson and K. Lake. Apart from the commentary proper it presents, in the two introductory volumes, a vast mass of material relative to the origins of the church. F. C. Burkitt's little book *Christian Beginnings* ought to be read in connection with this larger work.

Little has been written on the specific subject of the Nature of the Early Church, which is discussed in the present volume. The following books, however, are all, in their different ways, of first-rate importance:

Linton, O., *Das Problem der Urkirche.*
Porter, F. C., *The Mind of Christ in Paul.*
Dodd, H. C., *The Apostolic Message.*
Macdonald, A. B., *Christian Worship in the Primitive Church.*
Carrington, Philip, *A Primitive Christian Catechism.*
Heiler, Friedrich, *History of Prayer.*
Loisy, A. F., *La Naissance du Christianisme.*

To these may be added the writings of Nicolas Berdyaev, *The Destiny of Man* and *The Meaning of History,* which indirectly throw a real light on the constitutive idea of the church.

INDEX

Absoluteness of Jesus' teaching, 46, 178 f.
Acts of the Apostles, 7, 96, 121
Adam, Christ as second, 66, 150
Antichrist, 211
Apocalyptic, 32, 34
Apologists, 127
Apostles as teachers, 134
Apprehension, 132
Aquinas, St. Thomas, 141
Aristotle, 198
Athanasius, 151
Authority of church, 194

"Back to Christ," 20
Baptism, 82, 156
Baptismal confession, 120
Bernard, St., 151
Body of Christ, 64, 115, 153 f.
Bridges, R., 141
Brotherhood, 64

Cæsar, appeal to, 158
Caiaphas, 210
Calvin, 151
Case, S. J., 209
Catacombs, 82
Celsus, 220
Christian ethic, 196 f.
Citizenship in heaven, 157
Common fund, 105
Communal idea, 63 f., 149
Condemnation of Jesus, 209
Confession of Peter, 25, 192
Constantine, 216
Corinthians, 1st Epistle to, 154
Corruption of church, 19
Cotton, J., 74

Dante, 217
Deterioration, 15
Development, 11
Discipline, 185
Doctrine, 130 f.
Dodd, H. C., 36

Ecclesia, 30
Ecclesiastes, 225
Ecclesiastic, Paul as an, 148 f.
"Edification," 143
Eisler, R., 208
El Dorado, 102
Emmaus, Journey to, 28, 58
Empty tomb, 51
Enthusiasm, 80 f., 114, 165
Ephesians, Epistle to, 155
Episcopacy, 5, 107
Essenes, 114, 230
Eternal life, 35
Ethic, meaning of, 175
Ethical task of church, 172 ff.
Exclusiveness, 188 f.

Faith and reason, 139 f.
False teachings, 16
Fanaticism, 166
Federation of church, 167
Fellowship of saints, 191
First day of week, 73 f.
Forms of devotion, 86 f.
Forty days, 55
Founder of the church, 26 f.
Fourth Gospel, 17, 84, 188
Futurity of Kingdom, 37 f.

Galilee, political feeling in, 204
Gamaliel, 172

Index

Germany, 222
Gibbon, 96
Glossolalia, 78
Gnosticism, 228, 236
Grant, F. C., 32

Handel, 56
Hartley, 34
Hebrews, Epistle to, 13, 17, 18, 30, 84, 124
Holy Roman Empire, 217
Homer, 13
Hymns, 75

Ideal morality, 136
Ignatius, 80
India, 85
Individualism of Paul, 147
"Influences," 138
Initial period, 49 ff.
Institution, church as, 1
Instruction, 121
Internationalism, Roman, 216
Irving, E., 93
Islam, 72

James, 106, 184
John the Baptist, 32
John, 1st Epistle of, 188
Justification by Faith, 129
Justin Martyr, 142

Kingdom of God, 8 f., and *passim*
Koinonia, 152

Leaven, church as, 160
Lessing, 20
Liberty, 223
Liturgies, 81
Lord's Prayer, 37
Lord's Supper, 27 f., 57, 77
Love of the Brethren, 160
Luke, 7, 98, 146, 210
Luther, 234

Macdonald, A. B., 27
Marcus Aurelius, 173

Marriage law, 184
Message of Jesus, 25 ff.
Middle Ages, 6, 38, 216
Middle class, 198
Moderation, 198
Montanism, 15, 93
Morality and religion, 173 f.
Motive of right action, 176
Mustard-seed, parable of, 12

National religion, 203
New Israel, 29
New race, 2
New type of man, 66 f.
Newman, J. H., 101
Novalis, 66

Official ministry, 106
Opposition to Paul, 109
Order in the church, 165
Organization, 6, 96 ff.
Oriental mysticism, 97
Otto, R., 12

Palestinian mission, 108
Parable, 183
Paradox of Christianity, 21 f.
Passive obedience, 214
Pastoral Epistles, 111, 113, 149, 152, 234
Pentecost, 14, 27, 49 f., 78
Persecution, 219
Person of Christ, 131
Peter, 106, 120, 134, 193
Philip, 148
Philo, 83, 126
Pilate, judgment of, 209
Pliny, 76
Political attitude of Jesus, 206 f.
Prayer to Christ, 76
Private judgment, 194
Progress, 44
Protestantism, 234

Quakers, 94, 173
Qualification of Jesus' sayings, 184

Index

Rapture, 85
Rationalism, 126 f.
Reason and Revelation, 139
Reasonable service, 84
Restrainer, 213
Resurrection, 30 f.
Return of Christ, 99 f.
Reverence, 81 f.
Reward, 176
Roman government, 214
Rome, fire of, 169
Russia, 222

Sabbath, 73
Saints, 161
Sayings of Jesus, 181 f.
Scripture, proof from, 122, 196
Separateness of church, 159 f.
Sermon on Mount, 23, 174
Slavery, 187
Spirit, 6, 29, 77, 84
Spiritual gifts, 79
State, Christianity and the, 202 ff.
Stephen, 30, 123
Stoicism, 126
Synagogue, 71 f.
Synoptic Gospels, 8 f.

Tacitus, 210
Teacher, Jesus as, 119
Teaching in the church, 118 ff.
Temple, 71, 162
Tertullian, 93
Theology, meaning of, 132
Tolstoi, 20
Tongues, 78
Tribute-money, 206
Types, 86

Union of church and state, 217 f.,
   222
Universal religion, 216, 232
Universe as finite, 239

Virtues, Christian, 187
Visionary world, 238
Visions of Christ, 52 f.

War, 220
Way, Christianity as the, 181, 195
Wesley, 150
Wisdom of men, 128 f.
Women, Paul's attitude to, 168
Wordsworth, 34
Work, gospel of, 235
Worship, 70 ff.

War, Mutiny and Revolution
in the German Navy

War, Mutiny and Revolution in the German Navy

⚓

The World War I Diary of
Seaman Richard Stumpf

Edited, translated and with
an introduction by
DANIEL HORN

RUTGERS UNIVERSITY PRESS
NEW BRUNSWICK, NEW JERSEY

Preface

The text that follows is a translation of the complete version of the diary of Seaman Richard Stumpf originally entitled *Memories of the German-English Naval War on H.M.S. Helgoland*, as recorded in six thick notebooks of manuscript and published as Volume X, Part 2 of *Das Werk des Untersuchungsausschusses der Verfassungsgebenden Deutschen Nationalversammlung und des Deutschen Reichstages 1919–1928, Vierte Reihe, Die Ursachen des Deutschen Zusammenbruches. Zweite Abteilung. Der Innere Zusammenbruch.*

Since this version of the diary published by the Reichstag Investigating Committee omitted, for fear of libel suits, names of persons who were not outstanding historical personalities, I have, wherever possible, restored the names originally listed, including them in the text in brackets.

I have attempted to preserve the integrity of Stumpf's style by adhering as closely as possible to the author's sentence structure and vocabulary.

For the sake of authenticity, occasional technical errors in the designation of ship types and the rank of officers have been retained.

There is some variation in the opening of the various books of the diary. Stumpf prepared an abbreviated index of the contents of Book I which appears at the beginning of that section. For the other books he simply included a notation of the dates of his entries.

For reading the manuscript and making many helpful suggestions I am indebted to Professor Ralph Haswell Lutz of Stanford University and the Hoover Institution on War, Revolution, and Peace. I am also grateful to the Rutgers University Research Council for its financial support of this project and to Mrs. Roberta Weber, my departmental secretary, for her patience and accuracy.

For permission to use the illustrations included in this edition, I wish to thank the Militärgeschichtliches Forschungsamt in Freiburg im Breisgau and the Ullstein Bildarchiv in Berlin.

DANIEL HORN

New Brunswick, New Jersey
June, 1967

Contents

War, Mutiny and Revolution in the German Navy

Introduction

While I was engaged in research on my book on the German naval mutinies of World War I, I came across the war diary of Richard Stumpf. The diary of this ordinary seaman who served in Germany's High Seas Fleet on the battleship *Helgoland* was part of the interminably long and arid proceedings of the Reichstag Investigating Committee, which from 1919 to 1928 debated the causes of Germany's defeat and subsequent collapse during World War I. At first I was somewhat surprised to find such a personal document among the acrimonious, partisan, and polemical debates of that committee. However, when I had finished reading the diary and had an opportunity to compare it with the literature dealing with Germany during the war, I came to realize why the committee had accorded the Stumpf diary the distinction of being the only memoir to be published in its minutes.

Who was Richard Stumpf? Very little is known of his personal history. We do know that he was born in 1892, that he was a tinsmith by trade, that he was an ardent Catholic and belonged to a Christian trade union, and that he was quite nationalistic and conservative in his political orientation. Stumpf enlisted in the German navy in 1912 and served on the *Helgoland* as an ordinary seaman for six years.[1] In 1918 he was transferred to the *Wittelsbach* and the *Lothringen* and was discharged from the navy in November. On a superficial level one might well regard Stumpf as a completely undistinguished person, no different from the thousands of other enlisted men who served in the German navy.

Actually, however, Stumpf was a highly unusual sailor. Although he did not possess much formal education, he was surprisingly well read, extremely well informed, and had seen something of the world. He knew his Goethe, Heine, Schopenhauer, and Nietzsche. Somehow or other he had also acquired a smattering of Latin which permitted him to interject an occasional classical quotation in his writings. Above all, however, Stumpf knew a great deal of history. He was thoroughly familiar with German history and, even more surprising for a member of the proletariat, he was equally knowledgeable about such historical developments as the French Revolution, the Russo-Japanese War, British colonial policy, the modernization of Turkey, and the Franco-Prussian War. As a wandering journeyman, Stumpf had spent a year traveling and working in the Tyrol, had kept his eyes open and learned a great deal about the intricacies of the Austro-Hungarian Empire's nationality problem and Italian-Austrian relations.

Moreover, even during the war he strove valiantly and at considerable expense to continue his education. He bought such books as Friedrich Naumann's *Mitteleuropa*, frequented the public reading rooms ashore, attended the theater, taught him-

---

[1] *Das Werk des Untersuchungsausschusses der Verfassungsgebenden Deutschen Nationalversammlung und des Deutschen Reichstages 1919–1928. Vierte Reihe. Die Ursachen des Deutschen Zusammenbruches. Zweite Abteilung. Der Innere Zusammenbruch.* 12 Vols. Vol. X/1, pp. 43ff. Hereafter cited as *Das Werk des Untersuchungsausschusses.*

self stenography, and worked mathematical problems. In order to keep himself informed of the political and military developments of the war Stumpf became an avid but critical newspaper reader, closely followed the Reichstag debates, and maintained a general interest in happenings in all the belligerent countries. In short, despite his apparent obscurity and lack of formal education, Stumpf was an exceptional sailor, a perceptive observer, a shrewd political analyst, and an astute critic. Consequently he was well prepared to write a meaningful diary.

Endowed with far greater historical sensitivity than other enlisted men in Germany's armed forces, Stumpf realized shortly before the outbreak of the war that events of momentous significance were about to occur and therefore began writing a diary. During four long years of war, from its outbreak in August of 1914 to the collapse of the German Empire in November 1918, he recorded his experiences, his impressions and observations. Although he intended to write only a purely personal diary, Stumpf was keenly aware of what was happening around him in the navy, on the battlefields, on the diplomatic front, and in the minds of the German people.

Stumpf kept his diary, ultimately comprising six thick notebooks, solely for himself, in order to preserve the memory of the war and to while away the long hours. As far as he was concerned, it was not addressed to any audience; it served no political purpose. As a result, he failed for some time to realize the potential importance and significance of his work. Thus, although the German navy was convulsed by two mutinies, an abortive one in the summer of 1917 and one in November 1918 which led to the outbreak of the German Revolution, although Stumpf witnessed both and participated to a limited extent in the latter, although Germany collapsed and a revolution swept away many of her old political institutions and his beloved Kaiser, Stumpf made no attempt to bring his diary to the attention of the public. At the conclusion of the war he simply left the service, returned to his former trade, moved to Nuremberg, and resumed a normal and obscure civilian existence.

In 1924, however, a heated controversy broke out in Germany. The political parties and writers of the Right charged that the 1917–18 naval mutinies were the product of revolutionary subversion of the fleet by radical Socialists. The Right alleged that the Independent Social Democratic Party had conducted a propaganda campaign among the enlisted men of the navy and had incited a number of ringleaders to stage strikes and to overthrow the authority of the officers in order to bring about the conclusion of an early peace. The Left vehemently rejected these accusations and ascribed the origins of the revolts to bad food, the ill-treatment of the men, their war-weariness, and their refusal to uselessly sacrifice their lives to maintain the honor of the navy and its officers' corps.[2]

In 1926, when the Reichstag Investigating Committee on the Causes of the German Collapse began to examine the questions why the navy had been in the revolutionary vanguard in Germany and why the naval revolt had precipitated the outbreak of the November 1918 Revolution, Richard Stumpf, impelled by his sense of justice and his desire for historical truth, stepped forward and offered his memoirs as evidence.[3]

When Dr. Joseph Joos, the Catholic Center Party Reichstag deputy to whom Stumpf submitted his diary, read the manuscript, he was "surprised, astonished and shocked." He felt that the Stumpf diary was a document of such vital importance that it ought to be placed immediately before the Reichstag Investi-

[2] This controversy formed a vital part of the debate concerning the Stab-in-the-Back Legend. It began in 1924 when a number of former officers came forth with the allegation that Germany had not really been defeated in battle during World War I but had been stabbed in the back by the treasonable activities of the Socialist parties. Representative of this view as it applied to the navy are the articles of Vice Admiral Adolf von Trotha, "Der Dolchstoss auf der Flotte," *Süddeutsche Monatshefte*, Jahrgang 21, Heft 7 (April, 1924), pp. 49–54, and of Rear Admiral Magnus von Levetzow, "Der letzte Akt," *Süddeutsche Monatshefte*, Jahrgang 21, Heft 7 (April, 1924), pp. 55–71.

The debate was continued with mounting fervor at the famous Dolchstoss Trial at Munich in 1925. For this, see Ewald Beckmann, *Der Dolchstoss-Prozess in München vom 19. Oktober bis 20. November 1925* (Munich: Süddeutsche Monatshefte Verlag, 1925) and *Der Dolchstoss-Prozess in München Oktober-November 1925. Eine Ehrenrettung des deutschen Volkes* (Munich: Verlag von G. Birk und Co., 1925).

[3] *Das Werk des Untersuchungsausschusses*, IV, p. 210.

gating Committee.[4] So on February 9, 1926, Joos read a large number of excerpts from the diary into the minutes of the proceedings. Even this limited reading aroused the committee's interest. As a result, on April 29, 1926, Stumpf was invited to appear before the committee as an expert and consultant on naval matters.[5] He made his first appearance on June 25 of that year, read some selections from his diary, and indicated in a fifteen-page report what he considered to be the major causes of the naval rebellions.[6]

Although Stumpf presented an honest, straightforward, and objective report of his wartime experiences in the navy, the committee considered his diary far more valuable than his verbal testimony. His diary was clearer, more revealing, more trenchant, and much more immediate than what he could remember after a lapse of eight years. In fact, the diary presented so stark and violent an indictment of the navy that the impression it conveyed frightened even its author. Stumpf commented, "Upon leafing through these notebooks after eight years, I begin to tremble with fear at the violence of many of my expressions and at the way in which my attitude toward the old state and its authority was transformed." [7]

Deputy Joos proclaimed that the diary was "typical of the feelings of all crews" and insisted that everything which had been said before the committee in regard to the causes of the naval mutinies was "unified into a single answer by the diary." [8]

Another deputy asserted that the Stumpf diary constituted "a veritable manual for the treatment of troops . . . namely, the way they should not be treated." [9] Even the lone voice of opposition within the committee to the publication of the diary, Deputy Brüninghaus, a former naval captain, was forced to agree that the diary represented "very important evidence concerning the psychic attitude" of the enlisted men in the

[4] *Ibid.*
[5] *Ibid.*, p. 334.
[6] *Ibid.*, IX/1, pp. 43–58.
[7] *Ibid.*
[8] *Ibid.*, IV, p. 210 and IX/2, p. 528.
[9] *Ibid.*, IX/2, p. 523.

navy, that it was a "very unique phenomenon"; he merely refused to concede that it spoke for the attitude of all the men in the Imperial Navy.[10] Most important, however, was the judgment of Dr. Arthur Rosenberg, a noted historian and an authority on World War I, who went farther than the other deputies by contending that this was not the work of an ordinary witness and by predicting that the diary would become "the basic memoir for later historians." [11]

Although a drastically cut and edited version of the diary had been published in 1927 by Wilhelm Dittmann, a former member of the Independent Social Democratic Party who was allegedly implicated in fomenting the 1917 mutiny and who sat on the Reichstag Investigating Committee,[12] it was decided by an overwhelming vote on February 3, 1928, to include the Stumpf memoirs in their uncut and unedited version in the stenographic proceedings of the committee.[13]

What was it that the committee found so unusual about Stumpf's diary? Why did it respond with such great interest? Why did so renowned a historian as Dr. Rosenberg issue such a glowing appreciation? A partial explanation is supplied by the character and attitudes of the diary's author, his keen powers of observation, the almost clinical nature of his descriptions, and the comprehensiveness of his work, which encompasses the entire course of the war. Of even greater importance, however, was the psychological insight and understanding with which Stumpf had described his war experiences.

Stumpf had set out to write a purely personal diary and had somehow managed to impart historical meaning to his inner-

[10] *Ibid.*, p. 528.
[11] *Ibid.*, p. 525.
[12] For Dittmann's shortened version, see Richard Stumpf, *Warum die Flotte zerbrach. Kriegstagebuch eines christlichen Arbeiters* (Berlin: J. H. W. Dietz Verlag, 1927). Dittmann also wrote a polemical work (which incorporated large segments of Stumpf's diary) justifying the actions of his party and placing the blame for the mutinies on the naval authorities. See Wilhelm Dittmann, *Die Marine-Justiz-Morde von 1917 und die Admiralsrebellion von 1918* (Berlin: J. H. W. Dietz Verlag, 1926).
[13] *Das Werk des Untersuchungsausschusses*, IX/2, p. 539.

most thoughts and emotions. Thus he described in vivid terms his exultation and war fever at the outbreak of the war, the lassitude he experienced upon the prolonged inactivity of the High Seas Fleet, his growing resentment against short rations and ill-treatment by his officers during the terrible "turnip winter" of 1916–17; he narrated his exuberant reaction to the great naval battle at Jutland, his impression of the first sailors' mutiny in the summer of 1917, and his participation in the opening act of the German Revolution—the naval rebellion of November 1918.

On the basis of these qualities alone the diary would have merited the attention of the committee. However, the members of that committee sensed almost immediately that Stumpf clearly transcended the realm of the personal. As Communist deputy Putz, who had also served in the navy during the war, enthusiastically exclaimed to one of the committee members after reading the Stumpf diary in one sitting, "these are *my* war memories that are in this book. I experienced all these things. I could have written the same thing."[14] The committee realized that Stumpf had somehow managed to write the diary of all the thousands of sailors who never kept diaries of their own and that he had thus produced an invaluable historical source for the understanding of their individual as well as their collective mentality. Stumpf's lucid description of his emotions and reactions provided an understanding of how most of the men responded to the war, to conditions in the navy, to their officers, and what it was that had driven them to rebellion.

Moreover, the more intellectual members of the committee, who had read the mountains of memoirs that had been published since the end of the war, must also have recognized that the Stumpf diary was unusual in still another respect. Most of the war memoirs and diaries published in Germany up to that time had been written by officers or by prominent politicians who had either defended their strategic, tactical, and political decisions or attacked those of their opponents and were therefore so preoccupied with their self-justification before the

[14] *Ibid.*, p. 529.

tribunal of history that their writings were almost always exclusively military or political, highly technical, and hence of little use in explaining the fundamental causes of Germany's revolutionary upheaval.

Since very few former enlisted men had appeared before the committee and an even smaller number had published war memoirs, neither the committee nor the general public had thus far been afforded an opportunity to view the war from the standpoint of the common people, the ordinary sailors or soldiers. Thus far the war had not brought forth an exceptional kind of enlisted man, honest, nonpartisan, perceptive, literate, and analytical, whose testimony or writings might have aided the committee members to understand the way that that class was alienated and driven to revolt.[15] The one notable exception they found in Richard Stumpf, who had succeeded in writing a deeply moving history of the German navy and of German society at war from the much-neglected standpoint of the "little man."

This hitherto unknown sailor had filled the most conspicuous gap in German war literature by describing for the first time the response of the great masses of men in the army, the navy, and in industry to the social, economic, and political upheaval caused by the war. In short, Stumpf explained not only why the enlisted men of the German navy revolted against their officers, but also why Germany lost the war, why the Empire collapsed, and why it was overthrown by revolution.

The Stumpf diary can be read from a number of points of view. One may regard it, as did most of the members of the

15 The only other diary which meets even a minimal number of these qualifications but which falls far short of them in the area of honesty and nonpartisanship is that of Anti-Nautikus (Richard Willi Sachse), *Deutschlands revolutionäre Matrosen* (Hamburg: Verlag Karl Schulzke, 1925). However, Sachse's unreliability and lack of stability was notorious. He presented conflicting accounts on conditions in the navy and the causes of the mutinies as he shifted his political allegiance from the extreme Left to the extreme Right during the latter stages of the Weimar Republic and the early years of the Third Reich. See his fictionalized account, *Rost an Mann und Schiff. Ein Bekenntnisroman um Skagerrak* (Berlin: Traditions-Verlag Kolk, 1934), for a complete contradiction of his earlier work.

Reichstag Investigating Committee, as simply the eloquent testimony of an enlisted man on the causes of the breakdown of
the German navy. In that sense, Stumpf's naval diary makes a
signal contribution to history by refuting the thesis that the
mutinies in the navy were inspired by the propaganda and subversive activities of the radical Socialists. Stumpf presents in-
controvertible evidence that most of the men had no knowledge and certainly no sympathy for the aims of that party. He
makes it abundantly clear that the enlisted men's revolt in the
summer of 1917 and the fall of 1918 had far deeper causes. In
his opinion, the men rebelled because of hunger and starvation,
their mistreatment by the officers, and their intense desire for
peace.

By means of lengthy, occasionally tedious and repetitive but
historically correct and therefore indispensable descriptions,
Stumpf dramatically unfolds the dreadful effects of the perpetual monotony and stultifying routine under which the
sailors and stokers of the inactive High Seas Fleet were forced
to live.[16] Bored to distraction by their life on board their "iron
prisons," the enlisted men of the German navy in 1917 developed a sort of "prison psychosis" [17] that led them to wage an
"internal war" against their officers, who not only abused them
so shamefully but who also manifested a most callous disregard
for their sensibilities. Persisting in living in high style while the
enlisted men starved, the officers clamored loudly for a continuation of the war for the sake of territorial annexations and
ignored the agonizing war-weariness prevailing in the enlisted
ranks.

Stumpf's clinical analysis of the attitude of the men of the

[16] For the profound effects of this monotony, see the postwar com-
ments of Seaman Crisper, formerly of the *Friedrich der Grosse*, who
maintained in an interview that the monotonous routine which was so
characteristic of the High Seas Fleet vastly increased the men's hunger
and heightened their resentment of their officers. Moreover, Crisper also
claimed that he felt much more contented and less hungry when he was
transferred to the Naval Infantry Brigade in the muddy trenches of
Flanders, primarily because he was no longer so bored. Cited in Heinrich
Neu, *Die revolutionäre Bewegung auf der deutschen Flotte, 1917–1918*
(Stuttgart: Verlag von W. Kohlhammer, 1930), p. 13.
[17] *Das Werk des Untersuchungsausschusses*, X/1, p. 44.

High Seas Fleet succinctly sums up the reasons for the August 1917 mutiny: "High state of excitement caused by a total lack of confidence in the officers. Persistence of the fixed notion that the war is conducted and prolonged solely in the interest of the officers. Manifestation of bitter anger due to the fact that the enlisted men are starving and suffering while the officers carouse and roll in money." Stumpf goes on to explain how a man such as he, whose highest ambition upon entering the service was to become "body and soul a good sailor," who intended to emulate the conduct of his father who had served as a professional soldier for thirty years,[18] who was considered a "fanatic patriot," and who belonged to the conservative and annexationist Fatherland Party, could be transformed into a mutineer by the militarism and irresponsibility of the naval officer corps.[19] Even at the outbreak of the November 1918 Revolution, in which he was a reluctant participant, Stumpf's unalterable patriotism and loyalty compelled him to exclaim in horror: "My God—why did we have to have such criminal conscienceless officers? It was they who deprived us of all our love for the Fatherland, our joy in our German existence and our pride in our incomparable institutions."

As a political diary Stumpf's book is equally revealing. The author was neither a democrat nor a liberal, and certainly not a Socialist. As a Catholic trade unionist he was utterly opposed to all Marxist doctrines and the political propaganda of the Left. He consistently manifested a marked antipathy toward the "Jew Liebknecht" and the radical Independent Social Democratic Party.[20] Moreover, he was equally opposed to the "unruly crowd" in the Reichstag and its attempts to wrest control over foreign policy from the Kaiser. As late as the fall of 1917 Stumpf deplored the Reichstag's intervention and was "not at all pleased with the advent of the parliamentary system of government," which seemed to have begun with the appointment of Chancellor Hertling.

[18] *Ibid.*, p. 43.
[19] *Ibid.*, IV, p. 210 and X/1, pp. 48, 50.
[20] *Ibid.*, IV, p. 210 and X/1, p. 48.

At the same time, however, Stumpf experienced a sort of ambivalence. His innate nationalism committed him to the monarchy and the Kaiser, but at the same time he increasingly came to regard himself as a proletarian, "a coolie and a galley slave" [21] who had nothing to gain from a victory of the conservative forces in Germany. Thus at one point in 1917 he stated: "My present point of view—the convictions of an unpropertied proletarian—[does not allow me to] support an increase in the autocratic power of the Kaiser, of the army, of the navy! It is easy for anyone to talk who does not have to pay for it. I would rather be a slave to the English than a German soldier! My ideal is to approach the English-American form of government." Yet at the height of the mutiny of 1918 he felt that "political rights and privileges do not still one's hunger or create happiness," he opposed the Kaiser's abdication, and he was disgusted to march behind "this dirty rag" of a red flag.

Stumpf's strange transformation from an "outspoken Wilhelminian nationalist into an antimilitarist and republican" [22] was far from unique. A large part of the German population experienced a similar conversion as the war dragged on, as starvation and hunger became widespread, and as the ruling classes of Germany—the Junkers and the industrialists—successfully thwarted all attempts, even those of the Kaiser, to give the people a greater voice in the conduct of the government and to abolish the inequitable three-class franchise system of Prussia. The disillusionment and disappointment of the German masses is mirrored to perfection by Stumpf. Like most Germans, he wanted to remain loyal to the Kaiser and to Germany's singular form of government, but he could not understand why the country should continue fighting to maintain the privileges of a powerful minority which had no sympathy for the needs and feelings of the people. Hence he cried out in anguish in the spring of 1918:

[21] *Ibid.*, X/1, p. 52.
[22] *Ibid.*, IX/2, p. 569.

It almost makes me die for shame when I consider that even now our overconfident landed gentry deem it possible to deny the right to vote to the very people who protect their property with their lives. Do the Conservatives think that they alone would have been capable of rolling back the invading Russian hordes? What a shame that we cannot lay down our arms for at least a day and allow the Indians and the New Zealanders to run amuk on the estates of the Junkers. Maybe that would make them understand why the working classes are much less interested in our victory than the propertied classes.

The Stumpf diary thus constitutes a valuable source and a splendid record of Germany's response to the war and the domestic crisis which it created. For example, it would be hard to find a better description of the growing war-weariness of the German people than Stumpf's penetrating analysis of the home situation in July 1917.

I missed the lusty curses of the soldiers, the suspicious listening of the dock workers and the complaints of the women. Does this mean that things are now better in the land? I am afraid not. The people are so apathetic and without hope that it hurts my heart. It isn't so bad so long as the people still have the strength to vent their anger by cursing. Only when they have lost all hope and are totally depressed, do they appear as disconsolate and indifferent as they are nowadays.

Very properly Stumpf regards the war as more than merely an external conflict. He considers it increasingly as a conflict between the forces of democracy and reaction. Thus he alternates between the dread fear that the end of the war will spell the doom of the German monarchy and the destruction of the Bismarckian state which would terminate Germany's "short span of power and brilliance, of prosperity and confidence," and the hope that the new age about to dawn will be an "age of equality; an era of human rights" which will realize the "dreams and teachings of Voltaire and Rousseau."

On still another level one may read the Stumpf diary as a fascinating chronicle of the naval and land war, reporting as it does such important events as the Battle of Tannenberg, the naval action at Dogger Bank and off Helgoland, the tragic

Gallipoli campaign, the holocaust at Verdun, the German seizure of the Baltic islands of Ösel and Moon, the "black day" of the German army on August 8, 1918, and its evacuation of the Western Front. Here is a rich spectacle of virtually all the major developments of World War I, from the beginning of the conflict and the declarations of war to the conclusion of the armistice on November 11, 1918. It encompasses a variety of events which range from Italy's entry into the war, America's intervention, the collapse of Russia, the papal peace action of 1917, the Bolshevik Revolution, Germany's defeat in the West, to the culminating phases of the fighting, and finally the negotiation of the armistice. All of these events are seen through the slightly naive, but nevertheless astute eyes of a nationalistic sailor who thought deeply and intensely about what was happening in the world and who had a very keen understanding of the forces of history.

Despite the great volume of literature dealing with World War I there exists no other diary or any other kind of study that can tell us so much about the way in which the average German sailor or soldier viewed the war, the fighting, and how he responded to the political ideological and social changes created by that war. To this day Stumpf's diary remains unique in its poignant description of life in the German navy, the transformation of the German political temperament, and the deep-rooted causes of the German Revolution of 1918. There is only one other work in German that even begins to approximate the Stumpf diary in terms of its value as social history,[23] while nothing is available in the English language that transcends the narrow bounds of the traditional military or political memoir.

Fifty years after the events of World War I, Richard Stumpf's diary remains, as it was when it was written, a significant and fascinating historical document.

---

[23] See *Als Mariner im Weltkrieg* (Berlin: Karl H. Hennsel Verlag, 1955), the memoirs of Joachim Ringelnatz (Hans Bötticher), who saw the war as both an enlisted man and a naval officer and left a much more literate and polished account, which is, however, not nearly as authentic, stirring, and poignant as Stumpf's.

Author's Preface

In the following pages I have attempted to paint a true picture of my war-time experiences and observations on the battleship *Helgoland*. The thought of war was still remote when I began this diary. From that time on I recorded every happening. I kept a daily and even an hourly record of all the events that seemed of importance and deserved special attention. With the passage of time this book will grow into an ever more prized remembrance of the men with whom I served and at whose side I helped to defend our beloved Fatherland against its enemies.

One

A summer cruise to Norway · First rumors of war · Hasty return to Wilhelmshaven · War with Russia · The Kaiser declares war on France · First battles · English declaration of war · The first naval battle.

A warm and friendly sun shone on the muddy waters of the Jade as our proud ship [the *Helgoland*] left the canal locks [1] on July 10 [1914] and put out to sea leaving a broad wake. The families of our officers and petty officers waved their handkerchiefs at us for a long time. All of us felt happy and free of heart at this long-awaited change from the tedium of our usual duties. Once again we headed toward Norway, that wonderful country of sky-high mountains, perpetual glaciers and deep and mysterious fjords. At our visit last year we had the warmest possible reception from these serious, confident but friendly people. Once again we shall enjoy marching through the vil-

[1] Wilhelmshaven, Germany's chief naval base on the North Sea, is located in the northwestern part of Germany in the state of Oldenburg and lies in the bay formed by the mouth of the small Jade River. The German fleet frequently anchored in the locks of the Kaiser Wilhelm Canal, which connects Wilhelmshaven with the Baltic Naval Station of Kiel.

lages to the sound of music and climbing the cliffs to pick raspberries.

With my mind filled with such thoughts I stood on deck as we passed the Rotesand lighthouse and the shape of Helgoland appeared at a distance. Exercises had been scheduled for the first few days and nights: torpedo boat attacks, searchlight practice, as well as individual ship maneuvers. Night watches came often. As a lookout I had several opportunities to observe the fascinating spectacle of a torpedo boat attack. Our excellent submarines were active during the day.

Thus the days passed. In order to give the crews a day of rest, the entire fleet assembled at Skagen on Sunday. The liberty watch went ashore while those who stayed behind heard a very informative lecture about Norway and its people by the Squadron Chaplain. The next day we weighed anchor and conducted the same kinds of maneuvers in formation as the individual ships had practiced before. We continued our journey north all the while. The weather was lovely and gave no cause for complaint. Only then did we learn that our actual destination was Fjord of Songe, reputed to be the largest, longest and prettiest in all of Norway. We would soon see. The shape of the mountainous coast appeared. In order to enter the fjord we needed a pilot, but had to wait a long time until his arrival at 12:30 on Saturday night. The boat crew lowered a cutter to pick him up.

At its mouth the channel was fairly wide but soon became increasingly narrow. The cliffs were scattered and barely showing in the water at first but [as we went on] they became ever larger, higher and more imposing. Snow glimmered on the mountains. At dawn when we were closer we could see real glaciers up ahead. On a hill on our right side, or starboard as the sailor puts it, there stood a large statue which our Kaiser had built to commemorate the Norwegian poet Fritjof.

Every year the Kaiser comes to this pure and unspoiled natural setting to recover from his heavy cares and governmental affairs. The imperial yacht *Hohenzollern* arrived at Balholm several days ago. *Friedrich der Grosse*, the flagship of the fleet, and the light cruiser *Magdeburg* were also present. In order to extend a proper greeting to our Supreme War Lord, we held a parade and inspection on deck in our blue trousers and white blouses.

The fjord divides into two branches at Balholm. The *Hohenzollern* lay anchored in the left one. We passed by as slowly as possible and brought forth three resounding cheers. The Kaiser greeted us and waved as he stood on the bridge. Then our ship turned hard to starboard and proudly continued on its way. It took three hours before we reached the end of the fjord. A pinnace flying the English flag came toward us. It belonged to one of the yachts which was anchored there.

The water here is 97 meters deep. A hundred meters from the shore the mountains rise 1,000 meters high above the sea. The Chaplain was quite right when he told us that a natural cataclysm had suddenly plunged an entire mountain chain down. Then the water rushed in and flooded the former valleys. Pretty little red houses with pleasant paths leading up to them were clustered on top of the former peaks.

That day a Norwegian collier pulled alongside to deliver 500 tons of coal. Taking coal from a steamer is difficult and much more time-consuming than when barges are used. At 6 o'clock we were dismissed for supper. Rumors that Austria and Russia had mobilized against each other were heard for the first time. The captain had gone to the *Hohenzollern* with the motor launch. Somehow these things were related. We had just sat down to dinner when our uncertainty was ended as we heard the familiar call: "All hands on deck!" Korvetten Kapitän [Laffert], our First Officer, told us to gather around and delivered the following speech: "As you all know, three weeks ago at Sarajevo the heir of Austria was murdered. The assassins were Serbs and committed their crime with the aid and consent of their government.[2] Consequently Austria was compelled to

[2] On June 28, 1914, while on a military inspection, the heir of the Austrian monarchy Archduke Franz Ferdinand was assassinated at Sarajevo in Bosnia by Bosnian revolutionaries trained and equipped by the Serbian terrorist secret society Union or Death, which was headed by Colonel Dragutin Dimitrijevic, chief of the Serbian intelligence service.

demand certain guarantees against Serbia's activities. The accomplices were to be punished and certain societies and newspapers were to be suppressed. Our ally requested a reply to its demands within 48 hours; this time has expired with no answer. Thereupon the Austrian ambassador in Belgrade delivered a declaration of war in the name of his government and made his departure. The Serbian ambassador in Vienna has been handed his passport. Our alliance with Austria-Hungary goes into effect only upon the intervention of a third power—Russia.[3] At the present time there is no need to worry in the least over this. (How unfortunate, I thought.)

"Right now it is our job to finish loading coal as soon as possible. Each half hour is precious to us. Hence I have wired the Commander of the Fleet that we shall be finished by 9:15. Only if we devote all our strength to this task will this be possible. I shall pay each one of you one mark in cash if we are successful." A happy cheer rewarded the First Officer for his heartfelt words.

And now it began! I had never seen such speed and work before. The coal baskets seemed to fly as everyone looked excitedly at the blackboard on which our progress was recorded. And behold! Within an hour, 505 tons; at 8:30, 750 tons; and in another half an hour everything was finished. The coaling boat then headed to Balholm to deliver the coal needed by the flagship of the fleet. They worked through the entire night there while we went to sleep in exhaustion.

---

[3] Almost a month after the assassination, on July 23, Austria-Hungary delivered to Serbia an ultimatum so harsh in its demands that it was virtually bound to be partially rejected. Despite the conciliatory nature of the Serbian reply, which met nearly all of Austria's demands, Austria-Hungary rejected it as unsatisfactory, broke off diplomatic relations with Serbia, commenced to mobilize and issued a declaration of war on July 28.

According to the terms of the German-Austrian Alliance Treaty of 1879, which was later expanded into the Triple Alliance by the inclusion of Italy, Germany was to remain neutral if Austria-Hungary was attacked by only one power. However if that power was supported by Russia, Germany was bound to come to the aid of her ally. Since on that date Russia showed no signs of rushing to Serbia's rescue, it appeared as though a general war could still be averted.

On the following day, a Sunday, almost the entire crew got leave to go ashore from one to six o'clock. I used my time to stroll through the village of Börum. It goes without saying that our men crowded into the shops and the post office. Picture postcards and anniversary stamps were in high demand. Vainly I searched for a restaurant at which there was something to eat and drink. Alcoholic beverages are prohibited in Norway. Nevertheless I walked up to a small and somewhat secluded house and asked for "öl." This is their lovely name for beer. The woman nodded her head in agreement and went to fetch a bottle from the cellar. There was an inch of sediment at the bottom of the bottle. I poured myself a glass and gave it a cautious taste. Pfui Teufel! Sour apple cider!

There were several newspapers on the table and I tried to decipher the dispatches. 150,000 workers in St. Petersburg were on strike. The rebels in Ulster had launched an attack in Ireland. The Parisian mailmen were on strike. For that reason I thought that they would not risk going to war against us. On board, however, they seemed to be of a different opinion. We had orders to return to the ship at once if a shot was fired or if the sirens sounded. Since nothing of this kind happened, I was left undisturbed to enjoy the beauties of nature and to send off a few postcards to my dear ones at home.

The tiny post office as well as the local store soon sold out all their wares. Whenever sailors visit a foreign country for the first time they purchase the most incredible things to take home as "genuine articles." Thus I observed that some of the men were paying fifteen marks for a sheepskin merely because it came from Norway! On the pier at 5:30 I learned that the ship was to be ready to sail home by nine o'clock. Something is not quite right here, I thought to myself. What a shame! We had counted on a lengthy excursion for the following day. We came on board, hoisted the boats from the water and prepared for our departure. While we worked the band played the Norwegian national anthem, the "Byoneborganes March" and other "martial" pieces. A crowd of tiny boats had collected around our proud ship to listen to the music and to observe our preparations with gaping curiosity.

Up there in Norway they have a longer day than we. At 9:30, as the order to weigh anchor was given, it was still bright as day. Our 20 million kilogram colossus spun on its axis with ease. The narrowness of the channel made it appear to be very dangerous and we nearly collided with both banks. The people stood on the banks and shouted their Godspeed to us. Rockets were fired into the air from one of the buildings. We reciprocated by illuminating the houses with our search-lights and playing the lights along the shore. Darkness had de-scended in the interim. I remained on deck for a long time with a friend in order to allow the beauties of nature to sink in deeply. At about 11 o'clock as we passed Balholm, we were joined by another ship the *Oldenburg*. And now the two of us raced for home as fast as we could. Home! The Fatherland is in danger!

For the next two days I made no entries in my diary for nothing noteworthy transpired.

On Tuesday morning, as the people of Wilhelmshaven woke up, one part of the fleet was already anchored in the harbor while the others lay at anchor at the roadstead. What a trip we had! We sailed at full steam the entire time. An extraor-dinary achievement for our ships!

Today's date is August 1. Since no one any longer believed that there would be a war, there was little news about what had occurred while we were at sea. "Again all this excitement for nothing," was heard everywhere. Although there was talk of an ultimatum to Russia, nothing more specific was known. No one was allowed to go into town. During the course of the day we took some ammunition on board and put all the un-necessary gear over the side. At 5:30 in the evening the signal "All hands on deck!" was sounded again. Our Navigation Officer, holding a dispatch in his hand, announced curtly and tersely: "His Majesty has ordered that Germany will place her Army and Navy on a war footing tonight. You know what this means—war—and as of now, war with Russia." [4] The band struck up "The Watch on the Rhine," and everybody joined in enthusiastically.

"A war with Russia will not give our navy much to do. This is not a worthy opponent for us," we maintained. An announcement by the Commander of the Fleet on the bulletin board reported that the French, too, had ordered the mobilization of their army and navy. Nevertheless we were most concerned about what England would do.[5] Even France and Russia combined were no match for us. We built our navy against the false and treacherous English!

Our joy and excitement were boundless and lasted until late into the night. His Majesty the Kaiser sent the following telegram to the navy: "In this fateful time I send Imperial greetings to my navy. At this very moment it is preparing for the first time to enter the battle for the fame and honor of the Fatherland. As the youngest service in my armed forces, it shall go into battle filled with trust in God. In the great fight which lies ahead, let God be at its side." (That afternoon we had already primed our shells for firing.)

[4] Between July 28 and July 30 a number of frantic attempts were made to avert the outbreak of a general war, to localize the Austro-Serbian conflict and to prevent the intervention of the major powers. However, on July 30 Russia began to mobilize her armies. This prompted Germany to issue an ultimatum to Russia on the following day, July 31, demanding that she cease mobilization within twelve hours [noon on August 1] and to give Germany a distinct declaration to that effect. At the same time the Kaiser proclaimed that a "state of threatening danger of war" existed for Germany.

[5] On July 31 Germany sent a double ultimatum to France by informing the French government of the demand on Russia and giving the French government eighteen hours to decide whether it would remain neutral in the event of a Russo-German war. At noon on August 1 France responded that she would "act in accordance with her interests" and within hours issued an order calling for a general mobilization.

According to a secret exchange of notes between the British and French governments in November 1912, the British navy was pledged to protect the northern coast of France against any German attack while the French fleet, concentrated in the Mediterranean, would protect British interests in that area.

AUGUST 2

We are anchored at Wilhelmshaven Roadstead. We are about to go on war patrol today—real war patrol. Thus I wrote in my notebook on August 2.

Two rumors circulated everywhere at the time. One of them was that America was about to dispatch two billion dollars and two squadrons to our aid and the other asserted that Japan would give us moral support by demanding compensation for the war from Russia.[6] The future was to prove both rumors to be nonsense. We got no newspapers or information until 5:30 that evening when the Executive Officer called us together again and set our minds at ease.

"The political situation," he began, "has deteriorated to such an extent that we must count on the outbreak of a war with England. All telegraphic communication with England has been cut off since four o'clock this afternoon. You must know what that means. Furthermore an English fishing boat was discovered cruising around Helgoland this afternoon. One of our cruisers the *Danzig* ordered it to leave. The boat refused and consequently *Danzig* took her into custody. It is certainly very suspicious that this Englishman was snooping around Helgoland. Hence you know now that we are facing a war with England."

All of us breathed a sigh of relief. The very thing for which we had so long waited and hoped, the thing we had yearned for and feared, had come true. There was no doubt that the real cause was jealousy over our economic progress. Germany had grown great, strong and wealthy. The quality of German goods had deprived England of a large part of the world mar-

---

[6] Many Germans at the outbreak of the war felt that the economic rivalry and disputes regarding freedom of the seas between Great Britain and the United States of America would eventually cause the latter nation to come to Germany's aid while they felt that Japan would not permit Russia, her traditional rival in the Far East, to profit from any war without exacting either territorial or financial compensation in return for her neutrality.

ket. The reasons cited by the English that they wanted to protect Belgian neutrality are ridiculous. Would she also have declared war on France if it had violated the Belgian border? [7] However I don't wish to deal with events that occurred later. At that time Germany had not yet crossed the Belgian frontier.

I should like to add one more example to indicate how great the excitement was during those first days and how totally harmless incidents gave rise to the craziest rumors and suspicions. That evening while the starboard watch was busy painting camouflage, a great commotion arose suddenly and everyone ran to the top deck. There I heard that the *Oldenburg*, which lay next to us, had just fired five shots at English submarines. Some of the men insisted that they had seen and heard the shots quite distinctly. The next morning it turned out that none of our ships had fired. Twelve miles away, however, on the island of Wangerooge, a few blank shots had been fired!

At that time there was a general panic about spies. It was alleged that here alone eighteen of them had been captured and shot. I did not believe it. Then there was also the fear of enemy aircraft. The searchlights of some of the ships and of the coastal fortresses were continually playing in the air because of aircraft reports. The next day the newspaper announced that a bomb had even been dropped on the town hall. Later on this, too, was repudiated.

That same night while we stood at battle stations, we received a wireless message that our light cruiser the *Augsburg* had bombarded the Russian naval station at Libau, set it on fire and was now engaged in battle with [Russian] cruisers.

On the following day the official *Norddeich Zeitung* published the news that the French had already crossed the border. In addition, one of their planes had bombed the main

[7] Although England was morally committed to come to the aid of France by the Entente Cordiale of 1904 and by a number of other more specific agreements concluded after that date, this commitment had carefully been kept a secret from the people and even a number of Cabinet members. Hence the English government felt considerably relieved on August 4, when a German invasion of neutral Belgium provided it with an appropriate excuse to enter the war on the side of the French.

railroad track near Nuremberg. As a result, the Kaiser had declared war on France.[8] We had expected this news. It was inevitable. The center of our interest still focused on England's attitude. Would she merely rattle her saber again and sic the others on us? The next day relieved us of these fateful doubts.[9]

At that time I often wondered whether there were any objective reasons for England's intervention. As far as I could tell, the governments, scientists and labor leaders of both sides had tried very hard to establish friendly relations between the two countries. How long ago was it that the English war fleet was received with great honor at Kiel harbor? A few days! We were to pay them a return visit at this very time.[10]

Bitter thoughts rise to my mind whenever I recall that the cause of it all was probably envy and petty trade jealousy. But then the Kaiser had told us that they were Germans like us, of the same race and of the same blood. Blood is thicker than water. And the English?—My country right or wrong! The pursuit of Mammon has deprived that nation of its senses. Can they actually believe that they can conquer a Germany which stands united behind its Kaiser with their soldiers whom they pay ten shillings a week? Can they believe that?

It is my opinion that they do not know what they are facing. They do not know our army and navy. They probably expect a repetition of the Boer War.[11] One can forgive the French for going to war with us, the victors of 1870.[12] And the Russians? They are an apathetic, stupid mob who do as they are commanded. That poor shadow the Tsar may not even

[8] France had mobilized on August 1, the same day as Germany, but had also issued an assurance that the French armies would respect a zone of ten kilometers along the Franco-German frontier. Nevertheless, on August 3 Germany declared war on France on the false pretext that France had committed a number of border violations and that French aircraft had bombed Nuremberg.

[9] The English declaration of war on Germany came on August 4.

[10] On June 24, 1914, a British squadron under the command of Commodore Goodenough had visited Kiel to participate in the opening of the Kaiser Wilhelm Canal.

[11] A large and well-organized British army had subdued a Boer uprising in South Africa in a war which lasted from 1899 to 1902.

[12] The French were decisively beaten by Prussia in the Franco-Prussian War of 1870–71.

know that he has broken his promises.[13] Perfidious England, however, has stabbed us in the back with premeditation! This war is actually a racial conflict of the Germanic race against the Slavs, of culture against barbarism. Many prominent Englishmen understood this and have said as much.

I have failed to live up to my intention to present a chronological narration of the events. But these thoughts fill my mind and my hand must record them.

Earlier I wrote that the next day relieved us of our great anxieties. It was our captain, Kapitän zur See Lübbert, who told us of the English declaration of war on the evening of August 4. "We shall show them what it means to attack us," he cried. "Look at our wonderful ships all around. They shall all fight to the last man and so long as they remain afloat. Down with our enemies! Death and destruction to all those who break our peace. Join with me in giving three cheers to our Supreme War Lord! His Majesty the Kaiser!"

AUGUST 5

The first sentences I wrote today read as follows: "Everything is the same as it used to be. The monotony has a depressing effect. Expressions of disgust at our inactivity are heard everywhere."

During those early days all of us, including the officers, thought that our clash with the English fleet would have to occur almost immediately. It seemed almost inevitable to us that the English, having started the war, would also have to attack. And if they did not come, we would go and seek them out. Apparently our Executive Officer got wind of these feelings. He cautioned us to remain patient. He pointed to the numerical superiority of the British fleet and maintained that it would be stupid for us to allow ourselves to be lured from the

[13] Although the Tsar did not violate any specific agreement with Germany, he did break the long-standing tradition of friendship which had existed between the two royal houses. Moreover, Wilhelm II and Nicholas II were related as cousins and had in the past addressed each other by their respective nicknames Willy and Nicky.

protection of our coastal batteries to be ambushed upon the high seas.[14] Although many of us still retained some doubts, the atmosphere became calmer. A month and a half later when our cruisers *Köln* and *Mainz*, overcome by their ardent offensive spirit, allowed themselves to be ambushed and destroyed, it became apparent how correct he had been.

And thus we remained at anchor at the roadstead for several more days and I actually was unaware that our troops had marched into Belgium. Hence we were totally surprised to hear the reports of the storming of Liége.[15] What joy this great victory gave us! Of course the result was that we became all the more anxious to imitate our comrades in the army.

Italy proclaimed that she would remain neutral. We were outraged at this obvious disloyalty. But I could well imagine what reasons prompted her decision not to enter the war at this time.[16] The Austrians, too, have not committed them-

[14] The English Grand Fleet was superior to Germany's High Seas Fleet because she had twenty modern battleships and four battle cruisers to Germany's thirteen battleships and three battle cruisers. Although it might have been expected that the English commander Admiral Jellicoe should continue the Nelsonian tradition of seeking out the enemy and destroying him, England's worldwide naval commitments demanded that such a risky policy be avoided. As Winston Churchill so aptly put it, "Jellicoe was the only man on either side who could lose the war in an afternoon." Thus instead of seeking out the High Seas Fleet or of maintaining a close blockade on Germany's coasts, the English navy preferred to bottle up the German fleet in the North Sea by blocking its outlets from her northern bases at Scapa Flow in the Orkneys and Firth of Forth. Germany, on the other hand, avoided sailing out into a pitched battle because of her inferior numbers and the fear that her entire fleet might be lost in one engagement and that she would thus be deprived of an important bargaining point at the negotiating table at the end of the war.

[15] Liége was a Belgian fortress which stood directly in the line of march of the German First and Second armies in their sweep toward France. The fortress was attacked during the night of August 5 and 6 and was subjected to a murderous bombardment by heavy artillery. Nevertheless, the defenses of Liége did not totally collapse until August 17, and thus its fall delayed the German march considerably. When Stumpf refers to the fall of Liége, he means the heroic, single-handed seizure of the citadel by General Ludendorff, who drove up on the morning of August 7 and obtained its surrender.

[16] Before the outbreak of the war Italy had refused to adhere to the Triple Alliance by maintaining that Austria had acted as the aggressor against Serbia. On August 3, Italy issued a declaration of neutrality but nevertheless claimed that Austria's territorial gains in the Balkans entitled her to compensation in accordance with Article VII of the Alliance.

selves, although one could not for a moment doubt the Germanic loyalty of that brave nation.[17]

The days went by filled with impatience aggravated by the ominous persistence of uncertainty. In my diary there is a long list of mad rumors which circulated and were believed at that time. I don't find it worthwhile to jot them down any more.

On Saturday the ninth, the *Helgoland* sailed out to serve as patrol ship at the island fortress of Wangerooge. Since the enemy might be near we were ordered to keep a sharp watch. To make the harbor entrance secure, the following measures were taken: First of all, mines were sown everywhere. A chain of cruisers and torpedo boats stretched across the entrance. Additional torpedo boats and submarines were placed on patrol further out off the island of Helgoland. Every measure has been taken to protect us from being overrun. Even our engines are kept in a state of readiness day and night.

One of our cruisers brought in a Belgian sailing ship. Its small crew still did not know that there was a war. The minelayers *Pelikan*, *Nautilus* and *Albatross* sailed out heavily laden with mines. We learned later that they had been successful in mining a part of the English coast. The small coastal steamer *Königin Luise* penetrated as far as the Thames, where she was sighted by an English destroyer squadron and sunk. However their lead cruiser *Amphion* ran over one of the mines she had laid and sank at once. This news created great elation in our ranks. Although both of these events revived the happy spirit of the first days [of the war], nevertheless we received the news filled with repressed rage because there was no way for us to vent our anger. Terrible reports of atrocities against German citizens arrived from Belgium.[18] Our nation is not at all prepared for war, I thought as I read this.

[17] Austria did not actually declare war on Russia until August 6, and it was not until August 12 that France and England declared war on Austria.

[18] Although the Belgian government had warned its citizens not to offer any resistance to the Germans, a certain amount of *franctireur* or guerrilla activities on the part of the Belgians against the German invader could not be prevented. However, there is no evidence these activities were directed against German civilians. Moreover, German forces in Belgium retaliated by executing hostages and burning a number of villages.

At that time we began to receive daily reports of the events at the front from the large wireless station "North Coast." These were typed up in the ship's office and posted. Hence we were kept informed after a fashion. In addition, a huge map had been mounted in the forward battery which indicated the positions of the armies with little colored flags. The men crowded around and eagerly discussed the reports and the changes which took place.

In the interim we returned to our normal routines. Amidst grim comparison with the army, the much-hated calisthenics were resumed. Our first great victory at the Western Front went to the Bavarians, who repelled the attack of a French army corps at Belfort inflicting heavy losses.

On August 13 we sailed back to port to take on coal. I had pictured our return quite differently. All of Wilhelmshaven would have been at the shore to greet us if we had come back from battle, I thought. But to return like this! We were ashamed of ourselves. But our Executive Officer urged us to remain patient. "You will certainly hear something from our torpedo boats and submarines as soon as the days grow shorter and the nights longer. Our time has not yet come."

The men rationalized our inactivity by saying, "So long as we do not control Antwerp and Calais, we cannot take the offensive. Should we lose a major battle, our unprotected coastline would be at the mercy of a landing by a Russian or British army." This seemed to be a reasonable interpretation.[19] I knew from experience that in such questions the men of our ship were as well informed as the officers. Since our Executive Officer was not the kind of man to speak in riddles, we always knew how he felt. Hence we accepted the information he occasionally gave us as absolute gospel. He enjoyed the full confidence and loyalty of the crew. He had the reputation for

[19] This was actually the policy of the German navy. When the expected attack by the English Grand Fleet failed to materialize, Germany sought to wear down England's superiority in capital ships by using her torpedo boats, submarines and mines until some sort of equality had been established. Only if this actually came about did Germany's strategy contemplate engaging the English in a pitched battle.

being a fine man and a good officer from the day he came aboard.

It is my opinion that in such matters the men have an infallible instinct [for judging] even the highest-ranking officers. The men do not have a high regard for the Commander of the High Seas Fleet von Ingenohl. However the Commander of the First Squadron Admiral Lans is looked upon as a leader who will win at all costs.[20] We shall know one way or the other in the near future.

Right now we are not expecting any major operations. No one still believes that the English will come and attack us. Their fleet is much too dear to them for that sort of thing. The best we can hope for is that a defeat of the English army at the front will arouse public opinion to such an extent that they will be compelled to send out their fleet. The average Englishman is utterly convinced that his navy cannot be beaten.

Göben and *Breslau*, two of our cruisers, bombarded two towns in French Africa into a shambles. Then both ships sailed to Messina in order to replenish their coal and food supplies. The English got wind of this. When our ships departed, the English lay in wait for them with three heavy cruisers and a division of destroyers. The French also dispatched a cruiser squadron to ambush our ships. However they were badly mistaken. Despite the heavy fire *Göben* and *Breslau* sailed right through them and thanks to their high speed soon reached the protection of the port of Pola.[21] This uniquely daring feat

[20] Vice Admiral Friedrich von Ingenohl (1857–1935), as Commander of the High Seas Fleet, was unpopular among the men for his cautious policies and seeming lack of enterprise which were dictated by his orders from Berlin. Vice Admiral Wilhelm Ritter von Lans (1861–1947), however, had the reputation of being a daring commander. During the Boxer Rebellion in China in 1899–1900 he had commanded the gunboat *Iltis* and had been instrumental in the capture of Fort Taku.

[21] On August 3 the battle cruisers *Göben* and *Breslau* shelled Bona and Philippeville in Tunisia. Although the British Mediterranean Squadron was waiting for the two cruisers, they were not attacked but merely shadowed because Britain was still not at war with Germany. Stumpf is incorrect in stating that *Göben* and *Breslau* found refuge at the Austrian naval base at Pola. On the morning of August 4 the British battle cruisers sighted the *Göben* approaching from the west. Admiral Souchon in the *Göben* was able, however, to evade his British pursuers except for the

stirred up tremendous excitement all over the world. It was made possible by the fact that our two ships had better armor and were able to develop higher speeds than their opponents. Even the English papers expressed amazement at this outstanding feat of heroism.

On August 14 we loaded 400 tons of coal in two hours. That afternoon the free watch received shore leave until nine o'clock in the evening. Wilhelmshaven was crowded with reservists. They were billeted in all the houses and taverns. Many of them had only part of their uniforms or none at all. I nearly laughed myself sick over that. Just picture a man in a sailor's uniform wearing a top hat. Many of them had only been issued either a pair of trousers or a blouse at the supply depot. The taverns were all filled. Old friends celebrated their reunion by getting drunk.

The next day was set aside for resting. On Sunday, however, we sailed out again to the sound of the band. In contrast to our first departure, almost no one came to the locks [to see us off]. We briefly anchored off Wangerooge and then sailed to Cuxhaven to patrol the mouth of the Elbe. The usually lively traffic on the Elbe had virtually ceased. A double row of mines spanned the channel. In order to do everything possible to guard against the penetration of enemy ships, a strong chain and log barrier had been built. Cuxhaven was renowned as a fortress and was unusually well fortified. Light and heavy guns were emplaced on both banks. But we did not get to see the main fortifications.

Since we drew patrol duty in shifts every second day, things became considerably easier for us. An unusually fertile region of rich orchards surrounds Cuxhaven. The apple and pear trees bowed low under the weight of the autumnal harvest. The naval infantry was kept occupied erecting barbed-wire fences and digging trenches outside of town. Every farmer had men

Gloucester, commanded by Captain John Kelly. When Kelly was ordered to turn back at Cape Matapan, the two German ships succeeded in reaching the Dardanelles and Constantinople in neutral Turkey without further obstruction.

quartered in his home and the "defenders of the Fatherland" seemed to enjoy this very much. To my knowledge not a single one of them worked himself to death.

On the morning of the 18th the Executive Officer read a "secret" order from the Fleet Commander announcing that the German waters in the North Sea and the Baltic were now free of enemy ships.

> However, they are lurking off the Norwegian coast in the vicinity of the sixtieth parallel. Apparently they are hoping to lure us out in order to attack us with superior forces at a place of their choosing. We must not do the enemy this favor. Although we are all anxious to prove our determination to fight, we must remain very patient. In the end they shall have to come to us. Then, with God's help, we shall beat them.
>
> Signed: von Ingenohl

It seemed incredible to me that this order should be labeled a secret. Every last sailor knew all about it as a matter of course.

It seemed as if summer was about to return. But the constant shortening of the days heralded the approach of fall. One day was lovelier than the next. Our daily routine returned to peacetime conditions. In the morning we cleaned the ship, stood inspection and had battle practice. In the afternoon we cleaned the guns, worked or repaired equipment. I read in the newspaper that there was considerable unemployment [at home].[22] We may consider ourselves fortunate to have been inducted. None of the hardships and deprivations to which our army is subjected have as yet appeared here. We are much better off in this respect. Our life and activities on board are the same as in peacetime. Only those of us who have served in the Imperial Navy can tell that some of the old comforts are lacking.[23]

[22] At the outbreak of the war many industries producing for the civilian market had not yet switched over to war production, with the result that unemployment rose to a high of 28.7 percent in September 1914. Two months later it was down to 8.2 percent.

[23] The prewar navy had been called the *Kaiserliche Marine* or Imperial Navy, while during the war it became known as the *Kriegsmarine* or War Fleet.

AUGUST 20ʹ

This day shall go down as a day of everlasting shame in English history. Today Japan, in fulfillment of its alliance with England, delivered a note to Germany demanding the evacuation of Kiaochow and Tsingtao.[24] Our war ships are either to evacuate the port or to be disarmed. Only these yellow, slant-eyed Asiatics could make such an infamous demand. There is no doubt concerning our government's reply. An additional enemy [will provide us] with one more honorable cause. It is not yet known how the Americans will respond to this coup by their "yellow monkeys." I don't think that Brother Jonathan [25] will support us merely because he likes the looks of our honest faces. Not when there is no profit to be made. . . .

Be that as it may, our troops in the Far East shall give the thieving "yellow monkeys" a hard slap on the hand for trying to grab a German possession. The Commander of Kiaochow [Admiral] Meyer Waldeck sent the following telegram: "Am prepared to do my duty at all costs!" [26]

In one of the newspapers, *Der Tag*, I read the following poem which I find valuable enough to record. It goes as follows:

To My Fatherland

O my Fatherland, how they honor you
Seven countries with their armies
Courageously attacked you
Because it would be too much for six.

---

[24] On August 15 Japan implemented her alliance with England (the Anglo-Japanese Alliance of 1902 as revised in 1905) by delivering an ultimatum to Germany which demanded the immediate withdrawal of all German warships from Asia and the surrender of the territory of Kiaochow by September 15. Japan demanded a reply by August 23, and when none was received she declared war on Germany.

[25] A German nickname for America.

[26] In spite of Germany's determination to resist Japan, her Far Eastern Squadron, consisting of the armored cruisers *Scharnhorst* and *Gneisenau* and the light cruisers *Nürnberg* and *Emden* under the command of Admiral Graf Spee, was withdrawn from the area.

O my Germany, how strong you must be
How healthy to your innermost core
That no one has dared all alone
And seeks the aid of six more.

Germany how true must your heart be
O, how shining bright is your right
That the greatest of hypocrites hates you
That the Briton pales with rage.

Is it conceivable; could it happen?
Germany, could you be defeated?
Whoever faces a world of enemies
Is a conquering hero even in defeat.
But you shall grind them into the dust
Those who have crept up to you like thieves in the night.
Sweep clean the world of deceit
Let innocence triumph
Rush into the seven-fold turmoil.

Kill the devil and fetch from heaven
Seven garlands of humanity;
Seven suns of immortal fame.

Otto Ernst [27]

[27]   An mein Vaterland

O mein Vaterland wie sie dich ehren
Sieben Staaten mit ihren Heeren
Fielen tapfer über dich her
Den für sechse wär es zu schwer.

O mein Deutschland wie must du stark sein
Wie gesund bis ins innerste Mark sein
Dass sich's keiner allein getraut
Und nach Sechsen um Hilfe schaut.

Deutschland wie must du von Herzen echt sein
O wie strahlend hell muss dein Recht sein
Dass der mächtigste Heuchler dich hasst
Dass der Brite vor Wut erblasst.

Wär es zu denken, könnt es sich fügen,
Deutschland könntest Du unterliegen
Wer einer Welt von Feinden sich stellt
Ist auch im Sturze der siegende Held.

In the newspapers patriotic poetry bloomed very lavishly and occasionally put forth the most beautiful blossoms. I found many a highly patriotic poem whose author had formerly delighted in caricaturing and mocking Germany's political institutions. My fellow countryman ——— is an excellent example of this. I observed something even less gratifying in Cuxhaven. The show windows of the stationery stores displayed cards which depicted Russian, French and English soldiers as the most pitiful wretches. A German soldier [was shown] in the process of laying one of them across his knee, stating, "Don't push! You shall all get your turn." Other cards presented a rhyme which has quickly become popular: "At every shot, a Russian; every push, a Frenchman; every kick, an Englishman; and every slap, a Japanese." [28] While this was barely tolerable, there were others with such childish drawings that one felt sorry for their creators. So far as I know, no newspaper or government agency has yet expressed any concern over this trash.

One of our submarine flotillas has just returned from an unprecedentedly daring reconnaissance patrol along the English coast. Unfortunately, one of our ships the *U 15* was sighted by the British cruiser *Birmingham* and was sunk at once. According to the reports of German refugees, several wrecks of large ships [have been sighted] at the mouth of the Humber near Hull. Thus I would imagine that this reconnaissance patrol was not quite a total failure.

After an eight-day stay in the Elbe estuary we put out to sea

Aber du wirst sie zermalmen zu Staube
Die dich umschlichen zu nächtlichem Raube.
Fege die Welt vom Truge rein
Lass die Unschuld geborgen sein
Stürz dich ins siebenfache Gewimmel.

Morde den Teufel und hol Dir vom Himmel
Sieben Kränze des Menschentums
Sieben Sonnen unsterblichen Ruhms.

Otto Ernst

28 "Jeder Schuss ein Russ'—Jeder Stoss ein Franzos'—Jeder Tritt ein Britt'—und jeder Klaps ein Japs."

again. We conducted firing practice at targets and our guns were exceptionally accurate in their fire. If only they had been English ships. . . .

Thus came August 28th. On that day our *Helgoland* again took her post as ship of the watch at Schillig Roads. The weather had changed. A thick, impenetrable fog hung over the sea. In addition, we were all soaked to the skin by a light rain. I stood watch as a lookout in the crow's nest with one of our cadet officers. Under my breath I cursed the devilish rain which soaked through everything. One could hear the muted thunder of guns coming from the direction of Helgoland. I maintained that [the noise] was not from firing practice because the intervals [between shots] were much too short and the firing had lasted much too long. As I looked down I could make out groups of officers and enlisted men gesticulating excitedly and listening in the direction of the thunder. "Something must be the matter out there; our ships in the advance patrol are most certainly engaged in a battle," maintained the cadet. When I was relieved from duty and came down, I found out that three of our cruisers were engaged in battle with English destroyers. I jotted this down in my notebook. The engine room crew was ordered to raise steam immediately in all boilers for full speed. Oh, how our hearts pounded! How quickly we brought in the torpedo nets, raised anchor and set off in the direction of the enemy. Soon the stokers' shower room, where we washed ourselves, resounded to the song, "Proudly waves the flag black-white-red."

"Battle stations! Clear the decks for action!" came the order at 9:30. "Stretcher bearers in front of the sick bay." At last! At last! At last!

August 28th was a black day for the crew of the *Helgoland*. It shall always live as a bad memory. Try to picture the following situation: A few miles away from us our ships were in the midst of a heavy fight. We didn't know the size of the ships involved. However we did know that our sole cruiser stationed off Helgoland *Von der Tann* was refueling in Wilhelmshaven. Therefore our side could only muster light units, small cruisers and torpedo boats. The volume of the noise, however, indicated that heavy guns, either those of the enemy or our own howitzers of the shore batteries of Helgoland, were in action. Then on top of all that we got orders to drop anchor at once and wait to be relieved by *Thüringen*. Needless to say, we were immensely disappointed by this order.

We were overjoyed, however, when the heavy cruiser *Von der Tann* and the light cruisers *Köln* and *Mainz* sailed out at full speed in the enemy's direction.[29] We were never to see the latter two again.

I shall now attempt to describe the early phases of the battle and its later development. My story is based on the accounts of our First Officer and of a good friend of mine who lived through the battle on the *Ariadne* until its sinking. I want to make this clear because the press subsequently came out with a different description of the battle and for obvious reasons could not publish these experiences.

First of all our disposition: The light cruiser *Stettin* lay off the port of Helgoland. The Eighth Torpedo Boat Half Flotilla was in port. The light cruiser *Ariadne* lay a bit further out to the north, while *Frauenlob* stood off in the west. The torpedo boats of the First Half Flotilla formed our outermost guard. As I mentioned earlier, the visibility was extremely limited due to the bad weather. These conditions were of considerable help to the enemy and made his approach an unusually easy one. It all started when an enemy submarine was reported in sight. She fired two shots at one of our torpedo boats without scoring a hit. No other enemy forces were in sight at that time. Not long thereafter, however, a group of enemy destroyers escorted by a cruiser appeared near the First Half Flotilla. A wild chase ensued. Although the First Officer maintains that some of our ships did not have steam up in all their boilers, I can hardly

[29] The alertness of the German fleet had deteriorated considerably since the outbreak of the war. Thus on August 28, the day of the Battle of Helgoland, the German battle cruisers and battleships were tied up in port and could not head out to sea in time because of the low tide. While *Köln* and *Mainz* did participate in the battle, there is no evidence that *Von der Tann* ever reached the scene of the fighting.

believe it.[30] At any rate, the destroyers were faster and opened up with rapid fire. They failed nevertheless because they were chased away when *Stettin* came tearing to the scene in response to wireless messages for help.

In the meantime the Fifth Half Flotilla arrived. The boats were not [arrayed] in formation because the commanders felt confident that they were facing only one enemy vessel. Thus the leading boat *V 187* suddenly found herself surrounded by the enemy. Her only hope for salvation lay in flight. The boat was turning about to obtain maneuvering room when she received a well-aimed hit in the rudder and was crippled. Since her destruction was now a certainty, she tried to sell her life as dearly as possible. She fired her two guns until the moment she sank. At that point the English gave proof of their humanity in war by lowering their boats to save a number of our comrades swimming in the water.

Once again *Stettin* appeared in the thick of the fray. Although their superiority gave the enemy ships a chance to continue the fight, they chose to leave their boats behind and to make a rapid departure. Two of our seamen who had been rescued by one of their destroyers jumped into the water at the appearance of *Stettin* and thus escaped captivity.

In the meantime the light cruiser *Ariadne*, built in 1900, met her doom. She encountered her fate as she escorted one of our destroyer squadrons. Without the slightest warning she ran right into two of the most modern English heavy cruisers.[31] Each of them carried eight 34 centimeter guns as opposed to *Ariadne*'s ten 10.5 cm. guns. Nevertheless for a full half hour the brave ship fought back with heavy fire and scored many hits on both the opposing vessels. But what damage can a 10.5 cm. shell inflict on such giants? Soon her bow burst into flames. However it was not the steel but the paint, which was roughly a quarter of an inch thick from repeated applications, which

[30] Nevertheless, this contention appears to be true. Since the German ships did not have their steam up they were compelled to sail against the enemy one by one rather than in formation.

[31] Admiral David Beatty, the British Squadron Commander, had at his disposal five battle cruisers.

was ablaze. When the forward munition chambers were threatened by the fire, the Captain flooded them to prevent a fatal explosion. But this put half the guns out of commission. As the First Officer, Korvetten Kapitän ————,[32] was about to go below deck, a shell tore off his head. In the interval, the fire had spread over the entire ship. [The heat] was intolerable. Thereupon the Captain had the wounded brought on deck, handed each of them a life preserver, gave three cheers for the Kaiser and then ordered all hands to abandon ship. Within a half hour the ship listed to one side and sank beneath the waves. Almost every single one of the few survivors was awarded the Iron Cross. All this took place between ten and eleven o'clock in the morning.

As I mentioned earlier, we had dropped anchor at our usual position and had even spread out the torpedo netting. None of us knew the outcome of the battle. All sorts of ridiculous rumors made the rounds. No one enjoyed lunch. All of a sudden, at about three o'clock, we received the command: "Raise steam in all engines for maximum speed!" This revived us. An hour earlier *Seydlitz* had sailed out under full steam and was now probably face to face with the enemy. We still had to put all the unnecessary equipment over the side. The disposal tubes, the shell cases from yesterday's firing practice and the lockers and benches were still lying about. We signaled a boat at the dock to come and pick up this unnecessary but expensive equipment. In typically slow dock fashion she arrived after a lapse of an hour and a half. We were almost on the verge of throwing everything overboard. This time no one shirked his duty and everyone pitched in. Within half an hour everything was ready. The ship was ready for action. At 4:30 we received the order from *Ostfriesland* to raise anchor and to follow in a keel line. [We left] at full speed with *Ostfriesland* astern. The wind screamed through the rigging and foaming spray blew over the fantail. A storm was in the offing. Nevertheless in our anxiety to see something of the enemy and the results of the battle, we all stayed on the top deck.

[32] Name omitted.

Shortly before five o'clock we sighted the cruiser *Frauenlob* heading toward us. She had participated in the battle and appeared to have emerged unscathed. However as she drew nearer and passed us on the starboard side, we could discern her damage. Her aft smokestack was torn from its top to the middle and was shot through like a sieve with countless splinters. Amidship, near the top deck, a shell had torn a great hole and toppled a gun. Furthermore there was a direct hit on the stern near the waterline. Yet the cruiser sailed on proudly. Her engines must have remained unharmed. Her crew, like ours, lined the railing and we gave each other three resounding cheers. *Stettin* followed closely behind. Her smokestack, too, had been damaged but no other [damage] was visible.

Insofar as I could judge, the English guns fired shells without delaying fuses. At the least contact in their trajectory they would ignite and explode. This could be the only reason why they did not pierce or otherwise tear the thin metal of the smokestacks. Later on I learned that only half the enemy's shells actually exploded. A Dutch steamer who came into the line of fire was hit three times. Much later I read in the newspaper that an unexploded English shell was found in her hold. A similar shell was found on *Frauenlob*. An examination of the fuses and the powder revealed the interesting fact that their explosive power was sixty percent less than that of our own armor-piercing shells.[33] Of course this information had to remain a secret so that the English and their yellow monkeys would not think of acquiring new and better shells as they did ten years ago. At the Battle of Shantung the Russian ships hardly suffered from the Japanese fire. [However,] the Russian newspapers were so ingenuous as to inform the entire world that the Japanese fuses had failed to explode. By the Battle of Tsushima the Japanese had learned their lesson so well that they smashed the Russians to pieces.[34]

[33] Since the British navy continued to use black powder until after the Battle of Jutland in 1916, its shells were decidedly inferior to those of Germany.

[34] During the Russo-Japanese War of 1904–05, a Russian fleet of thirty-two ships was annihilated by the Japanese at the Battle of Tsushima Straits.

In my opinion our admirals and captains learned more from this one engagement than from ten years of maneuvers. Later on I shall have something to say about the sinking of *Köln* and *Mainz*. I am firmly convinced that it was the fault of the top echelons of the navy. Certain changes in commands seem to substantiate it. Although one would be punished for stating this in public, it filters down by word of mouth through quiet and secretive whispering. Be that as it may, we are positive that the right men shall be placed in the proper positions of responsibility.[35] This business of secrecy is ridiculous! We are forbidden to talk about things which on the following day are broadcast far and wide by the newspapers.

I return once more to our sortie against the enemy. A quarter of an hour after we passed the *Danzig* [36] we met the First Half Torpedo Boat Flotilla. Five of its boats were heading to port at great speed. I still remember vividly one of them which lay very low in the bow and rode heavily in the water. She had been hit in the collision room. Our Captain called down from the bridge: "Men, give them three cheers!" The officers and men who stood assembled on deck stared at us numbly. The rear was brought up by a hospital ship carrying the dead and wounded. It was a solemn moment.

Again no action! At 7:30 we received orders to drop anchor. The enemy had vanished. I don't want to attempt once again to describe the depression which this order created.

An hour later I was again on duty as a lookout on the bridge. After the day's excitement [I had a chance] to spend two hours in peace to collect my thoughts. Since we lay right off the locks at Wilhelmshaven, we were protected from the enemy. We could only be surprised from the air. I made my-

[35] The German fleet lost three cruisers and a torpedo boat and suffered 1,242 casualties, while the English lost only 75 men in addition to the damages sustained by *Arethusa*, which had to be towed home. The crews of the German light cruisers complained that they had been sent into an unequal fight with the English battle cruisers without any support and blamed their defeat on the alleged cowardly behavior of Admiral Ingenohl, the Commander of the High Seas Fleet. The loss of this battle had a severe effect upon the morale of the German navy.

[36] Stumpf probably means either *Frauenlob* or *Stettin*.

self comfortable, pulled in my legs and thought and dreamed mainly about the war.

How peaceful it was! The stars in the sky sparkled exceptionally brilliantly and were reflected a thousandfold in the water where myriads of tiny animals glowed in fabulous colors. How peaceful nature was! But man, the highest creature and the lord of the earth, is filled with hatred and fights with unparalleled ferocity.

We have been at war for forty-six days. Our enemies have treated us in an unimaginably abominable and cowardly fashion. They have cut our telegraph cable to inundate the world with a flood of lies. They have attacked our defenseless colonies and have destroyed everything that German industry and technology have created.[37] Without shame our enemies have instigated barbaric and semibarbaric nations against us even though these hardly know what it is all about. Two powers rule the world nowadays: guns and the press. While the English allow the first to remain silent, the latter is all the louder. It is astonishing how every bit of absurdity is believed these days. They lie and we—we win.

During the first few days after the battle it was absolutely impossible to find out how our two cruisers *Mainz* and *Köln* had been sunk. Several weeks later the Captain of the English cruiser *Arethusa* published a very interesting report about the sinking of the *Mainz*. The English cruiser subjected *Mainz* to such an [intense] bombardment that in a short time only one of its guns remained operational. Meanwhile a second [British] cruiser and a squadron of destroyers rushed to the scene. *Mainz* fought back against them as well as she could. In the end the decision was reached through the intervention of the great battle cruiser *Lion*, a ship of 30,000 tons with eight 34 cm. guns. *Mainz* was hit several times by the heavy guns at a very close

---

[37] Between the outbreak of the war and the end of September 1914, Germany lost the following colonies to the British: Togoland, Samoa and the Bismarck Archipelago, while the Cameroons, German Southwest and German East Africa were also invaded. A little later on, she was to lose the Marshall Islands, the Marianas, Palawau and the Carolines to the Japanese.

range of 4,000 meters and sank rapidly. *Arethusa* was severely damaged and had to be towed back to an English port. *Köln* evidently suffered the same fate. No official reports have been issued. It goes without saying that this ship, which was decorated by the Kaiser, fought no less bravely than her sister.

The experience that we gained from this defeat may well turn out to be a blessing in disguise. Since then only trawlers, torpedo boats, submarines and an occasional superannuated cruiser have been assigned to forward patrol duty.[38] In September an English submarine undertook a daring raid and sank the fleet tender *Hela*. All but three of her crew were saved. It seems that the English torpedoes do not possess great destructive power since they were unable to tear the old tub to pieces right away. We shall see how our own torpedoes perform in the future.

On August 31 *Helgoland* went into dock. The water was drained off and within a few hours the animals and mosses attached to the hull were scraped off. The band was assembled down in the dock. Amidst the strains of happy songs and marches the work progressed very rapidly. That same day we applied a new coat of paint and were able to leave the dock.

That evening I received a two-hour pass which enabled me to stroll through the town. The life on the streets had undergone a considerable change since the last time. There were no longer so many reservists on the streets. Everything was quieter. The people crowded around the shop windows and street corners to read the wonderful news from the East. "General Hindenberg's army has administered a decisive defeat to the Russians near the Masurian Lakes. As of this time we have captured 80,000 prisoners and 500 guns." Thus reported a tersely worded telegram from Great Headquarters. We later learned that about 100,000 Russians drowned in the

---

[38] The defeat at Helgoland deprived the German High Sea Fleet of much of its scope for action, for the Kaiser issued an order to the Commander of the Fleet to avoid further losses of ships at all costs and that all sorties or major attacks would have to be cleared with him in advance.

lakes and swamps and that an equal number had been wounded. General Hindenburg's name is on everyone's lips.[39]

We also won a great victory in the West. We defeated ten French army corps and captured 12,000 Englishmen. The latter news, in particular, created great joy. It was a deed worthy of the anniversary of the Battle of Sedan.[40] On that day we took the important fortress of Reims without a fight. As is well known, we lost it later on.[41]

The French government has deserted Paris for the warmer South amidst insipid excuses. . . .[42]

During our patrol on Monday night we received a wireless report that the strong fortress of Maubeuge had finally fallen. "40,000 prisoners taken; 400 guns captured," read the brief victory statement.

TUESDAY, SEPTEMBER 7, 1914

Today much of our time was taken up by the dreaded confusion of re-stowing. In order to maintain the ships in a state of battle readiness we shall have to dispose of many of the things making life comfortable. The dishes were packed up and placed

[39] Note the varied spelling of Hindenburg's name. General Paul von Beneckendorff und von Hindenburg (1847–1943) was living in obscure retirement when he was suddenly appointed to his eastern command. With the aid of his chief staff officer the brilliant Erich Ludendorff, the hero of Liége, he first defeated the Russian First Army at the Battle of Tannenberg (August 26–30). A week later (September 6–15) he led the German troops to another victory over the Second Russian Army at the Battle of the Masurian Lakes. In these two engagements the Russians lost an estimated 300,000 men and 650 guns. Hindenburg suddenly became the hero of the German nation and was rewarded for his victories by being promoted to Field Marshal and Commander in Chief of the German armies in the East.

[40] This must refer to the defeat of General Lanrezac's Fifth French Army at the Battle of the Frontiers on August 21–24 and the retreat of the British Expeditionary Force at the Battle of Mons from August 23 to August 26.

On September 2, 1870, Emperor Napoleon III surrendered his army to the Prussians. This was the greatest victory for Germany during the Franco-Prussian War and was celebrated as a national holiday.

[41] Reims actually fell on September 3.

[42] On September 3 the French government moved from Paris to Bordeaux on the eve of the Battle of the Marne.

in the forward petty officers' quarters, the benches and tables in the adjoining Compartment 14. The officers' cabins, the mess and the salon were emptied out altogether.[43] Endless confusion ensued as everyone milled about aimlessly in one place. As a result, we shall have to do the whole thing all over again.

U 21 passed by at about three o'clock in the afternoon and signaled: "Have disposed of my 'things.' " She had sunk the modern English cruiser *Pathfinder* with a well-aimed torpedo, thereby proving the usefulness of this modern and fearful weapon.

Every evening we took out the antitorpedo netting and brought it back in the morning. While the starboard propeller was still turning slowly, the end of a wire got entangled in the screw. A diver worked very hard for several hours to free the propeller but he did not succeed. We were compelled to go into dock once more where the repair was accomplished in short order. That morning when we peered through the port-hole, we were already at anchor at Schillig Roads. The weather was beautiful. Two of our newest battle squadrons lay there in keel formation in majestic peace and beauty. In viewing this tremendous battle power, I unconsciously thought, "Let them come." *L 4*, a naval airship, flew over the squadron and pre-sented a wonderful appearance all lit up by the sun.

That afternoon we practiced battle stations again but this time it went much more quickly than before. Almost the entire fleet participated in a forced march to the island of Helgoland. Of course we thought that we were sailing against the enemy. However nothing was to be seen in any direction. The Third Squadron was now up to full strength and was composed en-tirely of wonderful, brand-new ships: *Kaiser, Kaiserin, König Albert, Prinzregent Luitpold, Grosser Kurfürst, König,* and the flagship of the fleet [*Friedrich der Grosse*]. It is an un-forgettable sight to see these twenty-one monsters sailing in a

---

[43] Before each battle or whenever a state of alert was declared, the sailors had to remove all flammable material from the ship or stow it away in a safe place. This created a great deal of work for the men and made their lives very uncomfortable so long as the alert lasted.

line. How obedient they are! As soon as a colored flag whips out in front, they turn right or left, veer to the right or left, assemble in groups, form in rows and turn like a regiment of soldiers. At times like these one is reminded of the sailors' superstition that the soul of a ship is to be found in its every seam, plank and bolt.

These twenty-one battleships will be the ones who will deliver our main blow against the hated English. It is good to know that every single one of the men is convinced that our ships, our artillery, our torpedoes and armor are superior to those of the English. If this is not true, then we are lost. If the enemy were to lose the same number of ships as we, he would still have an equivalent number left over. This is without even considering the French and the Russian fleets. Even in the event our fleet should be destroyed, we would still remain a first-class military power on land. But what of the English? They are utterly dependent upon their sea power. But of what use will this be for them if we control the air and the depths of the sea? The British navy has suffered a greater percentage of losses than the German navy. England plans on starving us to death although our entire wheat supply remains unharmed! Should our merchant raiders ever succeed in interrupting, or even better yet, in severing England's supply lines, we shall see who will starve to death first.

Enough of that. I have already told how we made our first sortie into the North Sea. The perfectly executed exercise came to an end that evening. At approximately eight o'clock all the ships dropped anchor at Wilhelmshaven Roads.

On the following day, a Sunday, our Captain gave us a heart-warming "talk!" It was a pleasure to listen to his reply to the English charge that German ships had fired upon the English lifeboats during the battle. He also spoke very dramatically about the "ladies" who threw candy and fond glances at our prisoners. He ended his speech by making an appeal for economy and secrecy in all our operations.

During inspection I heard a muffled explosion coming from far away. Several hours later I discovered its source. An extremely audacious English submarine had penetrated as far as Helgoland and torpedoed the old cruiser *Hela*, which served as squadron tender and signal ship. She went under but her entire crew with the exception of three men who must have died in the explosion was rescued. This does not speak well for the effectiveness of the English torpedoes. Nevertheless the audacious raid merits recognition.[44]

While we remained anchored off Wilhelmshaven we did not have patrols at night. To make up for it our officers found other tricks to keep us amused. We had to unpack our seabags so that every piece of clothing could be subjected to the most minute inspection for its cleanliness and state of repair. In addition, as previously mentioned, they vigorously resumed the practice of killing us slowly with needless work. Hence we were all glad when we put out to sea. But we jumped from the frying pan into the fire. A terrible storm was raging outside. I shall always remember the experience as I stood at my post as lookout at the main mast. We were fortunate to be anchored in the German Bight. The wind whistled and howled in the rigging until we thought it might come down any minute. At about 11:30 the light cruiser H.M.S. *Blitz* passed by with its masts torn off. As wild as the storm had been, so peaceful again was everything that night. A great comet glowed in the starry sky and prompted all sorts of prophecies on the part of the "old wives." At that time I also received the shocking news that my brother Xavier had lost his life on the field of honor in France. Because of that I made no entries in my diary for four days.

Therefore I must resume with an event which created great excitement throughout the world, namely, the activities of our submarine *U 9*. We received this wonderful news on the wireless during the night of [September] 2d to 3d. A report from an English source announced that German submarines had torpedoed and sunk three armored cruisers *Aboukir*, *Hogue* and

[44] *Hela* was sunk by the English submarine *E 9* during a wild storm off the Frisian coast and Helgoland.

Cressy twenty miles northeast of the Hook of Holland.[45] At nine o'clock the next morning our First Officer gave us additional information about this remarkable exploit. According to him, only one German submarine the *U 9* attacked the three cruisers by turns at seven o'clock and sank them by means of six well-aimed torpedoes. Each of these cruisers had a displacement of 12,200 tons and was thus larger than our *Scharnhorst* and *Gneisenau*.[46] The casualty rate was terrific. 1,500 men are dead. The survivors were rescued by a Dutch freighter and taken to Imuiden. You can well imagine the jubilation, excitement and pride which this news created in our ranks.

On the following day Wednesday, it was announced that the victorious ship was expected to sail by around noon. We had just started to eat when the order came: "The band and all hands on deck!" Then it approached, a small white cloud of smoke and a long wake in the water. Nothing else was visible because the boat was painted the color of water. Next we heard the rousing cheers from the surrounding ships and then it was here, near us. Her two officers and the men, about twenty-two of them, stood assembled on deck. They waved at us and returned our cheers.

On Friday September 26, I wrote the following lines in my diary: Something of great importance is about to happen. The First and the Third Squadron have come in. Reveille is piped as early as four o'clock in the morning. We shall have to unload 300 tons of coal [from our ship]. What does this mean? Very simple! The English fleet (apparently) left port and will probably attempt to blockade the Baltic as well [as the North Sea]. We, however, shall go through the Kaiser Wilhelm Canal with all possible speed to give them a proper reception at

[45] Stumpf is mistaken in his dates. Actually the three ancient British cruisers were sunk during the night of September 22 by the *U 9* under the command of Captain Weddingen. Weddingen's exploit set a record which was never again matched by the German navy.

[46] *Scharnhorst* and *Gneisenau* were the two strongest ships in Admiral Spee's Far Eastern Squadron. However, the three English cruisers were very old and no longer fit for battle. This was the reason for their assignment to patrol duty off the Dutch coast.

Als Sound. Rumor has it that they have penetrated as far as the Great Belt. Confound it! That would be something!

Since we are now unloading coal and everything else that might weigh down the ship needlessly, I suspect that we are to sail through the canal at a very high speed. There is no other explanation for it. At present our ship has a draft of nine meters. After we have lightened her she will rise fifty centimeters. The canal is eleven meters deep. However we must consider that a fast-moving vessel always rides at an angle because its propellers dig into the water. In our case it would thus come to about a meter. Thus we shall have a gap of one and a half meters between the ship's bottom and the canal floor. Consequently a reduction in our draft is highly desirable.

The entire crew worked very strenuously all morning. By noon, when we had unloaded 120 tons of coal, the squadron flagship signaled: "Cease preparations." Once again terrific disappointment! All our work for nothing. Damn the English! Nevertheless it seems that we are extremely well informed about their fleet movements.

Nothing worth mentioning occurred in the ensuing days and weeks. Unimportant entries such as: We are the ships of the watch today—Visit from the *Oldenburg*—Antwerp has fallen—An English cruiser has been sunk—Japanese suffer heavy losses before Tsingtao—Military march held today, etc., fill my pages.

The beginning of the month brought a new chapter in the history of the war. Turkey and all of Islam have declared a holy war against their exploiters England and Russia. Although it did not come as a great surprise to those of us who are politically conscious, this report, nevertheless, was received with unimaginable joy.[47] We in the navy had even greater cause for rejoicing because of the activities of our two famous cruisers *Göben* and *Breslau*. After their breakthrough at Messina they first found refuge in and then were purchased by

[47] This was largely a rumor of German manufacture to enlist the aid of the Mohammedan peoples against the Entente. The rumor had it that the Kaiser had become a convert to Islam and that the Caliph was about to declare a jehad, or a holy war, against the infidel English, French and Russians.

Turkey. The *Göben* had been renamed *Sultan Selim* and the *Breslau*, *Mididilli*. Of course the German crews and officers remained on board. This did not please the Triple Entente at all. They demanded the removal of the men. The Turkish government replied: "No one shall prevent the men from leaving on their own volition. [But] Turkey strongly and decisively rejects any sort of intervention in her internal affairs." Upon this the diplomatic representatives of England, France and Russia announced that they did not recognize the sale of the ships and that they would be treated as though they belonged to Germany. [Then] three Russian ships loaded with mines tried to close off the entrance of the Black Sea. *Mididilli* arrived upon the scene and sank all three of them. Subsequently *Sultan Selim* and another cruiser bombarded Sevastopol, an important wheat shipping port. In the naval battle which thereupon ensued a Russian cruiser was sunk. This is the present state of affairs on November 2. We will obtain the not inconsiderable support of the newly reorganized Turkish army [in the future].[48]

According to all indications, they will attempt to sever one of England's vital arteries by occupying the Suez Canal. One may presume that the Mohammedan population of that country will also take the opportunity to overthrow the English despotism. What amazes me, however, is India's attitude. No other English colony has been so exploited and impoverished as this once-blooming land. Many high English officials have been murdered in the past. The last major uprising occurred in the year 1856. At that time the famed Sepoy regiments, estab-

[48] On August 10 the German Mediterrean Squadron of Admiral Souchon obtained Turkey's permission to enter the Dardanelles. Although this constituted a breach of Turkey's neutrality, it no longer mattered since Turkey had already decided to enter the war on Germany's side and had accordingly concluded a treaty to this effect on August 1.

Relations between the Turkish Empire and the Entente were strained to the breaking point when the German ships were incorporated into the Turkish navy. However, the Allies were reluctant to push Turkey into the war. When on October 29 some Turkish warships accompanied by *Göben* and *Breslau* bombarded not only Sevastopol but also Odessa and Theodosia on Russia's Black Sea coast, Russia declared war on Turkey on November 2. England and France followed suit on November 5.

lished and trained by English officers, rebelled.[49] At a later date Lord Kitchener ruthlessly suppressed the occasional uprisings. But talk of secret conspiracies and assassinations persisted. Especially those students and intellectuals who were educated in Europe and who were exposed to a taste of freedom bear an undying hatred for England.

Hence I believe that John Bull's active engagement in his first European war will cause the flames of rebellion to rise sky-high in all the suppressed nations. This is especially true of India but also of the Transvaal, of Canada and, finally, of Australia. By calculatedly exploiting the differences between the various religions and castes in India, England has cleverly managed to divide and conquer. 60,000 Japanese [soldiers] are employed in India to maintain peace. Native-born Mohammedan soldiers are used in the fight against Germany while Brahmins, Buddhists and Confucians are to be stationed in Egypt.

But this is not the place for all this; we shall have to help ourselves. The heroic deeds of our incomparable cruiser the *Emden* fill the entire world with amazement and admiration. She is reputed to have sunk fifty-four ships having an estimated cost of seventy to eighty million marks.[50] For two months now no English ship has dared to sail to the Bengal or India. By carrying a false fourth smokestack, she managed to surprise the Russian cruiser *Schemtschug* and a French destroyer and sank both of them with her torpedoes.[51] As a result, seventy cruisers have been assigned to capture her. But *Emden* merely laughed at these attempts, intercepted their wireless messages and always managed to elude them.

During her last escapade she appeared at the port of ———,

---

[49] The Sepoy mutiny occurred in 1857 and 1858 when the undisciplined and discontented native soldiers of the Indian army, fearing conversion to Christianity, sparked a revolt which soon spread through northern and central India.

[50] More realistic estimates maintain that *Emden* captured between thirteen and seventeen enemy merchantmen. However, she did bombard the important English oil depot at Madras and set half a million gallons of oil on fire.

[51] This took place on October 28 at Penang in Malaya. The French destroyer was the *Mousquet*.

which has an important English cable and wireless station.[52] She set a landing party ashore to destroy these installations. The [local] officials desperately wired for help in all directions. It arrived in the form of the Australian cruiser *Sydney*. While the landing party was hard at work, a signal to return was sounded. But it came too late; the men could not return in time. *Emden* accepted the fight with barely two thirds of her crew. A heated battle developed. Right at the beginning *Emden* scored two direct hits against her opponent. Then the two ships vainly tried to torpedo each other. However in the end the British cruiser with her much heavier guns gained the upper hand. *Emden*'s forward mast and her aft smokestack were shot away. The stern of the ship caught on fire. When the commander Captain Müller realized that he had been defeated, he drove the faithful *Emden* on the beach and surrendered. The casualties were enormous. Two hundred men met a heroic death.

The brave captain was rescued and has evidently been taken to England. All the neutral newspapers, and even the English papers themselves, are filled with descriptions of *Emden*'s heroism and the gallantry of her captain.[53]

The city council of Emden sent a telegram of condolence to the Kaiser. He replied:

> Grateful thanks for your telegram regarding the tragic but heroic defeat of my cruiser *Emden*. This brave ship has won laurels for Germany's war flag even in her defeat. I shall construct a new and stronger *Emden*. To commemorate the fame of her predecessor, the Iron Cross will be mounted on her bow.
>
> *Wilhelm Rex*

According to English reports, *Emden* was directly responsible for a loss of eighty-three million marks [in enemy shipping].

[52] Name omitted, but Stumpf means Direction Island in the Cocos, where *Emden* appeared on November 9.

[53] Since Captain Karl von Müller had always treated his prisoners kindly and no charges could be brought against him, he was allowed to retain his sword when he was captured.

During these November days the attention of the world focused not only on *Emden* but also on Kiaochow, that major outpost of German culture in East Asia. A handful of Germans defended this pearl of culture against the treacherous incursions of the marauding Japanese. Even the British took part in the attempt to recapture this oasis of culture from barbarism.[54] The reports from Tsingtao caused our hearts to swell with pride. Every attack by superior enemy forces was thrown back with great valor. Nevertheless the final outcome was never in question. The moment the Japanese received reinforcements and bore down with their heaviest guns, the bitter end would be near. After nine days of uninterrupted bombardment the fortress capitulated. All of her guns were out of commission and her stores of ammunition were totally depleted. The garrison was accorded military honors at its surrender and the officers were permitted to retain their swords.[55]

The report of a joyous victory by our Overseas Squadron provided a welcome contrast to this dreadful news. The squadron under the command of Admiral Graf von Spee had left the port of Tsingtao prior to the establishment of the Japanese blockade. It consisted of the heavy cruisers *Scharnhorst* and *Gneisenau* and several gunboats. The destination of the ships was unknown. At a later date the two of them bombarded a French port, sank one of the gunboats anchored there and once again disappeared for a considerable period of time.[56]

We heard from them again after they had won a victory over some English cruisers off the coast of South America. Admiral Spee had collected the rest of the Overseas Squadron, the *Nürnberg, Leipzig* and *Dresden*. The English squadron

[54] The Japanese launched their attack upon the German naval base on August 27. It was defended by a small garrison of 5,000 sailors and marines under the command of Admiral Meyer Waldeck. On September 23 a small English force under Brigadier General Barnadiston joined the Japanese.

[55] After the German garrison had lost about 2,000 of its men and most of the fort had been reduced to rubble by the bombardment, Kiaochow surrendered on November 7.

[56] On September 22 Admiral Spee bombarded Papeete in the Society Islands and from there sailed on to the coast of South America.

consisted of the armored cruisers *Good Hope* and *Monmouth*, the new cruiser *Glasgow* and the auxiliary cruiser *Otranto*. The battle lasted barely an hour. By that time the two enemy armored cruisers had sustained such damage that they sank with all hands. In the ensuing darkness the fast *Glasgow* and *Otranto* made good their escape but both were crippled severely.[57]

This wonderful victory generated tremendous jubilation in our ranks because our ships emerged virtually unscathed while our casualties came to a mere total of three wounded. Therefore we placed great hopes on our squadron. Soon thereafter we heard that Japanese ships were in pursuit and that English or Australian ships had joined the search. Nearly forty ships were involved in the hunt.[58] But our cruisers were everywhere and nowhere. They seemed to mock all of the enemy's exertions. For a long time no English merchantman dared sail in South American waters. The insurance rates soared to unprecedented heights. Now, however, the English were touched in their most sensitive spot—their moneybags—. They assigned two or three of their newest heavy cruisers to the pursuit and they were in luck. The German squadron allowed itself to be lured into a treacherous trap off the Falkland Islands.[59]

[The English] had posted several light cruisers at the harbor entrance while a number of heavy battle cruisers lay in hiding behind a rise near a high ridge. As soon as the German squadron came into sight, the fast English light cruisers went out to meet it. But no sooner had they come within firing range than

[57] Admiral Sir Christopher Cradock, the British Commander of the South American Squadron, realized that the Germans were much more powerful than he. Yet he had received orders from the Admiralty to seek them out and engage them. This he did at the Battle of Coronel off the coast of Chile with the result indicated above.

[58] Thirty ships would be more correct. Admiral Sir Doveton Sturdee, the Commander of the English fleet, had twenty-one ships under his command, and the rest were made up by the Japanese and the French. The English deemed the situation so serious that they separated three battle cruisers from the Grand Fleet—the *Invincible*, *Inflexible* and *Princess Royal*—to hunt down Spee.

[59] The Battle of the Falkland Islands took place in the South Atlantic on December 8.

they turned tail. Three of their newest battle cruisers (*Inflexible*, *Invincible* [and *Australia*]) came up from behind. Each was armed with ten 30 cm. rapid-firing guns. When Admiral Spee realized that he had walked into a trap, he ordered his light cruisers to disperse. But it was too late. *Scharnhorst*, the flagship, opened fire. According to the English reports her fire was amazingly fast and accurate. *Invincible* was hit twenty times. But the enemy may have been correct in asserting that our 210 millimeter shells failed to penetrate their armor and hence inflicted very little damage.

When the British received reinforcement in the form of another cruiser [actually pre-Dreadnought battleship] *Canopus*, *Scharnhorst*'s situation became desperate. Admiral Sturdee inquired if our ships wished to surrender. He got back the reply: "German ships do not surrender." The battle had already been raging for three hours. *Scharnhorst* had expended all of her ammunition and was slowly sinking. Those among her crew who were still alive assembled on deck and sounded three cheers. Not a soul was rescued. It went almost the same with *Gneisenau*. She, too, fought against several superior opponents. She managed to survive several hours longer and also used up her last shell.[60]

According to a letter which one of the surviving officers of *Gneisenau* wrote to his family, the ship blew herself up when her ammunition ran out. According to him, the top deck had virtually disintegrated [by that time]. All that was left of the ship was a shapeless mass of metal.

At the start of the battle Admiral Spee had ordered the light cruisers to leave formation and to make their escape. The English commander Admiral [Sturdee] sent a couple of his modern armored cruisers after them. They succeeded in catching up with *Leipzig* and *Nürnberg*. The English admiral reports that they fought back like the devil. Only *Dresden*, thanks to her high speed, managed to escape.[61] Hopefully she and *Karls-*

60 The German losses at the Falkland Islands were enormous. Admiral Spee, his two sons and 1,800 men perished. There were only 200 survivors.
61 It was not until March, 1915, that she was sunk at the island of Juan Fernández.

ruhe will long continue to terrorize the English merchant marine.[62]

Some recently published newspaper reports reveal that the English squadron suffered greater damage during the battle than they previously admitted. Four heavily damaged warships were tied up at Gibraltar. The *Glasgow* is said to have sunk, and her place has been taken by her sister ship the *Bristol*. I am inclined to regard this as true. *Scharnhorst* did not get the highest artillery award, the Golden Imperial prize, for nothing.

Something does not make any sense to me! How did our two battle cruisers find it possible to maintain such effective fire? Not only were the English capable of much higher speed but they also had the advantage of longer-ranging guns. According to the most elementary rules of artillery, they should have kept out of range of our ships. A 30 cm. gun has a range which is at least four kilometers longer than one of 21 cm. One plausible explanation might be that the English, as usual, fired very inaccurately. Thus they had to maintain a closer range to make their fire effective.[63] I can think of no other reason why the English would commit such a grave tactical error. Spanish sources indicate that *Invincible* sustained no fewer than twenty-one hits.

If the situation had been reversed and had our side possessed such a superiority, the battle would have lasted a mere five minutes. Nothing would have been left of the enemy. It is unbelievable that it should have taken the English with their thirty 30.5 caliber guns three to five hours to destroy a couple of old armored cruisers. Anyone having the slightest acquaintance with gunnery will agree that [had they been German ships] such a thing would never have occurred. A label of shame shall remain attached to this pitiful English victory for all time.

[62] The *Karlsruhe* blew up earlier, on November 4, in the West Indies.
[63] Not only was the fire of the English much less accurate than that of the Germans, but English shells were also much less powerful because they tended to explode immediately upon impact and thus failed to penetrate the German armor. At Falkland the English, despite their four-to-one superiority in firing power, expended practically all of their ammunition before they sank the German ships.

Christmas! Good God, today is Christmas! Who would have thought to live to see another Christmas! Although we were at sea, a freighter brought us a load of little Christmas trees. We decorated them as best we could and that evening we stood around the lights, bright-eyed like children. Each of us received a package of nuts and oranges.

The second day of Christmas brought us a visit from a flight of English aircraft. The extremely heavy fog prevented me from seeing anything but I could hear the noise of their motors quite distinctly. Our ships all fired at the invisible enemy with gusto. One of their dirigibles dropped two bombs on a cruiser-escort and a steamer and started a huge fire. Two of the aircraft were later fished out of the sea near Helgoland. We had probably shot them down.

We have had a very trying time lately. Since Christmas we have been on patrol every second day. Although we take no special pains to keep alert, still we have to stand at our posts. This virtually ruins a night's sleep. I cannot understand why half of our tables and benches have still not been returned to us. I find it difficult to write a letter or jot a note in my diary. However nothing worth mentioning ever happens. If I were to keep a record of my duties from day to day, it would always be the same. I understand that we are scheduled to go into dock as soon as it is vacated by *Nassau*. I shall be damned glad!!

On Sunday January [17] we did routine chores. First of all, we scrubbed the deck, shined the brass, and then—infuriating me all week long whenever I think of it—came a highly painstaking inspection in clean uniforms. Although we have been unable to replace our worn-out clothing at the ship's store for a long time because of the shortage of wool, our Division Officer examines every wrinkle and spot on our uniforms. He rejects every explanation with the stock reply, "Poor excuse!" My God, such behavior makes me sick of the navy! Most of us simply don't care any more. We are fortunate that not all officers are like that.

After this disgusting inspection (during which I wished that a plane would appear and drop a bomb on the "old man's" head) I consoled myself with the thought of spending a nice free afternoon, when the flagship signaled: "H.C. (code name for *Helgoland*) may go into dock this noon." Damn it! Another Sunday spoiled! The only consolation was that I would not have to serve as lookout that night.

Sunday afternoon was frittered away because we had difficulty in going through the locks. At dusk we tied up for the night. We did not get to the dock until Wednesday. Having made up my mind to shirk all hard work, I planned on enjoying myself while we were in dock. Everything went well the first few days. Because I had band practice all day, I had no part in the work details. But this joy soon came to an end. One day Smarting, the bosun, appeared smiling congenially and told the band to assemble on deck. That entire day we were compelled to help load ammunition. The very unmusical bosun assigned us to chipping paint on the hull as soon as the water was drained from the dock. In looking down from the top it appeared to be very dangerous to work on the swaying platforms. But we soon got used to it.

The week flew by. Today's date is Sunday January 24. Around noon we heard a rumor that our armored cruisers were engaged in a great battle with the English. At first I did not believe it. But then the Executive Officer called the other officers [to his quarters]. Surely this meant something. After lunch the rumors became more concrete. It was alleged that one of our heavy cruisers *Blücher* had gone under and that *Seydlitz* had sustained severe damages. An English ship of the *Lion* class also went down. I liked that part the best. We learned nothing more definite that day. [We lived] in painful uncertainty.

On Monday morning while we were assembling on deck for job details, the cruiser *Derfflinger* came sailing in. We gave her three echoing cheers. She responded in kind and tied up right next to us. The light cruiser *Kolberg*, which had also participated in the fight, went into the dock as well. She had been hit —a hit in the head! Glass splinters flew all around. Two men were killed and a third had his arm torn off.

As soon as it turned light I dashed over to *Derfflinger* to inspect the damage and to ask the participants what had happened. I noticed that *Seydlitz* was still in dock. Why? When I got on board the *Derfflinger* I observed a sizable hole on the starboard side near the third gun. Another hit was visible near the aft smokestack. I later discovered that she had also taken two hits below the water line. However these merely caused the armor plating to slip slightly.

The battle was described to me as follows: The First Reconnaissance Group, consisting of the heavy battle cruisers *Seydlitz, Moltke, Derfflinger*, and the armored cruiser *Blücher* were out on a reconnaissance patrol at nine o'clock in the morning when five enemy cruisers were sighted.[64] The ships at once cleared for action and opened fire at an unprecedented range of twenty kilometers. The German ships changed course immediately and increased speed to twenty-eight miles. *Seydlitz* was in the lead while *Blücher* took up the rear. The latter, an older ship belonging to the so-called transition type [of Dreadnought], could not maintain this speed and dropped behind. As a result, the other ships were forced to slow down. The battle closed in. Unlike in the past, the enemy did not concentrate their fire on the opposing flagship. Instead they selected the weakest ship *Blücher* with great success.[65] Within a short time *Blücher*'s engine stopped after taking one or more hits. She lay still, a convenient target for the enemy. Their destroyers mounted an attack and fired a large number of torpedoes at the helpless *Blücher*. Although she listed to one side, she defended herself vigorously and managed to keep up a very rapid

[64] On January 24, 1915, Admiral Franz von Hipper sailed out with his ships to destroy the English fishing fleet off the Dogger Bank. However, Admiral Beatty and the English cruiser squadron awaited him there. The English had obtained the German code book from the Russians, who had accidentally captured it in August, 1914, and were thus able to predict the movements of the German fleet by intercepting its radio messages.

[65] This was actually a grave tactical mistake on the part of Beatty's subordinates. By concentrating all their fire on *Blücher*, which was already crippled, they allowed the rest of the German squadron to escape. Beatty's flagship the *Lion* had been mauled severely and could not keep up. Hence the British Squadron Commander lost direction of the battle. This may also explain the illusion that he turned tail.

and accurate fire which hit and blew up two of the destroyers. But a number of their torpedoes must have found their mark because *Blücher* sank deeper and deeper. . . .

In the meantime, the other German ships directed their deadly fire on the English squadron. Two of their ships, the flagship *Lion* and the *Tiger*, had heavy lists (One battle cruiser [the *New Zealand*] sank beneath the waves). At that point Admiral Beatty thought it advisable to turn about and flee. *Lion* could not keep up and *Indomitable* took her in tow. It was foggy. As a result, one of our torpedo boats suddenly found herself right next to a gigantic and apparently badly crippled cruiser. She quickly fired a torpedo which did the rest and the cruiser went down.

All of this was observed by a Zeppelin cruising in the air, by *Moltke* and by a nearby submarine. Yet the British Admiralty has the nerve to talk about light casualties. It insists that no English ships were sunk and that only eleven men received superficial wounds.[66] Our newspapers are in an uproar. I don't know what to make of it myself. Some time ago when *Audacious* ran over a mine and sank, the English government not only kept this news a secret but denied the report.[67] Consequently I have reluctantly come to the conclusion that the English will stop at nothing to preserve the glory of the Union Jack. They keep the truth about their navy from the neutral nations at all costs. Whenever something happens they always keep their losses a secret. A while ago the Swiss papers reported that two English battleships *Thunderer* and *Queen Mary* had been lost. This news is too good to be true.

[66] Stumpf is mistaken. No English cruisers were sunk, and only the *Lion* sustained any severe damages. However, *Lion* alone had eleven wounded, so that the English casualties on all the ships must have been higher. In any event, the casualty rate for the English was incredibly small for an engagement of this size.

[67] *Audacious* had struck a mine on October 27, 1914, and had to be taken in tow by the liner *Olympic*. However, she blew up on her way back to port. Although the passengers of the *Olympic* had witnessed her sinking and some of them had even taken pictures of it, the English Cabinet decided to keep the matter a secret in order to preserve the morale of the people at home. Rumors of the sinking of the *Audacious* did not reach Germany until the end of the year.

The battle is discussed everywhere. We are all astounded that the superannuated *Blücher* should have taken part in this action. Not so long ago when we made our sortie against England, *Blücher*'s slowness and lack of maneuverability spoiled everything. However she does fire extremely well. Because of her faulty construction, she served as an artillery school ship. Hence she had the best gunners and artillery officers on board. All kinds of innovations and improvements were tried out on her. Thus for some time she had been equipped with a tripod mast and a range finder patterned after the English model. This made her very conspicuous. Her Captain, a very energetic and capable man, was taken prisoner. I have yet to hear a word of regret about the loss of this ship. It appears that 200 to 250 of her crew members were rescued by British torpedo boats. Anywhere from 600 to 650 men lost their lives.

Today on the Kaiser's birthday, *Seydlitz* buried 165 of her dead. A small number of coffins was sufficient to accommodate the remains of the unfortunate ones. *Seydlitz* was hit in a way which should never again be repeated in this war. A shell flew into a ventilator on deck and fell into her bowels. The heavy explosion ignited two shells in the elevator. These in turn set the ammunition in the aft gun turrets on fire. Within seconds both turrets were a flaming inferno. Their crews were burned to death in an instant. This created the horrible danger that the entire ship would explode if the munition chambers caught fire. A machinist's mate averted a catastrophe by flooding the threatened chambers. He was rewarded with the Iron Cross First and Second Class.

Some shipyard workers employed on *Seydlitz* told me that the men were found in the positions they occupied when death struck them. The man at the communication tube had his hands on his mouth and the tube as though he wanted to say something. The man at the range finder was still looking at his dials, while the master gunner sat in the turret seat. The most touching scene occurred in the gun room, where several men hung on the lock in an attempt to open it. At the first touch they all crumbled to ashes. *Memento mori!*

Now I understand why *Seydlitz* remained in the locks for such a long time. She had to pump the water out of her hold. Now she is in dock and will probably require three months to repair her damages. 16–24 January 1915.

We still don't know which English cruiser was sunk. England doggedly insists that she lost no ships. Yet we have the report of a Dutch fishing boat captain who distinctly observed a large ship sinking under the waves. Our most recent information indicates that it was the brand-new *Tiger*. We all hope so.

In the meantime we finished the work on our hull. The ship got three coats of red paint. Hence we were able to leave the dock. Our place was taken by the cruiser *Roon*. On Friday we conducted a net exercise in the harbor to test our new netting. Everything went off without a hitch. There were still a large number of shipyard workers on board. Almost all of them are dreadfully lazy. They "work" until nine o'clock every day and complain constantly. I wish I could send them into the trenches every fourteen days.

Our lovely stay in dock was over. We put out to sea again and lay at our moorings before the locks. The weather was tolerable. They seemed to have been waiting for us out there. No sooner had we arrived than it was our turn to go on patrol. Recently they issued a very sensible directive that only one ship shall be assigned this duty at any given time. Therefore our turn comes around only once every four days. This is very nice. Equally welcome is a squadron order giving the crews longer rest periods. Accordingly we have only one hour of cleaning guns, followed by equipment repairs in the afternoon.

This morning our patrol came to a close and we returned to the Jade at once. On the [February] 4th, His Majesty the Kaiser arrived in Wilhelmshaven. Important changes in command are in the offing. The Kaiser will no doubt also want to take a look at the ships that fought in the battle. He will have an opportunity to see all kinds of things on *Seydlitz*.

The Commander of the High Seas Fleet is to be removed.[68]

---

[68] Although the Commander of the High Seas Fleet Admiral Ingenohl had scrupulously obeyed the Kaiser's injunction not to jeopardize the

I saw him for the first time two days ago. I saw him walking about on deck of his flagship the *Deutschland* when we passed through the locks. The women of Wilhelmshaven have jeered at him on the streets on numerous occasions. The small boys sing:

> Rest in peace, dear Fatherland
> For the fleet is sleeping in port.[69]

It would serve these people right if a couple of airplanes dropped bombs on their homes. Then at least they would have cause to complain.

All in all, it is time we got a new and enterprising commander for the fleet. The name of Pohl is mentioned frequently.[70] The entire crew is agreed that he would be a likely choice. The reservists enthusiastically recall his daring conduct while he was still on active duty. His name has become world famous because of his announcement in the *Reichsanzeiger* declaring the waters around England a war zone. Any enemy merchant ship attempting to approach the coast in the future will be sunk.[71] This announcement was implemented at once. Much to the dismay of the English, several submarines turned up in the Irish Sea. Among them was the *U 21*, which had long been the terror of the Channel. Three or four large freighters

German fleet, the lack of success at the Battle of Dogger Bank and his unpopularity among the people prompted his dismissal early in February 1915.

[69] Lieb' Vaterland magst ruhig sein
   Die Flotte schläft im Hafen ein.

[70] Admiral Hugo von Pohl (1855–1916) had been the Chief of the Naval Staff up to that time.

[71] In retaliation against the English blockade, the German government on February 4, 1915, announced that a submarine blockade against Great Britain would commence on February 18. The note read: "All the waters surrounding Great Britain and Ireland, including the whole of the English Channel, are hereby declared a war zone. . . . Every enemy merchant ship found within this war zone will be destroyed without it being always possible to avoid attacks being made on neutral vessels in mistake for those of the enemy." The German decision to begin submarine warfare was soon to embroil that country in mounting difficulties with the United States and other neutral powers. Eventually it led to America's entry into the war against Germany.

were sunk. A troop transport also fell prey to her, and 244 men were killed. This must have come as a great shock to the shipping lines. Food prices have already risen by twenty percent and there is talk that a strike among the miners and railway workers is imminent.

The English and their allies are madly trying to discover how our daring submarines got into the Irish Sea. They thought that the presence of nets, mines and other protective devices made it impossible for the submarines to take the most direct route through the [English] Channel. They assumed that they went all around England by way of St. George Channel, a voyage of more than a thousand kilometers. The *Times* has termed it a milestone in the development of the submarine. I was quite convinced that they were wrong and that our submarines came through the Channel.

The papers were still filled with stories of the *U 21*, I myself was still of the opinion that she was up in the Irish Sea. Today on February 10, as we were eating chow, all of a sudden there came an order: "All hands on deck." A submarine was approaching, as fast as an arrow. Before we knew what was happening our Captain called from the bridge in a high voice: "Three cheers for the crew of *U 21*!" Our caps flew into the air and we saluted as did *Thüringen*, *Oldenburg* and the other ships. First Lieutenant von Hersing, the Captain of the *U 21*, has made it a practice to visit our ship before going to sea. He goes to the officers' mess and is entertained there by his friends. Those of his sailors and stokers who come aboard get coffee with bread and butter, while the petty officers and the deck officers receive the same treatment from their ranks. We therefore learn a great deal. Unfortunately we have never obtained permission to see the insides of the submarine.

On the surface she is powered by a gasoline engine and has a maximum speed of 15 miles. If the submarine wants to submerge, the engine is turned off and water is allowed to enter a tank. This is regulated in such a fashion that she can sail at any desired depth. The submarine operates under the water the same way as an airplane does in the air. The slightest upset in her balance can be very dangerous and may founder the boat. Thus, for instance, if a torpedo is fired in the forward tubes, the ship automatically lets in an equivalent volume of water to equalize the loss in weight. [Under the water] the gasoline engine is shut off and [the submarine is powered] by an electric motor fed by batteries. Waste gases are rendered harmless by means of chemicals and oxygen tanks supply fresh air. I have never noticed that the men look the worse for it. On the contrary! They all look quite healthy and contented.

If the submarine intends to surface again or to rise in the water, she simply expels some of the water she took on before. Whenever, as has occasionally happened, an engine failure renders it impossible [to expel the water], the entire crew dies a horrible death. To guard against such a contingency, a heavy leaden keel which can be detached is coupled to the ship's bottom. Then the submarine can rise to the surface despite the water. How this keel is attached and uncoupled is a secret. A floating object with a telephone attached enables the submarine to communicate with the surface. One of the most important pieces of equipment is the eye of the submarine, the periscope. From the outside it looks like an ordinary stovepipe. Inside there are lenses and mirrors that reflect the image of the surface on a glass plate.

In order to provide our lookouts with an opportunity to experience a submarine attack, the *U 21* performed a variety of exercises. We lay off Schillig Roads and knew the time and direction in which the submarine would appear fairly accurately. The sea was quite calm and the weather was clear. I must admit, however, that we would surely have gotten several torpedoes in our bowels because we first sighted her periscope when she was 150 to 200 meters away from us. I am convinced that any ship lying at anchor without torpedo netting would inevitably fall victim to this little monster's hellish torpedoes.

The sailors of the *U 21* told me some incredible things. Thus one of them said that they encountered an English cruiser division in the Channel one moonlit night. But they were under strict orders not to reveal their presence. "You may well imagine," he said, "our Captain's emotions at passing up such a fine opportunity." At one point the *U 21* sank a French merchantman (the *Malachite*) right off Le Havre. As the freighter sank in the water, a group of destroyers came up. Instead of fleeing, the brave submarine took up the challenge. She fired three torpedoes at her pursuers, dived beneath the waves and escaped. On another occasion the submarine had the misfortune of entangling herself in the wire netting guarding the entrance of an English harbor. It required thirty-six hours of strenuous labor before she managed to free herself again.

On the day of this writing, we sank another large English troop transport.

When we once again began making all sorts of preparations [to sail out] this was interpreted in various ways. There were some who maintained that enemy cruisers were approaching, while others insisted that we were going to sail to Kiel via the Kaiser Wilhelm Canal. The fact that we had not taken on coal for the past fourteen days gave support to the latter contention. This had to happen just when we were due to spend two days in port! The entire First Squadron raised anchor and set course toward Cuxhaven. No sooner had we passed the forward mine area than an impregnable fog descended. The Admiral therefore did not find it advisable to risk the mine fields off the mouth of the Elbe. He gave orders to drop anchor and to wait for clearer weather. However that took a long time. Before the fog lifted two days had passed. The continual clanging of the bells and the howling of the sirens almost drove one mad.

Finally, at last, we are to sail through the famous canal today. This is the first time a ship of our size has ever attempted it. I was anxious to see how it would go. Slowly we passed Cuxhaven, our beloved town with its many spires and dropped anchor off Brunsbüttel. On the following morning we saw the famous locks, the largest in the world. The *Ostfriesland* and *Thüringen* were already inside. Then came our turn along with the *Oldenburg*. Even the largest ships fit comfortably into the locks. For safety's sake they are equipped with double gates facing in the direction of the sea. The attendants live in low houses on the top. The process of entering the locks went faster than at Wilhelmshaven. The entrance of the canal is fairly wide but still not deep enough. We had to jettison quite a bit of drinking water to raise the ship a little. Inside a tugboat was waiting for us and nudged us over the sand banks. Soon, however, we were over and slowly our propellers began to turn to give us a speed of five miles. We were all curious to see the banks of the canal. The weather was tolerable. The February sun attempted a warm smile. At first there was little to see. Great mounds of black earth lined both sides. Now and again a strip of wintery, deserted flat land was visible. In an hour the view changed. I liked it better when some tree-lined ridges appeared on the left side. I was particularly struck by the farm houses of Lower Saxony. Surrounded by clumps of old trees, they stood in isolation. Their straw-thatched roofs almost reached the ground and their windows were tiny. These plain-looking little houses appeared all the more incongruous in contrast to the great modern industrial plants which had sprung up at their side.

Crossing right over the canal there was a huge half-finished railroad bridge. Its gigantic arches were supported by a lace-like web of iron cables and rails. At the bottom four thick columns resembling the paws of a lion were embedded in blocks of cement. With the same kind of awe and astonishment I had previously devoted to those relics of the past, the farm houses of Lower Saxony, I now gazed at this technological marvel. I noticed that no one was working on the bridge. The war needs men.

Our ship made steady and uninterrupted progress. Now and then [we saw] a Schleswig-Holsteiner on the banks waving a handkerchief the size of our top flag. Once a beautiful girl put her hands to her mouth and shouted over to us, "What kind of a ship is that?" "A steam ship!" promptly retorted a jovial fellow from Frankfurt amidst great howls of laughter.

At a distance we could already make out the famous high-span bridge of Grünthal. Here was a finished example of what we had seen before. Although I didn't know how long or how tall the bridge was, in any case it was as high as our church steeple at home. Our forty-three-meter-high masts did not create a problem here. To think that this bridge was built in the middle of the flatlands! To attain such a height huge quantities of earth had to be moved to the banks. I am convinced that it cost more to widen the canal than to dig the original bed.

About six months ago three English light cruisers sailed to the North Sea through the canal. A squadron of [English] warships was "visiting" Kiel at that time and also wanted to use the canal. But they did not get permission because the canal was not completed. I understand that our "dear cousins" planned on scuttling one of their ships in there. Of course the bad Germans would have been blamed for it. It would have provided them with a perfect excuse for going to war. Since they would already have been inside [the canal], they could have bombarded Kiel and Cuxhaven and cut off the entire Baltic fleet. Although this story may sound a trifle far-fetched after all that has happened, it seems quite plausible now. Had the plan succeeded, our fleet would have been split in half and the English could have finished off our few ships in the North Sea with ease. In fact part of the English fleet was lying off the Belt to ambush our Third Squadron as it returned to the North Sea. No doubt if the canal had not been completed, their sly plan would have worked. But by August 3 the Third Squadron consisting of eight ships of the line was back in the North Sea and the plans for the first great [English] victory went awry.[72]

There was a sharp contrast between the nervousness and excitement prevailing during the early weeks of the war and the present calm and confident state. We used to tie up close to the locks with our torpedo nets spread out and keep the guns on one side of the ship fully manned every night. The slightest incident gave rise to an uproar and a speech by the First Officer. Nowadays everything is changed. The ships take turns standing watch out beyond the mine fields every two weeks

---

[72] Although this is a completely unsubstantiated rumor, it illustrates the great hostility which existed between the two rival fleets.

and only on those occasions do they spread out the torpedo netting.

After our recent battle at sea not a single officer bothered to give us an explanation. Our uncertainty gives rise to incredible rumors concerning our losses. Even the dullest among us think, "Surely we would have heard from our officers if we had won. But they are told to keep their mouths shut." A small number among us who are more intelligent assert that we could gain a great deal by letting the enemy know the full extent of his losses. In my opinion we would be better off if our officers would relieve us of our monotony. We would be extremely grateful for a lecture on the enemy's strength and probable course of action, or a talk on the naval law, on torpedoes or on the various types of gunpowder. For my part [I would be happy to learn about] the development of British naval power, the importance of the Dardanelles or any other worthwhile subject. This would be a thousandfold improvement over stupid inspection of uniforms or the memorized recitation of lessons on "military courtesy, care of clothing, infantry rifle 98, sentry duty, articles of war, . . ." All of us are fed up with these things. What a shame! Every single one of us is interested in what is going on in the world.

By nightfall we had reached the high-span bridge at Levensau which is even taller and more imposing than the one at Grünthal. When we passed the town of Rendsburg the soldiers and the townspeople gave us a cheer and we responded in full voice. The entire canal was illuminated by electric lights. By eleven o'clock we arrived at the Kiel locks. When I stepped on deck the following morning, I was stunned by the beautiful panorama of the incomparable natural harbor. It had snowed during the night and everything was covered with a white blanket. The last time we were here the trees were in bloom and the birds sang along the lovely beaches. The great sails of the luxury yachts sparkled upon the waves and numerous pleasure boats filled with happy people sailed by. All this had disappeared. But the electric drills, saws and hammers of the Germania shipyards were as busy as ever. Not a single foreign ship was in sight. An old Dutch tub and a Danish motor cutter were all that remained. Everything was empty, even over at the "moth ball cemetery." The old ships of the *Kaiser* and *Brandenburg* class had been recommissioned and didn't look so bad after all. But there were some new things, too. Submarines no larger than a whale and equally tiny collapsible torpedo boats shot across the water. For the first time I had a chance to see the torpedo destroyers which we had built for Greece and Argentina. The light cruiser *Pillau*, built originally for Russia, was making her shakedown cruise. She was a pretty little ship, long and narrow like a blade. Mounted on her deck were four 15 cm. quick-firing guns. Her speed was presumed to be thirty sea miles.

As I surveyed all these small and yet powerful weapons, I kept thinking that the High Seas Fleet's function would be to serve as a mere trump card at the negotiation of peace. For this purpose it would have to be kept intact and at full strength. Presumably the English have the same intention. Only this can explain why no decisive sea battle has taken place. Although there is nothing wrong with the contention that we need a strong, battle-ready fleet at the end of the war, it means that our desire for action is never to be realized. If, as in 1870, the army succeeds in plucking all the laurels by itself, we will all be put to shame.

Nevertheless I still retained the hope that we would have a chance to fight with the big ships. What other explanation could there be for our exercises in the Baltic Sea? Every day we sailed out for torpedo practice. On Tuesday [March] 1 each of the different types of guns conducted firing practice with blank ammunition against target ships. We started firing at a range of 9,000 meters and fired about thirty rounds. We only got three hits; not a very brilliant achievement. Our new Squadron Commander Rear Admiral Eckermann observed the shooting from our ship. The weather was not especially good; there was a light fog. I noticed that we fired our torpedoes at an enormous distance of 12,000 meters. With what effect I don't know.

The next day we conducted especially interesting night-firing exercises. I was up on top at the searchlights. From below the bridge gave the order: "Attention, searchlights! Torpedo boats! Light at 30 degrees!" All at once eight beams of light shot into the darkness and played upon the surface of the sea. They pinpointed two black-painted targets (This is what happens when one prattles while writing! [73]) which represented cruisers and torpedo boats.

Once again from below came the command: "Range 2100! Fire salvo!" A bright hot stream of fire shot from the tubes, momentarily depriving me of my vision. The salvo lay to the right. The powder dust shone fiery red in the gleam of the searchlights. Quite a nice show, this night firing. The ship shook and trembled under the force of the detonation and all eyes strained to see where the shells would land. Our chemical explosive produces a hollow, heavy crack, which is followed by the howling and screeching of the shell that resembles a mighty storm. The impact shoots a fountain of water 40 to 70 meters high up in the air. Then comes the penetrating crash caused by the disintegrating steel. The shell had exploded. It sounded like subterranean thunder. What would it look like if a couple of squadrons let loose on one another? In that case it would feel good to stand behind a thick wall of armor and not to hear and see everything going on outside.

Although we had plenty of shore leave in Kiel, many of the men overstayed their passes by varying amounts of time. Each of them got ten "days" in Room 170 as well as the customary "sport" [of punitive exercise].

We were originally scheduled to spend several more weeks in the Baltic to serve as a target ship for the submarines. Hence we were surprised at our departure when the plans were changed. On March 10 at the crack of dawn, the ship was cleared to enter the locks; *Ostfriesland* and *Thüringen* went in ahead of us. The two locks at Holtenau are ———— wide, 11

[73] Explanation for an ink blot on the page.

meters deep and ——— long.[74] Right now there is no need to widen them since I strongly doubt that a ship of such size will ever be built. As was common elsewhere, torpedo nets were strung out along the sea side. On the whole the port of Kiel is amazingly well protected. The narrow fjord, surrounded on all sides by tree-covered hills, is ideally suited for defense even without the mines, the barbed wire and the underwater chain block. To my amazement many lovely stands of trees had been chopped down. From behind, heavy howitzer batteries stared out in a threatening manner. They had not been there before, when all one could see were the ancient forts with their parapets and moats and their 15 cm. mortars. If all this could be ———.[75] Here indeed was an example of what modern war technology could achieve in Germany.

An air defense system had been established. Every day they flew over us on the North Sea with great regularity. Often the dirigibles dropped to the surface and lowered an anchor. Many aquaplanes soared over our heads all the time. Here one could see what Germany's modern war technology had accomplished.

As early as 6:30 in the morning we were already moored in the left-hand lock. If we could count on traversing the canal in ten hours, we would arrive at Brunsbüttel between four and five o'clock. Paradoxically enough, the day before we had taken on two hundred tons of coal so that all our bunkers were full. Evidently the Squadron Commander wanted to find out whether our ships could make it through without difficulty at this draft. In the event we should touch bottom, twenty men were posted on deck at all times ready to drop the stern anchor. Thus the ship would be able to pull herself back with the aid of her engines. Fortunately nothing of this sort happened although our speed was higher than the time before. Most of the time we maintained a speed of six sea miles or eleven kilometers per hour. A special steersman from the First Naval Division who was a canal pilot in civilian life was stationed at the wheel.

[74] The dimensions are omitted.
[75] Remainder of the sentence is missing.

I now had a chance to see those parts of the canal I had missed during the night on the last occasion. Although it may be very attractive during the summer, this season of the year when everything is covered with snow does not speak well for it.

Near Rendsburg I made an interesting discovery. In order to attain the necessary height to cross the bridge, the train has to make two large turns just like the ones I observed near the Brenner Pass. As a result, the same train is visible three times at different heights until it goes over the bridge. Underneath the bridge a large suspension cable had been attached to carry people and vehicles from one side to the other. It was crowded with militiamen in their field-gray uniforms who shouted cheers and demanded some music. Of course the band as usual finally got ready to play just as Rendsburg disappeared from view. The Captain gave the Bandmaster a terrific dressing down for this which the latter accepted with his customary composure.

On either side of the locks there were some large fenced-in meadows. That morning we played such games as blind man's buff, fox out of the bag, etc. The best part came when we had a tug of war. The rope broke, and two hundred men fell down on their behinds all at once. The First Officer who looked on from the ship nearly died laughing.

After midday it suddenly became clearer, the sun broke through and dispersed the fog. We steamed out immediately but no sooner were we under way than the fog came down once more. Once again we were compelled to drop anchor. The fog disappeared as quickly as it had come and we took the opportunity to sail the remaining fifteen miles down the Elbe. Up ahead we were greeted by the many spires of Cuxhaven but we headed for Wilhelmshaven. At 11 o'clock we tied up at Voslapp Roadstead. 14 March 1915.

The next morning we ran into Wilhelmshaven Roads. The sight of that horrible, inhospitable town was not cheering. What a contrast with Kiel or Cuxhaven! There at least we had a change from our daily monotony. It is difficult to imagine our feelings on board. Deep disappointment mingled with boredom is rampant. The best and most intelligent of our officers have been transferred to cruisers, torpedo boats and submarines. They are urgently needed there. With a few exceptions those who have remained behind "don't have much on the ball." They are the ones who harass the men beyond the permissible limits. What purpose is served by making the men unpack their seabags so many times a day? As a result, a deep gulf has arisen between the officers and the men. The men are filled with undying hatred for the officers and the war. Everyone hopes for the return of peace. We don't even want to fight any more. We have had enough. Where is that wonderful enthusiasm of the August days? The ill-will of the officers has strangled and dissipated it shamelessly. But not all of them are responsible! No one could help but respect our First Officer! The recently promoted lieutenants and ensigns are the ones who make themselves important by harassing the men without reason.

Yesterday one of these gentlemen took his division into town for a walk. (Note: As a result of the shortage of older officers, a lieutenant is in charge of a division of 120 men these days.) He made them run in double time through the town and chased them up and down. It was supposed to be a military excursion! Our recreation consists of marching us up and down the dam in closed ranks and making us lie in the mud on the parade grounds. I am certainly not opposed to such physical exercise. Usually it is quite healthy if carried out in a reasonable and purposeful manner. Our comrades out there [at the front] also lie in the mud in bad weather but at least they know why. However we don't.

As has been the case in all of Germany, our food rations have been cut. But no one complains because this is how it has to be. If we are to hold out, we shall have to draw in our belts. Bread rations have been cut in half. If one considers the former importance of bread in our diet, it is going a bit too far. The only additional food we get with breakfast coffee and evening tea is some bread and butter. Nevertheless we will grow accustomed to it. A little suffering never hurt. Occasionally we receive a food package from home or from relatives.

Today [March] 16 we received orders from the flagship to maintain a state of alert. We got up steam in all the boilers and made all sorts of preparation for battle. We were to be prepared to sail out cleared for action by one o'clock in the afternoon. I could not tell what it was all about. One possible explanation might have been that the Commander of the Fleet wanted to find out how long it would take before the English heard of it. As I said before, this was a distinct possibility because all the orders were rescinded that very afternoon. That evening we sailed into Wilhelmshaven. The winter was making an attempt to stay; it snowed and hailed like mad.

The unhappy news from the Pacific is that the cruiser *Dresden* was sunk in a brief engagement with three English cruisers.[76] At present no further information is available. After this sad episode our attention turned to the fight for the Dardanelles. The straits were defended brilliantly and have held out despite the heavy bombardment by an Anglo-French fleet. Today I read in the papers that eleven of their battleships and cruisers had to be towed into the port of Lemnos. The main responsibility for the defense of the Dardanelles lay with our naval artillery. Recently while we were in Kiel, several hundred of our men were transferred there. They traveled through Rumania in civilian clothing. Hence it would appear that this country is inclined to be friendly to us. According to my information, some 35 cm. guns have been emplaced at the Dardanelles. Hence there is no cause for alarm. These guns have a range of 35 kilometers and the English will not be able to get through. I am convinced that neither the English nor the French will be able to force a passage. Our heavy artillery alone will suffice to prevent this. Moreover the straits are also sown with stationary and floating mines. According to what I hear and read, the Allies think that they can avert this threat by

[76] After *Dresden* had evaded capture at the Falkland Islands, she engaged in commerce raiding activities off South America until she was cornered at Juan Fernández and blew herself up on March 15, 1915.

floating wooden rafts ahead of them. This is not a bad idea. But in the narrow channel it will not be as simple as all that. It would slow down the ships considerably. Even the largest rafts would be torn to pieces by one or two mines. What would they do then? In addition, we have some mines anchored on the sea bottom. Stationed on shore we have lookouts waiting until an enemy vessel has reached a certain point and then they detonate these mines. Also our torpedo tubes are very lethal weapons, especially when they carry the stamp "Made in Germany." No ship afloat can defend itself against such powerful weapons. Therefore all calculations indicate that the Dardanelles are unassailable by sea.[77]

Thus far the English have lost three ships of the line and one cruiser. All the rest have sustained some damage in varying degrees. Two French war ships have either been destroyed or crippled severely.[78] Total casualties come to 6,000 men. Most of these reports come from Greece and past experience tells us that they are not too reliable. However all the reports agree in one respect, namely, that the Turks are putting on a brilliant defense. No wonder, since the ratio of Germans on the gun crews is four to one.[79]

Lately there has been much talk in the press regarding a recently invented torpedo-launching tube that can fire the greatest distance with amazing accuracy. This is probably the same type of system we have on our newest ships. It can even

[77] In order to open another front against the enemy and to open a supply route to Russia, Winston Churchill and a number of other influential members of the British Cabinet had long advocated an attack upon Turkey via the Dardanelles. In mid-February 1915 an Anglo-French naval force was sent to the Greek island of Lemnos to prepare for the invasion. However, on March 18, when the main blow against the Straits was launched, four of the Allied ships struck mines and three of them were sunk as a result. Since the Straits could not be forced open from the sea, a month later the fateful Gallipoli campaign was initiated with the landing of a British expeditionary force.

[78] The English lost *Inflexible* and *Ocean* while *Irresistible* was damaged so severely that she had to be beached. In addition, the French lost one of their battleships the *Bouvet*.

[79] Admiral Guido von Usedom and his German "advisors" had improved the Turkish batteries considerably. General Liman von Sanders did the same for the Turkish army.

fire at an angle. For awhile after launching the torpedo runs straight, until a clock inside stops and turns the rudder. As a result the torpedo turns at an angle and finally hits a ship by approaching from a different direction. This requires the most precise calculation and flawless operation on the part of the mechanism.

On Monday March 28, we were scheduled to take on coal again. Since we had only used a small amount, we were only able to load two hundred tons. The unseasonably warm weather was lovely. Work began at the very early hour of 7:30. After we had been occupied in this fashion for about an hour, the First Officer came on deck and told us to stop. We had already noticed that many ships were entering the locks and putting out to sea. First came the light cruisers and the so-called Sea Pig Squadron of old coastal cruisers. In contrast to the customary tempo of the docks, everything proceeded more rapidly than usual. The coaling equipment was quickly cleared and stowed away. Two wagons, one loaded with bread and the other with meat, came up at a full gallop. The still-grimy men all pitched in to bring as much food as possible on board. The top deck was hosed down and then the First Officer gave the command: "Let go all lines!" With incredible speed we entered and passed through the locks. No sooner had we emerged than the Captain ordered full steam and the ship sped forward at a pace which made everything tremble and shake. The ships of the *Kaiser* and *König* class forged ahead of us. The Second Squadron and all the heavy and light cruisers were also present. A torpedo boat sailed on either side of each ship of the line to protect it from submarine attacks.

The emergency crew stood by ready to assume their positions. It was a pleasure to be on lookout in this splendid weather. Soon we passed the ships which had preceded us, the Rotesand beacon and could see the red cliffs of Helgoland shimmering in the distance. But our course headed away from that island in the direction of the East Frisian Islands. Soon Sylt, Jiust and Nordeney came into sight. Our fleet looked lovely shining in the sun. In precise formation our twenty-one ships of the line sailed behind one another at 500 meter intervals. Up front the cruisers steamed in a semicircle like an unfurled umbrella to protect the ships from a surprise attack. It was especially nice when the ships formed in echelons and were all visible at the same time.

What was going on out there? Was the English fleet out there or were we going to flush them out in order to engage them in battle? Someone mentioned that the English had sent another contingent of ships to the Dardanelles and that we were thus taking advantage of the opportunity to score a coup. True enough, the time was propitious. Now that the English no longer outnumbered us so badly we had nothing to fear from an encounter. They have even sent the ships of the *Queen Elizabeth* class to the Dardanelles although they represent the newest and most modern type in the entire British navy.[80]

I was one of the optimists who felt that we would see something unusual by next morning. We could not hope to sight the coast of "old England" before that time. Since we cruised at a constant speed of 18 miles, by afternoon we had already made considerable progress. Two balloons and several aquaplanes accompanied us high up in the air. Until seven o'clock when the entire squadron turned back, we had all been in a happy and confident mood. We knew at once what this meant. We were going home again. Although no one said anything, every face showed boundless disappointment.

The darkness descended. It was a wonderful moon and starlit night. Not a breeze was stirring as I stood on the bridge silently immersed in thought and drank in the beautiful view. One could hear the muffled sounds of the engines and broad waves fell foaming over the bow of the ship. At ten o'clock we sighted two bright red lights on the horizon, the beacons of Nordeney and Sylt. I was relieved from duty at midnight and a little while later I heard the rattle of the anchor chains dropping in the water.

[80] It appears that only *Queen Elizabeth* was sent to the Dardanelles.

MARCH 29, 1915

It was Easter today. Spring was almost here. One could feel it everywhere. I sat in the dank casemates but the sun came streaming in through the doors and portholes amidst swirling clouds of dust. I went up into the air on deck and continued writing with my book held on my knee. It was difficult to think in this heavenly weather. I kept looking at the banks of the Jade. The grass had already taken on a lighter and greener coloration. All around on the earthen parapets were the batteries of Heppens, Rüstersiel and the Crown Battery. Further out to sea there were the fortifications of Altona. I was even able to make out the well-fortified island of Borkum, the Voslapp beacon and the fire ship at the mouth of the Jade.

If it were still peace we would be happy to be in port. We might have an excursion like last year or we would amuse ourselves by watching the people who came to visit the ship. Every Easter we had especially large numbers of visitors. They kept us laughing whenever they lost their guides and became confused. On occasion some of us would mischievously point to the door which led to the coal bunker. Once the lost soul was inside, we would put out the lights. Then there was the time when a Jew wanted to know what the munition elevator was. A sailor replied that it was a potato-peeling machine! The potatoes are put down here and they come out there! We had many such jokes.

In the past one of our nicest and most beloved Easter customs was a sailing party. But all this was no longer possible. The sails, masts and all the other paraphernalia had been placed in storage at the outbreak of the war. But we did have an Easter egg hunt. For all those whose birthday fell during the Easter week the First Officer hid a hundred eggs on the after-deck. Some of the men found twenty eggs and others only two. On the first and second day of Easter each of us received three eggs in addition. With a crew of 1,160 men this comes to a goodly number of eggs. Perhaps these eggs came from a Dutch freighter carrying a cargo of several hundred thousand eggs to England which was intercepted and brought to Zeebrugge by one of our torpedo boats. Its arrival there was greeted with great joy.

The band and the free watch went on an excursion on Easter Tuesday. Of course, we walked along the Ems-Jade Canal, which is the sole point of interest in the vicinity of Wilhelmshaven. Along the way I marveled at the accomplishments of our navy flyers. We passed right next to [an airfield]. They climbed and dived with apelike agility. We ought to be as proud of our flyers as of our submarines. The excursion lasted for three hours. At 5:30 we took the boat back to the *Helgoland*. 6 April 1915.

Today, on [April] 13, the same old thing happened again. Something was going on at sea. Early that morning three or four torpedo boats came into port in a sorry state. One of them was missing her forward mast, her bridge hung crooked and her bowplates were completely smashed in and bent. She had mounted a sail on her starboard side to prevent the water from leaking in. Some bow damage was evident on the other three boats. But all of them came in under their own power.

This incident stirred up a good deal of discussion. We were agreed that the boats must have had a fight with enemy ships. How else could they have lost a mast? We also remembered that a prize crew from our ship which had gone out with the torpedo boats four days ago had not returned. We knew that they had captured and seized as prizes twenty merchant ships. (Today I learned that they were Dutch fishing boats.) The crew included two officers, one reservist steersman, three petty officers, five stokers and six sailors from our ship.

At the ungodly early hour of four in the morning we were wakened to pull in the torpedo nets and to clear the ship for departure. The steam in our engines was set for a speed of 30 kilometers or 16 sea miles per hour. We waited expectantly for something to happen. After breakfast we made preparations which could only point to a battle. All hands were dressed in battle clothes, i.e., their best blue uniforms. The rest of the clothes were packed in the seabags and stowed away. At the same time we stored the tables and benches from the crew's quarters in a safe place. The officers' cabins were emptied and the chests placed in the storage compartment between decks. For a change the men were glad to do this work. The entire squadron was to be ready to sail out at eight o'clock that morning. Gradually we gathered all our ships. [We were surrounded] by heavy and light cruisers and a whole forest of thin tall masts of the torpedo boats. There were five flotillas of eleven ships each. We all sat around waiting for the order to sail out. By eight o'clock, however, we were still at anchor. Then it was announced that we would leave at ten. Only the devil knows why we lay there as though we were paralyzed. By noon we gave up all hope for action. The only thing which made this entire mess bearable was that we did not have to perform our regular duties. Since the sun was smiling down from the sky, we lay down on deck and lazily joked about the navy.

To put it bluntly, I no longer care if we get to fight or not. Once again our principal interest is food, extra rations and shore leave. Nothing has changed. The men often express the hope that there will be no battle. For whom should they allow themselves to be killed? For the wealthy? After the war we will receive the same treatment as in the past and we shall be the ones who have to suffer and pay for it. I ought to add at this point that these statements are caused by our discontent at our inactivity. Should it ever come to a fight, all of us would be eager and raring to go. The adage, "idle hands make the devil's mischief," sums up the situation quite well. One can get used to anything but it is extremely difficult to be kept waiting all the time in the knowledge that our tremendous power is being wasted. The atmosphere is strained and embittered. One can sense it among the officers and the men. Happy songs and joyful games are no longer in evidence. We are virtually at each other's throats. The happy spirit of camaraderie has vanished and has been supplanted by deep depression. No wonder all of us wish to leave the ship. Whenever there is a call for volunteers for the submarines or for [the naval infantry brigade in] Belgium, everyone steps forward. We are very envious of those few who have already departed. Formerly none of us wanted to leave and we were all afraid lest we be transferred. But now? Some time ago the Chaplain held a sermon on changing values. He could well have cited this as an example.

We have now been at war for nine months and everything seems to indicate that we are headed for some real action. I am convinced that our leaders will not hesitate for one moment to send the fleet in when the proper time arrives. Despite our impatience and cynicism, however, that moment has apparently not yet come. Perhaps when we obtain a real strong point for an operational base against England with the fall of Calais and Dunkirk, the proper time shall have arrived.[81] We were told, however, long ago that we would get going as soon as we seized Antwerp or Ostend.[82] But the first port would not do because of its proximity to Holland while the latter did not afford sufficient space for the German navy. In any event Calais is immeasurably more favorably situated in terms of geography than Ostend. Most importantly, the distance from Calais to Dover is only 33 kilometers. This would enable our 38 cm. naval guns to fire all the way there and even further

[81] During the First Battle of Ypres (October 30–November 24, 1914), the objective of the German army had been the seizure of Calais and Dunkirk. However, the salient at Ypres, which guarded these ports, was so doggedly defended by the British that the Germans were unable to advance.

On April 22, 1915, the Germans were about to launch another offensive on the same position in a fight which developed into the five-week Second Battle of Ypres. Although the German army threw all its might into the offensive, to the extent of using gas warfare for the first time, the British held on with as great determination as before, with the result that the two ports were not capured.

[82] On October 9, 1914, Antwerp, although courageously defended by the Belgian army and by a small contingent of British marines led by Winston Churchill, had fallen to the Germans after a heavy artillery bombardment had virtually reduced that city's defenses to a rubble. The port of Ostend had fallen to the Germans on October 15, 1914, but the other Channel ports were not taken when the British halted the German advance at Ypres.

inland. Moreover Krupp [83] has recently developed a 40 cm. gun which can fire a distance of 45 kilometers. (Their shells have a trajectory of 55 to 60 kilometers.) Consequently as soon as we take Calais we shall hold England in a vise. But we must first take it—. 13 April 1915.

For three weeks now we have been at sea without touching land. But it doesn't matter since we are used to it. For today, a Saturday afternoon, we had a military excursion scheduled. We had already changed our clothing and the boat which was to take us ashore was at the side, when suddenly we heard, "The excursion is canceled. All hands, prepare to take in nets!" A loud cry of joy greeted the order. The shipyard workers on board were quickly put over the side and we made ready to go to sea. What was going on? We knew that three of our Zeppelins had visited the English coast last night. Could it be that the English wanted to revenge themselves by sending a couple of their miserable planes against us? At two o'clock came the order: "Machine gunners and lookouts to your stations." Some enemy aircraft had been reported over Hanover. I took my lookout post in the forward crow's nest.

Two of our planes cruised over Wilhelmshaven to intercept the English. But nothing occurred despite the beautifully sunny and clear weather. Our three smokestacks began to bellow smoke. The ventilators sang and whistled. Most of our ships were already out at the roadstead and those still in port departed in a hurry. Even the battleship *Nassau* sailed out although she was in dock for repairs. Hence we concluded that we needed every ship and that a strong task force of English ships had to be in the vicinity.

At first we were told that we would sail at three o'clock. Hurriedly we fitted new safety firing caps on all our armor-piercing shells. During the last battle a shell had exploded in a gun barrel on one of our cruisers. The cause was a defective firing cap and therefore we replaced all of them with new and improved ones.

"Battle stations! Clear decks for action!" Indescribable chaos

[83] This refers to the famous German Krupp Munitions Works at Essen.

ensued. By 5:30 we had packed, stowed or unloaded everything, but we were still at anchor. The thermometer of our
hopes sank by several degrees. At last came an announcement
that we would sail at ten o'clock that night. By seven o'clock
our two battle watches stood ready on deck. Tremendous excitement was evident on all their faces.

I was profoundly shocked that none of our exalted gentlemen officers deemed it necessary to provide us with any sort of
explanation regarding the action which lay ahead. All they told
us was that we would maintain a greater than usual distance
[between ships] and that our torpedo boats had painted their
aft smokestacks yellow to facilitate distinguishing them from
the enemy. That was all.

Hammocks were issued to the free watch and the new watch
took its stations. A clear starry sky and a quarter moon made
it possible to see the bow of the ship. But nothing interesting
transpired. On the bridge no one was particularly attentive.
We sailed along the coast as on the previous occasion. It began to get light at four o'clock. From then on the men had to
keep awake at their battle stations. Our course alternated between North and Northwest. Our speed was 15 miles. When it
got lighter I noticed that we had been joined by the Second
and the Third Squadron as well as the reconnaissance ships.
What an impressive battle line!

The purpose of our sortie kept puzzling me. The only possible explanation for these exercises was that they kept the
fleet at a high state of readiness. But I seriously doubted
whether they would ever have an offensive purpose. Nevertheless [if the opportunity arose] we would certainly not avoid
engaging even the entire [English] fleet. According to my
calculations we had traveled a distance of 195 kilometers from
Wilhelmshaven. This was hardly halfway to London. Hence
we still had a chance to retreat, as our heavy cruisers had done
in January, to the protection of the batteries of Helgoland and
Borkum. (I might add at this point that *Seydlitz*, which had
been severely damaged at that time, had received a complete
overhauling three weeks ago.)

That morning we were kept busy maneuvering in different formations. I could observe the lovely battle formations from the main mast. I wish I could have taken pictures of these fascinating scenes. I was amazed at how quickly the formations dissolved at a given signal and seemed to break down in utter confusion, only to reassemble within seconds in the most beautiful keel, cross or step formations. If a ship made an error and did not respond or fell behind, the flagship would raise a black flag with the tactical number of the ship in question on it. Then the captain would know that [he had performed a] bad maneuver.

Of course whenever a squadron or a formation executed a maneuver very quickly and precisely, it would receive a sign of approval. In the more peaceful times of the past, the crews of the various ships used to compete with one another for this praise. At that time all the ships used to participate in the grand maneuvers. Each of us would be very proud if our ship finished three seconds earlier than the others. Later on the matter would be discussed in the taverns where the other sailors were taunted at their defeat. Thus brawls broke out. Frequently the sailors made up for their failure during the maneuvers with their fists. And that kind of a victory was more impressive than all the others. Even years later one could still hear the story how the *Helgoland* had thrown the *Oldenburg* out of a tavern, or the respect the stokers of *Rheinland* had earned among the different saloon keepers by wrecking an entire establishment three years ago. Yes, the class of '08, '09, and '10 was quite different from today's crews. There was one fellow, in particular—boy oh boy!—he cleared out the movie house single-handedly!!! These tales have become an integral part of the chronicle of each ship.

At dusk our squadron sailed into the German Bight while the ships of the *König* class were detached to the mouth of the Weser. We dropped anchor off the island of Wangerooge at about 10:30. Early next morning we came into Wilhelmshaven to replenish our diminished coal supply. Our trip had consumed three hundred tons of coal.

For the following Saturday a major military excursion to Blutjadingen at the other end of the Jade bay had been planned for us. We were all set. The men had already assembled on deck in their snowy white uniforms. Even the members of the band were all in place. A cutter lay alongside, ready to take us ashore. What was holding us up? We were scheduled to leave at one o'clock but it was already past 1:30. Maybe our trip would be canceled again by another alert? True enough! The Chief Engineer came out and told the stokers to maintain a state of readiness and to clear for sailing by four o'clock. A fine state of affairs; we were going out again. "This is all that ever happens lately. We sail out twice a week and then have to load coal!" grumbled the men. For my part I was very glad that the march did not take place because in my estimation it was no fun to run in double time for two hours.

Instead of leaving at four, as scheduled, it was not until twelve o'clock that we sailed out toward the west. Perhaps this time something will happen, I thought to myself as I took my lookout post. And why not? If we went as far out as last time, maybe we would run across the English. Up ahead the bait [in our trap] were calling back and forth on the wireless. Hopefully the English would intercept their messages and come out to find us. And then it would begin: crashes and thunder, splintering masts and a boiling sea. . . . "Stumpf, wake up! Pay attention!" called Kapitänleutnant [Zäschmar] the Duty Officer, interrupting my reverie. He was well-liked on board because of his droll personality. He cursed like a dockworker. Whenever someone responded with a joke, he nearly died laughing. Since he never took anything seriously, we could afford to take that risk. Whenever he ran out of words, he would usually say, "Go away! Go away, you stinking pig!"

Whenever someone got drunk, he was delighted because he liked to take a swig now and again himself. In port his constant companion was a dachshund who understood his master's every mood. During our last time in dock we painted the ship's bottom red. One of the sailors had some fun by painting some spots on the dog's back. With his tail wagging behind the dog went back to his master. He addressed him in the following words: "What have you done to yourself, you pig? Have you been playing with the sailors? Aren't you ashamed of yourself? You'll have to get rid of the paint by yourself, you Schweinhund. Go and stay with the sailors!" The dog seemed quite crestfallen. Ever since that time he never goes near the men. Later on two men removed the spots with some cotton and turpentine.

After that I stared into the star-filled night attentively and actually sighted a couple of tiny lights. When I reported this to the Kapitänleutnant, I once again returned to his good graces.

At daybreak I noticed that the fleet had come together. At about ten o'clock we passed a fleet of Dutch fishing boats which was busily engaged in sending up signal flags. I knew from reading the papers that they had been stopped and searched by our torpedo boats before. On this occasion we did not execute any maneuvers but sailed in the direction of England at a constant speed of 17 miles. By noon we had reached the Dogger Bank, where *Blücher* had been sunk. But at precisely two o'clock the entire fleet turned about and headed home. We arrived there at one o'clock that night. 23 April 1915.

I was lying sunning myself on the fantail of the middle deck at noon today and had almost dozed off when I noticed everybody crowding against the railing and pointing excitedly at an object moving in the water. It looked like a bushel of straw or rags. However when it came closer I discovered with dismay that it was the body of a drowned sailor. He must have been a crew member of the torpedo boat which was rammed by the *Hamburg* during the last exercise. We signaled a close-by hospital ship to fish the unfortunate man out and take him to port. Otherwise nothing else worth mentioning occurred.

5 MAY 1915

Once again everything was quiet. There were no sorties all last week. According to the newspapers a squadron of thirty enemy ships was sighted in the North Sea. Moreover some Norwegian ships reported that they observed a major battle during the night near Bergen. Such unconfirmed rumors were not unusual. Our troops have crossed the canal at Ypres and have seized quite a bit of territory. They then emplaced two 38 cm. naval guns and shelled Dunkirk.[84] Since this took place at a range of 35 kilometers the newspapers were astonished. These two guns were probably meant for the auxiliary cruiser *Hertha*, which is still tied up here. Because her guns are at the front, the work on the cruiser was progressing very slowly. If we only had six of this type of ship in commission, the English would be in for a surprise!

Once again we received the glad tidings that our submarines have torpedoed a great ocean liner the *Lusitania*. She was carrying twelve guns and a whole load of munitions. 1,300 people perished. Many among them were Americans (which makes me all the happier).[85] Two other ships of five thousand tons on that day learned that Germany does not deal in empty phrases. Hopefully [this will make] the despicable Italianos think twice before declaring war against her allies and pro-

[84] On April 22 the German Fourth Army gained a temporary victory and broke through the Ypres salient by means of a surprise gas attack.

[85] On May 7, 1915, the *Lusitania*, a British ocean liner, sailing from New York loaded with passengers and a consignment of small arms and ammunition, was sunk off the coast of Ireland by the German submarine *U 20* under the command of Kapitänleutnant Schwieger. Although Germany had warned the *Lusitania* against sailing, her captain failed to take any precautions and did not zigzag in the prescribed manner. Hence his ship fell an easy prey to the German submarine. 1,198 passengers, 139 of them American nationals, lost their lives. President Wilson lodged a strong protest with Germany on May 11, and a wave of anti-German feelings swept through the Allied countries and America. In England, for instance, German-owned bakeshops were sacked, and small boys went so far as to pelt dachshunds on the streets with rocks. However, the German people who resented America's violation of the laws of neutrality by continuing to trade with the Allied nations responded with jubilation to the sinking of the *Lusitania*.

tectors.[86] I have always felt a deep aversion against that degenerate nation. I only hope that despoilers of the Papal States share England's fate.[87] The newspapers are in a pessimistic mood. From day to day their headlines scream in huge letters: "Italy About to Decide."

7 MAY 1915

Italy is still making up her mind and has not yet acted. It almost makes one want to laugh.

John Bull has won a great victory. The night battle off Bergen which I mentioned before actually did take place. But it was not a fight between Germany and England, rather between the "British" and the English. The British lost the battleship *Superb* (19,000 tons) and *Warrior* (12,000 tons) is sinking. On the English side *Lion* was again mauled severely. A number of other ships were "merely" damaged.

I was still somewhat skeptical about this story. However if it turns out to be true, the English will be dishonored forever. In this case [Rabbi] Ben Akiba was wrong when he stated that everything has happened before.

We first heard the story on Saturday and on Sunday morning when we came into port the news was posted on all the street corners. "Great Sea Battle between British and English." The people crowded around grinning. This was simply too much! Up till now the British have managed to keep the disaster secret

[86] On April 26, 1915, after a good deal of diplomatic bargaining with both sides of the belligerents, Italy concluded the secret Treaty of London with England, France and Russia because they could offer more territory than the Central Powers. In return for entering the war the Allies promised Italy the Trentino, South Tyrol, Trieste, Dalmatia, Valona in Albania and the Dodecanese Islands. Moreover, Italy was also to receive a war indemnity, a share in the spoils of the Turkish Empire and compensation for the division of the German colonies. As a result, Italy announced her withdrawal from the Triple Alliance on May 3 but did not issue a declaration of war.

[87] In 1870 the Kingdom of Italy had seized Rome from Pope Pius IX and by the Law of Guarantees of 1871 took away control of Rome and the Papal states, leaving him sovereign only over the miniscule area of the Vatican. Thereupon the Papacy refused to recognize the existence of the Italian state until 1929 and the signing of the Lateran Treaty.

but it leaked out in a letter. The whole thing occurred the day after our first sortie on April 8. They were probably out to intercept us. Each of their squadrons must have thought that it had found the enemy. The entire incident seemed grotesque to us. Don't they have recognition signals and flags? One does not simply fire blindly into the night! [88]

INTERRUPTED ON 10 MAY 1915

The *U 20*, which was responsible for sinking the *Lusitania*, came into port today. We gave her the same kind of enthusiastic welcome we gave to *U 9* in her moment of glory. All the ships broke out with thundering cheers.

I might also mention that Italy's decision still hangs in the balance. Today, on May 18, we made another sortie up to Dogger Bank. *Danzig* ran over a mine but the damage was minor.

"Full steam to be raised in all boilers by 4:30. Prepare for maximum speed," our Captain told the Chief Engineer as he stood before him cap in hand on the afternoon of November 2.[89] We already suspected that something was going to happen either today or tomorrow. Our two destroyer squadrons and the large battle cruisers *Derfflinger, Seydlitz, Moltke, Von der Tann* and *Blücher* had sailed out. We made the usual preparations to clear the ship.

One man whispered, "We are sailing for England." "No," predicted another, "we are going to bomb Calais at the same time as our troops attack." At the onset of darkness the First Squadron in keel formation sailed out. All the ships' lights had either been extinguished or darkened with blue glass. Only one tiny needle of light gleamed on the jackstaff to guide the man at the wheel. While one watch stood at its posts the others slept fully dressed at the guns. The night was clear but pitch black.

[88] I have been unable to find any evidence to support this story.

[89] Stumpf is going back in time and describing the naval action attendant upon the bombardment of Whitby, Scarborough and Hartlepool on the Yorkshire coast on December 16, 1914. Hence his date November 2 is an obvious mistake.

Although *Thüringen* was hardly five hundred meters ahead of us, she was barely visible as a dark shadow. No other light or landmark was visible except the stars in the sky. According to our charts we passed by Helgoland at about eight o'clock. Our speed increased to 35 kilometers. I strolled throughout the ship from the bridge to the gun stations to see what the men were doing. They gave no sign of excitement! They just sat there smoking or reading, or playing skat or chess, while a few of them talked about the action to come. Over and over they voiced the hope that we would not merely bombard the English coast, but that we would also engage the English fleet in battle. I felt confident that the English navy could not tolerate a coastal bombardment without responding.

When I took a quick glance in the midship boiler room, I saw the burly stokers incessantly feeding coal into the glowing furnaces. The ship was absolutely silent. Now and then an officer would come down from the bridge, inspect the guns, whisper something to the petty officers, give an order and correct something or other. Many of the men had taken letters out of their seabags and were reading them with a smile. Then they put them away with a sigh. An almost inaudible whisper went through the ship, "If we could only get to go into action." The engines stamped their monotonous melody at a rapid rate, the walls trembled and panes of glass tinkled quietly. On the bridge the Captain paced nervously and the Officers of the Watch and the lookouts tried to penetrate the dark night with their glasses. The Captain had promised an Iron Cross to the first man to sight the enemy. The watch was relieved without a sound at midnight. Nothing was expected to happen until daybreak. In the wireless shack the operators sat and listened for signals. *V 87* sent the report: "SGK!" The Communications Officer took out his secret battle code book and informed the captain that *V 87* had wired: "Have sighted torpedo wake." "Gentlemen, did you hear that! Here we go. Submarines ahead! Keep alert!"

The wireless clicked again at about four o'clock. It was

Hamburg reporting: "Four destroyers off my starboard bow. Request permission to fire." "Yes," went out the answer.

The destroyers evidently thought that they had met some friendly ships because one of them shined her searchlight straight up in the sky. *Hamburg* replied with a broadside. She fired a second and a third salvo before the English had a chance to react. After she had fired five times *Hamburg* reported that one destroyer was sinking and the others were in flight. When this news circulated through the ship, it was greeted with great joy. Inasmuch as the surviving ships were bound to report our presence, we were now virtually certain to meet the English fleet.[90] One hundred kilometers ahead, our cruisers began to bombard Whitby, Scarborough and Hartlepool at dawn with their 8.8 and 15 cm. guns. They blew up a gas storage tank in one of the cities. The pessimists on our ship complained that there would be nothing left for us to do. And as usual, they were correct. We did not get into action.

Our cruisers reported: "Mission accomplished. Pulling back." Although some British contingents tried to cut off their retreat and although a few shots were exchanged, no decisive engagement developed. Thanks to their speed and the excellence of their leadership, our ships made good their escape. Only *Blücher*, because of her slowness, received a few hits. She almost spoiled everything. With a maximum speed of 24 to 25 miles she was fortunate to escape. *Moltke* covered her rear. I simply cannot understand how such a ship could be made to participate in a mission that depended on speed.[91]

We came across a number of floating mines during the day. We touched them off with our machine guns, or if that did not

[90] If Admiral Ingenohl had not withdrawn his battleships out of fear that his fleet's position had been reported to the enemy, the German fleet would most certainly have run into the Second Battle Squadron of the Grand Fleet under the command of Admiral Sir George Warrender. Since Warrender's squadron consisted of only six battleships, the German fleet lost a wonderful opportunity to score a great victory against an inferior opponent.

[91] The German battle cruisers engaged in a sharp artillery duel with the coastal batteries at Hartlepool. *Blücher's* slowness prevented her from getting away in time. She was subsequently sunk for that very same reason at the Battle of Dogger Bank.

do it, with our 8.8 guns. Whenever one of the light cruisers fired at one of the mines we thought that they were firing at a submarine. Then the sea turned rough so that even the heavy battleships began to wallow and rock. The light cruisers, and to a larger extent the torpedo boats, were sent flying. We maintained a high speed and kept zigzagging so as not to give [enemy submarines] a chance to fire at us.

It was clear but still windy that afternoon when we passed the islands of Helgoland and Borkum. A minor incident occurred there. Totally unexpectedly *Posen* began to sound her sirens and broke out of formation at full speed. "Have sighted a submarine," she signaled. It was very funny to see the great ship veer off all of a sudden with her sirens howling. I thought it looked like a tiger breaking into a herd of elephants. However it was probably not a submarine because the entire line of ships passed by without seeing anything. The "bone collectors" or hospital ships sailed in our wake.

We were all very glad to get back safely behind our mine fields, to hear the anchor chains rattle down and to sleep a whole night. The next day we headed into port to replenish our sadly depleted stores of coal. Major repairs were required on our rudder mechanism. Thus we would have a chance to spend a few days in dock.

End of Book I

Two

Begun end of May 1915 · Completed on March 29, 1916

Lovely Whitsun, the last of the religious holidays, is approaching and still no decision is in sight either on land or at sea. No matter how many times we sail out, all is in vain. Although our fastest light cruisers coasted very closely along the English shore during our last sortie, there was no movement or reaction from the enemy. What could we do? Several days later, however, about eighty enemy ships were reported in the North Sea. Hurriedly we mobilized every ship capable of sailing. All the old and new cruisers, including the ancient coastal gunboats of the *Beowulf* and *Fritjof* class, sailed out. Even the *Westfalen*, which was in dry dock, got up steam. In the evening the Kiel squadron arrived and the entire fleet sailed up to the mine fields and anchored there. Throughout the night we maintained battle stations and manned the guns.

The wireless station on board was locked and Lieutenant [Loebell] personally brought all the messages to the Captain.

Such things only occur at very important occasions. Hence tensions ran extraordinarily high.[1] It was rumored that the English would finally attempt an attack on our coast and navy in conjunction with Italy's declaration of war.

Yes, the Italian declaration of war. I almost forgot to mention this matter. Incidentally none of our "gentlemen" officers found it necessary even to mention one word regarding this momentous event. Our only source of information was the newspapers. Every evening in our talking session we made fun of [Italy's] constant delay and prevarication. We talked a good deal about Giolitti, Salandra, Sonnino and Garibaldi.[2] The most ridiculous notions came up. But all of us realized that Italy had compromised herself forever in the eyes of both her friends and enemies. We regarded it as very funny when she announced her determination to declare war on the 12th, then on the 20th, only to postpone it again. When it finally arrived on Whitsun Monday we responded with smiles of contempt. [Italy] had merely declared war on Austria and not on Germany.[3]

We were at battle stations at the time. The weather was

[1] During April and May 1915, the German High Seas Fleet sailed out on four separate sorties but invariably failed to encounter the English.

[2] This cannot refer to Giuseppe Garibaldi (1807-1882), the hero of Italian unification, who was long since dead. Perhaps Stumpf is referring to the flamboyant poet Gabriele D'Annunzio, who had become an ardent advocate of war.

[3] The Treaty of London (April 26, 1915) obliged Italy to declare war upon the Central Powers within a month. However, Premier Antonio Salandra (1853-1931) and his Foreign Minister Baron Sidney Sonnino (1847-1921), who were responsible for the conclusion of the treaty did not possess the required majority to pass a declaration of war in the Chamber of Deputies dominated by the noninterventionist veteran politician Giovanni Giolitti (1842-1928).

On May 13, the day when Italy was expected to declare war, Premier Salandra submitted his resignation and precipitated a governmental crisis that might have succeeded in ruining the treaty if Giolitti had won. At this point Gabriele D'Annunzio, the ardent nationalist leader, intervened by organizing mob demonstrations in the capital. The crowds chanted, "Death to Giolitti!" and so overawed his supporters that the King was able to reject Salandra's resignation. On May 20 the Chamber conferred full powers to his government to conduct a war. Finally on May 23, Italy issued a declaration of war on Austria but not on Germany. Although Germany broke off diplomatic relations with Italy at once, various financial and economic reasons caused Italy to postpone her declaration of war on Germany until August 28.

ideal. Several airplanes circled overhead. Then the Officer of
the Watch rang the aircraft alarm. But the men did not man
the antiaircraft guns quickly enough to please him. "All hands
on deck." We had not heard that signal for a long time. "Look
out. We are going to hear about Italy." Instead the Navigation Officer let loose a torrent of reprimands because he was
angry at our slow and slovenly response to the drill. This was
not surprising since the alarm was sounded daily for no apparent reason. No one runs any more because we all know that
it is only a drill. Should enemy aircraft actually ever appear, we
shall pay for this erroneous attitude. This is also true of our
submarine alarms.

On that Whitsun Monday we got another surprise in the
form of a uniform inspection. Our battle uniforms, in particular, were examined most minutely for dust or spots. All those
who did not pass had to report for several rounds [of punishment tour]. Since the outbreak of the war we have received
virtually nothing from the ship's store. Despite this, our
meticulous Division Officer, First Lieutenant [Kohrt], insists
that our clothing be spotless. He rejects all excuses by saying,
"Pay closer attention to your equipment and take better care
of it!"

There is now a greater gulf between the officers and the men
than at any previous period in my naval career. The fact that
the officers have made no sacrifices at all so far, contributes
significantly to this painful situation. While we have to content ourselves to live on half rations of bread, in the officers'
mess they hold feasts and drinking bouts at which six or seven
courses are served. No one objected to this in peacetime. But
is this proper at the present critical juncture?

The profiteering in the canteen is an additional cause for discontent. A half liter mug of beer used to cost 20 pfennigs. All
of a sudden, it now costs 30 pfennigs. But in the officer's mess
a half liter still costs 16 pfennigs. The situation is the same in
regard to sausage. A portion of a hundred grams which formerly came to 25 pfennigs has shot up to 35 pfennigs. What
has happened to our canteen fund? The men maintain that the

officers have eaten it up. Although I am not inclined to believe
this, [I am concerned] over the fate of such a large amount of
money. In former times, whenever we had a small feast or an
excursion, the canteen would pay the expenses. Its profits
amount to 2,500 marks per month. It distresses me greatly to
see the extent to which the formerly excellent relationship between the officers and the men has deteriorated. Perhaps once
we get into action it will all change. Isn't it scandalous that
although we have yet to fire a single shot, five of our officers
have already been awarded the Iron Cross. Does this not debase
the value of this cherished decoration . . . ?

Once again our battle at sea did not materialize. Throughout
the night we lay at anchor and returned to Wilhelmshaven
with a heavy heart the following morning. I still haven't found
out what actually happened.

A week later, on Trinity Sunday, we were again placed on
alert. The night before we had sailed out at ten o'clock on a
westerly course toward England at a speed of 15 miles. Six of
our new torpedo destroyers accompanied us for the first time.
They were almost the same size as our old light cruisers and
just like them were painted gray. After we had progressed
almost half way toward England, we turned about again at
nine o'clock in the morning. In all that time nothing conse-
quential took place. None of our cruisers hit a mine as the
Hamburg had done the last time out. By ten o'clock in the
evening we were back in Wilhelmshaven again. [Despite the
late hour] we had to lower two of the motor launches because
a number of our officers wanted to go to their homes. When
I finally got to rest it was already eleven o'clock and I had to
go back on watch at two. This is how we spend our Sundays
in the navy.

The following day we came into port and were cheered by
the lovely weather and plenty of shore leave. I went ashore in
the morning and am now recording this as I sit in the "old
man's" cabin. 1 June 1915.

On Thursday we loaded four hundred tons of coal. Then we
sailed out again the next morning. When will we get a chance

to go into the shipyard for repairs? The Captain, however, does not share our wish. He wants his ship to hold out longer than any other in order to establish a record. According to the engine room crew, we have already sprung a number of leaks in the boiler tubes. Moreover, the port engine is shaky and has already broken down several times. It is rumored that our condition is such that the shipyards will declare us unfit for battle. If this proves to be true we shall have to spend some time in dock whether we like it or not. This ought to be very nice. Then maybe we could get a few days of leave like the other ships. Now that summer is here, this would be especially welcome.

Derfflinger, the biggest and best of our battle cruisers, was anchored right off our bow. Two armed guards were stationed on deck. They say that something bad took place on board. We were gratified to hear that the First Officer [Max Fischer] received a thorough beating. When he was on our ship he was heartily despised for his unjust treatment of the men. In this case the major culprit was sentenced to eighteen years of imprisonment. Similar incidents have occurred on the other ships. I am certainly not surprised! When one sees how badly the men are treated, it is enough to make one's blood boil.

This summer is like the one of 1911. The weather is almost tropical with a temperature of 26 to 28 degrees. We go swimming over the side. Our Staff Doctor is of the opinion that the men still get too much food and sleep. As a result, we have reveille at five o'clock in the morning, then we scrub the decks and for breakfast we get a tiny piece of bread spread with butter or marmalade with our tea. During today's inspection the Division Officer said: "You still get too much to eat. Pieces of food, potato and unspoiled bread have been found in the garbage." Yet we don't hold these speeches against Oberleutnant [Kohrt]. May the Lord forgive him. . . .

Yesterday afternoon at two o'clock the signals flew back and forth between the ships and the flagship. We were ordered to raise steam at once. What was going on at sea? At exactly 4:30 all the ships weighed anchor and headed out to sea through the mine fields on a northeasterly course. We were not headed toward England. Where then? To Cuxhaven, the Elbe or the Canal? Since several minor engagements had recently taken place in the Baltic, this seemed quite conceivable. Perhaps we were to finish the job. But eighteen ships? It seemed incredible that we should strip the North Sea of all the ships. What if the English found out about it? Maybe it was only a ruse to lure them out. . . .

Instead of going to Cuxhaven or Kiel, we maneuvered for several hours off Helgoland. At eight o'clock we turned about, reached Schillig Roads at about ten and then dropped anchor. 10 June 1915.

The next morning we lay off the locks. On the following day we commenced our five days of advanced patrol duty. Nothing worth mentioning took place.

Then it really began to look as though we would put into the dock. The shipyard workers had already started some of the preparations. Among other things, they cut a long triangular piece in our armor casing. This way the guns will be able to move farther forward and achieve a longer range. At our only major engagement to date, the battle off the Dogger Bank on January 26, the medium artillery could not fire because its muzzles would not elevate high enough.

It is questionable whether medium and light artillery still perform a useful function on a battleship. On that particular occasion, the English fired at a distance of 20 kilometers and never allowed the range to fall below 14.5 kilometers. Many of the English battleships are armed only with heavy artillery. Therefore they can use heavier guns up to 38 cm. Only the future will tell whether or not [the retention of] our light artillery has been a bad blunder. Interrupted on 15 June 1915.

It is almost certain now that we shall go into dock on June 30. Then we shall get leave! Leave! All over the ship the men speak of nothing else but leave. The atmosphere has undergone a complete change; everywhere one sees friendly faces and humorous expressions. We all miss our dear homeland. Those among us who have gold currency [to convert] will get a few more days of leave than the rest.[4] There are many who have become so fascinated with the exchange rates that they spend all their time calculating the fastest way to get home.

On [June] 30, just as we were about to put into dock, there came the announcement we feared the most, a state of alert. The entire fleet sailed out and dropped anchor off Schillig Roads. Within seconds our happy spirit evaporated! Why did the *Helgoland* have to be so unlucky? We all swore that we would never again believe in leave until we stood at our mothers' doorsteps.

We stayed out under steam for three days. But once again John Bull contented himself with a petty air raid. We greeted the signal, "HC (*Helgoland*) to go in at six tomorrow morning" with great jubilation. We gladly got up at four o'clock, pulled in the torpedo nets and cleared everything to go into dock. Our leave passes were all made out. We would be free to go as soon as we pulled into the dock. Since that day counted against our leave, it was in our interest to hurry as much as possible. By eight o'clock we had finished everything.

"Men on leave, get ready!" Quickly we packed and dressed. But stop! Our Division Officer still had a surprise in store for us. He called the men to attention and inspected their "haircuts." And indeed, he picked out a few of his good friends who were not allowed to depart until they had their hair cut short. His cruelty enraged me beyond words.

How was everything at home? What did the people think of us and the war? I had never before been so excited and happy. 2 July 1915.

My leave is over! It took me a long time to force myself to take up my pen again and to write down my experiences and impressions. Today's date is already July 23. I shall nevertheless commit my impressions and observations of my trip on paper.

What a great and tremendous age we live in! My shut-up existence on board had not allowed me to form a true picture

[4] Since the government wished to obtain all the gold it could, such preferential treatment was widely used as an incentive in the navy.

of Germany at war. But I became aware of the effects of the war as soon as I had left Wilhelmshaven behind. When I passed through Bremen and stopped at the Station Commandant's office to have my pass stamped, I suddenly noticed a group of heavily wounded French and Belgian prisoners of war standing behind me. I had never seen a prisoner before and was somewhat frightened to see them standing right next to me guarded by only two men. The prisoners actually wore red trousers, blue jackets and red caps![5] And these fellows were as dark as Arabs! I felt great pity for the cripples who limped around on sticks and crutches. It struck me that all the Frenchmen were small and of slight stature. But among the Belgians there were some sturdy and intelligent-looking men. Many of the Frenchmen had enamel washtubs and cooking pots slung over their backs. They chattered and gesticulated in their vivacious way while their guards looked on benignly.

Since I had to wait three hours [for the next train], I took the opportunity of strolling through the town. One would hardly have known that there was a war if it weren't for the masses of soldiers in field-gray uniforms on the streets. At first I thought that I would not see any young men about, but there were so many of them on the streets that I often felt compelled to ask my traveling companions, "Say, can you tell that there is a war on?" At the famous market place they sold huge quantities of cherries at 25 pfennigs a pound. Everything seemed like last year; nothing had changed. They even had concerts and a theater.

At six o'clock in the evening we pulled into Hanover. I would have been happy to walk about the town for a while but had difficulty in obtaining permission. Consequently, I remained [at the railroad station] and made myself comfortable at the Red Cross. They had made all sorts of lovely arrangements for the servicemen. Since they had good, cheap food, facilities for washing and sleeping, the time passed pleasantly. The wounded men and those who had no money got every-

[5] These were the colors of French army uniforms at the outbreak of the war.

thing without paying. My train left at 7:30 and arrived at Nordhausen at eleven o'clock. The next train out was not until 5:30 in the morning, but Nordhausen had no facilities at all for us. There wasn't even any food. Therefore we went into town. But since the stores closed at twelve o'clock, I barely managed to get a glass of beer and a herring. There was no place to stay for the night. We had no choice but to return to the railroad station. A couple of officers sat in the Second Class Waiting Room—hence it was out of bounds for us. Therefore we tried to get a little sleep on a bench in the Third Class. We were used to this [kind of sleeping arrangement] from our war watches and everything went well. A friendly railroad official gave me a basin of water and some soap with which to wash myself.

Just as our train pulled out for Erfurt, a number of long freight trains loaded with artillery came rolling in. Because of the heat, the bearded soldiers stood in the open freight wagons and made merry. They had come from France and were going to Russia. They had decorated their wagons with birch leaves and branches. Of course, they had scribbled all sorts of funny drawings and poems over the train: "You are all finished, Nicolaievitch," [6] or "Insect powder is still accepted here." The Red Cross ladies brought out buckets of raspberries to refresh the thirsty soldiers. Soon the train began to move again and it sounded hauntingly beautiful to hear the men singing:

> When spring comes
> The lilac blooms and swallows
> Come back again.
> Courage then revives anew
> And all is well again.[7]

Yes, hopefully it will all be over by spring, you brave fellows. I was very touched by the open camaraderie of these

[6] "Nikolausewitsch mit dir ists ausgewitscht." This may possibly refer to Grand Duke Nicholas, the Commander in Chief of the Russian armies.
[7] "Wenn der Frühling kommt / Blüht der Flieder, und die Schwalbe / Kehret wieder– / Dann belebt sich neu der Mut– / Dann wird alles wieder gut."

wonderful men. One would expect that these men who had just spent forty hours on a train and had an even longer trip ahead of them, and were going from sunny France to filthy Russia, would appear sad and despondent. But on the contrary, they were all profoundly optimistic that we would win and all displayed a superb sense of humor. They regarded the French as a brave foe and respected them. I understand that the only thing they feared in Russia were the lice. I noticed with pleasure that they invariably addressed me as comrade and that they always used this genuine German expression whenever they talked among themselves. This word is never spoken in the navy. When I spoke to them I was almost ashamed to be a sailor because they maintained that we did nothing but lie in port and that we did not dare to face the English fleet. I did not tell them that this was virtually true. . . .

That afternoon at two o'clock I arrived at the lovely spa of Ilmenau and the house of my brother Hans. It looked about the same as last year, but then we were still at peace and now we are at war. . . . At that time we discussed the coming of the war without suspecting how near it really was. Here, too, everything seemed peaceful; the only indications that there was a war going on out there in France and Russia were the field-gray uniforms on the street. To be sure, the numbers of visitors at the local resort hotels and pensions had fallen off sharply, but this was only natural.

The next morning I was off again toward home. Schleusingen, Coburg, Lichtenfels, Bamberg. Now I noticed that I was back in Bavaria. Unlike Prussia, where soldiers are not allowed to travel with civilians, here everyone rode together. It was also evident from the blue uniforms of the soldiers. And the most important piece of evidence was that virtually everybody held a foaming beer mug in his hand. Here there was beer, there were no lengthy pass inspections and as a matter of course everybody rode on the D train.[8] Erlangen was overflowing with soldiers. Whereas two regiments had been stationed there

[8] In Europe, then as now, a D train is an express train.

before the war, now there were about eight thousand men. One was prompted to ask from where Germany got all these soldiers. In the East they were irresistibly advancing toward the Polish capital and in the West the armies of Crown Prince [Rupprecht] were making satisfactory progress. Then also there was the constant movement of soldiers on leave, carrying their equipment with rifle and pack. They were all happy to visit their homes. In addition, there were also many wounded men who would have to stay home longer to recuperate.

We had a three-hour stopover at Erlangen. The administration building, the university, and a number of schools were occupied by wounded soldiers. They had even taken over a part of the palace garden. Young women strolled up and down as if they had nothing else to do. Some talkative soldiers told me that they had formerly occupied the entire garden, but that they had abused [the privilege] by running around and carousing with the women. Therefore a high fence had been erected! When I ordered a glass of beer in a restaurant, I was surprised when the waitress replied that she could not give it to me since half of the beer went to the troops at the front. "Lemonade?" she asked. "Yes, please," I replied. As far as I could tell, this regulation and its intrusion in the private life of the people did not seem to engender any resentment. True enough, beer had become expensive. However, with a few exceptions, no one blamed the government, but rather the brewers. The war had taught the people to be patient and they accepted all of its hardships and restrictions without complaint. When the farmers had their wheat taken away from them while it was still in the fields, they merely said that this is how it had to be.

Speaking of wheat, it gave me real pleasure to look at the bountiful wheat crop all over the Empire. Everywhere, in Oldenburg as well as in Hanover and Thuringia, it was maturing full and heavy. They had already begun harvesting the wheat in Bavaria. But the barley and oats were not ripe yet. Those who think that it is possible to starve Germany to death could learn a good lesson by examining this bountiful harvest.

The war has made the people stoical. I found this to be especially true in speaking to people whose close relatives and friends were either missing in action or had fallen in battle. It seemed as though mothers who had lost their only sons were proud to describe the details. No one gave up hope for the men missing in action. There have been a number of cases where someone reappeared after four and even six months. As far as I could tell, the government did a good job in providing financial aid to the needy relatives of the fallen.

When I came home the first question I was asked was, "How long do you think the war will last?" I always answered, "As long as it has already taken." However, no one objected as I had expected. A year ago when the war broke out, no one thought that it would last past Christmas. Now, a year later, no one feels this way any longer.

I was amazed at my friends who were home on leave from the trenches or who were recuperating from wounds. They never looked so fresh and healthy. They told the most incredible stories. They did not brag or boast when they spoke of their pitched bayonet battles with Negroes, Turkos or Indians. . . . Their descriptions indicated how horrible, bitter and gruesome this kind of hand to hand combat really is. They also told me that the English forced line after line of Negro troops to charge forward until the barrels of our machine guns and rifles turned red hot and all our ammunition was exhausted. Then they went at it with knife and bayonet without mercy and pity. Our men never allow black or white English troops to surrender. As proof of their bravery a few of my friends were missing a couple of fingers on their hands. Yet they would still have to return to the front. But none of them seemed in the least frightened. These then are our quiet, patient Bavarians. Nevertheless the Prussians despise us and call us stupid. It was this "stupidity," however, that captured Przemisl [9] and that now stands like an iron wall at the Western

---

[9] A major German-Austrian offensive in Galicia against the Russian forces succeeded on June 3, 1915, in taking the important fortress of Przemysl, which had fallen to the Russians in March of that year.

Front.[10] Only when one compares the Bavarians with some of the others, does one realize how sturdy and strong they really are. Moreover these fellows are also friendly and helpful. In short, they make the best comrades in the world. For the first time I have come to a proper appreciation of the character of my fellow countrymen. I was told by a medical corpsman from Mecklenburg who was traveling to Hartmannsweide that Bavarians invariably stand out in every unit. This is true. I felt well and happy among these people. How different it was on board our ship where everyone makes one's life miserable.

While I was at home I visited many people and was received in the most friendly fashion everywhere. The worries of the war have changed the people. Money has lost its former importance. Everyone seemed eager to contribute to make things easier. It was quite heartening to see the way the farmers cared for their soldiers. They sent their best meat and largest sausages to the front. Some of them went too far and sent a package every day. They would rather not eat themselves than deprive our soldiers out there of anything.

I spent only one day in Nuremberg. The embankment at Dutzen was filled with all sorts of wounded soldiers. Although it was a work day, the large park was crowded. It was almost like peacetime except there was no music.

I spent my last two days of leave in the nicest possible fashion by staying at home. I was kept busy and did not lack recreation. Then came the time to depart. . . . It was no more difficult than usual. There was not much to say; a handshake and may God be with you. Otherwise, I would have broken down.

Accompanied by my sister and Frau Schrödel, I walked to Erlangen. I felt very apprehensive about my forty-eight-hour train ride to Wilhelmshaven. I found saying good-bye more difficult here than at home. I could not utter a word because

---

[10] This must refer to the Second Battle of Artois (May 9–June 18). Here the Tenth French Army succeed in making a breach in the German lines near Arras for a short period of time before its offensive was repulsed at the cost of approximately 400,000 men.

I was afraid that I might weaken. But then the train arrived. One more look and a wave and then I sank back in my seat, sad and exhausted. Although my traveling companions wanted to talk, I could not bring myself to say anything for the first hour. Again I passed dear old Forchheim, Strullendorf, the Main Schmor Forest and Bamberg. This is where I had waited for the express train eight days ago. I felt all different now. I bought a newspaper and the headlines announced that an Austrian submarine had sunk the Italian battle cruiser *Giuseppe Garibaldi*. This makes two within eight days. Good!

Staffelstein, Lichtenfels. Change trains! A black and white border post proclaimed that we were already out of Bavaria. The old fortress of Coburg winked at us from a distance. I traveled with a group of medical corpsmen from Nuremberg who had providentially brought along their beer mugs and refilled them at every opportunity. I was delighted to see the farmers bringing in their heavy golden sheaves. It was evident that most of the wheat had already been cut.

At 8:30 our slow train pulled into Coburg. The railroad station was crowded with soldiers in new uniforms and full field packs. They were going to the front in France. As we left, the band played the Prussian march, "Now Adieu, My Dear Native Land." Beyond the station and along the tracks a huge mob of people were waving their handkerchiefs and cheering. I was very touched by this impressive scene. It must have been like that all over Germany during mobilization. At last I got to see a real soldier's send-off. All the soldiers were very young and were going to the front for the first time. In their train compartments uninhibited gayety prevailed. When they began to unpack their parting gifts, I soon became infected by their happy spirits. There wasn't a man who didn't have a bouquet of roses or carnations. They had flowers stuck on their chests, their helmets, their rifle barrels and every other conceivable place.

The five hours to Eisenach flew by. My train did not leave until six o'clock the following morning. For a little while I slept in the Third Class Waiting Room. I spent some time in town and made a special visit to Wartburg.[11] Soon I was off to Bebra. I was enraptured by the lovely, dew-covered Thuringian forest. In Bebra I became so audacious as to board the express train to Göttingen. Although the conductor mumbled something, he did nothing about it. In Göttingen I had a three-hours' wait, but since it was raining I stayed in the station. There I met a reservist who had been shot in the knee. He told me a great deal about his experiences in the Carpathian [Mountains]. From the waiting room we could see a detail of Scotch Highlanders digging [a trench]. We were amused by the way they used pantomime and sign language in talking to their guard, a fat, good-natured militiaman. A train filled with Belgian medical corpsmen and wounded pulled in. Among them there were a number of intelligent-looking fellows. They seemed intensely interested in me. "Navy! Navy!" they called at me. But I did not give them even a glance. My reservist friend, however, nodded and greeted them as though they were old friends and acquaintances. Despite his crippled leg! Once again, without compunction, I boarded the express train to Hanover. It began to pour soaking rain. Thank God the weather had been so lovely at home.

At Hanover we were not allowed to go into town. However, they had good accommodations for staying over, waiting and eating. They even gave us a free plate of cherries. Here the majority of the men wore navy uniforms. Two gigantic Bavarian Guardsmen entered. I nearly fell over when I went to help one of them take off his pack. The thing must have weighed a hundred pounds. Right away they asked the Red Cross sister for some beer, apologizing that they were from Bavaria. They were distressed when the sister could only offer them some raspberry juice. But when they heard it was free

---

[11] The Wartburg is the castle at which Martin Luther found refuge when he was placed under the ban of the Empire after the Diet of Worms in 1521. In 1817, on the three hundredth anniversary of the Protestant Reformation, a group of liberal and nationalistic university students held a festival there at which they condemned the conservatism of the German princes, and they also burned a corporal's cane, a Prussian military manual and some conservative pamphlets.

and that they would also be treated to a bowl of cherries, they broke out into laughter. I was filled with admiration for these men who carried such heavy packs, but who still managed to retain their cheerfulness and sense of humor.

At five o'clock in the evening I arrived in Bremen. Since I was very tired and only had a wait of an hour and a half, I did not go into town. Later on I boarded the overcrowded express train to Wilhelmshaven. Upon my arrival at eight o'clock I had a glass of beer in town and then went on board.

It all seemed very strange and small! The ship had been torn up and there was thick dust all over. The sound of the hydraulic hammers and drills all through the day and night was enough to drive one mad. On my first morning back I did not report to the work formation quickly enough. "Mr. Churchill," our Detail Officer, responded by making me walk a punishment tour of two hours. Here was a great contribution to the "uplifting" of my morale. Because I had been punished, I resentfully shirked all work for four days. This is how we revenge ourselves against the excesses of the Imperial Navy.

One day *Helgoland* got orders to prepare for sailing within three hours. Although the work on the ship was still only half finished, the men from the shipyard went ashore leaving their tools behind. They believed that we were about to fight a major battle, but we had become accustomed to the old game and refused to get excited. And indeed, we merely sailed out and then dropped anchor at Voslapp Roads. We spent the night there in a state of alert and returned to the protection of the harbor on the following morning. During the night there had been an air raid over the North Sea which indicated that there might be a sea battle. Later on a small tugboat came in with a badly damaged aircraft in tow.

Since our ship's bottom had still not been scraped of barnacles and paint, it was rumored that we were to go into dry dock at the "South Sea." Unfortunately, however, on Sunday we had another alert with the attendant confusion of packing clothes and stowing away dishes, tables and benches. The First and Third Squadrons went on a shakedown cruise along the East

Frisian Islands at dusk. But nothing of unusual interest transpired during that time.

On Tuesday morning we ran in again and entered the dry dock. Since this was the first time we had ever done this since I entered the navy, it was all new to me.[12] As in any dock, the ship had to be tied fast at certain points so that the bottom fit precisely on the metal blocks. Even a slight slippage of a quarter of a meter might stave in the sides. Reinforcements were applied at the points of greatest stress. When all this had been accomplished, the pumps began to work and slowly the dock and with it the ship rose out of the water. After an hour the ship's bottom appeared above the surface of the water. The forecastle now afforded a view like the highest building. The walls of the dock were hollow and averaged a thickness of about three to four meters. They have built-in toilets, kitchens and washrooms and there is even an elevator to save climbing steps. To the left of the dock lies the Ems-Jade Canal and all around are the shipyards at which the new torpedo boats and submarines are built.

Among the vessels lying in the submarine pens there was the U ———, which had been attacked by a merchantman flying the Danish flag. Fortunately one of the shells was deflected by her conning tower but another one penetrated her ballast tanks. This was quite serious because the submarine was then no longer able to blow out the water. For just such an eventuality, however, a heavy leaden keel is attached to the submarine's bottom. It can be jettisoned to make up for the weight of the water. This is what saved the submarine. Immediately after this cowardly attack, she dived to a depth of sixty meters!, jettisoned her leaden keel, made it to the surface with no trouble and then headed back to Wilhelmshaven under her own power. 13 August 1915.

We spent the next two days scraping the bottom of our ship while the band played. As usual, we had to do everything over

---

[12] The *Helgoland* had been in dry dock before, but apparently this was the first time that Stumpf had taken interest in the intricate details of this maneuver.

three times. We wasted an incredible amount of paint in this fashion. When the paint had dried, the dock was half filled with water so as to enable the ship to sail out quickly. We remained that way for the next five days. But when we left the dock we were immediately placed on patrol at Schillig Roads. Before long we commenced preparations to go to sea. From the very outset rumors kept circulating that we were heading for Kiel. And this is exactly what happened! For the second time we traversed the canal but since it was midsummer everything was green and blooming along the banks. We passed through the entry lock at five o'clock in the evening. Inside the canal the Second Squadron was riding at anchor. *Pommern*, which was allegedly "sunk" by an English submarine, was also there. We crossed the narrow peninsula separating the North Sea from the Baltic at an approximate speed of 12 to 15 kilometers per hour. All along the shore people were waving flags and hand-kerchiefs at us. The band played until nightfall.

Some Russian prisoners of war were at work on one of the half-finished bridges. Their faces looked grim as our eight modern battleships proudly sailed by. No doubt they feared that we were about to attack their homeland. But what was our target? Were we going to attack Riga, Kronstadt, St. Petersburg or only the Russian fleet? None of us knew, not even the Admiral. But it was of no consequence so long as we got into action and could thus outdo the Third Squadron. We were all looking forward to the next few days. We arrived in Kiel at midnight and were lucky enough to be able to go to sleep without having to stand watch. In the morning when the sun rose shining over all the ships, the harbor looked truly lovely. Our light and heavy cruisers were all there. There were a few merchantmen as well and a number of school ships with gorgeous sails. And on all sides there were the pretty hills covered with beech trees. Behind them in trenches sat the howitzer batteries waiting for a chance to shoot at something. But they shall have to wait forever since the Russians will never dare to attack Kiel and the English are too far away. Our trade with the Scandinavian states, particularly Denmark, has returned to normal. As in the past, the three crosses of the Scandinavian flags are once again displayed alongside our black-white-red one.

We kept loading coal for three days until all our bunkers were filled to the top and the last hundred tons had to be stowed on the afterdeck. This convinced us that we were about to embark upon a lengthy and important mission. We expected the command to sail out at any moment. But four days passed; our cruisers ran out every morning and came back at night. Fourteen submarines of various kinds headed out to sea and did not return. Maybe something would happen after all . . . ? It seemed as though the good people of Kiel would not calm down until we had half of our navy assembled there. There was already some talk of maneuvers, firing practice and activities of a similar nature.

As usual, twenty of our men had overstayed their leaves. Consequently on Friday the port watch was led out [under guard] rather than being able to go out on their own. We were lying at anchor off the buoy near Kitzeberg and set off in the direction of that town. It was wonderful to be free for three hours. For awhile we marched through the lovely beech forest and then we spread out. The band played a number of its best marches and the trees listened attentively. When we turned back at six o'clock, we could tell that something was up on board even at a distance. They were preparing to go to sea! Fine brown smoke rose straight as an arrow from all three chimneys. This was true as well of the other ships. At last, we were going to have a change, thank God! We sailors would welcome staging a raid on Riga followed by a landing. We all felt that there was a good chance that we might attack the capital of Livonia. Since our troops were only a day's march from Riga after the fall of Warsaw, this was a distinct possibility.[13]

[13] Warsaw fell to General Max von Gallwitz's Twelfth German Army on August 5, 1915, thus opening the way for a further German advance into Courland and Livonia in early September. Riga is the capital of present-day Latvia.

There was a great commotion on board and a happy, lively mood which was reminiscent of the best times at the outbreak of the war. The battle cruisers set off at precisely 7:30 on Friday. *Von der Tann* was in the lead, followed by *Seydlitz, Moltke* and six light cruisers. Unfortunately *Derfflinger*'s engine troubles kept her in dock. All the ships' bands were playing their fastest and most stirring battle marches. In a joyous mood all hands stood on deck and looked on. A few civilian boats with their crews cheering madly sailed around us.

Then the whistle blew: "All hands, ready to make loose." The buoy lines smacked into the water and the gigantic ship slowly turned her bow to the sea. The entire First Squadron was with us. The nets were brought in and as it turned dark the first watch and lookouts were posted. The weather was mild and clear. But as we changed watches at twelve o'clock, it began to get foggy. At first there was merely a soft drizzle but the fog kept coming down thicker and heavier and by dawn it was pouring. This would not have been so bad if there hadn't also been a strong wind which dashed the rain into our faces like hail. Our slickers and oilskins were useless. Tiny streams of water flowed from our noses, ears and hair down our necks into our shoes and socks. Finally I gave up and allowed it all to run down, thankful that the waters of the Baltic were not as bitter as those of the North Sea. We passed the island of Rügen with its chalk cliffs and its renowned King's Throne at eight o'clock. But it kept pouring and pouring. . . . It certainly would have been preferable to be snug in dock than out here on war patrol. But by noon the worst of the weather was over and the farther East we got, the clearer and calmer it became. On the following day the sun shone brilliantly over a broad sea of small, foamy waves. We maintained a high speed of 17 kilometers day and night. As a result, we consumed enormous amounts of coal, 210 tons every twenty-four hours.

The Executive Officer defined the purpose of our mission in the following manner to the engine room crew: "We shall first blockade the Bay of Riga. After the mine fields have been swept clear, we shall come in closer to bombard the coastal fortifications and destroy all Russian shipping. The preparations of Admiral Schmidt's Fourth Squadron will facilitate our task considerably. By noon on Wednesday their minesweepers shall have cleared away all the mines. Then they will advance into the bay and destroy the three cruisers and torpedo boats located there.[14] However it is very likely that the main Russian contingent at Kronstadt will come to their rescue. But the first division of the First Squadron shall be waiting in ambush. In the meantime, *Ostfriesland*, *Thüringen*, *Helgoland*, *Oldenburg* and a couple of cruisers will move in and bombard the forts at Riga."

It was a fine plan. The Executive presented it so matter-of-factly that we were all certain of its success. The crew talked of nothing else. The men all seemed content now that we had at last found something to do. Nevertheless there were some unreformed pessimists who placed bets that nothing would come of the entire thing. However, we would have to see about that. 10 August 1915.

SWINEMÜNDE, 15 AUGUST 1915

Who would have suspected that we were headed for the lovely beach resort of Swinemünde! Since the shallow waters of Swinemünde made it inaccessible to ships of over 15 tons before the war, we had figured on going to either Danzig or Putzig. But something must have been done about it since that time. Our primary aim was to replenish our exhausted coal and food supply. Originally we only planned on staying for eight hours before going out to meet the dear Russians. Thank God, however, this proved incorrect and we were able to stay for several days.

We approached the harbor entrance at four o'clock on Tuesday afternoon. We were the last ship to come in and it took until 7:30 before we tied up. A seventy-meter-high light tower,

[14] The Fourth Squadron had been dispatched to the Baltic for this purpose as early as June 1915. However, when on August 8 it made an attempt to penetrate into the Gulf of Riga, it was repulsed by the Russians.

the symbol of the town, stands at the harbor entrance. Even from a long way off it makes the town look prosperous. The beach was crowded with villas. We sailed a distance up the Oder into town. Watching our arrival with curiosity and pleasure, people in colorful clothes lined both banks. Most of the people at the resort wore white clothes topped by brightly colored bathing robes. Around their heads they wore colorful cloths in peasant fashion. Most of the men were dressed in gayly colored beach wear.

Since the ship had to be ready on three hours' notice, we had to load a thousand tons of coal that very evening. The crowd was greatly surprised that we sailed in with our coaling tackle already rigged. When we tied up, the coal barges were already waiting for us. After we had eaten our dinner we were ordered to put on our coaling outfits. Much to the dismay of the watching tourists, our nicely dressed men in their white uniforms soon turned into half-naked and grimy Negroes. We began the loading at 8:30. The band had been told to play and to keep the intervals between pieces to a minimum. Our dusty work was watched with intense interest by ladies and gentlemen dressed in fragrant white clothes who rowed out to the ship. We were very pleased when in a short while these people turned as dark as we from the coal dust. This, however, did not deter them. They bought chocolates and cigarettes and threw them to the grimy crew. Then the searchlights were turned on to illuminate our work and we continued. We shoveled unceasingly and soon it turned eleven and twelve and all the tired spectators departed. Finally, by one o'clock the last of our eight hundred tons had disappeared into the insatiable bunkers. We were gratified to receive some sausages and bread and butter.

But the atmosphere of the entire ship was stupefying and suffocating. I kept waking up because it was so difficult to breathe. Finally, I crawled out of this nightmare up on deck and allowed the fresh air to revive me. The men were utterly exhausted. Many of them had fallen asleep where they had eaten. The heat and the annoyance of mosquitoes [added to the discomfort]. A layer of coal dust inches thick covered the entire deck.

Reveille was sounded at eight o'clock. It felt good to see the fire hoses play their heavy streams of water over the decks to wash away the worst of the dirt. At last it was possible to breathe without clogging one's nose. Thank God! After three hours of work our "tub" looked as good as new.

Then we put on our best uniforms, pulled on our monkey jackets and went ashore. The town was markedly different from Wilhelmshaven. It was small but nice. The people tried to be friendly and helpful in every way. On several occasions total strangers handed me some cigars and cigarettes for no apparent reason. The famous beach deserves a chapter by itself. There the wealthy sat in their beach baskets enjoying the wonderful sea air. Children romped in the incredibly white sand. The girls weren't shy with the sailors and our "blue-jackets" sat and flirted with the fun-loving sea nymphs as though it were perfectly natural. No one seemed to mind that the men had been black and dirty the night before. Around here we received even better treatment than the soldiers. However, if we "coolies" [15] were to stay around for about two weeks, the dear people of Swinemünde would no doubt soon change their minds!

At noon on Saturday, the fifth day of our stay, the *Ostfriesland* signaled: "Make ready to go to sea by five this afternoon!" The news of our departure spread quickly through Swinemünde and soon a large crowd of people had congregated at the shore to watch the show. Many girls looked across to us with yearning eyes to take a last look at their friends. Many couples found each other and shyly waved at each other. There was no end to the calling and waving as the lines flew off and the gigantic ships began to move out to the tune of the catchiest military marches of their bands. 23 August 1915.

As soon as we had left port, we posted lookouts and watches. It was not at all unlikely that the Russians or English would

[15] This was a common derisive nickname for the enlisted men of the German navy. Sometimes they were also called "the Kaiser's coolies."

take advantage of our stay to position a few submarines in our path. Since we had done nothing to conceal our presence, they would not be worth their salt if they did not try it. Consequently we zigzagged constantly and maintained maximum speed even at night. We all hoped that our work was not in vain and that we would get a chance to fire a few of our "heavies." Nevertheless, our persistent search and our desire for battle were unrequited. The enemy seemed fearful even in his own waters and kept out of sight in the Gulf of Riga and the Gulf of Bothnia. Hence we would have to go in and fetch him out.

It looked as though we were about to do that very thing on Tuesday. Our minesweepers, after three days of very arduous work, had succeeded in clearing a large number of the cleverly concealed mines and other obstacles which were planted at a depth of four to six meters in English fashion. Unfortunately, they blew up two of our auxiliary minesweepers and damaged another one severely despite the protection of the 15 cm. guns of *Bremen* and *Pillau,* two of our light cruisers. The next day *Posen* and *Nassau* fired ten covering broadsides at Fort Pernau and silenced its coastal batteries. Then, penetrating deeply into the bay, *Augsburg,* one of our light cruisers, accompanied by several torpedo boats, forced a fight on two Russian gunboats *Norejetz* and *Siiwitsch* and sank them both. *Posen* rescued about forty of their crew and took them on board. In the meantime, however, an English submarine torpedoed our great battle cruiser *Moltke.* According to my information, her forward torpedo room was flooded and the crew was killed, but she sailed on under her own steam. Thus we have gotten away with a trifling loss.[16] A German torpedo would have inflicted much greater damage.

Our first division left formation to refuel in Danzig. As usual, however, *Helgoland* had used up the least amount of coal, only about 120 tons a day. When they returned the following morn-

---

[16] In conjunction with an attack by the German army, the navy attempted to bombard Riga between August 15 and August 21 with minor success. Riga did not fall to the Germans until September 1917.

ing, *Elsass* and *Braunschweig* sailed off to Neufahrwasser near Danzig. By Friday our hopes of getting into action had sunk to a low point.

At this time I would like to record some of the wonderful orders which will illustrate the attitude of our officers' corps. Firstly, we are strongly forbidden—under penalty of imprisonment—to wear anything but a white uniform by day or night. (Note: The Captain has promised to punish any violators with five days of imprisonment.) Secondly, we are not allowed to bring coats, newspapers or books into the gun turrets. (To illustrate how insane this rule really is, it must be noted that we are not allowed to place our coats anywhere else either.) Thirdly, the Captain gave two of the men seven days of arrest for failing to wear their life jackets. (The Executive Officer punished six men with a six-hour punishment tour because their life jackets had become worn and had lost their buoyancy.) Fourthly, we are forbidden to hang our hammocks even where there are no guns. (I cannot fathom the reason behind this. Only deliberate nastiness could conceive of such a thing.)

The crew is constantly harassed by these petty pinpricks. It undermines our love and devotion to the service and on occasion even incites us to sabotage. Now and then something disappears or is broken. All of us wish that the *Helgoland* would run over a mine so that the officers' quarters would be torn to pieces. It is astonishing that all of the men have developed an interest in politics. We are unanimously agreed that the privileges of the officers' caste shall have to be abolished at the end of the war. It is quite evident that they wield much too much power. Each of them possesses the power of life or death over his subordinates.

There are some in the crew who don't hesitate to explain how this is to be accomplished. They argue most powerfully when they maintain: "What can 'they' do if we refuse to cooperate any longer? They can't put all of us in jail!" We often get into heated debates on whether or not Germany should retain some of the territories she has conquered after the war. Who would have thought it possible that these extreme Socialist views would ever crop up among us? No one seems concerned whether or not there are officers about while we hold these debates.

One concrete example of our resistance is the fact that about twenty of our men simply did not come back on board at Swinemünde. As a result, each of them got ten days' arrest. Among them were several petty officers [Gündel, Honholz, Mahnert]. Whenever the Articles of War are read, they are always greeted with scornful laughter and jeering remarks. Someone has posted a placard satirizing the Detail Officer in the canteen. The worthy [Martin Schultze] never fails to provide us with material for satire. Even though some of our officers are fed up with this kind of a life, they are not allowed to voice their true feelings.

On Saturday, [August] 21, we sent the War Supply Office in Swinemünde a request for twenty-five thousand marks in change and five mark bills. In addition, we ordered a certain amount of bread, butter and other food supplies and, most importantly, 1,700 tons of coal. What a thing to look forward to! At any rate, it meant that we would soon have to put in there. And considering the state of our nerves, this was very welcome news indeed. After all, we had been at sea for eight days with only an occasional snatch of sleep on deck while our engines worked incessantly. It was reported that the engines of the ships in the mine-sweeping division had broken down as a result of their herculean effort. Of course, their crews, too, were in urgent need of a rest.

When we sighted the snowy white dunes of the Baltic coast on Sunday morning, we became convinced that we were coming in. Nevertheless it was evening before we finally arrived at the harbor's entrance. Although it was Sunday, a large crowd of people had congregated at the shore. But it was by no means as large as last time. The height of the vacation season was over and many of the guests had already gone home. Something else had contributed to the mass exodus. Because of the outbreak of several isolated cases of cholera, we were forbidden to swim or wash our clothes in the Swine. But the situation must not have been critical since we were allowed to go where we pleased and wander freely on shore. On Monday morning, however, it was announced that we had to leave because of the danger of cholera. We all felt sorry to go.

We loaded coal from morning until afternoon but at five o'clock all of us received liberty. It was our last liberty because we sailed off on the following morning. Where were we headed? Some maintained that we were going to Kiel, others said that it was Wilhelmshaven, while the very clever ones insisted that we were headed for Riga. But we sailed toward Kiel and that was quite acceptable. 25 August 1915.

Having arrived at Kiel, we did not load coal, which meant that we intended to sail through the Canal. "Now we may resume our war in the Civic Garden at Banter," some of the sailors complained ironically. When I last went ashore at Kiel it took almost four marks to buy a filling meal. That was enough for me.

Our trip through the canal went smoothly and nothing worth mentioning occurred. However, as we went down the Elbe, our ship gave a mighty shake. We had hit a sand bar, but were lucky enough to pass right over it. That evening we passed Helgoland and three hours later our anchor splashed into the water off the mine fields in the German Bight. 28 August 1915.

Lieutenant [Meister], who had recently been badly wounded in the arm in a fight in the officers' mess, came back on board today. 30 August 1915.

First Lieutenant [Mildenstein] has been given four weeks of leave to mend his "hypersensitive nerves" after he had cursed a machinist in a most atrocious manner.

SUNDAY, 26 SEPTEMBER 1915

Virtually nothing worth recording has transpired during the past few weeks. But the entire world is in an uproar over the defeat which we dealt our enemies on the battlefields in the East and at the Dardanelles.[17]

We had thought that the First Squadron had been transferred to the Baltic Command and that we would no longer have to patrol Schillig Roads but our information proved to be false and we had to serve our usual round of patrol from [September] 8 to 13. On the 16th the fleet sailed out a good 150 miles. The weather was ideal. Our twenty-one armored giants looked incredibly beautiful as they rode into the night in the last rays of the sinking sun. But by evening we were back at our berths again and the Admiralty reported that we had not encountered any enemies. Once again we returned our life jackets and gas masks and fetched our seabags and eating utensils from the hold. Once again, for the hundredth time, all our work had been for nothing. The English, however, proclaimed that their fleet was now "ready" and that it would sink the German fleet as soon as it showed itself on the North Sea. We viewed these proclamations as the most hilarious joke.

The passive attitude of our commanders has engendered a great deal of adverse criticism. The men feel that while we do nothing, the enemy keeps building one submarine after the other. In my opinion our navy merely serves as a trump card for our diplomats to begin negotiations for a peace. At the outbreak of the war I felt that our navy could destroy the others, that it could disrupt the enemy's trade, that it could raid their towns and ports and that it might even protect a troop landing. But I have lost all hope after the experience of sixty weeks of war. All of our naval experts and prophets had predicted that a great sea battle would be fought between Helgoland and Borkum within the first few days of the war. All our training and peacetime maneuvers had been based on that assumption.

---

[17] Since July of 1915 the German armies and their Austrian allies had seized all of Poland, Lithuania and Courland from Russia in one of the greatest victories in military history.

The British had made another landing on August 6 at the Dardanelles but found that the resistance of the Turks was so strong that no headway could be made. In October the decision was reached to withdraw all British troops.

[We held all our drills and maneuvers] right off Helgoland and nowhere else. But by now it has become evident that the enemy will never dare to come within range of the island's howitzers and mortars on a clear day. And in bad weather the shoals, sand banks and mines constitute an even greater danger.

Our German submarines have overthrown all the theories of naval warfare. The only thing which prevents our enemies from realizing their ambition of launching an attack on us is their fear of our submarines. We all thought that the English fleet would come out when some time ago we announced our submarine blockade of England.[18] But it was of no use; they refused to sail out. We are now confident that something else, a troop landing on "old England," will bring us success. Surely this will make them react more forcefully than [our present tactic] of sinking some of their merchant shipping every day. For the time being, however, we cannot proceed with it since our two fronts need all the men we have. The French and the English are presently engaged in a desperate offensive in the West, and our tempo has slowed down on the Russian Front.

The English navy seems to be concealing something. It has forbidden all neutral vessels to depart from English ports. On Saturday [September] 25, we received orders to stand by to raise steam immediately. Our entire squadron, including the cruisers and the torpedo boats, ran out and lay off the mine fields under steam. Special measures were taken to guard against a possible air raid. In our resentment at the loss of another one of our Sundays we ranted and raved like heathens. We had been scheduled to come into port on Saturday. Nothing is certain in wartime. All day Sunday passed and we did not see a thing. At noon on the next day we received a message: "*Helgoland* may head in to give her crew three days of rest." Ah, then we came in, took on 500 tons of coal in the morning and graced Wilhelmshaven with our presence for two days.

What a rest that was! On the first day we took on 500 tons of coal. The weather was cold, rainy and windy. Typical

18 This took place on February 4, 1915.

weather for Wilhelmshaven. The next morning we were placed on work details. The weather had turned even worse. That afternoon we were finally given some liberty. But who wanted to go out in such weather?

Today we ran out again and resumed our patrol off Schillig Roads. Now, of course, the sun was shining.

30 SEPTEMBER 1915

No sooner had we arrived than we were placed on advanced guard. During our first night out we went on sea patrol. The men on the 15 cm. guns received permission to sleep at their stations while the 8.8 gun crews protected the Fatherland. Since I thus had to stand watch as a lookout for only one hour, it represented a considerable saving for me. When our patrol ended after five days, we resumed our place at the locks. This was not destined to last long, however, because on Wednesday we were placed on alert once again. Our gentlemen officers were just about to go ashore when we got orders to immediately raise steam for a speed of 14 miles. Such an order would formerly have delighted me, but now it infuriates me! Then we still prayed for action, gladly accepted the trouble of stowing things away and were willing to sacrifice our sleep. Now, however, we realize from the beginning that the whole thing is merely a bluff and that we are afraid to face a battle. The men maintain that if our officers could direct the ships from the shore we would long since have gotten into a fight. However there is a kernel of truth [even in] this senseless gossip.

It is rumored that [Grand Admiral] Tirpitz [19] has been dis-

---

[19] Grand Admiral Alfred von Tirpitz (1849-1930) was the Secretary of State of the Navy who was largely responsible for the creation of a large German navy. During the war Tirpitz became an outspoken advocate of a policy of unrestricted submarine warfare, a more active role for the fleet and extensive territorial annexations. Consequently, he became embroiled in conflict with Chancellor Theobald von Bethmann-Hollweg, the Kaiser and the Commander of the High Seas Fleet Admiral von Pohl, all of whom pursued a more moderate policy. This gave rise to periodic rumors that Tirpitz had been dismissed. This, too, was a false rumor, for Tirpitz remained in office until March 1916.

missed and has been replaced by his archenemy, the Commander of the High Seas Fleet Admiral Pohl. I don't know who is slated to take command of the fleet. A rumor is going around that the command was offered to Admiral Holtzendorff by the Kaiser, but that he rejected it by saying, "Your Majesty, I can do nothing with this kind of a fleet." [20] The only reason why I report this horrible story is that it is making the rounds right now and seems to be widely believed. It is not my intention to suppress unpleasant things.

Regardless of what one thinks of our excellent navy, we have committed an unforgivable error by retaining our 28 cm. and 30.5 cm. caliber artillery. The English have long since adopted 34 cm. guns; eight of their ships are even equipped with 38 cm. cannon. Given this kind of a situation, what can we hope to accomplish? We were under the impression that ours were the only guns that could fire a distance of 19 kilometers. But at the Battle of Dogger Bank the English commenced firing at a range of 21 kilometers. Our ships saw nothing but the flashes of their guns. Moreover, on that occasion the English only used their 34 cm. guns. They were positively brilliant in concealing the range of their artillery from us.

The shortcomings of our artillery are even more critical in the case of our light cruisers. A savings of a couple of millions has cost the lives of many brave men and has done untold damage to our trade and international prestige. Supposing that at the Battle of the Falkland Islands *Emden* had mounted even a small number of 15 cm. guns, what would have been the result? She could then have blasted *Sydney* right out of the water. And if *Leipzig, Nürnberg, Dresden* and *Königsberg* had even come close to their opponents in terms of artillery, they would never have stood by helplessly while they were being sunk.

Only recently have we begun to equip our ships with 15 cm.

[20] Admiral Henning von Holtzendorff (1853–1919) had been the Commander of the High Seas Fleet until 1913, when he was forced to resign his post in a disagreement with Tirpitz. In 1915 Holtzendorff served as Chief of Staff of the Admiralty and was widely regarded as Tirpitz's greatest rival in the navy.

guns (*Strassburg, Bremen, Pillau*). But I wonder if it is not too late. Right now an English destroyer is comparable to one of our light cruisers and in addition possesses far greater speed and maneuverability. Prior to the war the sea battle of the future was depicted in the following terms: The battle will commence with the heavy artillery. As soon as [the enemy's guns] have been silenced and we have closed in, our medium artillery will spew forth such a veritable hail of steel on the superstructures, decks, searchlights and other exposed parts of the enemy that he will not know what is happening. Our torpedo boats, which shall have kept out of the way until then, will then break forth at the proper moment and deal the enemy his death blow. After all, since the English are lacking proper medium guns, they shall not be able to put up an effective defense.

Our torpedo boats also merit a few remarks. This weapon was our greatest source of pride and hope before the war. When the war broke out their crews were delirious with happiness because they felt confident that they could sink the entire English fleet in the course of a single dark night. But they came back to port without having accomplished anything. For some unknown reason the English battleships felt more secure behind their fortifications at the Firth of Forth than in the German Bight. Nevertheless four weeks later on August 28, our "black ones" had an opportunity to show what they could do in battle.[21] But they achieved nothing. The English destroyers ran right over them, sank the lead ship (*V 187*) [22] and damaged several others severely. They came limping back to port with their tails between their legs and were no longer confident that they were unbeatable. Later on, however, a German-Turkish torpedo boat did make a brilliant attack on the [*Goliath*], which was lying at anchor.[23] Moreover it seems that one of our torpedo boats sank an older English cruiser and a destroyer.

---

[21] This refers to the Battle of Helgoland in 1914.
[22] V stands for Vulkan-Werft or Vulkan Shipyards.
[23] On May 12, 1914, the old English battleship *Goliath* was sunk with a loss of 520 men at the Dardanelles by a Turkish torpedo boat.

Then *V 5* sank the *Tiger*.[24] Nonetheless the English strongly deny these two victories.

While most of our torpedo boats are armed with 5.7 cm. caliber peashooters, the English have already introduced guns of 15 cm. caliber. But enough of this unhappy subject. Nothing else but this could be responsible for Tirpitz's dismissal.

Let me now return to our state of alert. No one seemed to know what was going on. But to be perfectly frank, there was really nothing happening. Throughout the night we lay hove to under steam and in the morning came the order to put out the fires. We were scheduled to come into port on Saturday and all of us looked forward to at last enjoying an undisturbed Sunday. But damn it! Just as we were about to dock, the flagship ordered: "All ships to replenish coal and to sail out." Good-bye, nice Sunday! At nine o'clock this evening we shall load 150 tons of coal and then run out again.

A wounded army lieutenant came to visit our ship. He wore a dashing monocle and viewed our activities on board with great interest. He had received a nasty bayonet wound in the leg. When the honorable "Sir Edward Grey," [25] his host and brother-in-law, saw the open wound, he fell into a dead faint. Surely we can entrust the command of our artillery in battle to such a man of iron nerves. . . .

Ever since the King of Greece has refused to continue to sanction the violation of his country's neutrality, the English have been feeling uncomfortable.[26] It is not unlikely that Eng-

[24] The old English battleship *Triumph*, not the *Tiger*, was sunk on May 26, 1915. But it was done not by a torpedo boat, as Stumpf contends, but rather by a submarine. On the following day the same submarine sank the *Majestic*. Since these waters were no longer safe for English warships, shortly thereafter all the larger vessels, including the *Queen Elizabeth*, were withdrawn from the Dardanelles.

[25] This was a nickname given to one of the *Helgoland*'s officers, possibly because he had as sensitive and melancholy a nature as the British Foreign Minister.

[26] On September 6, 1915, Bulgaria allied herself with Germany and Austria and agreed to attack Serbia. When Bulgaria began to mobilize on September 21, Serbia appealed to her Greek ally for support. The Greek Prime Minister Eleutherios Venizelos (1864–1936) had long since favored entering the war on the side of the Entente. He therefore concluded an agreement with England and France allowing the Allies to

land will respond to the success of our Balkan venture by invading the soil of our neighbor Holland. Therefore we have to maintain a constant alert.

On Saturday the entire fleet came together and sailed out. It was ideal weather for maneuvers. We fought a number of excellent mock battles and torpedo boat attacks. The part of the enemy, "the yellow side," was played by the Second Squadron. We did a good deal of shooting without ammunition and fought without bloodshed. The North Sea was clear of enemies! With this knowledge we turned about and without further ado dropped anchor in the Jade Estuary. 12 October 1915.

The most incredible thing happened today! It had long been rumored that a considerable number of Iron Crosses would be distributed among the crew. I really did not believe it; who among us had actually earned such a decoration? But this morning at inspection the Captain assembled the men on deck and delivered the following speech: "His Majesty the Kaiser has consented to award us a goodly number of Iron Crosses for our mission in the Gulf of Riga. All those whose names are called, step forward to receive your medals." This was followed by the names of all the officers with the exception of a few lieutenants, most of the deck officers,[27] the senior gun captains, several petty officers and a few seamen and stokers. A grand total of 65 [medals were distributed].

Repressed laughter broke out as each name was called. It was ludicrous and unworthy of the decoration to hand it out like a

land an expeditionary corps for the relief of the Serbs to be followed by the Greek entry into the war. However, King Constantine (1868–1923), who reigned from 1913 to 1917 and from 1920 to 1922, was married to Princess Sophie of Prussia, a sister of Kaiser Wilhelm, and was thus more favorably inclined toward the Central Powers than his Minister. At the last minute, on September 24, Constantine repudiated the agreement, compelled Venizelos to resign and refused an Allied request for a landing. Nevertheless, the Allies landed their divisions at Salonika over the objections of the Greek government. On October 6 a combined German-Austrian offensive led by Field Marshal August von Mackensen (1849–1945) was launched against Serbia. The Bulgarians attacked that country's flank five days later and Serbia was quickly overrun.

[27] A German deck officer was equivalent to a warrant officer, who occupies an intermediary position between a senior petty officer and a commissioned officer.

club insignia. We all hoped that the time would soon come when we could honestly say, "I have earned this cross in battle and not for good conduct." There is more than a little truth to the axiom that a healthy back is better than an Iron Cross.

I have just read in the papers that an English warship flying the American flag sank a German submarine which was fooled by the Stars and Stripes. The helpless sailors who were swimming in the water were finished off with machine-gun fire. Later on, five of the rescued men were shot down with Browning pistols. . . .[28] This is the outcome of the Kaiser's order to diminish our submarine blockade.[29]

This shameful incident has become the principal topic of conversation on board and all of us hope that we shall abandon our usual restraint. And why not? England has completely choked off our overseas trade. Why should we then unnecessarily restrain ourselves in regard to her commerce? It is scandalous that we lie here clenching our fists without doing anything about it. 16 October 1915.

[28] This refers to the famous and still controversial *Baralong* Incident of August 16, 1915. On that date a German submarine the *U 27*, commanded by Lieutenant Commander Neigener, was engaged in shelling the freighter *Baralong* which was carrying a cargo of mules and fodder to England. At that point another ship which looked like a freighter but was really the *Nicosian*, a disguised British auxiliary cruiser, appeared over the horizon. The German crew, thinking that she was simply another harmless freighter which they could despatch at leisure later on, ignored *Nicosian* and continued firing at *Baralong*. Thereupon *Nicosian* dropped her disguise, began shelling the submarine and sank her. About a dozen German sailors jumped off their sinking ship and started swimming toward the *Baralong* with the seeming intention of sailing off on her. The British captain Godfrey Herbert then sent on board the *Baralong* a party of Royal Marines who proceeded to massacre all the German sailors.

[29] The sinking of another ship the *Arabic* by a German submarine on August 19, 1915, with the loss of two American lives triggered an angry protest in the United States. It appeared as though the United States would break off diplomatic relations with Germany. As a result the German government on September 1 informed the United States that in the future German submarines would no longer sink liners without warning and without due regard for the safety of passengers, provided the liners did not try to escape or resist. The effect of this new policy was a drastic curtailment of the German submarine campaign. It must be noted, however, that this new policy was announced after the *Baralong* Incident and not before it, as Stumpf implies.

After a nasty argument with the Captain, our very able and beloved First Officer was transferred from our ship today. He was surprised when we gave him a resounding and heartfelt cheer [at his departure]. He is the fourth Executive Officer whom our Captain has ruined. Hopefully it will soon be his turn, that miserable slave driver.

Our new Executive Officer, who comes from the *Westfalen*, has a good reputation. He introduced himself with a speech which could not fail to charm the men. He promised that we could all come to his quarters with our problems. He said that he had inherited a model crew from his predecessor and that he wished to keep it that way but unfortunately it had come to his attention that nine men had overstayed their leaves and that one of them had shown disrespect to the Captain. He concluded his simple speech by expressing the hope that this was the last time that such a thing would ever occur.

Our new Executive Officer's actions are already making themselves felt. He went down to the galley, examined our food and ordered that it be improved. From now on we are to receive extra rations three times a week and twice weekly we shall get some warm soup in the evening. The men are absolutely delighted! Moreover we shall be able to sleep until 6:30 in the morning! If he will only be as generous in granting us leaves he shall have done everything that any good sailor might expect of his First Officer. We shall soon see how long this new broom continues to sweep clean. 19 October 1915.

At last our Captain has received his just reward. After ruining two First Officers, one Navigation Officer and a First Lieutenant, he is about to reap his reward. He himself will now have to go. [Von Laffert] must have submitted the necessary information to Berlin. In his parting speech the old war-horse did not conceal his disappointment at leaving his good ship. "I deeply regret," he said, "that I was not destined to lead you in battle. But I am convinced that you would have fought well and bravely. I am deeply and genuinely sorry to leave my work here unfinished and to hand over to a new commander a ship so well trained for battle and so staunch and eager a crew. Let me add just one more thing: When you get into battle, hit hard and never let the English out of your clutches."

His grim and wrinkled face lit up at these words. I knew how hard it must have been for him to give up his ship for a post at the Admiralty in Berlin after he had worked untiringly day and night to get it into fighting trim.

The new Captain introduced himself with five brief words. He was formerly in command of *Schwaben* and answers to the name of [von Kamecke].

The crew stood on deck and gave three cheers as the old man departed on the motor launch. But the cheers did not break down any walls. We did not respond when he waved his cap. It was quite different from the departure of the Executive Officer. [This time] none of the officers took command of the launch, proving that our officers' corps was only too glad to get rid of the old bastard. The only good thing about him was that he yelled as much at the officers as at the men. Our Division Officer in particular must feel as though a heavy weight had been removed from his shoulders.

On Saturday we had another one of our customary alerts. We knew that something unusual was about to take place because the officers' lackeys had been sent ashore to bring back as much laundry as possible. Thus we were fairly certain that we would not remain in the North Sea. Several other signs also pointed to such a conclusion: we did not lower all the boats as usual, etc. At eleven o'clock on Saturday night we headed out to sea on a northeasterly course. Thus we were not headed straight for England, but somewhere else. A lovely shimmering moon lit up the night. A fresh breeze was blowing. In the morning, just at dawn, a great new Zeppelin descended from the clouds. First it flew to the head of our formation and then turned back, in order to detect submarines from the air. Another Zeppelin, *L 11*, joined us at dawn. Now one of them took the point while the other guarded the rear. These airships outdistanced our fastest cruisers with ease.

At about two o'clock, one of our Zeppelins sighted an enemy submarine and issued a wireless warning to all the ships. We hurriedly turned eight points to starboard to escape from this underwater monster. I waited with bated breath for the first bomb to fall as the dirigible made its descent. But it dropped no bombs because the submarine either submerged in time or because the entire thing was a mistake. Lately we have sighted a number of submarines. Recently they sank one of our old armored cruisers, *Prinz Adalbert*, off Libau and despatched a half dozen of our iron ore vessels. But since our merchantmen do not sail in the North Sea, they have had no success in these waters. Nevertheless we sped back to the German Bight and Helgoland as fast as we could and by nine o'clock we dropped anchor in port. 23 October 1915.

We have been in the Kaiser Wilhelm Canal near Bruns-büttelkoog for two days now. At eleven o'clock on Monday night we raised steam and sailed into the Elbe at Cuxhaven and because of the ebb tide stayed there until morning. At flood tide we went up river and entered the locks. We tied up a little while later and were given a three-hour pass to visit the village. Because of the bitter cold I did not take advantage of the opportunity. Moreover it hardly paid to walk through this dull and flat countryside. It was utterly lacking in charm and had only an intermittent farmhouse or windmill to break up the monotony. An additional reason for remaining on the warm ship was that we were on a three-hour state of alert and our stay ashore could not exceed this time limit. Thus I sat in one of the rooms while the last weak rays of the sinking autumnal sun came shining through the porthole. Fall and even winter have arrived much earlier than anticipated. This morning, as well as the day before, the deck was covered with ice. The snow-white roof tops looked out over empty, brown fields. But despite the cold, every morning the band was made to play on deck for two hours.

We must not complain, however. Our comrades in the army will have to endure even greater cold and they would be happy if they could only have a roof and four walls over their heads.

Although it must now be bitterly cold in Russia and in Serbia, one still reads that we are advancing every day. In Serbia we have already made contact with the brave Bulgarian army.[30] Soon the most ambitious dreams of the German imperialists—an express railway line from Hamburg to Baghdad—will come true.[31] Right now there is a great deal of talk about our ambitions in Mesopotamia. Indeed the future looks very promising for Germany since all the things we are lacking, corn, silk, cotton, and tropical fruit, are raised there. Moreover the area is rich in copper and coal.[32]

KIEL, 8 NOVEMBER 1915

We were pleasantly surprised on Sunday when we suddenly got orders to sail to Kiel. But of course it also ruined our afternoon off and half the night. No one knew the purpose of our mission in the Baltic. Were we perhaps planning a raid on Riga? Could it be that an English task force was expected to

[30] The great German-Austrian offensive against Serbia commenced on October 6, 1915. By October 9, Belgrade had fallen. Two days later the Bulgarians invaded Serbia from the rear. By November 3 the combined German-Austrian and Bulgarian armies had routed not only the Serbians, but by early December they had defeated the Anglo-French expeditionary corps which retreated to Greece and its landing base at Salonika.

At the Russian front the German-Austrian offensive was meeting with equally great success. The Russians were retreating on Tarnopol in Galicia before an Austrian force and were barely managing to hold off the German thrust at the Battle of Dvinsk (September 9–November 1) before Riga. As a result of the Russian military disaster, Grand Duke Nicholas was relieved of the post of Supreme Commander, which was now assumed personally by the Tsar.

[31] In 1899 the Turkish Empire granted a German syndicate a concession to build a railroad line connecting Anatolia in Asia Minor to Baghdad and the Persian Gulf. This marked the beginning of German economic and political encroachment in Asia, and German imperialists looked forward to the building of a continuous stretch of railway connecting Berlin to Baghdad. However, the English opposed the project, and it was therefore still incomplete by the outbreak of the war.

[32] Germany's victory in Serbia gave rise to the hope that Germany could create a land connection to the Turkish Empire and might eventually control the rich and fertile area of Mesopotamia, which lies between the Tigris and Euphrates rivers and was the scene of intermittent fighting between the Turks and the English from the fall of 1914.

come pouring through the Danish Belt? Or maybe were the Danes up to some mischief? On the other hand, maybe it was merely ——— torpedo practice. Each of these alternatives found its advocates. I cautiously opted for the least dangerous so as not to be disappointed again later. But right now we were still in the canal, having just passed under the high bridge at Grünthal. We were scheduled to pass Rendsburg by afternoon and to arrive at the locks at Holtenau at ten in the evening.

The fall sun blazed away all day and made it a pleasant trip. To remind us that it was Sunday, we hauled up the coaling tackle from below so that we could start loading coal tomorrow morning. We had heard that a cholera epidemic was raging in Kiel and that no one would be allowed to go ashore. But that remained to be seen. When we arrived at ten that evening, we noticed that the blackout had been relaxed somewhat since May and that it was no longer effective. All the trees and hills had turned to autumnal yellows, reds and browns. It might snow any time now. In fact, today is All Souls' Day, the day of the dead. Although we had ample cause to remember our many dead, no one gave them a thought. Here we go by the principle that the living come first.

Oh, yes! A few days ago a court-martial was held on the *Ostfriesland* against the Chief Petty Officer of the First Division, Bosun's Mate [Klausen]. He struck my friend and countryman [J. Gassner] in the eye with such force that he had to be taken to the hospital. The doctor was appalled at the condition of the eye and reported the incident. We all thought that the Bosun's Mate would get a couple of weeks in the brig for it but, astonishingly enough, he was merely sentenced to seven days' confinement to quarters. *Suum cuique.* Thus the Bosun's Mate will now spend his time in the petty officers' wardroom reading all the latest papers and muttering a great deal.

But what would have happened if the reverse were true and it was a sailor who had struck a petty officer in the eye? The books say death by firing squad or maybe ten years in jail. This is justice! I hope when the war is over that a good, fresh wind will blow all these medieval laws away. If [Gassner] hadn't had a black eye as evidence and the testimony of the doctor, the guilty party would not have been punished at all simply because he is "a Knight of the Iron Cross!"

On Monday we loaded coal, three hundred tons of it! On Tuesday morning we headed out to the open sea. Torpedo practice has always fascinated me. Here is proof that the Captain represents the mind and the soul of the ship. He is the one who issues the orders to ready, aim and fire the torpedoes. At the command of "Go," a torpedoman pulls a lever, and a lightning streak of foamy white bubbles goes racing through the water. At one point, when we fired at an angle, the torpedo jumped out of the water like a shark and fell back to its designated depth with a thunderous clap. Once again it jumped up, barely missing the bow of a terror-stricken Danish steamer. Anyone who has ever seen one of our new torpedoes in action will admit that there is no such thing as a defense against them. I am convinced that our torpedo would have passed right through the Danish steamer. Hence we were not at all surprised to read that a German-Turkish torpedo had sunk the *Triumph* by penetrating through two layers of netting.[33] What amazes us the most, however, is that our bow tubes are capable of firing to the rear. The direction is controlled by a steering mechanism which enables the torpedo to describe a sharp turn and then to race on to its target regardless of its original direction. After a torpedo has been fired, a torpedo boat chases after it to retrieve it as soon as it runs down and returns to the surface.

Since the Baltic is presently menaced by a half dozen audacious English submarines, it is too dangerous to stop to take the torpedoes back on board. Therefore we take extra pains by heading into port and then run out again. This presents no difficulty in Kiel because there are no locks to negotiate.

Our routine in Kiel was pleasant. We would sail out at about

[33] This took place at the Dardanelles on May 26, 1915. See Note 24.

nine in the morning and fire our torpedoes and guns. By nightfall we were usually back in place and then we were free to go
ashore. On several occasions we had night practice, but it never
lasted later than ten or eleven o'clock. There was no sign of
the English submarines which had allegedly swept the German
fleet from the Baltic. As time went on, we worried less and less
and [even went so far] as to anchor out at sea to take on the
torpedoes. What a wonderful opportunity this represented for
an enterprising submarine pack.

The morale of our crew has sunk so low that we would all
be delighted if we got a torpedo in our belly. We all wish that
upon our despicable officers. If anyone had voiced such a wish
a year and a half ago, he would have received a good beating.
There is an evil spirit at work among us and only our good
upbringing prevents us from emulating the actions of the Russian Baltic fleet.[34] We all realize that we have more to lose than
our chains.

Since there is a copper shortage in Germany everybody, including ourselves, is saving scrap metal. The Captain set us a
good example by stripping his cabin of all unnecessary things
like doorknobs, clothes hangers, etc., and delivering them to the
docks. This was good! On each of our lockers there was a large
piece of tin imprinted with the name of the owner; these, too,
were taken down and collected in each division. If we had been
asked to deliver them voluntarily because of the metal shortage, goodness knows we would all have been happy to comply.
But compulsion leads to resistance and a few men refused to
give up their name plates. They justified themselves by asserting that they had paid for them out of their clothing allowance
and that they were thus their private property. As a result one
of them, Seaman [Fischer], was placed on report and got eight

[34] Stumpf does not mean the Russian Baltic fleet but the Black Sea
fleet, in which on June 14, 1905, the sailors of the cruiser *Potemkin* revolted against their officers by throwing them into the sea and assumed
command over the ship. Later on *Potemkin* sailed into the port of Odessa
flying the revolutionary red flag in the hope that the other ships of the
squadron would join her. When this did not take place, the mutineers
sailed off to Rumania and surrendered their ship.

hours of punishment exercise. Adding insult to injury, the First Officer suggested that he could always lodge a complaint. . . . We have long wished that this First Officer would go to hell. Immediately upon his arrival he established a drill squad and granted every officer the right to send his men to it. You can well imagine how the officers use this. At every opportunity they threaten us by stating, "Do you want to go to the punishment squad?" This is especially true of our Detail Officer. If he happens to see a washbasin, a brush or a sock [lying about] in the evening, the guilty party is sure to find himself on "guard duty" the next morning. The petty officers, too, of course, treat the common seamen with inconceivable cruelty. One stoker received eight days' punitive exercise merely for telling the machinist's mate that after four years in the engine room he did not have to be told how to do his job. Each day twenty to thirty men are made to run around with their rifles. Whenever the bosun's mate finds a man in the toilet while on duty, the sinner is at once remanded to the "foreign legion." My greatest ambition in life is to get away from all this stupidity and harassment! Although I was happy when I entered the navy, I have now come to detest it!

In Kiel I got ashore regularly and thus had an opportunity to revive my spirits. On Sunday I went to the Municipal Theater and saw two acts of *Lohengrün*. I am slowly learning to appreciate this great piece of music. It is a shame that I cannot attend such events more often. They make one feel like a human being and not like a useless beast of burden.

There are all sorts of rumors about our stay here. Some of the men insist vehemently that Denmark has made a deal with England and has gone so far as to sanction the landing of English troops. In fact, an army of 50,000 men has been stationed on the border. We have suspected for some time that the submarines which have lately been prowling in the Baltic must have come from Danish bases. In order to make certain of this, one of our gray [destroyers] sailed into Friederizia (?) and requested food and fuel. This was provided with no difficulty. There you have the proof! Our newspapers report that approx-

imately twenty English ships are cruising off the Great Belt.
The Danes are said to have cleared their mine fields. . . .[35] It
is quite possible that these ships may come out at any moment
and attack our Fourth Squadron, which is stationed at Libau.
Because of that threat six of our ships have recently returned
to Kiel.

13 NOVEMBER 1915

On Monday the commanders held a meeting on *Ostfriesland*
but I do not know what decisions they reached. I do know that
at nine o'clock that evening we were told to get up steam for
a trip through the canal. As a result, I lost my day of shore
leave, just when I intended to visit my friend ———— at the
barracks. This then was bad news. In addition, I was also unlucky enough to draw the deadman's watch from twelve to
four.

At precisely ten o'clock we secretly cast off our lines. Nonetheless we had all our searchlights turned on, as were the lights
at the locks at Holtenau. Still everything went well. It was a
dark but clear night. As we traveled along the canal, the lights
ahead of us were turned on and turned off as soon as we had
passed. At about 12:15, fog thick as pea soup moved in. As the
men put it, it was so thick that one could cut off a chunk of it
to save as a souvenir. We proceeded very slowly and cautiously. Soon, however, we had to tie up because our searchlights could not penetrate the fog. That took a bit of doing.
We could barely see. The men were delighted when everything went haywire on deck. They maintained, "It serves them
right for their damned secrecy. Now we'll have to wait until
morning anyway." It felt good to see everyone working at
cross-purposes. When the stern lines were drawn, the bow of
the ship turned forward. Then the bow lines became taut but

---

[35] This was merely a rumor. Throughout the war Denmark maintained a strict policy of neutrality and never removed her mines from
the sound. Moreover, the Danes knew that any breach of their neutrality
might result in a German invasion of their country and that they could
not expect any help from England.

the lines aft broke. Finally, after two hours of strenuous labor, we succeeded in tying the ship with four steel hawsers. We were all stiff and blue with cold.

By four o'clock it cleared somewhat and we were able to go on. I had just gotten warm again when they whistled: "Third Division out, prepare to cast off." Never before was I so happy to see a watch end as this one. At dawn we passed the fifty kilometer marker. This meant that we were halfway through. Good! Thus we could expect to be out of the canal by afternoon, but once again the fog ruined all our calculations. After a two-hour pause we proceeded once more and finally made it to the locks by six at night. We anchored at the Roads and waited until the other five ships had come through. Then we began the last leg of our trip to Wilhelmshaven and passed Cuxhaven at ten o'clock just as the starboard watch went on duty.

We knew right off that we were back in the North Sea because of the wind! It whistled and howled around our ears as if it wanted to tear every shred of clothing off our backs. At 11:30 the red beacon of the island of Wangerooge appeared over the horizon; we passed Minsener Sand and the Jade fire ship and then—it must have been midnight before I finally climbed down from the searchlight and joyfully collapsed in my hammock. 19 November 1915.

We set forth again in the morning, made our way through the last of the mine fields and anchored close to the locks. Only then did I begin to appreciate our stay in Kiel. There we had no long hours of division duty, inspections were rare and we were able to dress as we pleased. But all this came to a sudden stop here as we resumed our daily inspections and worked at our divisional duties all day long dressed in our thin linen fatigues. Christ, did we grumble about that! Fortunately we returned to port after three days to install two antiaircraft guns for use against dirigibles. We had made room for them a long time ago by removing two of our 8.8 cm. guns from the afterdeck. There were also rumors that we were to spend some time in dock during December. Bah! We'll have to wait until

May before that happens! At any rate, it is much more pleasant to be home in spring time than at Christmas.

One day I went ashore to buy a number of different items. All the local tradesmen complained that business was miserable. When I went to one of the better cafes in the evening, three customers, four musicians and five [waiters] were in the place.

Coinage has suddenly become very scarce due to the introduction of an iron five-pfennig piece. I suspect that the smart people are hoarding the coins made of nickel, while those who have five-pfennig pieces made of iron are saving them as souvenirs. . . . Since Monday morning we have been anchored at Wilhelmshaven Roads. If things go according to schedule, we shall have to go on watch for five days at Schillig Roads tomorrow. 23 November 1915.

An uneventful five days have passed. Although nothing happened here, out at the front a new chapter in the history of the world has begun. According to a report from Supreme Headquarters, our troops have conquered and occupied virtually all of Serbia. King Peter has found refuge with his friend King Nikita of Montenegro, but for how long? Soon this mountainous country, too, will vanish from the world map.[36] We began our campaign against Serbia on October 6, and despite all the natural and human obstacles, it took our [army] barely seven weeks to overrun the kingdom! The Serbs defended their country with desperate and death-defying courage. The expeditionary force sent by England and France to support Serbia has been routed by the Bulgarians. It is retreating by blowing up the bridges and anxiously searching the Gulf of Salonika for its ships. . . .[37]

[36] After the defeat of his armies, Peter I of Serbia (1844–1921) found temporary asylum with King Nicholas I (not Nikita) of Montenegro (1841–1921). However, in January 1916 the Austrians conquered this country as well, and both monarchs were compelled to flee. In November 1918, when Nicholas of Montenegro opposed the inclusion of his country in the new Yugoslav state, Peter repaid him for his former hospitality by having him deposed.

[37] See Note 30. At the insistence of the French government and of the commander of the expedition General Sarrail, the Anglo-French force was not withdrawn from Salonika until the summer of 1916. However,

Our bread rations have been cut again and our hunger is never stilled. The officers, however, still live and eat in luxurious style. Their mess serves big feasts with at least five meat courses almost every week. At yesterday's inspection three divisions complained about the smallness of the bread rations. The reply of the First Officer was short and sweet: "There is no more bread. The men at the front work harder than we and get even less bread. . . ." If this is true, why does the war continue? Our officers keep assuring us in their lectures that "we" (and here they mean the people) have enough food and money to hold out another year. Yes, indeed, the officers and high officials could even hold out for ten years. They get a fifty percent supplementary war allowance!

At home during the winter, at about four or five o'clock, when it is still too light to turn on the lights but too dark to work, comes the hour of the chickens when the hens go to sleep. Then the children and the old people like to gather around the stove to discuss the day's events, their plans for the next day and their various cares. Grandmother tells the children a fairy tale before they are put to bed. Grandfather tells the boys of his adventures in '70 or maybe even describes how his grandfather witnessed the burning of Moscow. Or, for the hundredth time, he tells how the townspeople of Reuter tried to hatch a horse egg and how they sowed their fields with salt. I used to look forward all day long to this brief quarter of an hour. But what does all this have to do with the events in my war diary? Come to think of it, it does not belong here at all. Hence I shall describe a different hour of the chickens that did not take place on the farm behind the warm stove, but which occurred here one evening in the darkness of the blacked-out casemates.

It gets dark at 5:30 these days; at six we eat dinner and then we write letters, play cards or play music until 7:30. Then it is time for "lights out." The lower decks are swept and cleared

the remnants of the Serbian army fought their way through to the coast of Albania from which they were evacuated by the British and Italian navies to Corfu.

and at precisely eight, the hammocks are brought out. It is usually 8:30 before the noise quiets down and all the hammocks are slung and then the chicken hour begins. Groups of three or four men sit in a corner smoking their pipes which taste all the better now that smoking is forbidden. And so we philosophize, criticize, gossip and discuss the war. Although a good deal of nonsense is spoken, on occasion some surprisingly intelligent and timely ideas are voiced as well. I like to keep quiet and listen because this is the time when all the men express their innermost thoughts and feelings. Often they continue spinning their yarns until eleven o'clock or until someone falls asleep. However, Felix [Krella] manages quite nicely to talk to someone who is asleep so long as the sleeper gives out a snore once in a while. Right now he is on leave to marry his beloved Maruschka. And he is also expecting the arrival of a little son— a baptism and a wedding at the same time—that makes it less expensive. 2 December 1915.

Thus it is often 11:30 or midnight before the ship is really at rest. Under ordinary circumstances seven hours of sleep are sufficient for an adult. Of course, this presupposes that he has plenty of clean, fresh oxygen to breathe. But my colleagues are so stupid as to seal all the windows air-tight every evening lest they catch a draft. It is difficult to describe how suffocating the air becomes when forty men are compelled to sleep in close proximity to one another in such a confined space. One wakes up with a headache; one's head is as heavy as lead and the rest of the body is tired and fatigued. Then, as is only proper, the men curse the navy. Only after we have washed ourselves up on deck and have had a chance to draw some fresh and pure morning air into our lungs do we really wake up. When we were recruits we always had to do half an hour of calisthenics in the morning. This proved to be a veritable cure for the lungs and the stomach.

The class of 1911 and the reservists are slowly being transferred from our ship to make room for younger men. Today fifty new recruits came aboard. Soon it will be the turn of the class of 1912. But where shall we go? Up till now most of the men have been transferred to patrol boats, another group has gone to the so-called contraband ships as dock workers, and a small number are still in the replacement company. Within the next few days we are going to send a transport of nine thousand men to Serbia and to Turkey. Although I really do not have it so bad for me here, I still wish that I were on it. It is very boring to stay on the same ship all the time and to perform the same duties over and over.

We have gotten a new Division Officer to replace our clumsy oaf of a First Lieutenant [K]. Thank God, he has left at last! His place is being taken by Lieutenant [Albrecht]. I understand that he is unusually learned in many fields. However in every other respect he is a bureaucrat and a stickler for detail who goes by the book. He refuses to recognize the existence of anything which is not in writing and does not bear an official stamp. He writes down every piece of trivia and never forgets a thing. If he would only translate his useless knowledge into practical action and teach us something, we would be delighted with him. First Lieutenant K. felt that we had no interest in anything but our jobs and that it was useless and inadvisable to educate us further. He exuded an air of superiority and like the Danish Junkers, his ancestors, he held the view that "the less educated a nation is, the easier it is to govern!" It will take a great deal of doing before we can teach his kind that the new German soldier is too smart to permit the officers' caste to lead him by the nose and to trample over him.

After the war . . . that is what we keep hoping. We are well aware that this would be the best time to do something to improve our conditions since the thunder of the guns has turned even the most conservative officials into Socialists. But if we abolished their privileges now, it might arouse false hopes among our enemies and thus might harm the Fatherland. Moreover we are also well aware that the officers do not represent the "German Fatherland." Should anything go wrong, they would be among the first to desert it by going into the opposition. And what would happen if we were to win? Then in all likelihood the ruling class will once more, as in 1812, push the masses back again.[38] So long as we small people remain divided, the Junkers and fifty thousand officers can afford to ignore us.

While the poorest people willingly surrendered every last gold coin in their stockings, the great merchants continue paying out hundreds of thousands in gold to foreign nations. Will we ever receive any reward for this? We have voluntarily rendered ourselves defenseless. Only fools place their faith in paper currency! One merely has to look at Serbia to realize that the paper dinar has virtually lost its entire value. After the war the price of real estate and of rents will soar up again. The advertising in the major newspapers is already pointing in that direction.

Why do such bleak thoughts keep churning through my mind? All my observations confirm my conviction that my predictions will come true. 8 December 1915.

My friend [Walz] was sentenced to a year and a half in prison by a court-martial for striking a petty officer in a tavern. . . . He is the kind of a person who would not harm a fly but for his drinking, his god-damned drinking! 8 December 1915.

Nothing worth mentioning occurred during the last eight days. 14 December 1915.

This morning when I walked by the Detail Officer on the afterdeck, he told me, "Your application for leave has been rejected!" "Yes, sir," I replied. His falseness disgusted me. I no longer care whether I get leave or not, since I can always find a better use for the money I have saved by spending it on books. Nevertheless many of my friends have left already.

We were scheduled to put into Wilhelmshaven at noon on Friday and I was already looking forward to a few days' rest. But we must have received an important message on Thursday evening, because all at once we heard that we had been placed

[38] In 1813 (not 1812) at the outbreak of the Wars of Liberation against Napoleon, King Frederick William III of Prussia addressed an appeal to his people to overthrow Napoleon and hinted that he might then reward them by granting them greater freedom and a constitution. However, after the defeat of Napoleon a conservative reaction set in, and the Prussian people did not achieve any of their promised freedoms or a constitution until after the Revolution of 1848.

on emergency alert. Sure enough, a little later the well-known order, "All hands stand by to take out nets," was piped. The order brought about an incredible uproar which resembled a scene from Walpurgis Night in *Faust*. Each one of us ran to get the best possible line. With a thunderous noise two thick and heavy booms were lowered from the mast. The chains rattled and clattered and the tackle weighing hundreds of pounds was flung down from a great height as though it were unbreakable and worthless. All at once ten voices shouted, "Warschau" as the order was given to lower the boats. But it was amazing how quickly order emerged from all this chaos and how few motions it took to drop the nets and to carry them out.

What was going on? No one knew for sure whether we were heading out to Kiel or were planning a sortie against England. Yes, that's right! A year ago today we had sailed over there and our cruisers had subjected three of their coastal towns to a thorough bombardment. But it was all different then; we were still idealistic. Our enthusiasm was such that each one of us would have been willing to lay down his life in battle. But now the very thought of a battle frightens me.

The port watch went on duty at eight o'clock. We requested permission to sleep at our battle stations in the gun turrets and after some delay the request was granted. I fell out of my hammock two times. An old woman would have regarded it as an evil omen. But I am not superstitious! At the unusually late hour of 6:30 we were wakened to discover that we had not sailed out after all. That morning we made our usual preparations: life jackets, gas masks and first aid kits were distributed; we packed our clothes and stowed them away and then we stood at battle stations. Although we had raised steam, a thick fog made it too dangerous for us to sail out that day. Therefore we stayed right where we were and had two hours of calisthenics in the afternoon. And for good measure the sirens and the foghorns howled all night while we slept at our guns. The next day we performed our divisional chores, did some more calisthenics and heard the same lecture over for the hundredth time. Another night passed without incident. In the morning we removed our seabags from the hold and thus returned to a peace status once more. 16 December 1915.

If the Third Squadron did not come back from Kiel by [December] 20, we would be compelled to be out on patrol at Schillig Roads on Christmas Eve. We did not relish that thought.

Christmas!! Once before this title has stood at the head of my diary but I would never have believed then that the war could last another year. In contrast to last year, the war has changed greatly in our favor. But this is only superficially true. At that time the Austrian invaders had just been thrown out of Serbia. The Russians had crossed the Uszok Pass in Galicia and the Hungarian steppes were overrun by Cossacks. In the West both sides were equal and the war had reached a stalemate.

Now, however, our original war aims have been achieved. Serbia has been punished severely, Russia has been defeated and only in the West does the fighting still rage in the same place. However our men returning from furlough tell us that long transports of Bulgarians and Turks are being despatched there for some future offensive. Our offensive, this is the magic word of the hour, simply has to succeed before the coming of spring and before the French and the English are afforded another opportunity to drive their black, brown and yellow soldiers [to the front again]. And if it fails . . . well, then I shall have to use the entry "Christmas" once again next year.

The morale of the people back home has not improved. Is it any wonder that anyone who has served for one and a half years without ever having come within sight of the enemy should lose all faith and confidence? I must give our Captain credit for having done much to make this a dignified and pleasant holiday. He brought aboard forty little trees, a whole wheelbarrow of decorations, sacks full of apples, nuts, oranges, chocolate and many other good things. The only thing found lacking was the morale of the men but then this was not something that could be bought. Only large rations of alcohol could possibly remedy this situation and this was not found lacking.

Of course we had an inspection on Christmas Eve, the main

objective of which was that all the men wear clean, white uniforms. The First Officer made a speech and admonished the men not to get drunk on the schnapps they had received from home. Otherwise he would be compelled to open all the packages in the presence of the Chief Petty Officer (who enjoys taking a good snort himself). Dire punishment and other consequences [were threatened].

At three o'clock came another inspection, followed by religious services. The Catholic chaplain delivered a stirring sermon and then [we sang] the usual Christmas carols.

The Petty Officer in charge of our division had a great deal of trouble making us decorate our tree, but after a while a few of the men gave in. After dinner we were politely asked to light our trees because the Captain was about to tour the ship. First came a messenger, then a cadet, then the ensign of the watch, then the Officer of the Watch in person, and finally First Lieutenant [Mildenstein]. We jeered and laughed at the first three but at last we complied anyway. I should devote a special chapter to our so-called transparencies. This was our only chance throughout the year to joke about our superiors' foibles with impunity. They were made of large cardboard sheets painted with pictures or, sometimes to make them more effective, we cut out the cardboard, filled it with transparent paper and lit a candle behind it. If the men wanted to embarrass their Division Officer without exerting their minds, they inscribed the following rhyme on the placard:

> We do not want wine and beer
> But would like a different Division Officer.[39]

This time, of course, the good Martin [Schultze] was the target of most of the fun. A placard depicted him standing on deck taking a food sample from the honorable first cook. Another showed him collecting washbasins in the casemates, holding a long pencil in hand, saying to a sailor: "Soldier, why are

---

[39] Wir wünschen uns nicht Wein und Bier
Aber einen anderen Divisions Offizier.

you wearing your boots?" Behind him, carrying a large pile of washbasins, stood his aide. Another one was directed at Kapitänleutnant [Belleville]. He had a habit of sending the men to the mainmast at every opportunity. Affixed beneath his picture were his words: "Get up there, you old owl!"

Another one of the placards dealt wtih the First Officer's unconscious habit of saying that the sailors ought to get twenty-five lashes on their rears each day. He made the best of it and laughed while the other officers joined in with varying enthusiasm. Most of the other placards showed a light tower whose beam carried the words, "Merry Christmas" or "God punish England."

That evening we had punch with some good sponge cake. However because the price of geese had risen to an incredible two marks per pound, we had to do without our customary roast goose. All the commodities which are not subject to price control are priced exorbitantly. 25 December 1915.

We have had a movie projector on board for several days and, since it was a novelty, all the showings were mobbed. What I have seen of it so far, however, does not suit my tastes because of the emphasis on "drama." But on occasion they do show some rather good films of the front.

My God, today is New Year's! But it doesn't feel like it at all because it is totally lacking in emotion. Nowadays even the holidays feel like regular work days. This would be a good time to review the year which will one day be regarded as Germany's most glorious age. I wish I were able to look into the future of the coming year in order to answer the questions: How will our dear Fatherland fare by next Christmas? How can we bring about a peace? However I am afraid that Mars still controls our destinies. All the New Year's cards I received expressed the hope that the coming year might bring peace and an end to this killing.

But on the other hand, there are still many people in Germany who do not want to hear of peace. Not only the army contractors and munition manufacturers, but many little people as well have derived considerable comfort and wealth from the war. While the great ones have benefited immensely, the little man has also turned a small profit. Naval officers, officials and shipyard workers are earning twice and three times their peacetime salaries. Nevertheless since it is dangerous to admit that one does not desire peace, they complain about these hard times.

But to get back to New Year's, nothing of any significance happened. Indicating that where there is a will, there is also a way, we had hot sausages and potato salad for dinner, followed later on by some punch. At midnight I was wakened by wild cheering. Happy New Year! Happy New Year!

In two days another seventy men from the class of 1911 will receive temporary transfers back to the replacement company. Having concluded their course in seamanship, our recruits will now be incorporated in the various divisions. When will it be my turn? In a half a year!

On New Year's Day we had an inspection with a short speech, followed by three cheers for His Majesty the Kaiser. Then I attended a rather disappointing Catholic service until 11:30. An order dated January 1, 1916, stated that we were to come in for a "rest" the next day. What a rest that was! The first day we coaled, the second day we cleaned ship and on the third we sailed our again. Since we were not permitted to go ashore, it hardly mattered!

It has come to our attention that our new squadron commander will soon inspect us for our battle readiness. What a joke, after eighteen months of war—a battle fitness inspection! But more was to come. We are going to hold a practice inspection on Monday. Much to the indignation of the officers' boys, the captain made us remove every stick of furniture from his own as well as the officers' luxuriously furnished quarters. Actually the whole thing was a swindle because the furniture was simply hidden away where the exalted commander would not find it. Since it was all placed in a huge pile, a single well-aimed shell would have taken care of the entire thing. That morning we were told to store our seabags in Compartment 15. This brought on a terrific uproar as we all pushed and shoved in every direction. The bags on the bottom, of course, were all crushed out of shape. Nevertheless if a man were to be spotted wearing a wrinkled cap or pair of trousers, he would never hear the end of it.

All these serious preparations were really quite funny. The divers stood around in their diving equipment, a few men wore smoke masks, the fire crew was on alert and the repair crew stood by with its beams, saws, hammers, mats and covers. Below deck the scuttling crew with its dynamite charges was assembled. The medics were ready with their bandage cases and stretchers, while the pump crew was prepared to flood the powder magazines and gun turrets in case of fire.

While this by itself was not so funny, it still made one laugh to think that it served absolutely no useful purpose. We were made to put on our life jackets and gas masks and had to wear our identification tags all the time. Then [we made believe that] His Highness accompanied by his staff had entered a turret and handed a damage report to the most intelligent man. "Stop!! Damage!!! Large fire in Compartment 14." As ordered, the Petty Officer shouted, "All hands, abandon compartment for flooding!" Everybody left but of course we merely simulated the flooding.

In another turret the order read: "Water! Repair leak!" Elsewhere there were "poisonous gases" or the lights went out. All these damages were repaired with lightning rapidity. His Excellency will write a very satisfactory report! But perhaps not! However, now that we are at war, I am certain that it "will all go well." Since we get all these extra rations, it could not be otherwise! No, no, everything will go smoothly and will be in tip-top shape for battle. . . .

Happily our practice general inspection was over. But the best was yet to come. On Friday reveille was sounded at five o'clock and then we cleaned the ship for an hour before breakfast. We made some last-minute adjustments. Here and there something was not correct; a beam had been lashed improperly, or worse still, a loose piece of equipment was lying about. Thus we waited and waited. . . .

At last, amidst resounding laughter came the announcement: "The inspection shall not take place!" In order not to be left out, [Martin Schulze] [40] added his own commentary by ordering: "Fatigue uniforms. The inspection will *probably* (emphasized) take place this afternoon."

We had gone to all this trouble for nothing. The men either laughed or cursed and got their seabags, the furniture, the dishes, the wadding material for leaks and the bandages back into place. A few days later we had another minor alarm, but sailed no further than Helgoland.

20 JANUARY 1916

This time we remained at Schillig Roads for eight straight days. It was rumored that we were almost certain to put into dock for repairs on [January] 20. It would be fine if we then got our furloughs. As far as I was able to tell, only those men who had not been on leave since our last time in dock will get to go. Boy, oh boy, this meant me! I looked forward to it like a child.

But curiously enough, instead of heading into port on [January] 20, we loaded coal. Fortunately it meant nothing. Three days later we entered the shipyard and then put into dock. Only forty men from each division were given leave and thus many of my friends had to stay behind. The first shift departed on the 26th.

In peacetime our stay in dock used to be the most pleasant time of the year for us. We usually stayed in for six weeks rather than two. Since our work load was no more extensive then than is now squeezed into two weeks, we all managed to get away with doing very little work. But now? Although I have lived through more than five dock periods, we were never so shamelessly driven and exploited as on this occasion. We even had to work until one o'clock on the Kaiser's birthday. Of course the officers had a big celebration at which the band had to play for five hours. Under the influence of champagne

---

[40] Note the different spelling of the name Schulze. Last time Stumpf spelled it Schultze.

the gentlemen were not at their best behavior but nevertheless they did sound out a loud and strong cheer for His Majesty. To make it an enjoyable day for the sailors as well, each of us received a cup of plain coffee with "milk." January 27, 1916.

One more day to go before my leave!

No matter how much it pains me, I still feel obligated to jot down a few lines about the inhuman work we were made to perform during those six days. I was sentenced to scraping rust in the coal bunkers. Then we scraped the sides of the ship. I have already described this type of work on an earlier occasion. But it makes a world of difference whether one has to do it in the bitter cold of winter rather than in warm weather. While it is tolerable in the summer, in the winter it turns into a real ordeal. It is almost indescribable how it feels to work on a swaying board 15 meters above the water. Moreover the work was highly dangerous, the tools were primitive, the dust from the rust was a health menace and there was a total absence of any protective devices. If it only had not been so bitter cold! Every noon and evening my hands and feet were frozen blue, drained of all blood and without feeling from the lack of proper exercise. My hands and face were all broken out from repeated washings with turpentine and pumice soap—the only way to remove the sharp ship's paint—so that I had to treat them with lanolin.

At night it was equally bad. Since they had removed the 15 cm. guns, we literally had to sleep in the open. Although I enjoy getting plenty of fresh air, it was not pleasant to wake up with a sore throat every morning. Thank God, it will all be over by tomorrow and I shall be able to put all this behind me once I am on the train. We shall finish the last of the painting by morning. After we have had a bath and a medical examination, we will pack our clothes and put away our seabags. And at nine in the evening, I shall be off. . . . 1 February 1916.

I have returned from leave! How it depresses me to say it! I am back again; back to this horrible dirt, hellish noise and the despicable people. It all felt so different fourteen days ago.

Even while I still painted the ship's bottom, in my thoughts I was back at home with my loved ones.

We sailors were off duty that last afternoon, while the poor stokers were still made to slave away in the boiler room until five o'clock. I was the only one from my unit [going on leave] and it seemed as though it would never turn eight o'clock. Finally, at long last, it was time. "Second shift of those going on leave, assemble on the starboard side of the middle deck." The bosun's mate called out the names in a loud voice. I felt greatly relieved when I held my pass in my hand. Yet we were still not permitted to leave! A half dozen times we got into formation without being able to speak or smoke, only to be switched around once more and then made to assemble all over again. The Officer of the Watch, Lieutenant [Oly], nearly kept back a few of the men who had spoken. How can one keep silent with such a full heart? After what I had seen and heard, I was fuming inside. But finally everything was worked out and the order came: "Line up. Right face. Forward march!" I took one last look at the gigantic black ship, passed through the dock gate and walked to the railroad station.

There the cook's mate in his wooden shoes put in a personal appearance to distribute some cigarettes to his "dear sailors and stokers." Most of the petty officers were drunk to the gills and behaved like silly schoolboys. But who cared? After all, we were going home! After a quick trip we arrived in Bremen shortly before twelve and almost immediately got permission to change to the train for Hanover. There we separated, the talk died down and sleepiness set in.

Hanover! I had just barely shut my eyes. Everybody out for the train to Göttingen! Twenty-minute waiting period. The local train to Göttingen was very slow and stopped every few minutes. We arrived there at five in the morning and boarded another local to Bebra! It was broad daylight before I arrived at the two-track station I knew so well. Old memories flooded back into my mind. Here was the place where I ate lunch when I was drafted. When I came back from leave the last time, I had stood there. In my happy mood I recalled how sad I was then.

Although it was only February 4, the weather was so beautiful that it felt as though it was the middle of summer. The lovely little town of Fulda flew by. I wish I could live in this wonderful area with its green forests and clean and aromatic air. When I looked out of the window, I almost thought that I saw a blue violet winking at me but it was still a bit early for that.

On the basis of the railroad schedule we had figured that we would arrive in Nuremberg by four o'clock. The passenger may think but it is the Railroad Minister who directs. By one o'clock we still sat at a railway siding before Elm with a three-hour wait ahead of us. Oh, yes! The main line was over-crowded and had thus spoiled the Prussian punctuality of the officials.

The station agent acted as though he had been expecting us all along. He took our baggage, explained the schedule to us and, most importantly, provided us with good food and drink. There were also toilet facilities for us. Along with some soldiers we took a twenty-minutes' stroll down to the pretty little town. There we had a row and drank and cursed to the stars.

The station master informed us that we were not to go by way of Würzburg, but via Schweinfurt-Bamberg. In Gemünden we had another half-hour stop. There I walked into the large waiting room to buy something. I knew right away that it was a typical Bavarian waiting room. First of all, there were the beer mugs, also impenetrable smoke, unbearable heat, and dirt; much dirt and noise. But the beer was excellent.

On the way to Schweinfurt we met a very nice young woman whose husband was also in the navy. It was night again when we finally arrived in Bamberg. But we would soon be home—nothing could happen now. The express to Munich stood waiting and off we went through the Hauptschmorwald. The names of the stations became more and more familiar: Strullendorf, Forchheim, Erlangen. I said good-bye to my comrades and went on alone. At Markgrafen I had an hour's wait and took the opportunity to eat a succulent piece of liver for dinner. The choice of food amazed me. And [the prices] were hardly more expensive than in peacetime.

Since it was the last day of the fair, the little train to Neukirchen was very crowded. The only light in the car came from two candles and we could barely see one another. But no one seemed to take this seriously. Uttemreuth, Weiher, Dormits, and finally, there we were, after a trip of twenty-four hours. Although I had arrived unexpectedly, my sister recognized me from afar. It felt wonderful to be back in the room where I had spent the golden days of my childhood. Every piece of furniture reminded me of them. What a pleasure it was to sleep in a soft bed, all alone.

Unfortunately my father was away. He had gone for a visit to Stadelhofen. Early next morning I called Stadtsteinach.

Things were very quiet at home. Virtually all the men from 19 to 40 were away. The girls and the women did all the work. However we were lucky that there was no food shortage. Flour, eggs, butter, shortening and meat were all available and priced reasonably. For example, a pound of butter cost 1.40 mark, an egg was 13 to 14 pfennigs, beef was 1.30 and pork was 1.50. Bavaria was truly lucky! When I told the men [back on board] the prevailing prices here, they refused to believe me. . . .

Since it was so nice and warm that afternoon, I rode over to Gräfenberg and part of the way toward Egglostein. On the return trip I visited some lovely people I knew in Weissenohr. What a lovely day! On Saturday I was so bored that I did not know what to do with myself. But in the afternoon Father arrived by train with Mrs. Sch——. She was the one who had helped me pass the time on my last furlough.

Everything went splendidly. On Sunday morning I went to church as usual. However, I soon tired of the priest's boring sermon and absented myself for its duration. In the afternoon I visited friends in Nuremberg. There was a large new cafe on the Königsstrasse which was unbelievably crowded with people, soldiers and women. . . . It was virtually impossible to get into the other places of entertainment. The theater and the movies were all sold out. At two in the morning I took the train back to Erlangen and walked home the rest of the way on foot. When I arrived, the people were just leaving for church. . . . After I had slept, I had to start thinking about packing up and leaving again. I paid one more visit of "only" two and a half hours to the local land agent, who was a navy buff.

Unfortunately I had to leave very early on Tuesday morning. As always, it was a short, hearty parting without much talk. My sister B. had accompanied me to the station and cried loudly as I bade her farewell. I had some difficulty holding back my own tears! By the time I had reached Erlangen my sadness had partially disappeared and it vanished altogether when a lovely girl I knew rode with me until Nuremberg. Since I had to wait for four hours until the next train, I took a stroll through the town. At the station commandant's office I managed to change my travel orders so that I was able to take the express by way of Halle.

The trip was unforgettably lovely that day. The train only stopped at the major stations. I was very familiar with the area until Bamberg and Lichtenfels. But I would never have believed that the Franconian Forest could be so delightful as far up as Probstzella. Here the train had to mount to a considerable altitude and heavy snow began to fall on the watershed. I was filled with admiration for this huge, dark but beautiful forest. Then a blue and white border marker flew by—we were back in Prussia. Nevertheless the area was rather nice. Rudolstadt! At the station we received the most luxurious treatment. There was coffee, tea, cake, apples, lemonade, and, in addition, there were the pretty smiling faces of the Red Cross sisters.

Numerous castle ruins in the vicinity served as silent reminders of a great and past civilization. Standing on a commanding height was Saalek [Salem?], which looked like a fairy tale castle. I suspect that it has been completely renovated. On the coal banks of the Saale the castles stand proud and tall. . . .

There were several noncommissioned officers and soldiers from France in my compartment. They told some interesting stories about the bravery of the French, of infantry charges, of mines and sappers. I really enjoyed myself and the time flew by. At Halle I regretfully parted from these vivacious Berliners.

I still did not know how I was going to proceed on my journey but I had plenty of time and could well afford to miss a train. At the Halle railway station I soon became acquainted with some soldiers who had come from the Üskub in Macedonia. From Üskub! [41] When the war started who would ever have believed that German soldiers would be fighting there? They readily described the difficulties and horrors, the knee-deep mud and endless rain of the Serbian campaign. For weeks on end they had no bread and ate only meat. Nevertheless they kept advancing day by day.

As I arrived at my next destination, Magdeburg, the shadows of night were again descending. Instead of staying on until Braunschweig, I made an error and changed at Stendal because I felt like spending the night there. For the first time since I had left home I drank a small glass of beer. (One could never consider this a full glass!) An exceptionally friendly railroad conductor advised me to take the next train to Hanover because it made better connections with Bremen. I complied and boarded a local train. The train was jammed with soldiers. Most of them were noisy Cologners whose speech was so repulsive to me that I could hardly stomach them.

Consequently I took a copy of Naumann's *Mitteleuropa* [42] which I had bought along the way and began to read. The book proposes a grandiose plan. Like all the other writings of

[41] The town of Uskub (Skoplje) in Serbian Macedonia had fallen to the Bulgarians on November 5, 1915.

[42] Friedrich Naumann (1860–1919) was a prominent leader and Reichstag deputy of the Progressive Party. He had started out in life as a pastor and rose to fame before the war because of his attempts to reconcile the German working class to the monarchy through religion. Naumann's book *Mitteleuropa* was published in October 1915. It proposed the establishment of a voluntary federation of Central European states around the core of the German-Austrian Alliance, which would eventually be joined by all the small states and nationalities of eastern Europe. The federation was to be primarily an economic union, but Naumann also envisioned the possibility it might grow into a political union at some later date.

this talented man, it reflects his enthusiastic temperament and brilliant powers of persuasion. However I think it would take a Bismarck to affect a permanent unification of Germany and Austria in the midst of a war. This idea of a Great Germany was the dream of the great men of 1848.[43] But according to Naumann, the unification of these two countries is to be merely a prelude to the inclusion of the other neighboring nations. Most important among these nations are the three northern monarchies, the southeastern states of Serbia, Bulgaria and Rumania (?) as well as France (Italy) and, farther to the east, Poland, Finland and Courland. Middle Europe is to be organized as a federation of states which would resemble the empire of Charlemagne or of Napoleon Bonaparte. Naumann's thoughtful analysis reveals what imponderable advantages are to be gained from such a union. However he also presents a fascinating appraisal of the inherent difficulties of this ambitious enterprise. In spite of that, his brilliant work was not received with exceptional enthusiasm apart from a momentary flurry of polemics in the press. Therefore it is my opinion that Naumann shall be condemned to remain a prophet in the wilderness. At one point, in referring to Bismarck, the author cried out: "Oh, if he were only here now."

Halfway along our journey the conductor entered our car and announced that we would all have to get off at the next station because the train had been reserved—for Russians. This is not bad at all, [to transport] Russian prisoners of war in a Third Class train. But why not even in Second or First Class?

Then they came in their fur hats and brown coats and I observed them closely. For the most part they came from the Kirghiz and the Tungus [44] and some of them had really loathsome and repulsive faces. At one of the stops I became curious to see what they were doing and looked through a window. It

[43] During the German Revolution of 1848–49 some of the members of the All-German Frankfurt Parliament had advocated the formation of a Great German (Grossdeutsch) state which was to encompass many non-German areas formerly associated with the Holy Roman Empire and the Austrian monarchy.

[44] This refers to territories located in Russian Central Asia.

was amazing! There they lay all stretched out on the benches and a few of them were playing tarock [backgammon] while the old militiaman who was guarding them peered good-naturedly over their shoulders. . . .

Finally we arrived at Hanover with its huge, drafty station which was bustling with traffic. A few of my acquaintances were already in the Red Cross waiting room. Nothing was any longer as cheap and as good as last summer. The enthusiasm had vanished. . . .

I looked in vain for a place to sleep. Everything had been reserved for a troop transport. They need sleep more than I do, I thought as I walked on. In my boredom I wrote a half dozen postcards but the time seemed to stand still. I tried to get a little sleep sitting up but found that impossible. It was two o'clock on February 15, 1916, but the express to Bremen was not scheduled to leave until 4:16. I tried to sleep a little on a cold bench but the fear of arriving late kept waking me every ten minutes.

Finally—four o'clock! I slowly walked to the train with my suitcase and waited. A goodly number of my comrades from the *Helgoland* were there. I was so depressed that I greeted no one. Nevertheless I looked forward to seeing the "Big Heinrich" [45] once more and longed to crawl into my hammock. Our train pulled into Bremen shortly after seven. I had to choose between waiting here for another four hours or taking the next connection to Oldenburg. I knew Bremen well enough. Hence I chose the latter [alternative] because I also wanted to investigate the stories about the people of Oldenburg and their big feet. What I saw was not very complimentary to the local ladies. Several young women were washing the floors in the waiting room, and boy, what kind of boots they wore! Oh, well. . . .

On the other hand, the new railroad station was rather pleasant and well executed. At first it reminded one of a church with a tower and a clock. The entire building was constructed of glass brick in a curious, winding pattern. Painted on the

[45] This was the crew's nickname for the *Helgoland*.

main facade was an enormous map of the little state [of Olden-burg]. Almost every house and tree was represented *in* life-like size.

After having had several glasses of beer and some bread with sausage, I made a little excursion into town in order to aug-ment my geographic and ethnographic knowledge. All in all, I came to the conclusion that the people of Oldenburg live in high style [auf recht grossem Fusse]. Unfortunately I did not get to see the famous Count and, since I was all by myself, I did not dare to sing or whistle the "Oldenburger Song."

I slowly made my way back to the station, where I met my comrades who had been arriving from all directions and told them of my adventures and observations. Now came the final stage to Wilhelmshaven. Oh, what a dismal, forlorn and monotonous piece of track that was! Whenever I looked out of the window, I was reminded of the Po Valley in Lombardy! The train stopped almost every ten minutes and the last fifty kilometers seemed to take an eternity. To add to my troubles, the compartment was filled with a lot of drunkards from Ham-burg. But then the familiar forts of Mariensiel and Rüstersiel came into sight and the *Helgoland* greeted us over the treetops.

Everybody out! As I gazed at the physically and mentally exhausted men, I though that they looked like swaying appari-tions. Aha! What was going on? "There he is, the gun cap-tain!" I heard someone say. We were shamefully rounded up and escorted off like a transport of prisoners of war.

"All the men from the *Helgoland*, report outside!" shouted the petty officers. We reported in but it took a long time until everybody had arrived. On the way [back to the ship] we met some shipmates who informed us that we were to sail out tomorrow morning.

> At Aachen on the shield of the Post Office
> Again I saw the bird
> Whom I hated so deeply,
> Full of venom he peered down at me.
> You monstrous bird,

Should you ever
Fall into my hands,
I shall pluck out your feathers
And hack off your claws.[46]

I felt just the way Heinrich Heine [47] must have felt long ago when I spied the huge Prussian eagle over the date at the dock yard. ". . . Full of venom he peered down at me. . . ."

There it was once more, that gray monster, our prison. We were back again in our world of iron and water. Now we ceased being human. . . . For how much longer?

Our usually clean ship looked dreadful! Although the major work had been completed, the marrow-piercing rattle of the air drills, hammers and saws was still resounding in full force in the casemates. Thank God, we would clean the ship and remove this horrible dirt tomorrow morning.

It seemed strange that we were placed on alert every time we left the shipyard. Maybe it was because of the torpedo boat raid we had scheduled for tonight. Another possible cause was that our newest auxiliary cruiser the *Wolf* might attempt to break through the English blockade. I wonder if she will be as lucky as the *Möve*? I hope so! The origins of that mysterious ship [*Möve*], its size, its commander and so on, still puzzled the newspapers of the world.[48] We were often compelled to laugh because they printed so much nonsense about her.

Nothing happened, although we stayed out on patrol under

46 "Zu Aachen auf dem Posthausschild / Sah ich den Vogel wieder /
Der mir so tief verhasst / Voll Gift blickt er auf mich /
hernieder. Du hässlicher Vogel wirst Du einst / Mir in die
Hände fallen / Dann rupfe ich Dir die Federn aus / Und hacke
Dir ab die Krallen."

47 Heinrich Heine (1797–1856) was a romantic poet and essayist who so despised the reactionary nature of the German and Prussian state that he spent his life in exile in France working and writing for the cause of German freedom.

48 Between January 1 and February 25, 1916, the auxiliary cruiser *Möve* under the command of Count zu Dohna captured a total of 15 steamers. Since *Möve* sent her prizes to such disparate ports as Norfolk (Virginia) and Teneriffe (in the Canary Islands), she succeeded in utterly confusing the English. Moreover, one of the mines she laid was responsible for the sinking of the warship *King Edward*.

steam for two days. It was rumored that we were soon to head back into dock to adjust our steering gear. We remained at Wilhelmshaven Roads for about eight days and then headed back to port for another three days. 20 February 1916.

The battle disposition of the fleet is about to be changed. From now on, one full squadron will be stationed at the locks for a ten-day period while the other rests up in port. This new directive probably came from the new commander of the High Seas Fleet (Holtzendorff?). The previous one, Admiral von Pohl, died in an automobile accident at Hanover.[49] The newspapers had little to say about his death and kept it secret that he had been Chief of the High Seas Fleet. When he was originally appointed, we had high hopes in him and felt confident that he would soon lead us into battle and victory. However he, too, either could not or would not accept the enormous responsibility of braving a superior British fleet.

The English press reports that there are signs that the "Hun" fleet is planning an attack. I am inclined to regard these reports as authoritative. The military editor of the *Times* Colonel Repington[50] has predicted a number of events which actually came true at a later date. I specifically recall that he forecast our offensive against Serbia long before it materialized. Actually, however, I am in the best position to determine whether or not we are really preparing an attack. Judging from external evidence, I would say that the answer is both yes and no. By and large, it would not be a novelty if we were to launch a sortie into the North Sea. This occurred rather more frequently last year than now. What remains to be answered is

[49] On January 8, 1916, Admiral von Pohl fell seriously ill. Subsequently he was transferred to a hospital in Berlin where he died. However, he was not succeeded by Admiral Holtzendorff but by Vice Admiral Reinhard Scheer (1863–1928), the audacious and enterprising Commander of the Second Squadron.

[50] Colonel Charles A'Court Repington (1858–1925), a former officer in the Rifle Brigade and British military attache to Brussels and The Hague, compelled to resign from the army as a result of a personal scandal. He became the military correspondent of the London *Times* in 1904 and acquired world renown for his brilliant reporting of the Russo-Japanese war. However, Repington also had a reputation for revealing military secrets through his indiscretions.

how long will the sortie take, how far will it be carried and how often will it be repeated. In my personal estimation, a sortie of three days' duration reaching as far as the Dogger Bank would inevitably draw the English fleet into the area. I can hardly accuse our leaders of cowardly behavior for not embarking on such a perilous enterprise. Gradually we have all come to conclude that even the most favorable outcome of a sea battle would not suffice to assure us an access to the open sea. Therefore the only way we can successfully wage war upon our enemy's trade is by means of small weapons such as submarines and torpedo boats. But think of the immeasurably more advantageous position that England and France enjoy in respect to Germany. Should the English feel so inclined, they can make sure that not a single German merchant ship will ever again pass through the Channel. Perhaps then, despite everything, France will be forced to assist us in cutting perifidious Albion down to size.

However, on the other hand, if things go badly and our fleet is beaten or even destroyed by the English, it would hardly affect the outcome of the war. Although the English fleet would thus gain greater glory, it would not deprive us of a single potato or a loaf of bread. This, above all, is the decisive factor. That power which manages to hold out the longest will win the war and will be able to impose its terms upon the others. . . .

I will now describe a sensational event which delighted us, namely, the triumphal return of the *Möve*. The entire North Sea Fleet lay at general quarters off Voslapp on March 1 and 2. On this occasion everything had been prepared for battle; even the officers' quarters had been stripped. The officers wore their pistols in case it became necessary "to put weight behind their orders." But during the night of March 3 to 4 we merely raised anchor and sailed out on a northwesterly course. My knowledge of navigation told me that we sailed past the East Frisian Islands of Amrum and [Sylt] and then steamed along the coast. No one knew the purpose of our trip. However we began to understand at eight o'clock the next morning,

when the following telegram was posted on the bulletin board
near the wireless shack:

> Welcome home!
> From the Chief of the High Seas Fleet to H.M.S. *Möve*!

Even the skies seemed happy and a benign sun smiled down
upon us. It felt good to stand at my lookout post on the bridge
in such fine, warm weather. It was gradually turning to spring
and it would not be long before we observed the second anniversary of the war.

Just as the starboard watch sat down to eat, the free watch
was called to the port railing! As I came rushing up, I could
hear loud cheering from the other ships. And there she was,
the *Möve*, the world-renowned *Möve*! I need hardly mention
that when the First Officer gave the order to cheer, we responded frantically at the top of our lungs. Across from us
Möve responded with equal vigor. In fact, a number of Negroes dressed in blue shirts and red caps stood on her deck and,
incredibly enough, they also cheered. (I discovered later that
they were natives of German colonies.) When *Möve* had
come abreast to the last ship, the entire squadron performed a
beautiful about-face. It was an indescribably lovely scene. A
short distance away, the island of Helgoland glimmered in the
golden rays of the sun, the sea was dark green and it appeared
as though fifty primordial monsters were dancing a triumphal
dance around the returning *Möve*. I deeply regretted not having a camera on hand on this occasion. If I were a poet, I would
have tried to describe this unforgettably lovely scene. I would
also have depicted in stirring language the full, pure joy in the
men's hearts. Soon after the ships had quieted down again and
had reassembled in two orderly lines, we spotted five tiny
black dots on the horizon approaching very rapidly. Airplanes!
They did not want to miss the reception and wished to partake
in the general jubilation. When they were directly over the
Möve, they pounced down like hawks upon a hare. Their
engines came to almost a complete stop and I could discern each

turn of their propellers. At the moment of greatest suspense, when I thought that they would surely plunge into the sea, their engines sprang up again and the mighty birds performed lovely, elegant circles around their namesake the *Möve*.

Whether intentionally or not, we increased speed to 17 or 18 miles and the *Möve* soon fell behind. An hour and a half later, while the entire First Squadron was anchored off Wilhelmshaven for refueling, the *Möve* passed us again and went through the locks. She lowered the flags of the fifteen ships she had destroyed and the high signal tower gave her a twentyfold salute. By eight o'clock we had completed refueling. It was rumored that we were to sail out again the next day.

Today when the Commander of the Fleet seemed as though he were determined to confront the enemy, the situation began to look serious. For fourteen hours we had been steaming in a westerly direction and it did not appear as though we intended turning back. That morning the wireless had announced that our Zeppelins had bombed Hull and the area around Kent and Essex. It was a very happy prelude of even greater events about to occur. At about noon the *L 15*, which had participated in the bombardment, passed our line. All but two of her engines had been knocked out and she flew very low.[51] She had wired that she would follow the prevailing winds and attempt a landing at Maubeuge or Namur. We had another Zeppelin with us for reconnaissance purposes. That night our cruisers were to attack the coast while we covered their retreat. I wished them success on their mission. 4 March 1916.

Again we did not see any action! As I write this we are back safe and sound in the Jade Estuary without having fired a single shot! I shall never again hope for anything! Our morale has sunken to a new low. One of our officers, (L.A.) [Lieutenant Albrecht] insists that we have again been betrayed. But is it

---

[51] Stumpf is mistaken in this instance. The Zeppelin he sighted could not have been the *L 15*, since she had not flown this particular mission. The dirigible he saw was probably the *L 14*.

any wonder, with our smokestacks belching smoke two days in advance?

The English have extraordinary ———.[52]

As I write these lines, the memory of the past two days and our two sorties into the North Sea is still fresh in my mind. The whole thing came as a total surprise. By last Friday our Detail Officer had practically run out of tasks to keep us busy. We could no longer scrub the decks because of the lack of soap, and even the guns could only be cleaned twice a week because cotton, emory and oil were all in short supply. Hence they invented a simple trick called detail exercise. In order to kill time, some minor change in the fire prevention or repair procedure was announced at a lengthy lecture. Then we practiced it over and over all afternoon, until it was changed back again.

The entire First Squadron refueled on Friday afternoon, raising the suspicion that we would sail out. But then we scrubbed the ship clean again. What would there be left for us to do on Saturday? Detail exercises, of course! First we had an inspection, then a little calisthenics and then it began. "The following changes have been made," announced the Detail Officer at the beginning of his lecture. "In the future, at the order 'secure bulkheads,' the ship's bell will continue to sound five short rings. Henceforth, however, these will no longer sound one right after the other, but will come at intervals of thirty seconds, so as to avoid confusion with the fire alarm signal." Although we had been through all that before, they constantly introduced these changes. Then off went the bells and the good man stood there, clock in hand, until all the reports were in. In spite of all that, however, the old system still proved to be better and more practical.

However at that point we were brought back to reality. Some important telegrams must have come in. While we stood assembled on deck, the Executive Officer suddenly appeared and shouted, "Men, today we'll see some action! The English are out and a number of their planes have flown over the island of Sylt. We shall sail out right away and if we are in luck, we

[52] Sentence left incomplete.

shall catch a few of them. Now pack quickly and stow away your seabags. In all likelihood we'll clear decks for action as soon as we have passed through the mine fields. You need not change uniforms now, but keep your battle gear handy. Dismissed!"

In happy confusion and with smiling faces we rushed to pack and stow our things away. Within a half hour the casemates were empty and the gun turrets were ready for action.

On the bridge the lookouts and their assistants scanned the sky and the water for the enemy. Every few minutes the captain nervously asked how many of our boilers had steam up. "Ten, Captain!" "Staff Engineer, how many revolutions can you make?" "87, Sir!" "This is not enough; pour some oil on the fires!" "Already being done, Sir!"

A messenger came up and reported: "*Thüringen*, running at 100 revolutions." "Damn it, Staff Engineer, you had better give it all you have, otherwise we won't keep up!" "Yes Sir, Captain!" The telephone jangled. "What is the matter?" The engine room reported twelve engines under steam. "Fine! How many revolutions are we making now?" "106, Sir!" "Very well!" The ship groaned and trembled as the screws drove forward. The Captain asked the Officer of the Watch if the men had eaten. "No, Sir, Captain!" "Have them feed the men one watch at a time!" "Yes, Sir!" The nice odor of mutton and cabbage came streaming up from the galley. But there was no sign of the enemy. Our watch was relieved at 1:30 and now it was our turn to eat the mutton and cabbage.

The weather was fine with a limited visibility of 10 kilometers. This operated in our favor. This was the only way we would ever have a chance to make effective use of our 30.5 cm. guns against the far longer ranging English 38 cm. artillery. As far as I could see, our flanking cover was rather poor since it consisted exclusively of old cruisers such as *Frauenlob*, *Stuttgart*, *München*, etc. Where the others were, I did not know. Probably in Kiel!

My navigational skill told me that we were headed toward England on a northwesterly course. Gradually the general excitement subsided when we had finished eating and had sailed out further and there was still no enemy in sight. Some torpedo boats off our port fired at some mines.[53] (But since they refused to explode maybe they were merely cans.)

Soon I felt certain that the enemy had once more beaten a timely retreat. Although we knew nothing regarding his air raid on Schleswig, we were sure that it had not been a success. A mission like that required more than mere talk. At precisely five in the evening we received the command: "Entire Division, turn about!" Thank God! We would thus be back in port by ten o'clock and could still get a good night's sleep.

On the next day Sunday [March] 26, we repeated the entire procedure. I thought that we might have better luck this time. In the past whenever we made a sortie, the English would always sail out on the next day. Then the English and especially the Dutch papers would report that a strong English squadron had been sighted on the way to Helgoland. This always made us very angry. I often thought to myself: "If we had only sailed out today, we would surely have met up with them." But we never sailed out two days in a row. . . .

The Reichstag is up to some wild things these days. I am not referring to the scenes created by the Jew Liebknecht [54] and his supporters, but to the major parties who have passed a unanimous resolution demanding that we use our submarines and air force more vigorously than in the past.[55] I am rather

[53] Actually, an encounter between the German torpedo boat and some English light cruisers did take place during the night. The English cruiser *Cleopatra* rammed and sank torpedo boat *G 194*, while another German torpedo boat, *S 22*, exploded upon hitting a mine.

[54] Karl Liebknecht (1871–1919) was one of the leaders of the left wing of the German Social Democratic Party, which he represented as a deputy in both the Reichstag and the Prussian Diet. During the war he opposed his party's cooperation with the government and in December 1914 became the first Socialist to vote against war credits. Subsequently, he and Rosa Luxemburg founded the radical, revolutionary Spartacist group. On May Day, 1916, Liebknecht led an antiwar demonstration in Berlin for which he was sentenced to prison for the remainder of the war.

[55] In fact, it was not the Reichstag, but the Senior Committee of the Prussian Diet which in February 1916 presented a resolution in favor of a policy of unrestricted submarine warfare. There was no mention of the air war in the resolution. It read as follows: "The Committee would regard it detrimental to the interests of the country if the attitude of the

shocked to see the Reichstag concern itself with such matters. Formerly all good Germans were content to leave these questions to the competent authorities in the Supreme Command of the army and the navy.[56] Whenever the French and English parliaments used to fight over these issues we were always astonished and maintained that ours was a much better system. But in truth our authorities are [presently] divided on this issue. It has developed into a conflict between boldness and caution and the latter has triumphed: [Admiral] Tirpitz has been forced to resign. . . .[57]

However the people do not agree with this and are demanding that we use all our weapons without restraint. In the future the presence of Americans on hostile ships shall no longer deter us. Some quarters in the navy have even gone so far as to propose that any ship entering or departing from an enemy port be sunk without mercy.[58] Ten of our Zeppelins are to fly across

government toward America were to result in a restriction of our liberty in waging, at the proper time, an unimpeded and therefore fully effective submarine war against England." When some of the parties in the Reichstag sought to pass a similar resolution, Chancellor Bethmann-Hollweg managed to squash the debate. Nevertheless, during February and March the German press held a very heated debate over the submarine issue so that Stumpf could well think that such a resolution had actually been passed.

[56] According to the constitution of the German Empire, only the Kaiser, in his position as head of state and Supreme War Lord, possessed the power to decide such military-political issues. Although the Reichstag lacked the legal power to intervene in these matters, the liberal parties had long challenged the Kaiser's prerogatives. Paradoxically, it was not the liberals, but the parties of the Right who wanted to press for a decision in favor of unrestricted submarine warfare. Traditionally, the conservatives and nationalists (and in this instance Stumpf may be ranked among them) had always regarded such actions as an infringement upon the Kaiser's prerogatives.

[57] Bethmann-Hollweg feared that unrestricted submarine warfare would drive America into the war against Germany. Hence he opposed Admiral von Tirpitz's demands for such a campaign and finally managed to persuade the Kaiser to dismiss the rebellious Naval Secretary from office on March 14, 1916.

[58] On February 11, 1916, the German government drafted an announcement stating that Germany would commence waging a campaign of "extended" submarine warfare as of March 1. Henceforth all armed merchantmen would be considered as warships and could therefore be sunk without warning. However, Germany pledged herself to protect the rights of neutral ships.

the Channel every day to bomb any installation which might contribute to prolonging the war. This will compel the English to give in somewhat and to allow a decisive battle to be fought at sea. Many of us believe that three months of such unrestricted warfare will bring the war to an end.[59] But I am of the opinion that our government is seeking to protect itself in case this kind of warfare leads to trouble with America. In that instance it would be an inestimable advantage for the government if it could turn to the Reichstag and say, "This is how you wanted it." [60]

A most vital right, the power to decide by what means the war is to be conducted, is thus slowly but surely falling into the hands of the Reichstag. Although I have no comment to make on this right now, I hope to God that the exclusive right to decide [these questions] will never be handed over to a representative body like this one. . . . 29 March 1916.

[59] This is an overly optimistic estimate. Even the Chief of the Naval Staff Admiral von Holtzendorff, who had now become a staunch advocate of submarine warfare, did not think that a totally unrestricted campaign could force England to sue for peace in less than six to eight months.

[60] This is not correct. Bethmann-Hollweg realized the danger which Germany ran in conducting this type of warfare and tried with all the power at his disposal to restrain the hotheads in the navy and the Reichstag from pushing Germany into an undesirable war with America.

End of Book II

Three

It looks like we have surmounted a serious food shortage, especially our shortage of potatoes. However the weather has warmed up nicely so this useful vegetable can once again be shipped by rail without danger of freezing. Of course there is no surplus but it does seem as though we are past the most critical stage. Hardly a day goes by without our sinking a half dozen English freighters or blockade runners. The English are in an uproar and the entire world has come to realize that Germany's great power is by no means exhausted. Our mysterious fish [the submarines] are even to be found swimming right in the middle of the English Channel.

In regard to the air raid on Schleswig, it has been announced that no fewer than three, about half of the [British] planes, have fallen into our hands. It seems very likely that one of their large destroyers the *Medusa* has run over a mine and has been sunk. One of our torpedo boats is also missing. I need hardly mention that we returned from Sunday's wild-goose chase without having sighted the enemy. To make up for our lost Sunday rest we got some time off Monday afternoon. On Tuesday we took on 500 tons of coal.

Something unusual seems to be going on in Holland. Her army and navy have been mobilized again and all leaves have been canceled.[1] This may well be the reason why we have to maintain a constant state of alert. Rumors abound in unprecedented volume. I personally feel that we have no cause for alarm since it is inconceivable that the Dutch would ever attack us. Of course we may not find it possible much longer to tolerate that the Rhine, our country's symbol, should flow to the sea through non-German territory. However I am confident that we shall be able to work out a mutually acceptable solution when the map of Europe is revised. But this is of no importance now. What is most important is that we obtain as much food as possible from this predominantly agrarian nation and that some of our industrial products make their way to foreign markets via Rotterdam. This ought to suffice to keep alive this little country's innate hatred of perfidious Albion. Since the Japanese are just looking for an excuse to get their clutches on the East Indian colonies of Sumatra, Java and Borneo, I wonder if they are not somehow responsible [for the present tension]. I hardly think that the English will invade the Netherlands. The Dutch would make it very uncomfortable for them. Besides, the lesson they learned at Gallipoli ought to stifle all such attempts.

This is ideal weather for our Zeppelins and they are making the most of it. On [March] 30, six of them crossed the Channel and bombed London.[2] The *L 15*, which had experienced engine trouble and had been hit on a previous occasion, was unfortu-

[1] On March 16, 1916, the Dutch steamer *Tubantia* was sunk thirty miles off the Dutch coast. Although the German government denied that any of its submarines had been operating in the area, the Dutch refused to believe this. There was much talk of war, and the Dutch parliament was called into session to discuss taking military precautions.

[2] At the end of March 1916, German airships flew five successive missions against England in as many nights.

nately hit even more severely this time and was forced to land in the middle of the Thames. Commendably enough, an [English] patrol boat rescued her entire crew (although this was by no means heroic). Then the triumphant English took the badly damaged balloon in tow as their prize. However our crew must have set the scuttling charges, for the ship blew up ten minutes later. After all, it must be kept in mind that she was manned by a German and not an English crew. The latter would no doubt have deserted their ship without ever thinking of destroying her. This is exactly what happened to three of their aircraft at Sylt. Two of them recently arrived at our local airport. They were brand-new machines built in America with English engines and they were painted in the French colors. Here was the entire Triple Entente all in one. Yet when our German planes chased after them, they went down and got hopelessly stuck in the mud. 2 April 1916.

Since our return to port we have been on alert every evening. This means that the ship has to be ready to go to sea within an hour. Hence after eight o'clock we maintain steam in eight of our boilers. During this time the entire crew, with the exception of the officers not on duty, has to remain on board. Our Zeppelins flew over for the third time last night and caused tremendous destruction in Yarmouth, London and Edinburgh. At about seven this morning I observed the return of our giant birds.

Although we are extremely pleased with this very vigorous conduct of the war, it is still not enough. We ought to send at least fifteen of them over every day. But this is easier said than done! Any day now we expect the English fleet to seek its revenge. And we wait and wait. . . .

Since it is impossible to keep thinking about the war all the time, our petty problems have risen to the forefront again. We spend most of our time worrying about our bellies. Not only the sailors but also the petty officers, the warrant officers and even the officers are embittered and dissatisfied with our present rations. Particularly the officers, who have not yet learned the meaning of suffering and hardship, complain the loudest since they no longer get their fried eggs for breakfast. But since they have always worshiped their bellies and other creature comforts, they hardly matter.

Nowadays we even complain about the most reasonable measures. Many of us have become so accustomed to complaining that we hardly notice it any more. It is true that our rations are no longer as good or as plentiful as before. I sometimes find myself leaving the table with a ravenous hunger. But many of us merely mutter and complain, refusing to realize that we are at war and that we have to conserve our food supplies. The only concern of this despicable rabble is their bellies. Since I often criticize these defeatists in strong terms, I have acquired a reputation for being "patriotic." In all fairness we must admit that we are still much better off than our troops in the trenches at the front. Interrupted on the afternoon of 4 April 1916.

Once again I am sitting here not knowing what to do with myself. Lately I have developed a strange aversion for any sort of physical or mental exercise. This was not formerly true when I used to work like the devil. Nowadays I start all sorts of projects without ever completing them. I began to build a ship [model] and now it lies discarded in a corner. I am no longer making any progress in stenography. For a while I was very enthusiastic about solving mathematical problems but I found it so exhausting that I could barely get up for reveille at 6:30. Although this may be due to the stale air, it never affected me this way before. The only thing for which I can still muster up some energy is to read the newspapers. I pick up any newspaper I can find. Right now the papers are filled with descriptions of the Battle of Verdun. This battlefield constitutes a burial ground for the French army. We seem to be less interested in taking the fortress than inflicting the greatest possible number of casualties upon the enemy. This is one of the innovations of this war.[3]

---

[3] The great Battle of Verdun began on February 21, 1916, and lasted until well into July. General Erich von Falkenhayn (1861–1922), the Chief of the German General Staff, adopted a new strategy which gave up the idea of breaking through the French lines in order to win the war. Instead he insisted that the same effect would be achieved by selecting a

But this is not the place for this kind of thing. Originally my diary was to record only my personal experiences and observations. But what can I do since I am in the navy and thus have no experiences and see very little? On the other hand, I would have a great deal to record were I to write about all the petty persecutions and injustices to which we are subjected by some of our officers. Hence I content myself with recording an occasional exceptional incident. Most of the time we bear it good-naturedly, laugh it off and then forget all about it. Let us act on the principle, "To understand is to forgive." We realize that you [officers] would have to be insane not to take advantage of the power which your stupidity, your birth and to a lesser extent your wealth, has conferred upon you. You do not demand that we honor and respect you or regard you as the saviors of our Fatherland. Instead you ask us to regard you as [useless] drones. Hence you will surely not be angry if we break your arrogance and topple you from the high pedestal upon which you have been placed by the ignorant masses.

Although this might be quite difficult to achieve, it is well worth the effort. I certainly do not oppose paying our officials and officers even higher salaries in the future. But they must do something concrete and positive for them so as to set a good

---

target which the French would have to defend at all costs for sentimental reasons, and for the retention of which, he figured "the French command would be compelled to throw in every man they have" until they were so exhausted that they would be forced to surrender. This is what Falkenhayn called his strategy of attrition. Although the Germans succeeded in taking some of Verdun's outer defenses, the fortress itself never fell. However, its stubborn defense cost the French army 460,000 casualties, while the Germans lost only 300,000 men.

Nevertheless, Falkenhayn's failure to capture Verdun led to his dismissal on August 29, 1916. He was replaced by the formidable military team of Hindenburg and Ludendorff, who assumed office as Chief of the General Staff and First Quartermaster General. The historical importance of their promotion cannot be overestimated. The two generals launched an immediate attack upon the conduct of the war and the foreign policies of the Imperial Chancellor von Bethmann-Hollweg, persuaded the Kaiser to issue his fateful order for the commencement of a campaign of unrestricted submarine warfare on January 9, 1917, and finally succeeded in July of that year in establishing their complete dominion over the civilian government of Germany by deposing Bethmann-Hollweg and having a more compliant successor appointed in his place.

example for our decent and hardworking people. A Kapitän-leutnant, for instance, earns a monthly salary of 650 marks. But what does he do for the state and the public? He cleans and polishes his fingernails, combs his hair and only performs his duties when we are at sea. Of course there are a hundred exceptions! There are certainly some praiseworthy, exceptional officers who concern themselves with our problems, who are a credit to their profession and who serve as models for us. But I can count them on half the fingers of one hand. Why should they behave in such a manner? After all, their positions are secure and they are promoted even if they do not demonstrate any intellectual prowess. What more could they want? One can become a lieutenant at nineteen and earn a salary in excess of 300 marks. Hence where can one find a better career than in the Imperial Navy?

Of course none of these noble gentlemen considers how much sweat has gone into their salaries when they get paid at the beginning of the month. They sneer at and despise the dockworkers and the miners even though they are the ones who pay for their golden stripes and buttons. In their eyes anyone who does not wear a star and gold braid is a plebeian and a ruffian.

I am not proposing that the salary of the average officer or official be reduced. But I would welcome the elimination of about two thirds of our top-ranking officers. There are about twenty superfluous officers on our ship. To name merely a few, there are the turret officers who do more harm than good, then there is the Navigation Officer whose job is performed by the helmsmen anyway, and the First Turret Officer who can be replaced by a petty officer.

Almost every day some sailor whose parents have requested that he be given leave is told that he cannot be spared from the ship. But this merely softens the blow. How can one reconcile this petty attitude with the following example: The Second Artillery Officer, who in the course of a battle is in charge of our entire medium artillery, received 16 (sixteen!) weeks of leave for the alleged purpose of regaining his health. In the interim a lieutenant took over his "functions" in addition to his own duties and his absence was hardly noticeable. Many of us have already forgotten that we ever had an extra Second Artillery Officer. Moreover just consider that this is one of our most important jobs which no one would think of abolishing. However I could cite numerous other examples.

Our Division Officer First Lieutenant [Kohrt] swallowed a fish bone and had to have his appendix removed. We all welcomed his absence. Now a half-grown ensign has been placed in charge of our entire division. He will thus have men under his command who have been in the navy since before he was born. . . .

Enough of this for today! There shall be plenty of other opportunities for me to write of the things which depress me and those which gladden my spirits.

During the past two weeks virtually nothing worth mentioning has occurred. We have become accustomed to being on a perpetual state of alert. This is due more to the personality of our new Chief of the High Seas Fleet Admiral Scheer than either the increased activity of the enemy or our own offensive preparations. Scheer is extremely cautious. Whenever our Zeppelins conduct a raid, he orders the cruisers to sail out while the battleships lie at the ready off the mine fields. We find it inconvenient to have to keep stowing our gear away. But as a result of one of his innovations, we now spend ten days on forward patrol, followed by five days at the roadstead and then five days in port. While we were delighted by this, the officers were less pleased because they could no longer sleep at home every night. On Easter Sunday we were scheduled to head into port but instead we were ordered out for five more days of forward patrol duty. However it hardly mattered to us, since we no longer cared whether we were at sea or in port. Ascension Thursday, 20 April 1916.

Today, Good Friday, while I am writing, the Great Procession is no doubt under way back at home. And here I sit in utter boredom. Outside the sun is shining with all its might and is turning the trees and shrubs to a delicate green. Ordinarily I would have been delighted to go for a stroll in this early spring weather. But not now! If I were now to go on deck the sun would still give me a friendly smile, but instead of the green foliage and the people in their holiday finery, all I could see would be the dirty yellow waters of the Jade and a few fog-enshrouded houses of Wilhelmshaven.

Good Friday! A picture of the past moved before my eyes. I could see a pious boy assisting with holy shyness and reverence at early mass. I could hear the sound of the gong which substituted for the broken bell in calling the congregation to church. I remembered the Good Friday when my blessed mother was on her deathbed and the one just before my first Holy Communion. I remembered piously and reverently kissing the cross in the Liebfrauenkirche in Nuremberg as a young man. [I recalled] Good Friday in Switzerland, Good Friday in Munich, and today for the fourth time Good Friday in the navy! Yes, each day of this horrible war represents a Good Friday for some unhappy family whose dear brother, father or relative has offered up his life for his fellowmen.

Today all music and singing is forbidden on board, giving me a chance to concentrate in peace on my reading and writing. Will it be as quiet and peaceful at Verdun [4] and Dünaberg,[5] at the Isonzo [6] and in Mesopotamia? [7] I fear not! There the soldiers will break Christ's commandment, "Thou shalt not kill,"

[4] The German armies launched a new assault on Verdun on March 6, 1916. The fighting raged uninterruptedly until April 10 and resulted in enormous casualty rates on both sides.

[5] This refers to the Battle of Lake Naroch (March 19–April 30, 1916), in which the Russians embarked upon an inconclusive offensive along the Eastern Front in order to relieve the German pressure on the French at Verdun.

[6] This refers to the Fifth Battle of the Isonzo on the Northern Italian Front (February 15–March 17, 1916), the product of an unsuccessful Austrian attempt to turn the Italian rear in the Trentino.

[7] In Mesopotamia the Turks (with a token German contribution), at the end of April, 1916, compelled the surrender of a British garrison at Kut-al-Imara.

and will do everything within their power to kill as many enemies as possible. Oh, what an unholy time we live in!

Mother Nature has done all she can to heal the wounds of the winter and of the war. Even the trenches which had soaked up so much warm blood are now bordered with white daisies, and blue violets bloom inconspicuously next to yellow primroses and red dandelions. The soil has become our ally against our enemies, who begrudge us our daily bread. Within her bosom she is nurturing a future crop of golden wheat, while even now radishes and spinach add a welcome change to the menu. Our most difficult time is over and hopefully this year will grant us a more bountiful harvest than the last. As soon as our people get enough food once more, their discontent and depression shall vanish like snow in the sun! However I hope that by next Good Friday we shall again bask in peace and that the nations will find it possible to conciliate their differences for the sake of their common culture and faith. 21 April 1916.

At six this morning all the ships in Wilhelmshaven sounded the general alarm. What could be the matter? Great clouds of smoke hovered over the town. When I climbed the foremast I discovered that it was our torpedo boats who were raising steam and causing the smoke. We were just spreading out our nets when we [received orders] to prepare to leave on a long trip by eight o'clock. What could be the matter?

EASTER 1916

Easter had come and the warm spring sun was shining brilliantly upon the wide, wide sea. The embankment near Schillig has turned green overnight. Although we sailed out for quite a distance yesterday, we soon changed our minds and turned about. Now we are back at our advanced stations. This is one of the very few days in the entire year when the whole North Sea was clear. The island of Wangerooge seemed to be close enough to touch and the great hotels at the beach could be seen down to the last detail. Yesterday's alarm proved to be a real fiasco. Seven warrant officers, six petty officers and a full dozen orderlies were still missing this morning. They had missed their train connection yesterday and wandered around in the North Sea on the fleet tender until four in the morning. Since we have ceased all battle preparations, the danger is apparently over. This morning we had an inspection in our third-class blue uniforms! The Imperial Navy cannot exist without inspections. The officers have planned a big dinner for this evening and have already reserved the band. 23 April 1916.

Recently they introduced a fine new measure which allows us to sleep until seven on Sundays. This time we even got two days in a row! On the second day, however, I awoke at six o'clock and dreamed of the folks at home, of girls, of the war and the future. Then I heard someone on the signal deck shouting, "Antiaircraft crew, rise and shine. Prepare to raise anchor." At first I thought it was an air raid. The shouting woke the men who, according to their respective dispositions, either muttered, laughed or cursed. "Everyone get up. Pack and stow gear immediately!" This was something more than an air raid. Since our breakfast was postponed until later, everything proceeded like lightning. Within less than an hour the entire squadron had sailed up to the mine fields and dropped anchor.

It was a glorious day, even nicer than the previous one. At eleven o'clock when all hands were summoned on deck, something very astonishing and unprecedented happened. What a beautiful scene! Four of our majestic Zeppelins flew overhead surrounded by a swarm of six aquaplanes. Our cruisers and their escorts were already under way. The men's faces reflected some of the enthusiasm which had been so evident at the time of mobilization. At first I thought that the Executive Officer had merely called us on deck to allow the loafers and skat players to inhale some of the delicious Easter air. But no! The captain himself appeared, stepped on a small gun and bade us to gather around. "I want to tell you," he began, "what lies ahead of us. We are on our way to England, where our cruisers will bombard the cities of Yarmouth and Lowestoft with their heavy and medium artillery. Yesterday a prize commando was sent out to capture all ships in the vicinity of the Dogger Bank.

Originally it was intended that a division from our squadron go along. But since our ships might suddenly meet the English fleet and everything will then depend on speed, this order has been rescinded. Consequently, we shall provide cover for our cruisers but maybe we will still be lucky enough to meet the enemy. . . . Nothing at all can happen to us . . . !" He uttered this sentence with such a serious face and with such deep and profound conviction that all of us laughed in agreement, "It is quite true," he continued undisturbed, "our ships are built so soundly that nothing can happen.[8] Just wait and see! While one watch is on duty, the other will sleep fully clothed at the guns. Tomorrow morning at dawn, however, we shall post both watches because we might unexpectedly stumble upon the enemy in the darkness. Then whoever gets to fire first will have the advantage. I shall again allow one of the watches to go to sleep as soon as it turns light. I want to warn all the gun captains not to be impatient and to remain calm. We must not fire one shot too many and must not miss! Dismissed! Hearty appetite!"

I must admit that I was very impressed by this short but confident speech. It felt good and it was fun to be informed in advance of what was going on. In my estimation, whenever our fleet sails in keel formation it presents an incomparably beautiful sight. Suddenly at about four o'clock we received a signal: "16 points to starboard," which really meant, "Entire division, about turn." Again we were deeply disappointed! However our disappointment vanished as soon as we received orders to resume our northwesterly course. Later on I discovered that the confusion developed when *Seydlitz* hit a mine and it was feared that it might be a submarine. I understand that the cruiser remained afloat and steamed home at a speed of

---

[8] Admiral Reinhard Scheer, the enterprising Commander of the German High Seas Fleet, hoped to accomplish two aims by means of his sortie of April 24. First, he wanted to bomb Lowestoft, a mine-laying center, and Yarmouth, an English submarine base. More importantly, he hoped thereby to lure some part of the English fleet out into the open to engage it in battle. Scheer's plan was uncommonly daring, for none of his predecessors had ever contemplated deliberately seeking out the English fleet in battle.

15 miles. This was our second accident in eight days. Last
Saturday afternoon *Graudenz* was towed in after she, too, had
hit a mine. These losses are very serious! Nevertheless we continued on our way. A large number of mines were floating
about that day and soon it thundered fore and aft as our torpedo boats commenced firing at these lethal sea roses.

It was an extraordinarily lovely evening as the sun sank in
the west. The deck vibrated softly to the tempo of the untir-
ing, booming noise of the engines. Gradually the shape of our
helmsman became darker and less distinct. Soon only the small
white light of the bow lantern remained to guide him. Even
though it had been a bright and clear day, the night was pitch
black. This meant that we had to be extra careful. Now and
then a night signal would flare up for three seconds, indicating
some change in our course anywhere from a quarter to a full
turn. From twelve to four I stood watch as a lookout on the
bridge. Needless to say, we all tried our best to penetrate the
darkness. At 3:30 when it began to dawn in the east, we suddenly caught sight of two Dutch fishing boats. Since we were
certain that they had been stopped before, we left them alone.
We kept up a speed of 15 miles and one of the boats raced with
us for half an hour.

Now the sky turned red and our tension reached a breaking
point. We might meet the enemy any second now. And indeed
several columns of smoke appeared on the horizon but they
were from our own cruisers and torpedo boats. Since it was
getting lighter now, our cruisers must already have started their
bombardment. Would their difficult mission be a success?
When would they send out their appointed signal for help?
Would we get to fight? Four o'clock! My relief was here!
"What's going on?" "Nothing much. Keep a sharp watch out
for mines and torpedoes. There is a cruiser off our port bow.
The torpedo boats are diagonally across from us and there is
a balloon at 30 degrees." "Nothing else?" "No. Have a nice
watch! Good night."

Now I quickly jumped into my hammock for two hours.

Perhaps we would be wakened by the alarm, "Clear ship for action." Soon I was in the soft arms of Morpheus.

A vigorous knocking on the bulkhead door roused me from my sweet slumber. I glanced at my watch. Seven o'clock! Nothing had happened! Feeling depressed and heavy-hearted, I tied up my hammock and climbed up on deck to wash my-self. There was nothing in sight far and wide. The visibility had become extremely good again. Once more the sun shone full blast and its light penetrated deeply into the transparent, dark-green water. What had happened to last night's beautiful sea glow? Where were the billions upon billions of tiny ani-mals whose phosphorescent lights created the illusion that the ocean consisted of shimmering and sparkling gems? I learned that we had just received a wireless message telling us that our cruisers had completed their mission and were now engaged in battle with some English light units. This was good news. Now the whole world would be informed that a "squadron of child murderers" had again attacked a defenseless English city and that an old man, a woman and a baby had been killed. But where was the English navy? Probably at the Firth of Forth!

Our trip home turned out to be as nice as the one out. Of course our sense of anticipation had disappeared but neverthe-less there was still a great deal to see. The English made an attempt to intercept us with their submarines on our way home. Our ships were forced to leave formation at least six times to evade onrushing torpedoes. At one point, just at twelve o'clock, a submarine came between us and the Second Squad-ron on our right. When they sighted it [they commenced firing] and suddenly shells began to land a thousand meters away from us. *Ostfriesland* narrowly missed being hit in the bow by a torpedo. Then the entire squadron quickly veered left and sped off at full speed. A torpedo boat stayed behind and fired twenty charges into the water but I don't know whether she scored a hit.

Soon we sighted the beacon at Terschelling, marking the entrance of the Scheldt into Vlisslingen. Antwerp was just be-hind. There is where Mr. Churchill's marines headed when they fled from beleaguered Antwerp. No doubt they spotted us and tomorrow there would be a report that a squadron of twenty-five German battleships had passed the heights of Terschelling. This must be near the spot where *Hogue*, *Aboukir* and *Cressy* found their final resting place after their encounter with Master Weddingen.[9] The Dutch islands of Baldrum and Hörnum appeared, then followed ————.[10]

I calculated that we could expect to be home by about nine o'clock. While this was not bad, it would be considerably less pleasant to have to stand the dogwatch tonight. We proceeded at a racing speed of 15 miles and soon up ahead rose the light tower of the island after which our ship was named. A patrol boat wired a report that an enemy submarine had been sighted ten miles away between Wangerooge and Helgoland. Hence we were ordered to raise our speed to 18 miles in this danger zone. Although we did not see anything, we arrived at the Jade Estuary an hour earlier than expected. Since the Second Squadron had sailed on to the Elbe, we had no activities scheduled for the next few days. Later we would have five days of patrol duty before heading into port again.

About an hour and a half after we had dropped anchor, our cruiser squadron slowly drifted in. First came *Lützow* followed after a slight distance by *Derfflinger*, *Moltke* and *Von der Tann*. Although these ships had met with greater success on this mission than ever before and must have left Yarmouth and Lowestoft in utter ruin, they were not received with cheers or rejoicing. They passed by very slowly as though they were mourning for their heavily damaged sister *Seydlitz*, which was refitting in dock.[11] They resembled a herd of utterly exhausted bulls returning to their pens.

Our prize crew came back on a torpedo boat. The men brought very good news that they had sunk *King Stephen*, the fishing boat which had been so lacking in mercy as to refuse to

---

[9] This incident took place on September 22, 1914.
[10] Sentence left incomplete.
[11] *Seydlitz* had a huge hole torn in her side, had taken on 1,400 tons of water, and eleven of her men had been killed.

help rescue the crew of our *L 15*.[12] They said that the English-men had begged for mercy and had assured them that they were not the same crew as the one of four weeks ago. Although this seemed rather unlikely, it was not totally impossible and there-fore our men gave up the thought of taking revenge.

All our ships were to refuel the next day. By nine that morn-ing we had cleared the ship, had sailed to Wilhelmshaven Roads and had already brought out the coaling tackle, when a telegram arrived [with the order]: "Cease coaling. Raise steam for speed of 15 miles." Aha! The English had come to repay us for yester-day's visit. Thus we repacked and re-stowed [the equipment] and had barely been under way for an hour when a counter-order arrived to resume coaling. So there! We went back again. Our bunkers were considerably lighter since our two sorties must have burned up from 700 to 800 tons which it took us until late that night to load. After the worst of the dirt had been removed, we all went to sleep.

As soon as we have completed our five days of forward patrol duty, our division will head into port. 25 April 1916.

This time we were in luck. We had incredibly lovely and warm summer weather. Now that everything was green and blooming, it was a pleasure to stroll about. But unfortunately, we were on a two-hour alert and could not go on longer excur-sions. In all probability we will have to put into dock for two days to repair the cylinder of our port engine. Then we are to take a long excursion to Varel or Nauen. 27 April 1916.

There was much discussion about the [recent] introduction of daylight saving time. The newspapers, lacking any other news to report, devoted long leading articles of varying intel-ligence to it. Since we were to set our watches ahead by an hour from eleven to twelve during the night of [April] 30 to [May] 1, it worked out to my advantage in that I gained an hour off from my duties.

On May 1 we went on the long trip that we had planned. The weather could not have been lovelier. We rode out on a chartered train while the band played. We did not demonstrate

[12] Stumpf means the *L 19.*

for the eight-hour day, for world peace, or for the franchise, but for something much more practical, something which made us happy and gay. The rare view of the freshness of May, of the green primeval forest and of the clean little Dutch-looking houses reminded us of home and we could not stop singing and rejoicing.

The enlisted men of the navy detest their officers and the state of Oldenburg and its people more than anything else in the world. I myself have always held this desolate land and its clumsy, ungainly people in contempt. But I have had to rescind most of my unfavorable and prejudiced views since I visited the Bockhorn and wandered in its unique forest. I had to admit that I had seen few such beautiful, real primeval forests in which no tree or shrub had been touched by man. The animals, especially the deer, were so tame that they allowed us to come quite close. I have already said that the tiny scattered houses were meticulously clean. But I was most amazed by the lovely and rare decorative shrubbery which surrounded the gardens. There were Japanese apricot trees with blossoms as big as a fist. Weeping willows and lilies alternated in a most delightful manner with apple, pear and plum trees in full bloom. It is quite possible that I found everything so beautiful because I rarely had a chance to see these things. Maybe if I had had an opportunity to meet the people I would have had to change my opinion of them, too. It seemed to me that people who nursed their gardens with such care and who maintained such clean homes could not possibly be as stupid and as clumsy as many of us imagined.

Today is the first of May! Perhaps this morning the sun discovered, upon arising, that the people of the earth had taken advantage of her by setting their clocks ahead to make better use of her light and her warming rays. Surely, however, she will not hold this against Germany and will continue to shine down on her grain and potatoes so that we may have the bumper crop which we all expect.

Our people seem slightly depressed at the present time. This is not due to the existence of a military stalemate on all our fronts. Instead it comes from the shameless food-profiteering which is going on. Despite all the sharp governmental and police regulations, this shameful profiteering still goes on in Germany. I read about it in the Berliner *Tag*, a paper which no one could accuse of sensational journalism. From now on all imported food will first have to pass through the hands of the Central Purchasing Agency [Zentraleinkaufsgesellschaft] in Berlin before it is shipped on to the rest of the country at a legally fixed maximum price.[13] For example, no one is allowed to purchase fats from Holland. Even if one were to receive some fat in a gift parcel, one would not be allowed to keep it. However it is quite evident that a small number of gentlemen at the Central Purchasing Agency cannot overnight do the kind of a job which was formerly performed by thousands of clever merchants. Since the Agency has committed itself to maintain its maximum prices, it will find it impossible to purchase all the food we require. The foreign nations will sell their pork and butter to the enemy because he is willing to pay a higher price. However the complaint of the nation, especially from the south, will not and cannot be silenced. Many of our larger cities receive only 100 kilograms of butter although they absolutely need 5,000 kilograms. This is the other side of the coin. Whenever a commodity is placed under price control, it soon disappears from the market. Therefore what good are meat-ration coupons when meat is unobtainable?

Another thing which is causing our good Germans a great deal of concern is the attitude which the President of the United States has taken against us.[14] I have already spoken out

[13] The Central Purchasing Agency was founded at the end of 1915 by Secretary of the Treasury Karl Helfferich (1872–1924) in order to improve Germany's bargaining position in the purchase of food supplies from neutral nations. By 1916 the personnel of the Z.E.G. numbered over 4,000 men and had succeeded in outbidding British buyers in Holland and Denmark.

[14] On March 24, 1916, a German submarine torpedoed the Channel steamer *Sussex*, killing and injuring eighty of her passengers. Although there were twenty-five Americans on board, only two were injured. As a result of the *Sussex* incident, President Wilson on April 18, 1916, sent a note stating that unless the German government "should now immediately declare and affect an abandonment of its present methods of

strongly about the disloyal Italians, the perfidious nature of England and the misguided French but all of them put together have not harmed us nearly as much as the Americans. In our last note to them we pointed out that hundreds of thousands of our children had been orphaned by American munitions and that millions of our families are in direst need because of America's toleration of the blockade. But our note made no impression at all. The Americans replied that "humanity" would not allow them to tolerate the stopping of merchant vessels upon the high seas and the transfer of the passengers to fragile boats. These [American] criminals always invoke "humanity" and "Christianity" whenever cutthroat competition and profits are involved. It is infuriating and drives one to tears to read these things. While the German lion is fighting for its life, America is trying to kick him in the pants. I was truly pleased to read the German reply, which in my opinion was forceful, dignified, confident and yet still open to negotiation. But I feel that it has merely postponed the outbreak of hostilities for another three months.[15] I suspect that the [American] "Republic" will copy the Portuguese gangsters by saying: "Although I am not willing to fight, I shall steal your ships." [16]

Speaking of stealing, I have several stories on that subject which I would like to write down. The first deals with the sudden disappearance of a cash box from the ensigns' mess. Since it contained 150 marks, it constituted sufficient grounds to make all the men unpack their seabags. But they found nothing

submarine warfare against passengers and freight-carrying vessels, the Government of the United States can have no other choice but to sever diplomatic relations with the German Empire altogether." It was this new and belligerent American attitude that worried Stumpf.

[15] On May 4, 1916, the German government issued the so-called Sussex pledge to President Wilson. It promised that in the future German submarines would no longer sink without warning and without saving of human lives any merchant ship unless these ships tried to escape or offered resistance. This pledge, however, was made conditional upon the lifting of the British blockade of Germany. On May 8 President Wilson replied stating that America refused to accept this last provision. In the light of this strong stand, the German navy, on May 10, felt impelled to stop its raids upon merchant shipping altogether.

[16] On March 9, 1916, Germany had declared war on Portugal after the seizure by that nation of all German shipping in the port of Lisbon.

except that one of our stewards had 150 marks in his possession which he claimed to have earned by selling cigarettes. The captain seemed to believe this strange story but he nevertheless punished the man and also confiscated his money. The second story is even more sensational and bears the title: "The robbery of the food locker."

On Wednesday morning the men in the galley discovered that someone had broken into the supply room. The center cover as well as the bulkhead door leading into the supply room had been forced open and two cheeses and a number of cans of sardines had been stolen. We all smirked upon hearing of it. Whenever anyone repeated the story, he would add that he thought that it was all a fake, that there had been no real break-in and that the cheese must have disappeared some other way. I thought so, too, because I well knew that certain men whom we called "cruisers" made off with a considerable amount of food.

The incident created a great sensation and the Executive Officer assembled the entire crew on deck and delivered a fulminating, thundering speech: "It is a crying shame that there are such thieves among you. One man could not have done it; at least twenty of you know who did it. I hope that we catch the culprit soon, otherwise I shall be compelled to take steps to prevent such crimes [in the future]. I shall post a guard in front of each door—six men, all told. However since I have no way of knowing whether the culprits were sailors or stokers—I am personally inclined to believe the latter—I shall order both [contingents] to provide one half of the guard. Furthermore I shall not issue any extra rations for eight days. In the future you will get these only twice a week, and no more than is coming to you!"

This touched the sailors where it hurt most. "What! Eight days of this dry garbage??!! I'll write to Liebknecht about that!" "He too eats dry slop because he is in jail," someone replied argumentatively.[17]

[17] The Spartacist leader Karl Liebknecht was arrested and confined to prison in May 1916 for leading an antiwar demonstration in Berlin.

In order to kill some time we conducted net maneuvers that afternoon. When I passed through the midship casemates I observed Bosun's Mate R—— and several other men rushing by in evident haste. What could be the matter, I thought to myself as I followed right after them. [I saw] one of the sailors reach into an airshaft and pull something out with a triumphant shout. "Aha! Here is one of the cheeses." Soon thereafter an order was sounded for the band to form without instruments at the starboard side of the middle deck. It was getting funnier all the time. Was the other cheese hidden in the bass drum? Although we were still in the dark, we all assembled with the exception of my good friend [Maxe]. Then he, too, made a sudden appearance. Everyone wanted to know what the band was doing. One of the comedians in the band asserted that the Detail Officer had taken a whiff of his instrument locker, had smelled his socks and thought that it was the cheese.

Then we were informed that the band could go but that a certain stoker was to see the Executive Officer. I said, "This can only mean that he will be interrogated." While we had been standing in formation the Detail Officer had one of the stokers look over the band to identify the guilty party. It was [Maxe]. The case was actually solved last night when this same stoker had spotted the thief climbing up the stairs carrying a bag. However he could only make out that he belonged to the band. The leader and his accomplice had formerly worked in the galley. Subsequently they both confessed and revealed that the other cheese was hidden in a hammock. I found most amazing, however, that the bag of sardines had disappeared without a trace. Someone else must have made off with it.

A similar incident took place in that same division about a week ago. During one of our periodic clothing inspections someone else's shirt was discovered in a young sailor's seabag. The Executive punished him rather mildly by giving him a few hours of "sport." However at noon when he was supposed to start his tour, he failed to appear. He did not come even after he was called. The Corporal of the Watch looked for him but could not find him. Had he committed suicide? Finally the entire engine room crew joined the search and after several hours found him. But where? He had crawled into the blades of one of the turbines between decks. If it had been turned on, he would surely have been chopped into mincemeat. Once again the Executive looked the other way and merely had him locked up for three days.

Now the fifth division is called the cheese division and has become the laughing stock of the entire ship. While the rest of us are mending our clothes, they have to perform division duties. I think that this stupid escapade will have serious consequences for both the guilty men. It is not likely that they will be shown any mercy if they are brought before a court-martial. The fact that they stupidly opened the bulkhead door and thereby endangered the safety of the ship will weigh against them heavily.

Nothing worth mentioning occurred while we were out at advance patrol. We never left our post and today, Sunday May 14, we have returned to port for a couple of days. To-morrow we will practice loading ammunition and on Tuesday we will conduct a major artillery drill. On Wednesday the free watch is scheduled to go on another excursion to the Bock-horn. I am really looking forward to that. 14 May 1916.

Once again I do not know where to begin writing. [Shall I write] of the lovely weather? No, I will need that to bail me out of trouble at some other time. Of the new Vice Chancellor Helfferich? [18] But this is not the place for that sort of thing. About the war at sea? In this respect we are at present enjoying a rest period! Then about the other battle fronts? Yes, at least about one of them. The focal point of the war has turned from the Meuse to the Adige. At this historic front the Austrians are rolling up the "organ grinders." [19] Oh, how terrible that is!

[18] Karl Helfferich was a former director of the Deutsche Bank. He became Secretary of the Treasury in 1915 and founded the General Purchasing Agency. In 1916 he was promoted to the post of Secretary of the Interior and Vice Chancellor.

[19] On May 15, 1916, the Austrians resumed their offensive against the Italians in the Trentino. Before their advance slowed down they captured Asiago and Arsiero on May 31. But when the Italian resistance stiffened, the promising offensive ground to a halt.

On May 23, the anniversary of their infamous breach of our alliance, Höfer [20] reported shortly and sweetly: "We have captured 24,000 prisoners, 188 guns and 101 machine guns since [May] 15."

(Nothing like this has ever happened to me before! All of a sudden I was overcome by an overwhelming drowsiness, placed my head upon my arm and when I woke up I had slept for two hours!)

I am following the developments on this front with special attention since I am very familiar with many of the places at which they are fighting. I once tramped on foot from Venice to Bolzano. Whenever I hear the names of Ala, Rovereto, Trent, Gorizia, it brings back all sorts of memories. Oh, whatever happened to my old journeyman's year? . . . Will it ever return, that golden time, so joyous and free . . . ?

I often sang that way in the silent valleys of the Tyrol. Even now I still yearn for its pink mountains and its golden wine. I still remember vividly how even then the Italians and Germans hated one another. There were many people in Bolzano who spoke good German but who would only answer in Italian. In the evenings the taverns were crowded with men with typical Andreas Hofer [21] faces who came to enjoy a glass of red wine while they proudly recalled their campaigns against the Katzelmacher [Italians].[22]

The situation has developed so well that the holy soil of the Tyrol is now free of all enemies. Even a layman could tell by glancing at the map that any further advance of the Imperial Austrian troops will jeopardize the northern corner of Italy.

---

[20] Franz Ritter Höfer von Feldsturm, of the Austrian war department.
[21] Andreas Hofer (1767–1810) led a Tyrolean revolt against Napoleon in 1809 during the Austrian War of Liberation. He was later captured and shot by the French but lived on as a popular hero in Austria.
[22] During the nineteenth century Austria waged a number of wars against Italy. In 1848–49 an Austrian army quelled the Italian Revolution. The process of Italian unification was attended by two subsequent wars, the war of Austria against France and Italy in 1859 and the Austro-Italian war of 1866.

Venice is especially vulnerable. Perhaps Conrad Hötzendorff [23] will repeat the triumphal march through Milan of Radetzky and Prince Eugene.[24] In my opinion the entire world, insofar as it still possesses any shred of decency and sense of honor, ought to welcome this. Ultimately treachery shall defeat itself!

And now something else. . . .

Once again we enjoyed our excursion to the Bockhorn, although we had even less time than before. On the way there our little train broke down, so that we did not arrive until four o'clock. Once again we danced lustily. Two days later our ship returned to its station on advance guard at Schillig Roads.

It was a peaceful time for us. Since the English seem to be hiding in their ports, I don't think that we shall embark on any major missions within the foreseeable future. Dollarika's [America's] hostile attitude has brought our submarine campaign to an end. One of America's most influential newspapers the *World,* which is friendly toward us, at the height of the crisis wrote that Germany was being offered an unprecedented opportunity to impress the entire world with her generosity. If we were to stop the sinking [of ships], maybe America would seriously reconsider her position. This might be more useful to Germany than the sinking of thousands of ships. I was unable to tell whether this was a promise in disguise or if it was merely a lot of hot air. The first part of the message seemed fascinating. Maybe our government would be sufficiently influenced by the second promise to cut back the full extent of our submarine campaign for a limited period of time.

But as yet there is no evidence of this serious reconsidera-

[23] Conrad von Hötzendorff (1852–1925) was the brilliant and belligerent Chief of Staff of the Austro-Hungarian army who had planned the Italian campaign and who made it his chief object to defeat the Italians.

[24] General Josef Radetzky (1766–1855) was the Austrian commander who defeated the Piedmontese army at the First Battle of Custozza (July 1848) and then occupied Milan.

This cannot possibly refer to Prince Eugene, who was the current Austrian Commander on the Balkan Front, or even to Prince Eugene of Savoy, the famous general who lived from 1663 to 1736. Stumpf means Archduke Albert, the Austrian victor of the Second Battle of Custozza in June 1866.

tion. . . . However I did read that America protested the seizure of her mail and parcel post but this is probably merely an attempt to circumvent the paper blockade.[25]

Even better yet, there is much serious talk of peace. It stems from reliable sources and is not based on astrological predictions or the prophecies of old women. Bethmann and Grey have been talking, as have Wilson and [King] Alfonso of Spain.[26] As of this time the leaders of the belligerent nations are still content to regale the representatives of the United Press with academic lectures and are still trying to foist the responsibility for the war on one another. But those who understand diplomatic jargon and who are able to read between the lines will detect a number of promising signs which might be used to negotiate a peace. Once again Bethmann, in his straightforward manner, has announced that he is prepared to conclude peace if our opponents would recognize the military status quo.[27] Although [this offer] was, of course, rejected emphatically by the enemy, they did not sound very confident and sure. But this foolishness will not deceive anyone who has the slightest acquaintance with history. After the fall of Paris and Strassburg in 1870, Gambetta [28] continued to

---

[25] The United States had recently protested Britain's policy of opening her mail, ostensibly in search of contraband being sent to Germany. Moreover, the English were also accused of stealing American trade secrets in this fashion.

[26] A number of tentative peace feelers were put forth in 1916, most notably the one of President Wilson, who sent his representative, Colonel Edward M. House, to England to propose the convening of a peace conference. House indicated at the time that if the Allies accepted his proposal and the Germans rejected it, America might be compelled to enter the war against Germany. Although the British gave this proposal some passing attention, it never actually materialized.

[27] On April 5, 1916, Chancellor Theobald von Bethmann-Hollweg announced in the German Reichstag that he was prepared to conclude a peace if Germany were permitted to retain the Eastern territories she had conquered and a measure of control over Belgium. This is what Stumpf must have meant by a peace on the basis of the military status quo.

[28] Leon Gambetta (1838–1882) was the leading member of the Government of National Defense during the Franco-Prussian War who tried to organize the resistance of France against the Germans. In spite of all of his efforts, France was eventually compelled to conclude the punitive Peace of Frankfurt.

announce proudly that he would not yield "a square foot of our soil or a single brick of our fortresses." In spite of that, he later talked very willingly. It is my general impression that all the countries except England are ready for peace. But how is peace to be brought about?

Today's newspapers are filled with reports of mad scenes of panic and despair in the North Italian cities of Padua, Venice, Viascenza and Verona. I read these reports with real relish. The weather has changed recently and there are many thunderstorms and much rain. But today Sunday, it is quite cool. This morning we returned to our advance station. 28 May 1916.

Finally, finally ——— At last the momentous event which for twenty-two months has been the object of our longings, emotions and thoughts has arrived. For many years we have hoped, worked and drilled with great fervor for this. I truly don't know how to begin! It all happened two days ago. I have just come back from taking a look at the ships which took part in it and the damage [which they suffered]. First of all, there is *Von der Tann.* . . . Stop! This will come later; first I have to tell how it happened.

As I mentioned before, the First Squadron was out on patrol. I was already looking forward to our stay in port which was scheduled to begin on Friday. We had no inkling that great things were about to happen.

The entire squadron had loaded coal on Tuesday. It was rumored by some that we "would sail for Kiel"; others maintained that we would remain here and still others [insisted] that we were to sail out for a small sortie. Hence nobody was very excited that evening when life jackets were distributed and the gear was stowed away. We went to sleep not knowing whether we would sail that night. At any rate, the Third Division was to stand the morning watch from four to eight. At about 5 A.M. the Officer of the Deck woke me with the words: "Come on, you are on the sounding lines. Get up. We'll lift anchor right away." At the same time [I heard] the boat crew being piped to raise anchor.

If we hurry we shall be back this evening [I thought] as we

got under way and passed the [submarine] nets. After break-fast we stowed our gear and bedding away, folded the loading booms and went through the routine of clearing the decks. At 10:30 all hands were called on deck. What was going on? I was soon to learn. The Captain stood on deck with two sheets of paper in his hand. Aha! Something is brewing!

"Close ranks; pay attention," he began. "We can look for-ward to something very special. We have recently discovered a heavy concentration of shipping up between the north of England and Skagen. We would like to take a look at some of the very interesting things being shipped there. The heavy cruisers will sail fifty miles ahead, will stop all the merchant-men they meet and bring them to Cuxhaven for a thorough inspection. Thus the first [objective] will be war against enemy shipping. However recently many warships have been sighted in that area and we would also like to give them a little tickle. A special surprise will await [the ships anchored] in port. Seven of our submarines are lying before the Firth of Forth." The captain continued to name ports and other instal-lations but unfortunately I can't remember them.

"Our bait, the light cruisers, will draw the stupid fools out to sea with their wireless messages. . . ." [29] He said this in such a droll Berliner dialect that everyone laughed out loud. The expression on the Captain's face while he said this was interest-ing. He appeared to be completely serious but his small gray eyes shone and blinked with such great delight that we found it impossible to suppress our laughter and chuckles. Turning to the gun commanders, the Captain reminded them to be patient, how to conduct themselves at night, and so on. I still remem-ber his final statement: "It will be mere child's play . . . and won't be bad at all for us."

Because of the fog we did not have air cover. Consequently we had to be doubly watchful, especially when it became

---

[29] It was the task of Admiral Franz Hipper's (1863–1932) battle cruisers, a squadron of light cruisers and torpedo boats, to lure the Eng-lish Grand Fleet into a trap off the Norwegian coast, where the main element of the German High Seas Fleet under Admiral Scheer would be stationed.

appreciably clearer and brighter. The visibility became excellent at about noon. If it was like this tomorrow, the British would commence firing at [a distance of] twenty-three kilometers. Then we'll really catch it. I had the impression that the area must be heavily mined because we kept changing course frequently. Our advance guard reported enemy cruisers at 6:30 and began to fire. As far as I could tell, *Elbing* fired the first shots. Nothing was in sight yet; but at a distance one could hear the dull thunder of the guns. However it came closer and closer quickly. A report came that six enemy cruisers were closing in.

I took the lookout on the forward bridge at four o'clock. It was apparent that something was approaching; the signalmen ran all around and removed the canvas bridge-rail covering. The Captain informed the lookouts that the enemy would be sighted in half an hour. Our battle cruisers had already engaged six large English ships.

Gradually our speed rose to 19 sea miles. How beautiful it was to see our twenty-one primeval elephants charging forward! Forward, forward, quickly toward the roar of the guns! Everything within me stormed and tossed in happy excitement. My mind already visualized the trained guns and the exploding shells all around. I was burning with impatience and it seemed to me that everything was happening much too slowly. Quickly, quickly staunch ship, up ahead our brave cruisers are already fighting and bleeding. If you don't hurry they will sacrifice themselves.

"There they are!" shouted the Adjutant. Sure enough, dim lightning could be seen through the fog off port. Clouds of smoke rose in the air. One, two, three, four, five, six, seven of them! "Bugler! Battle Stations! Clear for Action. Ta, ta, ta, ta." The men ran around like mad. In a minute and a half everyone was ready. "Lookouts down! Battle Stations!" yelled the First Officer. Pretending not to hear, I continued to look feverishly through the binoculars. I noticed that the lead ship had a triple mast. "Get going," came a yell from the command tower. I yielded and made my way down the ladder to the munition chamber of B Gun.

It was six o'clock. Down there the heat was already unbearable. With cheeks flushed with joy and excitement everyone was at work carrying shells to the elevator. "Don't be impatient," I said, "the enemy is still far off." Someone shouted back, "Did you see something?" The battle would start soon, I told them. At last count we had been thirty kilometers apart.

All of us were hungry. Hence the port side was ordered to leave stations to get supper. They obeyed with unprecedented speed. Everyone jumped to the upper deck or a porthole to catch a quick glimpse before going. It was still completely light. Because the English sailed in the fog, the light was against us at that point. Soon, however, we outmaneuvered them and had the evening sun ahead of us.

"Enemy has commenced firing. First volley 1,000 meters short. Third Squadron replying slowly," the bridge reported. We felt immeasurably relieved at these words. "We shall get to fight today!" "Pay attention, something is happening!" Long range fire off port! Damn it, why not on our side? Once again a shot—a cruiser—9,300 meters. Why don't we answer? There —our trained ear told us plainly—the forward gun had fired. A violent wind flew through the chamber, the gun tower shook. "Bang, bang!" Our first broadside was off. At first we thought that our B Gun had fired with the rest, but no. Bang, bang, another volley. We had hit a cruiser and a destroyer and they were burning. Both tilted over and sank.

What kind of a strange sound was this? "Crash, crash," the sound reverberated. Ah! It was the death cry of an English shell! I fell down on the deck and listened. I noticed that the floor vibrated slowly and sang at each crash. It was loud or quiet, depending on the distance from the point of impact. The engines shook like a machine gun. Before I left the bridge, I heard the captain tell the engine room, "In an emergency, use oil." Now I understood. As our tensions rose to the breaking point, our thirst became terrific. Fortunately we had a bucket of water and when it became empty we drank the water from the fire buckets. Later on these buckets served another, less pleasant, but nevertheless very important function.

The battle had already lasted half an hour. It was eight o'clock. Won't the enemy come to starboard? After all, this was the customary side for battle. We had practiced long-range firing from starboard for many years and now everything was different from what we expected. Slowly the battle veered to starboard. The enemy tried to turn our point! At last! Our gun tower turned slowly but our joy was short-lived. The ship suddenly shifted to one side. My first reaction was that we had hit a mine or something, although there was no loud explosion. But it was something else. We had turned hard rudder and the engines puffed their usual rhythm.

Once again the battle stood off port. We had nothing to do, so we yelled and carried on without restraint. Deep in our hearts we were all afraid and tried to still our fear by making noise. Once more I put my ear to the deck to listen to the crash, crash, crash. Suddenly I got a terrific slap. All at once everything became still. It was 9:19 P.M. The ship had been hit. "Thank God!" someone called out, "now we'll get leave to go home." He was silenced at once. "Shut up! Who knows how many got killed!"

"A hit in Compartment 15 above the waterline. No dead," reported the bridge at last. Everyone felt relieved. Then we began to discuss how long it would take to repair, whether we would get leave, and so on. The shells rained down like hail on the outside while the splinters dashed themselves to pieces against the armored sides of the ship.

"A lull in the battle! Enemy too far away. . . . But no one to leave stations because it can start once more any minute. . . ." And so it was. The guns began to roar again in less than five minutes. We fired very slowly with deliberation while the *Kaiser*-class ships in front of us shot like mad. Compared with the past, the range [of fire] was incredible. It fluctuated between 18 and 23 kilometers. Now the English were in an unfavorable position. The shining sun stood behind their backs while we had the dark Danish coastline in our rear. Before long, however, the firing ceased and the night lowered its merciful veil over the horror of the day.

While the others played cards I managed to doze off for an hour and three quarters. The most dangerous time for both us and the enemy had arrived: torpedo attacks. Perhaps at this very moment our famous black fleet [the torpedo boats] are engaging the enemy to demonstrate how German boats ride to the attack. Our friends on the torpedo boats who had thus far been denied an opportunity to demonstrate their offensive spirit and love of battle, will now be unleashed. As they passed by us during the first days of the war they had shouted triumphantly, vainly hoping that they would have a chance to fire their torpedoes at something that very night. 6 June 1916.

However they had to be patient like all of us. There were some people who insisted that torpedo boats had no value at all. Undoubtedly up until this time the submarine has been much more successful. Now, however, they [the torpedo boats] have had their day. Their attack delivered the death blow to a number of Dreadnoughts and caused the enemy much damage. The Ninth Flotilla attacked three times and fired all of its torpedoes.

At 12:30 I was placed on lookout duty once more. I wish I could describe my inner feelings as the grandiose drama unfolded before my eyes. A picture like that would have to be painted in the most brilliant of colors. It would have to record the most contradictory thoughts. Hence I am convinced that it is impossible for any human being to describe his feelings and thoughts as they actually race through his mind in the course of the baptism of fire. If I said that I was afraid, I would be lying. No, it was an undefinable mixture of joy, fear, curiosity, apathy and . . . love of battle.

What a sight unfolded before my eyes! Imagine a scene of pitch-dark blackness with flashes of light flaring up continually. There were two patches where the lights flashed with greater frequency—probably cruisers or destroyers. They must have been very far away because the thunder of their guns could not be heard. On the bridge loud talking was prohibited; the men spoke to their neighbors in quiet, secretive tones. Since at any moment [enemy] torpedo boats might attack through the darkness, all our nerves were on edge.

There they are! The beam of the stern searchlight swooped on a gray shape and held fast. Mighty flames shot from all our guns. One! Two! Three! The impact! Much too far away. Another broadside and [we had scored] a hit! I distinctly saw the pieces flying and in a moment flames jumped to the sky. That was a direct hit. Soon more torpedo boats would come. What ship was burning so horribly four stories high off our port? Was it one of ours or the enemy's? I stared through the glasses but could only make out an occasional fragment falling from the ship. Gradually its dark red glow was transformed into white-hot heat. If she didn't sink within fifteen minutes we would be there.

Within ten minutes enemy destroyers attacked once more. There were ten of them and each had chosen one of our battleships as its target. This meant their doom. They flew toward the lights like blinded moths; the roar of the guns nearly broke my eardrums. It was beautiful. On each ship seven medium guns commenced firing. The searchlights found their targets at once. Everything was over in two minutes. It all happened so quickly that it was impossible for the mind to grasp it. Its effect might be compared to a motion picture film composed of hundreds of little fragments jumping its track while the entire room [in which it is being shown] spins around and tilts to one side. It must have caused those who stood on the bridge a few worried minutes. Our ships scattered like a herd of buffalo struck by a bolt of lightning.

The quartermaster who had been standing at the wheel of the bridge for many hours asked, "Captain, Sir, where is the squadron?" "Three turns to starboard and full speed," [came the answer]. But what had happened to the half dozen destroyers? They lay astern like an aisle of fire all around us. Only one of them was not ablaze. She lay there like a dead sow emitting a white cloud of smoke from her belly. After a fourth broadside had been fired, she sank like a rock. The others burned like tinder.[30]

And now something incredible happened. *Nassau,* which steamed in front of us, left the formation without any apparent reason and hove to on our port side. Suddenly a beautiful destroyer with three smokestacks came into view and headed directly toward *Nassau.* The brightness of the searchlights allowed me to clearly identify its number as *A 41.* She disappeared behind *Nassau* before we had a chance to aim and fire our guns. Breaking off her masts and chimneys on *Nassau's* forward guns, she ran madly amidship and rammed the armored battleship squarely in the flank. Surprisingly enough, she managed to break loose and to turn around. Then she received a well-aimed broadside from the startled *Nassau* squarely in her belly. Now she was done for. A gun plummeted down from her upper deck, a volcano of molten iron flowed from her middle, two tidal waves from each side collided over her, and with a hiss everything disappeared in the water.[31] I observed this terrible spectacle from such close proximity that my knees began to tremble as I became aware that three hundred young men had just been roasted alive.

Something was happening astern. A large vessel, at least a cruiser, had broken through our lines without being recognized as an enemy. By mistake she must have taken us for English. However her peculiar behavior aroused suspicion and she failed to answer our recognition signal correctly. At once thirty heavy guns turned on her. Three of our volleys sent her burning to the bottom.[32] Her sole broadside landed short ahead of us.

It was now 2:30 and the height of the battle was apparently over. In the east a small stripe on the horizon gave evidence of the first signs of the coming day. For a short time everything

[30] The English lost eight destroyers during the course of the battle.

[31] The *Nassau* was rammed by the British destroyer *Spitfire.* However, it appears that she was not sunk and that she managed to escape.

[32] The British cruiser has been identified as the *Black Prince.* It strayed into the German fleet and was sunk in four minutes.

was quiet. Our mercurial captain who up till now had maintained his self-control and composure, now began shouting, "Donnerwetter—Damn it, what's happening? The ship is sinking! A mine!" Stepping toward the porthole, he yelled down the tube, "Heavy explosion! Check all compartments!" The answer came back in less than three minutes: "All compartments responding and tight." Thank God! Apparently we rode over a soft spot.

Three o'clock! Curious, how quickly these three hours have passed. In all the excitement I had not had a chance to glance at the clock. As I did so now, my first thought told me that it was time to be relieved. The shapes of the surrounding ships had become more distinct. Were some of our ships missing or by some miracle were we all still there? It was still too dark to tell. Over the wireless the casualty reports began to trickle in slowly. *V 31* reported she had lost her maneuverability. The small cruiser *Elbing* reported maximum speed 5 miles per hour. *Wiesbaden* heavily damaged! [33] The most important news came at 3:30: our newest battle cruiser *Lützow* approaching slowly. The report was too vague to disturb us. For the first time I noticed how cold it had become. Shaking with cold, the officers cowered sleepily and listlessly in wind-protected corners. The battle could break out anew at any moment. Sparks would fly again if the main body of the English fleet caught up with us. This was almost a certainty since the English had greater speed than we. We steamed at sixteen miles in order not to leave the heavily damaged *Lützow* too far behind.[34]

Now, close to four o'clock, full daylight had arrived but no sight of the enemy. Our scattered and crippled ships drew slowly together. Our division remained at full strength but the second division was missing one ship the *Nassau*. At the time no one knew where she was or what had happened to her. I

[33] The *Elbing* had been rammed by the German battleship *Posen* and was sinking. *Wiesbaden*, a light cruiser, had been heavily hit earlier in the evening and sank that night.

[34] *Lützow*, Admiral Hipper's flagship, had been heavily hit during an early engagement the previous afternoon. Hipper transferred to a destroyer, but the *Lützow* had to be scuttled later on.

was not in a happy mood when my relief came to spell me.

The first thing I did was to climb down to Section 14 to survey the hole and the damage.[35] Good God, how things looked down there! If I had not seen it myself it would have been impossible to picture the confusion which prevailed. The hole itself could no longer be seen because it had been patched up with mattresses, blankets, boards and beams. A hose had been laid to the stern battery, and most of the water had been pumped out. The water still stood about a foot deep in the compartment. Fortunately the sea was calm, otherwise this primitive patchwork would not have lasted long.

A piece of armor plate as big as a wagon wheel lay near the point of impact. Standing knee high in water, I tried to collect some small shell fragments but I gave up this dangerous game after I had stumbled repeatedly over things. The ship's tailor shop had been located in the room. Now it looked frightful. The tailor's sewing machine was a formless heap of twisted scrap iron, his large wooden trunk with its contents had been shattered and the clothes floated everywhere in a muddy swamp. I had to return to my battle station in a hurry and thus did not have time to form more than a hasty impression. Naturally the lookouts were bombarded with all sorts of questions [by the men]: "How was it? How many ships were sunk? Is this or that true?" Those who had witnessed the battle had to repeat the entire story over and over until each of the men was satisfied.

8 JUNE 1916

History will always regard this heaven-sent day as the day of the great naval battle between Germany and England. Very few of us, I realize, understand this momentous event although we lived through it and helped to shape it. This is only natural since the role of each individual was quite insignificant. The most vital tasks were performed by machines: electrical ma-

---

[35] Stumpf announced earlier that the *Helgoland* had been hit in Compartment 15.

chines, hydraulic machines and steam engines. The men merely stood by and pushed a lever, turned a wheel or threw coal into a furnace. They had performed these tasks in the same manner hundreds and thousands of times in the past. And even those who occupied more important positions—those who set off and hurled into the air hundreds of pounds of explosives—did they actually do more than turn a wheel or the rudder when so ordered?

Did they do more than that? It would certainly not seem so at first glance. In the final analysis, however, the spirit which dominates the machine decides the victory. During the battle I often thought that our ship was a huge live monster, while we humans might be regarded to be its soul. Indeed this must have occurred to anyone who watched the opposing fleets. The brilliant flags fluttering up high have always touched the soul and stirred the hearts of all men. The machines were willing to be used, to give their utmost and to obey. Whenever thick smoke and fog made observation impossible, the electric spark [of the wireless] sprang to our rescue and informed the commanders what had happened and what needed to be done.

The human imagination is incapable of coping with the tremendous power inherent in two modern fleets locked in battle. First of all, the very range of fire surpasses all previous dimensions. Giant guns fire at each other from a distance of 23 kilometers and when they hit they smash everything to pieces. What precision and exactitude is required of the instruments capable of such a thing? The function of these instruments is to destroy what has been created by years of labor of thousands of industrious hands. Those responsible for the destruction are overjoyed. And they promise once the war is over to rebuild everything which they have destroyed. Thus the havoc which they have wrought becomes bearable and can be regarded as unavoidable.

What might have been the decisive battle of the war did not occur on June 1. As far as I was able to judge, the enemy was forced to turn away by the increasing attacks of our brave torpedo boats. However possibly the enemy broke off the battle for the same reasons as we.[36] The English had used up more ammunition than we. Since we had entered the battle late and had fired sparingly, the First Squadron still had plenty of ammunition. But the ships of the *Kaiser* and *König* class had expended at least half of their stores of munitions while the battle cruisers were completely depleted. It would hence have been inadvisable to once more engage an enemy who possessed twice our number of undamaged ships.[37]

Our submarines and possibly the Zeppelins could finish cleaning up. Our dirigibles had not participated in the battle or in the previous reconnaissance patrols. If they had, we would no doubt have turned back in time. On the morning of [June] 1, I spotted the first of our Zeppelins diagonally across from us.

At six o'clock in the morning we suffered another serious mishap when the lead ship, carrying the flag of Admiral Schmidt, unexpectedly ran over a mine.[38] She veered off with a heavy list. We soon left her behind under the guard of two torpedo boats. Shortly past noon we sailed past Helgoland and at 1:30 we dropped anchor at Wilhelmshaven Roads. There we stayed for the time being.

We already knew that our magnificent *Lützow* would never return. Unfortunately that morning she had entangled her propellers in her tattered torpedo netting so that she became totally immobile. Ordinarily we might have towed her home, but one of the Zeppelins reported that twenty enemy ships were lurking about. Thus she and her escorts would have fallen an easy prey to the enemy. Regretfully we decided to scuttle the brave ship before she was discovered by the enemy. All the

[36] It was actually the German fleet which turned away. Admiral Scheer realized that he could no longer win the battle against the superior and faster British force. Under the cover of darkness he broke off the engagement while the British commander Admiral Jellicoe, cautious to the point of ineptitude, did nothing to prevent the Germans from escaping to their home waters.

[37] The British had entered the battle with twenty-eight battleships and nine battle cruisers against sixteen German battleships and five battle cruisers. There was an even greater disparity in light cruisers. Thus the British outnumbered the Germans almost two to one.

[38] The flagship of the First Squadron was the *Ostfriesland*.

survivors were taken aboard the torpedo boats. Then one of them fired two torpedoes and *Lützow* went to her grave about 120 miles from Helgoland.

For us this constituted an irretrievable loss. Now we were back to four battle cruisers, the same number we had when the war broke out. [On the other hand] we were only positive of having sunk *Indefatigable*, a battle cruiser of roughly the same size and fighting ability as our *Lützow*. However we had also observed and possibly contributed to the sinking of a number of light cruisers and a whole lot of destroyers. Hence one could by no means describe our spirits as happy or victorious. On the contrary, we were depressed. What had become of our cruisers, and *Ostfriesland* and *Nassau*?

After dinner [we saw] *Regensburg* arrive with a slight list. At first we thought that she too had been hit. But not at all! The ship was unharmed. Clinging like ants on her decks and superstructure, there were 1,200 to 1,500 men waving at us. They must have been the survivors of *Lützow* or *Seydlitz*. It was rumored that *Seydlitz*, too, had been mauled severely and beached herself at Amrum. We heard that *Rostock* had been sunk and that *Elbing* had been abandoned by her crew. Later on we found out that the ancient *Pommern* had after all gone down with all hands. She had been struck at night by three torpedoes and had sunk immediately. On the other hand, we heard that the badly crippled *Frauenlob* managed to save herself on the Danish coast.

An hour after the arrival of *Regensburg*, *Ostfriesland* came limping in slowly with her bow deep in the water. She must have taken on a great deal of water. She was in a sorry shape and would have to go into dock at once. Since we had not gotten any sleep the preceding night, we all looked forward to catching up on it that night. But unfortunately I had to stand watch until twelve o'clock. Filled with suspense, I waited to read the news in the next day's papers. The entire world was bound to hear and be excited by the news of this momentous battle. Even now we had a pretty fair idea of the enemy's losses.

At the inspection the next morning, the captain assembled all the men on deck and read the latest telegrams. "The English," he began, "have suffered even heavier losses than we anticipated. *Queen Elizabeth* has been sunk. (This proved to be wrong. He meant *Queen Mary*.) We are certain of it since we took prisoners. Then there is *Indefatigable*. We have picked up survivors from her as well. You will remember that she was the cruiser which burned so high and with a bright flame last night. Moreover, *Warrior* and the modern battleship *Warspite* were also abandoned by their crews. *Marlborough* was hit by several torpedoes and is not likely to remain afloat.[39] You are not to write home about the battle until the official report is released tomorrow. We may all be proud of ourselves and the victory we have won. I would also like to tell you how much I appreciate your exemplary behavior throughout the battle. Every single sailor and stoker performed his duties to perfection. The repair crew, especially, is deserving of praise for repairing the great gash in our bow while we were traveling at a speed of 15 sea miles. Dismissed!"

I am still somewhat uncertain about the number of casualties we suffered but according to our calculations they might add up to as much as 2,500 men.[40] *Seydlitz* is still out at the nets and appears to be in a rather helpless state. Since her high stern is submerged under 13 meters of water she can only move at high tide. However her engines seem unharmed and her chimneys are belching smoke as usual as she heads in assisted by *Pillau* and several other ships.

On Sunday morning we entered the dock to repair our damages. It would require about fourteen days. I immediately availed myself of the opportunity to view the damaged ships. On Saturday, while we were still in the southern Channel, we had a chance to take a look at *Von der Tann* as she lay right next to us. She had sustained a number of direct hits above and

---

[39] British losses came to three battle cruisers, three cruisers and eight destroyers, while the Germans lost one battleship, one battle cruiser, four light cruisers and five torpedo boats or destroyers.
[40] The German fleet actually lost 3,039 men while the British Grand Fleet suffered 6,784 casualties.

below the waterline. It is hard to imagine, without actually seeing it, the destruction and carnage which these had wrought below deck. In comparison to her, our ship looked perfectly unscathed. One hit had been particularly destructive. It was deflected from the aft command post through the top deck into the space between decks before exploding. When I was there the ship was still flooded with water; torn and broken steel was lying about everywhere. The base of an 8.8 cm. gun had been torn away and one could see the water underneath through a frightful hole. This was where stokers had kept all their gear and thus they lost everything save the work clothes on their backs. However by now they have found shelter in the barracks [ashore]. Another shell had penetrated the base of Turret C on the top deck and had made a great gaping hole. Miraculously the crew was spared when the shell failed to penetrate the armor because it had spent itself and exploded on the outside. But its fragments sowed devastation wherever they landed. While they could not get through the heavy armor, they did gouge angry holes, big as a fist, out of it. It looked as though someone had dug his hand into a clump of soft putty. I had never thought it possible that anything could bite through these diamond-hard walls and simply stood and gaped in astonishment at the holes and gashes. Despite all this, only eleven crew members of *Von der Tann* had been killed. Considering the material damage she had sustained, this was an incredibly small number.

Right next to her lay *Grosser Kurfürst*. She, too, was damaged and had three covered-up craters on her deck. In addition, shell splinters had turned her smokestacks into sieves. Fifteen men were killed.

On Saturday afternoon I went to the shipyard to inspect the hole in *Ostfriesland*. The workers were busy building a scaffolding all around it. A mine had exploded in a very dangerous but extremely well-protected spot, precisely over B Turret's munition chamber. A hole as big as a medium-sized barn door gaped in the outer shell; the torpedo bulkhead had been shattered as though it was a pane of glass and the vertical and horizontal ship's ribs stuck out like the bristles of a porcupine. At first I thought that it would never be possible to repair all this devastation. However when I saw how the acetylene and oxygen torches cut through the tattered and torn metal like butter, I really began to appreciate the tools of modern technology.

On Sunday we buried our dead comrades at the splendid new cemetery at Neuende. All of Wilhelmshaven was in mourning. From all over Germany people in funeral attire came to pay their last respects to a son or brother. Each ship contributed a thirty-six man honor guard. All off-duty officers had to participate in the ceremony. But only the relatives and the honor guards were allowed in the cemetery. Hundreds of individual coffins were placed in huge mass graves.

Since I knew that it would be very crowded, I chose to stay on board in order to write in my book and to take care of other pressing matters. Later on, some of my friends who attended told me what it was like. Mücke,[41] his whole chest covered with medals, was among those who had been there. Someone maintained that the Commander of the Fleet had not been present because he had sailed out with some ships of the *Kaiser* class to despatch a number of English vessels which were still helplessly drifting about. Right now I am not in a position to say whether there is any substance to this rumor.

Once again the men believe all the incredible rumors that are flying about. One rumor maintains that the British fleet has still not returned to port and, because of its fear of our submarines, is still at sea. It is alleged that the [English] sailors whom we captured have reported that they ate nothing but bread and water and they were very astonished when we fed them bread and butter. It is rumored that the Kaiser has paid us a secret visit to inspect the ships. Although the enemy's casualty lists have risen to astronomical proportions, Reuters [News Agency] is said to have reported that the entire German fleet, mouse and man, has been sunk.

[41] This probably refers to the much-decorated First Officer of *Emden*, Helmuth von Mücke.

Now that we have actually been in action, our imaginations are working overtime and some of us believe the most insane rumors. There are reports of hunger riots. The story is always the same. Some women and children marched on the town hall and along the way looted thirty to forty stores. The army was called out and was ordered to fire, but naturally refused. And now comes the most gruesome part: the youth militia was called in and fired mercilessly upon the women and children. The story is always the same, only the location, the time and the numbers varies according to individual taste. First this was supposed to have occurred in Brunswick, then in Leipzig, in Cologne, in Chemnitz and, finally, in Berlin. Several of us took the trouble to make further inquiries and found out that there had indeed been some rioting and mob scenes but all the rest was false.

While we were on watch on Monday, all sorts of things kept happening. The Kaiser arrived. He was accompanied by the Kaiserin,[42] von Capelle,[43] the War Minister [44] and a group of high dignitaries. Yesterday the newspapers had stated that the Kaiser was still at Hindenburg's headquarters, but he still managed to arrive here on the coast by special train today. There were no great formalities. His Majesty's train arrived at 9:30 and at once he went out by cutter to *Friedrich der Grosse*. Unfortunately it was a cold and rainy day. The Kaiser's morning was taken up by staff meetings and inspection of hospitals. He was supposed to come aboard our ship at 2:30 to view our hole. From there he was to go to *Ostfriesland* and then on to *Von*

[42] This was the title of the Kaiser's wife Augusta Victoria of Schleswig-Holstein.

[43] Admiral Eduard von Capelle (1855–1931) was the former Chief of the Navy office who succeeded Grand Admiral Tirpitz as Secretary of the Navy in 1916.

[44] This refers to the Prussian War Minister General Adolf Wild von Hohenborn (1860–1925).

der Tann, which was also in dock. At lunch time we got a little surprise which nearly made the Officer of the Watch jump right out of his skin. The Kaiserin drove up totally unexpectedly. Our Captain was informed of this at once and he hurried to her, kissed her hand and showed her around. It all took place so quickly that most of the men who were eating lunch did not even take notice.

At 1:30 we put on our blue uniforms and positioned ourselves on deck as we pleased, not at all in the usual parade manner. Since it continued to pour, many of the men kept disappearing below deck. The Captain had placed a small collection of grenade and shell fragments on a small table opposite the hole. Around it stood a dozen shipyard firemen and several detectives in civilian clothes. At the appointed time a car bearing an admiral's flag drove up. However it was merely the base commander, a very thin and fairly tall gentleman. Finally, twenty minutes later, three cars drove through the dock gates at a rapid clip. All three carried admirals' flags. The Kaiser, von Capelle and several other officers dismounted from the car in the middle. The Kaiser did not seem changed or aged since I had last seen him here two years ago. On the contrary, his joy at the victory of his navy, which he considered his very own creation, had made him younger by ten years. He wore a gray raincoat, a naval officer's hat and had a riding crop in his hand. He approached the table with a vigorous, confident step and called in a loud voice: "Good morning, sailors!" "Good morning, Your Majesty," responded a thousand voices. From the fantail sounded the sharp and high-pitched voice of the Executive Officer, "Three cheers for His Majesty the Kaiser and our Supreme War Lord!" Since we were all in high spirits that day we all cheered gayly. The Kaiser personally commented on the damage while the entire company looked on at attention. In his hand he held a drawing of the damaged compartments.

The rain gods were kind enough to spare us from further showers during those few minutes. With a vigorous, military step the Kaiser then returned to his car to inspect the neighboring *Ostfriesland.*

An order had been posted on our bulletin board [which announced]: "I hereby promote Vice Admiral Scheer to Admiral and award him and Vice Admiral Hipper the Order Pour Le Merite."[45] Our Captain will no doubt receive the Iron Cross First Class and it seems as though three hundred Iron Crosses will be distributed among the crew. This means that every third man will get one. I personally would be happier if I got ten days' leave at home and remained in good health. Unfortunately, however, my application was rejected. Only the range finders and the orderlies were sent home; all the others had to stay here.

The crew of *Lützow* received six weeks' leave. The men of the *Seydlitz*, which is still floating helplessly in the locks, got three weeks. *Derfflinger* is out at the dry dock. As I understand it, she, too, received more than two dozen heavy hits. However her acute list has made it impossible for the dry dock to drain her. About a hundred of her men were killed and it is said that there are still about twelve men caught in her forward boiler room who can only be supplied with food through a communication tube. But the story does not sound too plausible.

A similar story is told of *Lützow*. There, too, twenty-one men in the bow section were cut off from the rest of the ship by the water. They were told over the telephone to keep up their courage because it was hoped that they could be liberated from their involuntary confinement as soon as the ship made port. When the time came for the cruiser to be scuttled, the Captain assumed the heavy responsibility of informing the men that they would soon die. I need hardly describe the outraged reaction of the men. . . .

Vice Admiral Hipper and his entire staff were then transferred to a torpedo boat. The situation was critical. The faster English battleships had already formed a semicircle around us. Thereupon Hipper gave the decisive but almost suicidal order: "All fast ships, attack enemy's point!" They would even have

[45] The Order Pour le Merite was the highest decoration one could receive in Prussia.

had to ram if it became necessary. Our four battle cruisers along with the Sixth and Ninth Flotilla shot forward. And they actually succeeded in turning the enemy's point and in averting our danger of being encircled. At that point the English fleet still had two opportunities to cut off our homeward retreat by [laying] mine fields either at Horns Reef, or further on, at Amrum. The fact that it made no attempt to do so was proof enough of how badly it had been hurt.

Derfflinger is now in the shipyard and yesterday evening I found an opportune moment to take a look at her. What had happened to this proud ship! Even from a distance I could see the torn rigging hanging down. But the damage on her hull and on her insides was far worse than anything I had ever seen before. Back aft, it looked as though a volcano had erupted. An enormous, gaping hole had torn upward through the broken deck. Two 38 cm. shells had penetrated the armor close to one another and one of them had exploded inside. The other shell still lay unexploded in the cabin. The ship had also been struck below by two shells but they had failed to penetrate the rather weak armor at that spot. However they had burned off the paint over a large area. But elsewhere the armor had been perforated by perfectly circular holes. Here the striking grenades had found a more favorable location and had managed to penetrate. But the best example of the power of these shells was to be seen at the bow. One shell had entered the port side and had gone through the forward battery carrying an entire armor plate with it. Thereafter it may or may not have exploded on the outside. The superstructure looked like a madhouse; it had been rolled up, bent, torn and broken to bits. All the guns in the casemates had been ruined. The barrel of one had broken off completely and now resembled a howitzer. The one beside it had apparently been hit on the muzzle by a fragment which bent its barrel slightly. In spite of that, it was fired again with the result that the barrel had split asunder like a cat-o'-nine-tails. However elsewhere our armor had performed its function admirably. It had deflected hits on the command tower and the rear of the gun turrets with ease. But the damage was still very extensive.

Although it was forbidden to go on board, I still managed to sneak on without being discovered. It was well worth the effort. What I saw was really no longer a ship but something quite different. At several places looking down from the top deck, one could see the yawning water on the lowest level. The steps were gone; they had been squashed into mere rings and spirals of metal. The greatest damage, however, was to be found in the general storeroom. There the cans of paint had exploded and all the good leather, tackle, cleaning material, paper, cloth and glass had sunk into a quagmire of soft paint. The place looked as though a thousand devils had held an orgy there.

On the next day the heavily damaged ship sailed for Hamburg under her own power for repairs in the Blohm and Voss shipyard. But the repairs might take as long as seven months to complete. On our ship, too, the repair crews are hard at work, hammering, welding and caulking in order to cover our gash with an iron plate. They never stopped working, even at night or at Whitsun.

WHITSUN 1916

About three hundred of our men have received ten days' leave to go home. Also all the married men were given a chance to see their wives and children. Since the weather was miserable, I remained on board, nice and dry. Since I succeeded in avoiding doing any work, our time in dock constituted a vacation for me. By day I would stroll through the shipyards. I fearlessly walked through all the restricted areas and thereby acquired a great deal of useful information. Never before had I seen such magnificent iron-working machinery. With the greatest of ease it could bore holes through 30 mm.-thick steel plating. Other machines sawed, polished, bored, milled, cut and welded with almost unbelievable precision and accuracy. Even the largest of these gigantic machines was operated by no more than two or three workers. It was difficult to tell by looking at these metal workers what kind of jobs they performed. I would frequently have to wait until they started their machines [before I could be sure]. It made me feel very good to look at the achievements of these dedicated people. It was there that I began to realize that we were destined to become a leader among nations because our sons were better at working metal than any others.

There were a number of large Russian, English and American lathes and punching machines in the machine shop. Upon asking, I found out that they came from neutral ships which had been captured in the North Sea or the Baltic. I had never seen anything like those die-cutting machines. They were capable of turning, boring and cutting perfect bolts out of iron bars without any sort of human direction. This complicated machinery was operated mainly by war cripples or girls. While the machine was running, a thick stream of oil flowed on top over the entire mechanism. I also paid frequent visits to the metalshop, the carpentry shop, the armorer's shop, the stamping works, the artillery shed, etc. Almost everywhere large numbers of Russian, French and Belgian prisoners of war could be found at work and they were especially numerous at the construction site of the newly built ship *Helling*. Apparently this cruiser will be even longer and wider than the others.

The *Hindenburg*, which the English claim to have sunk, evidently will no longer get to participate in the war. This mighty ship, too, is merely armed with eight 30.5 cm. guns. If they had worked on her properly, she would have been ready a long time ago. How desperately we need her now! Hopefully *Bayern* and *Baden* with their 38.1 cm. guns will soon join us here in the North Sea. Then the English will get what is coming to them!!

I am told that *Bayern* was struck by a torpedo on her shakedown cruise. Now, however, she is fully tested and ready again for battle. She has an astonishing firing record. She hit the target fifty out of a hundred times when she fired at a range of 25 kilometers! The Baltic has again become a danger zone

J. H. W. Dietz Verlag

Richard Stumpf

The battleship *Helgoland*

Christie McFall

The North Sea and vicinity—area of principal German naval activity
World War I

eral jubilation at the
reak of the war in
many as reflected on
faces of reservists on
way to join their
s

Culver Pictures

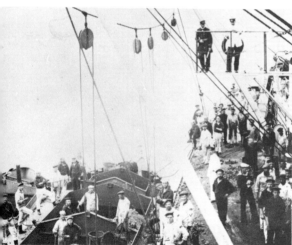

Ullstein Bilderdienst

Enlisted men of the fleet
pause for a picture dur-
ing the important but
arduous and dirty job of
loading coal

sthenics constituted
ge part of the mo-
nous routine aboard
in the German

Ullstein Bilderdienst

The Kaiser and his staff inspecting the cutting of armor plates in the shipyards at Kiel

Enlisted men of the German navy going ashore for liberty after action against the enemy

Officers and enlisted men at artillery practice

The battleship *Friedrich der Grosse*, flagship of the High Seas Fleet

Left: Stoker Albin Köbis of the *Prinzregent Luitpold*, executed on Se⟩tember 5, 1917, for mutiny

Right: Seaman Max Reichpietsch of the *Friedrich der Grosse*, one of tł leaders of the abortive mutiny of August, 1917, also executed on Se⟩tember 5, 1917

A gathering of naval personnel during the November 1918 mutiny Wilhelmshaven

Ullstein Bilderdienst

emissary of the Government, Majority Social Democrat Gustav
oske, addressing mutinous sailors in Kiel in November 1918

Historical Pictures Service, Chicago

Revolutionary sailors and soldiers in Berlin in November 1918

Revolutionstaumel in den Straßen Kiels

Abordnungen der Kriegsschiffbesatzungen marschieren zum Stationsgebäude Ostsee mit Plakaten, die den Bürger zur Ruhe mahnen

Der Vertrauensmann der Meuterer: Kuhnt

Ullstein Bilderdienst

A page of contemporary illustrations of the 1918 revolution in Kiel
Top: Delegations of men from warships marching on the Naval Station Headquarters bearing signs admonishing citizens to maintain law and order
Middle: Bernhardt Kuhnt, Chairman of the Council of Twenty-One, revolutionary council of Wilhelmshaven
Bottom: The November 1918 mutiny in the fleet. Crews of torpedo boats have hoisted the red flag of revolution.

and some English and Russian submarines have sunk several of our freighters there.[46] Apparently they don't give a damn for the territorial rights of Sweden or Denmark. On the day of the battle of Jutland the Russian fleet is supposed to have sailed out to escort an English squadron through the Belt. But we had posted our submarines there and *Bayern* lay waiting at the exit. Hence, from our point of view, it is unfortunate that at least some of them did not succeed in coming through. . . .

Some Russian destroyers engaged several of our torpedo boats in battle [at that time]. Our light cruiser *Memel*, which was on its shakedown cruise, rushed to the scene in response to wireless signals for help and had the misfortune to be torpedoed by a submarine. Did she sink?? (Either it is a secret, or it is not true. I am inclined to the latter view.) 10–18 June 1916.

Schillig Roads, 20 June 1916. We have been back here since Friday and have even been put on patrol again. The weather continues to be horrible. No news of any significance. Although our leak was repaired, it does not hold properly and the engine room floor is flooded each day. Perhaps we shall soon go back into dock.

We are now experiencing what the business world would call a "slack season." This is quite understandable since both sides are presently occupied with repairing the worst of the damage [of the battle of Jutland]. Nevertheless someone has predicted with "unerring certainty" that the next great encounter will take place on July 10. I find this hard to believe.[47] Perhaps [it might occur] on July 10, 1917.

[46] In mid-May three German steamers the *Kolga,* the *Bianca* and the *Hera,* were sunk in the Baltic by English and Russian submarines.
[47] Although the German High Seas Fleet had done much better than expected against a decidedly superior force at the Battle of Jutland, Admiral Scheer felt it his duty to admit to the Kaiser that "there can be no doubt that even the most successful result of a high seas battle will not compel England to make peace. . . . A victorious end to the war at a not too distant date can only be looked for by the crushing of English economic life through U-boat action against English commerce."

Our legendary three hundred Iron Crosses have not materialized. Instead a mere hundred of them were distributed on Saturday. Many of the men were bitterly disappointed. On the other hand, the rulers of the individual states will award their subjects a whole variety of medals for bravery and for achievements. The King of Saxony [48] has already been here to start the process.

My chances of obtaining leave have sunk to the vanishing point. We spent a few days in dock and now our cursed leak holds tight. Lately some of the days have been as cold as Christmas. This does not speak well for our imminent harvest. However I am told by the men returning from leave that the weather was quite good at the hay-harvesting time. The wheat is somewhat late but is standing up excellently. When I went home a year ago, the wheat harvest was already in progress. How hot it was then!

Now and then we read reports that corpses and pieces of wreckage from the battle have drifted ashore. We draw the most amazing conclusions regarding the extent of our losses on the basis of this evidence even though our side has issued a very authoritative report of the battle. However it is all over now; new events have superseded it. The world is trembling and holding its breath. I have often wondered why our enemies did not simultaneously attack us on all fronts. This is precisely what is happening now. The Austrian attack upon Venice has produced an Italian counteroffensive.[49] New millions of Russians have launched a terrific attack in the Bukovina and in the

Consequently, from that time on Scheer assiduously avoided engaging the Grand Fleet in pitched battle and increasingly demanded that the brunt of the naval effort be carried by the submarines and that the surface fleet be used to protect and cover their activities.

[48] Frederick Augustus III, King of Saxony (1865–1932), ascended the throne in 1904 but was forced to abdicate in November 1918.

[49] On June 17, 1916, the Italians staged a massive counterattack against the Austrians in the Trentino. The Austrians were under severe pressure in the East because of the Brusilov offensive and hence without adequate reserves. Thus they had to yield up most of their recent gains in that area.

Carpathian foothills.[50] Since the French were doing so miserably along the Meuse, the English have now been forced to throw their carefully protected army of three million men and their inexhaustible supply of munitions and steel against our well-entrenched front. The English have hardly bled at all up till now. Now, however, English blood has really begun to flow in streams. But it flows in vain because they shall not break through. They occasionally make a dent [in our lines], but nowhere is there a gap, a great, wide breakthrough, which would open up the road to Lille, Lens and the Rhein.[51] The situation is more serious on the Southeastern Front, in the Bukovina and in Galicia. There the Austrians are outnumbered by five to one and this time, for some unexplained reason, the Russians dispose of whole mountains of ammunition. In spite of that, their losses in terms of dead, wounded and prisoners are staggering even by Russian standards. They number two million men.[52] During the past ten days the English have lost half a million men. The French have suffered equally

[50] In order to relieve the Italians in the Trentino, General Alexei Brusilov, on June 4, committed more than fifty Russian divisions to an attack against the Austrians along the Eastern Front. The Austrian Fourth and Seventh armies were surprised and routed.

[51] The fighting along the Meuse centered around the heights occupied by the fortress of Verdun. At the end of June the Germans finally managed to seize the two outer defensive positions of Vaux and Thiaumont. Since the French were so heavily engaged at Verdun, the English had to bear the brunt of the Somme offensive, which began on July 1. Although the Germans were orginally outnumbered six to one, they were well fortified and dug in. The British troops stolidly marched in rank into the German machine-gun fire and were simply mowed down. At the height of the fighting the British lost over 60,000 men in one day. The Battle of the Somme raged on until November, at which point the Allies had penetrated the German lines to a depth of seven miles but had failed to gain a single major objective.

[52] During the Brusilov offensive some Austrian contingents were so overcome by despair and so completely demoralized that large numbers of their men deserted to the Russians. Finally, the situation looked so serious that Germany was compelled to withdraw troops from the West to bolster up her faltering ally.

Stumpf's figures on the Russian casualties are highly exaggerated. The entire Brusilov offensive, which lasted from June until September, 1916, cost the Russians about one million casualties. However, the cost of the Russian victory ran very high. At the end of the campaign, the morale of the Russian army was shattered and the troops were on the verge of rebellion.

high losses at Verdun.[53] Although these figures may sound a trifle excessive, they are by no means impossible.

However we [in the navy] sit by idly biding our time. How much longer shall we wait? How much longer?

I would also like to say something about [the possibility of] peace. Our soldiers returning from Verdun and the other [frontal] areas maintain that both sides have reached the point of exhaustion. They simply can no longer go on, even with the best of will. . . . Although we have heard this sort of thing before, it was never expressed with such fervor. (They have started to show a film right next to me and therefore I am closing off.) 5 July 1916.

Once again the great prediction did not come true. July 10, the day on which the great convulsion was supposed to occur, has gone by like any other day. I know that many of our men had staked all their hopes on it. The latest prediction postpones the conclusion of peace until August 15.

I have often written that the war has now reached its high point and has even exceeded it. But surely nothing in the past has approximated the intensity of the storm which is now raging against our lines along the Ancre and the Somme. The reports we get from there sound like [incredible] fairy tales. Within the past eight days the English have fired ten million rounds of artillery against our lines. But when the Englishmen in their khaki uniforms broke cover to attack, our German Maxim [machine guns] hammered away at them from every hole and crater. The English troops who had hitherto been so cautiously held in reserve were mowed down by the tens of thousands. Although a superior enemy force occasionally succeeded in seizing one of our trenches or in storming the ruins of a village, there is no longer any hope that they will advance up to Cologne. England is bleeding from thousands of wounds. Despite this, I am frequently reminded of Bismarck's predic-

[53] The entire Somme campaign produced about 400,000 **British and** about 200,000 French casualties. However, the French lost an additional 400,000 men at Verdun. All in all, the French and the British lost 1,200,000 men in 1916, while the Germans suffered 800,000 casualties.

tion that a future European war would last either seven or thirty years. Gradually I have come to the conclusion that there will be no victors and no vanquished [in this war]. I have come to accept the idea that we shall have to surrender all our conquests and that we will also have to forego a war indemnity. Every nation will have to pay its own debts and make an attempt to get along as well as possible with its neighbors. Then [after a while] each nation will become belligerent again and will commence to rearm as fast as possible for the next war.

This terrible war has certainly made a signifiant contribution to the progress of the idea of world peace. But this nebulous goal still lies in the far distant future, so that the very thought of it is a grisly joke. The overwhelming burden of taxation [after the war] is certain to keep the warmongers silent for the next ten years. But by that time we shall begin to forget. Then once again we will start railing against our hereditary enemies, the Russians and perfidious Albion. But when the sad time comes for our sons to join their regiments, our arsenals will be restocked not only with shells and guns, but also with copper and wheat, with cotton and nickel, with nitrates and fats. And when once more, God forbid, the tocsin of war rings out, we shall no longer have to face the dread specter of starvation. And with the experience of this war as our guide, we shall be able to move mountains. One thing is certain. If this war is not fought to a conclusion, but is broken off, it will be resumed again in less than thirty years.

Why have I written all this? It has nothing to do with my diary. That may well be true, but since one's memory cannot retain everything, I think it will later on prove to be instructive to occasionally read how we felt about these problems at this time.

Recently, when I took a three-day course in diving, I had much time to think about these matters. But then things looked much grimmer than they do now. Today, for the first time in a long while, we are enjoying glorious sunny weather. It is refreshing and restores one's optimism and faith. This entire month has been so cold and wet that there is virtually no hope that we can bring in the harvest in time. Although our newspapers predict that all of Germany may expect a magnificent harvest, I still recall that last year the very same writers said the identical thing. Then, too, they said: magnificent harvest, record year and so on. But later on, we discovered that we had three million tons less wheat than usual. And this year there will be even less.

For a long time now, our newest battleship *Bayern* has been scheduled to be sent to Wilhelmshaven. She has already been in commission for almost a half a year. When she finally arrived on [July] 17, we received her with immense enthusiasm. Her most important feature is that she is armed with eight 38.1 cm. guns. This represents great progress [for us]. She is even longer than *König*, has only a single tripod mast and two close-set smokestacks. If we only had a dozen like her. . . .

Although the King of Bavaria [54] was to come and inspect the Dreadnought on Monday, as usual we were placed on a state of alert on Sunday. Now that *Markgraf*, too, has been refitted, we are back to a strength of thirteen modern battleships. We sailed out as far as fifty miles west of Helgoland while *Bayern* took the rear. It may well be that the purpose of the whole mission was to accustom the new ship to the squadron in the same way that one accustoms a cow to a herd. It was rather foggy, but on the next day the weather improved. Nothing happened, but our Sunday was spoiled. 22 July 1916.

Today, for the first time in a long while, we are having real summer weather. I hope that it is not too late!

This morning our honorable old King made his appearance. All the ships in port sent the Bavarians in their crews to the southern port to give the prince a properly imposing reception. I estimated that two to three thousand men were present. We assembled in front of *Bayern* and thus had a wonderful opportunity to have a close look at this marvel of German technology. An old gray sea bear, a regular sea dog of an officer,

[54] This refers to King Ludwig III of Bavaria (1845–1921), who reigned from 1913 to 1918.

was in charge of the formation. It was a delight to see how he cursed at the officers. I think his name is [Häuser]. Then the Fleet Commander held a practice inspection, while an enormous submarine made a slow approach to show herself off to the King.

After we had formed and reformed our ranks about thirty times, the cars dashed up. A half dozen generals and other high officers, their chests covered with medals, dismounted. I regret to say that I noticed several typical Prussian faces among them. However most of them had a congenial [gemütlich] South German look about them.

The King was dressed in a simple field-gray general's uniform and he wore a single decoration, the Iron Cross. In looking at him, one might think that he was merely a trained privy councillor instead of a reigning monarch. As he slowly progressed from group to group, he shouted out a loud, "Good morning, fellow countrymen!" The men all responded heartily, while the officers introduced themselves. After the King had inspected our ranks, the sea dog of a Captain [Häuser] gave the King a proper military welcome. The King replied in an unostentatious way somewhat as follows: "Dear fellow countrymen, about six months ago I visited your comrades of the naval brigade in Flanders. Although all Bavarians, regardless where they are stationed, do their duty, they were sorry that they could not be with the fleet. You and your comrades from the rest of Germany have just won a brilliant victory. I never doubted that should an opportunity present itself, our navy would put up a magnificent fight. Therefore I am especially proud that so many of my country's sailors took part in it. Since you are Bavarians, you will be proud to know that for the past two years of this war you have become the terror of our enemies. His Majesty the Kaiser, our Supreme Ruler and War Lord, has invited me to visit his proudest possession, the navy, here in Wilhelmshaven. I was delighted to accept his invitation to be present at the commissioning of the ship which bears the name of our state. I am certain that she will preserve the ancient fame of Bavaria. Will you join me in giving three cheers for Our Supreme War Lord, the Kaiser."

The King's speech was splendid. However, those among us who had particularly keen ears could tell that he did not mention certain things. It was obvious that the ruler of a landlocked state [like Bavaria] could not be overjoyed that Prussia was the principal beneficiary of all our efforts. We South Germans are merely accorded the right to pay, but we get nothing in return. Not only are the ships built and provisioned in North Germany, but all the material for them is purchased north of the Main line.[55] Nevertheless there are many Bavarians in the navy and in the construction crews! But without exception they serve in a subordinate capacity as sailors, stokers and workers. While the navy, unlike the army, does not serve as a refuge for impoverished Junkers, they still preempt the majority of the best paid positions. Be that as it may, all of Germany was ecstatic over our victory at Jutland and hardly paused to reflect about the millions which Krupp and the shipyard made out of it.

After this digression, I must return to the subject at hand. *Bayern* turned and raised her guns into firing position in the most menacing way. The submarine surfaced once more and then we assembled to march off. Although this may have interested the old prince. I was quite bored with the whole thing. As soon as we got back, I sat down to write these lines. Afternoon of July 25, 1916.

I have promised myself to record everything of any importance in my diary and to omit nothing. I have come to the conclusion, however, that it will not work out the way I intended. One does not always have the time, the opportunity or the inclination [to write]. If I were to record everything as it passed through my mind, I would produce a shattering indictment against the military. Thus it may be for the best to allow one's temper to cool down right after some injustice has been committed, in order to gain a certain amount of perspective.

[55] The river Main represents the historical dividing line between North and South Germany.

Right now our ship is in dock because a large number of tubes in our boilers have sprung leaks and had to be replaced. Again about two hundred of our men obtained furloughs. But since they only got six and a half days, I refused to take my leave at this time. [I hoped to take it] later on when we went to Kiel for a "more extensive" stay in dock.

Here we have to abide by the most infamous dock regulations. They state that we may not leave our posts without permission from the dock officers, that we may not wander away more than a ship's length, and that smoking, bathing and the hanging of laundry are all forbidden. Although these regulations were meant to be broken, they offer our pettifogging officers hundreds of excuses to torture and harass us. It is simply shocking and more than one can bear without striking out that we have to ask a twenty-year-old lieutenant for leave to go to the toilet. Moreover he heaps insult upon injury by asking if it is an emergency or merely a pretext for not working. In the evening we are set free in small groups of ten men after our names are jotted down. The half-baked Lieutenant A. excels at this pettiness and made the men who left without asking him for permission scrub the decks until 11:30. It is scandalous that this young idiot, whom we knew when he was merely a midshipman, should possess such extensive powers. He chews us out most disgracefully. If any of us object, he places us on report or sends us either to the mast or gun turrets. However I must admit that there are others who are far worse than he in this regard.

Although our work is very strenuous, we get little food. This makes our stomachs grumble and reduces our capacity for work. While we toil and suffer, the officers are ashore in their comfortable quarters. But today they all showed up because it was payday.

I have been assigned to work in the engine room and find it no easy task to knock out and remove the tubes. We work seven and a half hours a day and all we get for lunch is a plate of soup! How can one bear this without grumbling? Thank God, this business will only last for eight days! 31 July 1916.

Thank God, the eight days are almost over now. The men who have gone on leave are to return tomorrow. We left the dock this morning and are now anchored at our old mooring at the supply pier. I am extremely glad that this dreadful interlude is over. On one of the days we were here I visited the dentist.

Fortunately we are now enjoying marvelous weather. We talked about the harvest a great deal and it gave our spirits a lift to learn that we might still be able to bring in all the crops. It is at times like these that even our city dwellers remember that they once came from the country. All of us have some sort of connection with the land. It will not hurt the city folks to learn to appreciate the farmers and to overcome their customary contempt for them. Nevertheless once the war is over, the old schism between town and country will grow deeper and wider than ever. It is discouraging that at a time like this there are food hoarders and war profiteeers in Germany.

Whenever one turns, inevitably the subject [of food] is raised as the people ask fearfully, "Will it go on like this after the war? Will an egg still cost 28 pfennigs and a pound of meat 2.50 marks?" It is difficult to predict. On the basis of the experience of our past wars, I would say no. But can one compare the past with the present? Did we have a population density of 220 people per square kilometer at that time? Not only has the population increased, but also the standard of living of the people has multiplied many times over. Hence I would not recommend looking at our future through rose-colored lenses, but by the same token, there is no cause for despair. Our submarine *Deutschland* has left Baltimore with a cargo of nickel, rubber and gold.[56] Her sister ship the *Bremen*, however, has vanished without a trace. . . . I hope that the rumor that we are soon to head for Kiel proves to be correct, because it is much more pleasant to be stationed there than here.

Our situation at the front has become very critical. Lloyd

---

[56] On July 10, 1916, the *Deutschland*, a German cargo submarine, arrived in Baltimore after a spectacular sixteen-day crossing of the Atlantic. She departed on her return voyage to Germany on August 1.

George's statement [57] that time is working for the Allies seems about to come true. Our enemies are hammering away at us on all fronts. Although we are still fighting on foreign soil, recently they penetrated deeply into the fertile Carpathian Mountains and the Bukovina. The daily reports from the Austrian army resembles those of the first phases of the war with their news of regroupings, positional changes and planned evacuations of villages and towns. But by now we know the correct meaning of these technical terms. The seizure of the bridgehead and town of Gorizia by the Italians came as a sudden and unexpected blow.[58] I never dreamed that this could happen. For us Gorizia symbolizes the power of Austria in the same way as the French regard Verdun. That it was the treacherous Italians who won this signal victory is virtually unbearable.

The recent glorious weather is responsible for the increased activity of our Zeppelins and submarines. Tonight eight of our Zeppelins assembled over the Jade for a bombing mission over England. Two of these were unusually large, with six or seven gondolas. These long-awaited great air cruisers of ours made the older models look like pygmies. I stayed on deck looking at these proud birds for a long time until they vanished over the horizon. In four or five hours they will make England resound with the howling of sirens and the barking of the antiaircraft guns, while the people cower in terror in their cellars. I hoped with all my heart that these aerial giants would bomb London.[59]

As was usually the case on such occasions, we waited in a state of alert, ready to sail out should an opportunity arise for

[57] David Lloyd George (1863–1945) was the British Chancellor of the Exchequer, 1908–15; Minister of Munitions, 1915–16; Secretary of State for War, 1916; Prime Minister, December 1916–22. On August 22 Lloyd George made a speech in which he asserted, "We are pressing the enemy back. . . . We are pushing the enemy on the Somme. . . . He has lost his tide. . . ."

[58] During the Sixth Battle of the Isonzo, General Cardona's Italian armies, outnumbering the Austrians almost three to one, finally succeeded in capturing Gorizia on August 9.

[59] During the night of August 8–9, German naval aircraft bombarded the English Midlands.

us to intervene. But nothing happened. The next morning, while we were having our breakfast, the first Zeppelins returned. Naturally we all rushed on deck to welcome our victorious ships who closed in with astonishing speed. The newspapers are very excited over the possibility that one of our Zeppelins may soon fly to New York. If that were only true! Interrupted on 9 August 1916.

I can't think of anything to write! Consequently the absence of important actions and events forces me to dwell on trivialities. But these are often quite interesting and well worth recording.

This morning the mistreatment of one of our enlisted men sent me into a towering rage. Lately our first division has had a great deal of physical training. They do a lot of calisthenics and bathe and shower every day. The above-mentioned sailor stood on line in order to learn how to swim in the ocean. It was evident that he was making a brave effort and that it must have taken great courage for him to jump into the water from the fantail. However [once he had landed in the water] the seaman who was holding him let go of the line. The poor fellow went under for about twenty seconds. When he finally came to the surface again, he climbed up the ladder and absolutely refused to go in again. Time and again, Lieutenant F. ordered him into the water, but he kept refusing and held on for dear life. He was trembling all over with cold. After making repeated encouragements and threats, the seaman came down and kicked him on the head, shoulders and hands with his heavy boots. There must have been at least a hundred men looking on. Some of them laughed while others openly shouted their disapproval, but with no result. The man [simply] would not go into the water any more. At last he was allowed to come up. Although he was blue with cold, he received a long dressing down and then was made to stand stark naked at A Turret for ten minutes. This incident brought to mind all the other cases concerning the mistreatment of men I had ever read or heard about.

What was going on today? We had cleared for action! Several Zeppelins were in sight. Were we going on another raid to England? Or were we merely going out, as some of the men maintained, to provide an escort for our returning cargo submarine the *Deutschland*? She had departed from Baltimore on [August] 1. According to my calculations, she should have been here already or was due to arrive at any moment.[60] With the exception of *Seydlitz* and *Derfflinger* the entire fleet lay assembled at Schillig Roads. We were fortunate to have *Bayern* join us as well, because she was equivalent to three other ships. Consequently, we were quite prepared to risk another encounter with the enemy. But I would have liked to have a chance to first go home for a little while. 17 August 1916.

SUNDAY AFTERNOON, 20 AUGUST 1916

We almost got into another sea battle yesterday, so I have a great deal to write. On this occasion [unlike the last time] the weather was lovely and clear and our aerial reconnaissance functioned perfectly. But as our Executive Officer told us this morning, [this time] the English knew all [about our plans] even before we did. But I shall return to that matter later. . . .

On Thursday all our ships slowly assembled at Schillig Roads. Many of them, such as the brave *Moltke* and a number of light cruisers, we had not seen for a long time. This in itself was sufficient proof that something unusual was about to occur. First our submarines put out to sea while our Zeppelins and airplanes circled overhead in the sky. The atmosphere on our ship was quiet but very tense. At five o'clock the previous night our jumpy Ensign had ordered us to stow our gear in Compartment 15. Later on he admitted with evident embarrass-

---

[60] When the *Deutschland* left Baltimore, a fleet of Allied warships were waiting for her outside the three-mile limit, but she managed to evade it and arrived in Bremen on August 23.

ment in a most friendly manner that he had acted too hastily and that we were to retrieve our gear. The men responded by showering him with curses which he pointedly disregarded.

We cleared for action the next morning. Here was additional evidence that something was about to break loose. Nevertheless nothing happened all that day. In the evening, however, it suddenly began again and once more we ran and scrambled all over the ship. Within a half hour we had cleared for sea and were ready for action.

Since two of our cruisers *Derfflinger* and *Seydlitz* were still in dock, a few of our fastest battleships had to substitute for them. Hence *Bayern*, *Grosser Kurfürst* and *Markgraf* joined the cruisers *Moltke* and *Von der Tann* when they sailed out at six o'clock. They were soon followed by two of our torpedo boat flotillas and their escorts. I still knew nothing of the destination or the purpose of our mission. Since I knew from past experience that whenever we sailed out in the evening we usually headed right back by dawn, I was not very optimistic about the entire enterprise. Despite this, all the signs indicated that we were about to embark on an important mission. We were issued life jackets and gas masks and we folded away the loading booms. At about eight o'clock all the battleships raised anchor and slowly formed themselves into a long line.

Last year at this time we were in the Baltic and spent some lovely days at Swinemünde. Then as now, the summer nights were magnificent. This kept going through my mind as we sailed into the uncertain darkness. Then, too, the glorious stars had shimmered in the heavens and their rays lighted the warlike activities of men on earth. Then as now, our morale was high. We forgot the usual complaints which saddened our daily lives. Our holiday made us forget the tedium of our everyday routine. Our officers probably felt the same way and did not abuse us with their usual threats. Most of the men gained a false impression from this. They maintained, "Our officers are frightened and therefore they have become friendly for a little while." Even though this may contain a kernel of truth, it is by no means the whole answer. In the event our mission should fail, it will have a depressing effect on both sides and the [old] hostility will rise up again.

A psychologist might conduct a most interesting study on the effects of external factors upon our morale. The narrow, confined atmosphere of the ship is extremely conducive to dreaming. On a monotonous tour of lookout duty when the ship is in no immediate danger, it is very easy to begin daydreaming. After the watch is over and one goes down to the overheated quarters, one can dream even better with one's head resting on the deck. The steady humming and pounding of the engines beat a hypnotizing rhythm which permits one's thoughts to be transformed into dreams. When we are dreaming about our sweethearts at home and are suddenly awakened by a call to battle stations, we cannot immediately find our way back to reality. None of us pauses to think that we could sink and die within a matter of seconds. We are all incapable of thinking of anything but our jobs. A little while later, when we are allowed to relax again, our thoughts resume the rhythm of the engines once more.

It was midnight by the time we sighted the Helgoland beacon diagonally across on our left. We sailed out slowly and our wake glittered like glowing diamonds. What was our destination this time? In all probability we were going to stage another raid on the English coast. But just then we were relieved from duty and we climbed down quickly to snatch three hours of sleep.

When I returned to my post at four o'clock, I heard the Officer of the Watch reporting, "Course, west-north-west. Speed, 17 miles." This was something new! I don't think we ever sailed on this course before. As it began to dawn we were instructed to keep a sharp watch for mines and submarines. Gradually the outlines of the surrounding ships became clearer and more distinct. Our speed had increased imperceptibly and we now raced along in a foaming wake at a hundred revolutions per second. Although an occasional plume of spray flew over our bows, it promised to be a glorious day. One of our Zeppelins emerged from a cloud bank and signaled to the flagship.

There was a sudden flurry of excitement when we received a signal announcing that *Westfalen* had spotted a torpedo. Several minutes later the ship reported that she had been hit on the starboard side and that three of her compartments were flooding. However her torpedo bulkheads held tight and she managed to maintain her place in line at a speed of 17 miles.

"Those most favored by God are blessed by running over a minefield!" mumbled our crew. "Why can't the *Helgoland* ever have such luck? Damn it, this bucket has barely left the dock and now she'll go right back. And then her crew will get leave again!" Just at that moment, however, the ship began to list to her right, compelling the flagship and *Friedrich der Grosse* to break formation and to rush to her aid. They reprimanded *Westfalen*'s captain for breaking wireless silence and finally ordered two torpedo boats to escort the ship back to port.

The actual purpose of our sortie was described to me as follows: Tonight our cruisers will bombard the town of Sunderland. They will avoid engaging strong enemy units but they have been instructed to seek out weaker units. Our assignment is to cover the cruisers and [should such an opportunity present itself] we are not to avoid a fight with the English fleet. This is quite a large order. If the English have not lost all their pride, we may expect that they will react very strongly. The weather is ideal for a battle at long range. But we shall have to wait and see what develops.

In the afternoon I observed the return of five of our cruisers. Did [this mean] that they had been forced to retreat before the stronger main body of the English fleet and that they had been unable to stage their raid on Sunderland? I did not know. In any event, I suspected that our daring plan had gone awry. Hence I was astonished when the Captain ordered us to remove the bridge covering. Was the enemy so close already? I soon learned what was going on. One of our Zeppelins had reported spotting fourteen enemy ships southeast of us. What a catch they would be for us! Our entire fleet raced to the designated area at full speed. Since the men who were not on duty had not been told of this, they sunned themselves on the top deck; the other watch was asleep. When general quarters was sounded, it was very interesting to see how the men jumped up and dashed about frantically. Within seconds all the guns were manned. Since we were still thirty sea miles away from the enemy, we could not expect to go into action for at least two hours. The men of the starboard side were particularly happy because they thought that they would finally get a chance to fire in this engagement. Bread and bacon were distributed [to the crew]. Time passed; one hour, two hours. We became impatient. Had the English scented their danger and made their escape?

No, it was something else. With fiendish cleverness the English had laid a dangerous trap for us. Fourteen of their ships acted as decoys, while some very strong squadrons waited on the flanks for us to enter the trap. But thanks to our Zeppelins, we learned of their plan. As a result, our entire division turned about and headed home.[61] Now the English would report sarcastically that they had driven us back to our home ports. Our trip home was uneventful. Since we sailed at very high speed, all the ships were back at Wilhelmshaven Roads by eight o'clock on Sunday morning. Sunday and Monday, 19 and 20 August 1916.[62]

What a surprise! No sooner had we returned to Wilhelmshaven from our sortie, than our squadron received a wireless order to sail to Kiel! Later on, however, our departure was postponed until Wednesday morning. At eight that morning we entered the canal locks at Brunsbüttel. I have already de-

[61] The main objective of the German fleet on August 19 was to engage parts of the English fleet in battle. Sunderland was merely a secondary objective. However, when Scheer suspected that he would have to face the main body of the English fleet, he beat a hasty retreat. He realized that Germany had nothing to gain by risking a new major encounter. For Scheer's views on this, see Note 47.

[62] Evidently at this juncture Stumpf had lost track of the days of the week. August 19, 1916, was a Saturday and August 20 a Sunday.

scribed the trip through the canal and this time it was no different from before.

Yesterday our First Officer flew into a rage when he was told that we had been issued double bread rations. The Quartermaster was on the verge of tears when he heard that we had also gotten some bacon.

By five o'clock that afternoon we reached the high bridge at Levensau with its lovely brick exterior and Kiel lay right behind. Since I was not on duty, I went ashore. Unfortunately, however, we had docked at eight o'clock and we had to be back at ten. 23 August 1916.

The next day we started our usual round of activities in Kiel. For an entire week we conducted torpedo and artillery practice. As an additional attraction, we fired at a hot-air balloon. On Friday we held target practice against the old *Bayern* with indifferent success. Each of our seven ships fired about twenty rounds, but since I did not observe any of them strike her, I could not tell how many hits we scored.

The lack of precaution in our movements in the Baltic astonished me. We acted as though there were no such things as English or Russian submarines. We casually lay at anchor for hours on end without spreading our torpedo nets. It was not even thought necessary to post lookouts and some of us were ordered to restow the coal bunkers. I spent eight hours on that job and got thoroughly filthy from it.

On Sunday I received a pass to go ashore and thus had a rare chance to drink in some of Kiel's scenic beauty. In the afternoon I visited the little theater and saw a very amusing new operetta, *The House with Three Girls*. The mere memory of such a joyous day is enough to sustain one for a long time. Since our coal supply had dwindled down to a thousand tons during the past ten days, we spent two days loading 1,600 tons. On Monday we learned to our dismay that Rumania had followed Italy's example by declaring war on Austria.[63] While

---

[63] On August 27, 1916, Rumania, long under pressure from France and Russia to enter the war on the side of the Entente, was cajoled into declaring war on Austria in return for a promise of territorial gains in the Bukovina, the Banat, and Transylvania. Germany retaliated by declaring war on Rumania on August 28.

we had merely smiled in contempt at the chestnut vendors' declaration of war, Rumania's actions encouraged our pessimists to point to "the inevitability of the impending doom." [64] Although it is indeed true that our situation is critical, there is as little cause to despair as there is for rejoicing. I am convinced that [Field Marshal] Mackensen in cooperation with the brave Turks and Bulgarians will succeed in teaching the Rumanians a lesson, and that ultimately these stupid and disloyal Rumanians will suffer the same fate as Serbia.

Still I have no wish to make predictions. It has become a difficult and thankless task these days. The issue is about to be decided by the force of arms along the Danube and the Sereth. It would be foolish to predict something which depends so heavily upon the outcome of the fighting.

On our ship we have ample cause for complaint and reflection. Our miserable food and ill-treatment had already resulted in open refusals to obey orders (on the part of the first division). Indeed our morale has deteriorated so badly that someone removed the safety pin from one of the guns and cut through one of the lines amidship. Consequently all the guns are now guarded day and night. Although the identity of the culprit remains unknown, our food has improved remarkably. And after all, this was the aim of the action.[65]

I understand that the older men in our crew are to be transferred and will be replaced by recruits.

Ended on 16 September 1916.

[64] These prophecies of doom were not unfounded. The Russian offensive had wreaked havoc with the Austrian army. However, since Rumania had delayed her declaration of war in order to bring in her grain harvest, her intervention lacked coordination with the Brusilov offensive. Therefore, Austria could still be rescued by the prompt despatch of German troops under the command of General Falkenhayn, the former Chief of the General Staff, to Transylvania.

[65] This may be regarded as the first overt manifestation of revolutionary activity among the enlisted men in the German navy.

Four

Begun 16 September 1916

Today I am somewhat depressed as I write in my diary. Actually I have no cause [to feel that way] because tomorrow, if God and the Executive Officer are willing, I shall go home on leave. But as is customary in these matters, I am still not completely certain and the worry and anxiety of waiting is worse than not knowing at all. Unfortunately, however, the men who are being sent home to work have always enjoyed a much higher priority and we propertyless proletarians have to take the leavings. This is the way it goes all over the world; those who have nothing, get nothing.

Nothing lasts forever in this world. Our enjoyable stay in Kiel ended all too soon. I would gladly have stayed for a while longer to search for knowledge and entertainment in the reading rooms of the great local public library.

We have now been back for ten days in the dirty waters of the Jade and are gazing philosophically at the "lovely" Oldenburger countryside. During the last days of our stay in Kiel there was considerable talk that a Danish declaration of war was imminent and unavoidable. Hence I hoped that we could stay on a while so that we would be right on the spot [when war broke out]. Since we departed precisely on schedule, I think that there was no factual basis to these wild rumors. Our presence seemed to be more urgently required in the North Sea. The news from Holland was not designed to awaken our hopes for peace. Recently thousands of our sailors were despatched to the border to dig trenches and fortifications. I understand that if war should break out [with Holland] there is a chance that a large part of that country will be flooded. I only hope that this will be enough to restrain the "Dutchmen" who have been egged on by the English.

Nowadays we treat these questions as casually as the weather. Even the death, drowning or burning of thousands of men no longer produces any pity or sorrow. It is remarkable how cheap human life has become. Every other commodity, however, has become extremely expensive even when there is no shortage.

Since we have had such limited contact with the actual war, we wage a sort of internal war among ourselves on the ship. The incident of the cut cable and the disappearance of the safety device [from one of the guns] has produced some unexpected results. The story was repeated in a barber shop by one of the biggest show-offs [on our ship] who came from Cologne. He must have said more than he actually knew because a Kapitänleutnant and a patrol came to arrest him. However he had already escaped and so the patrol arrested the stoker to whom he had told the story.

[Subsequently], at noon one lovely day, we were unexpectedly ordered to change into our dress uniforms even though it was a regular workday. We soon found out why. Several court officials and the stoker came on board to identify the culprit as we stood in array for inspection. Curiously enough, although the stoker identified five or six suspects, the real [culprit] was not among them. Only later did he reveal himself through his own carelessness. Now the stupid fellow has been placed under interrogatory arrest and he will no doubt be made the scapegoat for the entire affair.

Have just returned from leave!

I have returned from the longest and best leave I have ever had. It was a very special leave. [I find that it] was much easier to experience it than to describe it. Only when I was actually on the express train which brought me closer and closer to my beloved home with each passing second did I begin to feel happy. Then I dreamt how different everything would be back home and how anxiously they awaited my arrival. It is difficult not to talk when one is so happy and I told anyone who would listen about my happiness, my ship and its officers. I gossiped about the war and the coming of peace. I had promised myself that this time I would listen very carefully to what the soldiers said about [their experiences at] the front. Indeed it is imperative that one remain silent because whenever one asks curious questions, one is always regaled with lies which give an entirely incorrect picture of the situation.

At Kreiensen a civilian with a black and white ribbon on his chest got on the train. He looked pitiful and one could see right away that he was a war cripple. While we were conducting a lively conversation about the war, he painfully hobbled into our compartment on two crutches. The man then reclined in a corner, closed his eyes and said nothing. Only when our conversation turned into a heated debate and the question was raised whether France or Germany had lost more men in the war did the invalid chime in. He said in a quiet, confident voice: "Of course, France has lost more men." He sounded so certain that I risked asking, "Excuse me, but why are you so sure of that?" "I was there for eight months!" "Oh, and how were you treated there?" "Very badly. I was captured by the English after I had broken my legs. They bandaged them and then for three days left me lying totally unattended in a meadow. It was horrible! At last, a hospital train arrived and I and three hundred others were taken to a hospital near Calais. There the doctors treated my legs in such a fashion that the bones knit together crookedly." The poor man said this with such dead calm that cold shudders raced up and down my spine.

"But listen," I called, "the French could not possibly be so barbaric." "My legs are proof enough," he responded. "I was one of twenty men out of three hundred who survived. Then I returned to Germany through an exchange of badly wounded prisoners. Now the doctors will have to break my legs again and I hope that I shall thus learn to walk normally again." "The French must be fiends," someone stated. "Yes indeed! 'The Boche can either drop dead or become a cripple,' this is what their doctors say. Certainly this may not be true everywhere, but I have had a very, very bad experience," he concluded.

It was getting late and I tried to sleep but I kept waking up from the cold. At the first light of dawn I got up to wash myself thoroughly. At seven o'clock the shape of Frankfurt am Main emerged from the morning fog. We had a two-hour wait there and for a while I strolled along the Kaiserstrasse looking at the shop windows. I had been so careless as to leave my baggage on the waiting Munich Express and found it fully occupied a half hour prior to its departure. There were many Austrians on the train. In the next compartment I heard a man complaining loudly about the war. He carried things a bit far when he told his audience how happy he would be if he could only skin the usurers and the moneybags alive. He would confiscate the property of the millionaires, put them all in a sack and drown them at sea. Resounding laughter greeted this "joke." "God will surely see to it that they are punished!" [someone stated]. "God? But is there still a God? He got killed in the war!" [he retorted].

I walked over to the other compartment to take a look at the loudmouth. He was a typical Austrian noncommissioned officer with dapper, flowing mustache. I could not resist the temptation to egg him on by making a few pointed remarks. I was more successful than I had expected, for he seemed just to have been waiting for someone to challenge him who would also hear him out. He rose up immediately, went with me to my compartment and unburdened himself to me. He did not afford me a chance to say anything as he let loose a veritable torrent of words. His description of the conditions in the Austrian army sounded totally incredible. [He told of] the dreadful language difficulties, contradictory orders, cars colliding with each other, the panic-stricken flight of whole regiments, abandoned guns, and desertion of whole battalions to the Russians.[1] All this he rained down on me like a hailstorm. Whenever I attempted to introduce a cautionary objection, he immediately responded by raising another issue. The others listened quietly and merely shook their heads. He did clarify a number of things for me and thereby enabled me to view our ally's continual retreats and defeats in a different light. Everything that he had said was later confirmed by others. What a bleak prospect for the future! "Will the Austrians not conclude a separate peace?" was a frequent question. The German Austrians feel: "Why not allow the Russians to take all those [nationalities] who want to join them. This would enable the German Kaiser to annex [the territories] which are [rightfully] his." I could fill an entire book with this kind of talk. Is it any wonder that an army which still flogs its men should ultimately grow war-weary after two years?

Outside the vine-clad hills of Franconia flew by. Hence we were already on Bavarian soil. I saw the soil of my homeland and inhaled its delicious air. Our Bavarian officials are totally different from their North German counterparts. They answer questions with courtesy and friendliness and know their train schedules by heart.

Würzburg—Neustadt—Burgfarrnbach. Soon we would arrive in Fürth, where I had to change trains. "Go with God!

[1] The major difficulty of the Austro-Hungarian army was the nationality problem. About 75 percent of the officers were German-speaking while only 25 percent of the troops understood German. Even the Austrian official history admits, "It often happened that a platoon commander could not make himself intelligible to his motley collection of men. Ten separate nationalities fought in the army and many of them were of questionable loyalty. For instance, so many Czech soldiers deserted to the Russians that a legion was formed out of them to fight against Germany."

Auf Wiedersehen! Much luck!" the Austrian malcontent called after me. His eyes blinked as if to say, "Please, for heaven's sake, I didn't mean to make it sound so bad!" In Fürth I visited a lady friend and allowed myself to dally with her until the last train. As I strolled through the smoky and grimy taverns of the old Jewish ghetto, many old memories revived in my mind.

At Erlangen I met a number of people from home. [I met] a group of women returning from Altötting, where they had gone to pray for an early end of the war. A Jewish acquaintance of mine who was dressed in uniform cynically stated that this was perfectly useless because God had stopped caring for the human race. A little old lady snapped back, "Well, before the war the human race did not overly concern itself with Him!"

Bread ration coupons and meat coupons have gradually been introduced in Erlangen. Although it was still possible to buy virtually everything, here, too, prices have risen drastically. The major topic of conversation was the extremely high losses which the local 19th Regiment had suffered on the Somme. After the customary half-hour delay, my little train slowly set itself in motion. At the toll house station it began to fill up with Franconian farm wives. I was delighted at the sight of the people among whom I had lived as a youth and soon become so used to them that it seemed as if I had never left. Since I arrived unexpectedly [I figured] that my family would be in bed when I knocked on the door. On the train I entered into a lively conversation with a number of gentlemen whom I first took to be rabbis. However they were not rabbis, but their Christian counterparts. They were Protestant pastors going home from a conference in Erlangen. They were extremely friendly and spoke enthusiastically of the Kaiser, the navy, of the Fatherland and the war. Yes, it is easy to be patriotic while sitting comfortably at home [I thought to myself]. I kept these sentiments to myself because I did not want to hurt these simple, pious gentlemen.

Our engine with its four cars had in the meantime made the laborious climb up the mountains of Spardorf and Weihrig. Then as it wound through Dormitz, I took my package and stepped out on the platform. The air of home! All the lights were out save one small one at the Vasold Tavern. As the little train made its way to the station, the shrieking and moaning of its unoiled wheels sounded like music to my ears. The first houses! "Home, home! I shall love you always! You are beautiful beyond compare!" This song had been going through my mind all evening and as I now viewed the first houses, it resounded like an organ crescendo within me. Home, home . . .

I pulled the door bell. "Who is it?" "It is I, Father" "Good God, Richard, where are you coming from?" "From Wilhelmshaven, Father. Open up." "Are you hungry? There is some tongue in the kitchen." "No, Father, I am not hungry. But I am very sleepy. I have been on the train all night." From the hall came the voice of my sister Babette, "It must be Richard! Just like him to come without writing!"

"Where shall I sleep?" "In the outer room." "Good night, Father." "Good night; sleep well." Oh, what a delight it was to sleep in bed at home. And how wonderful it felt to wake up in the night and to be able to say, "You are not in your hammock, but at home, home. And there are still nine days left. Only one single day has gone by."

It was late, about ten, when I woke up the following morning. I went to the town hall and the mayor [to obtain] bread and meat ration cards. I was received most cordially and with many questions. The people were very busy with the potato harvest, which was in full progress. There were many Frenchmen and Russians employed at the harvesting. They had complete freedom of movement and many of them went about dressed in civilian clothes. There was not even a pretense of guarding them. On the following day, in order to make my trip complete, I cycled over to Gräfenberg to see my birthplace. On the way back I visited my favorite girl friend in Weissenhorn. I was especially pleased when she excelled herself in performing her loveliest piano pieces for me.

Although my brother Hans was expected to arrive on Saturday, I finally carried out my long standing resolve to pay a visit to my deceased brother's bride in Stadtsteinach. But the local train to Untersteinach took an eternity and it was almost night before I arrived. The dear girl was waiting for me and together we trudged for an hour on foot to reach distant Stadtsteinach. We exchanged fond memories and I learned to know and respect my deceased brother from an entirely new point of view. I was received in the most friendly fashion at her parent's home. Since they, too, were very busy, I did not want to be a burden to them. Hence the next morning, I climbed the nearest hill of the Franconian Forest all by myself.

I had come for the sole purpose of viewing my brother's belongings and the diary that he had kept so lovingly. It made me weep to read his last stirring words, "I shall have to die on the fourth." [2] He had splashed these words across the last page in a trembling hand as he lay dying. Although I had made up my mind that I would leave at the latest by Saturday afternoon, I could not tear myself away. Therefore I left on Sunday after attending morning services. As I bade farewell to the lovely people and the dear girl, I felt much different from when I arrived.

After a speedy two-hour journey I arrived at Erlangen, where my brother met me at the station. Then we naturally went into the nearby cafe. Since I had sent off a telegram requesting a five-day extension of my leave the day before, I awaited a reply with some anxiety. However it seemed as though it would never arrive. Monday came and went; then Tuesday—. When there was still no answer by Wednesday morning, I sadly packed my things together. Then I made my farewells and went to Erlangen with brother Hans. Before the express was scheduled to leave we decided to make one final telephone call to see if there was an answer. Hans called—and to my indescribable joy, the extension was granted. We went right back to the cafe and later fumbled our way home.

[2] This apparently refers to the date of death of Stumpf's brother Xavier, who fell in battle in France on September 4, 1914.

I had hoped to visit my godfather in Weiden, but found it inadvisable because the train connections were so poor that it would have required a day's travel each way. On the other hand, Friday was a holiday. It was Michaelmas!

As I sat amidst congenial company at the tavern on Saturday night, my brother-in-law suddenly barged in. He told me that a telegram had arrived for me and that I was to go home right away. Although I knew that it was bound to be bad news, I was staggered to read that a warrant for my arrest had been issued. [It read:] "Seaman Stumpf is absent without leave. He is to be arrested and delivered to Wilhelmshaven." In order to provide myself with an excuse, I went to the Post Office and sent off a telegram stating that my leave had been extended for five days by the Commandant. I returned home satisfied that I had done my duty. However, on Sunday it was time to pack up once more and to make my final departure.

The ride through the red-colored fall of the Franconian Forest was lovely. The train had to climb such steep slopes that it seemed as though it would grind to a halt at any moment. But at Steinbach vorm Wald we reached the highest point [before descending again]. The sight of the castles along the way made me hum, "At the bright shores of the Saale, the castles stand proud and tall. . . ." Saalfeld, Rudolstadt, Jena, Halle. Change trains for Magdeburg and Hanover! There I quickly drank two cups of chickory coffee at the Red Cross before the train came racing in.

It felt wonderful to cross Germany so quickly and so safely. Regardless of one's destination, one barely has a chance to look around before it is time to change trains at the huge station in Hanover. I had cut across three quarters of Germany in nine hours and there was only a relatively small distance to go to Wilhelmshaven. As I traveled through the night, I often had the feeling that I was going backwards or traveling in the wrong direction to Berlin, Cologne or Frankfurt. Consequently, whenever I passed a familiar place which assured me that I was on the right track, I always felt relieved. Brunswick —Königslutter—Hanover. I was always more talkative on my way home than in coming back from leave. As usual, the result was that I had no experiences worth mentioning. I only had a short wait before the Bremen Express pulled in. There, however, I was unfortunate to have to wait for six hours. Since the Red Cross was full up, I went to town to the Hotel Brema. 8 October 1916.

I worried [all night] lest the innkeeper forget to wake me on time. If, in addition to everything else I now returned belatedly, my game would surely be up. Hence when he came knocking at my door, [the next morning] I was already set to leave. I drank a cup of gruesome coffee at the station, which, as always, was crowded with sailors coming or going on leave. Soon I had put the last hundred kilometers behind me and the monstrous crane which was the symbol of Wilhelmshaven rose over the horizon. I fervently wished that I could go home again.

Exactly four years ago today, I arrived here as a new recruit. At that time my heart was still filled with high hopes and expectations. I wanted to be a good, efficient sailor. I would never have thought it possible that so many obstacles would be placed in the way of my good intentions. Nevertheless, I had decided that I would allow nothing to deter me. I was determined not to abandon my principles, even for the navy. I now realize how badly I have failed. I encountered such a great lack of understanding and ill will on the part of my superiors that I was at last compelled to give up the struggle. I grew tired, embittered and resigned. I was forced to look on without complaint while men with decidedly inferior minds practiced the vilest cruelties. But I could not remain silent. I lost my restraint and told those idiots what I thought of them. I told my persecutors why I did not recognize their authority, why I could not respect them as human beings, and I exposed all their failings with ruthless contempt. This is why, unlike most of my comrades, I have not yet been promoted to Seaman First Class. But that doesn't matter to me. However it would not be fair of me to neglect mentioning that there are some officers who are worthy of respect, admiration and love. But there are precious few of

them. [Most of them] have allowed the naval uniform to corrupt their character and morality.

Only the men who suffer every insult in silence and who
have no opinions of their own are considered to be good
sailors. Virtually nothing is done to develop our intellectual
capacity. Therefore I have often made myself unpopular at
lectures by objecting to the outright misrepresentation [of
facts] or by speaking out against the officially sanctioned
slander. I have on occasion behaved injudiciously and I often
acted as though I were addressing a union meeting. [As a re-
sult] I have been ridiculed and misunderstood by my comrades. However this does not trouble me and I merely feel very
sorry for them. I need hardly add that some of the officers consider me to be a regular "Red." It makes me laugh to think that
they may have entered such a statement in my conduct book.
But I do not regret my behavior in the least. I am only sorry
that I was so stupid during my early years here. In spite of all
this, I am filled with a genuine and deep love for the Fatherland. I am utterly convinced that Germany has a mission to
civilize the world. To my mind militarism and patriotism are
two contradictory phenomena which must be kept distinct
from each other. One has nothing to do with the other. Although I am in favor of universal military service, I am deeply
disturbed over the treatment of the men who wear the King's
uniform. Too many incompetent and useless people find a safe
refuge in the ranks of our officers' and noncommissioned officers' corps, leaving no room for honest and upright men. The
average man, who sees no distinction between the state and the
Fatherland, is all too prone to hold the Fatherland responsible
for every real or imagined injustice. Consequently many of
these people would be unhappy if Germany grew too powerful
and mighty—but I am allowing myself to be carried away by
politics and that is not my intention at all.

At the railroad station I learned that our squadron had
anchored at Schillig Roads that morning. Thus I first had a
cup of coffee at the Flagge Tavern (there does not seem to be
any prohibition against serving beer in North Germany) and

at eleven o'clock I boarded the postal steamer at the Nassau Bridge to take me out to the squadron.

It was a lovely, warm October day and one could see the gray ships from far away. On board the Bosun's Mate was waiting for me and immediately conducted me to the First Officer. However I was prepared for this and had documentary evidence to substantiate my testimony. He examined the telegrams for forgeries and erasures but they were authentic and in proper order. Several hours later I was summoned again and the First Officer asserted that I would not have left home in time if my application for an extension had been rejected. My irrefutable evidence allowed me to disprove this, too, and I was released once more.

A drastic change in the watch system had been instituted during my absence. The [traditional] six-watch division had been reduced to four. Consequently everything was in an uproar and no one knew where he belonged. There was much complaining; everybody was in a bad mood.

10 OCTOBER 1916

The smell of war was in the air. The Fleet Commander had just returned from Berlin; not a single one of our ships was in dock and certain nervous preparations on our ship all indicated that something unusual was about to happen. It was a shame that again every dock worker and sailor knew all about it. As a result, our cousins on the other side of the Channel were bound to be prepared and ready for us. It was my impression that we would already have sailed out if the weather had not been so bad lately. It was high time that we saw some action again. No one would have minded exchanging a few gentlemanly rounds à la Jutland. Moreover since we were long overdue to come in for some repairs, a good hit would be very welcome to us.

Last week a great sport festival was held to raise the crew's morale. But despite the promise of many prizes, the interest and participation of the men was negligible. Our professional athletes had no difficulty in collecting the prizes. Thereupon, of course, everybody complained loud and long. Interrupted on the afternoon of 14 October 1916.

There was no action on Saturday and it seemed that Sunday, too, would pass uneventfully. Since October storms were raging out at sea this came as no surprise. The lack of aerial reconnaissance was enough to prevent any undertaking. Yesterday afternoon the storm died down and the sun broke through the autumnal clouds. It turned into one of those truly lovely Sunday afternoons which are typical for this season. It all started as we sat eating our supper. As the last rays of the sun fell upon the sea and the foggy countryside, the searchlights of the flagship began to blink ominously. Suddenly word went all over the ship, "We are going into action today. *Ostfriesland* has just ordered a state of alert." We packed and stowed our gear with lightning speed. When even the officers cleared out their cabins, it became evident that we were on serious business. Hence it came as something of a surprise when we were told that we could sleep in our usual places in the casemates.

The night passed very peacefully without incident but the storms rose up again with new vigor. After breakfast we were told to get our seabags and to suspend all preparations for battle. I still did not know what was going on. 15 October 1916.

Last night after supper I sat in the forecastle writing letters. It felt very cozy to hear the waves dashing against the walls of the ship. The wind whistled through the rigging and the whole ship rocked and sang gently. This kind of weather relaxed my nerves and brought forth the most pleasant thoughts. My comrades sat around doing all sorts of things. Some of them were writing like me, many of them were playing cards and others were busy building little ship models. In short, no one wished to brave the nasty weather on deck.

All at once someone dashed in shouting, "How can you sit here playing cards when they are towing in some English prizes?" We jumped up excitedly and rushed on deck. It was a dark night with no moon or stars. But all the ships had turned on their top and flanking lights and in their dim glow we could distinguish a fairly large freighter passing by. I heard that she was a munition ship carrying artillery shells, trucks and airplanes to Archangel. What a wonderful catch! So this was the reason why we were on alert yesterday!! 19 October 1916.

The weather had cleared and the sun beamed down on a warm fall day. This meant that in London the alarm "Zeppelins approaching" would soon be sounded. On Wednesday morning, as we were loading four hundred tons of coal, I noticed that there was something strange going on. Not only were all the ships refueling at the same time, but while this was happening, the light and heavy cruisers, the torpedo boats and the minelayers all ran out to sea. I'll be hanged if something doesn't happen by night! As we finished coaling, two of our giant dirigibles, the *L 30* and the *L 31*, flew past in the sky. When it got dark, we were ordered to stand at general quarters and sail out by ten o'clock. Once again the decks were cleared like lightning. One might have thought that the English fleet was standing off Helgoland the way the First Officer shouted when we did not fold the starboard boom quickly enough to suit him. We were issued life preservers and there was every indication that we were headed on an important mission.

Since I would soon have to stand the middle watch, I fetched my hammock and strung it in the munition chamber of Turret B. I must have slept for three hours when I was awakened by the noise of the pumps. Aha, we were under way! I looked at my watch and saw that it was 11:30. It would soon be time to get up, but I wanted to get a little more sleep. "Everybody up! Lookouts and starboard watch get ready!" It was 12:45. I felt that I had slept much longer than that.

Because it was very windy on deck I put on my warm slicker. On the bridge the wind was blowing from all directions. Fortunately it was not raining. Could that circling searchlight be the island of Helgoland? No, the light was too weak and after each two turns it paused for a few seconds. It was the Jade fire ship. The shrouded silhouettes of the black ships and the net cranes appeared to the right and the left. In order to negotiate into the free channel we would have to pass between the red and the green light. Some time ago, when there were only two red lights, the *Yorck* had missed one of them by going too far to the right and had wound up in the middle of the mine fields.[3] She has been lying there for two years now—and only at ebb tide is there a small eddy to identify her grave. Half a dozen patrol boats have been sunk in the same place.

Across from us appeared the light tower of Wangerooge. We turned and continued on a northeasterly course. So long as we kept to this course which led straight toward England we were happy.

The entire sky was strewn with golden stars. Now and then a fleeting cumulus cloud would briefly hide the bright sickle of the moon. Tomorrow promised to be a glorious day. I drank fresh air into my starving lungs. Would there be another sea battle tomorrow? Or perhaps would we escort a couple of fat prizes back to port? Since our prize command had sailed out yesterday, this seemed very likely. While the early sun still fought to break through the gray banks of fog, two of our Zeppelins came out of the clouds and raced along the water's surface searching for submarines. But they did not spot anything. By noon we were at Terschelling, where we made a sharp turn toward Horns Reef. Maybe we could catch a couple of freighters there.

But we were out of luck this time and nothing came of it. At nightfall our light craft gathered up ahead and we headed back home on a southeasterly course. It was rumored that *Von der Tann* had been hit by a torpedo but that it had been deflected without causing any damage. *München*, one of our light cruisers, rode over a mine and one of her compartments was flooded. Although our trip used up a good deal of coal, we saw no action. At seven in the morning we ran into the Ger-

[3] On November 4, 1914, the *Yorck*, an old armored cruiser, had sunk on that spot.

man Sound and anchored between Wilhelmshaven and Voslapp. 20 October 1916.

That same day, a Saturday, we refueled and loaded four hundred tons of coal in an exceptionally short period of time. In the meantime, our Third Squadron had departed for Kiel. This meant that we would get a chance to rest up in the next two weeks. The light cruiser *München* came in with a slight list, but *Von der Tann*, which was moored right next to us, appeared entirely unscathed. I can't decide if this was a stroke of luck or a misfortune.

This time all of my predictions turned out wrong. There was a lot of activity on the North Sea. Had we captured some prizes again or was it the English? Since many of our prize crews sailed out early on Sunday morning, it appeared as though the first was the case. In a state of extreme nervousness we cleared for action again. The air seemed charged with electricity and it appeared that a major encounter could be expected at any moment.

We were heartened, however, to see that our submarine campaign was mounting in intensity. Every day our papers announced a growing number of freighters as casualties.[4] The Norwegian merchant marine had suffered extensive losses and [Norway] at the instigation of the English had despatched a protest to Germany. [For a change] we replied with refreshing insolence.

Our sortie on Sunday was very brief and we got no further than Helgoland with its bright red cliffs. I could not understand why our five battle wagons turned about with such suspicious haste. Was there a strong English force in the vicinity? It would have been sheer madness for such a small number of

[4] Actually, the German submarine campaign was rather quiescent at that time. German submarines operated principally in the Mediterranean and in northern waters, where they tried to sink the supply ships destined to Russia via Archangel. This was probably the reason for the Norwegian protest.

our ships to engage in battle. It is better to be a coward for a half hour than to die a hero's death.

Thus we felt greatly relieved on Monday, when we were ordered to come into port. Maybe now the overheated cylinder in our port engine would be repaired. The ship which *U 53* captured in the Arctic Ocean lay out in the southern [part of the] harbor. She looked very impressive. They say that she used to belong to the Hamburg-Amerika Line before she was stolen by the English. Since I had nothing more urgent to do, I wandered over to investigate her cargo as soon as our gang plank was down. I saw beautiful cases of smokeless gun powder for cannons and other explosive projectiles for three-inch guns. What a lovely and rare catch! Her cargo alone was supposed to be worth 40 million. How many of my countrymen would these projectiles have killed? There were 39 thousand such cases stored in her hold. How much was the ship worth? For once, reality had exceeded even the most fantastic rumors.

On two occasions when I went shopping for some small items in Wilhelmshaven I was outraged by the scandalously high cost of things. I observed eager women shoppers practically tearing an orange stand to pieces. Even the occasional butcher shops which sold ground meat at a mark a pound were mobbed. The sight of these things made my heart overflow with pity and made me realize how fortunate I really was. On my way back to the ship the newsboys shouted, "Extra! Cernavoda taken! The army of the Dobrudja has been cut off!" [5] This served to brighten an otherwise dreary outlook.

Today we put out to sea. 26 October 1916.

SUNDAY AFTERNOON, 29 OCTOBER 1916

It was a very somber fall day. When I went on deck I was reminded of how I felt in October 1912. It was still warm enough

[5] General von Mackensen, commanding a German-Bulgarian force, defeated the Rumanian army in the Dobrudja and captured Cernavoda on October 25, 1916.

so that one could go on deck without fear of catching a cold. Since I could not tolerate the tobacco-laden atmosphere below, I kept climbing up every half hour to breathe some fresh air. Those damned smelly pipes! They make me sick and ruin my appetite. As a result, I am delighted whenever I hear that the canteen has raised the price of tobacco.

What shall I write about now? Shall I describe our recent torpedo boat raid? But I only know what the newspapers reported. Since I did not experience it myself, it does not properly belong in my diary. However I am not smart enough to write a real history of the war.

We were having a quiet, peaceful interlude. I was just wondering why nothing ever happened anymore, so that I had to waste a lovely, free Sunday afternoon in writing, when the arrival of *U 53* solved my problems. *U 53*? Yes, the very same submarine that created such a furor in America not too long ago when she sent a half dozen English ships to the bottom. Today's *Kieler Nachrichten* reported that she and two other [submarines] had concealed themselves off the American coast. I immediately sensed that the whole story was impossible. What reason in the world did our gray submarines have to hide themselves there? [6]

But to continue with my story, I was shaken from my dreams by the call, "All hands on deck!" The officers stood at the railing gazing through their glasses at a small wake astern. Across from us, on *Ostfriesland* and *Posen*, the men started cheering and tossing their hats in the air. As she approached rapidly, [we could see] her entire crew assembled on deck. They wore oil slickers and their faces were beaming with happiness over our reception and in anticipation of a long leave at home.

[6] The *U 53*, under the command of Kapitänleutnant Rose, had actually been to America and had even docked at Newport, Rhode Island (there was no reason why she should hide, since America was still neutral). The purpose of her mission was to meet the cargo submarine *Bremen* and to guide her home. However, *Bremen* was lost at sea. Thus *U 53* took the opportunity on her homeward voyage to sink five ships, the *Strathdene, Chr. Knudsen, West Point, Blommersdyk* and *Stefano*.

Leave! We all thought of nothing else. Hopefully we would soon go into dock and then many of us would get a chance to go home. I wished I were on the *U 53*. . . . 29 October 1916.

It is so monotonous! What shall I do? Right now I have an overwhelming desire to do some work! But I am lacking the tools for intellectual labor; I have no books. However, I shall soon remedy that situation. I ordered a large number of books from Berlin.

If there were only not so much coal dust. . . . How can one enjoy working with this infernal coal dust crawling into one's intestines all the time? Oh! I wish peace would come! I wish it would come soon!

Did we really have such a good life when we were still at peace? Although it may seem that way now, we were not at all content then. I can recall that many of us kept hoping for a war—to bring us better times. Whenever I remember how finding a job, disputes over wages, and the long working hours would worry us, it makes our peacetime prospects seem less than rosy. Right now, however, it seems like paradise because we were able to buy all the bread, sausages and clothing we wanted. But what good was all this to the poor devils who lacked the money to afford these things! Perhaps the real crisis will come once we are happily at peace again? [What will happen] when all the price controls are removed, when state aid is suspended and when the millions of men come flooding back from the trenches wanting to return to their jobs at the store counter, the workbench, the loom, and the classroom? Unless we are careful in demobilizing, we could precipitate a catastrophe. Many people think that the death of a million vigorous young men will open up all sorts of jobs in public and private enterprise. But this is only theoretically true. In reality all the vital jobs have already been filled by women, older men and war cripples. Moreover there are many professions which will vanish completely after the war. After the war there will be no more hand weavers, coppersmiths, tinsmiths, hairdressers, soapmakers, and oil pressers. These are merely a few of the depressed handicrafts that will be wiped out. But even the livelier professions will decay or be sucked up by big business. These are the bakers, carpenters, butchers, brewers, millers, glaziers and many others. All the industries which are dependent on imported raw materials will long be depressed. But on the other hand, those industries which have been ruined or paralyzed by the war, by the shortage of labor and by worn-out machinery, will face a brilliant future. The shipyard workers, the machinists and the printers [will all be prosperous].

Once again I am losing myself in my favorite activity . . . [daydreaming]. But what can I do? There is no work to be done; virtually nothing ever happens; I am hungry, so that I think I am still best off to simply keep writing [about things] even though they do not belong in my book. Afternoon of 31 October 1916.

I have before me a red-bordered newspaper page with the following headlines:

POLAND A NEW CONSTITUTIONAL HEREDITARY MONARCHY!

To the people of the General Government of Warsaw:

His Majesty, the German Kaiser and His Majesty, the Kaiser of Austria and apostolic King of Hungary, confident in the ultimate victory of their arms and animated by the desire to create a bright future for the Polish territories which their brave armies have liberated from the Russian yoke at such great sacrifice, have agreed to construct of these territories an independent state with a hereditary, constitutional monarchy. A more precise definition of the borders of that kingdom will be proclaimed in the future. The new monarchy shall find the security it requires for the free development of its energies in alliance with both of the Allied Powers. The glorious traditions of former Polish armies and the memory of the brave Polish soldiers who fought at our side in this present war shall be perpetuated by the creation of an independent army. Its organization, training and leadership will be determined on the basis of common agreement.

The Allied Monarchs express the fond hope that they shall be able to fulfill the aspirations for national development of the

Polish Kingdom in accordance with the general European political situation and for the welfare and security of their own countries and peoples.

The neighboring Powers to the West of the Kingdom of Poland look forward with pride to the national flourishing of a free and contented new State. By the supreme order of His Majesty, the German Kaiser.

The Governor-General [7]

Thus the proud, victorious Central Powers have issued a document of worldwide historical significance for all to see. Twenty months ago the Tsar issued a similar proclamation to the people of the Bukovina and Galicia. In his picturesque, oriental language, he annexed these two areas to the Russian Crown under the name of Red Russia.[8] But on May 2, 1915 [Field Marshal] Mackensen began hammering away at the Byzantine Crown of the Little Father with such sledgehammer blows that he shook loose this pearl. Within three months, the vanguard of our armies stood before the forest region of Bielepol and the swamps [surrounding the town of] Pinsk with its spires and cupolas. We had crossed the borders of former Congress Poland and our troops had penetrated into the Ukraine and Russia proper.[9] As a result, we breathed a sigh of

[7] This proclamation was issued on November 5, 1916. Since Germany and Austria could not come to terms over which of them should actually rule the new kingdom, the powers and sovereign rights of that state were kept intentionally ambiguous. As a result, Marshal Pilsudsky's Polish Legion, which was recruited to fight for the new Poland, failed to materialize. Poland remained under German and Austrian military rule throughout the war. Moreover, this ill-considered and premature proclamation also served to shatter all hope of concluding a separate peace with the war-weary and tottering Russian Empire.

[8] During the early months of the war, Russia had proclaimed the establishment of a united and independent Polish kingdom under the Russian Crown and bade the Polish subjects of Austria-Hungary to come and join the united monarchy. When all of Galicia was conquered by Russia in the spring of 1915, Grand Duke Nicholas received a diamond-studded sword from the Tsar, commemorating the liberation of Red Russia, an ancient designation for Galicia. The Tsar made a triumphal tour through his new province in April 1915.

[9] Mackensen's great German-Austrian offensive reconquered Galicia from Russia. Shortly thereafter, Hindenburg and Ludendorff struck across the Narew, captured Warsaw and a number of other important

relief and felt that the end of the war was in sight. However, General Alexeyev's masterful retreat enabled a large part of the Russian army to escape beyond the Beresina to the plains of Volhynia. And by the following spring, with the aid of the French and English, a well-equipped new million-man army had been created. Once again they stood before Germany's iron walls. Mother Russia had called her sons and the Tsar's "brown little animals" came running from the Chinese Wall, from the Amur River, from the Caucasus and from the Black Sea.

Although Brusilov flung his masses with reckless daring against the German front, all was in vain. Here and there the wall gave in a little, but then sprang back with renewed vigor and mowed down the muzhiks by the hundreds of thousands. They [the Russians] failed to reconquer a single square meter of Polish soil. Thus the second gem in the Tsar's crown was finally lost.

There is no nation in the world which has held on to its nationality, its language and its religion with such phenomenal persistence as the Poles. They have often resisted their present rulers with slavelike determination, but this was due to the Russian knout and the extraordinarily depressed status of the population. Since I do not know these people well, I shall not be so presumptuous as to judge them, but it nevertheless seems to me that they have a greater respect for the whip than for learning. I only hope that we have now found a mutually acceptable solution for the "Polish Question."

If I am informed correctly, our submarines have sunk more enemy ships this month than in any previous month of this war. [They sank] 310,000 tons, which is more than all the enemy's and the neutral's shipyards can replace. If we continue like this, the English will soon sing a different tune about the "submarine menace." I might even venture to say that by this

cities and virtually expelled the Russians from Poland. This Russian defeat led to the dismissal of Grand Duke Nicholas and to the appointment of General Michael V. Alexeyev as Russian Chief of Staff in August 1915.

spring we shall not only succeed in blocking off all trade with England, but in cutting her off completely.

Interrupted. In any case, we are scheduled to come into port. Afternoon of 6 November 1916.

As I am writing, hundreds of hydraulic hammers are clattering away to the accompaniment of the unceasing activity of the drills and the electric elevators. Most of the noise comes from the construction of the new battleship across from us, but the hammering on the auxiliary cruiser *Wolf* alone would be enough to drive one to distraction. However one can get used to anything. After three days one forgets about the noise but it keeps straining the nerves. This is what it is like in dock. I can hardly conceive of it without a proper volume of noise.

The way we got into the dock was most surprising. On Sunday we still lay out at the locks suspecting nothing. It was a lovely afternoon. I was busily writing in this book when a friend sat down next to me and asked in a whisper, "Have you heard the latest news? No? They say that *Grosser Kurfürst* and *Moltke* were torpedoed at Horns Reef!" "You don't say?" I started. "This might mean that we could lose our turn in dock. . . ."

It was bad news. Mind you, no one was upset that two of our newest ships had been damaged. But we were all bitterly angry that they might have a chance of getting into dock ahead of us.

By Monday morning four ships of the *Kaiser* class lay peacefully off our side. Therefore we had already decided that it was merely another "Reuters Report." We all felt relieved. At noon we received a signal from the shipyard that *Helgoland* was to be ready for dock between [November] 9 and 11. And then, finally, that very same evening we got orders to come in immediately. The pace of events speeded up as order after order was issued. The division chiefs were already preparing lists of names of the men who were being considered for leave.

Kronprinz is in dock with a torpedo hit on her port bow at the first gun turret, but since her torpedo bulkheads were not pierced, the damage remained insignificant. *Grosser Kürfurst* suffered much more extensive damage and has been sent to Kiel. I understand that the mishap occurred in the following fashion: On Sunday morning the Third Squadron was on its way to Wilhelmshaven from Brunsbüttel when it received a wireless order to rush to Horns Reef to aid a grounded submarine. The squadron complied and by one o'clock the eight ships arrived at the scene. For some inexplicable reason, perhaps it was the suddenness of the order, the ships had no flanking cover. At that point both *Kronprinz* and *Grosser Kürfurst* were hit right one after the other, so that the English thought they hit the same ship twice. Unfortunately our ships failed to free the *U 20* and eventually she had to be scuttled by her crew. It is rumored that we also lost another submarine. In the light of these developments, November 5 may well be regarded as a black day for our navy.[10]

It is generally agreed that our time in dock has been extended until the beginning of December. The men will go on leave in two shifts and if nothing intervenes, I shall have the welcome pleasure of being able to go home again.

One can gain some interesting insights into human nature [around here] by keeping one's eyes and ears open. I concede that the poignancy of the story which I am about to relate stems from hunger. [It all began] today when I was a messenger on deck with instructions to watch out that no shipyard workers came on board to beg food from the sailors. Nevertheless each time the Duty Officer turned his back, I allowed a few of these poor fellows to pass. The misery and suffering of these hard-working men was clearly written on their faces. As they came back and tried to leave the ship undetected, each of them was hiding a small pot under his jacket. However they were spotted by Lieutenant K. He addressed the first one:

[10] *U 30*, the other submarine, managed to get away. However, *U 20*, the submarine that had sunk the *Lusitania*, had to be blown up. The near loss of two battleships angered the Kaiser to such an extent that he issued an order that the fleet not take such risks again. This would have condemned the High Seas Fleet to perpetual inactivity if Admiral Scheer had not been able to persuade the Kaiser to reverse himself on November 22.

"What have you got there under your clothes?" This fright-ened the old man out of his wits and he tried in vain to take the pot out. His fear made him appear suspicious and he was asked to present his identification. He had no pass, however, and could only stammer his work number. I then helped him to take out the dangerous object. Instead of being a bomb, as we expected, it was a half-filled pot of food scraps. The poor man was trembling all over and the Duty Officer quickly tried to calm him by saying, "But you don't have to hide it like that."

Although I am willing to concede that the officer had ample cause for stopping the man, the rough and unsympathetic way he went about it troubled me. I was even more outraged, how-ever, by the servile, fearful attitude of the workers toward the officer. These poor fellows don't possess even a shred of self-confidence and they are obviously ignorant of the fact that the golden buttons, the silver stripes and the fine cloth [of the officers' uniforms] have all been bought with the tax monies which they earned by their bitter sweat. How can we fight for the equality of our class with and for such people? No, they deserve to continue to be treated as disinherited proletarians!

Down below, a train filled with Russian prisoners of war passed by. Their similarity [to our men] saddened me. Evening of 8 November 1916.

We were fortunate to have such mild, lovely weather. Other-wise it would not be very pleasant to work on the turret deck, which had been partially dismounted to change the brake cylin-ders. Our guns were being lowered to enable us to shoot fur-ther in the future.

Within the next few days the recently completed auxiliary cruiser *Wolf* will head out to sea. She is an entirely new type of ship. Externally she bears a remarkable resemblance to a harmless freighter. In the event of danger, she can knock down her superstructure like lightning, thus exposing the rather formidable fighting power of her seven 15 cm. guns and her two torpedo tubes. She looks a good deal like the *Möve*!

As an experiment she will take a submarine along with her. Actually she will not carry the submarine in her hold but it will accompany her submerged beneath the water. I understand that the ship has been ordered to carry arms and munitions to our brave soldiers in East Africa.[11] She will [then turn to] large-scale commerce raiding and make the Atlantic and the Indian Ocean up to the Bay of Bengal unsafe for English shipping. That is, if everything works out as planned, but I have some serious doubts about that.

By February, the battle cruiser *Hindenburg*, which is under construction right near us, will also be ready. At this juncture almost all the work on her is being performed by women. At first one is prompted to laugh at the sight of so many women working in men's clothing. Nevertheless, these courageous and industrious women are certainly worthy of respect. 10 November 1916.

On Saturday afternoon we entered the dock. Our stern pointed forward to facilitate removing the armor plating which had been damaged during the battle [of Jutland]. The work on the forward compartments of the ship created such noise and smoke that it became impossible to stay, let alone to sleep there. We may consider ourselves fortunate that the weather has remained so dry and mild. It was particularly comfortable during nights when there was a full moon. It was almost bright enough to read a newspaper and one could even make out distant objects with great clarity and distinction. Last night, when two of our largest floating cranes tied up right next to us, it created an extremely imposing view. I once read that there exist certain machines and metal structures that compel one to admire the marvelous accomplishments of the human mind. As I saw these three dark and powerful technological masterpieces by the light of the moon, I was prompted to agree with Herr Naumann.[12] It was a scene which would have delighted

[11] In German East Africa, General Paul von Lettow-Vorbeck, beleaguered on all sides by the British under General Smuts, was in desperate need of ammunition. The munitions which *Wolf* brought him enabled him to undertake offensive operations in 1917 and to maintain the German resistance in that area until the end of the war.

[12] Although the author is undoubtedly referring to the Progressive leader, Friedrich Naumann, the connection is too obscure to trace.

an artist or a photographer. I, too, looked on with great wonderment. From a distance it looked even more imposing as the fine cablework of the cranes began to resemble a lace filigree. The sharply defined silhouette of the *Helgoland* stood in the foreground. She looked like a gigantic toy riding in a pool of mercury. . . .

I have seldom felt so fatigued and worn out as today. But I would still like to write a few lines, otherwise I shall go to sleep feeling that I have neglected something. My fatigue is due to the fact that I had been assigned to scrape paint over the side. In the words of an old sailors' joke, I had to scratch where it didn't itch. How unlucky for me! I felt so dizzy on the platform that if it were not for the line around my middle, I would have fallen off. My nose began to bleed when I washed myself. I already feel apprehensive about tomorrow. Am closing for the day, 16 November 1916.

Today I am feeling dreadful again. No wonder, since all the men are preparing to go on leave. I was originally granted a leave but then it was canceled. Although this in itself does not anger me too much, I still regard it as a setback. However it will pass. Since the men returning from leave are complaining bitterly about the food shortage [at home], I am once more content with my lot. It has turned freezing cold. I feel sorry for our poor soldiers in the trenches. We are still much better off than they! At least we still have a warm, dry bed. Nevertheless my hatred for the navy keeps growing. I now realize better than ever before, how stupid we really are to do all the work while those who merely look on get all the pay. We live in an unjust and evil world. Should the opportunity ever arise, I will be only too happy to make it better. Damn the officers! Never again shall they be allowed to drag us into a war! Let them either practice some honorable profession or drop dead! They shall no longer earn a living from our stupidity and grow fat on our money.

DAY OF FASTING AND PRAYER, 1916

I was not at all contrite. The weather was dismal! But I could not go ashore in any case. To our general amazement we were not given any work assignments this morning. Only the watch division was put to work hauling the boiler tubes out of the engine. I am now working on the ship's bottom. Thank God, I no longer have to sway on a plank. Yesterday we lit a huge fire and roasted potatoes. We have an extremely understanding petty officer in charge of us. Again I can't think of anything to write. We have just gotten the news that good old Kaiser Franz [Joseph] has passed away.[13] May he rest in peace!

If there were no war going on now, his death would have inevitably led to severe repercussions in the Danubian monarchy. In the final analysis, he was the only person capable of maintaining at least a modicum of peace among the various nations of his empire. They all used to say, "Just wait until the Emperor dies, then we will see who shall rule the land." Bismarck could well say of him, "When Kaiser Franz mounts his war steed, all of his peoples take their rifles in hand and ride along behind him." This is literally what happened [in this war]. In my opinion, the few isolated cases of treason, desertions to the enemy and that sort of thing were brought on by the traditionally bad food and ill-treatment of the Austrian soldier rather than hatred for the state. At the outbreak of the war, our enemies, especially the Russians, expected that the races living along the Danube and the Theiss would come over to their side.

No doubt our enemies look upon the death of this great personality as a victory. However they are making a grave mistake. For a long time the power of the state has ceased to reside in his strong but aging hands. Austria was all too often ruled

[13] Franz Joseph (1830–1916), Emperor of Austria (1848–1916), died on November 21. He was succeeded by his grandnephew Charles (1887–1922), the last Habsburg Emperor (1916–18).

by means of the time-honored Article XIV.[14] Her Parliament has long acted like a puppet theater rather than a representative legislature. The Austrians, Hungarians and Czechs have always shown greater respect for a strong man than for their own miserable and opinionated representatives. They used to rail against Metternich,[15] Kossuth,[16] Lueger [17] and Tisza.[18] However they were still glad that such men were available to pull the ship of state out of the nationality and parliamentary quagmire and to set it into motion again.

I had always looked upon Franz Joseph as a brother of our old William the Great.[19] What did this noble monarch not see and experience? What human suffering was spared him? His son Rudolf, the pride and hope of all of Germandom, died in bad company in a forester's cottage.[20] His wife the beloved Elizabeth died at the hands of an Italian assassin.[21] At an earlier date his ambitious brother Maximilian came to an inglorious

[14] The Austrian Emperor was empowered by the Constitution of 1867 to promulgate decrees that had full force of laws when parliament was not in session, provided that they did not violate the constitution and were ratified by parliament at its next session. This power made it possible for Franz Joseph to impose his will upon his unruly parliaments.

[15] Prince Klemens Wenzel Metternich (1773–1859), Austrian Foreign Minister (1809–48), represented the cause of conservatism and monarchism in Austria and Europe until sent into exile by the 1848 Revolution.

[16] It is not clear whether the author means Lajos Kossuth (1802–1894), who led the Hungarian uprising against Austrian domination in 1848–1849, or his equally nationalistic son Ferenc Kossuth (1841–1914), who wanted to abrogate the Compromise of 1867, which had established the Dual Monarchy of Austria-Hungary.

[17] Dr. Karl Lueger (1844–1910) was the founder of the anti-Semitic Christian Socialist Party of Austria and mayor of Vienna from 1897 to 1907.

[18] Stephen Tisza (1861–1918) was the Liberal Hungarian Prime Minister (1905–6 and 1913–17) who opposed the separatist tendencies of Kossuth and wanted to maintain friendly relations with Austria.

[19] Wilhelm I (1796–1888), King of Prussia (1861–88) and Emperor of Germany (1871–88), was commonly known as William the Great in Germany for his role in unifying that nation in the years 1864 to 1871.

[20] On January 30, 1889, Archduke Rudolf, the only son and direct heir of Franz Joseph, was found shot with his mistress Baroness Marie Vetsera at the royal hunting lodge of Mayerling. Various rumors blamed the shootings on Jesuits, Hungarian nobles and an outraged husband, but the official account maintained that it was a suicide, stemming from Franz Joseph's order to his son to break off the affair.

[21] Empress Elizabeth (1837–98) was stabbed to death on September 10, 1898 at Geneva by Luigi Luccheni, an Italian anarchist.

end as the Emperor of Mexico [22] when he was executed by Jordan Lopez.[23] As a loyal son of the Catholic Church, he must also have been deeply shocked by the robbery and imprisonment of [Pope] Pius IX.[24] The old gentleman has also been deeply hurt by several members of the Habsburg family.

Then there is the recent memory of the assassination of the heir-apparent and his wife at Sarajevo, which provided the immediate cause for the outbreak of this war. Franz Joseph most assuredly did not desire a war. Indeed he gave better proof of his desire to maintain peace than Kaiser Wilhelm II. After all, he was even willing to meet with the blood-drenched King Peter in an effort to improve his relations with that shameless Serb.

Still the Emperor must have experienced much joy in his youth and his old age. In spite of the fact that he lost two wars and two provinces to the vile Prussians,[25] he still saw the double eagle fly victoriously over many a battlefield. On the land, Radetzky beat the Italians at Custozza.[26] And [Admiral Tege-

[22] Archduke Maximilian (1832–67) of Austria and Emperor of Mexico from 1864 to 1867 through the intrigues of Napoleon III of France was executed by Mexican nationalists on June 19, 1867.

[23] Stumpf does not mean Jordan Lopez, but Benito Juarez (1806–72), the Liberal nationalist leader of the Mexican forces that ousted the French and Maximilian from Mexico.

[24] Giovanni Maria Mastai-Ferretti, Pope Pius IX (1846–1878), was deprived of his estates in 1871 by the Law of Guarantees promulgated by the newly founded Italian Kingdom. Although Pius remained unharmed and was left full enjoyment of his religious and sovereign powers, he considered himself the prisoner of the Vatican, refused to accept the law and instructed Catholics not to recognize the Italian state. Relations between the Papacy and Italy were not established until 1929 with the signing of the Lateran Treaty.

[25] Actually Franz Joseph only lost one war to the Prussians, the Austro-Prussian War of 1866 or the Seven Weeks' War. According to the terms of the Treaty of Prague which ended that war, Austria was forced to yield to Prussia the Duchy of Holstein, recently acquired from Denmark.

However, since Prussia had been allied with Italy in that war, Austria was also forced by the Treaty of Vienna of 1866 to cede Venetia, her last stronghold in Italy, to Napoleon III, who restored it to Italy.

[26] Stumpf is mistaken when he states that Radetzky's victory over the Italians occurred during the reign of Franz Joseph. The First Battle of Custozza took place on July 24, 1848, while Franz Joseph did not ascend the throne until December 2, 1848. Stumpf really means the victory of Archduke Albert at the Second Battle of Custozza on June 24, 1866, during the Austro-Italian War.

thoff] beat them at sea at Lissa.[27] On the occasion of Italy's declaration of war, he stated that this was the proudest moment of his life. In 1908 he was fortunate enough to increase the size of his empire by means of the bloodless annexation of Bosnia and Herzegovina.[28]

For sixty-eight years he reigned. The years of the reign of Kaiser Wilhelm pale into insignificance by comparison. When Franz Joseph ascended the throne, Bismarck had just begun to make a name for himself—a name which had not yet penetrated to the Hofburg.[29] He knew Tsar Nicholas [I] at the height of his power and when he was defeated in the Crimean War.[30] In 1848 [Louis] Napoleon was not yet President of France [31] and Eugenie was still Madamoiselle de Montijo.[32] He knew Queen Victoria,[33] Edward VII,[34] Palmerston,[35] Disraeli,[36] Gladstone,[37] Lloyd George, Churchill and the popes Pius IX, Leo XIII,[38] and Benedict [XV] [39] from the very beginning of their careers. Nations rose and sank before his eyes. He witnessed the rise of Prussia and Russia, the unification of Italy. More recently, he

[27] Admiral Wilhelm von Tegethoff administered a decisive defeat to the Italian navy near Lissa on July 20, 1866.

[28] The annexation of these two provinces, administered by Austria since 1878 but nominally under Turkish rule, represented a great diplomatic coup for Austria. However, since both Serbia and Russia had vital interests in that area, the Austrian annexation aggravated the ill-feeling on the part of these two countries and contributed significantly to the outbreak of World War I.

[29] The Hofburg was the imperial residence of the emperors of Austria.

[30] Nicholas I, Tsar of Russia (1825–55), died shortly after his defeat in the Crimean War.

[31] Louis Napoleon (1808–73) was elected President of the Second French Republic on December 20, 1848. From 1852 to 1870 he was Napoleon III, Emperor of the Second French Empire.

[32] Eugenie de Montijo, Countess of Teba (1826–1922), married Napoleon III on January 30, 1853.

[33] Victoria I (1819–1901) was Queen of England from 1837 to 1901.

[34] Edward VII (1841–1910), Victoria's son, reigned from 1901 to 1910.

[35] Henry John Temple, Lord Palmerston (1784–1865), noted British Foreign Minister and Prime Minister.

[36] Benjamin Disraeli (1804–81), British Conservative Prime Minister (1868 and 1874–80).

[37] William Ewart Gladstone (1809–98), British Liberal Prime Minister (1868–74, 1886, 1892–94).

[38] Giaocchino Pecci, Pope Leo XIII (1878–1903).

[39] Giacomo della Chiesa, Pope Benedict XV (1914–22).

also witnessed the victories won by his and his ally's armies.

Now we shall fly the Austrian colors for three days. Since the war began under that flag, I hope that it may also come to an end under that flag. 25 November 1916.

I have just lived through a difficult and trying week. On several evenings I tried to record my experiences on paper, only to have my pen literally drop from my hand from fatigue. Hence many a good story will not be preserved for posterity. I hope that posterity will not hold this against me. To be perfectly frank, I have never before needed food and sleep so much as this week. Yes, the food. There was much complaining about the food this week. Each day we got a soup mixture which was so thin and weak and so poorly prepared that I always felt hungrier after the meal than before it. As an additional treat, the soup was almost always burned. I pilfered potatoes whenever I could and cooked them over steam at night. I can well understand that our old, broken-down galley cannot produce anything better. We had to give away our lovely, shiny stainless steel cauldrons to be converted into nickel-plated steel armor by Krupp. "Break the pots, let fall the pans. . . ."

If one were to ask the men where on board this ship the most difficult work was to be found, in ninety cases out of a hundred they would answer that it was the ship's armory. This is quite true. We all agree that this is the place where we are given the most useless and stupid work to do. Recently I had a little taste of it myself. It is incredible how many half-wits there are among the armorer's mates. They regard anyone having more experience and know-how than they as an attack upon their authority and prestige. "You will do as I tell you even if you have to stand on your head" [they all insist]. I don't care how hard they work me. It will make things seem easier later on. Once I get the hang of the work, it should not be long before it becomes smooth and effortless for me. After all, I too know how to make a lot of hot air!

I did not go far when I went ashore last night. I bought some writing paper and then headed straight for my favorite chair at the reading room [in the library]. On the way there I noticed a sizable crowd in front of a delicatessen store on the Markt-strasse. My curiosity was aroused and I went to see what was going on. I only saw an unusually plump goose which was cleaned and plucked. The sign attached to it stated: "20 pounds. For sale." I could hardly believe my eyes—7.50 marks per pound. I calculated that this came to an even 150 marks. Next to it lay a meter-long, thick eel. The price was 8 marks. Not for the whole eel, mind you, but for a pound! This was the ultimate of cruelty, to make a cold-blooded mockery of the poor starving people who stood there with their great eyes. I would have regarded it as an act of justice if the people had broken the window and taken this object which incited them to class hatred. I overheard all sorts of bitter remarks about the wealthy classes, who could not only afford to buy such deli-cacies but who also had the nerve to display them so blatantly.

While the food shortage is causing us grave concern, the military situation of the Fatherland has improved on all fronts. Our invasion of Rumania has turned into a lightning advance. The people of Bucharest can already hear the thunder of Falkenhayn's and Mackensen's guns.[40] Every day we get re-ports that we have captured enormous quantities of foodstuffs, petroleum, wood, metals and other things. However we have only taken a relatively small number of prisoners. This might be explained by the fact that we have no desire to take in more useless mouths to consume food. [In addition] the Rumanians have recently conducted target practice on some thirty cap-tured members of our Life Guard Regiment. Once again the main theater of the war has shifted from the Somme to the Arges. Our enemies gaze in that direction as if hypnotized as they ponder how much longer they can hold Bucharest. They are hoping for a miraculous repetition of the Battle of the

[40] Falkenhayn's army had recently crossed the Vulkan Pass into Ruma-nia (November 10–14) and was moving down the Arges River while von Mackensen's troops crossed the Danube on November 23. Therefore Bucharest was assailed on two sides.

Marne in front of its gates.[41] However the only miracle in sight is the way in which the treacherous Wallachians will be beaten by Hindenburg's strong bolts of lightning. The Italians can already see what will happen to them as soon as we finish off the Rumanians. Our life could be a delight if only our women and children were not threatened by starvation.

We are about to witness the century's greatest social upheaval with the imminent passage of the Auxiliary Service Law.[42] We are about to realize Clausewitz's [43] prediction that a war can only be won by means of the total mobilization of all the emotional and productive capacities of the nation. Germany has committed all her energies to end the war by spring. I haven't the slightest doubt that our ambitious gamble shall succeed. Germany's power continues to mount even while the fighting rages. . . . In the meantime, the drama of Greece

[41] The Chief of Staff of the Rumanian army General Alexandru Averescu attempted a desperate counterattack on the Arges on December 1–5. Falkenhayn, however, managed to rout the Rumanians and captured 70,000 prisoners. Consequently, the Rumanian government evacuated Bucharest.

[42] On December 5, 1916, an Auxiliary Service Law, commonly called the Hindenburg Program, went into effect. Ever since his appointment as Chief of the General Staff in August 1916 (in place of the dismissed General Falkenhayn), Hindenburg had been calling for a massive extension of the war effort on the home front by harnessing the entire German labor force to a battle of production. He wrote that "we can only win the war if we provide our army with so much material that it can meet the enemy on equal terms . . . and if all the treasures of our soil that agriculture and industry can produce are used exclusively for the conduct of the war. But this maximum effort will only be attained if the whole people puts itself at the service of the Fatherland. All other considerations must come second. . . ."
The Auxiliary Service Law made employment compulsory for all males between the ages of fifteen and sixty, defined the possible types of employment and stipulated that workers could not leave their jobs without special permission. To coordinate this program, a Supreme War Office (the *Kriegsamt*) was established with powers to centralize and direct the entire German economic effort.

[43] Karl von Clausewitz (1780–1831), a Prussian army officer and military theoretician, headed the Prussian War School from 1818. He wrote a three-volume treatise on military strategy, *Vom Kriege* (*On War*), which stressed the interrelationship of war, politics, and economics. Subsequent generations of German military men, especially Ludendorff, were greatly influenced by Clausewitz and regarded his writings as the bible of military planning.

seems to be drawing into its final act. It is merely a matter of days before the monarchy is turned into a republic.[44]

Once again a few days have gone by without any important events. On Wednesday we ran out to sea to test our engines. Virtually the entire fleet had been assembled for this important practice run to Helgoland. Even *Derfflinger* with her tripod mast and the quickly patched-up *Kronprinz* were there. Our sixteen great battleships presented a truly imposing picture. However they no longer filled me with the same kind of enthusiasm as before. You useless, coal-consuming monsters, what are you doing here? Oh, if you could only be transferred for three days to the Black Sea or the Mediterranean! Then our position down there would change very quickly.

Bucharest has fallen.[45]

I became aware that the town's bells had been sounding for some time. Had we won a new victory or could it possibly be Bucharest . . . ? All at once my wishes came true. The Duty Officer was the first to know. "Bosun, announce to the ship that Bucharest has fallen!" [he ordered]. The casemates soon resounded with howls of joy at this news. The good Lieutenant [Klessel] beamed all over and he called down loudly to the mess, "Why haven't I heard any cheers?"

[Martin] went around hugging everyone he met. "Captain [Richter], Have you heard that Bucharest has fallen? Bucharest!" "He has gone completely mad," commented the mess steward. Then I bumped into [Martin], who detested me be-

[44] Fearing that King Constantine of Greece was secretly plotting to join the Central Powers, France and England issued an ultimatum to the Greek monarchy on June 21, 1916, demanding the demobilization of the Greek army and the establishment of a responsible government (preferably one headed by the pro-Entente politician Venizelos). Although Constantine acquiesced grudgingly, he refused to appoint Venizelos as Prime Minister. The latter replied by establishing a provisional government on Crete (September 29) and proceeded to declare war on Germany. In December 1916 it appeared as though England and France were prepared to march into Greece, to depose Constantine and to proclaim Venizelos president of a Greek Republic. However, this did not occur. Nevertheless, Constantine was later (June 12, 1917) forced to abdicate in favor of his son Alexander, and Greece formally declared war on Germany on June 29, 1917.

[45] Bucharest was occupied by German troops on December 6, 1916.

cause I [occasionally] forgot to salute him. According to him this is the most serious offence one could commit. [This time] I actually walked by him with my hands in my pockets. "Sailor," he purred softly, "I am sure that your hands will not freeze if you salute." [I replied] "No, Herr Kapitänleutnant, I shall have a better use for them later." He became highly indignant at my insolent response. I agreed [that I had acted improperly].

Recently while we were loading coal, he caught me as I stood at the railing eating something. I had enough presence of mind to throw it all overboard and to draw up at attention. The severe expression on his face became milder and milder and his thin mouth which was about to say, "Place yourself on report," turned up into a tiny smile as he brought forth, "Thank you, Seaman Stumpf." Thanks! "Kiss my a———!" I thought darkly, as I sprang in a most hypocritical manner to open the door for him. Thereupon he bowed to me and said once more, "Thank you. Thank you." "Get out of here, you old hag!" I thought out loud as he was leaving. I don't know if he heard me or not. I am still trying desperately to make up my mind about what kind of a transparency I shall draw of him this year. Or should I perhaps draw a caricature of [Lord] Grey? It is a difficult decision.

Now I shall go ashore for a while. 9 December 1916.

Yesterday, a Friday, we loaded 500 tons of coal. We had the morning off but began working right after lunch. It was terribly cold and by the time the last basket came flying up from the coal barge, my fingers were frozen stiff and blue. I had not noticed that two nasty accidents had taken place right near me. Someone by the name of [Kohl] fell backwards from the top deck onto the edge of the barge and was carried to the hospital in a state of unconsciousness. The doctor said that he had suffered extensive damage on the vertebrae of the neck and a concussion and had him transferred to the hospital on shore immediately. On the following morning we received the unhappy news that our poor comrade had died. At this point I should like to interject a little episode which was connected with this incident. Since the dead man had no parents, our First Officer wanted to send his sister the sum of 50 marks. When he discussed the matter with the Third Officer, the latter shamelessly replied: "Twenty-five would do very nicely, Herr Kapitän." How could anyone be so unfeeling?

At first the second accident looked even worse than the first one. However, it did not turn out so badly. When we were folding up the heavy coaling tackle, the heavy boom hit my friend [Nunidie Schlangele] in the face with such force that he looked as though he had lost his left eye. In spite of that, he is already running about again with a thick bandage.

The burial was scheduled to take place today. I would most certainly have attended it, but we are out on patrol. 12 December 1916.

Another fourteen days have passed, Christmas is just around the corner, but none of my predictions has come true. Greece was still "neutral," and even the Auxiliary Service Law did not seem to be able to bring the war to a quick end. The heightening of our effort simply called forth countermeasures on the opposing side.

"All hands, prepare to assemble on deck!" What could be the matter now? The most incredible rumors ran through the ship. Some of the men said that we had won an important victory in the West, others maintained that something had been stolen, while the very clever ones among us felt that we were about to embark on another important mission like the one to Jutland. A few of the men went so far as to assert that the First Officer had been transferred from our ship or that we were about to be awarded some Iron Crosses. There was one rumor, however, that kept reappearing with remarkable consistency. It claimed that we were either about to initiate peace negotiations or that the Kaiser was about to proclaim a peace offer. Although I found this [rumor] least plausible, it was true.

Utter silence prevailed when the Captain came out with a piece of paper in his hand and began, "I have been asked to read you the following order from His Majesty the Kaiser: 'In the light of our victories on all fronts, I have made a peace offer to our enemies. They shall have to decide whether or not to accept it. In the interim, it shall be your responsibility to continue to hold your present positions and to defeat the enemy if the need arises. Supreme Headquarters, December [12, 1916], Wilhelm II, Rex.' This order is to be read to all our armies and to the navy." [46]

When I heard these earth-shaking words, I was overcome with delight. In my initial excitement I could think of nothing else except that the coming of peace was now merely a question of time. Surely all the nations which were on the brink of disaster and ruin would gratefully accept our offer of peace. And surely men of good will all over the world would bless the man who first stepped forward with the olive branch. Now that twelve days have passed, I see [things] more clearly and am no longer blinded by my enthusiasm. But I don't want to get ahead of myself.

Since I wanted to learn more about the peace terms, I could hardly wait for the newspapers to come out. But I was rather disappointed when the papers merely printed the text of the proclamation in inch-high letters.[47] In the ensuing days, our tensions rose to the breaking point as we kept asking ourselves, "Will they accept it? What is the attitude of the neutral nations?" The first reports were not very hopeful. The *Daily*

[46] In order to capitalize on its one great victory of the year, the defeat of Rumania, six days after the fall of Bucharest on December 12, 1916, the German government issued a peace note. This note, however, was characterized by extreme vagueness and defiance; the German government made not a single concrete proposal concerning such major issues as the fate of Alsace-Lorraine, Belgium, or Serbia. The note ended with a belligerent tone: "If, notwithstanding this offer of peace and conciliation, the struggle should continue, the four allied powers [Germany, Austria-Hungary, Turkey, and Bulgaria] are resolved to carry it to a victorious end, while solemnly disclaiming responsibility before mankind and history.

[47] There were actually no peace terms. The German government refused to commit itself to any terms in advance and therefore merely stated ambiguously in its note that it felt "sure that the propositions which they [the Central Powers] would make . . . would be such as to serve as a basis for the restoration of a lasting peace."

Mail spoke in terms of a nation of predatory animals, robbers and murderers with which it was impossible to negotiate before it was beaten to its knees. *Le Matin, Novoe Vremia* and several others suspected that it was a trap. The Italian attitude was particularly amusing. [They insisted] "No peace at any price!" [48]

Every evening we would read out these proclamations. Then we would engage in lively disputes over them. Some of the men had the most fantastic ideas about what would happen if our offer was rejected by all of our enemies. Some of the men suggested in all seriousness that if this happened, we would start using gas bombs [of such power] that a single one of them could destroy all human life within the radius of a kilometer. This might very well be true. It was my personal opinion that we had made this offer to protect ourselves against the repercussions that might arise if we were to embark on a campaign of unrestricted, really unrestricted submarine warfare.[49] Several other developments confirmed my opinion. In the future our government will consider all armed English merchantmen as auxiliary cruisers. This is why Captain Blackie was pardoned.[50]

[48] The negative reaction to the German peace offer is best illustrated by Lloyd George's speech of December 19, 1916 in which he asserted, "To enter, upon the invitation of Germany proclaiming herself victorious, without any knowledge of the proposals she proposes to make, into a conference is to put our heads into a noose with the rope end in the hands of Germany."

[49] This is an extremely perceptive opinion. Chancellor Bethmann-Hollweg had drafted the note in an attempt to obtain a peace before the hotheads in the army, the navy and the Reichstag could force him into embarking upon a campaign of unrestricted submarine warfare which was likely to lead at the very least to a rupture of relations with America if not an actual declaration of war. Indeed, when the German note was not received without criticism, Hindenburg on December 23 demanded the immediate commencement of unlimited submarine warfare.

[50] It has proven impossible to unearth any reference to the pardoning of Captain Blackie. However, it may very well be that the author was really referring to the case of the British sea captain Charles Fryatt, who was sentenced to death and executed by a German naval court-martial on July 26, 1916 for attempting to ram his ship the *Brussels* into the German U-boat *U 33* when the latter ordered him to stop. There was considerable sentiment that Fryatt should be pardoned, but the German court-martial still condemned him to death because he had used his ship as an auxiliary cruiser in his ramming attempt without being a member of the armed forces of his country.

The consequences are unmistakable. Our submarines have grown larger and more effective. Hence they will no longer confine themselves to blockade the English coast but will range far out into the ocean. Out in the open stormy sea neither blocks nor mines, nor for that matter, destroyers, will be of any use. We shall simply sit back and wait. If we can only hold out until May, our enemies will be closer to starvation than we.[51]

Prepare for Christmas! I was really supposed to be cutting out paper designs and trimmings for our tree instead of writing. But none of us complied since we all felt that it was a waste of colored paper and glass balls and that it was more fun to play cards or to build ship models. I, too, was too depressed to have the slightest desire to do anything this year.

We were scheduled to load coal on Saturday and on Sunday or Monday we would go into dry dock to adjust our range-finder sights. I did not care in the least that this year's Christmas roast would not be too plump or fat. The weather was miserable; rain seeped in through every crack. 22 December 1916.

The only reason why I am writing today is to cheer myself out of my sadness and monotony. Nothing special has happened. I feel very depressed but it will go away eventually. Last year at this time I felt even worse. These few lines have already brought me some relief and lightened my cares. If I were all alone in the world, nothing would matter to me. But I had wanted to make my father happy. Oh, how I wish that I could tell him that now. I felt so certain that I could. At least my comrades are sensitive enough not to question me about it or to commiserate with me [about my leave]. Nothing matters to me any more, but whenever I think of home I feel like crying. . . .

While I was writing, three of my comrades were decorating

---

[51] The Chief of the German Admiralty Staff Admiral Holtzendorff had repeatedly asserted that an unlimited submarine campaign would bring England to sue for peace within six months. This news had been allowed to leak out to the public and engendered the overly optimistic hope that this would indeed come about.

276 ⚓ WAR, MUTINY AND REVOLUTION

the Christmas tree. Of course they went about it in the most tasteless fashion, with clumsy paper garlands, glass tinsel and balls. Although the rest of us did nothing to help, we all made fun of the three men. At four o'clock we were to attend religious services. Each man received a gift of four marks and six cigarettes. Those of us who did not get any packages in the mail also received a box filled with all sorts of useful trifles and some tobacco.

The First Officer ordered the men to assemble on deck. "I can well believe," he began, "that this year most of your placards will deal with the subject of food. If it were up to me, you would get more [food]. But we do not have any more to give you and hence we shall have to make the best of it." Whenever the Reichstag used to raise questions concerning the mistreatment of the enlisted men, this is how the War Minister responded, "If it were up to me . . . no one would be mistreated—after all, all of us are human. . . . We shall act with great firmness whenever such a case is brought to our attention, etc." The analogy came to my mind as I listened to this sophistry. I knew this sort of talk all too well to allow myself to be taken in by this holier-than-thou attitude. Such petty remedies can never cure the deep-rooted evil in our system.

Thereupon they called out the names [of the men who were going on leave] and once again my name was left out. I shall have to see what the next few days will bring. Christmas Day, 1916.

I was very happy when our three holidays were over. I could hardly get anything done with so much free time on my hands. Actually I could simply repeat my description of last year's festivities. But there were significantly fewer packages from home, and in general, we got less food. However it was still filling and it was served with good will. On the whole, our placards were witty and topical. Last year it had been the Detail Officer who was the butt of all the jokes, but now it was the turn of Quartermaster [Gasthaus]. Most often we made fun of him for his turnip marmalade. He was depicted preparing it by adding gigantic turnips, old rigging and fire hoses and every other conceivable way. Most of the poems and captions were unfortunate. One picture showed the Quartermaster vomiting violently after he had made the mistake of tasting some of his marmalade. Another humorless picture showed the Quartermaster, who had fallen overboard, being hit on the head with a gaff by a sailor. Our sensitive gentlemen officers must have felt insulted by a placard bearing the caption: "You must save [on food] so that we may feast." Below was a picture showing the enlisted men's galley, with a solitary cauldron of stew, while the "Lords'" kitchen was filled with hams, geese, sausages and the like. The stokers had dressed up a large doll as a sailor. It held a bucket in one hand and a piece of paper in the other. On it was written: "Where are you going?" "To the Quartermaster to fetch my marmalade." Most of the other placards expressed hopes for peace, "Merry Christmas," "God punish England," and other harmless sentiments.

While we were at dinner the Captain and his staff made the rounds. I must admit that he had a good laugh and a word of appreciation for each of the placards. He seemed particularly pleased when his officers were ridiculed. However many of them had an unhappy look about them. I overheard Oberleutnant [Kohrt] saying, "This placard is a scandal! Looks like something the First Division would do!!!" At eight o'clock we were issued some punch. However none of us managed to achieve the same happiness and exuberance which had been so common in earlier years. Each one of us was filled with his own sorrows. I don't even like to think of it

There was a big feast in the officers' mess. They had roast goose. The champagne corks kept popping. But I was not jealous. Let the gentlemen drink themselves into a stupor—if they would only leave us alone.

We slung our hammocks at nine o'clock but several of my drunken comrades made so much noise that it was impossible to fall asleep. I lay awake for a long time and thought of my loved ones at home who must now be on their way to Christmas mass. I had just managed to doze off, when in my sleep I heard everyone rushing up on deck. Filled with curiosity, I got up to see what was doing. I did not regret it. It was a clear, star-filled night. There was only a slight breeze but it carried the lovely and resounding song of a thousand men's voices singing, "Silent night, holy night. All is calm; all is bright. . . ." High above the singing one could distinguish the sounds of a trumpet. I was fascinated and filled with emotion as I listened to its solemn tones. Where did it come from? Ah, it came from the nearby *Thüringen*. At first I thought it was the music of a choir of heavenly angels. It sounded so solemn and so strange. I shall never forget this hour.

On the first day of Christmas we came into port, but I did not go ashore. It was rumored that we were going into dry dock on Wednesday. 26 December 1916.

And indeed this is precisely what happened. Our ship was towed into the dry dock very slowly. Its mighty pumps began to work and soon they had lifted us out of the water. Whenever I witnessed this marvel of human ingenuity, it always filled me with boundless admiration. Moreover it operated so quickly and quietly that even those who understood it were astonished when the red sides and bottom of the ship rose out of the water. Fortunately there was a constant fog. Ordinarily in good, clear weather, we would have been all finished by Friday. This meant that we would have refueled the next day and then wound up at Schillig Roads on New Year's. The weather, however, made it impossible to make out a church steeple at a thousand meters and therefore we were unable to make our exacting adjustments. Our officers did not mind the weather either. Despite all of their complaints about Wilhelmshaven, they were still happy to be in port. Had our former, hard-bitten captain still been in command, we would long since have been out of dock. Tomorrow will be New Year's. Will the new year bring this world conflagration to an end?

Although it was New Year's today, I was not in the proper mood. Four violins played in the casemates but each of them carried a different tune. Some of the men quietly played skat, while others filed and hammered away at their ship's models. It is incomprehensible to me how one can play cards all day and still retain an interest in life. However the men cannot understand why I am always writing when nothing happens. They think that I am copying our daily schedule. Each of us finds his own amusements. I could have gone ashore today but the weather was too unpleasant. In addition, I have no money, but that does not trouble me. Sometimes I find that I feel better when I have no money than when I do and spend it foolishly.

They have just piped, "All hands to receive punch." Therefore I must close. Prosit!

I have had a terrible headache since last night—but since I enjoyed myself so thoroughly, I do not mind it. For a change, I was happy and danced with abandon. I must have drunk a full liter of punch, which was enough to loosen my tongue. I am told that I sang very loudly and beautifully. Indeed I am still hoarse from it.

On the port side of the ship, the sixth casemate had been converted into a little theater. Two curtains, a table and a chair served as a stage. A professional comedian who served in the engine room gave the best performance of the evening. The loud bursts of laughter prompted me to take a look. I had to admit that it was great fun. However I soon was driven away by the clouds of tobacco smoke.

In our compartment, things had also livened up. Even from afar one could hear the tones of our favorite song: "Topsche, Topsche tralla Violina Draht kaputta." I sang and danced until I was dizzy. Then I had to get some fresh air before I could regain my senses. It was even livelier in Compartment 14. All the men there wore masks as they performed the most amusing circus pantomimes. One group presented a particularly amusing act entitled "How a giant boar lies with a sow." This sample of the program must suffice. It was not intended for sensitive people but none of us was offended. When the First Officer looked in for a while, even he was overcome with laughter. None of the officers, I must admit, interfered in the least with our merrymaking.

At the stroke of twelve, all the lights were extinguished and the most hellish noises from all sorts of instruments, noisemakers and voices resounded through every corner of the ship. A number of sneaky fellows took advantage of the general blackout to take a look at the contents of the officers' larder but I don't know what they took. Interrupted, 2 January 1917.

Since I have lost the point of the story and cannot seem to find it again, I shall not continue. Actually there is nothing more significant to report, so that I shall relieve my boredom by doing a little painting.

This time we were really in luck and stayed in dry dock for a full ten days. We were supposed to adjust our range finders. Every morning, however, a thick pea-soup of a fog descended, so that we could barely make out the town towers, let alone the one at Varel. Consequently we stayed on day after day. At last, when the sun penetrated through the wintery fog to enable us to take the necessary sightings, St. Peter sent us another miracle which kept us lying here idly for an additional two days. A violent storm made it impossible for us to run through the narrow channel leading out from the dock. The danger of being driven ashore was too great. I am still puzzled why our ship's bows did not block the channel altogether. What would have happened if we really had to get out? Under the circumstances, it is quite conceivable that we could have blocked off the entry to the submarine and torpedo boat pens.

However there was no hurry and thus we were able to stay on without any trouble for another two days. Finally, this morning when it had cleared up and there was no longer any wind, we ran out. We are about to get a new captain, if it hasn't already occurred. We were all sorry to hear that our "old man" had suffered a relapse of malaria and we hoped that the brave man would soon return to us. It looks as though our First Officer will also have to go because of the ramming of the *Hindenburg*. In his case, we did not feel so much regret. However I personally felt that his successor would not be an improvement. Interrupted, 6 January 1917.

Our wishes have been realized with astonishing speed. It seems that he [the Captain] is not so sick after all. He merely has a slight fever which can be treated on board. In any case, we are all presently forbidden to go on the afterdeck lest we disturb the old gentleman's rest. An elderly Fregattenkapitän has been sent to us from the Admiralty Office to act as his substitute and to familiarize himself [with the ship]. Unfortunately, for some unknown reason, our First Officer, too, is staying.

I gather from the newspapers that the English believe that they can sweep us from the sea even before they launch their "imminent offensive." But our naval command was not in the least disturbed by Mr. Beatty's threats.[52] We maintained our positions, relieved each other precisely on schedule and no unusual or exciting changes have taken place. But last Wednesday it did seem as though something was brewing. Totally unexpectedly, the entire fleet received orders to assemble at the outer roads by three o'clock. What was happening? Were we about to sail out on a mission of our own? Oh no, that would be too absurd! Although we made all sorts of preparations and paid the greatest attention to every last detail, we knew that nothing could happen so long as the officers did not clear out their cabins and the loading booms were not folded away.

As so often before, the fleet ran out to sea. Although it was overcast, there was almost no wind. The visibility was so poor that we almost ran into the island of Helgoland before it was sighted. Then the weather cleared, enabling us to perform a number of lovely maneuvers which were the primary purpose of our mission. I later discovered that a group of [visiting] Turkish and Bulgarian officers had observed our exercises. We had no luck this time; not a single one of our ships ran over a mine! At twelve noon, the flagship signaled that the exercise was over.

At Wilhelmshaven, "Batocky"[53] was waiting for us. (This is the name we had given to the supply ship *Dollart*.) She

---

[52] Admiral David Beatty (1871–1936) had commanded the British battle cruiser squadron from 1913 to 1916. After the Battle of Jutland he replaced Admiral Jellicoe as Chief of the Grand Fleet.

[53] Adolf Tortilowicz von Batocky (1868–1944) was the head of the recently established Ministry of War Supply.

brought us some fresh bread and some precious potatoes. Later on these would be served to us one at a time. In spite of the sharp vigilance of the "bacon cutter" (our nickname for the Quartermaster), several sacks of potatoes disappeared on their way to the bins. Thereupon the worthy man dashed off to register a complaint with the First Officer. Although every cranny [of the ship] was searched during rounds that evening, nothing turned up. However while we were at lunch, a few sacks were unearthed with much fanfare among the shelves on the port side, whereupon the entire port watch was placed on report. But the First Officer was in a good mood and he let the men off for lack of evidence.

These minor incidents do not affect our morale. We merely laugh and shrug them off with contempt. In general we are a very patient people. So long as we are free to complain, we can tolerate anything. However our shortage of soap is assuming catastrophic proportions. All we get for an entire month is a tiny little cake of 50 grams. Because of our filthy work, we run out of soap in two weeks no matter how sparingly we use it. Then we have to resort to soda and sand. In spite of that, our hands and fingernails are frequently checked for cleanliness at Sunday Inspection. The young gentlemen who still have a hundred cakes in their lockers are particularly adept at this. Whenever I see some of the old sailors extend their swollen hands to be inspected by these opinionated young thieves, I fly into a towering rage.[54] But the best is yet to come.

Our Kaiser's peace offer has been rejected with contempt. Even the conscience of President Wilson was touched and he issued an equivocal and vague note to the belligerent powers.[55]

[54] According to one of the later mutineers, Willi Sachse, the soap shortage and the resulting inspections had already led to a strike among the stokers on the battleship *Friedrich der Grosse*.

[55] The ambiguity of the German Peace Note of December 12, 1916 prompted President Wilson on December 18 to issue a note of his own which requested the belligerent powers to state their specific peace terms and which warned them that only a "peace without victory" could produce an enduring settlement. However, the reply of the Central Powers on December 26 was couched in vague language, mentioned no specific terms and called for a meeting to facilitate the exchange of views. On

Empty words. . . . This man has it within his power to compel the signing of a peace within a month. Indeed he could compel peace by placing an embargo on food and munitions. But gold is thicker than blood and also more valuable!!

What a miserable, boring and stupid life we lead! I would rather carry rocks all day long if I only knew that it served some useful purpose. But here! I dare not think how I waste my life here lest one day I suffer a nervous breakdown. Moreover, there is not the slightest hope that it will get any better.

Today I shall not complain, because my stomach is full. It is remarkable how modest my demands have become. Whenever I have a full stomach, however rare that may be, the entire world seems much brighter to me. Then I can even bear to see the cadets who entered in April strut about as arrogant ensigns. They are still only mildly surprised and outraged when a sailor who has already served for four, five or six years, neglects to salute them. But in another two weeks they will have learned enough to stop every "Schweinehund" and chew him out for this. It makes me laugh to see these seventeen-year-old little fellows order a bosun twice their age to report to them. It is a— No, I don't want to complain today.

I have noticed of late that we frequently get issues of fats instead of [our usual] marmalade. The answer is quite simple. Several barrels of this costly shortening have become spoiled and smell worse with each passing day. Today they put three barrels into the boilers to freshen it up again by cooking it with apples and onions. . . .

We only get potatoes once a week. On weekdays we get yellow, red and other varieties of turnips, alternating with

January 10, 1917, the Allies responded with even greater vehemence by asserting that they wanted the restoration of all territory conquered by the Central Powers, the evacuation of all occupied territory and the liberation of all Italians, Slavs, Rumanians, and Czechs from foreign rule.

Although Wilson was deeply disappointed with the meager results of his peace offer, he continued negotiating with both sides, but Germany in particular, until these negotiations were suddenly broken off by the German announcement on January 31, 1917, of the commencement of a campaign of unrestricted submarine warfare.

blue, red and green cabbage.[56] Consequently I am very glad that I was never spoiled at home. Maybe they will increase our bread rations. That would be fine. I am rather astonished at the prominence of food and eating in my war diary. Actually this is not at all surprising. Anyone who spent eight days here and became acquainted with the life of the sailors, would find that the most important question of the day is: What is there to eat today? The next important question is: What sort of work will we have today? It is only natural that we criticize the food. Our quartermaster would be the unhappiest man on God's earth if the curses we heap upon him after every meal would come true. Yet, despite all our curses, he remains unaffected. While it is quite true that anyone who is charged with feeding an entire crew is saddled with a thankless task, I have yet to hear of a retired quartermaster ever going bankrupt as a hotel keeper. But enough of that. . . .

We have been back in port since Sunday. Many of the men were granted leaves. Tomorrow, on Friday, we are going on patrol again.

Nothing new at sea. 18 January 1917.

Our First Officer has obtained a six weeks' furlough to enable him "to seek" a position in civilian life. Kapitänleutnant [Herzbruch] from the Admiralty has been appointed as his successor. He does not appear to be a very congenial fellow. I have already observed him chewing out the officers on several occasions. But he does not let us get away with anything either. He punished an entire work detail with six hours of "sport" because someone talked during formation. However he is refreshingly honest. When one of the cook's mates brought him some green

---

56 Premature frosts had spoiled the potato harvest of 1916 with the result that throughout the winter there existed a very grave food shortage in Germany. Hence the winter of 1916–17 became known as the "Turnip Winter" because the lowly turnip and other ersatz products had to serve as substitutes for more traditional food items. Moreover, the winter was also bitterly cold, the canals froze over and the overburdened railroads could not make their regular fuel deliveries. The food shortage, in combination with the fuel shortage, created great war-weariness in Germany not only among the undernourished and shivering civilian population, but also among the sailors in the navy.

cabbage to taste, he erupted, "Go to hell and don't bother me again with this stuff . . . I don't want my appetite ruined every day!!!!" He shouts like a lion. He has brought all sorts of peacetime practices from Berlin with him. Today, for instance, he woke the watch at every relief and made the men sleep fully clothed.

Recently our entire crew was weighed at the hospital. By and large, I think that there was a slight increase in our [average] weight. However certain individuals have lost enormous weight. I myself [lost] five kilos. When I and several other men were presented to the chief doctor, the following dialogue ensued: "You have lost five kilos. Have you any complaints?" "No!" "Don't you get enough to eat?" "No!" "Do you ever feel satisfied?" "No!" "Don't you receive any food from home?" "Oh, fairly regularly, eh?" "And you are still hungry?" "No!" "Aha, you probably don't finish what you get?" "Oh, no, Herr Doctor. I eat everything!" "Do you have an appetite?" "Yes, Sir!" "That's good. You may go now."

The entire Jade Estuary was covered with floating ice this morning. Large areas were even frozen solid. Somehow it seemed strange to see the otherwise perpetually restless sea so still and shimmering. Our gray ships looked like toys, like the little paper ships which we used to float along the Weiher as children. When our squadron ran out, we pushed the ice floes out of the way with ease. In this instance, technology still managed to control the powers of nature. The sailors insist that the ice does not drift in from the open sea, but that it is swept down by the Elbe and the Weser. At ebb tide it accumulates on the exposed sand bars, one floe piles on top of the other and thus very considerable deposits are built up. It will require some very strong spring breezes to melt these picturesque mountains. In looking at them from a porthole or from the top deck, they create the illusion that our ship is constantly moving at a slow speed. But this is not true. Actually, it is the snowy landscape that is moving. . . .

Under the circumstances, we found it impossible to maintain our [regular] communication with the shore by boat. It made us happy that the officers had to stay on board like the rest of us. Anyone who knows the navy will not be surprised that this situation should give rise to all sorts of jokes. One joke maintained that German industry was producing nothing but ice skates so that we could immediately launch a grand invasion against England. Our Detail Officer was said to have prepared a most painstaking plan for it. It would make the Kaiser very happy on his birthday to hear the news that his blue boys had invaded England on skates. All these fanciful stories were told with a broad smile and a total disregard for reality.

Something was in the air again. The atmosphere was tense and nervous. The cry, "Prepare for battle," was sounded at the least provocation. Even if one of our ships plunged forward a little bit faster than usual, there was an immediate response, "Aha, look over there, they are already increasing steam! Did you see that?"

Last night, while we were playing [music] in the forward battery, the alarm, "All hands on deck," was sounded. In our haste there was much shouting, the benches were knocked over and the dishes rattled. We were just halfway up to the deck when some of the men came running back shouting, "Stay where you are! S 53 has sunk an English destroyer-escort. . . ." The band went back to playing, but in half an hour we were again ordered to pack and stow our seabags away. Moreover I was unfortunate enough to be on guard duty until twelve o'clock and at four I had to assume my station as lookout. Luckily, however, there was no action. The orders were rescinded and I was able to sleep until seven in the morning. Then we were ordered to quickly retrieve our bags.

Much to our satisfaction, [we learned] that our new First Officer, whom we had named Lord Pfefferkuchenbruch, was about to be transferred. His place as First Officer will be taken by the First Artillery Officer [Captain Richter].

Our men possess a remarkable talent for being able to "scent" something brewing out at sea. They [nervously] anticipate the order for an alert and when it finally arrives, they feel visibly relieved to be freed from their enormous tensions.

Hardly anyone ever writes letters during this tense period. We merely pack our bags tighter, keep fiddling with our clothing and hide away our private possessions which will not fit into the bag. This is what happened yesterday. Early that morning we had a strange premonition that we would put out to sea. Maybe we planned to give the Kaiser a surprise gift for his birthday, or perhaps our cousins from across the Channel had one in store for him. At the stroke of two, our ensign came rushing in and told us to pack our gear away. Then the ventilators began to sing and to purr, indicating that we were raising steam in a hurry. After we had finished these initial preparations, our ship broke through the icepack along with the reconnaissance group. And then, naturally, we anchored once more off Schillig Roads. An hour later, the crew was again ordered to weigh anchor. We were astonished when we headed toward Wilhelmshaven instead of running out to sea. What was the meaning of all this? Could it be that the English were really out there??? No, not at all! We had to drag our things out of the hold all over again and we went about our business cursing profusely. 26 January 1917.

This is my fifth observance of the Kaiser's birthday in the navy. If it would only be the last one. . . . But there is damned little chance for that according to what K. told us on deck this morning. He stated that the coming year would be the most decisive in all of Germany's history. It would decide the outcome of the war and he felt that only the navy could bring about that decision. Therefore it would be our responsibility to gather up all our energies to administer the final blow to the enemy. . . . After we sounded the usual cheers the names of the few men going on leave were announced. No one in our division was included. . . . I felt simply dreadful. However my spirits revived a bit when I was able to fill my stomach at lunch.

I have just learned why we have been kept in a state of alert lately. Our torpedo boats have bombarded another English town. Henceforth everything will be fine again. 27 January 1917.

I was surprised when we ran into port to dismantle our remaining 8.8 cm. guns. We parted with them without regrets. The general monotony of this war has long since destroyed our loyalty for "our" guns. Familiar things disappear; the times change. . . . [Originally] these small-caliber, rapid-firing guns had been regarded as our major defense against submarines and torpedo boats. Two years ago if anyone had maintained that these guns were useless and ought to be dismantled, he would have been shot as a traitor. This was also true in regard to our protective torpedo netting.

Now that the silent guns have been carted away, I would like to say a few words of farewell to their memory. You [guns] will probably be sent off to lend your voices to the devil's symphony which is about to break loose in France and in Alsace. Since you might never have gotten a chance to fire at the English with us, this should make you happy. While we have already kept you waiting for thirty months to spew death and destruction at the enemy—there your wish will be realized. At Jutland you menacingly raised your muzzles against England's ships but you had to lower them because you could not reach far enough. Now, however, you shall fulfill your mission if each one of your rounds merely saves the life of a single soldier.

I have often maintained that we are living in great times. Sometimes our little worries and routine concerns make us forget that. Indeed, at times when we were hungry we have even cursed you, you heroic times. But men are fallible. However I don't think I am mistaken when I say that the war has reached another turning point. The whole world is holding its breath as Germany prepares to launch her final smashing blow.[57] It seems as though the clock has been turned back by a hundred years. . . . As in the early days, the God of War has worked miracles to bring his children to the front and to provide them

[57] No German offensive was scheduled for the early part of 1917. Instead, the German army was trying to consolidate its position in the West by constructing the so-called Hindenburg Line, which was designed to permit a limited retreat to more easily defended positions when the Allied offensive struck.

with munition, food and fuel. An order from War Minister von Stein [58] has canceled all leaves until February 19. However we did not complain. We all bowed before the imposing power of his spirit. We fervently prayed for victory.

No one will deny that these recent measures are not of great historical importance. But something else, something which affects us even more intimately, has been added. But I must first describe how my comrades and I found out about it. Yesterday morning the free watch went on a military excursion—where else is there to go hereabouts—to Mariensiel. On the way there [we went] along the dike and on the return trip we came through the town. These are the only two possible ways. The band was out in front. It was all very nice. The huge ice pack looked lovely and immensely powerful. Its glimmering beauty would not last much longer since the barometer has been rising constantly. As we returned from our meal, the Duty Officer called to us with the wonderful news: "Listen men, a telegram from Berlin. 'Starting today we shall commence a campaign [of unrestricted] submarine warfare.' " [59] This was a very pleasant surprise indeed. We were all extremely glad that we had finally taken this step. I had not even dared to hope that we would ever announce it officially. Yet it has happened. We spoke of nothing else on the ship. However I found it rather objectionable to evoke such high hopes among the people and the navy. It was as if we were pronouncing a final death sentence on England. Undoubtedly bread and meat

[58] Lieutenant General Hermann von Stein (1854–1927) was appointed to succeed Wild von Hohenborn as Prussian Minister of War in November 1916.

[59] On January 9, 1917, a top-level meeting of German military and political leaders was held at Pless in the presence of the Kaiser. The military, particularly Hindenburg and Ludendorff, insisted that the war could only be won by means of unrestricted submarine warfare. The navy gave assurances that England's resistance would soon collapse if Germany succeeded in sinking 600,000 tons of Allied shipping a month. It maintained that there was nothing to fear from an American declaration of war since it would guarantee that not a single American soldier would ever set foot in France. Although Chancellor Bethmann-Hollweg disagreed violently, he was forced to yield when the Kaiser opted in favor of his military advisers. Germany announced her decision to commence unrestricted submarine warfare on January 31, 1917.

prices will rise in England. But it would be absurd to think that the English people did not have enough of an instinct for survival to have stocked up their larders with food. Up till now we have merely disrupted their trade but we have by no means paralyzed it. Be that as it may, within four months we shall have a clearer view of the situation. I only hope that they will come to feel the same intense hunger as our people in Saxony or in Westphalia. Tomorrow morning we will run out to sea. 2 February 1917.

Never before has the Kaiser sent out so many messages of gratitude to his people as in the recent past. But none of these was warmer or more heartfelt than the one he sent to "his navy." Whenever he speaks of the navy, he becomes gentle and paternal and addresses his men as his dear children. Yesterday, when we published our declaration of unrestricted submarine warfare, the Kaiser's cabinet order was read out to us. It was addressed primarily to his submarine forces. But he instructed his surface fleet that it would be its responsibility to break the enemy's will to fight by waging the final battles with great vigor.

Although I am not a blind monarchist by conviction, I must admit that the Kaiser excels at communicating with his people. Moreover unlike the other heads of state, he did not wait until the war to turn social. He has been like that since he ascended the throne.[60] He has inspired the German people to reveal their best qualities of patriotism, selflessness and courage. But not even the Kaiser's optimism can convince me that unrestricted submarine warfare will lead us to victory. I cannot see how our sudden determination [to wage an all-out war] can make up for all the opportunities we missed because of our indecisive-

[60] From the very beginning of his reign in 1888, Kaiser Wilhelm II prided himself on his enlightened social and labor policies. He refused to extend the Bismarckian Anti-Socialist Law of 1878; he set up industrial courts to mediate wage disputes, limited the hours of work for women and children, prohibited Sunday employment, set up a system of factory inspection and established a labor department. Therefore he was sometimes called the "Labor Emperor."

ness and hesitation. Nevertheless I cannot help hoping that everything will turn out differently than reason and reflection lead me to believe. Since the enemy is prepared, the greatest power of this new weapon—the element of shattering surprise —will no longer be effective.

If this cold continues, the Jade will soon be frozen over entirely. Then we shall have to use our sturdy battleships as icebreakers. As an added nuisance, the ice floes have torn away our netting. Therefore we shall have to patrol the channel as in the early days of the war. It will be extremely uncomfortable in this damned cold. But there is nothing we can do about it.

4 February 1917.

I had just finished writing these lines when the mail came in. I received a newspaper and could hardly believe my eyes when I read the headline. The Reuter [News Agency] reported that America had severed diplomatic relations with Germany.[61] I almost suffered a heart attack when I read this terrible but not totally unexpected news. If America does not hesitate at the last minute and declares war against us, our situation, especially after the war, will be extremely critical. I have always looked upon the United States as a source of reserve strength for the world and hoped that it would give a decimated Europe a transfusion of new blood. We were all agreed that the United States would not significantly strengthen the military position of our enemies but that it would make them economically indestructible. Just think what enormous gold reserves they hold on the other side of the great pond!

What could we do under those conditions? Our submarines alone could not help us. Oh, if we could only cut despicable Albion's communications for six months! I am not thinking only in terms of food, but also of weapons, ores, wood, nitrates, metal, cotton and other war material. If we succeeded in achieving this, we would once again become the saviors of civilization and the dominance of the white race.

[61] On February 3, 1917, America broke off diplomatic relations with Germany over her announcement of unrestricted submarine warfare.

What will the Japanese have to say about all this? This is the crew's favorite topic of discussion. Although our opinions are divided, there are still some who believe that they [the Japanese] will take military measures against America.[62] But I cannot agree with these optimists. We all feel sad and depressed. It is even worse than September when Rumania declared war. But how do we look upon that threat now? The heroic deeds of Hindenburg have relegated that threat to the far-off, nebulous distance. Maybe four months from now we shall feel the same way about America. I shall have to pay very close attention to future developments. 6 February 1917.

Although America has moderated her threatening stance to some extent, our future still does not look bright. As far as I can tell, Wilson is trying to push the rest of the neutrals to take a stand.[63] I have still not made up my mind about this man. Is he really a cold-blooded, business-like Yankee, or is he, as the papers occasionally describe him, an impractical, humanitarian professor? [64] We do not have enough perspective to obtain a true picture of the President's mentality. Nevertheless it makes us angry to see his proclamations dripping with humanitarianism arrayed right next to the impressive statistics of America's arms exports.[65]

While I was occupied with my writing, one of our Zeppelins flew over with a thunderous noise. It blew away all my sad

[62] There existed a vain hope in some German quarters, even within the Foreign Office, that Japan would seize the opportunity to ally herself with Germany upon America's entry into the war. This was the purpose of the Zimmermann Note of January 17, 1917, which proposed the establishment of an anti-American alliance consisting of Germany, Mexico and Japan.

[63] When America severed relations with Germany, she appealed to the neutral states to follow her example. Brazil, Bolivia, and Peru did so immediately; the other Latin-American nations and China gradually emulated this action.

[64] President Wilson was professor of history at Princeton University from 1890 to 1902 and president of that university from 1902 to 1910.

[65] Before her entry into the war, the United States sold the Allies an estimated quarter of a billion dollars' worth of arms a year.

thoughts and worries. Its proud shape refreshed my heart and renewed my courage. Let the enemy copy this plane [if he can]! We already have thirty-nine of them. In this instance our factories have excelled themselves in producing something so grand and overwhelmingly powerful. I doubt that any plane can match this giant in speed. Although our ship was moving very fast, the shimmering giant soon vanished into the infinite distance. England, England, you are about to receive a surprise from the air.

I fluctuated between two extremes. My imagination and the power of suggestion soon changed what had earlier seemed so difficult and depressing into dreams of victory. O Zeppelin, please come more often to banish my sadness! 8 February 1917.

It was a wet but warm and springlike Sunday. The spring sun and the balmy breezes would soon melt away the ice in the Jade. Although it was warm, the fog was so thick that I could barely make out *Thüringen*'s smokestacks. The damp fog penetrated one's clothing as though it were rain. Something was not quite right out at sea. As a result we maintained a round-the-clock, three-hour alert.

I was delighted to follow the growing list of ships we sank every day. I estimated that we would reach the half-million [ton] mark for the first time this month.[66] We placed almost unbelievable hope in the outcome of the submarine campaign. Yesterday I visited the Dock Division Barracks, where the submarine crews are trained. The petty officers with whom I spoke all felt that we would starve England into submission by June. I found such optimism altogether outrageous. I only hoped that we would not be too badly disappointed. . . . In case it fails, we shall have given up one of our three remaining trump cards for nothing.

Strangers are never impressed with Wilhelmshaven. Even the natives detest the place. There are many reasons for this. First of all, the climate is wet and unhealthy, there is total lack of any natural beauty, and lastly, the population is very igno-

[66] During February 1917 German submarines sank 781,500 tons of shipping.

rant. In spite of all that, the town is better endowed with con-
sumers than any other place in Germany. Just think, the town
has sixty to seventy [thousand] sailors and then there are also
well-paid shipyard workers, officials, engineers and officers.
Nevertheless there is not a really modern department store, no
restaurant and no theater in the entire town. If one wants something special like a book, a tool or some chemical, the "businessmen" always refer one to Bremen or Hanover. What a fine
opportunity there would be here for an enterprising business-
man who wanted to open a really fine theater, department store
or a cafe. But since none of these are presently available, it is
virtually impossible to spend one's money in a decent manner.

What are these reflections doing in my diary? They don't belong here. I have recorded them only because I have nothing
better on my mind. I am also frequently annoyed by the sheer
stupidity of the local businessmen. Sunday, 11 February 1917.

Unfortunately once again I have to start off with a very,
very sad story. Although I have recorded a similar case at an
earlier date, I am repeating this story because it is even more
scandalous than the one before. As usual, a number of dock
workers crowded around our ship to beg for food scraps.
Among them was a crippled soldier with a stiff leg. One of our
men gave him a half portion of his turnips. Lieutenant [Kes-
sel], the Officer of the Watch, observed the incident and summoned the soldier to him. "How dare you beg food here?" "I
am hungry, Herr Leutnant," he replied. "I don't give a damn
about that. You have been informed that it is prohibited. Messenger! Take the food from the man and throw it into the
garbage." I could barely repress my rage as I accompanied the
man down the gangplank. All of a sudden the invalid's anger
exploded. "How stupid this is!" The dashing Lieutenant overheard him and summoned the poor man before him again, gave
him a terrific dressing down, took his work number and once
again ordered me to throw out his food. Fortunately the little

pot had a cover which enabled me to merely pretend that I was emptying the food.[67]

I cannot understand how an officer who is usually so good and devoted to his men can behave so cruelly. I feel that the fault lies in his upbringing rather than in his personality. He has probably never experienced hunger since he is the son of a surgeon-general. Even as a child he must have learned to despise all work. Hence he was probably satisfied with himself to present the gentleman's point of view so forcefully to the laboring classes.

On Sunday night we were surprised when a damaged torpedo boat which we recognized as the *V 69* passed near us. Several weeks before she had become involved in a hot fight with some English destroyers and was forced to run into Imuiden to escape. According to the rules of naval procedure, the Dutch were under no obligation to release her. That they nonetheless chose to do so was a sign of their good intentions toward us. It was a shame that we had to sail out this morning, otherwise I would have gone over to her and listened to her story. 13 February 1917.

Fog, fog, and again fog was our constant companion at sea. I hoped that our brave *Wolf* would manage to return home under its protection. Where could she be now that even the unfriendly American ports were closed to her?

Save coal! Conserve coal! This is the pleasant goal of our latest campaign. As a result, we now come into Wilhelmshaven every week and we no longer have to shovel so much coal into the hold as before. There are at least 300,000 tons of coal for the exclusive use of the navy in Wilhelmshaven. Therefore I kept asking myself if it was necessary for us to receive immensely long trains of coal every day when the civilian population was freezing and starving. It had long been rumored with mounting vehemence that the speculations of the coal syndi-

[67] According to the German health authorities, a worker needed at least 3,300 calories per day to maintain himself on a productive level. However, during the "turnip winter" of 1916–1917 the workers were reduced to 1,344 calories per day and by the summer of 1917 this was further lowered to 1,100 calories.

cates were responsible for the coal shortage. After all, it would not be right for the coal barons to restrain themselves when their colleagues in the steel, textile and paper industry were earning so many millions in war profits. Therefore they have found a convenient excuse by blaming it all on the very real shortage of railroad rolling stock. But I am convinced that there will be plenty of coal again as soon as its price has risen to three marks per hundredweight. Oh what sad, uncivilized times we live in!!

We were supposed to come in this morning but the fog made it impossible. I did not care. But the persistent ringing of the fog bells keeps interrupting my thoughts and hence I have to close. Sunday, 18 February 1917.

This damned, horrible fog! For two days now it has cut off our communications with the outer world. [We get] no mail, no news and no papers! This is totally unprecedented! Perhaps the war will end in the interim and we will not even be informed! Moreover any day now, that great event of the future, "our decisive offensive," may begin. Last year the fighting at Verdun started in February. Where will it take place this year? We are already worrying about it. It hardly matters whether it takes place at Verdun, on the Somme, in Flanders, in Italy— or off Helgoland—if it will only bring peace. 19 February 1917.

I don't know how the postal steamer managed to find us. In any event, she brought out the long-awaited mail. Nothing of special importance.

We were all set to come into port yesterday. Luckily the fog lifted somewhat at four o'clock and all seven of our ships headed full-speed toward Wilhelmshaven. The first three ships reached the locks before the fog descended again but we remained outside, holding the bag. At nightfall it cleared again somewhat and by eight o'clock the Captain decided that we would run in regardless of the consequences. We very nearly had cause to regret it. In my capacity as a messenger I witnessed the entire proceedings on the bridge. We were anchored two to two and a half kilometers from the locks. The channel lights appeared as dim points of light through the telescope.

In my excitement I wondered whether we could manage to find our way, which was elusive enough by day, through the darkness and fog. If it had been up to me, I would have given up the entire thing. If we merely strayed ten meters too far to either side we would either get stuck in the mud or ram into the wall of the locks. Our heavy ship was slowly and quietly inching into the lock when suddenly our bow began to spin toward the cement walls with alarming speed. We all caught out breath and held on to protect ourselves from falling backwards when we collided. "Forty meters, thirty meters!" the helmsman shouted fearfully from the stern. "Rudder hard port and three quarters reverse," called the Captain. Suspenseful seconds passed. Thirty meters, twenty meters, ten meters, five meters—and finally came the cry of relief: "Ship holding. . . . Ship reversing!" "Thank God! That was a close shave!" moaned the Captain. "Yes, it is all the damned tide," called the pilot. All at once our mood changed as we nodded with approval. By ten o'clock we were safely anchored in port.

22 February 1917.

We were scheduled to run out again on Sunday, but the fog came, left, came and disappeared again. Finally at seven o'clock in the evening the First Officer gave permission for the free watch to go ashore. But at noon on Monday we set out again despite the dank fog. By the time we had reached the locks, we realized that it was too risky to proceed further and we therefore remained hove-to for several hours. At last, toward evening, we arrived at Schillig Roads to relieve the ships of the *Kaiser*-class.

Today I was unbearably humiliated and annoyed. We were harassed unmercifully at battle practice in the morning. On top of all that, we had the devil's own grandmother as our Turret Officer. I had to suffer all sorts of unspeakable insults from gunner's mate [H]. "You have lost your mind! Take your hand off there," and so on and on. All this occurred in the presence of the gun captain. Truly, if I still possessed even a shred of honor, I would have had to jump at the scoundrel's throat. There may come a day when I shall lose control over myself. If it were not for my parents and relatives, I would long since have vented my wrath on one of these fellows who has done everything in his power to destroy my ideals, my love of the Fatherland and my sense of justice. Our military system has accomplished what no book, no newspaper and no Socialist could ever have done. I have learned to hate and despise its authority more than anything else in the world. This authority is not based on any distinctive superiority but relies solely on the fear of the paragraphs of the naval code of justice. August Bebel, for all your efforts on behalf of the poor, suppressed soldiers, I wish to thank you even in your grave. I misunderstood you and considered all your speeches on the military budget as vile exaggerations. Now, however, I look upon them as an act of patriotism for which all German mothers and sisters should bless you. . . . [68]

Our officers are bored. Hence we shall have more military drill in the future. We are getting too fat. . . . That's right, go on like this. You are making the seeds of hatred shoot up into sturdy plants. And when the time comes for the misguided proletarians to leave their trenches, they will turn their arms against those who have earned their hatred. When will that day of justice begin to dawn in my dark night? Although I am still trembling with rage, for the sake of justice I need some quiet contemplation. 26 February 1917.

We had two major robberies in one night. Nothing like this has ever happened before. Four stokers, acting on the principle that it is easiest to get away with a most audacious deed, broke into the Warrant Officer's larder. They seemed completely unconcerned that forty men were sleeping right on top of it. If the machinist on duty had not perchance happened to come by, their daring act would have gone undetected. However he noticed that the lock was open and when he played his

[68] August Bebel (1840–1913) was one of the founders of the Social Democratic Party of Germany and leader of that party's parliamentary group in the Reichstag. Before the outbreak of the war the Socialists consistently refused to vote for the budget.

flashlight on it, he saw a sack full of cheese, sausages, bread and other provisions [had been stolen].

The culprit in the second affair was not caught. One morning as the people in the canteen were about to start work, they found that their lockers had been broken open. Several packages of biscuits were strewn on the floor and 180 boxes of Flaggengala cigarettes were missing. The exact count was 17,800 pieces. Naturally all the men had to unpack their lockers but nothing was found. As if 18,000 cigarettes could fit into such a small container!

It was precisely this large quantity which aroused our suspicion. It was rumored quite openly that only an insider could have stolen the cigarettes or that it was possible that they had never been brought on board. I thought the latter conjecture was most sensible.

Of course the Canteen Officer was heartbroken (or at least he acted that way) and had all the munition chambers searched. [Moreover] he managed to persuade the Captain to raise the price of cigarettes by a pfennig apiece. Curiously enough, however, this new price was to be borne only by the sailors and not by the petty officers, ensigns or officers. This shabby trick deserves to be condemned in the strongest possible terms. All of us were highly indignant and agreed to protect ourselves against this profiteering by instituting a general boycott.

Our old First Officer has returned from his six-week furlough. There are also other changes among the officers. The most despicable of them all [Z.] has left. I understand that he has been assigned to the Air Force. We got a Flight Lieutenant to take his place. Right from the start on his second day here, he made it plain to us that he was dissatisfied with our division. It lacked polish, had no trace of military dash and behaved very slovenly. He announced that he would see to it that we spent more time on drill rather than on stupid artillery exercises. He announced that he would not rate his men on the basis of their conduct books but according to their behavior. Even a man with a miserable record could earn a good rating if he behaved himself properly. (I felt like shaking his hand for that.) He continued by appealing to our sense of honor and asserted that Germany had won her victories against a number of more powerful enemies solely on the basis of her discipline?? I think that Oberleutnant ———— is a competent, honorable officer and I shall not hesitate to honor him accordingly at all times. 27 February 1917.

We are admittedly enjoying a very peaceful interlude. Apparently we have no inclination to engage in any offensive action at sea. This pleased me greatly since I enjoyed the rest. Closing, 1 March 1917.

"All hands aft!" I had just sat down and rested my head on my hand to think about what to write when this happy incident came to my rescue. At first I thought that we were going to hear something about the rotten potatoes we had had for lunch. But no, it was something quite different. As I ran up the steps leading to the top deck, I heard cheering. Who would ever have expected it! *U 21*, the world-famous *U 21*, the savior of the Dardanelles, was running into port. Her long homecoming pennant fluttered proudly in the fresh breeze. How proud her twenty brave men must feel after their month's long voyage to see the light tower of Wilhelmshaven. Hersing richly deserved to eclipse the fame of Weddingen.[69] He had indeed accomplished the impossible. It was he who routed the English fleet into a frantic flight back to Malta and Samos by sinking the *Triumph*, which had been sent all the way from the Far East. The Turks could breathe again—the Straits were saved.[70]

Had this small gray vessel which just submerged beneath the waves accomplished all these things? Was it possible? Was it conceivable that such a small and insignificant vessel could disrupt the mission of an entire great and powerful fleet? The *U 21* was our first model of a new and improved type [of sub-

[69] Kapitänleutnant Otto Weddingen had sunk three British armored cruisers, *Cressy*, *Aboukir*, and *Hogue*, in September 1914.
[70] This had taken place at the Dardanelles in May 1915.

marine]. One of the major English newspapers wisely wrote of her, "We shudder to think what might happen if Germany had three hundred such submarines." And now? She has long since been superseded and outdated. Her engines no longer run noiselessly and are now outmoded for underwater cruising. She is much slower than ocean liners and battleships. Much has been changed and improved since then. It should make England groan all the louder. We know that her historic trip to the Dardanelles took six weeks. However we are also positive that she neither took on provisions nor fuel during that entire time. It is still a mystery how she managed to slip through the Straits of Gibraltar undetected and unharmed. But this is all in the past. Now we are all glad that the brave little ship has returned to Wilhelmshaven after her long trip looking so well.

How I envy the men in her crew! They will be able to go home for a long time with many a saved-up hundred-mark bill in their pockets. All the misery and wretchedness of my life in these "steel barracks" passes before my eyes as I think of it. . . . Allow me to present a small sampling of my life. Our cheers (rather pitiful ones) for the brave little ship had barely died down when the First Officer told us to gather around and addressed us somewhat as follows: "Once again a dozen men have come to me complaining that your potatoes were inedible. I need hardly assure you that you get twice as many potatoes as your relatives at home. In any event I tasted some of them. I found that they were a trifle sweet from being frozen a little and that they were also partially rotten. Men, I demand that you respect your First Officer's time and that you cease complaining about matters which he cannot remedy. If you do not like the potatoes this way—then don't eat them! If anyone complains again I shall have him locked up! Dismissed!"

Bang! I was speechless. . . . We would not have to wait long before the after-effects manifested themselves. Since everyone was on deck listening to the First Officer and there was no one to disturb them, several thieves took advantage of this singular opportunity by breaking into the Warrant Officer's larder. But all criminals make mistakes. This was true in this case. They hid their loot, a pair of lovely sides of bacon, in the emergency exit leading to A Turret. It was soon discovered there but we still don't know who did it.

One of our new destroyers passed by today. She was carrying Prince Max [of Baden] [71] and the Commander of the Austrian navy.[72] Tomorrow we shall have to provide these noble gentlemen with a proper show of maneuvers. Yesterday the ships of the *Posen* class came into port but had to run out again today. This pleased us immensely. Sunday, 4 March 1917.

I had just finished writing these lines when we were suddenly ordered to stow our bags. We cursed furiously and heaped all sorts of abuse on Prince Max. We had to hold a major battle exercise solely on his account. A proverb states, "Where there is much cursing, happiness does not abide." We found this true when our curses brought a misfortune upon us. But it serves our "superiors" right. Why do they plague us so needlessly?

At seven this morning our entire fleet raised anchor and steamed out into a friendly, but rather restless North Sea. From the direction of the Rotesand beacon came a devilish, piercing wind which whistled about our ears. Then we proceeded with our routine. None of us took notice when *Grosser Kurfürst*, which had just been beautifully refitted in Hamburg, hit the equally well-repaired *Kronprinz* in the flank. However both ships maintained their places in the formation. Only on the way home did it come to our attention that the ship which had been rammed had an enormous hole in her side. We all thought that it had been caused by a floating mine. Only later, when *Kronprinz*, too, passed near us did we realize what had actually happened. Strangely enough, when I first spotted the severely damaged ship with its crooked and bent nozzle, I burst out in unrestrainable laughter because of her funny appearance. The impact must have been terrific because her armored ram

[71] Maximilian Alexander Friedrich Wilhelm, Prince and Margrave of Baden (1867–1929), was commonly called Prince Max. In October 1918 he became Germany's first parliamentary Chancellor.

[72] The Commander in Chief of the Austro-Hungarian navy was Anton Haus.

was shattered to pieces. If we get into port within the next few days I shall have to take a closer look at her. 6 March 1917.

Yesterday I went ashore on duty for a brief while, but did not have an opportunity to carry out my plan. *Kurfürst* is already in dock while *Kronprinz* is at the shipyard. It is rumored that on the latter twenty men were killed (??).

It is Sunday again and my stomach is growling. But no, I would rather not ——— [complain]. Let me describe what we had for lunch today. Our quartermaster had concocted something completely new. Those of us who maintain that it was [merely] the week's leftovers are mistaken. I ascertained that it had the following composition: 75 percent water, 10 percent Oldenburger, 3 percent potatoes, 2 percent peas, one percent yellow turnips, one half percent beef, one half percent vinegar, one quarter percent fat, while the remainder cannot be analyzed. Floating on top there was—My God, my stomach!

We may soon sail to Kiel. That would be fine.

Today the Captain assembled us on deck and expressed grave concern over our recent lack of respect [for the officers] and the growing number of thefts. "I want to warn the older men in particular. You are in a very precarious position. I shall not hesitate to send an old man with six years of service home as a common sailor. And then the thefts! You do not seem to understand that it is your property that is being stolen. We can only requisition the amount of shortening and other foods specified by our stamps. Whatever is stolen from that cannot be replaced. Hence I want all of you to help us in finding the men who did it. After all, it is for your benefit! Dismissed."

We discussed his conciliatory statement at great length. It was generally agreed, and I concurred, that the Captain did not know of our sufferings and our condition. Sunday, 11 March 1917.

It all happened so quickly! The snow-covered hills of Kiel smile down on us as I am writing. It all happened suddenly last night. I had hoped that we would not go to Kiel for another month but it really doesn't matter. Our ship easily broke through the frozen surface of the canal and we accomplished the major portion of our journey during the night. At three o'clock this morning the port watch docked the ship. We shall see what the next few days will bring. 13 March 1917.

First day. Yesterday I went to the theater. It was a performance of *Tiefland*. The play was boring because it did not contain a single decent tune. However I may be mistaken because I was not watching very closely and paid greater attention to the girls [in the audience] than to the performance. Apparently there is no acute shortage of coal here because all the taverns were well heated and filled with happy people. Once more I amused myself without spending much money. I shall probably not be able to get out again before Sunday.

Several new warships have recently been commissioned to replace our battle losses. They bear famous old names which evoke the magic poetry of the first months of the war. They are the *Emden, Karlsruhe, Nürnberg*, and we will soon again have a *Blücher* and a *Gneisenau*. However, the most noteworthy type is the *Baden*. She is a first-class battleship and an exact replica of the English model. Her entire battle command post is located on the forward tripod mast and can easily accommodate twenty men. However performance is much more important than appearance. This principle seems to have been applied with the most fortunate results. All in all, we have built a powerful and truly imposing engine of destruction. An engine of destruction. . . . The thought that man should excel at this has destroyed the bliss of my happy dreams and my good spirits.

Does it have to be this way, that in the twentieth century all knowledge and technical improvement should be used to destroy the civilization of other nations? How many hospitals, villages and high schools could be built with the money it costs to construct a single one of these ships! But, one might object, in this war and even more so, in future wars, will not hospitals, villages and high schools serve a warlike purpose? This is quite true. One cannot win wars without these three things, in the same sense that one cannot win a war without artillery, steel, food and paper. An idea has just entered my mind. Why, I ask myself, can't we build such machines for use on land? I try to imagine what would happen if such a monster could race over the trenches along the Ancre and the Somme at a speed of 60 kilometers per hour. Nothing could withstand it; cities and fortresses would be reduced to rubble, the heaviest guns would crumble, fields of barbed wire would be pressed into the earth, and the people would die of fright. Has no engineer ever conceived such an idea? Or are the "tanks" merely a modest step in that direction? [73] This is quite possible. Consequently the next war will no longer be fought by armies and soft, perishable men, but by means of tanks and armored air ships. Each side will see to it that the enemy's industry, wheat fields and storehouses are quickly and thoroughly destroyed. What an enticing prospect for the pacifists and internationalists! It is a strange paradox that the most powerful weapons have been designed for the sea and not for the land. Here at sea, due to the triumph of technology, we already have mechanized warfare. Just imagine what a tremendous power potential this *Baden* could have as a land weapon; could not such a weapon decide the war in our favor? 15 March 1917.

Second day. Things are getting better all the time. The fog here seems even worse and more unpredictable than in Wilhelmshaven. No sooner had we cast off our lines than a game of hide and seek again. We came within an inch of colliding with the fire ship at Bülk, ramming into a torpedo boat and sinking a submarine. In every case, we averted disaster by the slimmest of margins. . . . No sooner had we dropped anchor, than as if to mock us, the weather turned bright again immediately. Then when we sailed out for a half hour, the fog came down again. One might have thought that we were at an October festival the way the sirens howled and the ships' bells

[73] The British had developed a tank in 1914 and had used it with indifferent success at the Battle of the Somme. The Germans, however, stubbornly refused to experiment with this new weapon. Yet it was precisely this weapon, the tank, that on July 18, 1918, broke the German lines at Soissons, marking the beginning of Germany's military collapse.

clanged all around us. Now the fog became even more stubborn and did not begin to disappear slowly until the afternoon.

There is a general rumor that "Willem" [74] will attend our maneuvers tomorrow. *Baden* has been designated as the flagship and will take the lead. We spent an entire night anchored in calm waters as though no [hostile] submarines existed. 16 March 1917.

Third day. Our flawless exercises were favored by the clearest of weather and the brightest sunshine. Our torpedo boats staged a simulated attack in the evening. One might almost believe that we were back at the outbreak of the war. We will probably refuel on Sunday, take on a thousand tons of coal and return to the North Sea on the following day.

Fourth day. Alternating fog and sunshine. We cruised through endless ice fields whose floes looked as pure and transparent as mountain crystals. A despatch steamer brought us our long-awaited mail. A full-blown revolution is said to be raging in St. Petersburg, Moscow and several other [Russian] cities. The [Tsarist] ministers have been deposed and imprisoned; the Duma has announced that it has assumed power. This was extremely good news for us [75] and it engendered a number of lively debates in which skepticism alternated with overwhelming optimism. I shall be very surprised if this small number of representatives manages to retain power. It would not require a Napoleon to disperse these fellows in a proper fashion.[76] I hope that the next few days will clarify the situation. 16 March 1917.

Fourth and fifth days. This horrible fog! It is so thick that no movement is possible. Our coal barges and a number of pretty girls are waiting for us in Kiel. If it is indeed true that

[74] A common nickname for Kaiser Wilhelm II.

[75] On March 8, 1917, strikes and riots broke out in St. Petersburg (renamed Petrograd in 1914). On March 10, the troops which had been called out to quell the uprising, mutinied and joined the rebellion. The next day the Duma, the Russian parliament, refused the Tsar's order to disperse and established a provisional government under Prince Lvov.

[76] On October 5, 1795, General Napoleon Bonaparte (1769–1821) dispersed an insurrection directed against the government of the Directory with his famous "whiff of grape-shot."

we are to refuel tomorrow and then sail straight on for Wilhelmshaven, we shall have had a most miserable stay in Kiel. Thus far we haven't even been able to fire our artillery or torpedoes. 17 March 1917.

Much to our relief we did not refuel on Sunday and were allowed to go ashore instead. Naturally, I stayed in the reading room until six o'clock, then I had a few mugs [of beer] at the Sailors' Home and went to the theater at 7:30. They performed my favorite piece, *Heimchen am Herde*. Unfortunately I had a very bad seat. After the play was over, I still had two hours but all the taverns were so crowded that it was impossible to get in. Therefore I took the eleven o'clock boat out to the ship. I did not regret it, for we were wakened at five in the morning to take on coal. In three hours we loaded 750 tons. We were given a small piece of bacon and some cigarettes as a reward. This was noteworthy indeed!

In the afternoon the entire fleet sailed out. We raised and dropped anchor three or four times. Otherwise nothing of any significance. 20 March 1917.

Overhead the ventilators were singing and humming and the whole ship vibrated from the even strokes of the engine. Although yesterday was the first day of spring, today a raw northeasterly wind blew whole clumps of new snow into the casemates. The icy air outside soon penetrated to the very marrow of one's bones. A single glance at the foaming waves and the glistening spray through the porthole was enough to indicate that we were back in the North Sea. The dirty yellow flood lapped against the ship's sides and made it impossible to look into the realm of the algae and the dolphin. We had just passed the locks at Brunsbüttelkoog and were riding downstream on the Elbe. I did not know our plan for the next day. But I must go back a bit because I forgot to tell how we left Kiel so quickly.

Everything was dreadfully confused. No one knew how long we were staying. One false rumor followed upon the other. Yesterday, on Wednesday afternoon, the port watch was just about to start refueling when we suddenly got word that the order had been canceled and that the free watch could go ashore. I was overjoyed and went ashore. It was bitter cold. Regardless of where one looked, even in Jacobsen's department store, the women had red noses. But it was warm in the reading room and I studied the papers with great interest. Although the papers were full of the Russian Revolution, I was unable to learn anything.[77] The conflicting welter of reports made it impossible to gain a true picture of the situation. One thing, however, was clear. Mr. Buchanan is about to harvest a most bountiful crop.[78] But perhaps a whirlwind may yet uproot the product of his labors. We shall have to wait and see. . . .

All hands had to be back on board by ten o'clock. Two hours later I was torn from my sleep as we cast off. Damn it, it was cold! Consequently we all worked feverishly, cleared the locks within fifteen minutes, and then wrapped ourselves in our covers once more.

As I glanced through the porthole I saw that we had just passed my beloved town of Cuxhaven. I felt compelled to step on deck for a moment. Old memories came flooding back. I arrived here in October 1913. Over at the pier a new fast steamer the *Imperator* had just tied up and I gazed at the latest marvel of German industry with shining eyes. At that time my heart was still not infested with dissatisfaction and hatred for the military and I took earnest pride in the products of German industry.

At a later date we passed by here on the day of the disastrous battle at Helgoland. The war was still young; I prayed for a German victory and was absolutely convinced that our

[77] On March 15, 1917, Tsar Nicholas II abdicated in favor of his younger brother Michael, who in turn abdicated to the Provisional government.

[78] Sir George Buchanan, the British ambassador to Petrograd, was widely regarded to be very critical of the incompetence and corruption of the Tsarist regime. He was opposed to the rule of the extremely conservative and pro-German government of Boris Stürmer (February-November 1916) and the influence of the monk Rasputin (assassinated on December 30, 1916). However, there is no evidence to support the contention of these elements, the probable source of the rumor, that Buchanan had fomented the March Revolution in Russia.

cause was just. My faith received its first gentle jolt that day when rumors of treason filled the air.

And the last time we passed by this lovely place I had just begun this book [of my diary] and I was overflowing with joy over my impending leave. Will this be the last time? If I can believe the rumors, we shall run into Wilhelmshaven sometime today. What a change! Yesterday we were ashore in Kiel and today we are in [miserable] Wilhelmshaven! The canal is truly a wondrous thing! (Time to eat.) 22 March 1917.

Of late I have been extremely lazy! And not because I had no time! No, there is another reason. I had to move. Forty new recruits came on board without notice and we old men were simply thrown out of our living and sleeping quarters with instructions to find our own accommodations. This lack of consideration depressed me for several days. However since all the available spaces had already been taken and the ship was already overcrowded, I hardly see what else could have been done. Indeed many of us who could not locate a place simply had to lie on the floor. I, however, did find a little corner to hang my hammock among the communication crew. But the bulkhead bounded on the bakery and the heat was almost insufferable. As a result I ran around all day yesterday but still found no home—another wasted Sunday. Today, however, I feel more comfortable in my new quarters because I have made provisions for some light and air.

I am just now beginning to realize why our entire fleet has been transferred to the Baltic. As we departed, the *Möve* came in with 600 new prisoners. This unimposing ship had sunk over thirty armed merchantmen and then managed to escape into the Baltic through the Sound.[79] I can still recall the uproar she caused last year upon her first return. But this year no one is especially excited, although she has accomplished twice as much and her mission was twice as dangerous. On the other hand, some of our submarines have sunk twice as many ships as

[79] The *Möve* returned from a four months' cruise on March 22 and reported sinking or capturing twenty-seven enemy ships, with a tonnage of 123,444 tons.

she within a month's time. The captain of *Möve*, Count Dohna, certainly deserves to be commended for his actions. (Interrupted.)

It is becoming too tedious for me to admit week after week that I am lazy. But this does nothing to improve the situation. I wonder if this can be due to my monotonous and uneventful existence or whether my mind has deteriorated to such an extent that I have become incapable of writing. To be sure, I no longer possess the high spirits, the enthusiasm, the sensitivity and the receptivity which I had during the first months of the war. On the other hand, I am convinced few men have kept up with their diaries like me. Although this does not constitute a great accomplishment, I felt a slight thrill when they gave up, one after the other. Occasionally my boredom compelled me to write and at other times it was my boredom which discouraged my writing. Incredibly enough, I did most of my writing when my duties kept me busy, while I wasted many a free afternoon [doing nothing].

I have neglected to record a slight incident which occurred recently.

The last time I was ashore I wandered around the docks with a friend. [We observed] a column of Russian prisoners of war with a few Englishmen and Frenchmen marching by, guarded by some naval infantrymen. All of a sudden, one of the Russians shot out of the formation like a hawk, threw himself over the edge of a rubbage ditch and began burrowing in the coal ashes with his mouth. "For heaven's sake, what is he doing?" I cried with disgust wrenching at my insides. What was it? Someone had thrown a few scraps of cooked turnips on the heap. It made me lose my appetite for a whole day. It is a shame that we cannot give these poor devils more to eat. How they must hate our country!

Who would ever have thought these dull people, this "gray mass," would be capable of such a violent overthrow of Tsarism? I would suspect, however, that the leaders of this revolution did not come from the black earth districts or the Siberian steppes. If I am not totally mistaken, the movement began on the streets of the large cities. Its adherents wore gold braid on their caps and had pounds sterling in their pockets. According to the latest reports, the [Russian] army will hold an election to decide the issue of war or peace.[80] A light cometh for the East. . . . There are numerous indications that the Central Powers will not be at all hesitant to offer the Russians an honorable peace. What a victory it would be for us and what a disaster for the French, if they were to accept it!! 4 April 1917.

Ended on Holy Thursday 1917.

[80] On March 12, 1917, the Russian Socialists established a Council of Workers' and Soldiers' Deputies, commonly known as the Petrograd Soviet. Unlike the Provisional Government, which wanted to continue the war, the Soviet was pledged to the early conclusion of a "general democratic peace." Fearing that the army officers were plotting a counter-revolution, the Soviet on March 14 issued the famous "Order Number 1," which placed all political decisions affecting the army in the hands of committees elected by the troops.

Five

Begun in Kiel on Palm Sunday, 14 April 1917

Will this book be thick enough? Will I fill it completely or only partially? Or will I again have to write the heading "Easter" over a section of my war diary? This is approximately the way I felt at this time last year as I prayed silently that it might be my last Easter. And since hope springs eternal in the human breast, I am [still] confident that I shall not have to describe any more wartime Easters.

But I must be brief. I still have to record what little news there is at present and I also have to catch up on the old news. I had filled up my old book, but because we were out on patrol I found it impossible to acquire a new one. Then, however, we unexpectedly returned to Kiel. We had practically no free time. But the lovely weather and the reading room at the library made me unusually eager to go ashore. Damn it! The Bosun just informed me that I was to get ready to go on watch. I am therefore closing for the day.

Easter! Nothing of special significance occurred either on Easter or on Good Friday. The weather was not interesting enough to describe. And the food? No, not that! Well then, how about the inspection, my work and my trip ashore? But none of these things interests me any more. What then? Ah, now I have it, I shall describe my mood. I hesitate, however, to describe my mood because my mind is in such a sorry state that I can hardly tell any longer what it means to be in a good mood. But if one is a self-proclaimed writer, one is obliged to write. . . .

I felt festive and happy as I strolled about on the first day of Easter, a glorious, sunny day. I held a copy of my beloved *Faust* in my hand and allowed its captivating text to take hold of me. I stood upon the bridge and did not look at the blooming fields and meadows, but at the silvery, diamond-studded North Sea. I communed with *Faust*. In my delight I kept returning over and over to the place where it said: "Oh keep singing, ye sweet, heavenly songs. A tear quivers in my eye— I return to the earth." I was in a gay mood. The magic of Good Friday made me happy and induced within me the kind of solemnity one usually feels upon entering a Catholic Church at this season with its smell of incense, shrouded crucifixes, glimmering candles and the silence of reverent prayer. I was not even overly disturbed when they served us meat loaf for lunch. I ate it. . . . And why not?

The first day had been bright and sunny but the second one was dreary and cloudy. Hence I put *Faust* aside and read Schopenhauer. Since I was on watch again I did not have much time. At the expiration of our five-day patrol we had sailed to Kiel. I would never have suspected that I would see it again so soon. I had expected the banks of the canal to be covered with green foliage, but no, everything was still as brown as at Christmas and the trees still raised their bare, naked branches to the sky.

This time around we had a crowded schedule of activities with a good deal of day and night artillery and torpedo practice. In addition, we also held various maneuvers, searchlight drills and other amusements. But they were considerate enough to give us plenty of liberty ashore. On Sunday I walked out toward Krönshagen. I felt human again as my lungs breathed in the country air and the smells of the earth. The people were busily at work in all the fields and gardens. It was truly peaceful and it allowed one to forget about the war for a little while. I went to an incredibly lovely and clean inn. A band was playing merrily and there was even dancing behind the stage. The people really enjoyed life out there. 16 April 1917.

On the following day, a Monday, we loaded heavy- and medium-caliber munition. Since the weather was so lovely, the band played in the area between the smokestacks. Below decks the torpedomen sweated profusely as they armed their torpedoes. This kind of weather made working enjoyable. . . .

The favorite activity of the crew is firing torpedoes. It allows the men to lie on deck, bask in the warm sun and only occasionally do they have to get up to hoist a torpedo back on board. We never tire of seeing our boats chasing after the silvery torpedoes.

On this occasion we did something totally new when we held target practice. It was a novelty in the sense that we fired from a distance which was formerly thought to be impossible. On our first run we fired at an initial distance of 19 kilometers, but this diminished somewhat as we neared the target. At the second run, however, the target (the old *Oldenburg*) was barely visible to the naked eye because the range was 20 kilometers. Later on it was increased to 23 kilometers. This constituted the maximum range for our guns. I don't know how many hits we scored, but there certainly couldn't have been too many. Nevertheless I did observe a characteristic black explosive flash three times.

Our torpedo firing went much the same way. Whereas in the past 13 kilometers had been considered just about the maximum range for our torpedoes, this time they ran 3 kilometers farther. I was almost tempted to condemn all this as mere foolishness and as a misguided attempt to break past records. It is as easy to hit a whale with a harpoon at a hundred meters as it is to hit a rapidly moving ship with a torpedo at 16,000 meters. Nonetheless these trials did reveal the inherent potential of our German armaments.

We conducted searchlight, torpedo-defense and gun-firing practice until midnight every second night. Consequently we found our duties very taxing. We complained and cursed a great deal about all this "nonsense." But on Saturdays and Sundays we were allowed to rest up, that is, if we were not on watch. One morning our launch took us out to Kitzeberg. There I bought myself a cup of coffee and it still hurts my stomach. The cup "merely" cost 50 pfennigs.

I don't know what is wrong this year. Although it is almost May, Mother Nature is not making any effort to put on her green dress. I am very interested to see what will come of the much heralded general strike of the workers.[1] I don't expect it will accomplish a great deal. Even the most effective strike cannot increase our bread supply by even a single loaf. Quite the contrary! Although I reject such methods, I can well understand that these hungry people feel quite differently than those who have a full stomach.

Will we go under in this war of starvation? It almost seems that way. I actually wish it would happen to certain classes. We have about a hundred people on board who still don't know the meaning of hunger. They have rolls with their coffee, they eat cutlets at noon and even for dinner they eat things which we would be delighted to have for noon.[2] These are the heavy laborers who spend all their time filing their nails and combing their hair.

[1] The reduction of bread rations on April 15, 1917, was followed the next day by strikers in Berlin, Leipzig, and a number of other cities. More than 200,000 workers struck in Berlin and refused to return to work until their food rations were increased. The strike in Leipzig assumed even more radical proportions. The strikers set up a workers' council and presented the government with a seven-point program which called for the introduction of equal franchise in all elections and the immediate conclusion of a peace without annexations. As one prominent Socialist leader put it, "the people wanted peace, bread and early democratization."

[2] In Germany it is traditional to eat the main meal of the day at noon while dinner is merely a light repast.

A current popular jingle states, "Equal food, equal pay—and the war would long since be forgotten!" [3] Although I have never had any liking for such generalities, I think this popular saying is unique to express such profound truth so succinctly. Although this statement deserves to be illustrated with a few examples and citations, I shall not do it. It would inject a note of hatred into my writing. Moreover it is common knowledge anyway. As Nietzsche once wrote: "Truth must be suppressed lest it scream too loudly."

In the beginning there was the word! It emanates from the trenches in the East and in its vibrant promise of power constitutes our only salvation. [4] Surely the Baltic Sea would not care whether it was the Russian or the German parasites which were to be drowned in its waters. [5] Germany might enjoy boundless power if it were not for the parasites that suck her dry. If she should lose this war, it will be the fault of the ever widening schism between her classes, between the mansion and the hut and between the educated [minority] and the apathetic masses. If it were not for this depressing conflict between the rich and the poor and, above all, between the officers and the men, a Germany which was led by a king of the people would be unbeatable.

It has just been announced that the loyal Prussian people's yearning for freedom will be rewarded by a slight reform of their franchise system after the war. [6] If our Kaiser were not a

[3] Bei gleicher Lohnung, gleichem Essen—Wär' der Krieg schon längst vergessen!

[4] The Russian Revolution had a profound and immediate effect upon German politics. Within days of its outbreak, the parties of the Left began to clamor for a reform of the government and the introduction of democracy in Germany. For instance, one radical Socialist in the Reichstag, Deputy Kunert, openly called Germany a "Russian Tsardom" and maintained that he would "be proud if Germany had made the political progress which the Revolution in Russia has brought about."

[5] Admirals Viren and Nepenin and a number of other Russian naval officers were executed by mutinous sailors at the naval bases of Kronstadt and Helsingfors during March 1917.

[6] In response to the discontent of the lower classes in Prussia and fearing a repetition of the Russian Revolution in his country, Kaiser Wilhelm II issued his famous Easter Message on April 7, 1917. The message promised the Prussian people that the inequitable three-class fran-

man whose word was his bond, I would be tempted to cite the many promises the Hohenzollern [7] have broken in the past. The Kaiser's Easter Message is a masterpiece of confident strength and inspiring faith. "Yes, indeed, if the Kaiser only had his way, everything would be different," the enlisted men keep repeating.

Despite my reservation, I was extremely pleased to read his Easter Message. It proclaimed a truly refreshing and positive new attitude. I only wish that the opposition (if one may be permitted to use such a profane term) possessed a mere fraction of his temperament and spirit. When William II says, "It is my will," or "I hereby order," his power is simply overwhelming. Thus a recent proclamation by the Russian Workers' and Soldiers' Party stated, "William II is not the same sort of miserable wretch as the Romanov whom we have just ejected from power."

More than anything else, this war has demonstrated the need for skepticism. The soaring hopes we had placed in the Russian upheaval have been dashed to pieces. It was inevitable! At this point the two opposing parties [in Russia] are busily building up support for their cause while the German Michel and the Austrian Schani [8] stand by with their hands in their pockets. I would be willing to bet right now at ten to one odds that things will not work out in our favor, that we shall be unable to conclude a separate peace and that our government will be severely criticized for it. Why did we not pluck the ripe fruit at the propitious moment by launching a decisive attack upon Dorpat and St. Petersburg? Because the German

chise system would be abolished and that a more democratic electoral system would be introduced when the war was over. However, the Kaiser did not specify whether or not this meant equal, universal, and direct franchise. At any rate, the Easter Message calmed the strained political atmosphere in Germany for awhile.

[7] The Hohenzollerns were the ruling dynasty of Prussia from 1417 to 1918. Members of that dynasty, in particular King Frederick William III (1797–1840) and his son Frederick William IV (1840–1861), had repeatedly broken their promise to grant their people a constitution.

[8] These were the common caricatures of the German and Austrian people, much in the same way that John Bull or Uncle Sam represent the English and American people.

Michel is in the habit of ruminating [endlessly] before he acts
(to ruminate about everything he does or plans).

After this mental excursion into the realm of world politics,
I find it difficult to descend again to the petty matters of our
everyday affairs. I should like to do what has not been done for
a long time, namely, to write an account of my morale during
my long years in the navy. I am convinced that many of the
men share my feelings. However their more immediate daily
problems and concerns will soon make them forget all about
it. Nevertheless there are some men who would not have forgotten the humiliation and mortification to which they were
subjected. However their mouths have been closed for all time
by death.

If all of us were to commit our innermost thoughts and
wishes to paper, what a whirlwind it would raise up against
our monstrous militarism! How can we perpetuate a system
which deprives the working people of their rights and freedom? I would feel proud to be a German if I had been treated
as a human being during my five years of service, rather than
an animal. But I see this band of thieves carousing and loafing
on their beds all day. Yet at the first of the month they take
their pay as if it were merely a down-payment on their labors
or a mere pittance. I do not begrudge anyone his pay for his
physical or mental labor. Nothing impresses me more than a
person who combines intellectual ability with manual dexterity.
But when I see that even the simplest tasks are beyond the comprehension of our officers, my admiration changes into ordinary contempt. For example, not too long ago our Division
Officer, Lieutenant [B] indicated that he did not know that all
German workers have to have Sickness and Accident Insurance.[9] And the whole point of the lecture he was delivering

---

[9] The German Imperial Insurance Code of 1911 consolidated, improved,
and extended all previous social legislation into one uniform code which
covered all industrial workers and a large percentage of white collar
workers.

was designed to convince us how generous and advanced Germany's social system really was. He would have been better advised not to praise it so highly. His intentions served only to make me feel depressed. . . .

When I reflect what miserable failures these high and noble gentlemen would be in civilian life, I keep wishing that they all be dismissed [from the service] without pensions at the end of the war. This would surely result in an unexpected upsurge in membership for the Socialist Party. And it would also solve the shortage of traveling salesmen in wine and cigars, lottery collectors and insurance agents for a long time. Certainly there are some wonderful people in their ranks; men who are very impressive. But only a few of them are left now that the battleships have become the refuse heap of the navy.[10] Here there has been an increase in stupidity and pride. . . .

Today about ten of our oldest men were transferred. I watched them go without knowing whether I should envy them or feel sorry for them. There could be nothing better for an intellectually and physically lazy sailor than a soft berth on one of our big ships. I certainly cannot complain in this respect. No mental or physical exertions are demanded of me here. But this is precisely what nearly drives me to the point of distraction. If I could only find something to keep me busy, I would not be half so embittered and depressed. I become insufferable, especially when pay day rolls around. I harbor no exaggerated respect for money. However it is a necessity for making one's life more comfortable and it is also indispensable if one wants to continue one's education. How often have I stood before some shop window yearning to buy a book if I could only afford it? Thus I find it rather strange when some petty officer who earns more than a hundred marks a month comes to borrow a book from me.

The thought that I am forced to work here for nothing

[10] Since most of the younger and more enterprising naval officers were urgently required for service in the submarine and torpedo boat fleet, the inactive High Seas Fleet came increasingly to be staffed by either very young and inexperienced officers or elderly and frequently incompetent officers.

preys on my mind. The Chancellor's promise of "careers open to talent" [11] fills me with bitterness. But enough of that!

We spent a full seventeen days in Kiel and now I am almost glad to be back here in peaceful Wilhelmshaven. [In Kiel] I visited the theater five times but I must confess that it has deteriorated frightfully. All the [performances] were shoddy war productions and even the actresses were poor. I hope that by the time we return here there will be no more beer. That which presently passes by that name is merely adulterated water.

The first of May has arrived with glorious sunshine. I do not think that the workers went on strike.[12] It was encouraging to read the figures of our submarine sinkings. I think that we can expect roughly a million tons to be sunk this month.[13] This is enough to inspire our courage and raise our hopes. Fortunately we have just survived several highly critical weeks. Many of us had lost our last shred of hope when the Entente succeeded in drawing Russia back into the war [14] and when the deliberations of the Socialists wound up in failure.[15] Happily the weather has at long last turned warmer. This has two in-

[11] In an effort to improve the sagging morale of the German people and to stimulate their interest in the war effort, Chancellor Bethmann-Hollweg proclaimed during the early part of 1917 that he would introduce a "New Orientation" in German political life by opening up careers to talent and by giving the lower classes of the population a greater share in the running of the government.

[12] It was traditional before the war for the highly unionized and socialistic German workers to stage an annual strike or demonstration on May Day.

[13] During April 1917, German submarines sank an estimated total of 1,091,000 tons of Allied shipping, most of it English. However, the British Admiralty soon introduced a highly effective convoy system and thus effected a drastic reduction of losses by autumn.

[14] Germany's hope that the Russian Revolution would remove Russia from the camp of her opponents was shattered in May when Paul Milyukov (1859–1945), the Foreign Minister of the Provisional Government, announced that Russia intended to honor her treaty obligations to France and England by pursuing the war to the full extent of her power.

[15] On April 22, 1917, some neutral Socialist leaders extended invitations to all Socialist parties to send representatives to Stockholm in order to discuss the means by which peace could be reestablished. Although the German and Austrian Socialists accepted with alacrity, the French and English refused to attend. This is what the author must have meant by the failure of the Socialist's deliberations. However, the conference did convene in June although not all of the countries sent representatives.

estimable advantages. Firstly, it allows the farmers to work on the land and secondly, the townspeople are no longer so hungry. I can personally attest to that. 16 April to 10 May 1917.

Living on an undeviating routine makes it very difficult to keep a diary. Nothing much interesting can come of that! Or have my senses grown so dull that I can no longer feel any distinctions? In any case, our recruits have many more impressions than we old-timers who have been doing the same things here for five years. I have just about as much lust for life left in me as a dog who turns a spit. Whenever I recall our artillery practice this morning it makes me shudder. For God only knows the how many thousandth time, came the command: "Prepare to load charges—load—eject!" The very sound of these words is enough to drive me to distraction. I am astounded at how the old gun captains, who have been doing the same dirty job for twenty years, can stand it without going insane. But maybe they are missing a few marbles in their heads! It may also be possible that they regard a hundred mark bill as an adequate substitute for mental stimulation.

I read a good joke in yesterday's *Hamburger* [*Fremdenblatt?*]. In a debate on naval affairs [the Secretary of the Navy] Herr von Capelle announced that the officers and officials of the Imperial Navy had volunteered to forego an increase in their rations because of the general reduction in bread rations. . . . And the Reichstag deputies responded with wonder and awe! I do not express myself well enough to write an adequate refutation of this monstrous statement. My angry mind could only stammer, have we really sunk so low? I would never have believed that the Secretary of the Navy could tell such a horrendous lie. This small illustration reveals how simple it is to deceive the gentlemen with the title of Member of the Reichstag. However I would still like to read the comprehensive report which will be issued today.

I am very impressed with our new Division Officer Oberleutnant [Dreckmann]. He is very open and truthful in telling us about what is going on at the front. He has had a great deal of experience as a flyer and in my judgment he treats us as human beings. He has never yet prevented a man from protecting himself nor has he ever voiced the attitudes of the ruling class. It was extremely nice of him to remove some of my comrades from report even though he did not know them. He is one of those officers who can gain the absolute confidence of his men without hardly ever punishing them. If only the majority of our officers were like him, things would be quite different.

Someone has placed an announcement on the canteen bulletin board warning us that certain elements are trying to sow distrust and dissension among the German people. Every good German is obliged to cooperate in the unmasking of these traitors. All those who provide information leading to the arrest and trial of one of the ringleaders will receive an award of 3,000 marks. This is an old trick used by criminals to blame someone else for their crimes. The criminals who have undermined our love for the Fatherland with their snobbishness and whose arrogance and injustice have nearly driven us to despair are now searching for ringleaders. *Difficile est satiram non scribere!*

What a wonderful opportunity [this represents] for informers (there is no other word for it)! It will give every scoundrel a chance to ruin his neighbor for a mere slip of the tongue. In truth, no dark foreign powers are needed to drive the most patient and the most disciplined people in the world to desperation. I have often wished that our officers would carry their madness to such a point that we could overcome our reluctance to stage an uprising. So far, however, they have always been clever enough to relieve the pressure before it reached the breaking point. Thus far the pressure has not risen high enough to set off a liberating explosion. Will it ever come to that in this war? No!

We have irretrievably lost an incomparable opportunity to join the democratic wave which is sweeping the world. Germany and not Russia should have taken the lead. I feel that the Kaiser would be much more powerful in a monarchical republic than he is now. Now he merely reigns. But he could [really] rule if he had the support of his people. Just think how President Wilson would have reacted. Such a reform would have deprived the Anglo-American world of a potent weapon. Speaking of America, a new thought has just entered my mind. I am not intelligent enough to cope with the previous subject.

It is rumored that an American fleet has been sent to England and may already have arrived. I don't know whether our Division Officer was serious or not when he told us that our Admiralty was pleased about this news. Be that as it may, I seriously doubt that the Yankees have sent their battleships. Since it is primarily a question of smaller units of the destroyer type, we need not trouble ourselves too much.

Last Sunday one of our submarines, the *U 93*, came in with a huge gash in her side. Luckily she had been struck a half a meter above the water line, otherwise she would have been lost. Nevertheless I understand that Captain ———— and several crew members were killed. I really don't know whether the story I am about to tell is true. (*Se non vero e ben trovato.*) However even if it is not true it still makes a good story. According to what I heard here on board, on her way home the *U 93* became entangled in a net and despite her frantic efforts could not free herself for several days. By the time she did manage to come to the surface and continued on her homeward journey, her meager supply of food was exhausted. Then, as if by magic, she ran into a deeply laden sailing ship. The starving men were so preoccupied with getting some food that they threw all caution to the winds. But to their dismay they found that the sailing ship was really an auxiliary cruiser who opened up on them with its two 15 cm. guns from a very close range. The submarine was forced to crash-dive. All of the men on her decks drowned miserably. As I have already mentioned, she was hit right in the vicinity of the conning tower and the English thus had ample cause to presume that they had sunk her. Later on when she surfaced, nothing was in sight. She wired for aid and was soon rescued. Since we have been on a continual alert for the past few days, it is possible that this incident may have had something to do with it. 14 May 1917.

If I were to describe how I really feel right now, it would make for a very dismal chapter. I imagine that these pages are full of this anyway. Hence I would like to put aside my anger, bitterness and disaffection to make room for a brighter subject. A lovely May sun is shining and glittering everywhere. For this one day I should like to return to the early stages of the war and forget our petty concerns and problems so that I may concentrate on the really serious and earnest problems of these fateful times. But the combination of our barbaric military system and the perfidy and bigotry of the officer class has slowly but surely driven this kind of thought out of my heart. I keep hoping that we might lose the war so that we could dispense with all the people who wear epaulettes and all the weapons of destruction. *Tempora mutandur.* Thus do the times and man's attitudes change!

Inevitably militarism will destroy itself. Only those who are unfamiliar with it admire it. But those who suffer under its refined system of suppression have grown to hate and despise it. Sometimes when I see a warrant or a petty officer lounging about on deck, I often wonder what sort of satisfaction these people can derive from their existence. I am not referring to the officers because they were born as drones and have always considered any kind of work (even intellectual work) fit only for the lowest elements. But the members of the former group all came from our class.[16] Hence I would be curious to know whether they derive any joy and happiness from their useless lives. Perhaps the friend with whom I recently discussed this matter hit the nail squarely on the head when he stated that "the officers regard work as the exclusive province of the proletariat while the noncommissioned officers consider it fit only for the stupid!"

I have long noticed the suffering and hardened expression on

---

[16] Senior noncommissioned officers of the German navy were frequently promoted to the intermediate rank of warrant or deck officers after many years of service.

the faces of the older men [of the class of 1910–13]. This was not caused merely by poor food. Such mundane things as food and drink cannot impart a spiritual expression to a face. Even hungry and undernourished men have a more lively and spirited look than these totally dejected sailors.

Sometimes when my comrades complain about our situation I ask, "Now what would you do if you were in charge? How would you begin to remedy our sad situation?" They have some wonderful ideas. "Conclude an immediate peace" is the most frequent response. "Dissolve the army and the navy and send the men home! Make Scheidemann Chancellor and Liebknecht War Minister!" [17] Many similar ideas are also voiced. But my experience tells me that most of these people haven't the vaguest notion how to conduct a war. If I were to be appointed War Minister or Food Minister, I would either drop dead in my tracks or I would be compelled to do what Kerensky is currently doing in Russia,[18] namely, to leave things as they are for the time being. . . .

Oh my God, what have I done! I have complained and muttered for four full pages. I had planned on reserving that for now. Obviously I cannot overcome my own temperament. Whenever I start off with [talking about] the sunshine, I ultimately wind up discussing Prussia. 20 May 1917.

We are in port right now and have just finished an important exercise loading the guns with blank ammunition. Thank God it is over! The loading itself was child's play, but the prepara-

[17] Philipp Scheidemann (1865–1939) was a prominent leader and Reichstag deputy of the moderate Socialists. Shortly before the November Revolution he became a member of the Cabinet of Prince Max of Baden and in 1919 became the first chancellor of the Weimar Republic.

Since it was impossible for a Socialist to be appointed to any high office in the government at that time, let alone the crucial office of War Minister, the nomination of Scheidemann and of the much more radical Liebknecht provides a good indication of the discontent and revolutionary temperament of the enlisted men.

[18] Alexander Kerensky (born 1881), a democratic Socialist, was appointed Minister of Justice in the Russian Provisional Government in March 1917. In May he became War Minister and the leading spirit of the government. However, Kerensky did little to ameliorate Russia's chaotic internal affairs. Instead, he devoted his energies to reviving the fighting spirit of the army in order to launch a new offensive.

tions that went into it were enough to drive one crazy! To-morrow we will refuel and in the afternoon we are scheduled for an excursion to the Bockhorn. I am already dreading it!

I had to serve six hours of punishment tour because some-one stole my blue blouse. But I was not placed on report. The First Officer simply punished me at his own discretion. Actu-ally, I have grounds for lodging a complaint, but— I had better be careful. Fortunately our excursion is over. It was not at all as bad as I had feared. Although the officers lorded over us again, with time one can become immune to anything. During our free time several of them requested that we take them on a special tour. The thought of paying us for it never entered their minds. Not even a word of thanks! However I hasten to mention two of them acted differently. One of them gave us five marks and the other paid ten. The officers' rude, over-bearing attitude ruined my whole day. They treated us and our class with such obvious disdain that I no longer cared about the few glasses of lousy beer [which their money would have bought]. On the way home one of our chief petty officers con-fided in me that he felt the same way.

We had to leave port and go on forward patrol on the first day of Whitsun. Now I am sitting in the casemates, my head filled with sad thoughts as I recall the gayety of former Whit-suns. My heart is near the bursting point as these fond mem-ories pass before my eyes.

Although it is Whitsun today, the stokers are madly ham-mering away in the coal bunkers. This had gone on all night, but no one bothered to ask us if we could sleep or not. Many of my comrades complain that they often don't get to sleep until midnight, but fortunately my nerves are so healthy that I usually fall asleep by nine o'clock. This morning about a dozen men were promoted to Stoker First Class. They all be-longed to the class of 1915. I could not help feeling bitter about it. I was almost ashamed of myself and terribly upset. The present state of my soul leaves much to be desired. Sometimes when I wake up at night in my hammock and reflect upon my misery, I cry hot tears of impotent rage. It is strange that I find my only solace in my beloved *Faust*. I have become disgusted with religion. I am almost convinced that priests are merely officers in civilian dress. And perhaps they have even more to gain from the ignorance of the masses than the officers. Our so-called religious services are a blasphemy and a mockery of the relationship between God and man. First thing in the morning on Whitsunday we were led to "Easter confession." In order to raise our morale and in deference to the holiday, Kapitänleutnant [Kohrt] placed some thirty odd men on report for being late on formation. As a consequence, the confessional was, of course, deserted. Out of approximately four hundred men, a mere ten percent took Holy Communion.

At present it is rumored on the ship that we are about to bring in a large prize. It is said that one of our former First Officers, Captain Laffert of the auxiliary cruiser *Vineta*, captured her. Her cargo is said to consist of several thousand horses. But I shall wait until I hear a more detailed report.

When will peace finally come? I would give a great deal to know that. . . . If one may believe the confident speeches which Lloyd George has been making, it would seem that a winter campaign is inevitable. But on the other hand, there are also some concrete indications that our enemies may soon be willing to treat for peace. The specter of the Russian Revolution looms threateningly over Asquith's [19] and Ribot's [20] shoulders and is compelling them to publicly retract their insane plans of conquest. I was also immensely impressed that the King of Greece told an American reporter that our submarine campaign would force the Entente to sue for peace within two months. I still remember vividly his predictions regarding our victorious offensive against Rumania. As the Kaiser's brother-

[19] Herbert Henry Asquith (1852–1928) was the Liberal Prime Minister of England from 1915 to 1916. He was ousted from office by the more energetic and ruthless Lloyd George.

[20] Alexandre Ribot (1843–1923) was the French Prime Minister from March to September 1917. He continued on as Foreign Minister in the succeeding Painlevé government.

in-law [21] he must know a great deal, even if he will not reveal everything he knows.

Tomorrow we are scheduled to celebrate the anniversary of the Battle of Jutland. This will give our good citizens and the old ladies a chance to express their delight in our wonderful navy and the brave boys in blue by offering us a couple of baubles. Those of us who have thus far not participated in the first outpouring of medals will receive their little crosses tomorrow. A few barrels of beer have been set aside for us plebeians and our cheers will certainly sound the louder for it. At any rate, they will be louder than the ones we gave three days ago at the departure of the Second in Command of the squadron [Engelhardt]. I was delighted that only three to five men responded when a cheer was ordered for him.

Our new First Artillery Officer is a very rare specimen. He has a bad stomach and therefore can only eat eggs, cocoa, roasted meats and other fine foods. On occasion he can outswear a full-blooded sailor. Yesterday he delivered a speech to the crew of the heavy artillery at the aft gun turret. Suddenly he stopped, stared sharply at one of the men and without changing expressions uttered the fine words: "I shall spit on your head until you get flat feet!" Once, during a searchlight drill, I heard him shriek, "When this war is over I shall send this entire crew to Hagenbeck [Zoo] and the monkey's cage." But he insulted the Detail Officer [Martin] most of all. He asked him what idiot had written in the order book!! [Martin] made an indescribably indignant face and ran off to tell the captain of his superior officer's *fait accompli*.

Today we had a proper celebration of the anniversary of the sea battle by adhering to our usual Sunday routine and holding a major inspection. The Captain delivered a speech on the origins and the course of the battle. But he presented nothing new. Toward the end of his lecture he changed his pace by discussing the war aims of our enemies. I strongly suspect that the usually genial man had obtained his manuscript from one of

[21] King Constantine of Greece was married to Princess Sophie of Prussia, the sister of Kaiser Wilhelm II.

the secretaries of the Agrarian League.[22] He did not hesitate to state that "our enemies pursue one particular goal, namely, to break the bonds between our Supreme War Lord and his army and navy. Once the Hohenzollern are expelled, they will impose upon us a parliamentary system of government resembling that of England and France. Then we shall be ruled by merchants, lawyers and journalists just like them. Any time they tire of some general or military leader over there, they simply dismiss him. But we shall need an even stronger army and a larger navy after the war. You must oppose all those who want to introduce a parliamentary system of government in Germany and must never forget that Germany's greatness stands and falls with the existence of its Imperial dynasty, its army and its young navy. Remember one thing: The Social Democrats of all the nations we are fighting wish to destroy us. They are extremely nationalistic; only our Socialists are internationalists.

"I am utterly convinced that we shall meet the English fleet again and that when this occurs, we shall teach them an even better lesson than before. It looks as though they are about to concentrate their attack on our home ports and our Flemish ports. They have no other alternative. In order to halt our submarine campaign they will first have to beat our fleet and stop up our ports. So far the enemy has been content to sow mines in the North Sea. Under the cover of our fleet, however, we have always managed to clear the sea and to open up a free channel for our submarines. So far, our German conscientiousness, our thoroughness and our discipline have made us triumph. This is the threefold combination which our enemies call militarism.

"A year ago today 2,400 of our comrades gave up their lives for their Kaiser and their country. Let us pay our respects to them by giving three cheers for 'His Majesty, our Supreme War Lord!' "

[22] The Agrarian League, or Bund der Landwirte, was a large and powerful landlord's and estate owner's association. It was particularly close to the Conservative Party and tried to prevent Prussia and Germany from becoming too liberal.

Twenty Iron Crosses were distributed. At the express order of His Majesty they were to be awarded only to those among us who had participated in the battle. Just now!! I find it difficult to describe the emotions which stormed through my heart after this speech. The enthusiasm which burned in the Captain's eyes almost made me feel despite myself that much of what he said was true and as a loyal servant of the Kaiser that he could not have spoken otherwise. If I were an officer I would agree wholeheartedly. But my present point of view— the conviction of an unpropertied proletarian—[does not allow me to] support an increase in the autocratic power of the Kaiser, of the army, of the navy! It is easy for anyone to talk who does not have to pay for it. I would rather be a slave to the English than a German sailor! My ideal is to approach the English-American form of government. I do not fear parliamentary government. Just look at its success!! Virtually the entire world is fighting against us. Why? Because it regards Vienna and Berlin the last strongholds of autocratic absolutism. Despite all of my sympathies for these two monarchs, I want them to gradually relinquish their power. The peoples of Europe must rule themselves so that we may avoid any future wars. Regardless of how peace-loving any of these rulers might be, they simply cannot stand against the tide of the war interests. . . .

Although I could continue to berate this theme for hours, I should like to pause for a while in order to sing the praises of Lloyd George's genius, Briand's[23] vitality and Kerensky's abilities. But is this the proper place for such things? There shall come a time when one will be able to voice these thoughts in public and when the hatreds of war will no longer make us conceal the praise-worthy motives of our present enemies. All the participants in this horrible and bloody conflict ought to

[23] Aristide Briand (1862–1932) was a former Socialist who had broken with his party by entering a bourgeois government. He was both Prime Minister and Foreign Minister of France from October 1915 to March 1916 but is best known for his part in negotiating the Locarno and Kellogg-Briand pacts after the war.

learn to accept good things regardless of their origin. 31 May 1917.

Sometimes when my friends discuss the sad plight of the sailors and the proletarians, I enter the argument by saying, "Listen here, we don't deserve anyone's help so long as we persist in our [mutual] antagonisms, our disunity and our bootlicking. Our situation will have to grow much worse before we are able to develop a certain amount of self-respect. So long as we are willing to do anything to gain their favor, so long as we do not stop the unequal treatment of the various ranks of sailors, so long as a friendly smile from our oppressors transports us into delight, so long as we make scapegoats of each other by complaining to our so-called superiors over every trivial quarrel and call upon their advice—we do not deserve better treatment." Yesterday these views of mine were borne out a hundred times over.

Our officers held a great carousal and feast in their mess which did not reach its high point until midnight. For the enlisted men a few barrels of thin beer were broached in the canteen. At night there was a party on deck for the crew. The Officer of the Watch condescendingly threw us a few friendly glances from the bridge and even laughed several times. I don't know whether he laughed at our silly jokes or at our stupidity. But the sailors who noticed it went into ecstasy over the honor and outdid themselves in their clowning. As chance would have it, I was on lookout on the bridge until midnight and thus witnessed the whole disgusting affair. The [officers'] mess resembled a madhouse. It was even more scandalous how the sailors begged these drunkards for beer, cigarettes and schnapps. I could have cried at the way they debased themselves. A few of them lost all control and assured the officers that they were good sailors and good Prussians. As a reward they received an extra glass of beer. Finally they even went so far as to cheer the generosity of the individual officers. The debauchery lasted until four o'clock in the morning when I fell asleep. 1 June 1917.

Lately there has been a revival of enlisted men's parties. God only knows what has come over the men that they feel that they must dance every evening. Our men must possess an indestructibly healthy spirit. As soon as their stomachs are full and they have a little money they forget all about the past. I would even wager that they will join the Army and the Navy Leagues[24] [after the war]. Consequently it would be wise to keep this in mind and not to expect that these people will fight the entire world for their rights and defend their interests.

We are currently spending a good deal of our time debating whether or not it would benefit the German people if we lost the war. I am in a difficult dilemma. I feel like Dr. Faust and must confess with him that "two souls dwell within my breast." Unfortunately, I cannot separate them.

As a good German and as a Catholic, I hope that we might emerge from this war with a total victory. From that point of view I simply cannot conceive how the degenerate French, the brutal English, or for that matter, the stupid Russians, could defeat our brave troops. God only knows why, but I still possess enough national pride so that I regard the Germans as the most decent and honest people on earth. I am utterly convinced that Germany's spirit must triumph for the betterment of the world. From the opposite point of view everything is different. Then I am not a German but a proletarian, and as such, I hope for a great, but not an annihilating defeat [for Germany]. Why should I feel this way? Past experience tells me that the lower classes stand to benefit from a defeat while the rich stand to lose. I cannot conceive of the achievements of the Young Turk Revolution without the background of the battles of Plevna and Shipka Pass.[25] Mukden and Tsushima

[24] The German Army League and Navy League were pressure groups, usually associated politically with the Right, who demanded large armaments and an aggressive foreign policy.

[25] The Young Turk Revolution of 1908 in the Ottoman Empire stemmed from the dissatisfaction of young liberals and army officers with the repressive regime of Sultan Abdul Hamid II, who had abrogated the Turkish Constitution of 1876 and who refused to modernize his country. However, neither the Battle of Shipka Pass nor the Battle of Plevna, which had occurred during the Russo-Japanese War of 1877–1878, had anything to do with the revolution.

brought the Russian people liberty and a free press [26] while the disasters of Tannenberg and Brest-Litovsk broke down the last remnants of tyranny and oppression.[27] If we had not been beaten back at the Marne, if the enemy had not closed the world seas to us, and if we had retained our colonies, we would long since have won the war. But one thing is equally certain! [Our victory] would have inevitably led to the assumption of power by a strong man who would have abolished our equal franchise.[28] Moreover an excuse would have [then] been found to deprive the working class of its past social protection and benefits. It would have made the sort of attitude which the Kaiser expressed in his Easter Message totally impossible. Thus everything in the world has its good side—even a long war.

Today I would like to write about something other than the war. The story I am about to tell was an outgrowth of the war but it made me laugh and cry at the same time. It was a real tragicomedy. One might entitle it, "How a sailor nearly drove his ship to rebellion."

This is the way it happened. Aboard our ship there was a reservist by the name of [Sänger]. Since he was a range finder, he had not yet been transferred. He was an absolute genius at making himself seem mysterious. He always knew the latest

[26] Russia's military disasters during the Russo-Japanese War at Mukden and Tsushima straits in 1904 led directly to the Revolution of 1905 and the promulgation of the October Manifesto by the Tsar, which established a representative assembly, the Duma, and granted a number of civil liberties.

[27] Russia's defeat at the Battle of Tannenberg (August 1914) and her expulsion from Poland (in which the German seizure of Brest-Litovsk on August 25, 1915 forms a vital part), undermined the people's confidence in the Tsarist regime and paved the way for the outbreak of the Revolution in 1917.

[28] Prussian Conservatives maintained a constant clamor throughout the war that the franchise for elections to the Reichstag was too liberal and hence ought to be modified in a more conservative sense. Many of them insisted that it was more important for Germany "to have militarism than parliamentarism," thus creating the fear that if Germany won the war, the political rights of the working classes would be drastically reduced.

gossip, always smiled knowingly and delighted in confusing the men. He made himself important by contending that he earned a great deal of money without having to work for it. Now he asserted that he had a really big plan which would make him rich as soon as he was released from the navy.

He invented the slogan "Germany, show your teeth!" He had some leaflets printed in Berlin stating that he managed to subsist on half or a third of his previous diet now that he no longer simply swallowed his food, but ground it up finely. One day in June of 1914 he had a brainstorm as he gazed at a dung-heap. He asked himself why the flies kept hovering around it and had elicited the aid of a chemist to explain the phenomenon. Thus he learned that it was the undigested food [in the dungheap] which attracted the flies so irresistibly. He went back home with this knowledge but from that time on he chewed his food more and more thoroughly. One fine day he had the products of his digestive tract examined and lo and behold!! There was nothing left for the flies [to eat].

He therefore concluded that mankind would be eternally grateful to him if [it would learn to] chew up each mouthful of food thoroughly. This prank resulted in the most amazing effects. Proclamations reminiscent of those of the Russian Workers' and Soldiers' Councils appeared on every corner. They began with the salutation "Comrades!" and ended by stating "Down with the traitors!" Filled with dismay, Seaman [Sänger] tore down one of these proclamations and presented it to the First Officer. But the officers did not take the matter too seriously.

After that our noble [Sänger] no longer enjoyed a moment's peace. His quarters were always crowded with curious people. At lunch we held [mock] lectures on chewing, we made up insulting jingles and all sorts of other foolishness. A band was quickly gotten together and it incessantly played [the song] "You are insane, my child. . . ." That evening the sailors held a party on deck and once again [Sänger] was the target of all the jokes. Since the stokers had decided to give him a sound drubbing, he was forced to find refuge in the sick bay that night. On the next day the uproar was even wilder. Under the circumstances, it seemed advisable that he be transferred as soon as we came into port. When he [finally] walked down the gangplank, a hundred voices jeered after him, "Chew! chew!"

In the past I have often had ample cause to feel that our officers were inhuman. However our Division Officer is certainly most human. Moreover he is also a very likable fellow. Unfortunately he will not long remain like that on our ship. During the current heat wave he took his men out for a sailing party dressed in their bathing suits. He wore one himself and he brought along his accordion to play for the men. Has there ever been anything like it? The world stood still!!

Today, on a Tuesday, we took on coal. As usual, Oberleutnant [Dreckmann's] division was finished first. *Qualis rex talis grex!* But the first division had to shovel from the shore which was, of course, more awkward and more time-consuming. Despite this, Oberleutnant [Oly] subjected his division to an hour of drill when it was finished. He made the poor men hold knee-bends for minutes at a time, made them throw themselves down in the coal dust and marched them around until they were all bathed in perspiration. While this was going on, a column of prisoners of war marched by. I was never so ashamed of myself in my entire life. Is this what Bismarck meant when he said that no other nation would ever succeed in copying our Prussian lieutenants?? 12 June 1917.

Today, on Sunday, Admiral Schmidt, our Squadron Commander, was to inspect us. Whenever [Lieutenant Martin] shows up we always have to salute him by shouting "Good morning, Your Excellency!" Then we nearly die laughing when he starts swearing like the devil. Of course we prepared for Admiral Schmidt's visit days in advance by having our uniforms inspected, our posture corrected and by rehearsing all the questions which he might ask us. We were politely instructed to answer very loudly in the event His Excellency should greet us with a "Good morning, Sailors." So that it might proceed more smoothly, [Martin] practiced it with his division. He began, "Imagine that I am the Squadron Commander and I greet you with 'Good morning, men!!' " No one answered. Once again he said, "Good morning, men!" A voice from the rear came. "Good morning, Your Excellency!" Uproarious laughter ensued. "Gather around! There is nothing to laugh about. I can't understand how you could be so childish to laugh about it. Dismissed!" Now, suddenly, everybody shouted, "Good morning, Your Excellency!"

Admiral Schmidt was here this morning but he did not greet us. This was too bad, for we had secretly made up our minds not to respond. But he just strode along our ranks without uttering a sound. I could not understand why all this had been necessary. Maybe the honorable gentleman merely wanted to find out if he would soon share the fate of his colleague, [Admiral] Kolchak [29] of the Black Sea Fleet. Sometimes it pays to find out from what quarter the wind is blowing.

In general our prospects are not very bright at the present time. Our troops are decidedly on the defensive on all fronts. The effectiveness of our submarine campaign has fallen drastically. Hardly a day goes by without some damaged submarine coming into port. It is rumored that many more of them have been sunk. Our air raids on England have entered a new phase. We now have to rely solely on our great air cruisers to carry the initiative. Unfortunately during last night's raid one of our Zeppelins was shot down. Just yesterday we heard that L 43 was missing. She was shot down by an English naval force which must have been particularly well equipped with antiaircraft guns. Must close now due to unbearable heat. 17 June 1917.

---

[29] Admiral Alexander Kolchak (1870–1920) was the Commander of the Russian Black Sea Fleet during the *Potemkin* Mutiny of 1905. During the Russian Civil War Kolchak for a time was the commander of all the counterrevolutionary armies.

As a reward for our good performance in coaling, our Division Officer obtained permission to take each of his sections on an additional excursion. We sailed along the Ems-Jade Canal up to Knyphausen in our motor launch. About an hour inland there stood the magnificent castle of the Prince of Knyphausen. But now it belongs to Count Wedel.

Unlike the rest of the Junkers, the Prince of Knyphausen did not make his fortune as a highway robber, but as a sea pirate. During the Napoleonic Continental System, ships flying his flag sailed on all the seas. Even later, when Lord Palmerston still looked upon the North German Confederation's flag [30] as that of a pirate, he continued to respect the flag of Prince Knyphausen. We romped through his magnificent park, the band played and we were all happy and gay. Unfortunately our time was all too short because we were standing on a six-hour alert basis. Our Division Officer played the accordion beautifully. All in all, it was a lovely day. 17 June 1917.

Today was Midsummer Day. According to what our newspapers predicted four months ago, England should now be on the verge of starvation, or at the very least, should have reached the end of its capacity to resist. At that time we gladly believed all that because we all hoped that it would come true. But now rumors are circulating throughout Germany that huge amounts of wheat have reached England and that an American convoy of sixty ships had no trouble in slipping through our blockade. I do not know if this is true but there is an old saying which states, "Where there is smoke there is fire." On the other hand, we do know that during the past eight days our submarine sinkings have shot up again. Just a while ago one of our newest submarines passed by. She must have been traveling at a speed of at least 20 sea miles per hour. Interrupted on 24 June 1917.

[30] The German states lying to the north of the Main River formed the North German Confederation in the years between 1886 and 1871. The Confederation was the immediate predecessor of the German Empire, which was founded in 1871.

I don't know what has come over me lately. A terrible bitterness and hatred rages within me. The first thought which comes to my mind upon accosting our First Officer is "I could cut his throat." At this point I would be capable of doing such a thing in all seriousness. The injustice to which others are subjected enrages me more than that which affects me personally. The way he [the First Officer] distributes leaves of absence is sheer favoritism. He is a typical Junker in all respects. My own leave has been delayed for months. However he always assures us that he grants as many leaves as he can. He always promises the crew high-sounding and meaningless things. For example, if the band happens to play on the after deck and the sailors stand around to listen, he rarely neglects to say, "Play on the middle deck. After all, the music is for the men." What a hypocrite! For us good music; for them good food. I would much prefer to have a real bastard. However we are fortunate to have two such decent division officers.

We now sail for Kiel. I can't fathom what we are expected to accomplish there. Surely the continued presence of our squadron cannot be regarded as a threat against Denmark? Very edifying news reaches us from the [Russian] Baltic fleet. When Kronstadt refused to obey the orders of the present regime, the ships of the *Gangut* class were ordered to shell the place. They responded by flinging their hated officers overboard.[31] Bravo! Whenever I think of those courageous fellows, my heart beats joyfully. We Germans ought to imitate them. Despite their reputation for dullness and patience, the Russians have accomplished what might be regarded as one of the best deeds of the war. This ought to act like lightning to clear the atmosphere in all the belligerent countries and to pave the way to peace for all the suppressed peoples. But such hopes are very

[31] Kronstadt was the island naval base off St. Petersburg. Its sailors had been prominent in the overthrow of the Tsarist regime and now refused to obey the orders of the Provisional Government, which with Alexander Kerensky as War Minister tried to instill "revolutionary discipline" among the armed forces.

dim at the present. All the countries are on the defensive; nowhere is there a ray of hope. The Reichstag has just approved another 15 billion [war loan]; a good harvest is expected. All these are factors which will prolong the war. The entire world is a madhouse. The oldest dynasties have fallen or now hide fearfully from an increasingly restless and fuming volcano. . . .

Will wonders never cease? Since early this morning the entire fleet has been chasing madly around Helgoland. It was almost like peacetime. While this in itself was not so unusual, it was really amazing that we did not have to stow our gear and furniture. If [Rabbi] Ben Akiba were still living, he would have regarded this as an unprecedented miracle. Our festive activities were intended to honor our ally Prince Ferdinand of Bulgaria.[32] Many of our planes flew overhead and filled the air with deafening noise. Our twenty-four great battleships presented a truly imposing sight with their bristling guns and their tripod masts which looked much more effective than the single conventional ones. Before the war our naval architects' ideal had been to build their ships as low as possible so that they would not present much of a target in battle. But that brilliant idea has been superseded by the enormous range at which we commence firing nowadays. Since we do our sighting from the tops of the masts, the side with the highest masts has quite an advantage. This principle was discovered by the English before the war. Consequently they equipped their ships with tripod masts to which they transferred their entire fire control section. We are just now trying to emulate them.

I calculated in my mind how much coal our little excursion had cost us. With 24 ships of the line using 200 tons apiece, this amounts to 4,800 tons. If the light cruisers and torpedo

[32] Ferdinand I (1861–1948), Prince of Bulgaria from 1887, King from 1908, forced to abdicate in October 1918, was paying a visit of state to Germany in order to obtain the Kaiser's permission to annex the Dobrudja. However, the discussions were inconclusive and it is not entirely clear whether or not he actually witnessed the naval maneuvers that were conducted in his honor.

boats are added it will reach about 5,000 tons.[33] This excludes the oil and lubricating material which were also expended. What an expensive ally! While the German people cannot obtain any coal at all, here we waste it recklessly. If this ever became widely known, it would stir up a great deal of ill will. Late that evening we returned to port. We were in luck, however, insofar as none of our ships got rammed or hit a mine.

Last Tuesday, July 5, 1917, I went for an evening stroll in town. A large number of people returning home from work clustered around a newly posted placard. I thought, surely a new chancellor has been named. But upon coming closer, I was surprised to hear that equal franchise had been proclaimed for Prussia.[34] The people's talk and expression reflected profound satisfaction. My own feelings are mixed. The whole thing is nothing but a common political deal to gain approval for the next war loan. It is disgusting! (Pfui Teufel!)

Our "Sailors' Council"[35] played a big trick on our First Officer. He had kept the First Division up the night before. Hence someone took the order book and wrote in it: "Reveille at 7 A.M.!" The Duty Officer was taken in by it and let us sleep until seven o'clock. Ninety hundredweight of our flour has turned bad. Although we tried to bake it into bread, it would

[33] There is an error in the author's calculations and therefore he lists the amount of coal expended as half a million tons.

[34] Stumpf's date is incorrect. This did not occur on July 5, but on July 12, 1917. On that day the Kaiser announced that he intended to modify his promise of the Easter Message by granting the Prussian people equal franchise at the end of the war. This most important concession to the democratic forces in Germany was made in order to revive the sinking morale of the German people.

Chancellor Bethmann-Hollweg did not retire until July 14.

[35] In the spring of 1917 the German navy established Food Complaints Committees (Menageprüfungskommissionen) for the enlisted men. Originally their function was quite modest. They were created to register the complaints of the men concerning food and living conditions. However, on many ships the authorities resisted the establishment of these committeees with the result that they became more radical, met in secret, began to concern themselves with political matters and were eventually to play a prominent role in organizing the sailors' mutiny in August. Occasionally the committees were called "Workers' and Sailors' Councils" by the men as well as by the officers. However, no actual workers' and sailors' councils were established until November 1918.

not rise. The First Officer said that it would have to be returned as soon as we got into port.

While we lay at anchor at the roadstead we were surprised
by an order to come into dock for compass repairs. This
pleased me very much. We were thus able to get rid of the
flour right away. When the sailors manning the cutter received
orders to this effect, they refused. Threats proved useless.
Finally a deck officer strapped on his side arms and drilled the
thirty men who had refused to obey. What would the consequences of such behavior have been in peacetime? At least a
court martial and the brig. But now, at the time of the
"Workers' and Sailors' Council?!!"

At long last the sailors of the watch changed their mind
about the flour. With three men to a sack they dragged it on
deck. It is a pity to allow so much flour to spoil. However our
new-found unity is highly gratifying. It proves that we can
do anything if we are united. I had always thought that conditions would have to become considerably worse before we
would overcome our timidity.

The newly formed Food Complaints Committee (Menageprüfungskommissionen) is progressing in a very successful and
energetic manner. It causes the First Officer untold annoyance
every day. We recently discovered that we have been swindled
out of a third of our rations. It is not yet entirely clear who
the culprit was, but our suspicions point to the quartermaster.
This incident brought the narrow-mindedness and cruelty of
our men out into the open. They regard every innocent remark or action as grounds for an accusation. For example, not
too long ago the quartermaster called to the driver of the supply truck to "bring the auto around!" Several of the men overheard him and informed the First Officer that the quartermaster was on a "per du" [36] basis with his driver because they
had heard him call, "Otto, bring it around!" Others maintained
that they had seen or heard that Otto had a piece of bacon in
his pocket. Occasions such as this provide the best illustrations

[36] In Germany only very close friends address each other in the familiar
form (Du) rather than the more formal form (Sie).

of the bigotry of the plebeian. I utterly detest these denunciations.

I respect the Food Committee for its good work. Indeed noticeable improvements are already apparent. We have been issued additional rations several times and the ordinary meals are much tastier than before. I imagine that this will continue until the uproar dies down again. We still have a long way to go before thoroughgoing and basic changes are made. However judging from the talk of the men, one might almost believe that the events in Russia are about to be repeated here. Much has yet to be done to merit such a comparison. God willing, I shall go on leave tomorrow. Hence I close my book for ten days. Again, I have had to wait for almost a year. Under the circumstances, however, I am in a happier mood today, 17 July 1917.

I have been back for two days. With my book open before me, I transport myself back to the spirit of its last pages. I can't quite succeed, however. The great contrast between the present mood and that of the past does not allow me to make the transition with ease. I must confess that I did not return in a happy frame of mind. It is difficult to say why. The trip in itself was very tranquil. Many of the things which formerly made the trip so interesting and stimulating did not occur. There were no blood-curdling stories, no secret predictions of things to come or discussions concerning the possibility of peace. I missed the lusty curses of the soldiers, the suspicious listening of the dock workers and the complaints of the women. Does this mean that things are now better in the land? I am afraid not. The people are so apathetic and hopeless that it hurts my heart. It isn't so bad as long as the people still have the strength to vent their anger by cursing. Only when they have lost all hope and are totally depressed do they appear as disconsolate and indifferent as they are nowadays.[37]

[37] Stumpf's description is very perceptive. During June and July of 1917 a deep wave of war-weariness gripped all classes of the German

If anyone were to confidently assert that he knew and understood everything which went on in his village, home town or
state, he would be exaggerating. Such a thing is hardly possible under normal conditions; how much less so in chaotic
times like these. Prior to going on leave I would have wagered
that it was impossible in the near future for the men to unite
solidly. I even thought that we would be unable to organize a
hunger strike, even though they had met with great success on
the other ships and bore so little danger for the individual.[38]

I soon discovered how easily unexpected events can overturn formerly accepted notions. A Food Inspection Committee
was established to act as a safety valve for the dissatisfaction
of the men. But it did not work out this way. Their long-pent-
up anger, having found a small opening, continued to boil full
force. It would have burst the furnace had it not found other
ways to escape. Our men, united and resolute, stood up and
demanded the right to inspect the food account books. Although the demand was turned down because it smacked too
much of control by the crew, we were promised a considerable
improvement in rations. Next the entire crew requested more
leave. The First Officer maintained that this represented an
organized and illegal plot. Then, however, he pretended as if
he had long ago decided to grant more leaves. "In order to
show you, however, that you will accomplish nothing with
your stubbornness, I shall postpone this ruling for eight days,"
he asserted. The ill-concealed laughter of the sailors revealed
how well the men saw through this disguised retreat. What is
most significant, is that we shall get three times as much leave
as before. Starting on July 3, in addition to the regular work
leaves, each division will send three men on leave.

population. Despite the Admiralty's promises of February 1917 that a
campaign of unrestricted submarine warfare would soon cause England
to capitulate, the war continued and the hopes for an early peace became
ever dimmer. The disaffection of the people manifested itself in the form
of more urgent demands for the establishment of a democratic government and the immediate commencement of peace negotiations.

[38] The crew of *Prinzregent Luitpold* conducted two successful hunger
strikes on June 6 and July 19, 1917.

The code of military justice has only one designation, "conspiracy to mutiny," for the events which have transpired on the other ships. I shall wait until I am certain that they are true before writing them down. This chapter requires greater caution than any other. I adjusted to the new situation more quickly than ever before. The level of morale was much higher than I had anticipated. Considering the present circumstances, our food is excellent. What is even more heartening is the fact that men have learned through experience what can be achieved with a bit of energy and a united front.

The triumphal victory of our army in East Galicia was the high point of my leave. When the reports from the front announced: "Stanislau taken—Delatyn occupied—the border has been reached," I was reminded of the days of Gorlice and Hermannstadt.[39] Thus right before our eyes, formerly unknown names become the keystones of history. 31 July 1917.

Today's date is August 2. It is the third anniversary of the declaration of war on France and Russia. I tried to recapture the spirit of 1914 by recalling my impressions. The feverish excitement which then gripped our emotions has vanished completely. I still tremble whenever I think of the events of three years ago. Those who were the most enthusiastic supporters of the war are now to be found in the camp of the pessimists and defeatists. On August 2 we regarded such great events as the outbreak of a two-front war as unimportant in relation to the fateful question: what will England do? It seems almost incredible to remember that at the time we felt "that the war would be no fun without England."

However now the war is no fun even "with" England. All of us ought to beat our breasts and confess *mea culpa*. I am utterly convinced that England is no more responsible for the

[39] On July 1, 1917, Russia launched her last desperate but massive offensive against the Central Powers in East Galicia. The German First Southern Army and the Austrian Third Army successfully repelled this new Brusilov offensive and drove the Russians out of Galicia by the end of the month.

In May 1915 a spectacular German-Austrian offensive had liberated the same area of Galicia from the Russians and had captured the towns of Gorlice and Hermannstadt (Yaroslav).

war than we. We provided England with the best rationale for its intervention by our injustice to Belgium.

All the statesmen who participated in igniting the powder keg are no longer in office. The Kaiser's well-intentioned servant, the honorable philosopher of Hohenfinnow, resigned recently.[40] He has been succeeded by a Bismarckian mind [Georg Michaelis], a man who is deadly earnest in [his intention to] obtain an early and honorable peace. In his most impressive speech he stated: "I do not know what will happen. But I cannot conceive of the misery resulting from an unexpected announcement that Germany does not have enough food to last until the next harvest!" These words from such an important source electrified all of Germany. He was Director of the War Wheat Control Administration. In my opinion, this is the only organization which has completely fulfilled its responsibilities without mismanagement. He is Germany's first bourgeois chancellor.[41]

[40] Theobald von Bethmann-Hollweg, the German Chancellor and Prussian Minister-President since 1909, resigned from office on July 14, 1917, as a result of the so-called July Crisis. That crisis was precipitated by the great war-weariness of the German people and their feeling that not even the unrestricted use of the submarine could win the war. This general depression was reflected in the Reichstag where the Center, the Progressives, the Social Democrats, and briefly the National Liberals banded together to draft the famous Peace Resolution, a document calling for the end of the war by a peace without annexations and indemnities. When it appeared that Bethmann-Hollweg would support this resolution, Field Marshal von Hindenburg and General Ludendorff, long dissatisfied with the Chancellor's inability to control the parties and to wage an all-out war, intervened decisively. The two generals presented Kaiser Wilhelm II with a harsh ultimatum that demanded the immediate dismissal of Bethmann-Hollweg. In the event the Kaiser was unwilling to comply, they threatened to resign. At the same time the army summoned the Crown Prince of Prussia to Berlin to commence negotiations with the Reichstag parties to drop the chancellor. When Bethmann-Hollweg was informed that the parties no longer supported him, he had no choice but to resign.

He was called the philosopher of Hohenfinnow because of his interest in Kantian philosophy and his estate at Hohenfinnow.

[41] Georg Michaelis (1851–1935) succeeded Bethmann-Hollweg as Chancellor on July 14, 1917. He had made a reputation for himself as a strong-willed administrator who did not mince words. In his most famous speech prior to assuming the chancellorship, Michaelis had announced in the Prussian Diet that he would run his sword through anyone who dared to oppose his administration of the War Wheat Office.

Since the army was largely responsible for his appointment to the chan-

If I were called upon to render a medical diagnosis of the present state of feelings among the enlisted men, it would read something like this:

> High state of excitement caused by a total lack of confidence in the officers. Persistence of the fixed notion that the war is conducted and prolonged solely in the interests of the officers. Manifestations of bitter anger due to fact that the enlisted men are starving and suffering while the officers carouse and roll in money.

Is it therefore any wonder that the men should now inevitably turn to revolt as a means of improving their sordid lot? As far as I have been able to tell, the mutiny raged most strongly on the ships of the *Kaiser* class, especially on *Prinzregent Luitpold* and *König Albert*. Apparently the Captain bears most of the blame. He arrested a stoker for collecting subscriptions to *Vorwärts*.[42] The joint protests of two crews of stokers compelled the Captain to set him free again. The next morning the Captain was missing, his body was found later floating near the submarine nets. . . . No one knows what happened; whether

cellorship and he was utterly dependent on it for support, Michaelis quickly became known as a willing tool of the Supreme Command. Therefore, although he was compelled to accept the Reichstag's Peace Resolution on July 19, he immediately qualified his endorsement of that resolution by stating that he would implement it "the way he understood it." Because of this defiance of the Reichstag and his total lack of political skill, Michaelis did not last long in office. He was dismissed at the end of October 1917.

All the previous German Chancellors, Bismarck, Caprivi, Hohenlohe, Bülow and Bethmann-Hollweg, had been members of the aristocracy. Hence Michaelis was Germany's first bourgeois chancellor.

42 *Vorwärts* was the official journalistic organ of the moderate, majority Social Democratic Party. It consistently demanded a negotiated peace without annexations and indemnities and urged the immediate introduction of domestic political reforms such as broadening the franchise, parliamentary government, and ministerial responsibility. Because of this and its internationalist views before the war, the paper was highly suspect in the navy. Hence Admiral Bachmann had issued an order banning the reading or circulating of socialist literature among the crews. There is no evidence that anyone ever got arrested for reading *Vorwärts*. The order was not uniformly enforced on all ships. Most importantly, the order tried to stem the circulation of the much more radical Independent Socialist journal, the *Leipziger Volkszeitung*.

it was murder, suicide, or an accident.[43] At any rate, it constitutes a warning to all officers.

These unpleasant events were discussed at a commanders' meeting on the *Posen* on Friday morning. Afterward our Captain assembled the crew on deck and gave an explanation. Some very unfortunate things had occurred on *Prinzregent Luitpold*, he said. "Three days ago one of the watches was scheduled to go to the theater, but for some reason the production did not take place. Instead they were to see a film. As the showing began the projector failed to function properly. Since it was too late to start anything else, the next day's schedule was substituted. The men were marched to the drill field for military exercises. A large number of the crew refused to obey and left the field without permission. Later on, 350 of the men were found at Fort Schaar. They rested there, got hungry and returned to their ship. There is evidence that foreign agents were involved (outraged muttering from the men). At a time when thousands of your comrades lay down their lives for the Fatherland in Flanders and are about to drive the Russians out of Galicia, it is tragic that you should entertain such ideas. This is precisely what our enemies desire. Our internal dissension and hatreds will give them what they could not achieve in honorable battle. I feel sorry for these unfortunate, misguided people; they will suffer the full consequences of the law. Dismissed!" [44]

[43] There exists no evidence to substantiate the incident.

[44] These events constituted the "sailors' mutiny" in the eyes of the naval authorities. However, the Captain's report on the happenings on the *Prinzregent Luitpold* are not entirely correct.

On August 1, forty-nine stokers left the ship in protest over the cancellation of their recreation period. On the following day, when the stokers were given disciplinary punishment for their action, the crew of the *Prinzregent* staged a sympathy strike. Six hundred crew members left the ship without permission, marched to a tavern in the neighboring town of Rüstersiel, where they had some drinks and listened to speeches. Some violent expressions were used in these speeches and one of the speakers shouted, "Down with the war! We do not want to fight this war any longer!"

Thereupon a solitary police sergeant appeared on the scene and tried to arrest the men. However, they refused to obey him and on their own volition began marching back to the ship in formation. On the way back

Thus once again it is England's fault. What a ridiculous notion! These gentlemen have no idea what a tremendous guilt they bear. What a convenient excuse to say that the enemy is responsible! This is what always happens when something goes wrong in Germany. One might almost laugh if it weren't so terribly serious. Before these people will admit their guilt a few heads will have to roll. What a shame that a good and industrious nation like Germany is ruled so miserably. I wish I could exterminate this corrupt band which leads the people astray and embitters their lives. Is there nobody to whom a free and happy Germany can look to with confidence and pride? Even the Kaiser's pure image and noble intentions are ruined and corrupted by the evil deeds of his officials and "trusted advisors." Kaiser of the people, I call upon you! Sunday, 2 August 1917.

The First Squadron has been in port for three days. I have heard so much about the mutiny since then that my head reels with confusion. As yet I have been totally unable to separate truth from falsehood. Hence I can only record what happened here.

I am convinced that an actual revolutionary situation exists in the fleet. Even the Kaiser seems to have been notified. His imperial train arrived yesterday without any fanfare.[45] Some of our gentlemen will not like that at all. He is not likely to distribute decorations on this occasion.

While I was on watch on Wednesday evening I was informed by a friend that 20 members of our crew had been arrested. At first I refused to believe him and told him that he was mistaken. "No, no, I even know some of the names," he said. I still did not believe the story. Soon, however, I changed my mind. Around ten o'clock an officer from the Judge Advocate's Office and a First Lieutenant came on board. They

they were met by one of their own officers and refused to allow him to arrest them, but still they returned to the ship. This was the extent of the mutiny. The *Prinzregent* was placed under a state of siege and the ringleaders were imprisoned.

[45] Here Stumpf asserted, "I later discovered that this was not true." This constitutes the only footnote Stumpf ever wrote in his diary.

searched the possessions of a number of men and left carrying an assortment of books and letters. What had happened? The whole thing was actually quite simple.

About two dozen men had attended a meeting at a tavern in Banter to hear a lecture by [Seaman First Class Linke] concerning the Balkan Wars, the origins of this war and the current situation. I don't know if it was an intelligent discussion. In any event, all of a sudden fifteen policemen appeared. They declared the meeting closed and arrested all participants. Apparently the men refused to leave when ordered. After a telephone call had been made, a section of marines arrived. With loaded rifles!! they marched the prisoners first to Headquarters and then to the courthouse. The interrogation lasted a long time. Nevertheless, at 11 o'clock the first three were released, at 3 A.M. three others, while three "ringleaders" are still there. They must be the stupid ones.[46]

Today our youngest lieutenant shouted at one of the participants: "You ought to be shot!" Moreover, the First Officer amused himself by asking one of the men if he wanted to overthrow the German government. I am sorry that I didn't hear this; I certainly would not have kept quiet. Meanwhile the members of the "peace conference" are confined to the ship and are allowed to walk about only when accompanied by a guard. *Difficile est satiram non scribare!*

I would like to add a personal observation. Had I known of this matter and intended to participate in it, I would have insisted that the meeting take place in the open. In this fashion undesirable listeners would have been excluded. At intervals I would have struck up some patriotic songs. However things always look easy in retrospect. No one knows who informed the police. I would suspect that it was the innkeeper. In any case, the court scribblers now have their hands full. Certainly all the prisons are filled to overflowing. Hence I

---

[46] This occurred on August 8, 1917. A number of men from the *Helgoland* were arrested when they held a meeting at which, it was alleged by the naval authorities, they discussed plans for the liberation of their imprisoned comrades.

might recommend that some churches be used for this purpose. Interrupted, afternoon 16 August 1917.

I have been trying in vain for the past half hour to resume my interrupted train of thought. But regardless of how much I think, nothing fitting comes to mind. Recently, however, I was in a proper mood and would have been able to write for hours on this subject, but so much has happened in the interim that my thoughts have wandered off in an entirely different direction. One can never recapture even a moment's loss. What shall I describe first today? [Shall I write] of the fine sermon of Pastor [Bode] of Bremen, or of the good food we have been getting lately, or for that matter, of the fact that while I am writing this we are back again in the Baltic? Let me therefore take up these matters in their original order.

In a praiseworthy effort to provide us with some diversion and perhaps also to root out the vestiges of the "revolution," our command has engaged a pastor from Bremen to lecture to us. I must admit that the gentleman performed the job brilliantly. He delivered an exciting and infectiously enthusiastic speech which made me resolve to look at the brighter side of the future. He had a masterful and fascinating way of interweaving anecdotes and his personal experiences. But in my opinion he really excelled at justifying the very things we detested the most. For example, he presented such a convincing argument in favor of drill that none of us was able to contradict him. However, under ordinary circumstances, we are very quick to condemn this "invention" and to dismiss it as being totally useless and harmful.

A saying which has become so popular during this war that every little boy can recite it, states "It is better to be a coward than a dead hero." Surely this popular saying is supported by ample evidence. Nevertheless the pastor proved that just the opposite was true and that the German troops would rather die than act like cowards. He was able to cite case after case to support his contention. I felt that he was capable of proving anything. For emphasis his speech was punctuated with unusually lively gestures.

Now something about our menu! Since it has become the center of interest not only of the sailors [but of the entire population], it has become more highly prized than the ballot or stock certificates. I am pleased to be able to comment favorably on it. An immeasurable improvement has occurred so that it is now even better than before the war. Our new cook is very capable and can convert even white cabbage and barley groats into a tasty meal. Even on ordinary workdays we receive plums, apples or tomatoes for dessert. This was not the case when we were still at peace. One evening, after we had had an especially good meal, the First Officer came around to ask the men if they were satisfied now. They all answered affirmatively. *Panem et circenses!*

There are a few things which I have forgotten to note of the Kaiser's visit. A while back I wrote that the Kaiser had visited Wilhelmshaven incognito. But since he has just now paid an official visit to his "boys in blue," I would tend to doubt this. I shall not comment on our preparations for his visit. . . . Everything went famously. The day before, the entire fleet had assembled at the mouth of the Jade and the following morning we weighed anchor in glorious "Hohenzollern weather." First the flagship carrying the Kaiser reviewed all the ships. He stood there dressed in a Grand Admiral's uniform and saluted us with impassivity. Our cheers sounded rather pitiful since only the officers and cadets participated. After the review we sailed out for maneuvers. Approximately twenty airplanes buzzed around the big ships. We were followed by innumerable light cruisers and torpedo boats. The Kaiser left the flagship at Helgoland but in the afternoon he sent us a wireless message expressing extreme gratification at all he had observed.

On August 19, precisely the same day as last year, we steamed through the Canal. I am still puzzled about what we were expected to do in Kiel. At any rate there must be some truth to the rumor that the whole thing was merely a diversionary tactic to raise our morale. It was even rumored that we were about to embark on a summer cruise.

Our suspicions were confirmed right away when we first put into Apenrade and then at Sonderborg. We were given ample liberty ashore. When I went ashore and strolled inland, I detected no signs of hostility on the part of the people. Although they almost always spoke in Danish among themselves, I noticed that they all seemed ready to answer in German. [This was true] even at Loitkirkeby, which is commonly regarded as the stronghold of Danish nationalism.[47] At their scattered homes the farmers all seemed willing and eager to sell the sailors fruit, eggs and butter. I simply cannot understand this perpetual struggle of nationalities. But I doubt that it has developed any strong roots among these healthy people. In Sonderborg we anchored off the historic Düppel fortifications,[48] but unfortunately I was on watch that day.

For several days now I have tried to describe a crime which in its horror defies description. In vain I sought to compare it with other countries and periods. But this proved to be impossible. It is impossible to compare this war in terms of its geographic dimensions, the number of those engaged in combat, the volume of material or the length and intensity of its battles with anything known previously. Thus I am unable to find past precedents for the current brutality of the courts. If, in the past, someone had told me that it was possible for people to be sentenced to jail or to be executed in Germany without having committed a crime, I would have looked upon him as a fool. Now I gradually realize why some people fight the

[47] The duchies of Schleswig and Holstein were annexed by Prussia as a result of the war against Denmark (1864) and the war with Austria (1866). Nevertheless, the Danish population of these two provinces continued to desire affiliation with Denmark. Consequently, after the war a plebescite was held in 1920 and Northern Schleswig was returned to Denmark.
[48] The fortress of Düppel was the last Danish outpost in Schleswig to surrender to the Prussians during the Prusso-Danish War.

military and its system with such determination. Poor Karl Liebknecht! How sorry I feel for you now.

And now, down to specifics. Several days ago two of the men whom the police accused of being "speakers" were tried at a court martial on the Königstrasse. We all thought that they would be released or that at worst they would get disciplinary punishment. None of the many witnesses produced any incriminating evidence. And yet, despite all this, both men were sentenced to ten years in prison, five years' loss of citizenship and dismissal from the navy. I still cannot believe that such a thing could happen here. The judge's statement is characteristic of the entire comedy: "I shall dispense with the testimony of the witnesses since it will not reveal anything incriminating!" This statement is more revealing than any number of thick volumes. No matter what, the court felt obliged to set a terrible example. It is quite possible that an organization desiring to obtain peace by means of direct action exists in the navy.[49] However to connect the harmless meeting at the "saloon in Banter" with it is certainly a miscarriage of justice. None of those present at the meeting intended to do anything which might come under the heading of treason. The actions of the "speakers" can readily be interpreted as an example of human vanity.

Such distinctions, however, are not taken into consideration by a German court-martial. If the Archangel Michael had testified to the innocence of the accused, I don't imagine that the prosecutor would have believed him. All the more so if he did not produce any "incriminating" evidence. The prison

---

[49] An organization of this type had actually been created out of the Food Complaints Committees of *Friedrich der Grosse* and *Prinzregent Luitpold*. When the crew members' grievances concerning bad food and ill-treatment were ignored by their officers, a few of the men established contact with some Independent Socialist Reichstag deputies in the hope of obtaining information and material for agitation. They became members of that party, tried to enroll others and in a very vague sort of way discussed plans for staging peace demonstrations and a strike. All in all, it was a confused and embryonic movement which lacked leadership, organization, and mass support. In spite of the navy's subsequent allegations, there was no conscious plan to organize a mutiny. This was particularly true of the *Helgoland*, Stumpf's ship where no organization existed.

terms as well as the death sentences were all ready before the tribunal had even met. One of the lawyers who interrogated my friend [Belz] made a very interesting remark: "Be careful and tell the truth. One [conviction] more or less, doesn't concern me!"

That a sailor [from the *Prinzregent Luitpold*] should have been sentenced to death in 1917 for saying to a friend, "Won't you come along,"—conspiracy to mutiny—will no doubt be regarded as a curiosity in some future age. I wonder whether the five death sentences will be carried out. If a firing squad would agree to carry out this [sentence], it would besmirch the honor of the whole navy.

It is difficult to predict the consequences of such brutality. Half of the men are apathetic; a quarter of them regard this as an outrage and feel sorry for the poor devils, while fewer than another quarter are ready to act and seek revenge. Maybe everyone is convinced that the "criminals" will be given their freedom by an amnesty at the end of the war. I am too skeptical to share this view. I would rather depend on a revolution, or the loss of the war, or possibly, either an earthquake or fire. . . .

As I was sitting writing, the news arrived that our troops had taken Riga. Naturally this meant that there was no longer any reason why we should remain here [in Kiel]. Some of the men began insisting that we would head there next, but we shall have to see about that.

We thus left Kiel much earlier than anticipated. Today we are once again lying off Wilhelmshaven. Many of our men who had planned to visit Hamburg or who had arranged "dates" ashore were very disappointed. It was positively cruel for us to depart on a Sunday morning. We traversed the canal on a magnificent sunny fall day. Would it be the last time?

I neglected to mention something a few days ago. Last week I was busy scraping rust in the bunkers. But I received double rations, 10 pfennigs an hour and was also released from all other duties.

One afternoon all hands were called on deck to hear the Captain read out the sentences which had just been handed down. Of the five death sentences "only" two had been carried out, while the rest were "pardoned" to life imprisonment.[50] In addition, the majority of the jail sentences have been greatly reduced. The two men from our ship will thus serve six rather than ten years. There is no hope for additional pardons since amnesty proclamations do not apply to cases of treason. Thus the gruesome drama came to a (temporary?) close.

Those of us who have remained behind, however, now reap the benefits of the sacrifice. Since it was discovered that a full stomach is not conducive to violence, we now get plenty of food. It is the old trick all over again: the stick and the carrot. The men in jail have virtually been forgotten. From now on [only] five of us will get to share an entire loaf of bread.

We were highly amused to read of our navy's participation in the seizure of Dünamünde and Riga in the newspapers.[51] In their flashy style they described the outstanding bravery of our young navy. For those of us who know what actually happened, this will serve as a good lesson of with what care one must read all their other reports. I knew that our big ships anchored at Kiel during the battle and that very few of our submarines were in the Gulf of Riga. They were unable to prevent the Russian fleet and numerous troop transports from breaking out and reaching Reval. But the newspapers report just the opposite. . . .

[50] On August 26, 1917, Admiral Scheer in his position as Commander in Chief of the Fleet, pronounced the death sentence on the sailor Max Reichpietsch of *Friedrich der Grosse* and the stoker Albin Köbis of *Prinzregent Luitpold*. Three other men, Sachse, Weber, and Beckers received fifteen years imprisonment. On September 5 the execution was carried out at Cologne by an army firing squad. The executions were widely regarded as a callous judicial murder and created deep resentment and hatred among the men.

[51] The Russian fortress of Riga in Latvia was forced to surrender to General Oskar von Hutier's Eighth German Army on September 3, 1917. In his brilliant assault upon the city, von Hutier had used an amphibious landing on Riga's offshore islands and an unprecedentedly heavy and well-organized two-day artillery bombardment. Since Russia was soon convulsed by the Bolshevik November Revolution, the engagement before Riga was the last major battle between the German and Russian armies in World War I.

In general I have become rather disgusted with the news-papers. Certain well-informed sources have long insisted that they [falsely] build up our nation's hopes for an early peace before each bond drive. I cannot understand how it can happen time and again. At present all the newspapers maintain that England has just put out a new peace feeler. Although there has been an official denial of this, they have cleverly asserted that [certain] well-informed private sources insist that it will still materialize. Hence poor Michel thinks that it must be true and plunks down his money. . . . Nevertheless I seriously doubt that the war loan will again amount to 12 billion.

I am very puzzled at the high hopes which the [usually] calm Protestant North Germans have placed in the Pope's peace move.[52] If he should indeed succeed in bringing peace to the war-torn nations, he will make the position of the Papacy secure for all time. Surely he must have been divinely inspired. I even regard it as possible that the Russian and other Eastern Orthodox Churches might find their way back to Rome. What a truly earth-shaking prospect! As a result, the influence of the Papacy would reach unprecedented heights. It would constitute a visible manifestation of God's intervention and would compensate the Papacy for all the humiliation and insults it has suffered at the hands of the secular world. But one would be well advised to wait a while before exploring all the various possibilities this has raised.

Today I went ashore at Wilhelmshaven. Everywhere the sailors talked of nothing else but the forthcoming naval action

---

[52] Pope Benedict XV, on August 1, 1917, sent a peace note to all the warring nations requesting them to conclude a peace and imploring that they make "a complete restitution of all occupied territories." The Papal Peace Note was received with great enthusiasm by the war-weary German people and found only a slightly less favorable reception in England and France. However, the Allies made it clear that they would refuse to negotiate so long as Germany did not renounce her hold over Belgium. This renunciation, however, was not forthcoming, since Chancellor Michaelis, for religious reasons (he was an extremely devout Protestant pietist) as well as for political reasons, refused to issue the necessary declaration. Thus by September the Papal peace appeal had failed, shattering perhaps the last hope that peace could be attained by other than military means.

in the Baltic. After winnowing out all the rumors, I came to the conclusion that the following might be true: It seems certain that parts of our fleet, or perhaps the entire fleet, will take part in seizing from the Russians and occupying the island of Ösel in the Gulf of Riga. I understand that six of our troop transports are being outfitted for this in Hamburg. Moreover the men in the replacement companies have been recalled from leave. These facts alone, however, do not warrant such far-reaching conclusions. Nevertheless a mere glance at the map will indicate that we must gain control over Ösel if we wish to secure ourselves in Pernov or Riga.

Although none of us any longer is very eager to fight and to [win] victories, this plan is extremely popular. We would all like to give the Russians a thorough beating, not only because they so shamefully insulted us during the summer of 1915 over their wireless [A message which was intercepted at that time read: "Germans love to gorge on ham and sauerkraut"], but for a number of other reasons as well. I need merely mention the names of Danzig, Langfuhr, Libau, Swinemünde and Ahlbeck to indicate what I mean. It is a shame that the year is already so far advanced. I personally feel more secure in the North Sea, where a wide belt of mine fields serves to protect us against surprise attacks by the enemy.

Recently I overheard a group of my comrades discussing the imminent seizure of Ösel. Toward the end they raised the question of what the Commander of the Fleet did to keep himself occupied all day. "Oh," said one of them, "a great deal! He paces up and down all day long on the deck of *Kaiser Wilhelm II* counting the buttons on his coat while he mumbles: 'Shall we stay here? Shall we sail out? Stay here? Sail out?' As soon as he is finished, he begins all over again. This explains why he issues different orders every five minutes. I would gladly cut off one of his buttons so that he could finally decide one way or the other."

I thought that this was a wonderful joke which describes our present situation to perfection. Right now it looks as though we will "stay here." We have interrupted our forward patrol, have returned to Wilhelmshaven and have refueled. All of us were certain that we would head for Kiel the next day. But no such luck! In the morning we discovered the reason for it when our Zeppelins came flying in. One of them performed a very curious maneuver. First she stood on her head and then on her tail. We feared that she would crash any minute. When she came closer I saw what was wrong. A round hole in one of her ailerons indicated that she had been hit by English anti-aircraft fire. If the hit had landed a few meters farther forward, it would have been all over for her. As she flew by she signaled: "Everything went well." What an optimist, I thought to myself. 25 September 1917.

Stay here? Sail out? Our future still fluctuates between these two alternatives. No one knows anything of our immediate plans and why we are standing by on a perpetual alert. We are lucky that our portside loading boom has gotten stuck, because this made it necessary for us to come in and we have been placed on a six-hour stand-by alert. The talk about Ösel has still not died down and it assumes new and more fantastic proportions with each passing day. The number of our troop transports has already risen to forty and it is said that 80,000 troops are to participate in the invasion!! I no longer believe the whole swindle. We are merely being chased around in circles.

Inside Germany the war-bond drive is obtaining a great deal of publicity. There is hardly a fence or a street corner that is not "decorated" with a picture of Hindenburg with a facsimile of his handwriting underneath stating, "The best birthday gift you can give me is to buy war bonds. . . ." There is something truly magnificent in the adulation which the entire nation showers upon him. One might without fear of exaggeration say that the fate of all of Central Europe rests upon his shoulders. There is virtually nothing that he cannot demand of us. I doubt whether we could have surmounted this spring's hunger crisis without our hero. We are just beginning to realize how really horrible that turnip winter was. We would have collapsed physically as well as mentally if it had not been for our unshakable confidence in our [ultimate] victory. In spite of all our enlightened views and sophistication, we still need an idol to worship.[53] Today, on the seventieth birthday of our savior, all good Germans wish him much luck, success and a long life. 2 October 1917.

The Fleet Commander seems finally to have decided that we are to stay here. Since it is extremely unlikely that we would have emerged with glory, I approve of his decision. Some evil tongues are wagging that we will now have to wait until the Russian fleet is frozen in again and that we might then try it on ice skates. But I would insist [that we shall have to wait] because our staff officers would not be able to escape quickly enough and because the shells do not pay any [special] respect for sleeves with gold braid. . . .

For the first time in this war our flyers have succeeded in destroying an entire enemy city. This is the fate which befell Dunkirk and today's report from the front announced that all of the immense supply stores of the Anglo-Belgian armies have been destroyed. This is merely a small foretaste of the wars of the future. How lucky we are that we are not fighting on our own soil and how proud we may be that we Germans have the industrial potential [to construct such weapons]. I keep reading that the Americans will send 10,000 to 100,000 planes to crush Germany. But what are we doing about it? We produce!! 3 October 1917.

I have just been on deck to get a whiff of fresh air from the October storm. The Jade basin was exceptionally clear and the red roofs and spires of Varel winked across the choppy waves. I almost felt that I could reach out to touch them. I took delight in defying the howling storm and enjoyed the whistling song of the wind in the rigging. Old memories revived on my mind; my mother's fairy tales of dark forests, bad robbers and deep seas. Does not the groaning of the wireless

[53] Field Marshal von Hindenburg had indeed become the idol of the German people. In order to sell war bonds the German government would erect huge wooden statues of the hero of Tannenberg and the people who purchased a war bond were given the privilege of driving a nail into it.

antenna sound like the cry of an abandoned child? Was it a kitten that just cried out so pitifully? Imagination, go away! I am no longer a child. . . . I am an apprentice, a journeyman —no, I am a sailor who has spent a fifth of his life behind these gray, iron walls. Five years ago a similar storm was blowing from the northeast. I trod these very same planks as an enthusiastic recruit and my head was filled with airy dreams. But then we were at peace and were unable to peer into the future. To be perfectly frank, I cannot recall a single person who did not look forward to a little war like the one of 1870.[54] The workers were not well off at all: there were no jobs and a merciless struggle for survival was raging. However in retrospect we all feel that we used to live in paradise when a pound of butter or meat cost one mark, an egg seven pfennigs, a kilogram of soap sixty pfennigs, and a pair of good shoes twelve marks. And everyone could buy as much as he wanted. Was it really like that? Why then did you not stock up all these good things? You could be a wealthy man now if you had a hundred kilograms of soap! Very true! Did you do it? Unfortunately no! Well, then.

I believe that there is hardly a single person between Helgoland and Orsova who does not secretly regret that he did not foresee all this and that he did not enrich himself in the ensuing inflation. None of us is content. Even those who have already made a million would like to add another ten million to it. I for one, however, have very little respect for people who made a fortune behind the safety of our borders while millions of their fellow countrymen were dying and impoverishing themselves at the front. It would only be fitting and proper that all of these excess profits be confiscated and divided among the soldiers. 9 October 1917.

Recently the buttons of the Fleet Commander must have pointed to "sail out," for on Saturday we suddenly received orders to raise steam in all boilers. Aha, something was going on in the Baltic! Unmistakably we were heading toward the

[54] This refers to the Franco-Prussian War of 1870–71.

mouth of the Elbe. We took along all of our boats and even the mail wagon. Even our fleet tender received orders to follow. Hence it could be neither Kiel nor Helgoland.

Within a few hours we had covered the short distance to Cuxhaven. The warm sun of Indian summer had changed the Elbe into a brilliant sea of diamonds. It was sheer joy to see our armored keels cut through its glimmering beauty. Who had time to watch out for the floating mines which one of our lookouts had reported? When we sighted the island of Neuwerk with the Störtebeck tower in the distance, I nearly felt sorry that my watch was over. Our beloved Cuxhaven was still covered with fresh green foliage and large herds of cows grazed on its fragrant meadows. Yes, indeed, herds of cows at the very place which our gray theoreticians had once designated as the critical location in the naval war between Germany and England. . . . I was just about to start writing when we were ordered to stow away our gear. Closing for today. 16 October 1917.

It is a shame that my writing was interrupted so suddenly yesterday. I had a free afternoon ahead of me and my mood was just right. I think it is quite curious that my mind seems to work best when it is least needed: shortly before falling asleep, when I wake up at night and just before getting up in the morning. At these times my fantasy works wonders and I have often wished that I could somehow record these thoughts. Then my diary would contain more intelligent ideas than at present.

Slight causes—major results. By and large, the mutiny which I have described cannot be regarded as an event of worldwide significance. But it was turned into one through the unparalleled clumsiness of the Secretary of the Navy and the Chancellor. As was to be expected, the whole story was aired before the Reichstag. Thus I learned that three deputies of the Independent Social Democratic Party were implicated. . . . After I had read the report I believed that it was the politicians who had incited my comrades [to rebel]. When the men were tried they cowardly left them in the lurch. I expressed this opinion quite openly. But after I had reconsidered the matter, thought about it calmly and, above all, after I had received further reports, I discovered that the guilt lay on the other side. Before the Reichstag Herr von Capelle maintained that the rebellious sailors had conspired to refuse to obey orders and to force the conclusion of a peace by paralyzing the navy.[55] The Independent Social Democratic deputies had provided them with [propaganda] materials to aid their criminal agitation.[56]

Inevitably every thinking person will ask if these three deputies had been summoned before the court for abetting treason. This is only natural. But no! These gentlemen did not even receive a report [of the proceedings], let alone an invitation to serve as witnesses. A lynch court was convened; it stopped up its ears when the witnesses for the defense testified and merely paid attention to the testimony of a few frightened men. I know that many of them said much more than they actually knew. A few of the men (especially [Gleinitz] [57]) said everything that their inquisitors wanted to hear in the expectation they would be pardoned if they acted like repentant sinners. But they dug their own graves. In the certain knowledge that these intimidated souls were capable of reversing their evidence, the court turned the tables on them and converted the major witnesses into the major defendants.

[55] On October 9, 1917, Chancellor Michaelis and Admiral von Capelle appeared before the Reichstag and maintained that Deputies Dittmann, Haase and Vogtherr of the Independent Social Democratic Party had instigated the sailors to mutiny. Consequently, the Chancellor asserted that he would no longer regard that party as legal and threatened indirectly that he would try to proscribe it.

[56] The Independent Socialists had indeed provided the sailors who visited them with propaganda material, but this material consisted of perfectly legal Reichstag speeches. Moreover, Dittmann in particular had cautioned the sailors not to transgress naval laws and was unaware that the men were thinking of organizing demonstrations and strikes.

[57] No sailor by the name of Gleinitz was ever implicated in the mutiny. The author is probably referring to Max Reichpietsch of *Friedrich der Grosse*, the man who established contact with the Independent Socialists in the Reichstag and who was the nominal organizer of the abortive movement among the crews.

Of course the other defendants, especially Sachs[58] of *Friedrich der Grosse*, cooperated in this. The final outcome is that the "major witnesses" have been sentenced to death and are to be shot.

Now that their mouths have been shut and they have been placed behind prison walls, the Chancellor came along, threw their testimony at the feet of the Independent Social Democrats and declared that in the future he regarded them as standing outside of the confines of the law. Fortunately his unscrupulous [maneuver] gave rise to almost universal indignation and criticism. Deputy Naumann, in particular, went right to the heart of the matter.[59] Although I am personally as opposed as can be to the "Independents," in this instance they are completely in the right.

Von Capelle has had to pay the consequences for his error and has already resigned.[60] Slight causes—major results. 18 October 1917.

Our projected invasion of Ösel, which I have already described, materialized very suddenly. We were greatly astonished one evening as we were about to go to sleep, when a telegram was posted informing us that our army and navy had just seized a strong bridgehead on the island. We greeted this news with universal satisfaction. In spite of all our war-weariness, we could not help feeling a little bit envious of the Third and Fourth Squadrons for participating. When we put out to sea on the day before yesterday, we were convinced that we

[58] This refers to the sailor Willi Sachse of *Friedrich der Grosse*, who managed to escape the death penalty by cooperating with the prosecution. After his release from prison by the November Revolution, Sachse drifted into the Communist camp. Later he collaborated with the Nazis and then was finally executed in 1944 for being a member of the anti-Hitler conspiracy.

[59] The Reichstag remained unconvinced by Michaelis' vague allegations and demanded that the navy present concrete evidence of the Independents' complicity in the rebellion. Friedrich Naumann stated, "After what the Chancellor has just said we are all compelled to support this party and its existence."

[60] This is incorrect. Although Michaelis tried to place the blame for his repudiation by the Reichstag on the Secretary of the Navy, the latter did not resign until the entire government was reorganized in October, 1918.

were headed for Riga. But no! Instead we anchored in the Elbe off Altenbruch. For the next two days everything was peaceful, until we were unexpectedly called to general quarters. We reacted with great enthusiasm but our excitement abated when we entered the canal and tied up at Brunsbüttel-koog. Once again I went ashore in the loveliest weather. Moreover I expected that it would be no different the next day. But this did not come about. There seemed to be something brewing in the North Sea. Two of our cruisers *Bremse* and *Brummer* raced by on Tuesday night while four large but empty freighters steamed toward Kiel.

Our idyllic existence had been disrupted. Hence we were not surprised that very same evening when we were told to pack our seabags and prepare for battle. The last time we did that was fifteen months ago. It was rumored that we were to patrol off Amrum Bank to cover our minesweepers. But I also suspect that our new Squadron Commander, our former Captain [Freiherr von Dahlwig] wanted to make a name for himself. At any rate we sailed in a northeasterly direction for 120 sea miles. It was unusually windy and most of the recruits became violently seasick. Our two [torpedo boat] escorts were bounced about like Ping-Pong balls. I felt sorry for them. These conditions made it impossible for our minesweepers to work. Consequently we were somewhat disappointed to return to Cuxhaven. Therefore we were quite astonished when we heard over the wireless that during the same night our light cruisers had attacked and destroyed a thirteen-ship convoy and two modern destroyers off the Shetland Islands. What a fine coup! *Bremse* and *Brummer* had struck! Nevertheless we sailed out again in the same direction on Saturday night. This time the sea was not as choppy but again there was no trace of our minesweepers. Maybe we were merely creating a diversion. In the afternoon we loaded 600 tons of coal. It was a bright, clear day and a light breeze ruffled the mirrorlike waters of the Elbe. I stood on the searchlight deck and looked on as the insatiable mouths of our bunkers swallowed up the black coal.

That day the traffic in the air was particularly heavy. A

number of Zeppelins were constantly cruising overhead. The old former *Hansa*, now serving as school ship *L 16*, caught our attention because of her daring tricks. I thought, now we are using a school ship in battle! What next? . . . There was something strange about her forward gondola. It looked as though it were made of wire. We thought nothing of it when she suddenly turned at a sixty-degree angle and began to descend. But we all stopped working and watched her with fascination as she came down to fifty meters above the water. Until the very last I thought that she was doing this deliberately. However when her stern jolted into the water I soon learned otherwise. Our motor cutter raced to the scene of the disaster. A searchlight lit up and signaled: "Explosion in forward gondola!" Helpful boats raced to the scene from all directions, but the water was so shallow that only the smallest of them could approach her. Hence the dirigible was allowed to drift toward the shore. When she suddenly shot up into the air, we realized that she was out of danger. Later on I learned that she had landed safely at Brunsbüttel and that her entire crew emerged unscathed.

The following night we were again ordered to make clear for sea. At about one o'clock we slowly headed out toward the open sea. This time a major air raid on England was on. The conditions seemed just right for it. There was a new moon, only a light breeze and a thick cloud cover. At daybreak we were lying off Sylt when to our consternation we discovered that the weather had undergone a radical change. An impenetrable blanket of fog descended and the waves lapped restlessly against our sides. It kept getting worse all the time. Only an act of God could now save our Zeppelins. The Captain received a constant stream of wireless messages. From a distance I heard him say that several of our aircraft had lost their bearings and that their engines had stalled. This was alarming news.

Since even we found it impossible to make any headway in this pea soup of a fog, we dropped anchor and stayed where we were for the rest of the day and the night. At long last we received the bad tidings. Four of our Zeppelins had run out of fuel, were compelled to make a forced landing in France and had to be destroyed by their crews. This was unfortunate indeed. Nevertheless it was still comforting to know that our dirigibles had not fallen prey to the enemy, but to the higher powers of nature. 20 October 1917.

After the strenuous and tiring days which we had just experienced, I was very glad to get a chance to rest up in peace and quiet under the protection of the shore batteries of Wilhelmshaven. As much as we complain about Wilhelmshaven, it still remains the best place to serve. However even if only half of what we hear about our losses before Ösel is true, we might as well forget about our spell in dock. According to these reports, *Bayern* is in critical condition at Kiel, *Kurfürst* has hit a mine and *Markgraf* has been torpedoed. There is a persistent rumor that our squadron will be sent out in relief. This is quite possible. I can well imagine how tired the men of the Third and Fourth Squadron must be.

While I was writing, our crew was busy loading provisions for a full six weeks. The steward, the carpenter, the sailmaker, and the bosun have also received orders to stock up for six weeks. Furthermore we had to exchange all our old Russian rifles for new M. 98's. Hence it looked as though we were really serious. To be perfectly honest, I must admit that I was excited by the prospect of going into action against the enemy. Of course it also meant that we lost our turn in dock but that is no great calamity.

Up on the top deck the First Officer was raging with anger because our flour and bread had gotten soaking wet. It is simply scandalous that we cannot use a covered boat for the purpose [of food deliveries]. As a result, we will have to eat much chopped food and bread soup from now on.

I find nothing more comforting than to lie in my hammock at night and to waken to the sound of the monotonous, soft pounding of the ship's engines. It is comforting to know that other men are on watch and at work. Although I know that it is possible that we may be blown up any minute, I still retain a feeling of great security. My fear of these dangers is dulled by the knowledge that the command of the ship is in capable hands. With a deep sigh I turn over and fall asleep again immediately. . . .

We have very rarely steamed without interruption for thirty-six hours during the last few years. We cannot subject our engines to such a strain too often. I did not think that it would take us so long to sail from Kiel to Danzig. After all, the Baltic was free of danger and we did not even have to post a war watch until we reached Rügen. Sunday was a wonderfully clear day and we were filled with anticipation as we sailed toward the East. I was informed that we would refuel first at Putzig and that we were then to occupy the harbor of Ahrensburg at Ösel. Throughout the night we sailed past the hilly, wooded coastline. The almost full moon shone so brilliantly that it was possible to read the signal book up on the bridge. Our "Little Fritz" was now in the happiest of spirits and whistled all day long. At about one o'clock we sighted the light tower at Rixhöhe and at dawn we anchored at Putziger Wick. (Which is notable for the fact that on August 15 *Moltke* was torpedoed here.) On the following day both of our watches loaded coal and transferred 700 tons into our hold, while an additional 60 tons were stored on deck for the torpedo boats. At the time of this writing we are enjoying a day of rest in compensation for our lost Sunday. . . .

An important consequence of this long-drawn-out war has been to make us more modest [in our demands] and more contented [with our lot]. This is not only true of our food requirements. During the first months of the war we were spoiled by the immense number of prisoners [we captured] and if we did not seize a fortress a day we began grumbling about our slowness and lack of initiative. But nowadays we regard even a thousand prisoners as significant. I would never have expected to relive the days of Tannenberg and Ivangorod. But in spite of that, here they are again. According to our army reports we have captured 100,000 Italians during the past five days. Our joint offensive with the Austrians has beaten the Italians and our troops are already standing before the Undine and the headquarters of the Italian army.[61] Fortunately we have a wireless, otherwise we would not have known anything about this great event. We have not received any mail for the last five days. I never before missed not being able to read a newspaper so much.

I think that there is not a decent man in this world who is not pleased that we beat the Italians. I am elated at the thought that we Germans were fated to win this victory. Now I understand why time is operating in our favor. What would have happened if we had concluded a peace without this victory??!!

I shall not forecast the consequences of this victory. I would merely like to note that we greeted it with universal satisfaction. 30 October 1917.

I have to keep running back to the bulletin board to read these wonderful victory announcements over and over again. It is simply too overwhelming. The maps of the front are in a state of constant flux. A mere glance serves to indicate what immense possibilities might result from it if we continued our offensive. Our front from Asiago, or better yet, from Schlegen to Venice would run no more than a hundred kilometers. Today our troops are already standing before Tagiamento.

Yesterday the Captain assembled all hands on deck and announced that we would soon head into one of the harbors on Ösel. However the channel which had been cleared of mines was very narrow and by no means safe. There were still two English submarines in the Gulf of Riga who might make things uncomfortable for us. Four additional English and two Russian submarines have been sighted in the Finnish Gulf and the Gulf of Bothnia. Hence we would have to maintain the strictest discipline on our ship and beyond it. We would get a chance to go ashore on Ösel but we were to resist the tempta-

---

[61] On October 24, 1917, six German and nine Austrian divisions broke through the Italian lines at Caporetto and routed the demoralized Italian army in one of the greatest military victories of the entire war. The Italians retreated all the way to the Piave River before they managed, with the aid of French and English forces, to halt the German-Austrian offensive. It is estimated that Italy lost 300,000 men in the Caporetto campaign and that an equivalent number of men deserted.

tion to bring back "small souvenirs" such as pigs, helmets and rifles.[62] This is the way Cossacks behave, but not Germans.

Unfortunately most of the rumors concerning our heavy losses were confirmed. *Bayern* sustained the most extensive damage. A mine and a torpedo hit crippled her so severely that she had to be beached for emergency repairs. When we met her three days ago, she still had a heavy list because of the 3,000 tons of water in her holds. She will probably head to Kiel for repairs. Less damaging were the two mine explosions suffered by *Grosser Kurfürst* and *Markgraf*. Moreover we have also lost four torpedo boats. But by and large this was not too heavy a price to pay. 1 November 1917.

Just as I was finishing this, a telegram was posted announcing that we had captured 180,000 Italians to date. 1 November 1917.

How time flies! I have neglected my diary for six days. This always happens to me in Kiel. On Sunday we were placidly at rest in the Bay of Danzig when we were suddenly ordered to sail out immediately. Where were we headed? East or West? Since we had refueled so recently, it could only be the latter. I heard that we were to have our bottom scraped in Kiel and then were to come back here right away. This serves to illustrate why we are having a coal shortage. In this fashion each of our ships merely expends a thousand tons of coal.

At about four o'clock on Sunday we weighed anchor. Along the way our fleet tender caught up with us to deliver our men returning from leave. After we had passed the triple blocks we raced back at full speed. By nightfall we sighted the great docking facilities at Schichau. For a long while I continued sunk in thought to gaze into the distance. . . . Twenty-five hours later we sailed past the light tower at Bülk. However we soon learned that in all of Kiel there was not a dock free which

62 The island of Ösel had already surrendered on October 16.

was large enough to accommodate us. Therefore the only solution was to go on to Wilhelmshaven. However before sailing home again to the North Sea we remained in Kiel for a couple of days. We all hoped that we would be able to spend a few days in dock there. 8 November 1917.

Nothing had changed in our "beloved" Wilhelmshaven. Unfortunately time did not allow us to undertake any other repairs than to scrape our bottom. But I happily escaped being assigned to this noxious work. 12 November 1917.

Our victories in Upper Italy have improved the Fatherland's military position but its domestic outlook remains bleak. With some justice we have until now regarded our highest officials' long tenure in office as proof of the essential soundness of our governmental system.[63] When Chancellor von Bethmann-Hollweg resigned three quarters of a year ago, we were dismayed at this unfortunate change in the highest leadership of the Empire in the midst of a war. We disapproved because we knew that any new Chancellor would have to follow in his predecessor's footsteps. Then came Michaelis, "the man with a Bismarckian head." The magic sound of his name made all of Germany breathe a sigh of relief. Prince Michael, the patron saint of Germany! The Bible states somewhere that St. Michael will slay the seven-headed monster. I confess that I, too, entertained these hopes. But to my boundless regret, I soon learned that it was a false hope. The Chancellor was a disappointment from the very first time he appeared before the public. Apparently he found the burdens [of office] too heavy and we were extraordinarily fortunate that we had [Foreign Secretary] von Kühlmann[64] to save the situation. It is my impression that the Chancellor never manifested any independence and allowed the Reichstag majority to bully him into making any declara-

[63] Since the founding of the German Empire in 1871, there had been only five governments, those of Bismarck (1871–90), Caprivi (1890–94), Prince Hohenlohe-Schillingfürst (1894–1900), Bülow (1900–09) and Bethmann-Hollweg (1909–17).

[64] Richard von Kühlmann (1873–1948) was the German Ambassador in Turkey before his appointment as Foreign Secretary in August 1917. He was the only minister of any stature in the Michaelis government and stayed on even after the Chancellor's resignation.

tion it desired. This was particularly evident in his attitude on the so-called Peace Resolution. Instead of curbing the unruly crowd [in the Reichstag], he became its tool.[65] The man who had once uttered the proud statement, "Those who know me will understand that I shall never allow the leadership to be taken out of my hands," [66] [was completely overwhelmed].

In my opinion we suffered a great moral setback when our first bourgeois Chancellor proved to be such a fiasco.[67] Now a Count will once again have to retrieve the reins of the errant chariot of state which have been dragging on the ground to bring it back on the proper road. The Junkers may well congratulate themselves. They could hardly have found better proof for their constant contention that government is "their" profession. Now a seventy-five-year-old man has been placed in charge of the destinies of the Empire. I wish the clever professor all the luck in the world.[68] But damn it, is there no young man in this nation of ours with its seventy million people who is capable of assuming this great responsibility? I am not at all pleased by the advent of the much-heralded parliamentary system of government.[69] But one must

[65] It merely seemed that way. Although Michaelis accepted the Reichstag's Peace Resolution of July 1917 expressing Germany's willingness to conclude a peace of understanding without annexations and indemnities as his official foreign policy, he worked behind the scenes with Generals Hindenburg and Ludendorff of the Army Supreme Command to undermine that resolution and to acquire extensive annexations. In addition, Michaelis refused to implement the Kaiser's promise of equal franchise for Prussia and was a steadfast enemy of the Reichstag and its striving to obtain power over the government.

[66] Michaelis had made this promise in his first Reichstag speech as Chancellor on July 19, 1917.

[67] On October 30, 1917, the Reichstag forced Michaelis to resign from office. On October 9 he had delivered a speech before that body in which he accused the Independent Social Democrats of having fomented the mutiny in the navy. However, he was unable to produce concrete evidence to that effect and was therefore compelled to resign.

[68] Count Georg von Hertling (1843–1919), a former professor of philosophy at the University of Munich, a former leader of the Catholic Centrist Party and most recently Minister-President of Bavaria, succeeded Michaelis as Chancellor on October 30, 1917. He was seventy-four years old at the time.

[69] Hertling was appointed to the chancellorship after a period of protracted negotiations with the parties of the Reichstag. He was forced to accept a five-point program of democratic reforms and was also com-

remember that no unfinished product ever looks beautiful. Therefore I fervently hope and pray that under the aging, but nevertheless strong hands of Count Hertling a new, united and peaceful Germany may arise. 13 November 1917.

Day of prayer and repentance 1917. I am as unrepentant in spirit as I was in 1916. The terrific pressure under which we have been living for the past few days has made this holy day seem more irrelevant than ever. While we were peacefully at rest we were attacked by an English cruiser squadron. Naturally they did not notify us in advance. If they had, the staff and the officers on *Ostfriesland* would not have gotten themselves involved in a chase. According to regulations the entire First Squadron should have been on duty outside of the harbor. However our flagship [the *Ostfriesland*] always received special privileges and was thus tied up in port. As a result, we arrived too late. The Helgoland batteries were already firing in the distance.

Naturally the wildest rumors were making the rounds on our ship. The ships of the *Kaiser* class were supposed to be heavily engaged while *Nürnberg* and *Königsberg* were said to have been trapped between the mine fields and the English force. Furthermore it was rumored that the enemy had disrupted our wireless communication so that we had been out of contact with our *Kaiser*-class ships for the past hour. Our Captain wisely ordered us to stow the tables, benches and seabags and at about three o'clock (on November 17) our five puny ships sailed out, *Posen* in the lead. Needless to say, we soon turned about again. Apparently it was still too dangerous for us out there. As we passed by the outer blocks we met the two flagships *Ostfriesland* and *Baden*. At two o'clock we sailed out for a sortie to avoid giving the appearance that we were remiss in our responsibilities. We might just as well have chased the moon. However the next day it enabled our Admiralty

pelled to appoint a number of prominent party leaders into his cabinet. The unorthodox nature of Hertling's appointment (in the past the Kaiser had simply named a chancellor without troubling to consult anyone) was widely regarded by Germans as signifying the advent of the parliamentary system of government.

staff to issue a triumphant statement that the English had withdrawn in the face of our superior force.[70] The English were in the happy position of being able to issue a similar report. Consequently both sides spent the remainder of Sunday in a state of highest bliss.

Since our gear remained stowed away, we concluded that we would soon embark on a mission of our own. I served as a messenger on the deck and had to present our sailing orders to the Officer of the Watch. Beneath the heading "Purpose of sortie" there were a number of question marks. The Officer of the Watch muttered under his breath, "Evidently there is no purpose!" "But on the contrary, Herr Leutnant," I responded impertinently, "our purpose is to save coal!"

At dawn our trip became more interesting when we began to encounter a number of floating mines. I marveled at one of the officers on *Ostfriesland* who kept firing at the mines without ever hitting any of them. It required the expenditure of a good deal of ammunition by our torpedo boats before these dangerous "sea roses" were sunk. In the evening we returned to Voslapp Roads without any further losses. But I understand that about twenty crew members of *Königsberg* were killed. Now, however, we are back at peace and we can rest on our laurels for a while. 21 November 1917.

About two months ago an incident took place on *Westfalen* which sums up our current state of feeling to perfection. It occurred at about the time when the shameful sentences for the mutineers were handed down. These men were not in the least intimidated by this draconian measure. In fact the entire crew refused to load coal. Of course this crisis, too, was precipitated by inadequate rations. Although I tried to discover some more immediate and related causes, I came up with nothing. Moreover it will serve no useful purpose to reiterate all the ridiculous rumors which are being spread about it. *West-*

[70] The naval action of November 17 took place at the line of mines formed off Horns Reef and Terschelling when some German minesweepers unexpectedly ran into an English light cruiser and destroyer squadron. Neither side inflicted any damage, and the English force turned away before German heavy units could rush to the scene.

falen's crew is extremely suspicious because some of their men were implicated by detectives masquerading in sailor's uniforms. However I am certain that prison terms of forty years and six death sentences were handed down. It is said that three of the men have already been executed(?).[71] This will no doubt raise quite an uproar at the next session of the Reichstag. In today's newspaper I read that a request for new war credits has already been submitted. If it is approved, the Imperial Navy could use its share of the funds to build a number of new prisons.

If all goes well and we are lucky, our ship will go into dock [for repairs] on [November] 28. Tomorrow morning, however, the entire fleet will conduct major maneuvers to honor some visiting Austro-Hungarian journalists. Hence we shall once more waste an incredible amount of coal. All our battleships with the exception of *Bayern* and *Thüringen* are again in a state of battle readiness. We all hoped that nothing would happen to any of the other ships so that we would be able to go into dock.

We just met two torpedo boats carrying the reporters. It would serve them right if the sea was a little rough. We all wished that the reporters would come down with a little dose of seasickness. 23 November 1917.

Seldom, if ever, has such an evil wish come true so quickly. Without fear of exaggerating I can honestly say that in all my years in the navy I have never seen such a raging tempest upon the North Sea. If the storm does not cause any destruction we may consider it as a blessing because it shall have saved us an enormous quantity of coal, many tons of lubricating oil and other expensive materials.

It was a regular tempest and we had a great deal of difficulty in reaching port. Since the strong winds buffeted our ship in

[71] On August 16, 1917, the stokers on *Westfalen* staged a strike because they had not received extra rations for coaling. When the leaders of the strike were arrested, the ship's captain was threatened with violence. On October 30 four of the ringleaders were sentenced to death on the basis of evidence supplied by *agents provocateurs*, but these sentences were commuted to long-term prison sentences on November 19.

all directions, we were fortunate to pass through the locks without damage. I shall not soon forget this experience. There were times when we were in actual danger of being swept overboard. With the greatest effort we [finally] tied up at the pier. A number of times it looked as though we would be driven against some other ship in the harbor. If any one of our cables had snapped under the terrific pressure we would now most certainly be in dock. What a shame!! This way we are still not sure whether we will go in. [However,] much to our satisfaction, the reporters have left without being able to gape at the navigational skill of our commanders.

In another two weeks it will be a year since the Kaiser so generously made an offer of peace to our enemies. In the momentary excitement of the time we all felt that peace was just around the corner. But our sincere peace move was rudely rejected by France and England. Thereupon the Kaiser called upon our troops to steel themselves [for the final assault]. We were all convinced that the Kaiser would now overcome his humanitarian scruples and allow us to use our new secret bombs. I even heard our First Officer, now Captain ———, say, "In two months the English shall come crawling to us on their knees begging for peace. . . ."

Now we are cured of these fantastic hopes. Our campaign of unrestricted submarine warfare and the Russian Revolution are our only hope now. Why do I repeat all this? This disappointment has made the entire population skeptical about any new hopes for peace. How would we have felt a year ago if our peace offer would not have worked to our benefit but that of Russia? However it seems as if the impossible has come true. The new Russian government has just extended Germany an offer of a peace of understanding.[72] We received official word of this happy event a half an hour ago. Right now they [the

[72] On November 7, 1917, one day after assuming power, the new Bolshevik government of Russia issued its Peace Decree inviting all the belligerent powers to conclude a peace without annexations and indemnities. When the Allies failed to respond to the offer, the Russian government began to take steps to negotiate a separate peace with the Central Powers.

Russians] seem to prefer [to treat with] our Austro-Hungarian allies but surely they will not negotiate without our consent.

Currently there is much talk that we are about to launch a great offensive against the West. I am quite willing to concede that this sounds more plausible than last year's story about the gas bombs. Now that the Austrians should be able to hold the Eastern front by themselves, we will be able to devote our undivided energies to beating the enemy in the West before the Americans have a chance to step into the breach. 30 November 1917.

I had just finished writing the above entries when the whole crew was summoned on deck. Naturally we all thought that it had something to do with the peace offer. Instead we were greatly disappointed and our happy mood vanished when the Captain read out the jail and death sentences which had been pronounced against our comrades on *Westfalen*. Sentenced to death . . . Ten years imprisonment . . . Twelve years imprisonment . . . Fifteen years imprisonment. . . .[73] Oh what fateful times we live in! Also on 30 November 1917.

The surface of the North Sea is hardly ever as flat and calm as a freshly polished mirror. I can only remember five such lovely days as this. [After all] the North Sea is justly famed and feared for its wildness and its unruliness. But I have never before witnessed such a violent storm as the one that raged yesterday and last night. The storm-tossed waters tore into the ground and changed the basin of the German Sound into a mad, seething witches' cauldron. Real tidal waves kept slamming against the sides of the ship and made it shake and rock like a baby's crib. It was comforting to know that our thick iron walls could withstand this attack of the elements. I kept climbing on deck to gaze at the powerful and lovely play of the ocean breakers. But I was careful not to stay too long because the whistling northeaster penetrated to one's very bones. In any case, however, I shall long remember this fantastic

[73] See Note 70.

scene on the North Sea. I found it much more exciting than its mirror-polish calmness.

I was busily at work writing when I heard the boatman of the watch shout something which was greeted by cries of jubilation. I stepped closer. What was it? An armistice with Russia? Yes, an armistice had just been concluded by the commanding general, Prince Leopold.[74] Thank God! At last a glimmer of light in these dark times. However a general peace is still a long way off. 3 December 1917.

Everywhere I go there is talk of the Russian-Rumanian cease-fire.[75] Most of the men feel that a general peace will be concluded in a matter of months. The men always object vehemently when I enter the discussion and insist that the war will last at least another three to four years. I am quite willing to concede that we may be able to force a few nations, maybe Italy and France, to surrender. Many of the men feel that it will not be too difficult after that to defeat the English Empire and the great American nation. But will they not find it possible to construct three million tons of shipping a year? I am sure that they will ultimately find a way to prevent our large-scale sinking [of their ships]. Greater things than that have already been accomplished. In order to obtain a true picture [of the situation] I try to look at things from the point of view of the English, the Russians and the Americans. If I were one of them, I would take out a world map and say to the German peering over my shoulder: So you want to beat us? Just compare our population and the extent of our territory to yours. Look at our forests, our fields of grain, visit our steel mills, our gold-mines, take note of our herds of cattle and our tropical plantations and compare them to what you have to offer. This

[74] On November 28, 1917, the German government announced its willingness to negotiate a peace with Russia. On December 3 pre-armistice talks commenced at Brest-Litovsk and two days later a cease-fire was concluded by Field Marshal Prince Leopold of Bavaria (1846–1930), the Commander in Chief of the Eastern Front.

[75] Rumania signed an armistice with the Central Powers on December 9, 1917.

should open your eyes and give you a better picture of our relative power. Although you may well still win a few more battles and defeat a few more countries, we shall nevertheless win in the end. We English will cut you off from the sea until you are ready to recognize that the world belongs to us and that you merely deserve to play the role of a policeman in our worldwide empire. Later on if you mend your ways and give up your ambitious plans, we may return you to your prewar status of a junior partner in our English world. This is the only way I would think if I were an Englishman or a Yankee.

By the same token the Russian, too, can point to the huge area and wealth of his country. Undoubtedly he, too, will recognize that our army has accomplished a number of miracles. And although one imperial and five royal crowns are wallowing in the dust, [he may nevertheless still maintain] that we only occupy a few hundred square miles of his soil. Our armies have only captured a few advance outposts, the main columns of the Anglo-American world empire still stand strong and unshaken. And this is something which most of the people of Central Europe do not realize.

When I express these thoughts to my comrades, they merely laugh at me and regard me as insane. Admittedly there are a number of factors which might militate against such an infinitely long war. However so long as the present situation remains unchanged, I regard the factors which I have just enumerated to be much more significant. Although a worldwide revolution or a general collapse might well alter the situation, it is not advisable to hope for miracles. 4 December 1917.

Today we went out on patrol again. I hoped that it would be my last one. If we are in luck, we will finally head into dock on [December] 17. We have generously been granted fourteen days of leave. I hope that it will be my last one on H.M.S. *Helgoland*. Our older men are gradually being transferred and thirty new recruits have already arrived [to take their places]. There seems to be a plan in the offing to introduce a new—

rather the old–spirit in the navy. The discipline of the men who have already served five, six and seven years has deteriorated greatly. Our lieutenants do not feel that they are as respected as they should be. Hence they are reviving the stupid [routines] which ruined my devotion to the service even while we were still at peace.

Now the Captain will resume inspecting our lockers; we will have an overabundance of absurd lectures, rifle drills and stultifying battle practice. Consequently I shall be extremely glad when I am transferred. I would rather go to the trenches in Flanders than to bear this spiritually stultifying routine for another year. I would rather do the hardest work if it only had some visible reason or purpose behind it. Best of all, I would prefer to be stationed in Turkey, Bulgaria, or Rumania or some other foreign country. But in all probability I shall conclude my naval career with a mine-sweeping division, a harbor patrol boat or some trawler. But I would welcome any change. 10 December 1917.

As I write these lines I am breathing the sweet air of home. This will be the last chapter of this book. Moreover the next section will also bear a different title than "My Experiences on H.M.S. *Helgoland*." In a few more hours my lovely Christmas leave will vanish for all eternity. Each of its hours flew by with lightning speed. How long has it been since my nice visit to Günzburg and Krumbach? As soon as I return to Wilhelmshaven, I shall depart from the old and beloved ship on which I spent so many sad and so many happy hours. However since I realize that I am easily replaceable, I shall not find it difficult to leave. No mental efforts are demanded and none are given on His Majesty's ships. Hence I can safely close the story of a fifth of my lifetime without any sorrow. Maybe at some later date I shall again have a more favorable opinion of the navy but it will take a long time for my bitterness to disappear.

The rays of the wintery sun are slowly sinking behind the Kalchreuther mountain.

End of Book V

Six

Begun on Candlemas Day (February 2), 1918.

I must now fill the longest gap in my diary. Since I expected to be transferred any day, I did not think that I would have to start describing my experiences on *Helgoland* again. When I began the last book I asked the question: Will it suffice? Will I fill it completely or only in part? Of course I was referring to the end of the war. Since that time nine months have flown by and now I hardly dare to ask the same question again. It would be foolish to maintain that we have not made considerable progress in the direction of peace. Still the end is yet nowhere in sight. While the guns roared on the battlefields the mysterious progress of history has converted former allies into foes. Our unparalleled military victories have paved an easy road for our negotiators to Brest-Litovsk. And the German armies are now moving toward the West to accomplish the greatest feat in the history of the world.

What a striking contrast! The representatives of the German military autocracy sit haggling over the green negotiating table, arguing over the future outlines of the map of Europe with Jews and Jacobins.[1] But one cannot escape from reality. I understand that we are demanding land, fertile, black soil of the Russian colossus. However Trotsky [2] cleverly inundates the world with his well-conceived speeches and distributes glistening gold among his cohorts in Central Europe. Not without success. The lower classes are seething with discontent. If there were only someone who could channel that discontent, a great eruption would become virtually inevitable. But as it stands right now, the pressure from below noisily erupts here and there and soon dissipates itself. When it began in Austria it looked rather serious but then it quieted down again.[3] By subterranean means it then spread north and at present Berlin and Hamburg are the focal points of the disturbances.[4] But the harshness of life, the impact of events and the threats of the

---

[1] The Russian delegation at Brest-Litovsk at first included two Jews Adolf Joffe and Leo Kamenev. In January 1918 another Jew Leon Trotsky took over the leadership of the delegation. The German delegation consisted of General Max Hoffman, Baron von Rosenberg and Major Brinkmann. Later the German Foreign Secretary, Richard von Kühlmann, assumed leadership over the German contingent.

[2] Leon Trotsky (1879–1940), a brilliant revolutionary and chairman of the Petrograd Soviet, was also Commissar for Foreign Affairs. He very cleverly sought to delay and protract the negotiations at Brest-Litovsk by engaging in long harangues and disputations on the "right of self-determination of peoples" while Bolshevik propaganda was disseminated throughout Europe and especially among the German and Austrian armies.

[3] In January 1918 Austria's munition workers went on strike over the prolongation of the war and a reduction in their bread rations. The strike was particularly intense in Vienna and seemed so ominous that the Austrian royal family fled from Vienna to the protection of the army. Later on that month, the strike spread to the dock workers at the Austrian naval base at Cattaro, where it resulted in a rebellion among the ships of the Austrian navy which were lying in that harbor. The crews hoisted the red flag and placed their officers under arrest. Finally, the naval revolt was suppressed by the timely intervention of German submarines, which threatened to blow the mutineers out of the water.

[4] On January 28, 1918, a major strike erupted among the munition and metal workers of Berlin, 180,000 of whom laid down their tools. In subsequent days the strike spread to Hamburg, Leipzig, Cologne, Breslau and Munich and involved more than a million workers. The most important reasons for the strike were the failure of the Prussian franchise reform, the imminent breakdown of the peace negotiations at Brest-Litovsk and the inequitable distribution of food.

mailed fist will soon put a stop to it.[5] Then our energies will probably swing around in the form of Mackensen's battalions to threaten the Balkans and Hindenburg's picture will rise up from the trenches between Nieuport and Belfort. And then as soon as these equally vainly spent energies are restored, they will flow toward some other place where they are urgently needed. . . .

But stop! I am again making predictions which will soon become laughable. I would rather stick to the facts and to write only about the things that really exist and happen. Why make excursions into Utopia when the present is so interesting?

The *Helgoland* has now been in dock for a full eight weeks and the dirt becomes more unbearable every day. One can hardly touch anything without soiling one's hands. The major part of our work is finished and eighty percent of the men have nothing better to do than to keep an eye out for the comings and goings of the Detail Officer. Although he is a wonderful person, it would not do to be caught sleeping by him. I have rarely had it so easy and earned so much money. Since I enjoy making shoes out of hemp, I earn a considerable amount of money. I have set up a workshop for myself in the bakery and can barely keep up with the demand. Everyone is excited about politics. But I consciously avoid becoming involved. I have long since concluded that all attempts to improve our lot are bound to fail because of the stupidity and evil ways of my fellow proletarians. Here everyone has to look out for himself. . . .

Last week, on Thursday morning, like wild fire the news spread through the ship that some Socialist leaflets had been discovered. Within minutes we knew all about it. Groups of men crowded around the find and the leaflets were passed from hand to hand. In my opinion the leaflets contained much truth

[5] The government refused to bargain with the strikers. The army intervened, militarized many factories, and called upon the workers to return to their jobs on penalty of desertion. The police were ordered to break up demonstrations and the more radical workers were either arrested or inducted into the army. These harsh measures—the mailed fist—caused the strike to peter out at the beginning of February.

with which was interspersed a motley mixture of silly plati-
tudes and phrases. "If Germany is not to be ruled by the saber,
you must prepare for a general strike!" [6] Of course the leaflets
were unsigned and bore no place of publication. However they
did create a considerable stir and by noon the Captain knew all
about them. He made us assemble on deck and had the Division Officers warn each one of us not to participate in this sort
of nonsense. On the other hand, he expressed gratification that
the leaflets were handed over to him immediately and asked us
to continue to do so in the future.

Everything appeared normal on deck. The workers did not
seem any lazier than usual and only as I passed close by did I
hear one of them call, "Starting tomorrow we shall stop this
hammering." He did not mean the hammering of the tools but
the fighting at the front. Evidently he believed that our troops
would soon lay down their arms. On Friday we had to assemble on deck once more. The Captain announced that the mass
meeting and the resulting disturbances compelled him to can-
cel all shore leaves.

At noon almost all the workers downed their tools. They did
it very quickly and with great assurance. The sailors were delighted and advised the workers never to come back again. At
1:30 we all waited on deck to watch the arrival of the strike-
breakers. As was to be expected, the twenty-five-man work
crew which boarded the ship was made up primarily of old
men and young boys. But since it was a lovely springlike day,
a considerable number of them disappeared during the course
of the afternoon. . . .

We have received grave news from some of the cities. Even
the workers of the Imperial Navy Yard in Kiel were on strike.
However I felt confident that it would not develop into a general strike. The most important requisite for it, an empty,

[6] The January strike of 1918 was largely directed against the army and
the domination by the military of the government. The Socialists held the
army responsible for the failure to obtain an early peace at Brest-Litovsk.
They also resented the army's maintenance of a state of siege, its censor-
ship of the press and its political interference and opposition to reform.

grumbling stomach, was lacking. Now it grumbles very softly. Last spring things were much worse. Moreover this time we realize what they are up to and therefore will not support them. On Saturday morning all the workers returned to work. They maintained that the government's reply had been post-poned until Monday morning and that if it turned out to be unsatisfactory they would resume their strike. But we shall have to see about that.[7] 2 January 1917.[8]

One can hardly recognize our *Helgoland* since three days ago. One's feet no longer stick to the floor, the walls and the decks are painted glistening white and one can even touch the decks without getting one's hands all black. I think that it is simply lovely. Although it meant working for three days, it was well worth the effort. One's ear nerves refuse to believe that the mad hammering of the hydraulic riveters is over. But our time in dock is also over. Right now our sights and directional sys-tems are being adjusted and in a few days we shall start our trip to Kiel. I shall not go along because my transfer is ex-pected momentarily.

Today is a day of historic importance. We have just signed a peace treaty with the new Ukrainian Republic. Regardless of how one may feel about it, it is of inestimable economic and military value to us. As a result, next fall we shall have bread and plenty of butter to go along with it. Rumania averted our collapse last year; this year the fertile black soil [of the Ukraine] will serve this same purpose.[9]

But what is happening up north between Brest-Litovsk and Petrograd? I fear that the Prussians will have to step in to

[7] The harshness of the military measures forced the workers to resume work on February 5 despite the government's refusal to negotiate with them.

[8] The author's date is incorrect. It should not read January 2, but February 2, 1918.

[9] On February 9 the Central Powers signed a peace treaty with the newly formed Ukrainian Republic which provided for the immediate delivery of wheat to the starving populations of Austria and Germany. The Ukrainian peace was therefore frequently called the "Bread Peace."

establish some law and order.[10] Maybe then some of our fleet
will tie up at Kronstadt and Reval while the banners of our
cavalry wave over the Peterhof.[11] What useless fantasies!
8 February 1918.

PEACE WITH RUSSIA![12]

If our newspapers had printed this headline a year ago, all of
Central Europe would most certainly have gone berserk with
joy. But what is Russia now? At this time last year the oldest
imperial throne of Europe was completely undermined in cold
blood because the ruler [the Tsar] toyed with the idea of coming to terms with his enemies. Inevitably a comparison with
the French Revolution comes to mind. If I am not wholly mistaken, we are already facing the last act—Marat[13] or the guil-
lotine. Robespierre[14] and Danton[15]—in this case, Kerensky and

[10] The impotence of the Soviet Russian regime enabled nationalists in
the Baltic states of Courtland, Estonia, Latvia and Lithuania to rise up
against their former masters in an effort to win their independence.

[11] This was the name of the Tsar's summer palace on the Gulf of
Finland.

[12] This was not an actual peace, but an attempt to implement Trotsky's
famous formula "neither war nor peace." On February 10 the Soviets,
incensed at Germany's signing of a separate peace treaty with the Ukraine
and the German demand for the liberation of other nationalities from
the former Russian Empire, declared that they considered the war over
even without the formality of a treaty. The German army replied by
resuming its offensive and beginning to march on Petrograd on February
18. Since the Russians were in no position to offer any resistance, it seemed
as though the German armies might well occupy the Russian capital.

[13] Jean Paul Marat (1743-93), a French physician, made a name for
himself during the French Revolution by his appeals to violence. He was
largely responsible for the massacre of the inmates of the Parisian prisons
in September 1792 and at the time of his assassination by a royalist sym-
pathizer was about to proscribe the more moderate revolutionaries
belonging to the political faction of the Gironde.

[14] Maximilien de Robespierre (1758-94), the ruthless leader of the
radical Jacobins of the French Revolution, waged a reign of terror against
the enemies of the French Republic from 1793 to 1794. When even the
radicals felt threatened by Robespierre, they instigated a plot against him
and arrested and executed him during the Thermidorean Reaction.

[15] Georges Danton (1759-94), a right-wing Jacobin leader during the
Reign of Terror, fell out with Robespierre when he wanted to call a halt
to the Revolution and sign a peace with England. Robespierre used
Danton's financial indiscretions to hail him before the revolutionary tribunal and had him and his supporters executed for treason on April 6, 1794.

Lenin—have already played out their parts. And in this case, Wilhelm II will play the role of Napoleon in terminating this revolution.

Within hours after Lenin [16] had signed the demobilization order, the [Russian] prisoners of war marched singing through the streets of Wilhelmshaven to buy themselves souvenirs. The bells tolled, a few flags were flown, but otherwise there were no signs of raucous and exuberant jubilation. When we heard that the Russians refused to sign the peace treaty, we all felt dreadfully depressed. What was the real meaning of this refusal to go through with this formality? Virtually all of our newspapers were skeptical and regarded it as a delaying action on Herr Trotsky's part. Just now we have come to realize how sound this interpretation was. I have always puzzled why we kept postponing our offensive against the West. This is probably the reason for it. Therefore we shall again have to revert to our system of "offensive defense" to keep our enemies off our necks. Thus my theory of a second Seven Years' War is again borne out. . . .

During our last few days in dock everything proceeded smoothly and swiftly because we were eager to depart for Kiel. On the last day we loaded up on coal. The weather was miserable. The rain poured down on the hard-working men for eight hours. I, too, emerged without a dry stitch of clothing on my body. In spite of that, we sailed out that very same evening. For a change, I almost looked forward to seeing the brown tidal waters of the German Bight. Yet I was glad when we sighted the bright lights of Neuwerk because this signified that my watch was over. At two o'clock in the morning we passed through the locks at Brunsbüttel. We sailed at an even speed and by dawn we had put about half of the canal's length behind us.

[16] On February 10, 1918, Vladimir Lenin (1870–1924), the architect of the Bolshevik Revolution, as the head of the Council of Peoples' Commissars announced Russia's refusal to abide by Germany's harsh peace terms, proclaimed that the war was over for Russia, demobilized her armies and implemented Trotzky's "neither war nor peace" formula in the hope that Russia's territorial losses could thus be minimized.

For our first assignment in Kiel we had a thirty-six-hour shakedown cruise to test our engines. Thank God that the friendly Baltic is now the most peaceful and secure waterway in the world. It is a real pleasure to sail about without concern or worry. The "left lobe of Germany's lung" is free of all harmful bacilli. If this were only true of the right one as well. . . .

It has been a long time since we cursed, swore and muttered so profusely as in the past few days and yesterday in particular. It seemed as though we were all possessed by a devil. We were all so nervous and irritable that we behaved atrociously. Once more the demand that we perform useless and senseless work thoroughly undermined our morale. Every once in a while one of our higher officers takes it into his head to revive some of the nicer tricks which were practiced in peacetime. Thus yesterday they tried out one of their most effective tricks by making us go to all the trouble connected with clearing the ship for action. Surely no one will deny the usefulness of practicing battle stations, especially when we are so out of practice. But when it is conducted as it was yesterday, it turns into a cruel and inhuman harassment. They subjected our lockers to the most painstaking inspection, checking that they contained no other articles than those stipulated by the regulations. Our officers don't give a damn if our favorite and valued possessions are ruined in the seabags. [Consequently] everything is carelessly thrown into the storage hold. Invariably everything which winds up near the bottom of this great pile is either squashed or broken. No wonder we are all fed up with this vile nonsense. We all muttered bitterly about the senselessness and wastefulness of this procedure. However other factors also contributed to the creation of an explosive situation on board. We were kept on duty from early in the morning till late at night and when the Executive Officer [was informed of our complaints] he said with apparent helplessness: "Yes, after all, the First Artillery Officer needs the men." However so long as our rations remain tolerable, nothing will happen.

At present the German people are again manifesting incredible patience and discipline. Without a murmur they accept the fact that our armies have again begun to roll eastward. When [the Russians] failed to sign our peace treaty, we abrogated the cease-fire. The reports from the front sound wonderful: "Reval occupied; Minsk has been reached, Dünaburg taken, 1,400 guns and 8,000 prisoners captured"—what more could one want? Our newspapers are filled with cries [for help] from the Ukrainians, the Balts, the Estonians, the Latvians and the Finns.[17] I must admit that I find these developments immensely gratifying, primarily because they so clearly reveal the failure of the Communist system. For a time it seemed as though the Socialist tree would sprout up to heaven. Now, however, its lush growth has been cut back and the gardener who did it was Ludendorff. How this would delight me, if the lack of understanding by our "superiors" did not spoil it all!

Here I am and I can already count the hours which I will have to spend on *Helgoland* on the fingers of my hand. My transfer arrived this morning. All my things are packed; only pen and ink remain to be thrown in on top. I leave without sorrow and regret. Where will my destiny take me? First thing tomorrow morning I and twenty-nine others shall go by train to Wilhelmshaven and [report to the replacement] center.

on h.m.s. *Wittelsbach*

Yes, this is the way it is. According to my reckoning I shall serve out my inglorious military career on H.M.S. *Wittelsbach*. I am writing these lines in the lovely reading room of this

[17] On February 18, 1917, the German army began a virtually unopposed march into Russia in an effort to compel that country to sign a separate peace. Germany's advance was greeted as a blessing by the subject nationalities of the Russian Empire, who appealed for aid in liberating themselves from their former master.

ancient decommissioned ship. Although there is no longer any point to recording my personal experiences, I really should not ignore my new impressions and the new atmosphere [in which I find myself]. Possibly I ought to be thankful that I have found myself a "bombproof shelter," but I find it difficult to allow my restless spirit and energies to go to waste while I laze peacefully in bed. I would have been happier to have found a berth on one of our troop transports heading for Finland. I might even have arranged this if it had not been for—shall I call it treachery or luck—the chief petty officer of *Lothringen*, who was looking for members for his band. Somehow he must have found out that my friend Jub and I were awaiting assignment in the Second Company. He appeared at the Personnel Office before noon and despite our loud objections put in a request for us. Thereupon I volunteered for an auxiliary cruiser [lying] in Geestemünde and it almost worked. I was properly paid, was issued some rations and a railroad ticket. I was just about to take my bag down to the railroad station, when an office orderly arrived and asked for Seaman First Class Stumpf. He informed me that I had to stay here because an order from the Division had just arrived which assigned me to the *Lothringen*. "All right, let's go to the *Lothringen*," I said but I first had to return my money, my train ticket and the bacon.

Today my conscience compels me to acknowledge an institution which is commonly held in disrepute. I am referring to our holy bureaucracy. During my brief stay here in the [Replacement] Company, I acquired something bordering on respect for its achievements. Despite all the confusion, the contradictory orders and the daily changes, it seemed to function flawlessly. Although each one of us tried to arrange things to his advantage, to fake, to malinger, everything still functioned smoothly. Or at least everyone pretended that the job he had been assigned was the one he had wanted all along. Many of the practices which I formerly condemned as useless and incomprehensible now appear in an entirely new light.

Moreover I was also amazed how quickly the enervating dullness which depressed the spirits of my comrades who lived in the deadening atmosphere on the ships vanished. I never experienced such friendliness before and it seemed to me that my new environment was responsible for fostering an entirely different outlook on life. Seldom before have I ever laughed so much as during my one day's stay in Hamburg. The impudent behavior of some of the females of that city was simply unbelievable.

The grand and imposing business buildings, however, made a more lasting impression upon me. As I stood before Herr Ballin's [18] domain, the huge palace of the Hamburg-Amerika Line, I was overcome by melancholia. It was a shame that its many hundreds of windows were all boarded up. Hamburg had been harder hit by the war than any but the front line areas. The business activities and the food situation of this metropolis are in desperate straits. Hamburg has been completely cut off from the outside world. So far as I know, she does not possess any significant war industries to make up for that loss. An unnatural silence prevailed in all the offices and the empty, yawning warehouses. Nevertheless when my train left Hamburg, I carried away the impression that a brilliant future lay ahead for this important metropolis. At nine o'clock I arrived at the familiar railroad station at Bremen and was none too pleased when I saw a poor devil in irons—a deserter—being marched off. At the stroke of two our fast-moving column reached the new Rüstringer Barracks. As might have been expected, nothing had been done to prepare for our arrival. In spite of that, we soon fell into a deep and peaceful sleep on the hard wooden floor.

What would become of us now? Would I be in luck, or was I fated to continue plying the seas on some trawler? I could hardly have cared less. Any change would have been welcome

---

[18] Albert Ballin (1857-1918) was the president of the Hamburg-Amerika shipping line, one of Germany's largest shipbuilders and a close personal friend of the Kaiser. He committed suicide during the November 1918 Revolution.

to me. I tried to make myself as inconspicuous as possible. The sergeant at the Personnel Office, however, acted unusually important and secretive. He asked all the men about their trade, how many years they had spent in the service, the number of times they had been punished, etc. Then he snapped, "All [able-bodied] seamen step forward." Only Justav Heidke stepped forward with decision. "Are there no more of you? We need some experienced hands for Finland." Now suddenly we all volunteered and insisted that we had experience. "No more than eighteen men!" he shouted. Thereupon I and one other man at the end of the line stepped back. . . .

The men harbored all sorts of strange notions about their "trip to Finland." Although none of them possessed more than a capital of ten marks, each of them felt that he would strike it rich there. As the Berliner saying goes, they all wanted to do some "pilfering."

I was not at all pleased with the food [we were served at the barracks]—turnips again. In the afternoon we fetched our bags from the railroad station. At muster on the following morning a few more comrades were taken away. The men who had already received their assignments were issued gas masks, rifles, woolen blankets and other good things. But I got nothing. At noon the petty officer whom I have already mentioned appeared and asked for the "two musicians." "I don't feel like going," said I, but he replied sternly: "I don't care whether you like it or not, I shall go to the Personnel Office and will have you transferred." "I don't care. Good-bye," I responded.

[Later on] an orderly came and asked if there were still any unassigned Seamen First Class present. I volunteered with alacrity. But my enthusiasm declined somewhat when I found out at the Personnel Office that it was an assignment for a fairly large ship. Nevertheless I agreed to everything, confident that I could still escape the clutches of the chief petty officer. I have already described what happened after that.

Right now I am on *Wittelsbach* and don't feel too comfortable. In contrast to our reception in the [Replacement] Company, we were badly received here. It required a considerable effort on our part even to obtain our bread rations. Still, we are not raw recruits and know our way about. I am not at all pleased with the very long hours of duty, although they are not at all taxing. Here we only get the afternoon off on Wednesdays and Saturdays. And patrol duty! Every second day. I had nearly forgotten what this was like on the *Helgoland*. Still, there are a number of advantages, above all the room in which I am presently writing. It was formerly the officers' mess and is now used as a reading and writing room for the crew. Also the ship is very quiet and there is plenty of space. Each of us can have as many lockers as he pleases. What I appreciate the most, however, is the abundant supply of fresh air everywhere. Now I no longer wake up with a headache and a sore throat every morning. We are virtually the only ones who sleep in the forward battery. The only drawback is that I have to serve in the band. 8 March 1918.

If at some future date someone were to read my diary, he would surely be astonished at my omission of the peace which we concluded with Russia eight days ago.[19] On the other hand, this may also serve as proof how unimpressed we were by this great event. Our grandchildren will be amazed that we did not burst with pride and self-confidence after our victories over five kingdoms and the largest empire in the world. They make the glories of the Napoleonic campaigns pale into insignificance. I wonder if there will be another Ranke or a Treitschke[20] with sufficient facility in the German language to write a worthy memorial of them. To me this represents an even more difficult task than what our two divine heroes Hindenburg and Ludendorff have accomplished. Only our grandchildren and our great-grandchildren will really appre-

[19] The author is referring to the Peace of Brest-Litovsk of March 3, 1918, by which Russia surrendered Poland, Lithuania, Estonia, Latvia, Finland and the Ukraine to German control. To Turkey, Russia ceded Kars, Ardahan and Batum.

[20] Leopold von Ranke (1795–1886) and Heinrich von Treitschke (1834–96) were two of Germany's most renowned historians. They were both highly nationalistic and supported the warlike manner of Germany's unification by Bismarck.

ciate what occurred during the years between 1914 and 1919. It requires a certain amount of perspective to overlook the small details and insignificant events.

I am confident that the German troops could have performed even more brilliantly if the men and the officers were not so divided. If the private and the lieutenant had been able to march into battle with common ideals, it would have been simply magnificent! If each of our soldiers knew that he was fighting for his home and his own land, then we might have fought even more valiantly than the Serbians. How sad it is to realize that our class will still be homeless after the war and that we shall again be at the mercy of the landlords. If we could only manage to shorten the war by twenty days, it would save millions which could be used to give every soldier a little cottage and a square kilometer of land. But this land would have to be inalienable and free from all debts so that the speculators could not snatch it away from us.

Our great foe Lloyd George is planning something like that for the English soldiers. If one may believe the newspapers, he wishes to spend a billion marks to build homes for the soldiers. I simply must take off my hat to such a man! All honor to the statesman who understands the temper of his times. Without a doubt, the English example may serve as a potent catalyst for us. However it is precisely in this matter that I would like to see our leaders seize the initiative. If they did this our men at the front would not always grumble bitterly: "Why am I doing all this? For whom am I suffering and risking my life? For my home, my workshop, my office? No! For the Junkers, the capitalists and for the military autocracy!" Unfortunately one hears this sort of talk everywhere. And it is true. Unfortunately, it is all too true!

A horrible easterly wind has been blowing all day. If it were not for the fact that the sun manages to break through now and then, it would be impossible to stay out in the open. Fateful and foreboding storm clouds are drifting from East to West and are concentrating ominously over Nieuport and the Sundgau.[21] If I am not mistaken, the storm will break loose at any time. I hope that it will all end well. 9 March 1918.

We have a remarkable Executive Officer here on the *Lothringen-Wittelsbach*.[22] He is completely immersed in politics and gives us weekly lectures on that subject. Although he is uncommonly serious about everything he says, he is not at all convincing and I frequently feel an urge to contradict him. The content and point of view of his lectures seem to come straight from the headlines of the *Deutsche Tageszeitung*.[23]

In his first lecture he discussed the Prussian electoral system. He took great pains not to mention its faults, but kept repeating over and over that it would be a crime to divide the people over this issue at the present time. There would be time enough for that after the war. The worker was much more concerned with such matters as food, clothing and better wages. . . . I could have disproven his superficial arguments with ease since they depended on the ignorance of his audience. A single reference to the Easter Message would have been enough to refute him thoroughly.

The second lecture, delivered by a gentleman from the League for Land Reform, was altogether different. Although it was not lacking in barbs aimed against the Reichstag, these barbs were well justified. This old and insignificant-looking little man was a brilliant speaker and each one of his arguments struck a responsive chord in my heart—and as I observed—in the hearts of others as well. We owe our Executive Officer a debt of gratitude for this lecture. 10 March 1918.

[21] The cessation of hostilities in the East permitted General Ludendorff to move the bulk of his armies westward to launch an ambitious spring offensive against the English. Ludendorff hoped that his troops would manage to effect a breakthrough and that the war could thus still be won.

[22] Stumpf had been assigned to an ancient, decommissioned battleship, the *Wittelsbach*, which was part of a flotilla of several such vessels under the command of the *Lothringen*. Ships of that sort were frequently commanded by one set of officers and it was not uncommon for the crews to be transferred back and forth. In fact, Stumpf was later assigned to serve on the *Lothringen*.

[23] The *Deutsche Tageszeitung* was a Conservative, Pan-German newspaper published in Berlin, which generally opposed all proposals for political reform.

Once again our entire attention is focused on our great offensive in the West. And once again, gas, that famous blue and yellow gas,[24] will lead us to a total victory. Hindenburg himself indicated that we now possess a superiority in men as well as in guns, shells, tanks and gas. This revived our courage and made even the suspicious ones among us open their pockets to buy the new, eighth series of war bonds. However I am convinced that the moral stamina of our allies, and maybe even our own, will collapse if our offensive fails. This offensive and the submarine are the last and strongest trump cards in the hand of Central Europe.

"HOLLAND IN DANGER," reads the latest headline of the *Wilhelmshavener Tagesblatt*. Indeed this small but wealthy nation faces the most difficult predicament imaginable. The small neutral powers are being ground up between two great millstones. First England threatens them. Germany acts reassuringly. Then the roles are reversed. From our vantage point, England's actions seemed damned close to an act of desperation. But it may constitute the most effective way for England and America to make up their frightful losses of shipping. Maybe it has something to do with their fears of our general offensive. At any rate, the crisis should end within the next few days or weeks. 18 March 1918.

One of the current vices I find most objectionable in many of our people is that they no longer possess the ability to react to important events with open admiration or revulsion. I cannot understand their indifference. How can anyone simply shrug his shoulders, or still worse, belittle all of Germany's great accomplishments? I might even go further and consider

---

[24] Gas warfare on the Western Front was initiated by the German army during the Battle of Ypres on April 22, 1915. At first the gas, chlorine, was simply released from cylinders and had a devastating effect largely because it was such a novelty. However, the British were quick to retaliate and launched their first gas attack at Loos in September 1915. Moreover, gas masks and other protective devices soon made chlorine obsolete. Therefore in 1917 German scientists developed mustard gas or "yellow cross," which blistered the skin rather than attacking the lungs. A year later, an even more frightful gas, phosgene, was invented. This was twice as effective as chlorine and is undoubtedly the gas to which Stumpf was referring.

this as a sign of illness and disease. I have always felt that it was good to praise greatness and to call despicable acts by their proper name. But now almost no one objects when the Father-land's good name is besmirched, while those who extol its virtues and noble qualities find it difficult to maintain their position. Curiously enough, however, all of the men deem it an absolute duty to sacrifice their lives for the German Empire. Is it because of the categorical imperative? Most probably, yes. But our lack of self-confidence and pride in our achievements also has something to do with it.

Why [did I write] this introduction? I find it difficult to express what I would now like to say. Today's army report, as if it were the most natural thing in the world, stated, "Today we shelled the fortifications of Paris from a distance of 120 kilometers." [25] Was it a premature April-fool joke? This was my response at first until Havas News Agency issued a similar report. 120 kilometers? Why doesn't the whole world go mad? I simply cannot understand how this is possible.

For some weeks now a wonderful spring sun has been beam-ing down on Mother Earth and has brought all the green, growing things back to life. Our troops who are presently engaged in a most horrible, ferocious and bloody battle with the English and the French can certainly use this magnificent weather. I think that even the most apathetic people could not help but jump for joy when it became known yesterday that we had already captured 45,000 Englishmen, that we had seized an immense booty and that we had broken through on a sixty-kilometer-wide front.[26] The report mentioned old familiar

[25] In March 1918 a new weapon, an 8.26-inch naval gun, developed by the German scientist, Dr. Eberhardt, began to shell Paris from Saint-Gobain, a distance of approximately 75 miles or 120 kilometers. On March 29, a shell from one of these guns hit the church of Saint Gervais in Paris, killing 88 people and wounding 68 others severely. Shortly thereafter the French began to bombard the German gun position; the guns wore out and had to be withdrawn by May 1.

[26] On March 21 the German offensive began with an extremely heavy bombardment and gas attacks on the English lines along the River Somme. Within a few days the momentum of the attack breached the English-held front and enabled Ludendorff's troops to penetrate to a depth of forty miles.

names from the [first] Battle of the Somme. "Perrone has been reached. Bapaume has been taken. Our troops are standing before Noyon," etc. Just like at the outbreak of the war we waited for the papers with baited breath and reread each word ten times. Of one thing, however, I am certain. If our attack does not succeed in capturing the lung of France at Calais, then our hundreds of thousands [of soldiers] shall have died in vain. The war can only be brought to an end if we not only defeat but annihilate the enemies' million-man armies.

I should now like to add a word about something that I mentioned at an earlier occasion and shrugged off with contempt. [It concerns] our gas bombs. They are capable of wreaking horrible devastation upon every form of life. Even though I still am not prepared to believe all the fantastic rumors about them, I do know that they exist and that they have also been used. Even the semiofficial Wolff [Telegraphic Service] reported that many English gunners were found gassed to death at their places. Thus there must be some truth to it. Oh, how wonderful it would be if we were able to obtain a peace this year! 25 March 1918.

Once more a cold wind has blighted our hopes of spring. Although it would be incorrect to assert that the frost has destroyed all our blossoms, the people act as though we had already suffered a second defeat at the Marne.[27] In my view such pessimism is completely unwarranted for no other reason than the fact that we now no longer need to worry about Russia. On the contrary, I assume that Hindenburg has not given up hope and that we must expect the slaughter on the Western Front to continue. However I did overhear a group of smart alecks who maintained that it was all a show to get the eighth war bond drive launched. . . .

Good Friday and Easter have come and gone, but I was not in a very festive mood. The world is growing more dismal all

[27] The spectacular German breakthrough compelled the French to rush all available reserves to the aid of the reeling English troops. They managed to halt the Germans by March 25. However, a new German attack was to be staged shortly near Lys and Ypres.

the time and there is no longer any joy in our holidays. Or does it just seem that way? Actually it all depends on one's surroundings. Bleak and dismal Wilhelmshaven, however, at no time ever allows any Faustian Easter Morning thoughts of "hopefulness and happiness" and of "educational strivings" to arise. Every day of the year is a workday here. The spirit of Good Friday becomes especially meaningful when one reflects that Germany's youth has sacrificed its best years solely to destroy and kill men, the creations and images of God. In place of a single Calvary, our generation has millions of them.

Although fifty days lie between Easter and Whitsun, in that entire time I have not written a single line in my diary. [Was it because I had] no time? Oh yes, I have had ample time, but my ever-increasing boredom admits no noteworthy experiences. However I must not neglect to mention the most important thing, that during the course of that time I had fourteen days of leave. How wonderful it felt to travel in the happy May sunshine and to admire the budding green beauty of large stretches of the German countryside. I visited Berlin twice, both in coming and going, and I must admit that I was delighted upon seeing that wonderful city for the first time. I consider myself fortunate to have spent a few enchanting days there. Since blooming shrubbery and people in festive dress have always transported me into a cheerful mood, I viewed everything in a most pleasant light. I came to understand why Berliners are so justly proud of their home town. I was treated most cordially there. Although Berliners are unusually clever and intelligent people, they are also very businesslike. I had several opportunities to find that out for myself. The hotels charged dreadfully high and inflated prices. I mention them only for the sake of curiosity. For example, just a plain morning coffee with nothing added came to 2.25 marks. Everything else was priced accordingly. But enough of these horror stories! At 3:30 in the afternoon I boarded the express train at the Potsdam railroad station and twelve hours later I gratefully sank into my old hammock. 21 April 1918.

The little ship *Germania,* which belonged to the munition

depot was anchored near us. The very top of her mast was decorated with a large bush of birch twigs. Fresh greenery had been placed all along her railings and superstructure. Even after four years of war these people had not lost their sense of beauty, I thought to myself. Why else would anyone bother to risk his life climbing the high mast top? Just as pussy willows symbolize Easter and the fir tree stands for Christmas, so do birch twigs represent Whitsun. Which of these is the nicest holiday? It would be a thankless task to express some sort of preference. Each of the three in its own unique way is equally lovely. Yesterday, in ideal weather, the petty officers went on an excursion to Neustadtgöden and the palace of the Prince of Knyphausen. The wonderful old park was incredibly lovely. For a long time I stood enraptured under the mighty chestnut trees which had just sprung into pretty bloom. The smell and the color of the lilacs was enough to make one drunk. Their blue, red and white blossoms intermingled with the green leaves to form an indescribably beautiful symphony of color. And nothing can compare with the rich and wonderful aroma [they exuded]. I simply could not understand how our men could spend their time dancing in the hot and humid hall.

In its May costume the Oldenburger countryside which is usually so devoid of charm was unbelievably pretty. A vast green carpet [of grass] stretched as far as the eye could see. Tiny red-roofed farm houses were strewn about here and there. Each of them was bordered with a ring of ancient chestnuts and elms. Large herds of meager cows testified to the wealth of the population. I would have been completely overwhelmed by my delight with nature but for the dissonance of my growling stomach. Also I found it unpleasant to think that I would have to load coal until noon the next day. 19 May 1918.

I wish it were already noon. This damned nuisance! Today *Moltke*, which has already lived through this sort of thing several times, was towed into port with a torpedo hit back aft.

The rest of the fleet seemed rather nervous. Our staff evidently expected repetition of the [attack] on Zeebrugge.[28] Our ships assumed their advance stations and had to maintain continuous patrols. This made me appreciate my peaceful existence here. It was rumored that our fleet would go into action the next time Hindenburg launched an offensive. [But] I cannot believe that!

I have been transferred from the *Wittelsbach* to the *Lothringen*. I am well content with the change since what I have thus far seen of her officers would seem to indicate that they are quite a decent lot. Second day of Whitsun, 1918.

I have a whole free afternoon ahead of me, but nothing of any importance comes to mind. There is virtually nothing to report concerning my own experiences. It seems to me, however, that the fleet's nervousness has abated somewhat. After all, it would be ridiculous for the English to try to blockade Wilhelmshaven.

Whatever the navy may be lacking in daring is abundantly compensated by our army. After an almost unbearable pause of four weeks, our shock troops are again storming out of their trenches. Today, on the fourth day of our offensive, the vanguard of the Crown Prince's army is standing before the Marne.[29] I wonder if our advance will again grind to a halt at this famous river. I would not think so in view of the fact that this time there are no Russians on German soil and the treacherous Italians can no longer stab us in the back. Granted that America has joined the ranks of our foes; however this cannot make up for their losses in the East. In another year this might well be possible. Thus if we should fail to defeat our enemies now, we shall lose the war by next year. . . .

If that should prove to be the case, only Prince Lichnow-

[28] The British conducted a surprise commando raid upon the German-held submarine base of Zeebrugge on April 23 in which they sank a number of blockships in the channel of that port to prevent further excursions of enemy submarines.

[29] On May 27 the German armies renewed their onslaught on the Western Front in the Battle of the Aisne and pushed the French back to the River Marne only thirty-seven miles from Paris.

sky [30] will be capable of assuring us of a junior partner's position in a world dominated by England. The course of history may well point in that direction, but I would not consider it an intolerable solution. Up till now we have been lacking in the qualities necessary to become a world power. Much, all too much, has transpired in Germany and in our colonies, to make us ashamed of ourselves. It almost makes me die for shame when I consider that even now our overconfident landed gentry deems it possible to deny the right to vote to the very people who protect their property with their lives.[31] Do the Conservatives think that they themselves would have been capable of rolling back the invading Russian hordes? What a shame that we cannot lay down our arms for at least a day and allow the Indians and the New Zealanders to run amuck upon the estates of the Junkers. Maybe that would make them understand why the working classes are much less interested in our victory than the propertied classes. It is very depressing to realize that all our work is in vain and that after four years of fighting and sacrifice we are now worse off than ever before.

But a tiny glimmer of hope still burns in our hearts that Hindenburg's sword may still pave our way to a brighter future. All Germans still retain an indestructible confidence in their own invincibility and maybe this is the secret of our success. Be that as it may, we shall still need all the luck in the world for the impending battles in the West. 1 June 1918.

A dreadfully dismal and boring Sunday afternoon has caused me to bring forth my diary again. Although I do not know [what to write], I prefer it to darning socks or washing shirts even though this would undoubtedly be much more useful. I have just said farewell to a good friend with whom I had planned on going to Finland this March. He has "earned" 3,000

[30] Prince Karl Max Lichnowsky was the former German Ambassador to England. Before the war he had worked for friendship between the two countries and later on published a report which blamed the Kaiser for the war and called for a reconciliation.

[31] The Prussian House of Representatives (*Abgeordnetenhaus*) on May 2 voted down the government's franchise bill, which would have given every Prussian male the vote.

marks cash to send home to his family. The memory of my own bad luck pained me deeply. Although I have no complaints about my present life, I would not mind working like a horse if it would only help to establish myself. But what are 3,000 marks today? They will hardly buy as much as 300 marks in former times. At any rate, it makes a big difference whether one has money or not. It is strange that we all should feel that we are born businessmen. All of us have invested in something or other, whether it be sewing yarn, soap or pepper, and all of us want to realize a hundred percent profit on it. Indeed many people who never had a cent before now throw great sums of money around very liberally. I wonder where all this will lead. This is a time of unprecedented opportunities. Although at present we are all hungry and have nothing to wear, at a later date we shall come to look upon it as "the good old times."

There has been no talk of peace for a long time. We have to content ourselves with Hertling's formula: "This is the time for action and not for words." In fact our advance in the West has progressed so well that the newspapers are already beginning to talk of the battle "before" Paris.[32] Hence it would not come as a surprise if the French responded to our peace feelers. Our government ought to make an announcement declaring, "We can hear, but cannot speak. Hence it is now your turn to speak!" I am firmly convinced that the fate of Paris will be decided within three months. However this would still leave unresolved the problem whether or not France is in a position to conclude a peace. Even if we assume that she might follow Russia's example [and sign a separate peace treaty], it would do nothing to revive our economy in the ensuing trade war. It is unthinkable to conceive of what would happen if our soldiers left the trenches only to find that there were no jobs and food for them at home. It would precipitate a most acute crisis and would compel us to declare war again immediately. Only

---

[32] Subsequent to reaching the Marne, the German armies made a hasty attempt to attack Paris. However, since the attack had been ill prepared it was soon repulsed.

time can tell whether this last gamble of the Anglo-Saxons is correct. 10 June 1918.

I am frightened to look at the date [of my last entry]. I have not written anything for almost two months! What kind of a diary is this? In a certain sense it might indicate that I am fairly content with my present existence, I would surely have already filled up this book if I had experienced as many outrages and injustices as before. I may even consider myself to be incredibly lucky since I have had twenty-eight days of leave within six months. I just returned from home four days ago. Everything seemed very optimistic on my way back. Everybody [on the train] was buzzing about our impending grand offensive and the soldiers' rucksacks and baggage were stuffed with loot from our latest advance. When they opened them I saw some wonderful things. There were chocolates, corned beef, rum and biscuits. I was also shown rubber raincoats, woolen blankets and boots. Some of the most incredible things are imported into the country in this fashion. [But] only a small part of the population is able to supplement its food and clothing rations in this way. A paymaster told me that our men are now looting like the Russians; they take everything from silver spoons, bed covers, to cigarettes. And why not? Otherwise all these things would be shot to pieces by the artillery.

He told some dramatic and exciting stories of our advance along the Chemin des Dames.[33] [He said that] "the French and the 'Tommies' ran away like mad from our gas attacks. They were completely surprised. They fled in terror. We drank the still-warm coffee they had left on their tables." When I asked if they still had real coffee "over there," he gave a cautious smile [and said,] "They have an abundance of all the things which we can only vaguely remember." All of the men who took part [in the battle] were amazed how we managed to seize these heights and fortifications. It was a miraculous accomplishment.

[33] This refers to the Battle of the Aisne (May 27–June 6) in which the German armies overwhelmed the unprepared French at the lightly defended heights of Chemin des Dames and progressed to the Marne.

When I asked the soldiers where we would most likely attack the next time, with mystifying confidence they all pointed to the area east and southeast of Rheims. They even specified that it would take place on July 16. And, in fact, this is exactly what happened! [34] We were so confident that we could not understand why we should not capture everything we required, even Paris. But it is a different matter, whether or not it was worth the effort. I had the general impression that the common people were unconcerned with the struggle over war aims. They thought, let us beat them first and then let's worry about the rest. I was in agreement with this and regarded this attitude as proof of their implicit faith in our government. I was reminded of the similarity to the "Knight of Lake Constance." [35] Most of the people did not realize the insecurity of our [military] position and the extent of our commitment. After all, we Germans are a good, unpolitical nation of servants and bureaucrats. Even now, as we enter our fifth year of war, most of us still view the world through blinkers, gaze with fascination at [developments] in the West and believe that the food situation constitutes our gravest problem. Indeed if our [worldwide] reputation and our overseas possessions would grow as fast as potatoes, it would be a great relief.

My journey to Würzburg went very quickly but then Bavarian conviviality set in and the express train began to travel somewhat slower. The blue caps [of the officials] were not the only sign that we were in Bavaria. Here the local officials did not stand at attention at their stations but sat on a bench smoking their pipes with their beer mugs in hand. The conductor did not even make a conscientious effort to check

---

[34] In a last desperate attempt to reach Paris, Ludendorff on July 15 threw his tired troops into the fray once more near Rheims in an engagement which is frequently called the Second Battle of the Marne. Although initially the Germans managed to actually cross the Marne, their progress soon halted when they ran into stiff French and American opposition.

[35] This refers to the ballad "Der Reiter und der Bodensee" by the early nineteenth-century German poet Gustav Schwab. In the ballad the knight, without realizing it, performs an incredible feat by riding his horse over the frozen but treacherous Lake Constance. When he finally reaches safety he is informed of his amazing exploit and dies from shock.

our tickets. He merely asked, "Have I checked all your tickets?" When everyone responded affirmatively he was satisfied and moved on.

At Nuremberg I treated myself to a 28-pfennig measure of beer. Then I walked home on foot from Erlangen and arrived at my village at about one o'clock at night. The air was pure. How good it felt to be home! Everything seemed in order although all the lights were out and nothing was stirring. Here was the little garden where I had planted some beans last spring. I pushed my hand through the fence to feel how high they had grown, but alas, I merely felt bare stalks. The next day my father informed me that they had been blighted by frost three times. But the sunflowers stood as high as a man and along the sides of the garden the pumpkins grew fat. When I knocked against the barn door I heard some angry groans and high-pitched shrieks. Aha, father was raising pigs, young geese and chickens. Was it time to call out that lovely word "father"? No, first I wanted to go back a little way and sit on the bench beneath the blooming linden tree. My heart was so full of joy that I felt like shouting the song I had heard that morning:

> Great forest and sunshine
> Far away at the Mohrin strand
> My dearest Fatherland
> I think of you. *

I felt as emotional as a Crusader returning home [from the Holy Land]. Was this not a different sky; a different and milder air? And to think that twenty-four hours ago I was in Bremen, five hundred kilometers away! The nonstop express train has really shrunk our planet!

But now I had to ring the bell. The door still creaked just like it used to when I was a child. Soon I heard my father's concerned voice. "Who is down there?" "It is I, Richard." "Who?" "Richard, Father." "You? From where are you com-

---

* Waldgrün und Sonnebrand / Fern an der Mohrin Strand / Herzliebstes Heimatland / Denk ich an Dich.

ing?" "I am on leave, Father. . . . Fourteen days." "Come on in. You must be hungry." "No, only sleepy. I must sleep until 10 o'clock!" "Well, sleep well! Good night!"

Where was I? My God, I recognized that picture of the Madonna up there. Was I in bed? Yes, that's right, I was home and not out with the minesweepers at Horns Reef, as I had just dreamed in my nightmare. I was home—still home—for another thirteen days. . . . The day was sunny and bright. A whip cracked, the birds twittered and from across the way at the school came the students' monotonous recital of their morning prayer. Eight o'clock! Much too early in the day! Get back to sleep! Once again I was on the North Sea, which was filled with dangerous black mines. They came extremely close. I could almost hear their metallic sound. . . . I had heard it before. . . . Once again the picture of the Madonna came up. . . . I let loose a sigh of relief. It was only a dream; my imagination. I was home in my warm bed!!

I pulled back the curtain and let the light and the sun flood in. The sparrow's nest still lay in its bowl on the dresser as it had decades ago. But where was the tree with its finch's nest? Otherwise everything was as I had seen it through my childish eyes. Only the faces of the peasants were more deeply lined and the unoiled axles of their carts shrieked more piercingly than ever. The war has done it. But I no longer wanted to know anything of war and misery, of Wilhelmshaven and the North Sea. For fourteen days I did not give a damn about that. . . .

Two months of my life—an eternity—have flown by since that time. I feel terribly war-weary. My former optimism is giving way to ideas which I have always rejected with disdain. However all of Germany is dejected. It all started when the French threw back our offensive and gained the upper hand. We have lost our strongest card. The news that we had lost our hold on the enemy's territory shattered our confidence in our ultimate triumph. Although we did win some unparalleled victories in

the past, we also have suffered some extremely serious dis-
appointments. They began with the Italian proclamation of
neutrality. Then came the Japanese [declaration of war], the
Battle of the Marne, and Austria's defeat by the Serbians and
the Russians. This was followed by our own failure at Verdun,
the Battle of the Somme, our difficulty in Flanders, the failure
of our submarine campaign, America's declaration of war and
most recently, our general retreat from the wastelands along
the Somme.[36] This last event dealt our self-confidence its
harshest blow. None of us believed that we would ever surrender this territory for which we had paid such a bloody
price. We have gradually come to learn what the army reports
mean when they state, "We have assumed a new and more
favorable position." The people back home know of the American shelling of Metz [37] but the official newscasts still keep it a
secret. All these things have had a very adverse effect on us.
I regard it an insult that our high-handed bureaucrats do not
consider the German people mature enough to face the truth.
Our critical situation on land and at sea is shamefully and
stupidly misrepresented in the Reichstag. I am astonished that
the people [who are responsible for this] are not given a sound
thrashing.[38] But apparently the patience of the German people
is inexhaustible.

[36] On August 8 the British with 450 massed tanks broke through the
German lines at Amiens and penetrated to a depth of eight miles. The
German troops were completely overrun; Ludendorff called it "the black
day of the German army." Two weeks later, on August 21, in the Second
Battle of the Somme, the British and French continued their successful
offensive and hurled the Germans back to the protection of the Hindenburg line and compelled them to relinquish all their recent gains.

[37] The first significant American action in the war took place on June 4,
1918, at Château-Thierry. However, it was not until the Battle of St.
Mihiel Salient, of which the Battle of Metz was a part, that Americans
in large numbers fought independently under their own commanders. On
September 12, 1918, the German-held fortress of Metz was reduced to
smoldering rubble by a concerted artillery barrage of one million rounds
and a huge aerial attack in which 1,400 planes participated.

[38] As early as July 18, 1918 when the French began their series of
counterattacks in the West, General Ludendorff realized that Germany
could no longer win the war. On August 4 he drafted his first defensive
order and ten days later officially notified the Kaiser and the government
that his offensive had failed and that the war could no longer be won.

Appropriately enough, I have entitled the next section [of my diary] as follows: *Peace Is in Sight!*

I am somewhat puzzled by the intensity of our sudden desire for peace. We all feel that peace is inevitable and that it will come very soon. Surely our change in government alone cannot be responsible for this miracle. We all discuss the enemy's peace terms with terrifying calm.

Bulgaria has suddenly collapsed; Turkey is in grave danger.[39] Who knows if Austria, too, will not soon surrender upon any terms.[40] We have virtually lost the war overnight. As is commonly the case in these matters, the German people were kept totally ignorant of these events. Now all at once we, too, have collapsed and even the best of us are completely despondent and without hope.

Somehow or other I feel that we should not give up all hope. There will be no peace simply because the conditions which led us to war are still in existence. So long as our industrial apparatus remains intact, so long as our mighty battleships still cruise the North Sea and the old inequalities [among nations] persist, England will not grant us any mercy. Hence we have directed our appeal for an armistice to [President] Wilson, although we have never understood him and held him in contempt.[41] He

This news quickly became known to many prominent members of the Reichstag. Moreover, anyone who was capable of reading a map realized this as well. However, most Germans, among them many of the members of the government and Reichstag deputies, did not realize that the end would come so soon. Therefore they were stunned to hear from the army on October 2 that Germany's exhaustion of her entire manpower reserve obliged her to seek an immediate peace because the front could crumble within twenty-four hours.

[39] By the end of September 1918 both the Bulgarian and the Turkish armies were decisively beaten. The Bulgarians concluded an armistice on September 30, and the Turks were soon to follow suit.

[40] The Austrian monarchy was in a rapid state of disintegration. Czechoslovakia had established her independence, and the other nationalities were about to follow her course. Food was in short supply and her armies could no longer go on fighting. Hence the Austrian Empire had sent out an appeal to President Wilson on September 15 asking him to arrange for a cessation of hostilities.

[41] The collapse of the German armies at the Western Front made Generals Hindenburg and Ludendorff aware that the war was lost. Therefore they insisted that the government be reorganized on a more democratic

is, after all, the only man at present who is in a position to decide these questions of war and peace. His orders shall dampen France's lust for conquests, his words shall open the seas to all the nations and his judgment shall force us to rectify the injustice we have done to Belgium. What a responsibility for one man to bear! Although he was not born a nobleman, he is an aristocrat of the democratic age. Is an age of equality, an era of human rights in the offing? Will the dreams and teachings of Voltaire and Rousseau actually be realized? [42] Will this new age bring us hope for a better life and a more humane existence?

I wish that Wilson's face would reveal these answers! But by the same token, [this new age] could just as well bring us more sorrow, more bloodshed and an even more miserable existence! I am not concerned why this should be so—but I would like to know for how long this [era of misery] will last.

If we workers were compelled to lead the same miserable lives as before, we could not bear it. I hope that it will not come to pass that we shall ever yearn for war again. [Oh, new era], bring us peace, bread and good fortune! 3 October 1918.

Just about a year ago all our newspapers reported triumphantly that the English were concentrating their insane attacks against our submarine pens in Flanders. For weeks on end they charged with lowered horns and still they failed. . . .

This introduction is necessary. It will provide a proper back-

basis so that an armistice could be concluded. On September 30, Count Hertling resigned and was succeeded by the liberal Prince Max von Baden as Germany's first parliamentary Chancellor.

On October 4 the German and Austrian governments sent an appeal to President Wilson for an armistice and accepted his Fourteen Points as the basis for peace. For Germany this meant giving up her control over Belgium, Poland and various parts of the former Russian Empire as well as Alsace-Lorraine. However, it was widely felt that Wilson's idealistic program and his commitment to democracy would at least preserve Germany's national integrity and would bring about a peace which would not be overly punitive in nature.

[42] François Marie Arouet de Voltaire (1694–1778) and Jean Jacques Rousseau (1712–78) were probably the two most outstanding thinkers of the French Enlightenment and were popularly regarded as the leading exponents of liberalism in the battle against the forces of conservatism and obscurantism.

ground of the shattering effect of what follows: A week ago on Thursday, one of my comrades told me that our torpedo boats and submarines stationed in Flanders had fled from Ostend and Zeebrugge. They were now on their way here and might already have arrived. I merely laughed at him and cautioned him not to believe every latrine rumor. On the following day, however, I stopped laughing when more and more of the bad news came filtering in and I found out that he was correct. Our bases had been completely destroyed by intense naval and aerial bombardment and therefore any [further] activity was impossible. Thousands upon thousands of shipyard workers have recently arrived here. Our torpedo boats suffered another mishap during their retreat. One of them was torpedoed and another ran upon a mine. I understand that all our military installations, shipyards, docks and piers in Zeebrugge as well as in Ostend were blown up. But this has not yet been confirmed. According to different accounts, the only reason why the workers were evacuated were some serious cases of treason.[43] Be that as it may, the result remains the same. Yet none of the newspapers has been allowed to print a single word about this. Only after this news had been exaggerated a thousandfold did the people find out about it. However it is still too early for me to tell if it means the end of our submarine campaign. 5 October 1918.

The mood of my comrades is grave, very grave indeed. Many of our younger men have had their heads turned by Bolshevik ideas. Many of them are seriously discussing how they will soon conduct themselves as [members] of a Red Guard. But what will happen if all our efforts to negotiate a peace should fail and we are left no other choice but to fight it out to the bitter end? This would not be the first time that a nation has risen up in great wrath against its foes when driven

[43] Before their complete abandonment between October 17 and 20, the German naval bases at Zeebrugge and Ostend were gradually evacuated. There is no evidence at all that the bases were abandoned because of treason or sabotage. However, the workers and sailors arrived in Germany in such a despondent mood that they must have conveyed the impression that a calamity had taken place.

to desperation. Without a doubt Central Europe still possesses tremendous vitality. But where is the Napoleon capable of gathering all these disparate sources of strength together and of focusing them at one point? It is very depressing to read, "Germany begging for peace." Despite the unprecedented duration of the war and the shattering of many of our hopes, we all felt that ultimately it would be the enemy and not we who would have to come and beg for peace. Our confidence as well as our faith in the justness of our cause have suffered a staggering blow. A report by Schulze-Gävernitz [44] maintaining that our government acted dishonestly in regard to President Wilson's [mediation attempt] at the beginning of 1917 has stirred up a great furor. His contention that we could have obtained the present peace terms at that time sounds almost unbelievable to me.

Our communications with Turkey have been cut. The French have occupied the Bulgarian capital. The heroic Serbian people are about to liberate their land from the enemy. Thus the outer ramparts of the "German Fortress" have fallen but our interior defenses are stronger than ever. At this juncture a successful sortie might work wonders. Now that our troops are concentrated in a smaller area, it is quite conceivable that we might break out with a terrific force. But all the signs seem to indicate that we shall try to save lives by surrendering the territories we conquered at such great cost.

If peace is concluded, the diplomats will have their work cut out for them. A number of immensely important problems and questions still remain to be solved. I am most concerned about the fate of our navy. Moreover, it seems to me that Wilson's proposals come nowhere near removing all the sources of contention in Europe and that they may even create a whole series of new ones.[45] It would be intolerable for us if German

[44] This refers to Gerhart von Schulze-Gävernitz (1864–1943), professor of economics at the University of Freiburg, who had long advocated coming to terms with the Allies

[45] President Wilson's Fourteen Points contained a number of provisions which were bound to appear troublesome from the German point of view. They demanded the evacuation of Russian territory, the evacuation and

Lorraine and an even more Germanic Alsace were to wind up in the hands of the French. In this instance the German proposal for [the establishment of] the complete autonomy of these territories seems more correct. Since there are so many other disruptive factors, I have very little faith in an early triumph of the angel of peace. 12 October 1918.

Again I am forced to ask how we could develop such great despair? It merely goes to show that it is impossible to make an absolutely correct judgment of our nation's psychology. Although our people were by no means optimistic a month ago, no one would have expected such a precipitous drop in the barometer [of our hopes]. A part of our nation now kneels submissively before Wilson and accepts all his dictates with resignation. "Evacuate the occupied territories, rectify the injustice done to France, compensate Belgium, chase out your Emperor. . . ." [46] —our faint-hearted people are willing to agree to all these things if it will only bring peace. But I simply refuse to believe that it will always be that way.

Will this brief period between 1870 and 1914 really constitute our entire historical life? Is our short span of power and brilliance, of prosperity and confidence really over? My faith in divine justice makes such an end unbelievable. I never felt that we had the capacity to impose our will upon our enemies. But we did demonstrate our abilities in test after test before the whole world in a way which even the most optimistic would never have thought possible. However we have now reached a point from which we can no longer go on. But is there not also a saying which states that it is better to die than to become a slave? The greatest spiritual blow which a nation can be dealt is to compel it to overthrow its leaders and its

restoration of Belgium and northern France, the righting of the wrong done to France in the matter of Alsace-Lorraine, the division of the Austro-Hungarian Empire into a number of autonomous states, and the creation of an independent Poland with free and secure access to the sea.

[46] President Wilson's note of October 14 hinted that Germany would only be able to obtain the armistice which she so desperately needed if the Kaiser, whose "arbitrary power" might jeopardize the peace of the world, were deposed.

monarch. I know of no example in history which would indicate that a great nation ever yielded to such a demand. However [there are cases] of nations choosing death over slavery.
I do not say this out of love for the Hohenzollerns. Quite the
contrary, but I confess that I am convinced that all our power
and our respected position [in the world] stems from the
Empire.

Most of the people who kowtow to the orders emanating
from America praise Wilhelm II's flawless character, his peace-
loving nature and his incomparable abilities as a ruler. However they frequently object, "Yes, the Kaiser may be fine but
he is surrounded by a group of Junkers who keep undermin-
ing him." I am in no position to judge the validity of these
objections but every right-thinking person will agree that all
of the Kaiser's actions and proclamations point to the opposite
conclusion. Just remember how bitterly the Conservatives
attacked his Easter Message and how they subjected every one
of his conciliatory diplomatic gestures to contempt and ridicule. Nevertheless even when the responsible Chancellor was
forced to admit that his negotiations with England had broken
down, the Kaiser exclaimed, "This was not my desire. We have
only drawn our sword to defend ourselves." [47]

Now that all our efforts are directed toward liquidating our
bankrupt [policies], certain hotheads in Germany are clamor-
ing with outraged blame. Furthermore the dark elements of
every defeat are already arising. Our newspapers are already
shouting "Bring the guilty before the state tribunal" in a
fashion which is reminiscent of the ravings of the Parisian
Communards.[48] Our petty mentality is manifesting itself just
when dignity and confidence are more necessary than ever.

I have seizures of horrible depression whenever I read of our

[47] This is a paraphrase of the Kaiser's speech of August 4, 1914, in
which he stated that Germany had gone to war merely to defend herself
and that she did not seek to make any territorial conquests or annexations.
[48] In 1792, during the French Revolution, the ruling body of Paris was
the Commune. When France was invaded by Prussia and Austria and
Paris was in danger, the Commune purged all people suspected of disloyalty before a revolutionary tribunal. In addition, the Commune was also
influential in bringing about the trial and execution of King Louis XVI.

planned evacuation at the front. What wonders a military victory could work now! I no longer believe that our retreat is planned. Our troops can simply not go on any longer. This places the common soldier in an incredible dilemma analogous to grain being ground up between a soft and a hard millstone. He probably reasons as follows: If our side wins, we shall have to suffer the insolence of our own government. On the other hand, if we are defeated, Wilson's henchmen will deprive us of all our freedom.

We have recently made a courageous attempt to remove the upper millstone.[49] I hope and pray that it will succeed. However before we launch any major [attack], we must dispel the idea that we are doing it for the sake of the capitalists. If after all these tribulations, we could manage to overthrow our exploiters by a triumph of our will, we would stand in history as God's chosen people. I am utterly convinced the strength to do such a thing lies dormant within our nation despite all the years of bloodshed. But where is the man who can exploit this treasure?

In the event we should give in to the demands of the cold-hearted plutocrats from the other side of the Channel and the ocean and overthrow the Kaiser, I shall be ashamed for all eternity that I was ever a German. Only an immature mind could believe that our enemies would content themselves with that. They want us to have a weak and incompetent government, in which case it would hardly matter if its head were called Wilhelm X or Karl Liebknecht. The Australian Prime Minister summarized their feeling most succinctly [when he stated], "The only good Hun is a dead Hun."

For the longest time I refused to believe in the existence of such satanic cruelty. As a good German I was accustomed to look at the brighter side of things and never suspected that the

---

[49] No doubt the author is referring to the formation of the new parliamentary government of Prince Max of Baden, which included a number of prominent democratic politicians as cabinet members. He may also be referring to the program of constitutional revision which the Baden government introduced in the Reichstag on October 5 and which was designed to turn Germany into a democracy.

English, the Americans and the Australians were criminals rather than ordinary people. This January [Chancellor] Hertling declared that he regarded Wilson's Fourteen Points a practical basis for peace. Moreover our new government of Prince Max accepted them without any reservation. But what happened? Wilson put up five new points.[50] Although we accepted these, too, with a certain amount of trepidation, the latest American [note] shamefully demands unconditional cessation of submarine warfare, evacuation of the occupied territories without guarantees and payment for all damages caused by the war.[51] I have the distinct impression that they always spit on our hand whenever we stretch it out in peace. I wish I could glimpse into the workings of Providence so that I might learn if such an outrage can go unavenged!! In my opinion this is a greater crime than any of those which led up to the war. I hope that the near future will finally produce a solution which will resolve this impossible dilemma. 16 October 1918.

The Kaiser's possible abdication as a result of American pressure and the breakdown of Germany's morale is the most-discussed question of the day. Since it is hardly likely that the Hohenzollerns' proud tradition of divine-right rule will permit them to give up their prerogatives to the people piecemeal, I am almost ready to believe it. The Kaiser would no doubt find it easiest to give up his exclusive prerogative over ques-

[50] Prince Max's note of October 4, 1918, made it clear that the German government accepted Wilson's Fourteen Points and the President's subsequent pronouncements, especially the one of September 27, 1918, frequently called the "five particulars," stating that no leagues or alliances would be tolerated in the future and that the ensuing peace settlement would have to be implemented impartially without any considerations for national interests.

[51] On October 14 President Wilson dispatched another note, which demanded the evacuation of all occupied territory, the immediate cessation of submarine warfare, and reiterated the suggestion that Germany alter her form of government. Although Wilson's note did not specifically demand payment of war damages, it called for an end to Germany's destruction and spoliation of property in the occupied areas, which raised the possibility that Germany would have to pay reparations.

tions of war and peace. But could he place the General Staff under the control of the Reichstag? And worse still [permit the army] to swear allegiance to the constitution?!! This is virtually inconceivable! [52] What would he then have left? Germany [would be left with] about as much monarchical government as England, Denmark or Norway. Has our young Empire actually outlived its purpose already? This amounts to an admission that the attempt to graft a young twig on an old tree has been a failure. If the German nation has already outlived its youthful energy, then the period of 1870 to 1914 can merely be regarded as the belated blooming of a tree in autumn.[53] Now a young and much to be envied nation will rule over us. Who knows whether it will not uproot all the trees of Europe? What am I talking about? No, there is no real cause for such pessimism. 24 October 1918.

The greatest drama of all times is at its height. . . . I live through it without strong inner feelings. At this very moment our Kaiser may already have followed the Tsar's example and signed his abdication. What an unprecedented sacrifice for the welfare of his people. With deep emotions his people look forward to this second Golgotha. It seems incredible to me how anyone could exude hatred at this parting. Only a base nature could conceive of such a thing. I fear that the raging sea will no longer content itself with this grandiose sacrifice. The greatest of our generals Ludendorff resigned the day before yesterday.[54] In the depth of my despair I recall the biblical analogy to the stricken shepherd and his herd. Why did the days of Jena and Auerstedt have to strike the German people

[52] Nevertheless, all of these changes were enacted into law on October 28, when the Kaiser and the Bundesrat assented to the conversion of Germany into a democratic parliamentary monarchy.

[53] Bismarck had created the German Empire in 1871 by grafting a federal government onto the old system of independent states. Consequently, the strength, vigor, and power of the new Germany were the result of this relatively recent union.

[54] General Ludendorff was compelled to resign on October 27, 1918, because of his insistence that Germany continue to fight a war which he had previously given up as lost, and because he would not agree to the Baden government's acceptance of Wilson's prearmistice conditions.

for a second time? [55] We stand amazed like children at the ocean. Why do the waves swell, why?

Who would have believed that our army, standing deep on enemy soil, would be forced to beg for peace? This ungodly war bore a fateful legacy from its beginning: it would not be won by force of arms. Ludendorff's mistake was not to have understood this. However it must not be forgotten that not only he, but our entire nation, believed in the victory of our arms. Our soldiers did everything that was humanly possible. Those who formerly were loudest in their praises (hosannahs) now stand before the gates and clamor, "To the cross with him! " [56]

Just like the first days of the war, one rumor follows another. Everything is believable, be it that Hindenburg has turned senile or that the Kaiser has committed suicide. Even a very dispassionate observer must conclude that this city [Wilhelmshaven] resembles a bubbling volcano. Mass refusals to obey orders have become routine; one talks about them the same way we used to discuss a horse race.

On Sunday (October 26) the *Strassburg* was to put out to sea. Some of her stokers deserted and went on shore. Those who remained put out the fires [in the boilers] and tried to sink the ship by opening the flood gates. On a ship of the *Posen* class, a lieutenant was beaten to death.

However the following is much more serious: It became evident last Monday afternoon that the fleet was about to sail out. Apparently an Anglo-American fleet of a hundred and fifty ships was sighted off Helgoland.[57] We all knew within

[55] In 1806 Napoleon routed the Prussian army at the battles of Jena and Auerstedt. As a result, Prussia was punished severely and virtually ceased to exist as an independent state. It was the greatest disaster in Prussian history.

[56] Ludendorff's insistence on a total victory for Germany and his refusal to enter into negotiations with the victorious Allies engendered so much resentment among the people that the General was shortly compelled to flee to Sweden wearing a disguise.

[57] This was merely a rumor. However, preparations were under way for the German fleet to sail out for a last desperate engagement with the English fleet before the imminent armistice suspended all belligerent activities.

our hearts—today is the last time we shall ever see many of our ships. My mind contemplated what would happen if we engaged and destroyed the enemy fleet. I toyed with the most grotesque possibilities. In the final analysis this might still result in our victory. Soon, however, an impregnable veil of fog descended upon the sea. The weather made any thought of sailing out impossible. In the sea of fog and fine rain one could no longer make out the stern of the vessel from amidship.

Soon thereafter we heard that the stokers on three battle-cruisers had deliberately allowed the fires to die down and had even extinguished them. At this time about a hundred men from *Von der Tann* were running loose about town; *Seydlitz* and *Derfflinger* were missing men. Thus the fleet could not have sailed even if there had been no fog.[58]

It is sad, tragic that it could go so far as this. But somehow even with the best of intentions I cannot suppress a certain sense of frantic joy (Schadenfreude). What has happened to the almighty power of the proud captains and staff engineers? Now at last, after many years, the suppressed stokers and sailors realize that nothing, no, nothing, can be accomplished without them. Can this be possible? After having lived for such a long, long time under this iron discipline, this corpse-like obedience (Kadavergehorsam), it appears hardly possible. As late as a few months ago I would have laughed at anyone who suggested that our people would simply throw up their hands at the approach of our enemy.

Long years of accumulated injustice have been transformed

[58] Although the war was practically over, the German Admiralty wanted to strike one last blow at the enemy to preserve the honor and reputation of the High Seas Fleet, which had lain idle so long while the army had done all the fighting. On October 29 and 30 orders were issued to the fleet to sail out for a final engagement with the English off the coast of Flanders. The men, however, felt that this maneuver was designed to disrupt the armistice negotiations and to prolong the war. They correctly suspected that the government knew nothing of the projected battle. In addition, they feared that the officers had planned a suicide mission in order to preserve their honor by seeking a glorious death in battle. For all these reasons, the sailors and stokers refused to obey the order to weigh anchor and sail out. Thus began the mutiny which was soon to develop into the first act of the November Revolution.

into a dangerously explosive force which now erupts with great power all around. My God—why did we have to have such criminal, conscienceless officers? It was they who deprived us of all our love for the Fatherland, our joy in our German existence, and our pride for our incomparable institutions. Even now my blood boils with anger whenever I think of the many injustices I suffered in the navy. "Every injustice shall find its revenge." Never has this old motto been truer than now.

On the *Thüringen*, the former model ship of the fleet, the mutiny was at its worst. The crew simply locked up the petty officers and refused to weigh anchor. The men told the captain that they would only fight against the English if their fleet appeared in German waters. They no longer wanted to risk their lives uselessly. Six destroyers and a submarine were summoned, and aimed their guns at the ship. A company of naval infantry then occupied all the compartments and arrested three hundred men. Reports of similar happenings come from the *Helgoland*.[59]

At any rate the authority of the officers has vanished.[60] They surrender in droves and have changed greatly. Our Division Officer has become friendliness itself. The new Captain alone remains unyielding and incorrigible. It gives me great pleasure to watch how he stops the sailors who do not salute him and how quickly they knuckle down. This happened to me today.

[59] *Thüringen* and *Helgoland* were the first ships to hoist the red flag in Wilhelmshaven on October 29. However, on October 31 the rebellion was suppressed when a submarine and a single torpedo boat drew up next to the ships and threatened them into submission. Boarding parties were sent on the ships, and 600 men were arrested on *Thüringen*, 150 on *Helgoland*, 200 on *Grosser Kurfürst*, and 150 on *Markgraf*.

[60] In order to quell the rebellion, to divide the men and to preserve its authority, the Fleet Command had sent the Third Squadron to Kiel on October 31. On their arrival in that city, however, the sailors continued the mutiny, demanded the release of the prisoners, paraded in the streets, formed Workers' and Sailors' Councils, and by November 4 succeeded in assuming control over Kiel. Surprisingly, the officers offered very little opposition to these developments. Except for one isolated street battle, there was no organized resistance to the rebellion. Admiral Souchon, the Station Commandant of Kiel, simply gave up and surrendered his authority to the Sailors' Council.

This morning when he asked me in his paternally mild voice why I did not salute him, I could hardly answer for shame over my arrogant behavior. Many will feel as I do when they come to realize that political rights and privileges do not still one's hunger or create happiness. Now, however, it feels wonderful to demonstrate our power, to ignore orders and to assert ourselves. Napoleon, that great observer of human nature, once said that it was virtually impossible to keep a victorious army unemployed for years [and maintain its morale]. This is precisely what happened here [to the German navy].

HOW DID IT HAPPEN?

This question should not have been placed here, but at the beginning of my diary. By "it" I mean the mutiny or revolution, which is greeted with horror by most people, by many as the fulfillment of their ideals and by a small group as the reward for their work. Now the revolution has arrived! This morning I heard the first flutter of its wings. It came like lightning. Unexpectedly it descended with one fell swoop and now holds all of us in its grip.

Even though I was in the midst of things, I did not realize how quickly word spread this morning to "prepare to demonstrate on shore." The Division Officer, the First Officer and the Adjutant came down to our quarters and asked us in a crestfallen manner what it was that we wanted. We replied, "We have nothing against our officers. Nevertheless we shall parade in the streets to obtain our rights." However each one of us looked upon these "rights" as the fulfillment of his own wishes. Since things seemed to be getting interesting, I put on my parade uniform and went along. "I can't stop you," the First Officer commented with resignation.

Hardly any of the men stayed behind. At the Old Port Barracks a long line of marines armed with rifles stood assembled. At our approach they broke out in a loud shout of joy and gave three hurrahs. People streamed in from all sides. Within a matter of minutes a huge crowd of sailors had gathered on the parade grounds. Occasionally someone tried to address the crowd. At last we decided to march to the flagship in order to enlist its crew in our demonstration. The only interesting part of the entire story occurred at this point. A verbal duel ensued between the Captain of the ship and several spokesmen of the demonstrators. The crew of the *Baden*, which stood assembled on the top deck, would be the reward for the victor. Had the Captain been a reasonably accomplished speaker, our spokesmen would have been forced to depart without a single man. However both the deathly pale officer and the Sailors' Council handled themselves badly. Consequently roughly a third of the crew joined our ranks.

Later on I saw more. Since it was difficult to maintain order in the huge mob, loud calls for music rang out. The harbor band and several of us fetched our instruments and played the old military songs and marches. The mighty throng, more or less inspired [by the music] moved along the docks. At the Peterstrasse we were met by a forty-man patrol led by an officer. The men came over to our side with their weapons. It was very comical to watch the lieutenant when he realized suddenly that he was all alone. Because of the music we received large reinforcements from all directions. At first I thought that we would release the imprisoned sailors at the jail. But I soon realized that we lacked leadership and that the crowd was driven along by sheer mob instinct.

The great gate at the Marine Barracks was bolted. In an instant the gate was off its hinges. An elderly major blocked the way. He thrust a pistol against the first sailor who broke in. He was disarmed immediately, hands reached for his sword while others tried to tear off his epaulettes. My sympathy went out to this unfortunate man who courageously tried to do his duty, and disgust at such brutality rose in my throat. I felt like shaking his hand.

The seemingly endless procession moved along the sides of the great drill field and joined at the center.[61] Hastily a

---

[61] It has been estimated that 10,000 men participated in this demonstration.

speaker's platform was erected. Then all at once twenty men began to speak. It was an excellent opportunity to study the thoughtlessness of the mob in action. Even the most ridiculous demands were greeted with stormy applause. A demand to hang the Kaiser could easily have been pushed through. I must admit, however, that there were also repeated demands for order and discipline. This is somewhat encouraging. It indicates that the radical, irresponsible elements have not yet gained the upper hand. I hope it remains this way. Then I will not be sorry that I participated.

We next moved in the direction of the Torpedo Division. I was able to observe the gradual rise of bestiality [in the mob]. Every woman was greeted with coarse remarks and whistles. Incredibly red cloths waved in the air. In the place of a banner someone carried a red bedsheet on a pole. It was certainly no great honor to march behind this dirty rag. But because it was the first day of our new freedom we gladly ignored these superficialities.

It was evident that we received little support from the townspeople in their windows. Surely the shortage of handkerchiefs alone could not have been responsible. The townspeople understood quite well that the collapse of the fleet meant the end of the growth of their city. In the future Wilhelmshaven will remain an insignificant medium-sized town.

Relentlessly the procession moved across the drill field toward the Teichbrücke and the torpedo boats. Everyone there applauded us but no one joined us because—it was lunch time. When the mob began to grumble at this, a crew member yelled across to us: "Calm down, friends. We've put out the fires long ago, but now we're having lunch." Lunch—everyone began to feel pangs of hunger. In nervous and planless haste we moved on.

An hour later we stood assembled in front of the Station Headquarters. A statue of Admiral Coligzy [Coligny?], drawn dagger in hand, towered over us. Breathless silence prevailed when a speaker arose from the crowd. He announced that

Admiral Krosigk [62] had agreed to accept the demands of the Kiel Sailors' Council.[63] Rousing applause. "All political prisoners in the fortress are to be released." The mob resisted: "We want all [prisoners] released, all! Down with Kaiser Wilhelm." The speaker handled all these protests very effectively by ignoring them.

Now a dockworker stepped up to speak. The man had a typical, classic criminal face, I thought. Only from such a face could come the demand for the establishment of a "Soviet Republic." I felt sorry for the fellow even moreso for the crowd which applauded these stupidities.

When the first speaker rose again and suggested that we return to our posts immediately, he was met with resounding laughter. But then everyone disappeared in the direction of the nearest kitchen. The revolution had triumphed bloodlessly.

In order to stage a proper celebration, a great triumphal meeting was organized the next day. Although the [rest of the] fleet had still not arrived and its attitude was still questionable, we ignored these problems. Our representatives wrangled throughout the night about which of them should be elected to the so-called Council of Twenty-One.[64] It was not a pretty scene. Naturally each of them wanted to see his signature affixed to some proclamation, especially since no risk was in-

[62] Admiral Günther Krosigk (1860–1938) commanded the North Sea Naval Station at Wilhelmshaven.

[63] On November 4 the Kiel Sailors' Council had issued a thirteen-point program demanding the release of the prisoners of *Thüringen* and *Helgoland* as well as the mutineers of 1917. In addition, it demanded equal rations for officers and men, the formation of new food committees, and the creation of new complaints committees of the enlisted men to supervise court-martial proceedings, a more equitable distribution of leaves, a relaxation of discipline which would abolish the saluting of officers in town or off duty and which would permit the men to address an officer as "Sir" only once in the course of a conversation. The demands of the Wilhelmshaven sailors on November 6 coincided with these demands in all important respects.

[64] The Council of Twenty-One, established on November 6, was to be the revolutionary ruling body of Wilhelmshaven. Each ship's company and each land company was to elect three representatives to the Sailors' and Workers' Council, which in turn would elect the Council of Twenty-One.

volved. Early the following morning a broadsheet listing all the gains we had already made was distributed.

This time I scornfully refused to join the demonstration and went into town all by myself. Things were even more hectic than on the previous days. This time most of the demonstrators were civilians and shipyard workers, but I also noticed some officials and a sprinkling of deck officers without their swords. Red flags abounded and they were in better condition than yesterday. In order to simplify the matter [of identification] each of the flags indicated the organization it represented. The procession lasted for twenty-eight minutes. A speaker in a flowing cloak and with gesticulating hands was already talking in the square. Could it be [Reichstag] Deputy Noske? [65] But no. In his first sentence I heard him say that the Reichstag deputies had accepted bribes from food speculators and the war profiteers. "I also know their names," shouted the speaker. "Yes, I know who they are. Deputy [Giesberts of the Centrist Party] [66] is one of them." At that point I began to realize who had instigated the whole uproar. There was a long pause while the band played a few selections. In the meantime a Seaman First Class amused the gathering by reciting his family secrets and personal problems. Today a soldier's wife with her five children had been to see him. Her application for an increased allowance had been rejected. "All of you must be aware of whom I mean?" A voice from the rear, "The mayor!" "Yes, indeed, he is the one." (The same voice again) "Away with him! Away with him! Pfui, pfui!" echoed the voices of

[65] On November 4 the government in Berlin dispatched the Right-wing Socialist deputy Gustav Noske (1867–1939) and Secretary of State Conrad Haussmann (1857–1922), a deputy of the Progressive Party, to Kiel to obtain control over the sailors' rebellion. Since that rebellion lacked leadership or a cohesive program, Noske succeeded in establishing his authority almost immediately. He was elected governor of the port, and Admiral Souchon resigned. Consequently, Haussmann was enabled to return to Berlin almost at once. Noske, however, stayed on, but he did not make an appearance in Wilhelmshaven.

[66] Johann Giesberts (1865– ?), editor of the *Westdeutsche Arbeiterzeitung*, represented the town of Essen as a Centrist deputy in the Reichstag. In October 1918, Giesberts was appointed Undersecretary of State in the Reich Labor office. There is no evidence that Giesberts either offered or received any bribes.

thousands in the audience. I was astonished at the patience of the crowd, for it allowed the loudmouth to repeat the story all over again. But when he attempted it for a third time, the band drowned him out ingloriously.

Thereupon a sailor stepped onto the platform and informed the "honorable party members, comrades and workers" that the principal objective [of the revolution] had thus far not been implemented and that the Kaiser and all the federal princes should herewith be deposed. "True, true!" they shouted to the sky with the same sort of fervor they had manifested over the misdeeds of the mayor. All those who accepted this demand were told to raise their right hands to signify their approval. About one half [of the people in the crowd] managed to raise their hands, the same hand which had once sworn loyalty and obedience to the head of state. Now I was overcome with disgust. I wandered around for a while longer and then departed.

While I was busy recording these impressions, a terrific noise interrupted my thoughts. Someone stuck his head through the door and bellowed: "All hands to receive rifles and ammunition!" I stopped the first man I met and asked, "What's going on? Why the rifles?" "Treason," he gasped, foaming with rage. "The loyalists are firing on us at Rüstringen!" Someone else shouted, "The Tenth Army Corps is marching against us. We shall shoot them down like dogs!" That I would like to see. The uproar was terrific. Everybody called for the Executive Officer and the armorer. Then the first men carrying rifles and bayonets came out. I said to myself, this means blood will be spilled; these people are absolutely insane. The streets were like a madhouse. Armed [men] ran through the gates from all directions; there were even a few women dragging cases of ammunition around. What madness! Is this the way it has to end? After five years of brutal fighting, shall we now turn our guns against our own countrymen? Since even the most reasonable and stable of the men I saw were in a state of semihysteria, only a miracle could prevent a disaster.

But the miracle occurred. With the same care of planning

and direction that had gone into spreading the rumor, the "Soldiers' Council" now saw to it that order was restored. Men in cars and on bicycles spread the word that it had all been a "false alarm." Later on one of the representatives even admitted that this was merely a stratagem to obtain possession of the weapons. At any rate it was certainly not a proper way to behave. It was an unbelievably reckless playing with fire. By evening, however, everything was peaceful and quiet once more. 8 November 1918.

Within the past two days an unbelievable change has taken place within me. [I have been converted] from a monarchist into a devout republican. No, no! My heart—I no longer understand you! Truly, it must have stopped.

(I find that I can no longer devote even fifteen minutes to my work. Spectacular events occur in bewildering succession. This veritable witches' sabbath has completely upset my mental equilibrium. Never before has Wilhelmshaven looked like this! Thousands upon thousands of flaring rockets rise in the air, all the sirens howl, the searchlights gleam by the dozen, the ships' bells clang madly and the guns of the fort roar out their salute. This is really too much all at once.) 10 November 1918.

I think that the time has come for me to reorganize my thoughts. But since my mood keeps vacillating every hour between extreme exultation and deathlike despair, I find it extremely difficult to narrate my impressions and feelings in a sensible order. Although I wrote earlier that I have become a convinced republican, I came to regret my decision within a matter of hours.

November 10 may perhaps turn out to be the most significant day of this war. At least this is the way I felt on Sunday morning as I gazed down upon a mob of "a hundred thousand." For the first time I felt somewhat solemn. A springlike sun was shining and the happy and gay faces of the men indicated that they welcomed the arrival of the new era with open arms. Although the procession had already lasted two hours, a constant stream of new battalions of sailors and soldiers came streaming from the center of town. Amidst wild cheering

Stoker First Class Kuhnt [67] introduced himself as the first president of the Republic of Oldenburg. Low-flying aircraft dropped down bundles of handbills. To the thunderous applause of the mob, the huge Imperial war flag was lowered and the red flag of liberty, equality and fraternity rose up over the barracks. I could no longer resist and was swept along by the mass hysteria.

All my qualms of conscience evaporated when the Kaiser abdicated [68] and my Bavaria proclaimed itself a Republic.[69] I felt as if a heavy weight had suddenly been lifted from my heart, particularly when I learned that the revolutionary movement had spread to the French-Italian front.[70] This automatically signified the conclusion of an armistice. The proletarians of all nations would embrace each other and the capitalists, of course, they would pay the price. . . . Was this not an exhilarating and an infectious prospect?

Thus far I have not taken advantage of my ample opportunities to go on leave because I would rather record my impressions. Hence on Sunday night I was engrossed in my work when I was suddenly disturbed by joyous shouting, hurried running, bright lights and the explosion of a volley of signal rockets. Thousands of them rose up like red, green and white stars in the clear sky. Rifle shots cracked from the barrack windows and soon the guns of the neighboring forts joined in

[67] Bernhard Kuhnt, a former local secretary of the Social Democratic Party, was elected head of the Council of Twenty-One of Wilhelmshaven. As the revolution spread to the surrounding countryside, the Duke of Oldenburg abdicated, and Kuhnt had himself proclaimed president of the new republic.

[68] On November 9, 1918, Prince Max of Baden announced the Kaiser's abdication in order to obtain the armistice which Germany needed and to avert an impending revolution. Actually, Wilhelm II had not abdicated. He continued to cling to his power and even contemplated finding an honorable death among his troops at the front. Only when confronted with Baden's *fait accompli* and the army's decision not to obey him any longer, did Wilhelm II flee to exile in Holland.

[69] On November 7, 1918, the Socialists Kurt Eisner (1867–1919) and his supporters abolished the Bavarian Monarchy and established a socialist republic.

[70] For a short while this, and many other unfounded rumors regarding the outbreak of revolutions, was believed by the gullible revolutionary sailors.

with their thunderous roar. To add to this hellish noise, the sirens joined in full blast. A little more decorum would not have done any harm.

No one knew precisely what the joyous noise was all about. At first I thought that it was an air raid; then it was rumored that the English fleet was approaching. Finally it became known that it was to announce the proclamation of the newly established International.[71] This struck the civilians with fear and terror. I heard one old woman say, "These wild sailors will stop at nothing." The hellish music had not yet ceased when a delegate from the Sailors' Council with a very crestfallen face ran up on the gangplank and wordlessly handed me a broadsheet bearing the ominous title: The Terms for a Cease-Fire. I read the fateful sheet with bated breath and growing amazement. What were the terms? Evacuation of the left bank of the Rhine as well as the right to an extent of forty kilometers. . . . 150,000 railroad cars. . . . 10,000 automobiles. . . . 5,000 heavy guns. . . . the blockade to remain in effect. . . . the navy to be surrendered. . . . 10,000. . . . 5,000. . . . 30,-000. . . .[72] It can't be. This is ridiculous. . . . It means a fight to the end. . . . What a sudden change from the joy we had felt that morning! "This is what you get for your God-damned brotherhood [of nations]," I shouted to the suddenly silent spectators. It was too much for me to bear and I hurried off to grieve in a lonely corner.

The last of the rockets exploded; one siren after the other turned silent; but within me the storm still raged as I was convulsed to the very core of my soul by a deep and terrible anguish. It is sheer madness to subject an industrious and undefeated nation such as ours to these shameful terms. Just this morning we demonstrated our eagerness for peace by destroy-

[71] The Third International was not actually established until March 1919.
[72] According to the armistice of November 11, Germany pledged herself to surrender to the Allies 5,000 guns, 3,000 mortars, 1,700 fighters and bombers, 5,000 locomotives, 150,000 railroad cars, and 5,000 trucks. The navy had to deliver for internment 10 battleships, 6 battlecruisers, 8 light cruisers 50 modern destroyers, and all of its submarines.

ing our most powerful weapon [the navy]. And what did we get in return? They responded by spitting in our face. 11 November 1918.

No pen in the world could possibly describe my emotions these past three days. I looked on with grief as our fleet was hurriedly prepared for surrender [to England].[73] When I saw the alacrity with which the men performed their tasks, I was [momentarily] reminded of the days of 1914. Until late into the night the shells were sent hurtling down the chutes and cranes into the damp coal dust of the hold. These were the very same shells which we had handled so gingerly, on which we had inscribed [our hope] that their explosive power would destroy England's world empire. But Germany's situation has changed much too precipitously for me to adjust to it so soon.

Nowhere in Germany was there greater enthusiasm and confidence [in our cause] than in the fleet. Just a few months ago our ships penetrated as far [north] as Bergen and no one complained about having to stand strenuous watches while we were out minesweeping. To be sure, the present developments have put many things in a different light. In my opinion our sailors reacted with almost unbelievable patience to harassment by their superiors. If, for instance, some dumb lieutenant was out carousing half the night with his friends on another ship, he would wire at two o'clock in the morning that a boat be sent to take him home. Consequently the watch division was aroused to lower the pinnace. The men were then made to wait until it returned. In freezing cold, in snow and in rain they stood and shuffled their feet straining their ears to pick up the roar of the returning boat. A half hour would pass, a whole hour, but still no sound. The noble lieutenant had changed his mind and now wanted to stay another hour. But he would not give a second thought to the 150 sailors whom he deprived of their sleep, who were freezing and also probably hungry. . . .

[73] Article 29 of the Armistice demanded that all German ships be disarmed and that those scheduled for internment be readied for their journey by November 19.

Sunday inspection: The division would stand assembled on deck for half an hour before the Oberleutnant would condescend to inspect the men. According to plan, every tenth man was made to fail the inspection. "Bosun! This pig shall have to clean the sirens. This one shall report to the petty officer of the watch every hour this evening in parade dress! And this young pig? He is to unpack his equipment for inspection at twelve o'clock!" And so it went on and on.

The Executive Officer would find a few potatoes in the food slops. He summons the quartermaster, who agrees that the crew still gets too much to eat. At inspection the Division Officer would then announce in his harshest tone, "You are still living too high on the hog. Otherwise you would not waste potatoes. From now on you will get less to eat until nothing is found in the garbage."

One could recite these incidents by the hour. Each one of them, however, loosened a brick and was thus responsible for the overthrow of the military autocracy. We will lose many good things this way. Some of the older men will miss the educational function of the barrack parade grounds. However it will be a notable improvement if the honor of our men is no longer sullied as before. Perhaps providence has fated us to be not only the most industrious nation in the world, but also the freest. 17 November 1918.

Now that the revolution has actually arrived, it does not bear the slightest resemblance to Kautzky's [74] glowing predictions. Neither his predictions nor Bebel's description of the war of the future have materialized. But in the final analysis, both men were correct. The proletariat did rise up and the war did collapse. They were merely mistaken about the details.

Although we have now been free for ten days, we are still not in a state of bliss. Worries about the future dampen our spirits. Very few of us have regular or well-paying trades. But

[74] The leading orthodox theoretician of German Social Democracy Karl Kautzky (1854–1938) had insisted before the war that revolution was inevitable in Germany until the proletariat wielded all the power in the land.

we have more than enough defeatists among us who paint the future in the darkest colors. Some bad news concerning the lawlessness of our retreating armies has come to our attention. To be sure, there are large numbers of men among them who are merely waiting for a signal to start plundering. Then the business people had better watch out. Since they have always exploited the soldiers, they are thoroughly detested by them. Fortunately the men's desire to go home and to escape from all this is presently diverting their attention and making them forget everything else. As if everything depended on a couple of days, they connive and stop at nothing to get away. Since the Soldiers' Councils do not possess any real authority, they have no alternative but to agree to everything. They would merely make themselves look ridiculous if they seriously tried to oppose any demand. One thing is certain. We could not have conducted a war for even four months, let alone four years under such a regime. The pressure of circumstances has forced some of the former authorities to assume power again. But in everything else, those who shout the loudest and make the most radical demands are still given a chance to rise to the top.
18 November 1918.

Today is a very sad day for me. At this moment *Friedrich der Grosse* and *König Albert* are in the locks and the other ships are ready to follow. They are assembling at Schillig Roads for their final difficult voyage.[75] The submarines will also go along. Now and then the wind carries a snatch of their sad songs over here. It is like a funeral. We shall not see them again. Impassively holding their seabags, the men who are being left behind stand at the pier. At the last minute they feared for their lives and threw down their weapons. I, too, feel too disgusted to remain here any longer. I wish I had not been born a German. This despicable act will remain a blot on Germany's good name forever. Even Nebogatov's surrender of

[75] The ships designated for internment to England left Wilhelmshaven on November 19 under the command of Admiral Reuter and arrived in England on November 21. They remained at the English naval base of Scapa Flow until they were scuttled by their German crews on June 21, 1919, to prevent their sale or incorporation in the British navy.

his "floating coffins" to the Japanese pales in comparison.[76] Although our army is still much respected by foreigners, the actions of our High Seas Fleet will live on with shame in history. It is a wonder that Graf Spee [77] does not rise up from his watery grave to lay a curse upon his cowardly compatriots. On the whole I am not sorry to see these instruments of destruction disappear from our waters. I might even consider it a blessing for all humanity if all the nations copied our example. Unfortunately, however, the much-heralded brotherhood of all mankind has failed to materialize. Thus our own ships will help the English navalists to once more enslave us and other nations.

Why don't the English send some of their warships to Wilhelmshaven? Probably they are afraid that their men will fraternize with us and hoist the red flag in place of the Union Jack! I recently paid a visit to the printing shop of our "Republic" and saw whole stacks of appeals addressed to the comrades of the Grand Fleet. Since victorious troops are not very susceptible to Bolshevik ideas, I doubt that they will do much good. I cannot shake off the impression that our enemies are merely waiting for our complete collapse. This would provide them with a splendid excuse to come in and plunder us. Only then will the men who threw down their arms so lightly, realize what they have done.

I shall be discharged in another few days. But I had always pictured it entirely differently. There will be no flowers, no wreaths, no tolling bells and no gay receptions. Although the future looms sad and dark before us, as a perennial optimist, I refuse to believe that Germany's days as a historic nation are over. 18 November 1918.

I am in a strange mood today as I take pen in hand for the last time to conclude my memoirs. I wish they could end on a happier note, that I did not have to describe our despair and the licentiousness of our new rulers. Our situation has undergone a

[76] This refers to Admiral N. I. Nebogatov's surrender of the reinforcement contingent of the Russian Baltic Fleet to the Japanese after the Battle of Tsushima Straits.

[77] Graf Spee was the Commander of the German Pacific Squadron who met a heroic death at the Battle of the Falkland Islands in 1914.

complete change since the departure of most of my comrades. The new recruits stand all the watches, while the older men hardly stir a finger anymore. Now we have more than enough to eat. In fact we are issued punch three times a week. All of this comes from the stores of the former officers' mess. Moreover there was also enough whiskey left over for the members of the Sailors' Council to drink themselves into a stupor. They prowled around the ship the whole night. What was it that one of the speakers said on the second day of the Revolution . . . ? "We have rebelled . . . because we were treated like children . . . !" Like children. . . .

Fortunately, tomorrow I shall be able to turn my back to all this.

My Fatherland, My dear Fatherland, what will happen to you now? 24 November 1918.

Index

ABOUT THE EDITOR-TRANSLATOR

Daniel Horn graduated from Brooklyn College and obtained his master's degree and doctorate from Columbia University. Now assistant professor of history at Douglass College of Rutgers, The State University, he has also taught at the College of the City of New York and Temple University.

His interest in the history of World War I may not be unrelated to the fact that he was born in Vienna. In his research he interviewed German admirals and visited areas along the coast of Europe described by Richard Stumpf—descriptions he found invariably accurate and sensitive.

Dr. Horn is currently working on a history of the German naval mutinies of World War I.